**Prashant Dhingra**
**Trent Swanson**

# Microsoft® SQL Server 2005

# Compact Edition

## Microsoft SQL Server 2005 Compact Edition

ISBN-13: 978-0-672-32922-7

ISBN-10: 0-672-32922-0

*Library of Congress Cataloging-in-Publication Data*

Dhingra, Prashant.

  Microsoft SQL server 2005 compact edition / Prashant Dhingra, Trent Swanson.

    p. cm.

  ISBN 0-672-32922-0

  1. Client/server computing. 2. Microsoft SQL server. 3. Database management. I. Swanson, Trent. II. Microsoft Corporation. III. Title. IV. Title: SQL server 2005 compact edition.

  QA76.9.C55D585 2007

  004'.36--dc22

                     2007020219

Printed in the United States of America

First Printing July 2007

### Trademarks

### Warning and Disclaimer

### Bulk Sales

Sams Publishing offers excellent discounts on this book when ordered in quantity for bulk purchases or special sales. For more information, please contact:

**U.S. Corporate and Government Sales**
**1-800-382-3419**
corpsales@pearsontechgroup.com

For sales outside of the U.S., please contact:

**International Sales**
international@pearsontechgroup.com

---

**Editor-in-Chief**
Karen Gettman

**Senior Acquisitions Editor**
Neil Rowe

**Development Editor**
Mark Renfrow

**Managing Editor**
Gina Kanouse

**Project Editor**
Andrew Beaster

**Copy Editor**
Laurel Road Publishing Services, Inc.

**Indexer**
Brad Herriman

**Proofreader**
Laurel Road Publishing Services, Inc.

**Technical Editor**
J. Boyd Nolan

**Team Coordinator**
Cindy Teeters

**Book Designer**
Gary Adair

**Production**
Laurel Road Publishing Services, Inc.

---

**Safari** BOOKS ONLINE ENABLED  The Safari® Enabled icon on the cover of your favorite technology book means the book is available through Safari Bookshelf. When you buy this book, you get free access to the online edition for 45 days. Safari Bookshelf is an electronic reference library that lets you easily search thousands of technical books, find code samples, download chapters, and access technical information whenever and wherever you need it.

To gain 45-day Safari Enabled access to this book:

- Go to http://www.samspublishing.com/safarienabled
- Complete the brief registration form
- Enter the coupon code **SCMG-RGCL-ZUW1-FPLK-PRUP**

If you have difficulty registering on Safari Bookshelf or accessing the online edition, please e-mail customer-service@safaribooksonline.com.

# Contents at a Glance

# Table of Contents

# About the Authors

## Prashant Dhingra

Prashant Dhingra, Lead Program Manager at Microsoft, has been working in the software industry for the past 14 years. He has had a diversified experience working on mobile and embedded device applications to large enterprise applications. Prashant has used database extensively in his career ranging from Multi Terabyte Data warehouses for enterprises to a few MB of compact databases on mobile devices. At Microsoft, Prashant worked as Product Manager for SQL Server Mobile Edition Product from 2004 to 2005. Prashant has also architected one of the world's largest mobile device implementations. His earlier career includes designing and developing compilers and enterprise applications. Prashant has published articles on MSDN and presented mobile device and database technology at conferences.

## Trent Swanson

Trent Swanson, a program manager at Microsoft, is working with partners and customers to design, develop, and deploy solutions on the Windows Mobile Platform. He has gained experience and in-depth knowledge of Microsoft SQL Server Compact Edition by helping customers and partners migrate and design managed as well native mobile applications leveraging SQL Mobile.

# Dedication

*I dedicate this book to my parents, my wife Mamta and my son, Desh.*
*Thank you for your love and your patience.*

*—Prashant Dhingra*

# Acknowledgments

I would like to express my gratitude to various friends who helped me conceptualize my ideas, encouraged me to write, and participated in writing this book. I would also like to thank my current team at Microsoft who helped me to keep a balance among product development assignments and book writing.

I met Trent Swanson during MEDC in Las Vegas where the concept of this book originated from our initial discussion. First, the content writing and MEDC teams at Microsoft helped me in publishing a white paper on SQL Server Compact Edition replication. After the good response and feedback on the white paper, Trent and I decided to write this book.

Thanks to the members of the SQL Server CE team who provided help and advice. Special thanks to Alok Goyal for answering technical queries. I would also like to thank the following people who gave their feedback and advice: Arif Kureshy, Arun Mehta, Syed Yousuf, Dan Shaver, Asim Mitra, Amrish Kumar, Abhishek Mishra, and Shrinath Shanbhag.

During my interactions with customers, MVPs, consultants, and the support team, I was able to learn where the market is headed and what kind of scenarios customers want to build using a compact database. Most of what I learned emerged from community forums on SQL Server Compact Edition.

I would like to thank the Sams publishing team who provided me the opportunity to write a book on a subject of which I am most passionate. Special thanks to Neil Rowe and Mark Renfrow who made this book a reality.

Finally, special thanks to my parents, my wife, Mamta, and my wonderful son, Desh.

*—Prashant Dhingra*

# We Want to Hear from You!

As the reader of this book, *you* are our most important critic and commentator. We value your opinion and want to know what we're doing right, what we could do better, what areas you'd like to see us publish in, and any other words of wisdom you're willing to pass our way.

As senior acquisitions for Sams Publishing, I welcome your comments. You can fax, email, or write me directly to let me know what you did or didn't like about this book—as well as what we can do to make our books stronger.

*Please note that I cannot help you with technical problems related to the topic of this book, and that due to the high volume of mail I receive, I might not be able to reply to every message.*

When you write, please be sure to include this book's title and author as well as your name and phone or fax number. I will carefully review your comments and share them with the author and editors who worked on the book.

**EMAIL:**  feedback@samspublishing.com

**MAIL:**  Neil Rowe
Senior Acquisitions Editor
Que & Sams Publishing
800 East 96th Street
Indianapolis, IN 46240

# Introduction

The main objective for IT enterprises today is to add strategic value to business and provide greater return on investment. As prices fall and technology improves, technology architects have the opportunity to build innovative solutions. The architects first built intelligence into enterprise IT systems. Later they built intelligence as well as logic into the devices that connect to enterprises. For example:

- Mobile device applications provide up-to-date information and notifications to the in-field work force.

- Vending machines can order new inventory when stock reaches a threshold level and even call for support when not working.

- Weighing machines at airports, railroad stations, etc. can automatically update a central system.

To build the logic into individual machines and devices, you either need permanent connectivity between the stand-alone device and the enterprise system or you need a local store that synchronizes data with a backend enterprise system. Permanent connectivity is not always possible and can be very expensive. To use a local store, developers need a database uniquely designed for embedded systems.

To fulfill their unique requirement, embedded developers started building their own local data-management system. Building a reliable and robust custom data store had its own challenges. Being a product company, Microsoft developed the SQL Server Compact Edition database for embedded systems in mobile and desktop applications such as Pocket PC, Smartphone, and Windows CE based devices. Microsoft has written SQL Server Compact Edition from scratch while considering the unique requirements for these embedded devices. Although SQL Server Compact Edition is a new product, scratch developers can still use their existing SQL Server knowledge and enhance it for SQL Server Compact Edition.

When using SQL Server Compact Edition, it will appear as an embeddable scaled down version of SQL Server 2005. Its database has features compatible to SQL Server 2005 as well as unique features needed for Smart devices and in-proc databases.

Similar to SQL Server 2005, SQL Server Compact Edition is a standard relational database and is integrated with SQL Server 2005. You can use the SQL Server Management Studio tool to manage SQL Server Compact Edition and also synchronize the data between SQL Server 2005 and SQL Server Compact Edition. SQL Server Compact Edition supports the subset of Transact-SQL. You can also use your existing ADO.NET knowledge to develop ADO.NET and OLE DB applications for SQL Server Compact Edition. SQL Server Compact Edition is integrated with Visual Studio 2005, enabling developers to instantly develop SQL Server Compact Edition based applications.

SQL Server Compact Edition has a light weight engine making it suitable for Smart devices and in-proc databases. It provides an updatable result set for faster performance on an embedded database. It also supports Merge Replication and the Remote Data Access mechanism to synchronize data with a backend SQL Server.

This book presents SQL Server Compact Edition concepts and the overall environment that you will be using to develop and deploy SQL Server Compact Edition based applications. You will also be able to transfer your existing programming knowledge to write applications for SQL Server Compact Edition.

This book is written for the architect, designer, developer, technology consultant, and project manager. No matter what your title is, if you are responsible for applications using an embedded database, this book will provide you with the main concepts and feature details of SQL Server Compact Edition. By providing step-by-step instructions and examples for designing, developing, and deploying SQL Server Compact Edition based applications, this book will help you understand the SQL Server Compact Edition concepts and programming interface.

This book has two main objectives: (1) to teach you SQL Server Compact Edition concepts, and (2) to provide information on how to build and deploy SQL Server Compact Edition based applications using .NET Compact Framework, SQL Server Management Studio, and Visual Studio. After reading this book, you should be able to build effective applications using SQL Server Compact Edition best practices.

# Overview of the Book

### Chapter 1: Getting Started with SQL Server 2005 Compact Edition

Chapter 1 introduces the SQL Server Compact Edition feature set and how it meets the design goals. Also discussed are the SQL Server Compact Edition architecture components that you will need in the development and production environment. An overview of features and high-level detail of architecture components will paint the overall picture. Liken this to understanding the role of each card before playing a card game. The chapter will also provide a history of SQL Server Compact Edition and explain the difference between versions 3.1 and 3.0

### Chapter 2: Platform Support and Installation

This chapter will explain the software installed in your development and production environment as well as the hardware and software requirements for installing SQL Server 2005, Visual Studio 2005, and SQL Server Compact Edition. In addition, this chapter will help you build a development environment on your computer including Windows Mobile 6.0 and Windows Mobile 5.0.

### Chapter 3: Getting to Know the Tools

Presented in this chapter is the information on the correct usage of SQL Server Management Studio, Visual Studio 2005, and the Query Analyzer user interface. We will discuss the usage of Device Emulator Manager, Device Emulator, and ActiveSync. Also, in this chapter you will learn how to connect to and manage the SQL Server Compact Edition database.

## Chapter 4: Managing the SQL Server 2005 Compact Edition Database

Chapter 4 discusses how to create, secure, verify, compact, and shrink the SQL Server Compact Edition database. By providing you with information on all these options, it will also demonstrate how you can complete these operations using SQL Server Management Studio, Query Analyzer, and by writing programs.

## Chapter 5: Defining Database Structure

In this chapter you will learn the Transact-SQL syntax for defining tables and indexes for the SQL Server Compact Edition database. By using SQL statements, you will create tables, columns, and indexes. In addition to SQL statements, you will use SQL Server Management Studio, Query Analyzer, and Visual Studio dialogs to create and *modify* tables, columns, and indexes. You will create a database project to manage SQL Server and SQL Server Compact Edition scripts.

## Chapter 6: Manipulating the Database

In this chapter you will learn how to access and manipulate data in the SQL Server Compact Edition database using SQL Server Management Studio, Query Analyzer, and the SQL syntax. We will also discuss the usage of the SQL Server Integration package to populate the SQL Server Compact Edition database.

## Chapter 7: Programming SQL Server 2005 Compact Edition with ADO.NET

Chapter 7 shows how to use ADO.NET to connect to the SQL Server Compact Edition database as well as how to read, update, and merge the changes back to the SQL Server Compact Edition database. You will learn how to create desktop- and device-based projects using SQL Server Compact Edition. You will also learn how to use Sqlclient name-space to develop device-based applications that directly access a remote SQL Server.

## Chapter 8: Introducing Native Access

Here you will learn how to access and manage the SQL Server Compact database using nonmanaged programming. First you will learn Engine object method in order to do common database management tasks. Secondly, you will learn how you can use the OLE DB provider for SQL Server Compact Edition to manager and access the database. In conclusion, the specific properties and interfaces for the OLE DB provider for SQL Server Compact Edition are discussed.

## Chapter 9: Using Operators in SQL Server 2005 Compact Edition

SQL Server Compact Edition supports most of the operators supported by SQL Server. In this chapter you will learn Arithmetic, Assignment, Bitwise, Logical, Comparison, String Concatenation, and Unary operators.

## Chapter 10: Using the Built-In Functions

This chapter explains in detail the functions supported in the SQL Server Compact Edition database. SQL Server Compact Edition supports a subset of built-in functions that SQL Server supports. You can utilize these functions for calculations, string manipulations, and date manipulations.

## Chapter 11: Upgrading from a Previous Version

In this chapter you will learn how to migrate the SQL Server CE 2.0 database file to the SQL Server Compact Edition 3.0 database file. Also, you will learn how to convert a .NET CF 1.0 project into a .NET CF 2.0 project. Additionally, you will be presented with information on how to migrate a Visual Studio 2003 project into a Visual Studio 2005 project.

## Chapter 12: Synchronizing Data with Merge Replication

Here you will learn Merge Replication features. You will also learn how to synchronize data between SQL Server 2005 and SQL Server Compact Edition. In addition, you will learn how to set up a publication on SQL Server, set up a subscription on SQL Server Compact Edition, and synchronize data with a backend SQL Server.

## Chapter 13: Synchronizing Data with Remote Data Access

Chapter 13 introduces another method, Remote Data Access, to synchronize data between SQL Server and SQL Server Compact Edition. You will learn how to pull the data from the SQL Server to a device and manipulate the data on a device and push the changes to SQL Server. Also you will learn how to submit an SQL statement from a device to the backend SQL Server.

## Chapter 14: Securing the SQL Server 2005 Compact Edition Database

In this chapter you will learn about SQL Server Compact Edition's security features. You will learn how to secure an SQL Server Compact Edition database on a client device as well as how to securely synchronize the data between SQL Server and SQL Server Compact Edition.

## Chapter 15: SQL Server 2005 Compact Edition Performance Tuning

In this chapter you will learn the factors you should consider in SQL Server Compact Edition database design and when to create an index on your tables for performance improvement. You will also be presented with performance improvement tips for programming. Finally you will learn the performance improvement guidelines for data synchronization.

# How This Book Will Help You

The power of the .NET compact framework has made mobile and embedded application development easy. This book starts off with easy examples and builds a learning curve to cover the more advanced topics. You will be using the SQL Server Compact Edition database as a Database Designer, as an Application Developer, as an Administrator, or as a System Architect.

## Defining Architecture

An architect needs to choose the right technology and define the evolutionary path. As an architect you need to know whether the product features meet your requirements and whether they provide security requirements to suit your enterprise. You need to consider the integration and scalability that a product provides. If you are using SQL Server Compact Edition on a device, you need to make an important decision about how to synchronize the data between the device and backend server.

Finally you also want to ensure that architecture is not only suitable for development but is also the right one for deployment, operations, and maintenance.

This book provides an overview of SQL Server Compact Edition features, the architecture components, available tools, integration with Visual Studio and SQL Server, support for T-SQL, programming languages, security features, and most importantly, the connectivity features.

## Designing Database

SQL Server Compact Edition database has a small footprint. At run time it only takes 5 MB of memory space. The database size is limited to 4 GB. This book will help you to understand the limitation of memory. Chapter 15, *SQL Server 2005 Compact Edition Performance Tuning,* gives you the insight of query execution and explains the trade-offs you should consider while designing the database. It will also help you in determining when to create an index and on which columns. Chapter 3, *Getting to Know the Tools,* demonstrates SQL Server Management Studio and Visual Studio 2005 user-interface usage for defining SQL Server Compact Edition database structures.

## Developing Application

A developer can leverage his existing knowledge to develop SQL Server Compact Edition based applications. The learning curve for developing SQL Server Compact Edition application is very small. SQL Server Compact Edition supports the subset of T-SQL and most of the built-in functions and operators supported by SQL Server. This book has dedicated chapters for ADO.NET programming, OLE DB Programming, SQL Server syntax for writing queries, operators, and built-in functions. If you are an experienced SQL Server developer, you will find it extremely easy to understand the commonality between SQL Server 2005 and SQL Server CE. These chapters will explain the features that are not supported in SQL Server Compact Edition and will also call out additional functionality provided by SQL Server Compact Edition that is not available in SQL Server 2005.

SQL Server Compact Edition also supports ADO.NET and OLE DB interfaces for programming. SQL Server Compact Edition is tightly integrated with Visual Studio 2005. The integration with Visual Studio allows rapid application development. Visual Studio allows a developer to create new SQL Server Compact Edition databases or add existing SQL Server Compact Edition databases into Visual projects. You can use Visual Studio Server Explorer to browse SQL Server Compact Edition database objects. Visual Studio also has the Data Source Configuration Wizard to easily manage database connections. Chapter 3, *Getting to Know the Tools,* provides an overview of the Visual Studio feature and demonstrates how to utilize these features for application development.

Merge Replication and RDA chapters are extremely useful for application developers. These chapters dive into the pros and cons of two synchronization methods. Both chapters have step-by-step guides to program Merge Replication and RDA.

Chapter 15 highlights the performance tuning techniques for SQL queries and ADO.NET programming. This chapter also shows you how to get insight and examine the execution plan that the SQL Server Compact Edition database engine is using.

## Administrating Server and Client

The Server Administrator is focused on managing SQL Server, Web Server, and a large number of clients that connect to a backend server. This book explains the tools and features that help you in deploying the application as well as managing a Web Server and backend servers. Chapters related to Installation, Security, Merge Replication, and RDA show step-by-step instructions and explain how to install, secure, configure, and manage the replication and RDA set-up environment.

# Getting Started with SQL Server 2005 Compact Edition

Over the last few years, mobile devices have evolved rapidly. There is a lot of expectation in the industry regarding the scenarios and applications that can be built on these devices. Microsoft, being a product company, is focusing on building platforms, tools, and databases to enable developers to create truly distributed applications. When you build distributed enterprise applications on mobile devices, the main challenge is to define the strategy for transferring data between the enterprise server and the mobile device running the application that consumes and manipulates the data. The other challenge is providing rich data management functionality along with a small footprint.

SQL Server 2005 Compact Edition (earlier known as SQL Server 2005 Mobile Edition) is a compact and embedded database in the Microsoft SQL Server family. SQL Server Compact Edition provides rich relational database features in a small footprint. The focus of this book is to provide you with the knowledge for building applications for mobile devices and embedded applications for the desktop. In 2005, Microsoft released .NET Framework 2.0, .NET Compact Framework 2.0, Visual Studio 2005, SQL Server 2005, and SQL Server 2005 Compact Edition. This book describes how to use these technologies to build data-aware applications. It will also explain the SQL Server Compact Edition database features, programming techniques, security, and data synchronization mechanisms as well as the SQL Server Management Studio and Visual Studio features useful for building SQL Server Compact Edition based applications.

# Design Goals

Mobile devices such as laptops, ultra mobile PCs, and converged mobile phones such as those running Microsoft Windows Mobile, have grown significantly in popularity over the last several years. More and more businesses are beginning to realize the benefits of mobilizing their line of business applications such as improved productivity, application adoption, as well as improved team collaboration. The bottom line is that businesses want to bring the functionality from their enterprise applications down to the small and easily portable mobile devices. Mobilizing an application can, however, present a number of very unique application design and development challenges.

## Support Data Synchronization

In an ideal client server model, all client machines are connected to backend data and have access to the most recent data. Mobility gives you the freedom to work anywhere. When you want to work from anywhere, it won't be appropriate to have guaranteed connectivity to backend data. Given the transient nature of wireless networks, mobilizing applications often require that the application needs to be capable of functioning when disconnected from a central data store needing a local copy of data, and then be able to synchronize changes with a central data store. In a disconnected solution, the client device needs to download data from a central server. The application on a device should be able to work on local data. A suitable interval application can connect back to a central server and synchronize data with a backend server.

## Providing Rich Functionality with a Small Size and Footprint

Information is generally a key component of any solutions architecture and a critical asset, thereby making data consistency and security high priorities within most firms. Most applications have a need to manage data and are quite often the reason for the application entirely. Persisting, querying, securing, replicating, and maintaining the integrity of the data are some of the fundamental tasks that any application must address. Be it a stand-alone application or a connected application, data management is quite often an integral part of solutions design and development. The challenge with client data management—especially with small mobile devices where resources such as storage, battery, bandwidth, and clock cycles can be very scarce—is in balancing features or the ease of development with resource limitations. This is where a compact, in-process database management system such as Microsoft® SQL Server™ 2005 Compact Edition (SQL Server Compact Edition) is useful.

## Rapid Application Development

One of the critical factors in technology success is the ease of use. SQL Server Compact Edition is written from scratch to support mobile device and embedded database needs. The needs of mobile device architecture are different. On top of the architectural and connectivity challenge, there is an additional challenge for the training developer and administrator. With new tools and programming languages, enterprises will have to spend more time and money in building a new generation of mobile and embedded applications. To reduce the learning curve, Microsoft has integrated SQL Server Compact Edition with SQL Server and Visual Studio. As a designer, developer, or system administrator, you will use the same set of tools for SQL Server Compact Edition that you use for SQL Server.

# Features

SQL Server 2005 Compact Edition is a lightweight but feature rich relational database. You can use SQL Server Compact Edition database on desktops, Smart devices, and on tablet PCs. SQL Server Compact Edition delivers necessary relational database functionality to the client, such as an optimizing query processor, support for transactions, indexes, referential integrity, and various data types. Merge replication and remote data access ensure data from a backend SQL Server database can be delivered reliably and securely, and the data can then be manipulated offline and later synchronized to the backend server. SQL Server Compact Edition database integrates with Microsoft Visual Studio 2005 and offers support for the Structured Query Language (SQL), providing a development model consistent with Microsoft SQL Server. You can manage SQL Server Compact Edition database on a desktop computer or a device using SQL Server Management Studio, providing the same experience as users connecting to SQL Server 2005 and SQL Server Compact Edition.

In this section you will become familiar with SQL Server Compact Edition features. In the upcoming chapters you will learn and create example exercises using these features.

## Relational Database Functionality in a Small Footprint

SQL Server Compact Edition delivers relational database functionality in a relatively small footprint, offering data management services such as a robust data store, optimizing query processor, and reliable, scalable connectivity capabilities. SQL Server Compact Edition database supports primary keys, indexes, and foreign keys. The tables can be related using a primary key and a foreign key relationship. To maintain the referential, the integrity database also supports cascade updates and deletes.

The SQL Server Compact Edition database engine packs a lot of features into a 2.2 to 2.6 MB disk space footprint, depending on the processor of the target device. Balancing the footprint with a rich set of functionality is a key design requirement in SQL Server 2005 Compact Edition, and as you will soon discover there is a lot of functionality wrapped up in a very small package.

## Transaction Support

Using API or SQL statements ACID, you can start and end ACID transactions.

## Robust Data Support

SQL Server Compact Edition database protects data by supporting atomicity, consistency, isolation, and durability. Microsoft has written SQL Server Compact Edition 3.x from scratch.

## Small Footprint

SQL Server Compact Edition takes only 2.2 MB to 2.6 MB of space depending on the processor of the target platform. At run time SQL Server Compact Edition takes up to 5 MB of memory space. The small footprint of SQL Server Compact Edition makes it extremely useful for Smart devices and as an embedded database on desktop applications. Maintaining a small footprint, and componentization along with the right balance of features were critical to the design and success of SQL Server Compact Edition. The functionality in SQL Server Compact Edition is very highly componentized, allowing a further reduction in overall footprint and only deploying the components that are necessary to the solution.

## Security Features

At rest or in motion, data security is quite often important to most solutions and should not be overlooked. SQL Server Compact Edition enables data encryption at a local store through password protection and RSA 128-bit file encryption, and when in motion, data synchronization can be done over SSL. SQL Server Compact Edition does not support the notion of users and roles as the other SQL Server 2005 Edition products do. Instead it uses a shared key that is used to encrypt/decrypt data stored in a single file.

Security is most important concern for Smart devices. Chapter 14, *Securing the SQL Server 2005 Compact Edition Database,* is dedicated to this issue. In the chapter you will get expert advice about the various options available to make your data secure on a device as well as transferring it to and from an SQL Server.

## Multiuser Access

SQL Server Compact Edition supports multiple connections to the database, enabling multiple threads or processes to be working with a data file at the same time. Having multiple connections allows for scenarios such as a client application being able to work with data while data transfer is happening in the background. To support the multiuser access, SQL Server Compact Edition provides a locking mechanism. Date synchronization may not succeed if appropriate locks are not acquired during synchronization. SQL Server Compact Edition uses a database exclusive lock, a row exclusive lock, and DDL locks to prevent synchronization failures.

## Integration with SQL Server 2005 and Visual Studio 2005

You can manage an SQL Server Compact Edition database using SQL Server Management Studio and Visual Studio. SQL Server Management Studio UI, dialogs, and wizards can be used to manage the SQL Server Compact Edition database as well. You are provided with the same user experience to manage both SQL Server and the SQL Server Compact Edition database. A Query Analyzer tool is available to manage the database on Smart devices. With Visual Studio you can create the SQL Server Compact Edition database, design schemas, and update the data without even writing SQL queries.

In Chapter 3, *Getting to Know the Tools,* you will learn the features of SQL Server Management Studio, Query Analyzer, and Visual Studio. Later you will be utilizing these features to build exercises outlined in book.

## Common Programming Model

SQL Server Compact Edition supports a subset of T-SQL. The syntax of the SQL statement in SQL Server Compact Edition is similar to SQL Server statements. Included are ADO.NET support and OLE DB provider support for the SQL Server Compact Edition database. This means you can access the database in the same way as you do for SQL Server. You can leverage your existing knowledge of developing database applications and quickly start developing ADO.NET and OLE DB provider based applications for SQL Server Compact Edition.

## Single Data file

The SQL Server Compact Edition database is stored in a single data file. Having a single file allows you to easily deploy the database onto Smart devices. The SQL Server Compact Edition database file can be password protected. The recommended file extension for the SQL Server Compact Edition database file is .sdf.

### NOTE

The SQL Server Compact Edition database has a limit of 4 GB. The SQL Server Compact Edition database file including schema and data can be up to 4 GB.

## Easy Deployment

SQL Server Compact Edition supports a **ClickOnce** deployment feature. ClickOnce deployment technology is used on desktops and on Tablet PCs. It makes deployment of Windows forms based applications similar to Web applications. You do not need to touch each client, you can just update files on a server.

Visual Studio 2005 SP1 has a ClickOnce feature and enables the packaging and deploying of the application to be much simpler than it would be otherwise. You can select the prerequisite for your application. Regarding prerequisites, Visual Studio will generate a bootstrapper file. During deployment, the bootstrapper will install all the required files. You will learn more about the ClickOnce feature in Chapter 3, *Getting to Know the Tools*.

### NOTE

The ClickOnce deployment feature is added in SQL Server Compact Edition 3.1. The feature is not available with SQL Server Mobile Edition 3.0.

## Data Synchronization

The SQL Server Compact Edition database provides two powerful mechanisms to synchronize data between SQL Server and the SQL Server Compact Edition database. Using Remote Data Access or RDA you can get data from an SQL Server table and store it in a local table in SQL Mobile on a device. You can also update the table locally and later on update the modified records back to the SQL Server table. By using Merge Replication, you can update the data both on the server and the device and synchronize the data between SQL Mobile and SQL Server. Merge Replication functionality is extremely useful when multiple clients or devices need to subscribe data, make offline changes, and subscribe data back to a backend server.

Not only does SQL Server Compact Edition have features to synchronize data, it also ensures that overhead data transmission is minimal. During the synchronization, only modified data is transferred. The transmission can be further optimized by sending only the modified columns and not the complete rows. Merge Replication includes features such as: Wizards, download only articles, filtered articles, Column Level Tracking, and Support for Multiple subscriptions.

It is possible for the same record to be modified on a local SQL Compact Edition database and a remote SQL Server. The SQL Server Compact Edition synchronization mechanism allows you to detect such conflicts and take corrective actions.

Merge Replication and RDA are the most important features of SQL Server Compact Edition. Chapters 12 and 13 are dedicated to both these topics.

## Locking and Isolation Levels

SQL Server Compact Edition provides a locking mechanism at row level, page level, and table level. It also supports a lock escalation process to convert fine grained locks into coarse grained locks.

SQL Server Compact Edition also supports three isolation levels. An increased isolation level means more protection against data inconsistency but a decrease in concurrency.

## Result Set

SQL Server Compact Edition provides an updatable, scrollable cursor. Using this cursor, you have the performance of DataReader and a similar functionality of the DataSet. It also requires less memory as it does not perform double buffering of the database as DataSet does.

## Named Parameter

Named Parameter is supported in .NET Compact Framework provider for ADO.NET. Named parameter was not supported in SQL Server CE 2.0.

## Cost-Based Query Optimizer

SQL Server Compact Edition has a cost-based Query Optimizer. SQL Server Compact Edition Query Optimizer evaluates the options for executing a query and determines the execution plan. A number of possible ways to execute a query is generated, and their estimated execution time is calculated. The plan that is fastest is used for the actually query execution.

## Integration Services Support

You can use the SQL Server Integration Service Package to extract and transform data from SQL Server Compact Edition. Using SQL Server Integration Services, developers can export or import data from various data sources such as XML, flat files, MS Access, Oracle, IBM DB2, and so on.

# Evolution of SQL Server Compact Edition

Microsoft released SQL Server 2005 Mobile Edition version 3.0 in 2005 with SQL Server 2005 and Visual Studio 2005. In the beginning of 2007, Microsoft released version 3.1 of SQL Mobile Edition and officially changed the product name to SQL Server 2005 Compact Edition.

## SQL Server Compact Edition Version 1.0

SQL Server Compact Edition 1.0 was released in 2000 before the release of .NET Compact Framework. The version 1.0 had a small footprint of 800 KB.

## SQL Server Compact Edition Version 2.0

Microsoft released SQL Server CE 2.0 in 2002. Microsoft also released .NET Compact Framework version 1.0 during this time. The powerful combination of .NET Compact Framework and SQL Server CE started an era of developing applications for mobile devices using Visual Studio.

## SQL Server Mobile Edition Version 3.0

In 2005 Microsoft released SQL Server 2005 and Visual Studio 2005. The next generation of SQL Server Compact Edition 3.0 was released with SQL Server 2005 and Visual Studio 2005. SQL Server Compact Edition was then renamed SQL Server Mobile Edition.

Version 3.0 was written from scratch. The database engine was optimized for mobile devices and embedded applications. The main highlights of version 3.0 include the following:

- Improved reliability for mobile devices

- Multiuser database

- Multiple subscriptions

- Column level tracking

- Tight integration with SQL Server 2005 and Visual Studio 2005

You will be learning details of these features in upcoming chapters.

## SQL Server Compact Edition Version 3.1

In January 2007 Microsoft released version 3.1 for SQL CE. SQL Server Compact Edition 3.1 is the next edition of SQL Server Mobile Edition 3.0. SQL Server Compact Edition 3.1 and SQL Server Mobile Edition 3.0 use the same database engine as well as other components. Other than the name change, the main difference with version 3.1 is that Microsoft has removed the restriction to use SQL Mobile only on Smart devices and Tablet

PCs. Now you can use SQL Server Compact Edition to develop Smart devices, Tablet PCs, and on Windows Platforms. Here is a summary of the differences between SQL Server Mobile Edition 3.0 and SQL Server Compact Edition 3.1

---

**NOTE**

You can use this book with SQL Compact Edition 3.x. The examples will work with both SQL Server Mobile Edition 3.0 and SQL Server Compact Edition 3.1.

---

## Naming Convention for SQL Server Compact Edition

The chapters in the book will refer to SQL Server Mobile Edition as SQL Mobile. For SQL Server Compact Edition, we will use the term SQL Server Compact Edition or SQL Server CE. For SQL Server Compact Edition 2.0, the term SQL Server Compact Edition 2.0 will be used.

The book also has pictures of SQL Server Compact Edition and SQL Mobile dialog boxes. The SQL Server Compact Edition dialog boxes refer to the names SQL Server Compact Edition and SQL Server 2005 Compact Edition.

## Obtaining SQL Server Compact Edition 3.x

SQL Server 3.x is available with SQL Server 2005, with Visual Studio 2005, and as a Web download. Table 1.1 provides a quick summary about the SQL Server Compact Edition versions available.

**TABLE 1.1** Versions

| SQL Server / Visual Studio Version | SQL Server Compact Edition Version |
| --- | --- |
| SQL Server 2005 | SQL Server 2005 Mobile Edition 3.0 |
| SQL Server 2005 SP1 | SQL Server 2005 Mobile Edition 3.0 |
| Visual Studio 2005 | SQL Server 2005 Mobil Mobile Edition 3.0 |
| SQL Server 2005 SP2 or later | SQL Server 2005 Compact Edition  3.1 |
| Visual Studio 2005 SP1 or later | SQL Server 2005 Compact Edition 3.1 |

# Differences Between Versions 3.1 and 3.0

Microsoft SQL Server Compact Edition version 3.1 is the next version of Microsoft SQL Server Mobile Edition version 3.0. The SQL Server Compact Edition 3.1 extends the database functionality to the desktop as well. The new version also provides features for Data Directory and ClickOnce.

If you have started using version 3.0, you will not be impacted. The version 3.1 and version 3.0 database components are the same, the database format is the same, and database features are the same. You don't have to worry about the brand name change from SQL Mobile to SQL Server Compact Edition. While changing the brand name, Microsoft changed all the strings on the dialog titles and error messages but there is no functional change.

## Desktop Restrictions Are a Thing of the Past

You can use SQL Server Compact Edition on mobile Devices and Tablet PCs, as well as on Windows based PCs. In earlier versions, Microsoft placed a restriction and SQL Mobile was only available for Tablet PC and Mobile devices. You could use SQL Mobile on a desktop for development but you were not allowed to use it on a desktop in a production environment. The restrictions are gone with the new SQL Server Compact Edition 3.1. SQL Server Compact Edition 3.1 is ideal for many desktop-based applications where applications need to store data locally. A desktop-based application can store financial assets of the user. In the past, the possible choices were SQL Express or Microsoft Access. If you do not require SQL Express power, SQL Server Compact Edition's small foot print and relational database capability are ideal. You can also transfer the SQL Server Compact Edition database file onto a mobile database and view financial transactions on a mobile device.

SQL Server Compact Edition can also be used for applications that get data from a server and store it locally. For example, Outlook stores email in a .pst file. In the future, an email client can download data into an SQL Server Compact Edition database file (.sdf) instead of using .pst file. The advantage of using a .sdf file is that you can use relational capabilities of a database to find information in the database. The .sdf file can also be transferred to a mobile device and emails can be viewed on mobile devices as well.

## Data Directory and ClickOnce Deployment

In SQL Server Compact Edition 3.1 the Data Directory feature is introduced. With this feature you do not have to hard code the full path of the database in a connection string. ClickOnce functionality allows easy deployment for managed applications. You will learn more about these features in Chapter 3, *Getting to Know the Tools*.

## Branding

Microsoft has branded the version 3.0 database as SQL Server Mobile Edition. In January 2007 version 3.1 was released with the name SQL Server Compact Edition. If you are using version 3.0, all dialog boxes, error messages, and other strings will refer to the product as SQL Server Mobile Edition or SQL Mobile. If you are using version 3.1, dialog boxes, titles, error messages, and all other strings will refer to SQL Server Compact Edition.

SQL Server Compact Edition is available with SQL Server 2005 and Visual Studio 2005. SQL Server 2005 SP2 or a higher version will install SQL Server Compact Edition 3.1. SQL Server 2005 RTM version and SQL Server 2005 SP1 install SQL Server Mobile Edition 3.0.

Similarly Visual Studio 2005 Service Pack 1 installs SQL Server Compact Edition 3.1. Visual Studio RTM version has SQL Server Mobile Edition 3.0 version.

### Difference in SQL Server Dialogs

The SQL Server 2005 earlier version (RTM and SP1) will present the SQL Server Compact Edition dialog box as an SQL Mobile Edition dialog box. The various dialog boxes will use terminology such as SQL Server Mobile, SQL Server 2005 Mobile Edition, SQL Mobile and SQL Server Mobile Edition. Let's examine a few commonly used SQL Server Management

Studio dialog boxes to help you see the difference. You will learn the usage of these dialog boxes in Chapter 3, *Getting to Know the Tools*.

### Server Type

When you connect the database, you choose the database type. As shown in Figure 1.1 the Server Type appears as SQL Server Compact Edition if you are using SQL Server 2005 SP2 or higher.

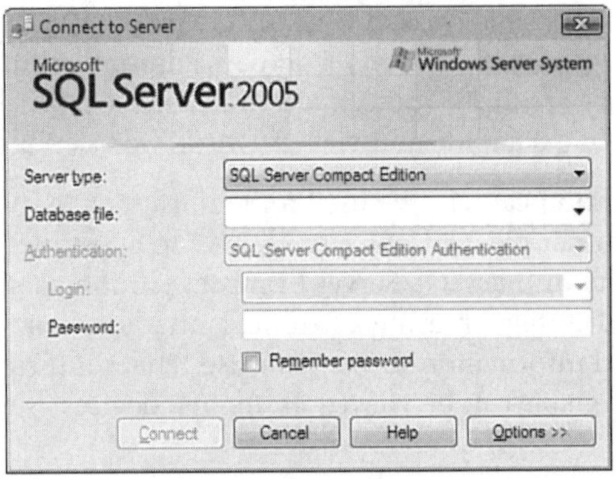

FIGURE 1.1    Connecting to SQL Compact Edition 3.1

If you are using the SQL Server 2005 RTM version of SQL Server 2005 SP1, the Server Type available is SQL Server Mobile as shown in Figure 1.2.

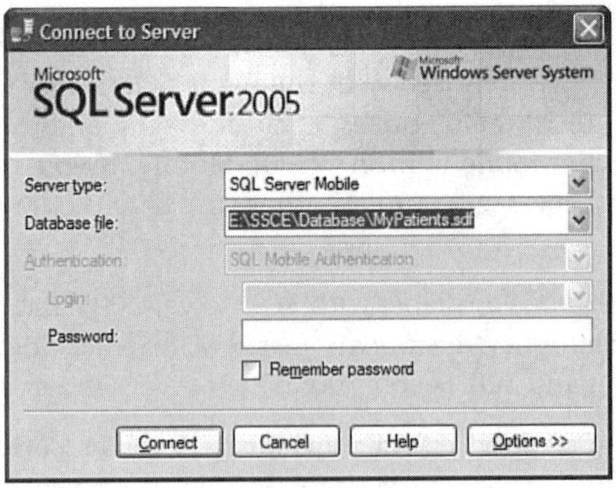

FIGURE 1.2    Connecting to SQL Compact Edition 3.0

## Strings

Similarly, while using SQL Server 2005 SP2 or higher, in the Browse for Files dialog box it will show a message string and refer to the database as SQL Server Compact Edition database as shown in Figure 1.3.

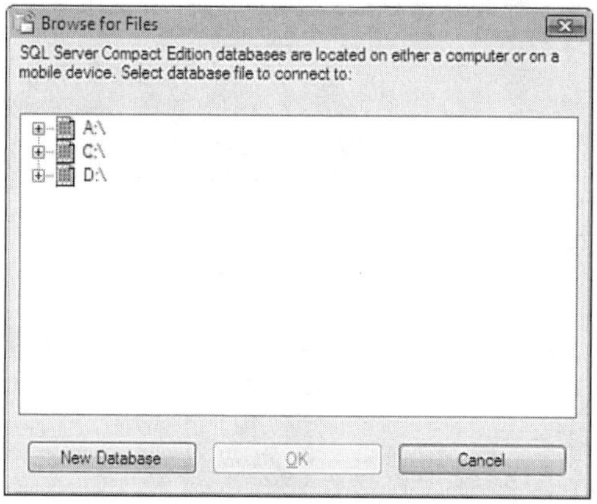

FIGURE 1.3    Browse for Files in SQL Compact Edition 3.1

The same dialog box in SQL Server 2005 RTM version and SQL Server 2005 SP1 will refer to the database as SQL Server 2005 Mobile Edition as shown in Figure 1.4.

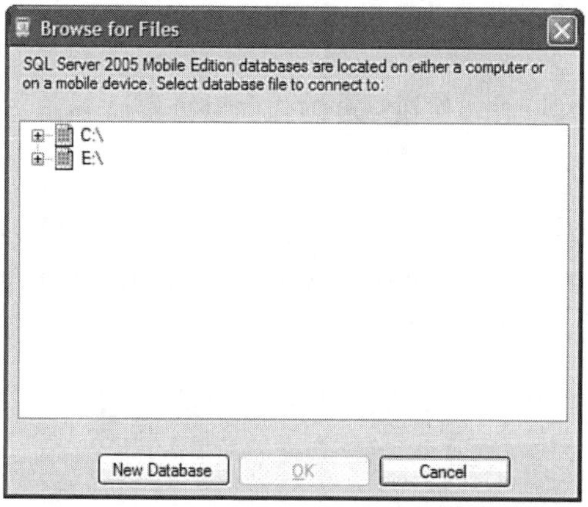

FIGURE 1.4    Browse for Files in SQL Server Compact Edition 3.0

## Tabs

The Object Explorer displays the database type. As shown in Figure 1.5, for SQL Server Compact Edition version 3.1 or higher, the Object Explorer will refer to the database as SQL Server Compact Edition.

**FIGURE 1.5**    Object Explorer in SQL Compact Edition 3.1

For SQL Server Mobile Edition 3.0 (available with SQL Server RTM and SP1) the Object Explorer will show data type as SQL Server Mobile as shown in Figure 1.6.

**FIGURE 1.6**    Object Explorer in SQL Compact Edition 3.0

**Tool Tips**
You will notice similar differences in the Template Explorer. As shown in Figure 1.7, when you move your mouse over SQL Compact Edition icons in Template Explorer, the tool tip will shown SQL Server Compact Edition.

**FIGURE 1.7**    Template Explorer in SQL Compact Edition 3.1

If you are using earlier versions of SQL Server 2005 (RTM or SP1), the tool tip will display SQL Mobile on moving the mouse over icons in Template Explorer as shown in Figure 1.8.

**FIGURE 1.8**    Template Explorer in SQL Compact Edition 3.0

### Summary  Heading

You will see similar differences in the Summary dialog box. In the topmost part of the Summary dialog box, the database type is displayed. As shown in Figure 1.9, when using SQL Server 2005 SP2 or a higher version, the dialog box will display SQL Server Compact Edition.

The same window in the SQL Server 2005 RTM version of SQL Server 2005 SP1 version will display SQL Server Mobile (see Figure 1.10).

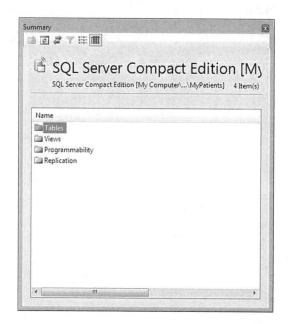

**FIGURE 1.9**    Summary in SQL Management Studio for SQL Compact Edition 3.1

**FIGURE 1.10**    Summary Tab in SQL Management Studio for SQL Compact Edition 3.0

## Connection Properties

The dialog box to create or modify tables specifies the database type, database path, and database filename. If you are using SQL Server 2005 SP2 or higher (having SQL Server Compact Edition 3.1), the dialog box will specify the database type as SQL Server Compact Edition as shown in Figure 1.11.

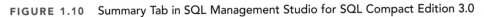

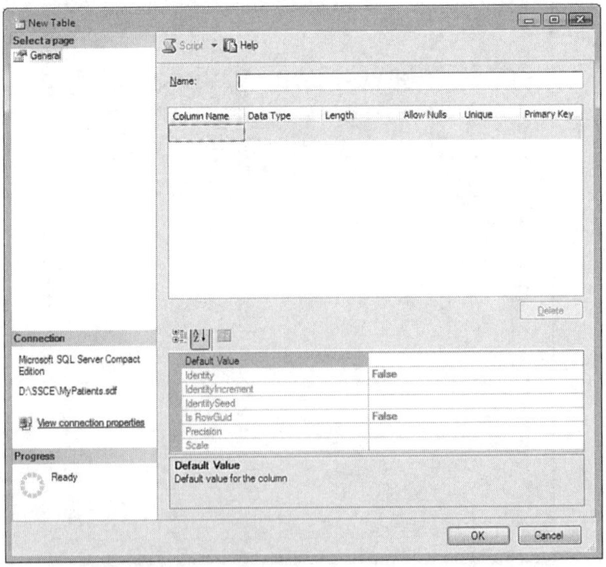

**FIGURE 1.11**    Connection Properties Dialog Box in SQL Compact Edition 3.1

For earlier versions of SQL Server 2005 (RTM or SP1), the dialog box will display SQL Server 2005 Mobile Edition as shown in Figure 1.12.

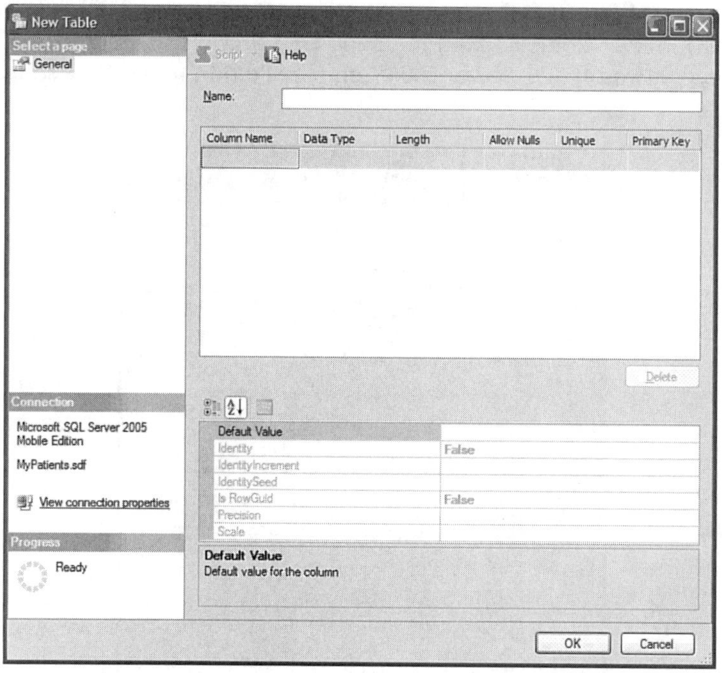

FIGURE 1.12     Connection Properties Dialog Box in SQL Compact Edition 3.0

### Differences in the Visual Studio 2005 Dialog Boxes

In this section we have displayed a few dialog boxes that you will use quite often. In Chapter 3, *Getting to Know the Tools*, you will learn in detail the usage of these dialog boxes. In this chapter you should notice the difference in the appearance of dialog boxes in SQL Mobile and SQL Compact Edition.

You may see similar results from figure to figure based on whether Visual Studio 2005 RTM version or Visual Studio 2005 SP1 or a later version is installed on your system. You will notice that in the RTM version, SQL Compact Edition is referred to as Microsoft SQL Server Mobile Edition and in later versions SQL Compact Edition is referred to as Microsoft SQL Server Compact Edition.

### NOTE

You will be using various examples shown in the book. Simply remember that SQL Mobile and SQL Compact Edition are the same databases. If the examples in this book show results as SQL Server Compact Edition and on your computer it shows SQL Server Mobile Edition, you should still treat them the same.

### Data Source

Use the Add Connection dialog box in Visual Studio to enter information to connect to a data source. You can click on the Change button to see a list of data source types and data providers. Choose Microsoft SQL Server 2005 Compact Edition and .NET Framework data provider for SQL Server Compact Edition. If you are using Visual Studio 2005 SP1 or later, you will choose Microsoft SQL Server 2005 Compact Edition under Data source as shown in Figure 1.13.

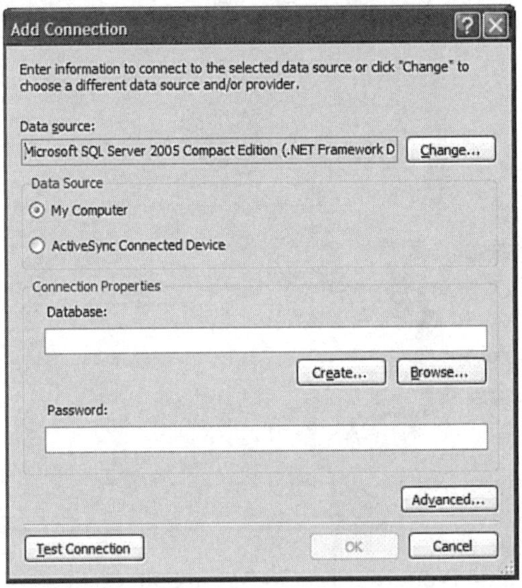

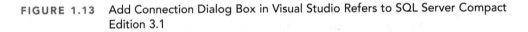

**FIGURE 1.13**    Add Connection Dialog Box in Visual Studio Refers to SQL Server Compact Edition 3.1

For Visual Studio 2005 RTM version you will choose Microsoft SQL Server Mobile Edition as shown in Figure 1.14.

Clicking on the Change button in the Add Connection dialog box brings the Change Data Source dialog box. For Visual Studio 2005 SP1 version, you will choose Microsoft SQL Server 2005 Compact Edition as shown in Figure 1.15.

For Visual Studio 2005 RTM version you will choose Microsoft SQL Server Mobile Edition as shown in Figure 1.16.

You can add an SQL Server Compact Edition database file in a Visual Studio project. Visual Studio 2005 SP1 or higher installs SQL Server Compact Edition onto your computer. Earlier versions of Visual Studio 2005 (RTM) install SQL Mobile Edition on your computer.

Similar to C# or VB.NET classes, it is possible to add an SQL Server Compact Edition file as an Item in Visual Studio. For SQL Server Mobile Edition the file type is called SQL

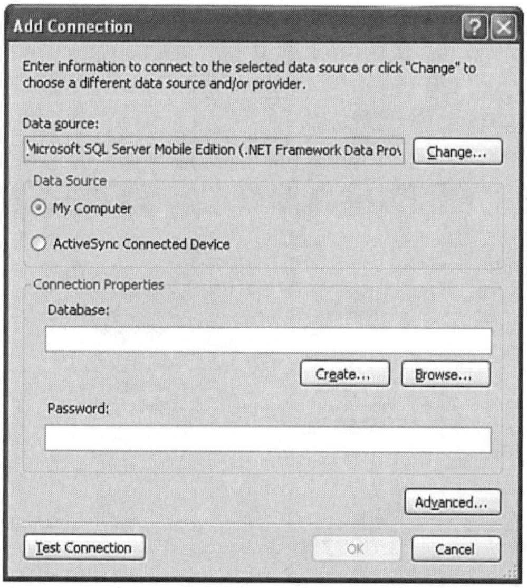

**FIGURE 1.14**    Add Connection Dialog Box for SQL Server Compact Edition 3.0

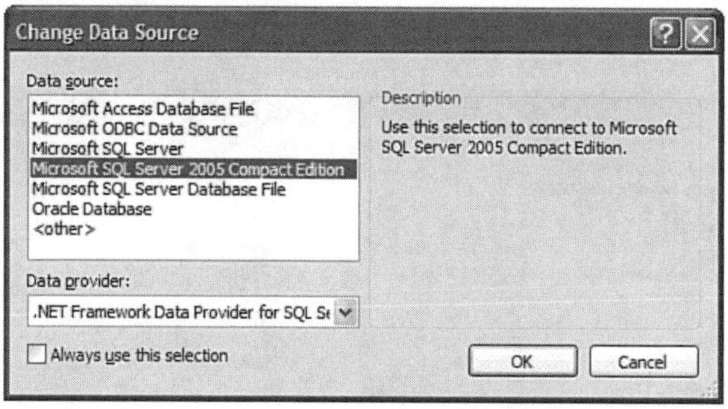

**FIGURE 1.15**    VS 2005 SP1 Change Data Source Dialog Box

**FIGURE 1.16**    VS 2005 Change Data Source Dialog Box Database File

Mobile Database and for SQL Server Compact Edition, the file type is called Database file as shown in Figures 1.17 and 1.18. Similarly, if you are using Visual Studio 2005 RTM version, you will select the SQL Mobile Database type to add SQL Server Compact Edition database as shown in Figure 1.18.

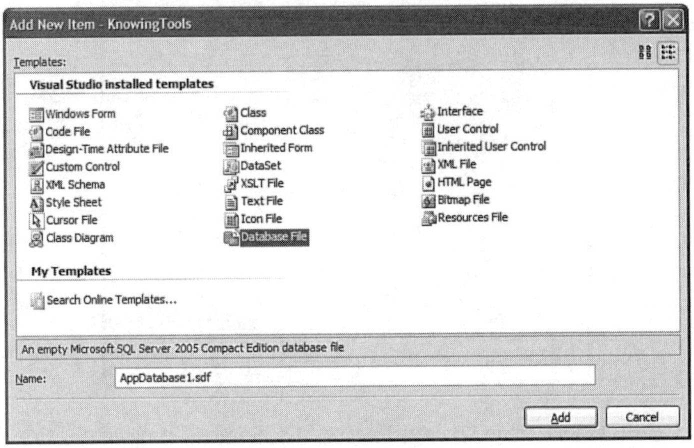

FIGURE 1.17    VS 2005 SP1 Add New Item Dialog Box

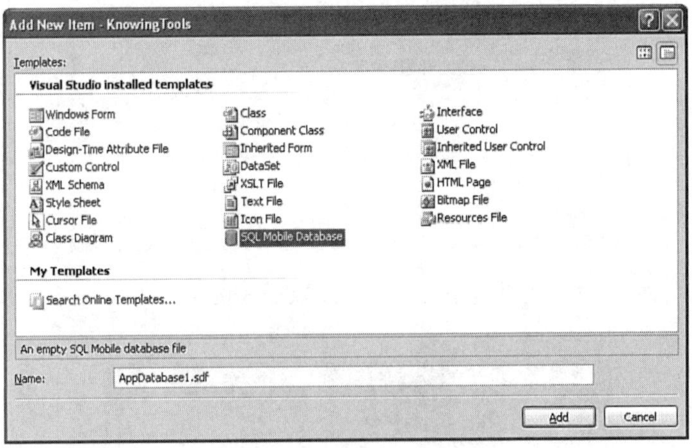

FIGURE 1.18    VS 2005 Add New Item Dialog Box

The next section explains in detail the type of changes you will notice in SQL Server and Visual Studio dialog boxes due to the SQL Mobile name change to SQL Server Compact Edition. Server Type, Strings, Dialog headers, Nodes in Explorer, Tool tip, etc. have all been changed to reflect the new name. The name change will not have any impact on functionality.

# Architectural Fundamentals

This chapter uses multiple concurrent views to describe the SQL Server Compact Edition architecture. In an enterprise application, SQL Server Compact Edition is one component that interacts with Web Server and SQL Server. An application architect responsible for a client application wants to know the data access architecture on a client machine or device. A developer writing an application for a Smart device or client device will be more interested in knowing the in-depth component details that SQL Server Compact Edition has and their relationships. Deployment engineers and support engineers want to know how SQL Server Compact Edition and other solutions are deployed in a production environment. End-users, project managers, and senior managers want to understand the simple and abstract form of architecture.

SQL Mobile 3.0 and SQL Compact Edition 3.1 have the same architecture.

## Logical Architecture

Figure 1.19 shows a use-case view or scenario of logical architecture. There are a number of client devices and client machines. All client machines have local storage and use SQL Server Compact Edition as a database. In addition, the clients using SQL Server Compact Edition can synchronize the data with a backend SQL Server through a Web Server.

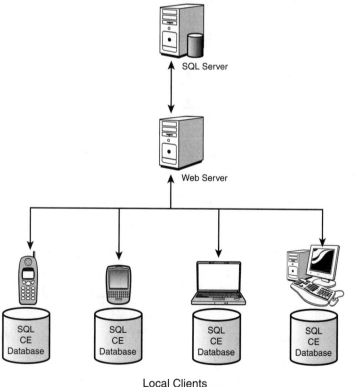

Local Clients

**FIGURE 1.19** Scenario View

The Web Server and backend SQL Server can be present on one computer. This is termed a *Single Server Environment*. In a *Multiple Server Environment*, a Web Server is installed on one computer and an SQL Server on another computer on the network.

For security and scalability, a Multiple Server Environment is recommended in enterprise production. For completing the sample exercises in the book you can create a Single Server Environment.

## Connectivity Components View

We have decomposed the architecture further as shown in Figure 1.20 and depict the SQL Server Compact Edition components used to synchronize the data with a backend SQL Server. The SQL Server Compact Edition Client Agent and SQL Server Compact Edition Server Agent are the primary components used in connectivity. You use the SQL Server Compact Edition Client Agent on each of the client devices and the SQL Server Compact Edition Server Agent on a Web Server. The SQL Server Compact Edition Client Agent interacts with the SQL Server Compact Edition Server Agent to synchronize the data.

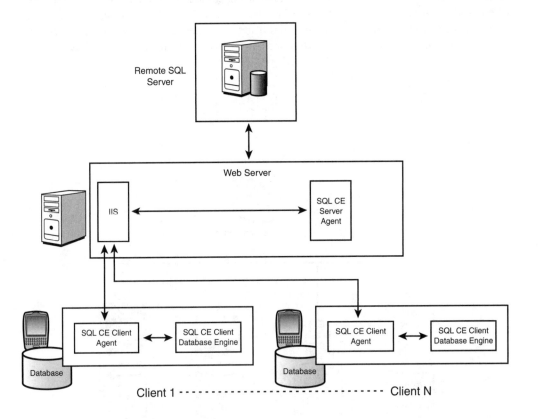

**FIGURE 1.20**   Connectivity Components View

Merge Replication and Remote Data Access are two built-in mechanisms to synchronize data between the SQL Server Compact Edition and SQL Server. For more information on both Merge Replication and Remote Data Access exercises, see Chapter 12, *Synchronizing Data with Merge Replication.*

---
**NOTE**
_____

You can synchronize data with SQL Server 2000 or SQL Server 2005.

### Client Agent

The SQL Server Compact Edition Client Agent component is available as `sqlceca30.dll`. The Client Agent will interact with the SQL Server Compact Edition Server Agent and the database engine. You will be using the Client Agent method and properties to implement Merge Replication and Remote Data Access. The Client Agent and Server Agent components use data compression. Compression reduces the amount of data transmitted and encryption ensures the safety of sensitive data. Replication can be performed over wired, wireless local area networks (LANs), and wide area networks (WANs) such as GPRS. Client Agent has following responsibilities:

- Managing database subscriptions.

- Enabling change tracking in the storage engine.

- Resolving conflict during synchronization.

- Securing transmission of data during synchronization.

- Compressing data in synchronization.

### Server Agent

The SQL Server Compact Edition Server Agent is deployed on a Web Server. You deploy the Server Agent separately. The SQL Server Compact Edition Server Agent receives an HTTP request from the SQL Server Compact Edition Client Agent. The SQL Server Compact Edition Server Agent interacts with the SQL Server and returns the results set back to the SQL Server Compact Edition Client Agent. The Server Agent components run as an ISAPI extension and use the authentication, authorization, and encryption services present in IIS to secure communications with the replication agent on the client. In Chapter 12, *Synchronizing Data with Merge Replication,* and Chapter 13, *Synchronizing Data with Remote Data Access*, we will discuss in detail the interaction between the SQL Server Compact Edition Server Agent and the SQL Server.

### The Storage Engine

The SQL Server Compact Edition database engine manages the database. For data synchronization, the engine does a special task of tracking. With every record in a table it maintains information to track whether a record is added, deleted, or updated.

## Client Components View

In the previous architecture diagram you have seen components that are used in connectivity. On a client computer or on a client device, the application will use an ADO.NET or OLE DB provider for the SQL Server Compact Edition to access and manipulate the database. Figure 1.21 demonstrates the component used in programmatic access.

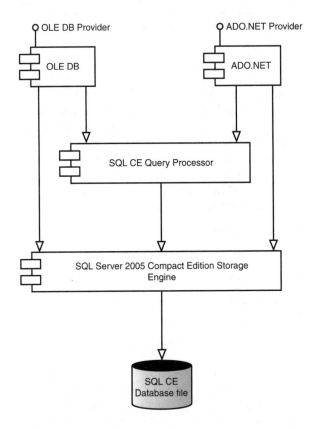

**FIGURE 1.21**    Client Components View

### SQL Server Compact Edition Database Engine

SQL Server Compact Edition database engine manages data. The database engine allows you to store, access, secure, and maintain data. The database engine has two parts:

- Storage engine

- Query processor

### Storage Engine

The storage engine is the lowest component in the stack and it directly interacts with the SQL Server Compact Edition database file and is encapsulated in `sqlcese30.dll`.

The storage engine is responsible for managing data, metadata, transactions, and database constraints. Optimized for mobile database and embedded database requirements, the storage engine is the foundation and lowest layer in the SQL Server 2005 Compact Edition stack. To meet the performance and size requirements of the SQL Server Compact Edition, there is a lot of functionality packed into the 400K database engine, more than most traditional storage engines.

The storage engine uses a main shared memory section along with a number of shared memory segments providing a variable sized lock pool to coordinate between multiple connections of the same database from different processes. Although the SQL Server Compact Edition allows for multiple connections, you can open the database exclusively if you do not want other connections or applications accessing your database at the same time.

To provide access to multiple users, the storage engine uses a shared buffer pool. The storage engine maintains information about database pages and has the following responsibilities:

- Exposing operations to create, update, and delete records from tables.

- Exposing operations to read and iterate records from tables.

- Exposing operations to create, update, and delete indexes.

- Exposing operations to traverse indexes.

- Maintaining and enforcing constraints for primary key, unique keys, and foreign keys.

- Providing ACID transactions.

- Providing encryption and compression functionality.

- Providing a mechanism to track inserted, updated, and deleted records.

### NOTE

The storage engines are different in SQL Server Compact Edition 2.0 and SQL Server Compact Edition 3.x.

### Query Processor

The goal of the query processor is to compile and execute SQL queries. The query processor component is encapsulated in `sqlceqp30.dll`. The query processor parses, compiles, and optimizes SQL queries. The query processor is also responsible for providing statistical information on the process of compiling and optimizing a query into an execution plan—a sequence of operations that produces the results. By providing useful insight into query costs and optimization, application designers can better optimize their data access techniques.

Your ability to tune SQL queries depends on your knowledge of the query processor. The following list describes the various stages of query processing:

- Parse the SQL queries.

- Validate SQL queries and expressions.

- Compile and optimize the query.

- Do query optimization on indexes and joins.

- Create and use statistical information.

- Generate query execution plan.

- Execute the query.

- Return the results of query.

### OLE DB

Object Linking and Embedding Database (OLE DB) is an API designed to access various kinds of data stores in a uniform way. OLE DB is a set of COM interfaces and consists of a consumer and a provider. Consumers are the applications that need to access data and the provider component implements the interface and provides data to the consumer.

The OLE DB provider for SQL Server Compact Edition implements the OLE DB interfaces. OLE DB provider for SQL Server Compact Edition exposes the data stored in the SQL Server Compact Edition database. Chapter 8, *Introducing Native Access,* lists complete details about the OLE DB provider for SQL Server Compact Edition as well as the differences between the OLE DB provider for SQL Server Compact Edition and general OLE DB interfaces.

### ADO.NET

ADO.NET is part of .NET Framework and .NET Compact Framework. ADO.NET exposes data access functionality in .NET languages. Using the data providers you can connect to a database, execute queries, and retrieve results. Managed applications can programmatically access SQL Server Compact Edition databases on supported devices using the ADO.NET data provider in the System.Data.SqlServerCe namespace.

ADO.NET consists of two providers:

- .NET Compact Framework data provider for SQL Server Compact Edition.

- Compact Framework data provider for SQL Server.

The ADO.NET data provider interacts directly with the query processor and storage engine that were initially designed to work well with managed code.

ADO.NET consists of two parts: Data Provider and Data Sets. In Chapter 7, *Programming SQL Server 2005 Compact Edition with ADO.NET,* you will learn the two parts and classes available.

## The Development View

The Development architecture view shown in Figure 1.22 demonstrates that you can write managed and native applications to access and maintain data in the SQL Server Compact Edition database. The architecture shows an SQL Server Compact Edition component deployed in a development environment. Apart from explaining the static structure of a development environment, Figure 1.22 also shows how to invoke SQL Server Compact Edition components.

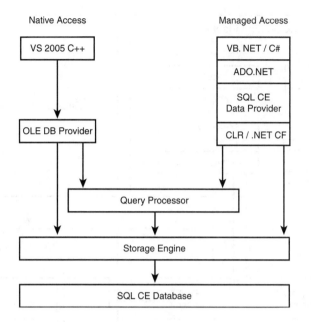

**FIGURE 1.22**    Development View

Developers can programmatically access data and features in Microsoft SQL Server 2005 Compact Edition by using C++ in an unmanaged application or in one of the .NET programming languages in a managed application. By utilizing the SQL syntax, OLE DB provider interfaces, and the ADO.NET programming model common with other SQL Server 2005 editions, SQL Server Compact Edition allows developers to apply their existing skills. Chapters 7 and 8 will explain managed and native programming and take you to the next level of abstraction.

## Deployment View

As discussed, SQL Server Compact Edition database is deployed on a client device or desktop as a local store. In order to synchronize data with a backend SQL Server you also need to deploy IIS Web Server. Figure 1.23 shows the distribution of the SQL Server Compact Edition components across a developer machine, a client machine, and a Web Server.

Figure 1.23 summarizes the installation of a database file, storage engine dll, query processor dll, and client agent dll on a client device. You will need ADO.NET or Managed Provider and dlls related to a client on a developer machine. You will install Server Agent and Replication provider dll on a Web Server.

Under the \Program Files\Microsoft SQL Server Compact Edition\v3.1 you will find the dlls shown in Table 1.2. Each dll represents one component.

In addition you have an Error dll, SQL Server Compact Edition name space, and a Compact utility installed on your machine.

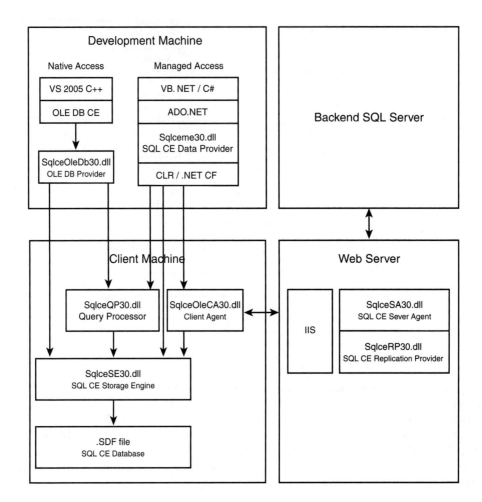

FIGURE 1.23    Deployment View

TABLE 1.2    **SQL Server Compact Edition components**

| Dll Name | Component |
| --- | --- |
| SqlCese30 | Storage engine |
| SqlCeqp30 | Query processor |
| SqlCeca | Client agent |
| SqlCeOLE DB30 | OLE DB provider |
| SqlCeme30 | Native dll used by managed provider |
| SqlCeer30en | Error |
| System.Data.SqlServerCe | Sql Server Compact Edition namespace |
| SqlceCompact30 | Compact utility |

# Compact Edition Features Related to SQL Server 2005 Features

Although SQL Server Compact Edition shares a lot of common features with SQL Server 2005, it is still an embedded process database engine and a partial subset of the Microsoft SQL Server. First, they are completely separate code bases and unlike SQL Server 2005, Compact Edition does not support views, triggers, or stored procedures. Security features in the SQL Server Compact Edition do not include role-based security, and password and encryption are at the database level only. However, SQL Server Compact Edition does come with great .NET language support such as user-defined types, and user-defined functions, and supports a subset of data types. There is no binary compatibility between SQL Server and SQL Server 2005 Compact Edition though. SQL Server does offer some additional features such as ADO.NET `SqlCeResultSet` object, allowing fast direct access to data in a database. There is also no unnecessary overhead, like caching, since the database and the application are in the same process on the machine or device.

## Choosing SQL Express *Versus* SQL Server Compact Edition

Microsoft SQL Server is available in Workgroup, Standard, Enterprise, and Express editions. SQL Server 2005 Express Edition is a free version of SQL Server 2005.

> **NOTE**
>
> Oracle and IBM also provide Oracle Express and DB2 Express.

The free Express Edition version enables the developer and small business to use relational database functionality on a desktop. When the business grows and needs to move to a model where multiple users connect to a central database, it can easily migrate to a higher-level edition of SQL Server 2005.

Both SQL Server Express Edition and SQL Server Compact Edition can be used as a free relational database for local store. You should choose SQL Server Express Edition or SQL Server Compact Edition considering your application needs.

SQL Server Express Edition is a restricted version of SQL Serve 2005. SQL Server Express Edition uses the same database engine as used by SQL Server 2005. SQL Server Compact Edition is a database written from scratch to meet the requirements for mobile and embedded databases. The footprint of SQL Server Express Edition is high compared to SQL Server Compact Edition. SQL Server Express Edition has 50 MB of footprint, whereas SQL Server Compact Edition has 1.5 MB of footprint. Both SQL Express and SQL Server Compact Edition support Merge Replication. SQL Server Compact Edition also supports the Remote Data Access mechanism. Remote Date Access functionality is not available in SQL Server Express Edition. SQL Server Compact Edition has a feature for a small footprint database such as SQLCEResultSet.

The biggest advantage with SQL Server Compact Edition is that it works on both a desktop and on a mobile device. SQL Server Compact Edition is stored in a single database file and you can move it from a desktop to a device and vice versa.

Both SQL Server Express Edition and SQL Server Compact Edition are free products and work on a desktop. SQL Server Compact Edition is suitable for an in-proc database. SQL Server Express Edition runs as a service and is suitable when you need the functionality of server platform.

## Summary

The need to mobilize a line of business applications is a fast growing trend in the market as it is quickly becoming apparent that the future of the computer industry is at the edge of the network. Mobilizing applications can offer a number of unique challenges, one of which is managing application data on a device and securely moving that data in and out of the enterprise.

SQL Server 2005 Compact Edition is a compact feature-rich database engine that can be utilized in applications that need to extend enterprise data management to the desktop and mobile devices. SQL Server synchronization technologies can be leveraged to address the challenge of developing highly available, occasionally connected mobile applications. We have also covered the components that make up SQL Server Compact Edition, their roles, and their interaction with one another to deliver this set of features.

At this time you probably have various questions—how much data to store on SQL CE, how to access and manipulate data on SQL Server Compact Edition on a memory constraint device, how and when to transfer the data between a backend server and SQL CE, what kinds of conflict can occur while synchronizing data? These are all critical parts of an enterprise mobile application.

In the upcoming chapters we will examine these questions in detail. Not only is SQL CE successful in meeting the final goal of building mobile applications and embedded applications, but it also has additional features that make the development processes much easier.

# Platform Support and Installation

Microsoft released SQL Server Mobile Edition 3.0 at the end of 2005 and then released SQL Server Compact Edition 3.1 in January 2007. The main difference between versions 3.0 and 3.1 is that the 3.1 licensing allows you to use SQL Server Compact Edition on both desktop- and laptop-based applications.

SQL Mobile 3.0 has restrictions that allow you to build only Smart devices and Tablet PC applications. Building a desktop-based application using SQL Mobile was not allowed. The SQL Mobile restriction on desktop is history now and SQL Server Compact Edition 3.1 can be used on desktop, tablet PCs, and mobile devices. In this chapter you will understand the desktop and mobile devices operating systems on which SQL Server Compact Edition is supported. You will also learn how to set up a development environment and how to deploy your application and required components in a run time environment. When you complete the chapter you will have SQL Server, Visual Studio, SQL Server Compact Edition, IIS Web Server, and Windows Mobile SDK installed on your computer. You can then use this environment to complete the exercises presented in the book.

## Software and Hardware Requirements

This section lists the platform you can target to build SQL Server Compact Edition based applications. In a run time environment, the application and SQL Server Compact Edition are installed on a device or on a desktop. Also discussed in this section is the prerequisite operating system that is required on client machines.

The development environment consists of Visual Studio, SQL Server, SQL Server Compact Edition, and IIS Web Server. Included are the operating system and the hardware needed for SQL Server, Visual Studio, and IIS.

## Platform Support for SQL Server Compact Edition

Microsoft released SQL Server Mobile Edition 3.0 for the mobile information worker. In versions 3.1 and higher, Microsoft also added support for desktop-based systems. You can now use SQL Server Compact Edition in a desktop-based application.

It is interesting to know the history of SQL Server Compact Edition and how platform support has been expanded over the years. SQL Server 2000 Compact Edition (SQL CE 2.0) is a relational database for mobile devices. To manage an SQL CE 2.0 database you need to use the Query Analyzer tool on a device, or write a program and execute it on a device. To make the development easier, Microsoft integrated version 3.0 SQL Server Mobile Edition with Visual Studio 2005 and SQL Server 2005.

To use SQL Server Mobile Edition 3.0 within Visual Studio 2005 and SQL Server 2005, Microsoft added desktop support with SQL Mobile. The desktop support was restricted and you could use only SQL Mobile if you had SQL Server 2005 or Visual Studio 2005 installed on the same computer. The x86 support and tight integration with Visual Studio and SQL Server 2005 Management Studio made the management of the database easier. SQL Server Mobile Edition and SQL Express are both free databases. Microsoft positioned SQL Mobile for Mobile devices and SQL Server Express for the x86 based system. Due to SQL Express positioning on an x86 based system, SQL Mobile had a restriction about its usage on an x86 system. Development was allowed on a desktop with SQL Mobile but production was not.

### NOTE

Microsoft received a lot of feedback from the user and MVP communities and finally decided to remove the restriction. Now SQL Server Compact Edition Database can be used on mobile devices, tablet PCs, and on a desktop.

Following is a list of operating systems available on desktop, Tablet PCs, and mobile devices on which SQL Server Compact Edition is supported.

### Mobile Device

SQL Server Compact Edition is a relational database with a small footprint making it suitable for Smart devices. One of the following operating systems is needed to run SQL Server Compact Edition on a Smart device:

- Windows Mobile Pocket PC 2003

- Windows CE 5.0 or later

- Windows Mobile Pocket PC 2005 or later

• Windows Mobile Smartphone 2005 or later

Windows CE 5.0, Windows Mobile Pocket PC 2005, and Windows Mobile Smartphone 2005 have a common Windows CE 5.0 kernal.

Additional requirements for running SQL Server Compact Edition are .NET Compact Framework version 2 and a minimum of 1.5 MB of storage space.

### NOTE
To check the operating system version, click on the device's Start | Setting menu option. In the Settings dialog, choose System Tab and double click on the About icon. The version tab will display the Window Mobile OS version and the device processor.

### Tablet PC
Tablet PCs have processing power and memory similar to desktop-based systems. The Ink support on a Tablet PC makes it usable for the office or mobile worker. For example, an employee can walk around with a Tablet PC and enter the inventory data into a Tablet PC-based application. The application needs to connect to a central database which is not ideal for mobile workers; a local data store is better suited for mobile worker scenarios. SQL Server 2005 Compact Edition is suitable in these scenarios as it provides a relational database a with small footprint and it is not necessary to buy an SQL Server 2005 license copy for each mobile worker.

The Windows XP Tablet PC Edition operating system is needed to run SQL Server Compact Edition on a Tablet PC.

### NOTE
Server Mobile Edition 3.0 is not supported on a desktop.

### NOTE
SQL Server Mobile Edition 3.0 is supported on a Tablet PC. SQL Server Compact Edition 3.1 and higher versions will be supported on a desktop.

### Desktop
You can use SQL Server Compact Edition 3.1 on a desktop. Desktop applications that need local data storage can use SQL Server Compact Edition database 3.1. SQL CE 2.0 was supported only on mobile devices. One main limitation in the SQL CE 2.0 version was the need to manage the database on a device. To allow rapid application development SQL Mobile 3.0 has desktop support. However there was a restriction in SQL Mobile version 3.0. You were allowed to use SQL Mobile 3.0 on desktop only with Visual Studio or SQL Server 2005.

Desktop support also enables you to develop applications in which desktop, laptop, and mobile devices can use the same database. You can also develop applications for mobile workers that use desktop, laptop, Tablet PC, or mobile devices as a client machine.

SQL Server Compact Edition is a relational database similar to SQL Server and is built with few dlls. You need to reference these dlls and provide the database file path. SQL Server Compact Edition usage is similar to an Access database but different from an SQL Server because the SQL Server needs to run as a background service.

SQL Server Compact Edition support on the desktop enables many useful scenarios such as the following:

- When you want to share the same database among multiple types of client desktop, Tablet PC, and mobile devices.

- When you require local storage on desktop or laptop clients.

- When using applications in conjunction with SQL Server Express or Microsoft Access.

On a desktop you can use SQL Server Compact Edition on Windows XP, Windows 2000, Windows 2003, and Windows Vista. One of following operating systems is needed to build an SQL Server Compact Edition based application on a desktop.

- Windows XP Professional Edition SP2

- Windows XP Home Edition SP2

- Windows XP Media Center Edition 2002 SP2

- Windows XP Media Center Edition 2004 SP2

- Windows XP Media Edition 2005

- Windows XP Tablet Edition SP2

- Windows Professional 2000 SP4

- Windows Server 2000 SP4

- Windows Server 2003 Enterprise Edition SP1

- Windows Server 2003 Datacenter Edition SP1

- Windows Server 2003 R2, Standard Edition

- Windows Server 2003 R2, Enterprise Edition

- Windows Server 2003 R2, Datacenter Edition

- Windows Vista

## Platform Support for SQL Server

In this book you will create an exercise to build an SQL Server Compact Edition application and synchronize data with a backend SQL Server 2005. The following hardware is needed to run SQL Server 2005:

- Intel or compatible Pentium 600 MHz or greater processor (recommended processor speed is 1 GHz or greater)

- Recommended 512 MB of RAM or more

- Recommended hard disk space of 250 MB

SQL Server 2005 is available in the Developer Edition, Express Edition, Workgroup Edition and SQL Express Edition. Each edition has a different Operating System requirement. You should refer to the SQL Server 2005 Help to determine the hardware and software needed for SQL Server 2005. In general, SQL Server 2005 can run on the following operating systems:

- Windows 2000 SP4 Professional Edition

- Windows 2000 SP4 Server

- Windows 2000 SP4 Advanced Server

- Windows 2000 SP4 Datacenter Edition

- Windows XP SP2 Professional Edition

- Windows XP SP2 Media Edition

- Windows XP SP2 Tablet Edition

- Windows 2003 or later

- Windows 2003 Enterprise Edition or later

- Windows 2003 Datacenter Edition or later

- Windows Small Business Server 2003 SP1 Standard Edition

- Windows Small Business Server 2003 SP1 Standard Edition

- Windows Vista

## Platform Support for IIS

You will need to set up a Web Server to synchronize data between SQL Server Compact Edition and a backend SQL Server. You will also need to install IIS 5.x version or later on a Web Server. One of the following operating systems will also need to be installed in order to run the Internet Information Server:

- Windows XP

- Windows 2000 SP4 or later versions

- Windows Server 2003

- Windows Vista

Additionally, you will need .NET Framework version 2.0 or later on a computer running IIS.

## Platform Support for Visual Studio

You can run Visual Studio 2005 on Windows XP, Windows 2000, Windows 2003 Server, and Windows Vista. One of following operating systems is needed to run Visual Studio:

- Windows XP Media Center Edition

- Windows XP Professional

- Windows XP Tablet PC Edition

- Windows 2000 Professional SP4 or later versions

- Windows 2000 Server SP4 or later versions

- Microsoft Windows Server 2003

- Windows Vista

# Obtaining SQL CE

SQL Server Compact Edition 3.x is available as a Web download and is also available with SQL Server 2005 and Visual Studio 2005. Table 2.1 provides a quick summary about the SQL Server Compact Edition versions available.

TABLE 2.1    SQL Server Compact Edition Versions

| SQL Server/Visual Studio Version | SQL Server Compact Edition Version |
|---|---|
| SQL Server 2005 | SQL Server 2005 Mobile Edition 3.0 |
| SQL Server 2005 SP1 | SQL Server 2005 Mobile Edition 3.0 |
| Visual Studio 2005 | SQL Server 2005 Mobil Mobile Edition 3.0 |
| SQL Server 2005 SP2 or later | SQL Server 2005 Compact Edition 3.1 |
| Visual Studio 2005 SP1 or later | SQL Server 2005 Compact Edition 3.1 |

### NOTE

You should visit the SQL Server Compact Edition site to check for updates.

http://www.microsoft.com/sql/editions/compact/default.mspx page contains an overview of the SQL Server Compact Edition product.

http://www.microsoft.com/sql/editions/compact/downloads.mspx page contains the download information for the SQL Server Compact Edition product.

## SQL Server Compact Edition Packages

You can install SQL Server Compact Edition packages from the Microsoft Download Center. SQL Server Compact Edition is available in ten languages. The EN string in the package name denotes the English language. You should download a corresponding MSI if you want SQL Server Compact Edition in a different language.

Table 2.2 provides a summary of installer packages available for the SQL Server Compact Edition.

**TABLE 2.2    SQL Server Compact Edition Packages**

| Packages | Purpose |
| --- | --- |
| SQLSERVERCE31-EN.MSI | Installs SQL Server Compact Edition Engine and Core component. |
| | This file is also placed in <disk>\Program Files\ Microsoft SQL Server Compact Edition\v3.1\SDK\bin\Desktop folder. |
| SSCE31SDK-ENU.MSI | Installs SQL Server Compact Edition Developer Software Development kit. These components are useful for developing and deploying applications for mobile devices. |
| SSCE31VSTools-ENU.exe | Installs SQL Server Compact Edition tools for Visual Studio 2005 SP1. |
| | Visual Studio RTM deploys SQL Mobile (SQL CE 3.0). This download comes with the Visual Studio Service Pack 1 and upgrades the Visual Studio UI. After the upgrade, Visual Studio refers SQL Server Compact Edition related dialog as SQL Server Compact Edition. Without this upgrade, it refers dialog as SQL Mobile. |
| | This package also installs DataDirectory and the ClickOnce feature. These features make deployment easy. |
| SQLCE30SETUPEN.MSI | Installs the SQL Server Compact Edition Server Tools. |
| | The server tools should be installed on the Web Server. The server tool components are required to synchronize data between SQL Server Compact Edition and SQL Server. |
| SSCE31BOL-EN.MSI | Installs the SQL Server Compact Edition Books-on-line. |
| | The file is also placed in <disk>\ Program Files\Microsoft SQL Server Compact Edition\v3.1\SDK\Docs\EN folder. |

# Setting Up the Environment

In Chapter 1 you learned about the development and deployment architecture. To use SQL Server Compact Edition at run time, you need Storage Engine and Query Processor. To access the database using a managed and native provider, you need ADO.NET and OLE DB provider. You also need Client Agent and Server Agent to synchronize the data between a backend SQL Server and an SQL Server Compact Edition client.

Also needed are additional Development Tools components to use SQL Server Compact Edition at design and development time.

The following section provides in-depth details of packages, cabinet files, and dll that are installed on a developer computer and on client devices. Each piece of the game and what it does are explained.

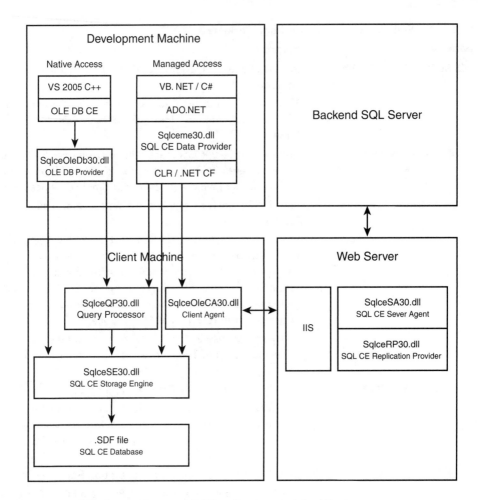

**FIGURE 2.1**    SQL Server Compact Edition Deployment Architecture

As shown in Figure 2.1, Visual Studio, Windows Mobile SDK, ActiveSync, and SQL Server Compact Edition client components are set up on a developer computer.

## The Development Environment

Visual Studio provides a single development environment to create the SQL Server Compact Edition database, design mobile, and desktop-based application. You can manage the SQL Server Compact Edition database and also design SQL queries using Visual Studio. Visual Studio 2005 is the primary component for your development environment. You will enhance Visual Studio 2005 for devices by installing Windows Mobile SDK for pocket PC and devices.

You should also have SQL Server Management Studio to manage the SQL Server Compact Edition database on the developer computer. You can tune queries for better performance query plans in SQL Server Management Studio.

**NOTE**

If your application needs to synchronize data with the backend SQL Server, you will also set up an IIS Web Server. You also need to install SQL Server Compact Edition Server Tools on a computer running IIS. In Chapter 12 you will set up an IIS Web Server and install the Server Tool component on the IIS Server.

To set up your development environment and to complete the book exercise, you need to install SQL Server 2005, Visual Studio 2005, ActiveSync, Windows Mobile SDK for Pocket PC, and Windows Mobile SDK for Smartphone.

You can install all the above components on one computer or on separate computers. If you are working alone and learning SQL Server Compact Edition, you can deploy Visual Studio, SQL Server, SQL Server Compact Edition, and IIS Web Server on a computer and complete all the exercises available in this book. You can build a full-fledged project on one computer.

If you are working as part of a team and developing a project, you can deploy Visual Studio and SQL Server Compact Edition components into each developer machine. The Web Server and backend SQL Server can be common for the whole team. You can deploy Web Server and SQL Server on the same machine or onto two different machines.

## Production Environment

After you complete the development of SQL Server Compact Edition, you will deploy the application in a run time production environment.

There are three main components of a run time environment:

- Client device or computer
- Backend SQL Server
- IIS Web Server

### Client
You will deploy the SQL Server Compact Edition based application, SQL Server Compact Edition, and .NET Compact Framework on devices. You also need to deploy the cabinet files specific to the platform and processor of your device. You can deploy the .NET compact Framework, SQL Server Compact Edition, and applications separately or you can package and deploy them together onto your client.

### Backend SQL Server
You can use Merge Replication or RDA to synchronize data with backend SQL Server. In Chapters 12 and 13 you will learn how to use Merge Replication and RDA.

### IIS Web Server
Merge Replication and RDA communicate with the SQL Server Compact Edition client using IIS Web Server. On a Web Server you need to deploy IIS and the SQL Server Compact Edition Server Agent component.

# Installing SQL Server Compact Edition

Now you know the hardware and software requirements for a developer computer. It is time to go through the steps for installing SQL Server 2005, Visual Studio 2005, Windows Mobile SDK, and SQL Server Compact Edition.

## Installing SQL Server Compact Edition with SQL Server 2005

SQL Server Compact Edition is available as installation components with SQL Server 2005 and SQL Server 2005 Express. Installing SQL Server 2005 installs SQL Server 2005 as well as SQL Server Compact Edition. If you are installing SQL Server 2005 RTM version or SQL Server 2005 SP1, SQL Server Compact Edition version 3.0 (SQL Mobile) will also be installed on your computer. Installing SQL Server 2005 SP2 or higher installs SQL Server Compact Edition version 3.1.

> **NOTE**
>
> The SQL Server Compact Edition Developer Software Development Kit is not installed with SQL Server 2005.

You should refer to SQL Server or SQL Server Express Edition instructions for installation.

## Installing SQL Server Compact Edition with Visual Studio 2005

Visual Studio 2005 provides support for mobile device development. Visual Studio 2005 Standard, Professional and Team System Edition includes SQL Server Compact Edition. Visual Studio installation CS includes an installer package for SQL Server Compact Edition. When you install Visual Studio, you can choose to use Default or Custom installation. The default option automatically installs the SQL Server Compact Edition Developer Software Development Kit. In custom installation there is no option to check or uncheck the SQL Server Compact Edition Developer Software Development Kit. Custom installation has options for Smart Device Programmability for various languages. The SQL Server Compact Edition Developer Software Development Kit is installed if Smart Device Programmability is checked as shown in Figure 2.2.

Once the installation is complete you can verify it in the Add or Remove Program applet. The Add or Remove Program applet shows the following:

- SQL Server 2005 Compact Edition
- SQL Server 2005 Compact Edition Books Online
- SQL Server 2005 Compact Edition Developer Software Development Kit

If you have installed Visual Studio RTM, the following SQL Mobile versions (SQL Server Compact Edition 3.0) will be installed on your machine:

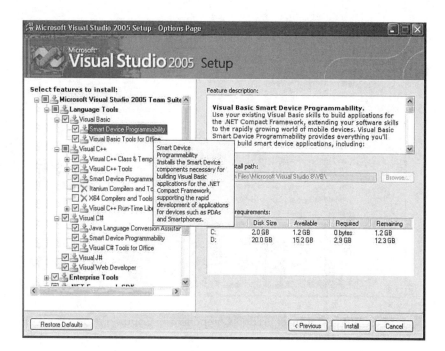

**FIGURE 2.2**   Visual Studio Setup

- SQL Server 2005 Mobile Edition
- SQL Server 2005 Mobile Edition Books Online
- SQL Server 2005 Mobile Developer Tools

Table 2.3 summarizes the SQL Server Compact Edition version that is installed with Visual Studio 2005.

**TABLE 2.3**   SQL Server Compact Edition Versions

| Visual Studio Version | SQL Server Compact Edition Version |
|---|---|
| Visual Studio 2005 | SQL Server 2005 Mobil Mobile Edition 3.0 |
| Visual Studio 2005 SP1 or later | SQL Server 2005 Compact Edition 3.1 |

VS 2005 installation does not have an option to install/uninstall SQL Server Compact Edition components. You can install/uninstall SQL Server Compact Edition components using the Add or Remove Program applet on the computer. To uninstall SQL Server Compact Edition components, you can use the Add or Remove Programs dialog box. Figure 2.3 shows how to remove the Microsoft SQL Server 2005 Compact Edition Developer Software Development Kit.

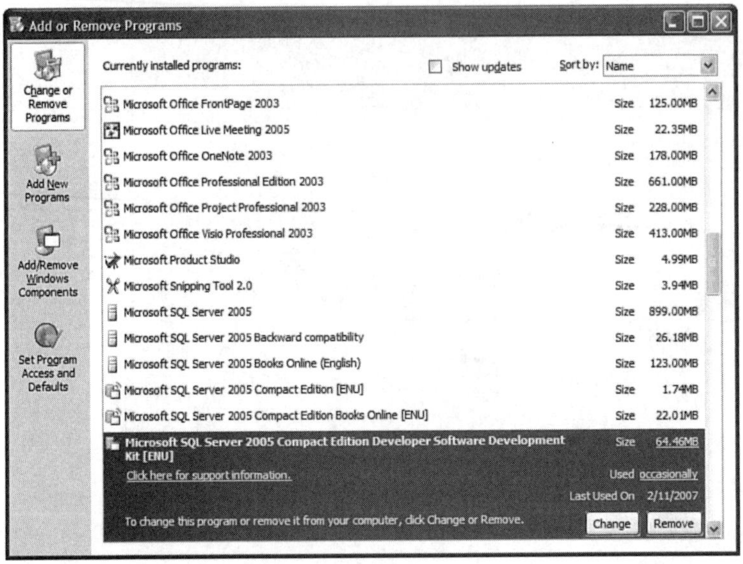

**FIGURE 2.3    SQL Server Compact Edition Component in Control Panel**

To install the SQL Server Compact Edition Developer Software Development Kit again, access the SSCE31SDK-ENU.MSI package and install.

---

**NOTE**

In version 3.0 SQL Mobile components were packaged in SQLMobile30DevTools.MSI.

---

### Installing Windows Mobile SDK

The Windows Mobile SDK extends the Visual Studio capability and enables you to develop managed and native applications for Pocket PC and Smartphone. To write an application for Pocket PC and Smartphone you should download and install corresponding Windows Mobile SDKs for Windows Mobile Pocket PC and Windows Mobile Smartphone.

### Windows Mobile Branding

The branding has also changed between Windows Mobile 5.0 and Windows Mobile 6.0. Windows Mobile 5.0 uses Pocket PC and Smartphone SDK terminology. Windows Mobile 6.0 uses Professional Edition and Standard Edition terminology. The Professional Edition is equivalent to the Pocket PC Edition and the Standard Edition is equivalent to the SmartPhone Edition.

The code sample in this book uses both Windows Mobile 5.0 and Windows Mobile 6.0. The example in this book can be used on Windows Mobile 5.0 or Windows Mobile 6.0.

TABLE 2.3    Windows Mobile SDK

| Packages | Purpose |
| --- | --- |
| Windows Mobile 5.0 Pocket PC SDK | You can create a .NET CF application for Windows Mobile 5.0 Pocket PC and later. |
| Windows Mobile 5.0 Smartphone SDK | You can create a .NET CF application for Windows Mobile 5.0 Smartphone and later. |

Windows Mobile 5.0 and Windows Mobile 6.0 SDK for Pocket PC and Smartphone are available on the Web at the Microsoft Download Center.

In Visual Studio you choose the project type that you want to build. After you install Windows Mobile SDK for Pocket PC and Smartphone, Visual Studio will begin to show you the following two new project types ( see also Figure 2.4):

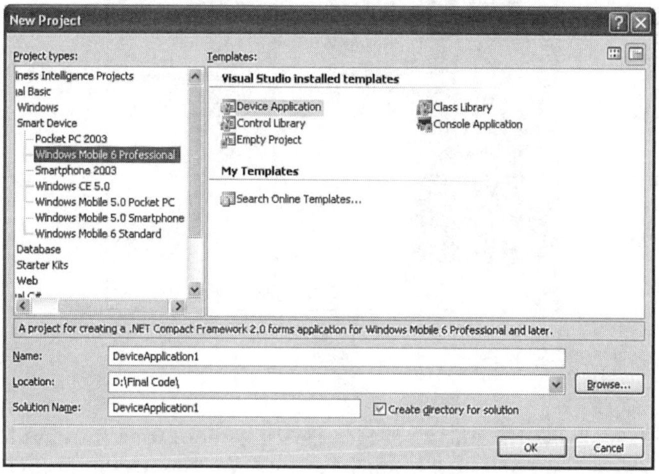

FIGURE 2.4    Project Type for Pocket PC and Smartphone

- Windows Mobile 5.0 Pocket PC and Windows Mobile 6.0 Professional Edition
- Windows Mobile 5.0 Smartphone and Windows Mobile 6.0 Standard Edition

You will be using these two project types for completing the exercises in this book.

### Installing Windows Mobile 5.0 Pocket PC
The installation steps are very simple. Go to the Microsoft Download Center and download Windows Mobile 5.0 Pocket PC SDK. You will be directed to a File Download dialog box as shown in Figure 2.5.

Click the Run button to initiate the install.

Click the Next button to initiate the installation as shown in Figure 2.6.

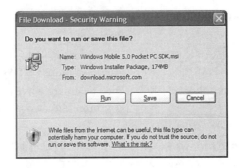

FIGURE 2.5    Download Windows Mobile Pocket PC SDK

FIGURE 2.6    Pocket PC SDK Setup

The next dialog box shows the End-User License Agreement for Windows Mobile 5.0 Pocket PC SDK. Once you have read the license, click on the Accept radio button as shown in Figure 2.7 and click Next to proceed with installation.

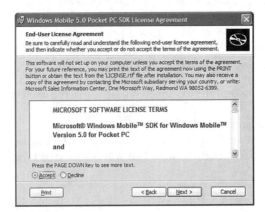

FIGURE 2.7    End-User License Agreement

Enter your and your company's names onto the Customer Information page as shown in Figure 2.8. Click Next to proceed.

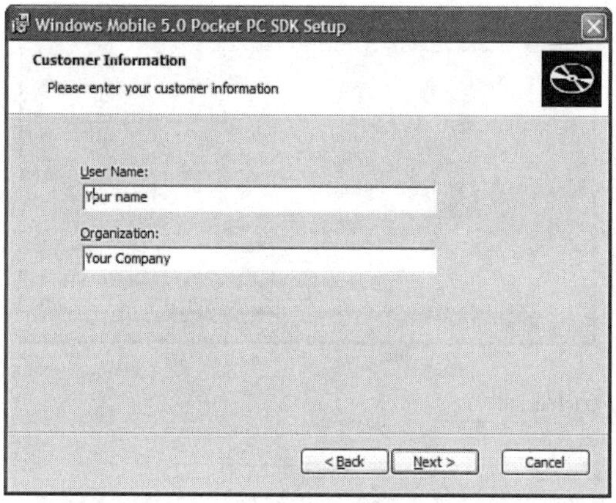

**FIGURE 2.8**    Customer Information

Specify the location to install Windows Mobile 5.0 Pocket PC SDK as shown in Figure 2.9 and click Next.

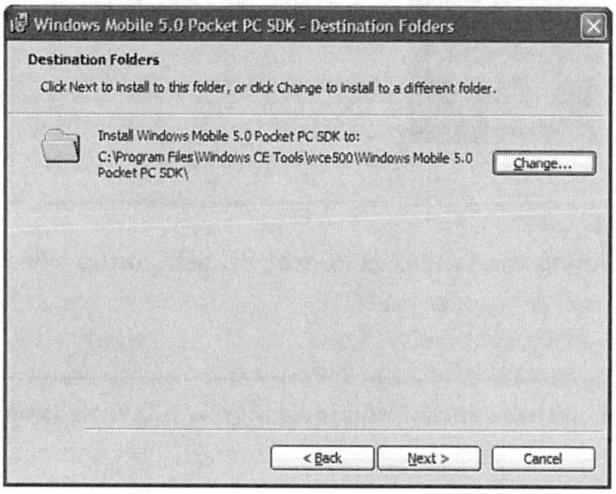

**FIGURE 2.9**    Destination Folders

Click Next to begin installing Microsoft Windows Mobile 5.0 Pocket PC SDK as shown in Figure 2.10.

As shown in Figure 2.11, click the Finish button once installation of Windows Mobile Pocket PC SDK is completed.

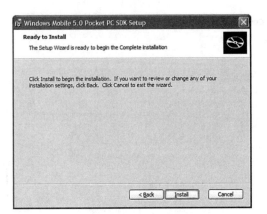

**FIGURE 2.10    Ready to Install**

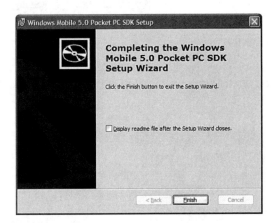

**FIGURE 2.11    Completing the Windows Pocket PC SDK Setup Wizard**

<u>**NOTE**</u>

You can follow similar steps to install Windows Mobile 6.0 Professional Edition.

### Installing Windows Mobile 5.0 Smartphone SDK

To install Windows Mobile 5.0 Smartphone SDK, go to the Microsoft Download Center and download Windows Mobile 5.0 Smartphone SDK. Figure 2.12 shows the File Download dialog box. Click the Run button to initiate the install.

Click the Next button to initiate the installation as shown in Figure 2.13.

Figure 2.14 shows the End-User License Agreement for Windows Mobile 5.0 Smartphone SDK dialog box. Once you have read the license, click on the Accept radio button and click Next to proceed with installation.

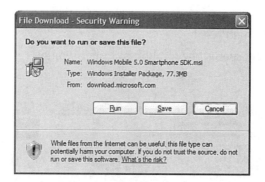

**FIGURE 2.12**    Download Windows Mobile Smartphone SDK

**FIGURE 2.13**    Smartphone SDK Setup Wizard

**FIGURE 2.14**    Smartphone SDK End-User License Agreement

Enter your and your company's names onto the Customer Information page as shown in Figure 2.15. Click Next to proceed.

As shown in Figure 2.16, specify the location to install Windows Mobile 5.0 Smartphone SDK and click Next.

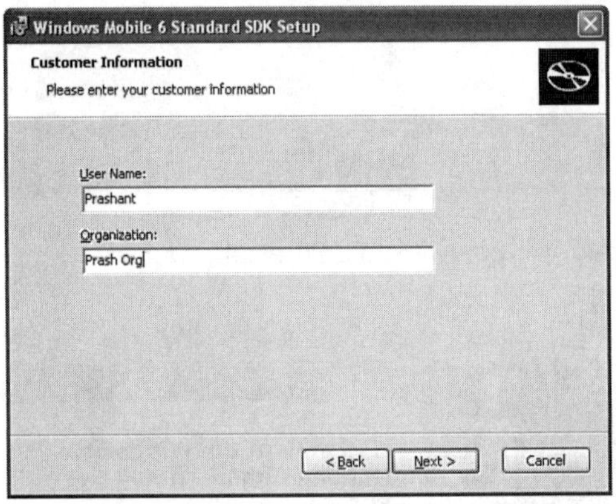

FIGURE 2.15    Customer Information

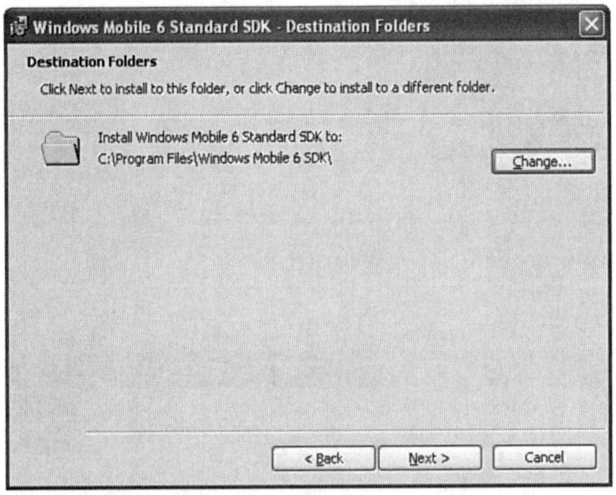

FIGURE 2.16    Destination Folders

As shown in Figure 2.17, click Install to begin installing Microsoft Windows Mobile 5.0 Pocket PC SDK.

Allow Window Mobile Pocket PC SDK to install.

Click the Finish button once installation of Windows Mobile Pocket PC SDK is completed as shown in Figure 2.18.

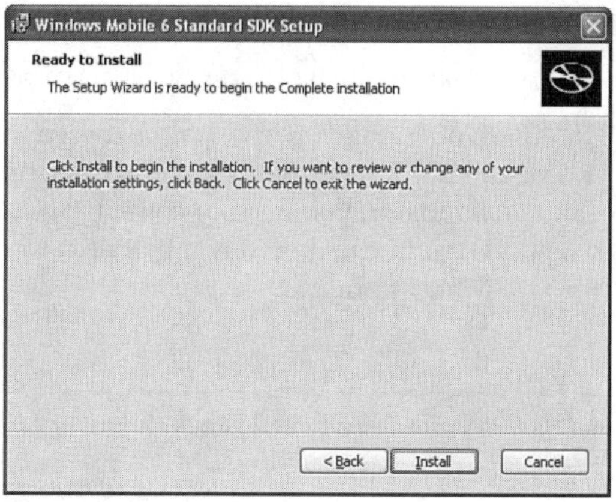

**FIGURE 2.17** Ready to Install

**FIGURE 2.18** Completing the Smartphone SDK Setup Wizard

**NOTE**

You can follow similar steps to install Windows Mobile 6.0 Standard Edition SDK.

## Installing ActiveSync

ActiveSync allows your Windows PC to communicate with a Windows mobile device. Using ActiveSync, you can synchronize emails, documents, pictures, and so on, between a device and a PC. You will need to install ActiveSync in a development environment. In a production environment, a Smart device can connect to an enterprise backend over internet/intranet. However, in a development environment, you need ActiveSync to deploy and debug an application. To install ActiveSync, download ActiveSync version 4.1 or later.

Details of the ActiveSync download and troubleshooting guide is available at

`http://www.microsoft.com/windowsmobile/activesync/default.mspx`.

Once you have installed ActiveSync, set up a partnership between a device or emulator and your PC. You can choose to have a standard or guest partnership. To synchronize data between a desktop and an emulator, you need to configure ActiveSync. Click on File | Configuration settings. Select DMA in the drop down box next to the "Allow Connection to One of the Following" option.

> **NOTE**
>
> Visual Studio supports DMA channel to communicate with Emulator.

## Installing IIS and SQL Server Compact Edition Server Tools

You need to install SQL Server Compact Edition Server Tool components if your application synchronizes data with SQL Server 2000 or the SQL Server 2005 database. SQL Server on a server machine and SQL Server Compact Edition on a client machine need to communicate with each other to synchronize data using a replication and RDA mechanism. The communication happens using the IIS Web Server. You need to deploy the SQL Server Compact Edition Server Tool component on the machine running IIS. This component is installed using `SqlCe30Setup[lang].exe` executable. The SQL Server Compact Edition Server Agent is available as a Web download and also with SQL Server 2005.

> **NOTE**
>
> SQL Server Compact Edition Server Tool installer packages are also available as Web downloads, with SQL Server 2005, and with Visual Studio.

Depending on your backend SQL Server version, you need to install a Server Tool package specific to the SQL Server version. Table 2.4 summarizes the Server Tools installer package.

**TABLE 2.4    Server Tools Component Packages**

| Package | Description |
| --- | --- |
| Sqlce30setupen.MSI | Server Tool components to synchronize with SQL Server 2005 |
| Sql2kensp3a.MSI | Server Tool components to synchronize data with SQL Server 2000 SP3a |
| Sql2kensp4.MSI | Server Tool components to synchronize data with SQL Server 2000 SP4 |

Depending upon your backend server, you need to install one of the packages listed in Table 2.4 on a computer running IIS.

You need to install the Sqlce30setupen.MSI package if your backend server is SQL Server 2005. It does not matter whether you are using RTM, SP1 or SP2 of SQL Server 2005; you should still use the Sqlce30setupen.MSI package.

You can also use SQL Server 2000 SP3 or SQL Server 2000 SP4 as a backend database. To synchronize data between SQL Server 2000 and SQL Server Compact Edition, you need to use the SQL Server Compact Edition installer package specifically meant for the SQL Server 2000 Service Pack. For Service Pack 3 of SQL Server 2000, use the Sql2kensp3a.MSI installer package. For Service Pack 4 of SQL Server 2000 install the Sql2kensp4.MSI installer package. All these packages are available from the Microsoft download center.

If you installed SQL Server 2005, you can find the SQL Server Compact Edition Server tools for SQL Server 2005 at

```
<Disk>\Program Files\Microsoft SQL Server\90\Tools\Binn\VSShell\Common7\IDE\.
```

If you install Visual Studio 2005, it also copies all these SQL Server Compact Edition Server Tools installer packages on your computer. These three packages are copied at

```
<Disk>\Program Files\Microsoft Visual Studio 8\SmartDevices\SDK\SQL
Server\Mobile\v3.0.
```

# Getting Familiarized with SQL Server Compact Edition Components on a Developer Computer

Now you have completed the installation of all the components necessary for development and your development environment is ready to develop and deploy an application. Before you move further you should become familiarized with various folders, packages, and cabinet files that Visual Studio has placed on your computer.

The knowledge you gain will help you understand how to deploy your application in a development environment and in a production environment.

## SQL Server Compact Edition Client Components for Desktop and Tablet PC

When you install SQL Server Compact Edition on a development computer, the components shown in Table 2.5 are installed.

On a developer machine, the components are installed on

```
<drive> \Program Files\Microsoft SQL Server Compact Edition\V3.1
```

---

**NOTE**

If you remove the program SQL Server Compact Edition using the Add or Remove Program applet, the installation will be removed.

**TABLE 2.5     SQL Server Compact Edition Components**

| Component | Dll |
|---|---|
| SQL Server Compact Edition Storage Engine | Sqlcese30.dll |
| SQL Server Compact Edition Query Processor | Sqlceqp30.dll |
| SQL Server Compact Edition Manage Provider | Sqlceme30.dll |
| SQL Server Compact Edition OLE DB Provider | Sqlceoledb30.dll |
| SQL Server Compact Edition Client Agent | Sqlceca30.dll |
| SQL Server Compact Edition Compact Utility | Sqlcecompact30.dll |
| SQL Server Compact Edition Namespace | System.Data.SqlServerCE.dll |

## SQL Server Compact Edition Readme File

The SQL Mobile Readme file is in HTM format. You can find the Readme file
`ReadmeSSCE_ENU.HTM` in

```
<disk>Program Files\Microsoft SQL Server Compact Edition\v3.1
```

The SQL Server Compact Edition Readme file provides information about the Microsoft
Download center where you can download the product. The Readme file also has information about the platform supported. It is a good idea to read this file available with your
installation.

## SQL Server Compact Edition End-User License Agreement

The End-user license agreement file is located at

```
<disk>Program Files\Microsoft SQL Server Compact Edition\v3.1.
```

The name of the file is `EULA_EN`.

SQL Server Compact Edition database is used as a local database for Smart clients and as a
local data store where data is pulled from a backend SQL Server. You can develop a Smart
device application using SQL Server Compact Edition. You can freely distribute SQL Server
Compact Edition 3.x to Smart devices. You only need an SQL Server License if you use
SQL Server as a backend Server to synchronize data with an SQL Server.

## SQL Server Compact Edition Cabinet Files for Devices

You will develop the managed or native applications for SQL Server Compact Edition
using Visual Studio. At design and development time, the binaries corresponding to the
x86 system will be used. When you deploy the applications onto devices, you will need
binaries corresponding to the platforms and processors for your devices.

Visual Studio installs SQL Server Compact Edition binaries for all supported platforms and
processors on your developer machine. At the time of installing the SQL Server Compact
Edition Developer Software Development Kit, SQL Server Compact Edition binaries for

various platforms and processors get installed onto your developer computer. You can get the SQL Server Compact Edition components at the following location:

```
<Disk>\Program Files\Microsoft SQL Server Compact Edition\v3.1\SDK\bin\
[PLATFORM]\[PROCESSOR]
```

For example if you are deploying an application on Windows CE 5.0 and the processor type is x86, the path of binaries will be similar to what is shown in Figure 2.19.

```
<Disk>\Program Files\Microsoft SQL Server Compact Edition\v3.1\SDK\bin\wce500\x86
```

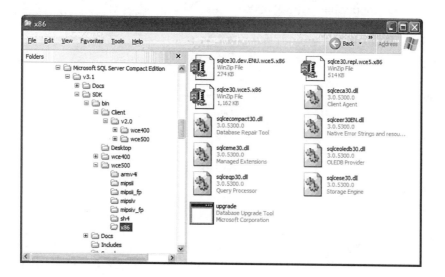

FIGURE 2.19    Platform and Processor Specific Files

As shown in Figure 2.19, there are three cabinet files in the folders:

- Sqlce30.wce5.x86

- Sqlce30.repl.wce5.x86

- Sqlce30.dev.ENU.wce5.x86

You have already learned that there are separate folders for cabinet files for each platform and processor type. The subdirectories under

```
<Disk>\Program Files\Microsoft SQL Server Compact Edition\v3.1\SDK\bin
```

are named according to platform and processor.

Within each subdirectory the cabinet files are also named according to platform and processor. Table 2.6 shows the convention for two types of platforms supported for devices.

TABLE 2.6    Cabinet Files for Supported Platform

| Supported Platform | Folder | Label Used in Cabinet File Names |
| --- | --- | --- |
| Windows Mobile Pocket PC 2003 | Wce400 | Wce4 |
| Windows CE 5.0 | Wce500 | Wce5 |
| Windows Mobile Pocket PC 2005 | Wce500 | Wce5 |
| Windows Mobile Smart phone 2005 | Wce500 | Wce5 |

Table 2.7 shows platform and processor combinations for which SQL Server Compact Edition binaries are installed with VS 2005.

TABLE 2.7    Binaries for Platforms and Processors

| Platform | Processor |
| --- | --- |
| Wce400 | Armv4 |
| Wce500 | Armv4i |
| Wce500 | Mipsii |
| Wce500 | Mipsii_fp |
| Wce500 | Mipsiv |
| Wce500 | Mipsib_fp |
| Wce500 | Sh4 |
| Wce500 | x86 |

When you initiate the deployment of a manage application that refers to the System.Data.SqlServerCE namespace, Visual Studio copies the SQL Server Compact Edition client components onto the device or an emulator.

SQL Server Compact Edition components are packaged into self-extracting cabinet files as shown in Table 2.8

TABLE 2.8    SQL Server Compact Edition Cabinet files

| Cabinet File | Dll |
| --- | --- |
| SqlCe30.platform.processor | Sqlcese30.dll |
| | Sqlceqp30.dll |
| | Sqlceme30.dll |
| | System.Data.SqlServerCE.dll |
| SqlCe30.repl.platform.processor | Sqlceoledb30.dll |
| | Sqlceca30.dll |
| | Sqlcecompact30.dll |
| SqlCe30.dev.lang.paltform.processor | Isqlw.exe |
| | Sqlceerr30lang.dll |

---

**NOTE**

For SQL Mobile (SQL Server Compact Edition 3.0) the path of cabinet files is
`<Disk>\Program Files\Microsoft Visual Studio 8\SmartDevices\SDK\SQL Server\Mobile\v3.0\[PLATFORM]\[PROCESSOR]`.

---

# Deploying and Distributing SQL Server Compact Edition Applications

Everything required to deploy the SQL Server Compact Edition application is available on your development machine. You have learned what packages and cabinet files Visual Studio has deployed onto your developer machine. After your application development is complete, you should deploy the application, SQL Server Compact Edition database, appropriate SQL Server Compact Edition components, and .NET Framework or .NET Compact framework components on the target platform.

## Deploying on a Desktop and Tablet PC

For deploying the application on a desktop and on a Tablet PC you need to install SQL Server Compact Edition components. To install the SQL Server Compact Edition components, you should install the package SQLSERVERCE31-EN.MSI. The file is also available at

`<disk>\Program Files\ Microsoft SQL Server Compact Edition\v3.1\SDK\bin\Desktop`

## Deploying on a Device

For deploying the application on a device, you need to install application SQL Server Compact Edition and .NET Compact Framework libraries. You need to choose the SQL Server Compact Edition CAB file specific to the Windows Mobile version and processor architecture of the device.

### Deploying a Managed Application

When you develop and deploy a Smart device application that references the `System.Data.SqlServerCe` namespace, VS2005 automatically checks whether the device or emulator has SQL Server Compact Edition client component and .NET Framework. If the components are not already there on the device, Visual Studio deploys .NET CF2 and SQL Server Compact Edition client components onto the emulator or onto the device.

To deploy an application onto a device, create a Smart device project. Once the project is complete, click on the Build | Deploy menu option. Visual Studio will ask you whether to deploy onto the emulator or onto the device. Choose the target platform. Visual Studio starts deploying the required files:

1. .NET Compact Framework

2. SQL Server Compact Edition Client components

3. SQL Server Compact Edition Database file

4. Managed Application

You can check out the cabinet files that are getting deployed onto the device or emulator. As shown in Figure 2.20, the bottom bar of Visual Studio displays the name of CAB files getting deployed at the emulator or onto the device.

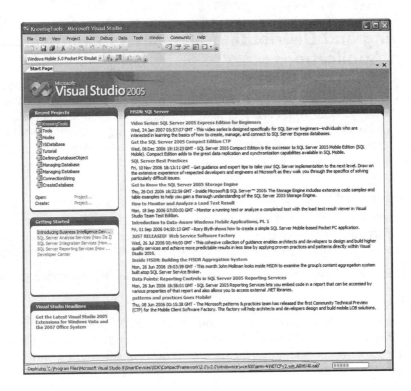

FIGURE 2.20    Deploying Cabinet Files

### Deploying a Native Application

Visual Studio does not automatically deploy SQL Server Compact Edition components while deploying a native application. When you develop SQL Server Compact Edition based native application in Visual C++, you should deploy the SQL Server Compact Edition components yourself.

You should manually copy the SqlCe30.platform.processor and SqlCe30.dev.lang.palt-form.processor cabinet files to the device root directory. You should also copy SqlCe30.repl.platform.processor cabinet files if you need to use Merge replication, RDA, or Compaction utility. You can find a copy of SQL Server Compact Edition components  at

```
<Disk>\Program Files\Microsoft SQL Server Compact Edition\v3.1\SDK\bin\
[PLATFORM]\[PROCESSOR].
```

Visual Studio installation also copies SQL Server Compact Edition components onto your computer. You can also find a copy of SQL Server Compact Edition components at

```
<Disk>\Program Files\Microsoft Visual Studio 8\SmartDevices\SDK\SQL
Server\Mobile\v3.0\
```

## Packaging the Application

You can package .NET Compact Framework, SQL Server Compact Edition components, the SQL Server Compact Edition database file, and your application into a self-extracting CAB file. You can build the CAB files using Visual Studio. In Chapter 3, *Getting to Know the Tools,* you will get detailed instructions for packing an application into a CAB file. You have learned which dlls need to be deployed depending on the platform and processor type of each device. You have also learned which folder and cabinet file contains the dll for your platform.

## Summary

In this chapter, you looked at the software used for developing applications with the SQL Server Compact Edition database. You learned that SQL Server Management Studio, Visual Studio 2005, and Windows Mobile 5.0 developer kits are needed for Pocket PCs and Smartphone. You examined the folders, cabinet files, and dlls that get placed when you install Visual Studio and SQL Server Compact Edition on your development machine. And in conclusion, you learned how you will deploy and distribute your application and required SQL Server Compact Edition components on a target platform.

# Getting to Know
the Tools

One main limitation of the SQL CE 2.0 database released in 2002 was the need to manage the database either using a query analyzer tool on mobile devices or by running a program to manipulate data on a device. To allow rapid application development, Microsoft has added tight integration between SQL Server Compact Edition 3.x, SQL Server 2005, and Visual Studio 2005.

Using SQL Server Management Studio, developers and administrators can manage the SQL Server Compact Edition database located on a device or on a desktop. You can design tables, columns, constraints, and indexes using SQL Server Management Studio.

Similarly you can use Visual Studio features to create, design, and manipulate the SQL Server Compact Edition database. Visual Studio also helps you to deploy a database on a device.

In this chapter you will be familiarized with the available tools. You will also learn how to use SQL Server Management Studio and Query Analyzer to manage and manipulate the SQL Server database. You will become familiar with the Visual Studio interface and will learn how to include SQL Server Compact Edition in your project. You will also learn how to set up a connection with the SQL Server Compact Edition database and finally how to deploy the application on platforms.

# Using SQL Server Management Studio

SQL Server Management Studio provides an integrated environment to manage the SQL Server family of databases. Using SQL Server Management Studio, you can manage SQL Server 2005 database, SQL Server Compact Edition 3.x database, Integration Services, Analysis Services, and Reporting Services.

SQL Server Management Studio is installed on your computer along with the SQL Server 2005 installation. By default the `SqlWb` executable is installed at `C:\Program Files\Microsoft SQL Server\90\Tools\Binn\VSShell\Common7\IDE`.

> **NOTE**
>
> SQL Server Management Studio is also known as Management Studio, SSMS, or Work Bench. Many developers also use the term Work Bench for SQL Server Management Studio.
>
> SQL Server Management Studio has replaced Enterprise Manager and Query Analyzer. Using SQL Server Management Studio, you can also manage SQL Server 7 and the SQL Server 2000 database.

The biggest advantage of SQL Server Management Studio is that you do not need to learn a new interface for managing the SQL Server Compact Edition database. If you are already using SSMS for managing SQL Server, you can use the same interface for managing the SQL Server Compact Edition 3.0 database.

## Starting SQL Server Management Studio

You can start the SQL Server Management Studio by clicking on Start | All Programs | Microsoft SQL Server 2005 | SQL Server Management Studio. Using SSMS you can create a project and a solution. The project contains a connection to a database and the corresponding SQL scripts. A container solution contains related projects. A project provides a mechanism to organize files, not the database objects. To create a new project and solution use the File | New menu option and specify the project and the solution name.

The SSMS user interface provides two types of windows—component windows and document windows. Component windows display windows listed under the View options such as Object Explorer, Registered Server, Solution Explorer, and so on. Document windows are used for queries, scripts, and files. The SQL Server Management Studio windows are shown in Figure 3.1. You can use various options to customize SSMS windows by using the Tools | option.

This section will describe these windows. The Bookmark feature is a new feature that you can use to create a shortcut to a line in a project file. To create a bookmark, choose Toggle Bookmark from the Edit menu.

## Getting Connected to SQL Server Compact Edition Database

When you start SQL Server Management Studio, it starts with the Connection dialog box. In this dialog box you will specify that you wish to connect to SQL Server Compact

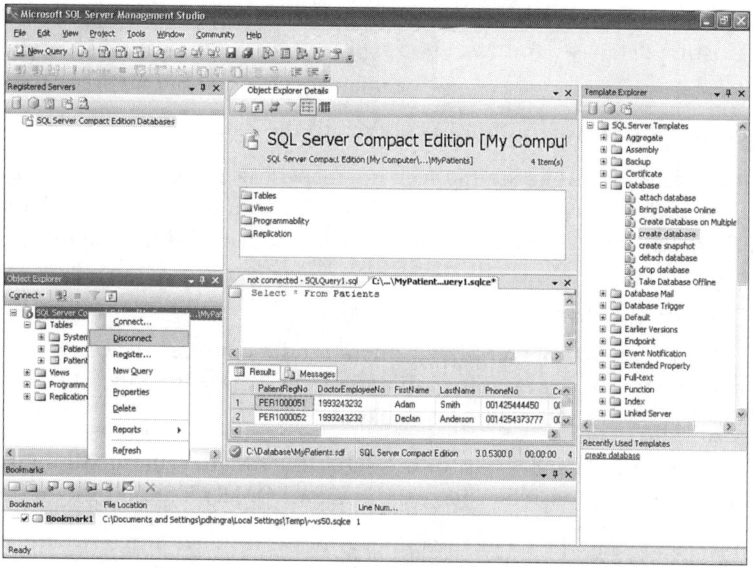

FIGURE 3.1    SQL Server Management Studio Windows

Edition database. You need to specify the path of the SQL Server Compact Edition database file and initiate the connection. To connect to the SQL Server Compact Edition database follow the steps given below:

1. Start the SQL Server Management Studio. The Connect to Server dialog box will appear as shown in Figure 3.2.

2. Select SQL Server Compact Edition Server Type.

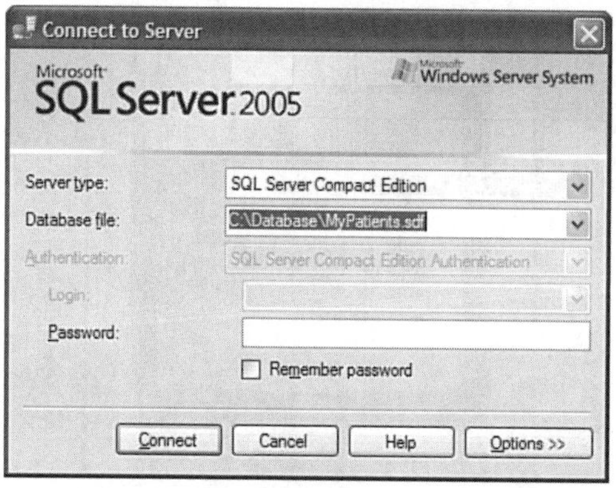

FIGURE 3.2    Connect to SQL Server CE

3. Specify the name of the SQL Server Compact Edition database file in order to open an existing database. You can choose Browse for More options to browse the database file.

4. Click on the Connect button to connect to the database.

This example demonstrates a simple scenario—opening an SQL Server Compact Edition database. Using the dialog box shown in Figure 3.2, you can open a password-protected encrypted database and create a new SQL Server Compact Edition database.

## Using Object Explorer

Object Explorer is an SQL Server Management Studio component. Using this component you can connect to SQL Server, Integration Services, Analysis Services, Reporting Services, and an SQL Server Compact Edition database.

Object Explorer is displayed as part of the SQL Server Management Studio user interface. If Object Explorer is not visible, click on the View | Object Explorer menu option.

As shown in Figure 3.3, the Object Explorer window displays a tree structure view for all the objects. For each server type, Object Explorer displays a different set of nodes. For an SQL Server Compact Edition database, it displays Tables, Views, Programmability, and Replication nodes.

Figure 3.1 shows a connection to both SQL Server database and the SQL Server Compact Edition database. All available connections are shown in a tree view. You can expand the tree nodes to see underlying objects. Object Explorer can display up to 65,536 objects.

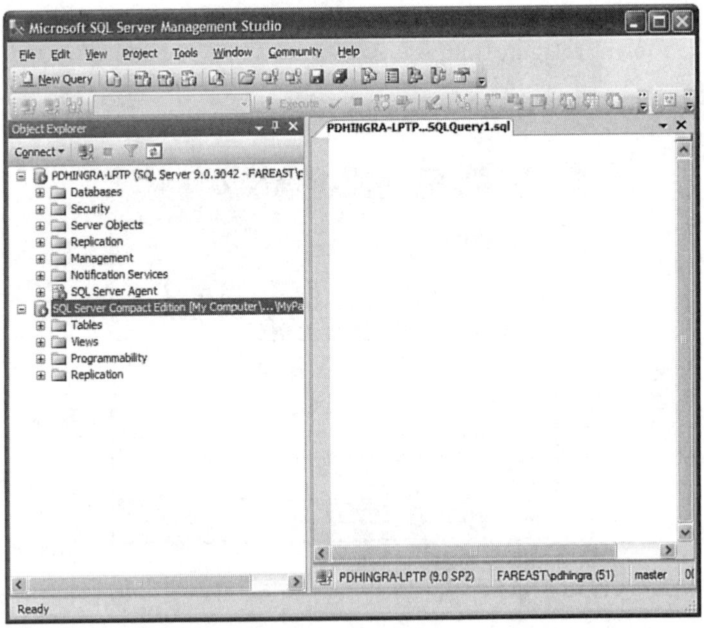

FIGURE 3.3    Object Explorer

You can right click on any node revealing a list of operations that can be performed on the object. For SQL Server Objects, the Filter option is available to allow filtering of objects. For SQL Server Compact Edition, the Filter option is not available.

### Disconnecting from the SQL Server Compact Edition Database

To disconnect from the SQL Server Compact Edition database, simply select the database. Right click and then click on the Disconnect option.

After disconnecting from the SQL Server Compact Edition database, Object Explorer is refreshed. You can use the Tools | Options menu option to customize a window layout of SSMS as shown in Figure 3.4.

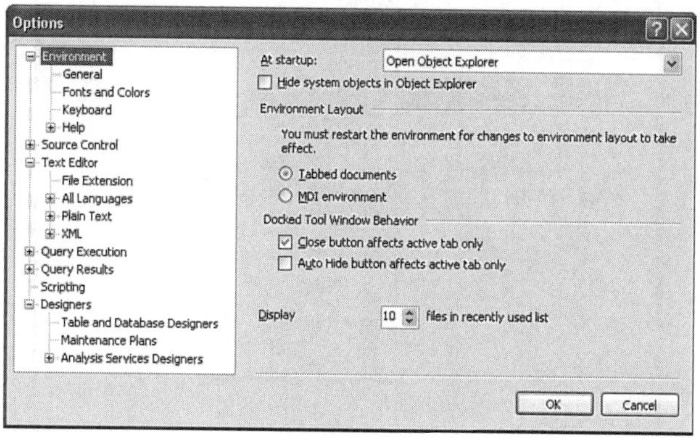

**FIGURE 3.4    Object Explorer**

### Connecting to SQL Server Compact Edition Database from Object Explorer

To reconnect to the SQL Server Compact Edition database, click on the Connect button in Object Explorer. You will be shown options to connect to SQL Server Database Engine, Analysis Services, Integration Services, Reporting Services, and the SQL Server Compact Edition database. Select the SQL Server Compact Edition database option.

You will be shown the Connect to Server dialog box. Specify the path of the SQL Server Compact Edition database as you did earlier, thereby connecting to the SQL Server Compact Edition database.

### Registering a Database Server

Using the Register Server option you can store the connection information. While connecting to an SQL Server Compact Edition database that is already registered, you do not need to resupply all the connection parameters. The Register Server Option is useful for connecting to databases that you connect to frequently. Use the Register Server Option to store connection information for SQL Server Compact Edition, SQL Server, Analysis Services, Integration Services, and Reporting Services.

At the time of registration, you store the connection information in SQL Server Management Studio. To store this information, use the Register a Database Server option.

1. To register a server, select the SQL Server Compact Edition database in SQL Server Management Studio Object Explorer.

2. Right click on database and click the Register option as shown in Figure 3.5.

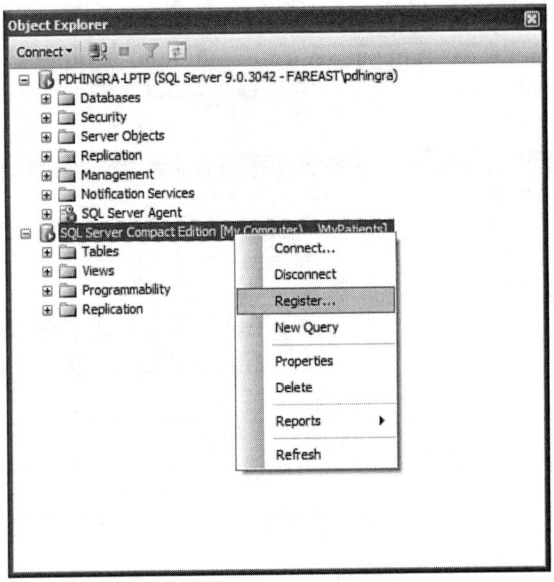

FIGURE 3.5    Register a Database Server

3. In the Register Server dialog box, specify where you want to place the database in the Server Group box. By default the SQL Server Compact Edition database is selected in Figure 3.6.

4. To create a new group, click on the New Group button.

5. In the New Server Group dialog box, enter a Group name and Group description as shown in Figure 3.7.

6. Click Save.

7. The new Group name is entered under SQL Server Compact Edition database.

8. Click Save.

## Connecting to a Registered Database

You can view all registered servers and connect to one of the registered databases. You can access all the Registered Servers by clicking on the View | Registered Servers option.

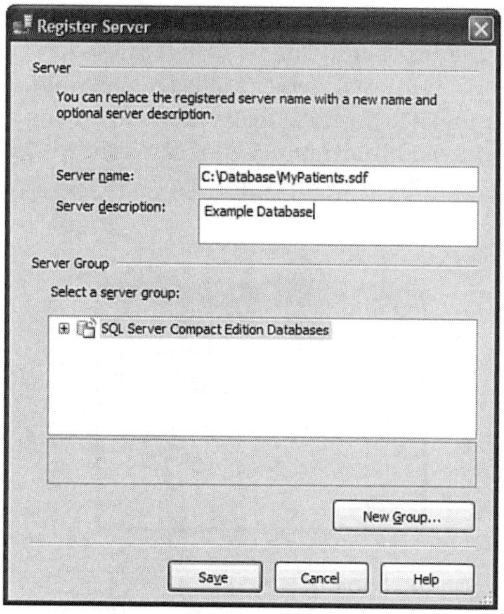

FIGURE 3.6    Specify a Server Name

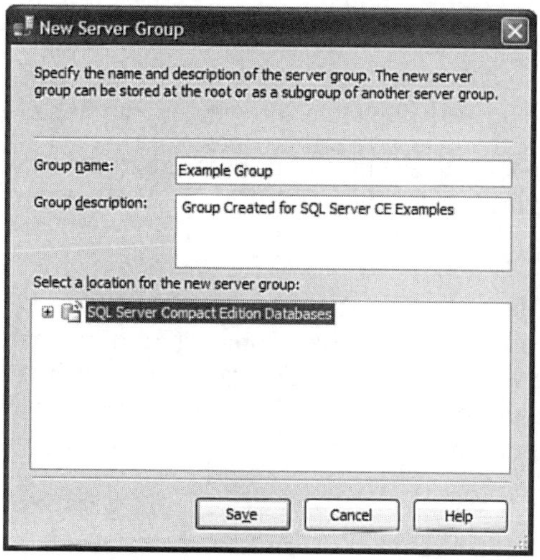

FIGURE 3.7    Specify a New Server Group

Clicking on Registered Server will start the Registered Server Explorer tab. Register Server Explorer has five tabs in the top menu. The five tabs correspond to five types of database server that you can connect using SQL Server Management Studio. Earlier in this chapter you learned that when using SQL Server Management Studio you can manage the SQL Server 2005 database engine and Integration Services. As shown in Figure 3.8, select the tab for SQL Server Compact Edition to access the Example Registered Server Group that you created earlier.

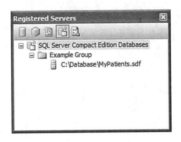

**FIGURE 3.8    List of Registered Servers**

Select your Database Group and Database and click to connect.

### Using Tables Node
You will be using the Tables node to define the tables and columns structures. You can right click on the Tables node and use options to create new tables. You can expand the Tables node by right clicking on any existing table and view/modify the properties of the table.

You can also expand the table to see the columns. You can see the column properties by right clicking on all columns.

### Using Views Node
SQL Server Compact Edition provides INFORMATION_SCHEMA views to help you obtain metadata information about the SQL Server Compact Edition database. The INFORMA-TION_SCHEMA view gets included in each SQL Server Compact Edition database. You can click on views folders to see INFORMATION_SCHEMA views available. When you click on Views, your result will look similar to one shown in Figure 3.9.

### Tables
The Tables view contains one row for each table that is accessible to the current user.

### Columns
The Columns view contains one row for each column that is accessible to the current user.

### Indexes
The Indexes view contains one row for each index that is accessible to the current user.

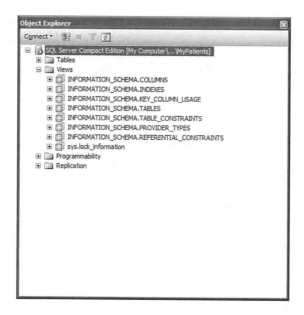

FIGURE 3.9      Information Schema Views

### Key_Column_Usage

The Key_Column_Usage view contains one row for each column that is defined as key in the current database.

### Table_Constraint

The Table_Constraints view contains one row for each table constraint in a database.

### Referential_Constraints

The Referential_Contraints view contains one row for each foreign key constraint in a database.

### Provider_Types

The Provider_Types view contains the data type supported in SQL Server Compact Edition.

In the upcoming chapters you will learn how to utilize these views for problem solving.

### Using the Programmability Node

The programmability node is more useful in SQL Server 2005. In SQL Server 2005 this node contains subnodes for Stored Procedures, User Defined Data Types, etc. In the SQL Server Compact Edition database, Programmability nodes display the data type available in SQL Server CE.

### Using the Replication Node

Merge Replication is a mechanism to synchronize data between SQL Server and SQL Server Compact Edition. In Merge Replication, SQL Server acts as Publisher of data and

SQL Server Compact Edition as Subscriber of data. In the Object Explorer of the SQL
Server Compact Edition database you have a Replication node. The Replication node will
have a Subscriptions subnode. This node will show the subscriptions available for SQL
Server Compact Edition database. If you have set up the subscription, this node will
display the subscription information as shown in Figure 3.10. You can check out the
subscription properties by right clicking on the subscription.

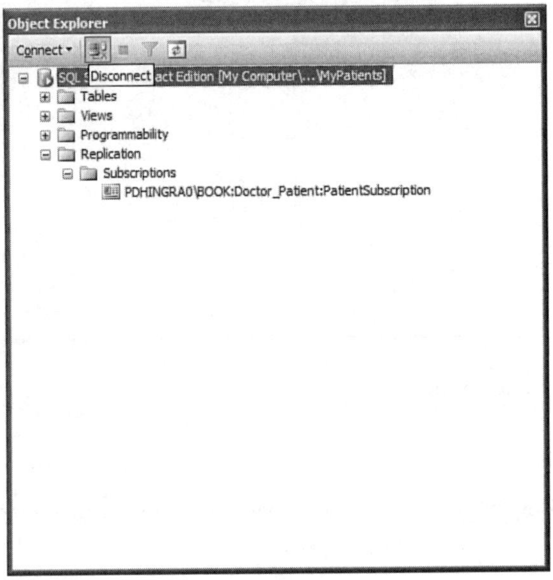

**FIGURE 3.10**    Replication Node

If the SQL Server Compact Edition database has not been configured to act as Subscriber,
the Subscription node under Replication node will be empty.

You will learn more about Merge Replication and Subscription in Chapter 12.

## Using the Query Editor

SQL Server Management Studio has a query editor. To write queries for SQL Server CE,
click on either the New Query button or the File | New Query menu option. Clicking on
New Query will start the new query editor or ask you to specify a connection. Query
Editor can be connected or disconnected to an SQL Server Compact Edition database.
Query Editor color highlights query syntax and provides tracking indicators.

You can also open existing queries using the File | Open | File... option.

From Object Explorer you can select the SQL Server Compact Edition database, right click,
and select New Query to open a query editor.

The Query Editor has an upper pane in which you can write queries. The lower pane displays the results of query execution. The results displayed are read-only. In the results pane there are two tabs: Results and Messages. The Result tab displays the data after successful execution. The Message tab displays an error message if the query has errors or it displays a message indicating the number of rows impacted as a result of a query. You can click on the Message tab to see the message. The track changed indicator in Query Editor shows which lines of an SQL script are changed.

**NOTE**

SQL Server Compact Edition supports a subset of Transact-SQL commands. SQL Server 2005 supports complete Transact-SQL commands. Chapter 5, *Defining the Database Structure*, and Chapter 6, *Manipulating the Database*, provide the syntax and examples of Transact-SQL that are supported in SQL Server Compact Edition.

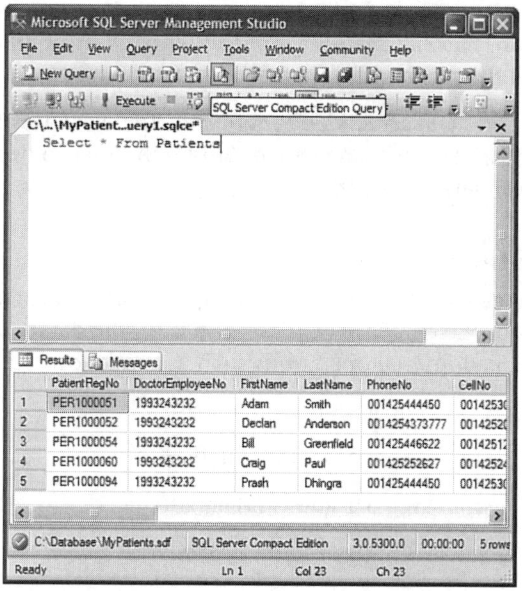

**FIGURE 3.11    Query Editor**

The results are displayed in the Results section as shown in Figure 3.11.

**NOTE**

SQL Server Management Studio provides a query builder feature to design queries. For an SQL Server database, use the Design Query in the Editor menu option. You will not see this menu option when you write queries for an SQL Server Compact Edition database. The Query Builder feature is not available for an SQL Server Compact Edition database.

## Using a Graphical Execution Plan

When you write an enterprise application, it is very likely that you will want to isolate and tune performance bottlenecks. SQL Server Management Studio fulfills this key objective and helps you to understand where the most time is used in query execution. SQL Server Management Studio provides a solution to seeing the execution plan for queries. The query execution plan gives you insight and enables you to tune queries.

### Using the Estimated Execution Plan

The Estimated Execution Plan option parses the query and then generates the execution plan. In this option, SQL Server Compact Edition does not execute the query but generates the execution plan. You can see the graphical representation of the execution plan with Query Display Estimated Execution plan.

### Using the Actual Execution Plan

The Actual Execution plan generates the query and then shows the plan used by SQL Server Compact Edition. You can see the graphical representation of execution plan with Query | Include Actual Execution plan.

In Chapter 15, *SQL Server Compact Edition Performance Tuning*, you will learn how to exploit this feature of SQL Server Management Studio in order to debug and tune SQL Server Compact Edition database queries.

## Managing the Database

Using SSMS you can create a new SQL Server Compact Edition database. Not only can you modify the properties of the database, you can also drop the database. With Management Studio you can even do additional operations such as the following:

- Verify the SQL Server Compact Edition database.

- Repair the SQL Server Compact Edition database.

- Shrink the SQL Server Compact Edition database.

- Compact the SQL Server Compact Edition database.

In this section you will also use SSMS interface to complete these operations.

## Using Replication Wizards

For enterprise applications you will be synchronizing the data between SQL Server and the SQL Server Compact Edition database. The SQL Server Compact Edition database provides a built-in mechanism Merge Replication and Remote Data Access to synchronize the data with SQL Server. To implement Merge Replication you need to configure a Web Server, set up the Distributor, set up the Publication, and set up the Subscription.

Before using a Merge Replication you need to provide configuration details—central database, remote database, Snapshot agent folder, security mechanism, etc. You can set up this configuration either programmatically or by using Wizards. SQL Server Management

Studio provides tools and wizards to set up publication, subscription, and a snapshot folder. It even generates a template code that can be used for Data Synchronization. The set of wizards remains the same whether you are setting up Merge Replication between two SQL Server instances or between SQL Server and SQL Server CE database.

### Using the Publication Wizard

For database synchronization between SQL Server and SQL Server CE database, SQL Server first needs to publish the data. The database instance publishing the data is called Publisher. By using the SQL Server 2005 Publication Wizard you can specify the Publisher, Publication type, snapshot folder, and articles to publish.

### Using the Subscription Wizard

The SQL Server CE database synchronizing data with backend SQL Server is called Subscriber. The subscription wizard allows you to create and manage subscriptions for SQL Server and SQL Server CE databases. You can use the properties dialog box for modifying properties of existing subscriptions.

### Using the Configure Web Synchronization Wizard

You need to set up a Web Server for both Merge Replication and Remote Data Access. SQL Server Management Studio provides a Configure Web synchronization wizard. This wizard helps you to specify the Web Server, virtual directory, and authentication mechanism.

To use Web Synchronization Wizard, Publication Wizard, and Synchronization Wizard, you first need to learn the Merge Replication and Remote Data access features. You will learn how to use these wizards in Chapter 12, *Synchronizing Data with Merge Replication.*

### NOTE

You can run the Configure Web Synchronization Wizard from SSMS or by running the executable `Connwiz30.exe`.

# Using the Query Analyzer

You have probably already used the SQL Query Analyzer tool to execute a query against an SQL Server 2000 database. Microsoft developed a device version of Query Analyzer, similar to SQL Server Query Analyzer, to manage the SQL CE 2.0 database on a device and SQL Server Query Analyzer functionality is extended to devices too. With SQL Server Compact Edition 3.0 you can manage the database using SQL Server Management Studio on a desktop. With SQL Server Compact Edition 3.0 you also get the Query Analyzer tool to manage the database on a device and on an emulator.

Query Analyzer allows you to not only execute queries but it also allows you to view database object information and manipulate database objects.

## Installing the Query Analyzer

On a desktop, you have SQL Server Management Studio tool to manage an SQL Server Compact Edition database. On a device, you will use the SQL Server Compact Edition Query Analyzer tool. The Query Analyzer gets installed when you install SQL Server Compact Edition on a device or on an emulator. If you are a developer and deploying an application using Visual Studio in debug mode, both SQL Server Compact Edition and Query Analyzer are installed.

You can also manually install SQL Server Compact Edition and Query Analyzer onto a device. To install the Query Analyzer on a device you should install the .NET Compact framework and the SQL Server Compact Edition database. The procedures for deploying . NET Compact Framework and SQL Server Compact Edition database is explained in Chapter 2, *Platform Support and Installation*.

## Getting Connected to the SQL Server Compact Edition Database

Query Analyzer is a graphical tool that manages an SQL Server Compact Edition database on a device and on an emulator. With SQL Server Compact Edition 3.x you can use Query Analyzer version 3.x. As discussed earlier, SQL CE 2.0 also provides support for Query Analyzer. Query Analyzer for SQL CE 2.0 and SQL Server Compact Edition 3.x are different executables. Both versions can exist on the same device. Query Analyzer for SQL CE 2.0 will not connect to an SQL Server Compact Edition 3.x database.

Start the Query Analyzer on a device or emulator by clicking on Start | Query Analyzer as shown in Figure 3.12.

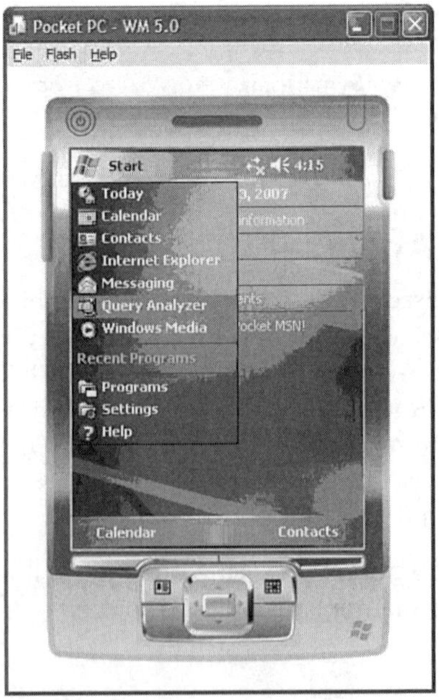

FIGURE 3.12    Start Query Analyzer

**NOTE**

You need to use Query Analyzer for SQL Server 3.0 to open and manage an SQL Server Compact Edition 3.x database. When you click on an .sdf file on a device or emulator, Query Analyzer for SQL Server Compact Edition opens the database. In case you have installed Query Analyzer for SQL CE 2.0 and SQL Server Compact Edition 3.x, the Query Analyzer installed last will open the .sdf file.

Figure 3.13 shows the layout of Query Analyzer. It has four tabs—Objects, SQL, Grid, and Notes.

**FIGURE 3.13    Connecting the Database**

1. To connect to the SQL Server Compact Edition database using Query Analyzer, click on the Connect button inside the rectangle as shown in Figure 3.13.

2. Specify the path of the database and click Connect as shown in Figure 3.14.

The database is open. It has Objects, SQL, Grid, and Notes tabs as shown in Figure 3.15. Under the Objects tab you can browse the database objects. Under the SQL tab you can write SQL queries. You can view the results of SQL queries under the Grid tab. The Notes tab shows remarks such as errors in executing query, time taken to execute queries, and rows impacted.

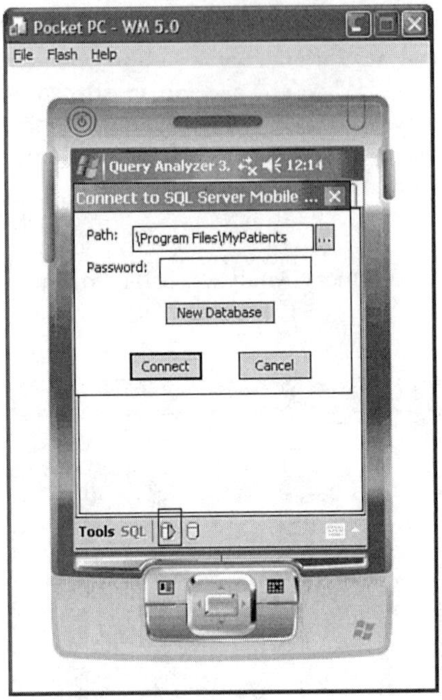

**FIGURE 3.14**    Specify the SQL Server CE Database File

**FIGURE 3.15**    Tools Menu

## Using the Tools Menu

At the bottom of the Query Analyzer dialog box there is a Tools option. The Tools option is available under all four tabs. As shown in Figure 3.15, the Tools menu has subitems—Refresh, Logging, Fonts, About, and Exit.

### Refresh

The Objects tab displays the tree view of the SQL Server Compact Edition database object. You can click on the Refresh menu to refresh the tree view.

---

**NOTE**

In SQL Server Management Studio, you refresh the tree view by right clicking on tree and clicking Refresh.

---

### Logging

Logging is an interesting option. You can click on Logging to enable and disable this feature. After enabling logging, any DDL or DML operation that you do using the Object Explorer Graphical menu option is logged in the SQL tab. The SQL statement equivalent to your action is logged in the SQL tab. For example, if you use the New Table menu option, the Create Table command logs into the SQL Tab.

The statements logged or written in SQL Tab are not saved automatically. Use the Save menu option if you need to save the statements for future usage.

1. Click on the Tools I Logging option as shown in Figure 3.16.

**FIGURE 3.16**   Logging Option

2. Select a table. Click on the Execute Query button.

3. Clicking this button while a table is selected shows the content of the table as shown in Figure 3.17.

4. You can check the statement that Query Analyzer has executed. Click on the SQL tab.

5. The SQL tab shows the "SELECT" statement as shown in Figure 3.18. If you drop a table, column, or index, you will see an equivalent statement in the SQL tab.

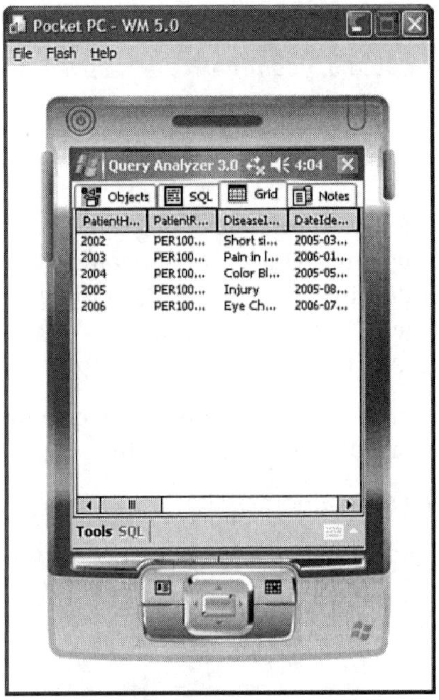

**FIGURE 3.17**    Table Content

Using the Logging option, you can record the SQL statements corresponding to actions that you do using the graphical tool. If you need to insert one hundred rows into a database and you are not keen on writing SQL Statements, you can generate the first few SQL statements by using the Logging option and then copy and paste to convert them into a hundred rows.

### Fonts

You use the Font option to change the setting in Query Analyzer. Click on the Font menu option to change the font in the Font dialog box as shown in Figure 3.19.

### About

The About menu option displays the current versions of Query Analyzer and the SQL Server Compact Edition database.

FIGURE 3.18    SQL Statement

FIGURE 3.19    Font Dialog Box

### Exit

The purpose of the Exit menu is to close the Query Analyzer. Clicking on X in the right-hand corner only minimizes the application and leaves it running in the background. In the Visual Studio Tools section you will learn to use the MinimizeBox property to change the default behavior.

## Using Tabs

The tabs on the Query Analyzer allow you to access and manipulate database definition and data contents. You can use the Object tab for a database object and the SQL tab for writing SQL queries. The Grid tab shows the results of queries. The Notes tab contains information regarding query execution time and number of rows impacted.

### Objects

The Object tab shows the tree view of database objects such as the one shown in Figure 3.20. This relates to Object Explorer in SQL Server Management Studio. At the top of the tree is the Database node. The Database node shows the available connection. The open database connection will have a green icon and a closed database will have a red icon. Under each database there are tables, columns, and indexes.

Clicking on the Tables node displays a set of icons as shown in Figure 3.21.

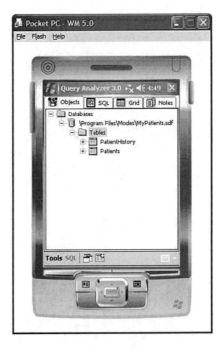

**FIGURE 3.20**    Database Objects

**FIGURE 3.21**    Icons with Tables Object

The second icon is for displaying and hiding system tables. You can toggle the option by clicking on it. Figure 3.22 shows a Hide System Table. Clicking on the Hide System Table icon hides the table.

**FIGURE 3.22**    Hide System Table

Figure 3.23 shows a Show System Table. Clicking on the Show System Table button shows system tables.

**FIGURE 3.23**    Show System Table

The icon with a plus sign shown in Figure 3.24 is used to create a new table. The icon is shown when you select Tables node.

**FIGURE 3.24**    Create New Table

You can click on a specific table in Object tree. When you select a table in Object tree, icons appear at the bottom as shown in Figure 3.25.

**FIGURE 3.25**    Icons with Table

Clicking on the button shown in Figure 3.26 displays the content of the table you have selected.

**FIGURE 3.26**    Execute Query

Clicking on the button shown in Figure 3.27 opens a dialog box for adding a new column object.

**FIGURE 3.27**    New Column

Clicking on the button shown in Figure 3.28 opens a dialog box for adding a new index object.

**FIGURE 3.28**    New Index

### SQL

The SQL tab shown in Figure 3.29 is an editor to write and execute SQL queries. This relates to Query Editor in SQL Server Management Studio.

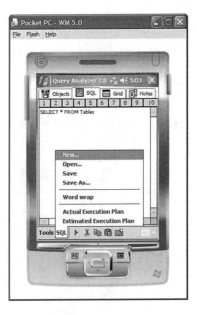

**FIGURE 3.29**    SQL Tab and Menu Options

When you move to the SQL Tab, the Query Analyzer shows the SQL menu option on the lower left-hand side. The SQL option has suboptions to open a new query, open an existing query, save a query, and to show the execution plans. You will be using these options in upcoming chapters.

The Word Wrap option is specific to Query Analyzer. The Word Wrap option is useful for the small screen and wraps an SQL statement to the visible part. A similar option is not available in SQL Server Management Studio.

Next to the SQL menu option there is the Execute icon. (This icon is shown in Figure 3.27.) Use this function to execute queries.

On the right side of the Execute icon you have standard Cut, Copy, and Paste icons as shown in Figure 3.30. These are standard features and you can utilize them while writing queries.

**FIGURE 3.30     Cut, Copy, and Paste Buttons**

The icon on the far right as shown in Figure 3.31 is the Preset button. This saves a frequently used SQL statement.

**FIGURE 3.31     Preset Button**

You will be using the Preset button in conjunction with ten SQL statement buttons. These ten buttons are shown in Figure 3.32.

**FIGURE 3.32     Ten SQL Statement Buttons**

You may have noticed these ten buttons at the top of SQL Query Editor.

The Preset button allows you to save up to ten frequently used SQL statements. By clicking on one of these buttons you can invoke an SQL statement.

**Saving SQL Statements**
To save SQL statements, click on the PreSet button. It will start the Button Presets dialog box. Type the SQL statements and click OK. Figure 3.33 demonstrates a scenario in which two SQL statements are written.

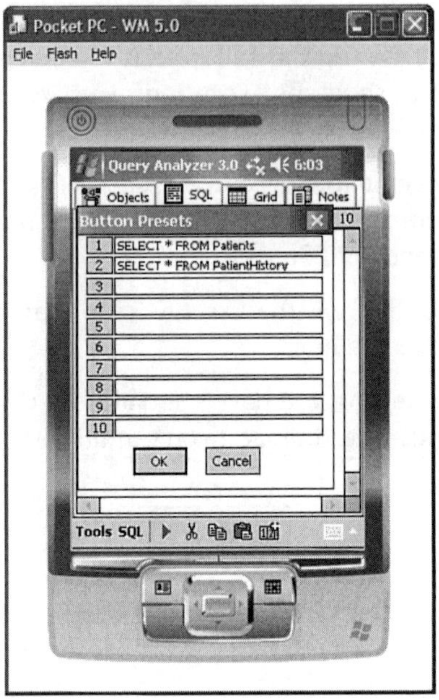

**FIGURE 3.33    Button Preset Dialog Box**

Type an SQL statement. Highlight the statement as shown in Figure 3.34 and then click on the Preset button.

**FIGURE 3.34    Highlighted SQL Statement**

The Preset dialog will open. Click on the button number where you want to store an SQL statement. The example shown in Figure 3.35 stores a statement at number three.

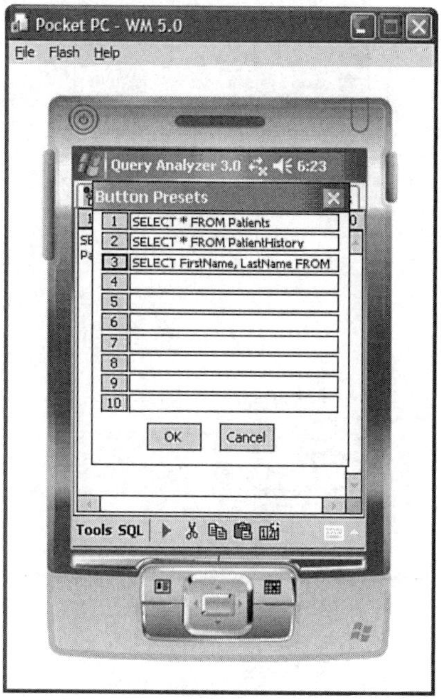

**FIGURE 3.35**   Adding SQL in Button Preset

### Using a Saved SQL Statement
Once you have saved SQL statements, you can retrieve them by simply clicking on the button on top of SQL Query Editor. The SQL statement corresponding to the button number will be copied to SQL Query Editor.

### Grid
The Grid node displays the results of query execution. When you double click on the Execute Query button, the Query Analyzer automatically activates the Grid tab and displays the results. If the query has an error, the Notes tab will activate. Figure 3.36 demonstrates the Grid tab.

### Notes
When you execute a query, the Notes section contains the amount of time it took to execute the query similar as shown in Figure 3.37. In the event the query has an error, the Notes tab will display the error message.

Now you know how to utilize Query Analyzer functionality. In the next three chapters you will learn more about the SQL Server Compact Edition database and you will use Query Analyzer interface for other operations such as creating, compacting, and deleting the database.

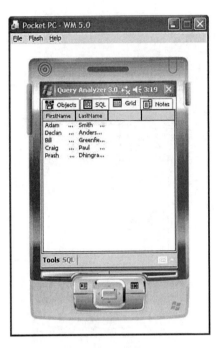

**FIGURE 3.36    Grid Tab**

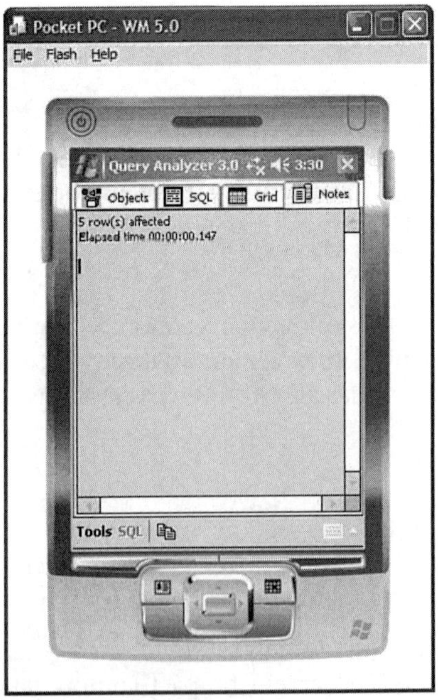

**FIGURE 3.37    Notes Tab**

# Using Visual Studio

SQL Server Compact Edition database is fully integrated with Visual Studio 2005. The integration enables rapid development of SQL Server Compact Edition applications. In this section you will create a Visual Studio project. Once the project is created, you will then explore the user interface of Visual Studio.

> **NOTE**
>
> Using Visual Studio 2005, you can create managed applications in C#.NET and VB.NET. In Visual Studio, you can create native applications using Microsoft Visual C++. Microsoft Visual C++ is also known as an embedded Visual C++ 4.0. Microsoft Embedded Visual Basic is not supported by SQL Server Compact Edition.

## Creating a Smart Device Project

One primary goal of Visual Studio integration with SQL Server Compact Edition is to provide a single development environment where a developer can create a database, design forms, and write code to access and manipulate the database. Using Visual Studio 2005, you will do the following:

- Connect to an SQL Server Compact Edition database on a desktop or on a device.

- Manage an existing database or create a new database.

- Design SQL Queries with Query Designer.

- Automatically deploy SQL Server Compact Edition and .NET Compact Framework binaries onto a device.

The following example demonstrates the Visual Studio 2005 features that help the development of a Mobile devices application using SQL Server Compact Edition.

1. Start Visual Studio. Click on File | New Project

2. The New Project dialog starts. The dialog allows you to choose project types—Visual Basic, Visual C#, Visual J#, Visual C++, etc. In the example shown in Figure 3.38, Visual C# node is selected.

3. You can build Windows, Smart Device, Database, or Starter Kits projects. In this example, select Smart Device. The Smart Device project can be built for Pocket PC 2003, Smartphone 2003, Windows CE 5.0, Windows Mobile 5.0 Pocket PC, Windows Mobile 5.0 Smartphone, Windows Mobile 6.0 Professional Edition, and Windows Mobile 6.0 Standard Edition. Select Windows Mobile Platform.

> **NOTE**
>
> You need to have Windows Mobile 5.0 SDK and Windows Mobile 6.0 SDK installed in order to have the Windows Mobile 5.0 and Windows Mobile 6.0 project options available.

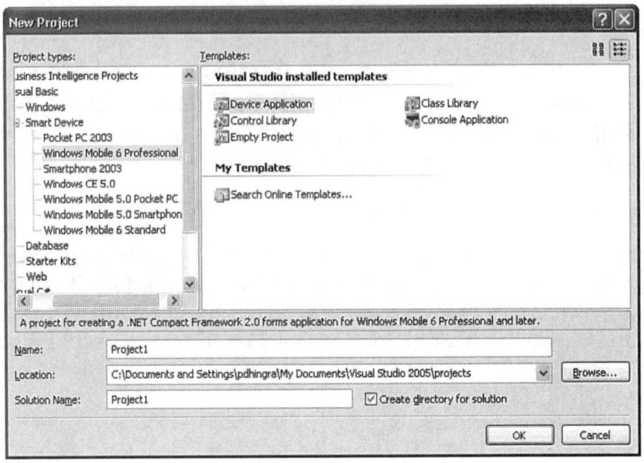

FIGURE 3.38    New Project

4. Select Device Application from the templates.

5. Specify the project name and click OK to create the project.

You will get a blank form. Using the Tool box you can add various controls to the form. In Chapter 7, *Programming with ADO.NET,* you will create examples and build a user interface for an SQL Server Compact Edition based application.

### Setting Up References
Every project has a reference file that contains the run-time requirement of application for which the project is built. You should add a reference to SqlServerCe dll in your C# or VB.NET program. To add a reference, right click on References in Solution Explorer and choose Add Reference. The Add Reference dialog box shown in Figure 3.39 allows you to browse and add components. Under the .NET tab, select System.Data.SqlServerCe dll and click OK.

Once you have set up the reference, you need to add System.Data.SqlServerCe namespace in your program as shown in Listing 3.1.

LISTING 3.1    Include namespace C#.NET

```
using System.Data.SqlServerCe;
```

LISTING 3.1    Include namespace VB.NET

```
Imports System.Data.SqlServerCe
```

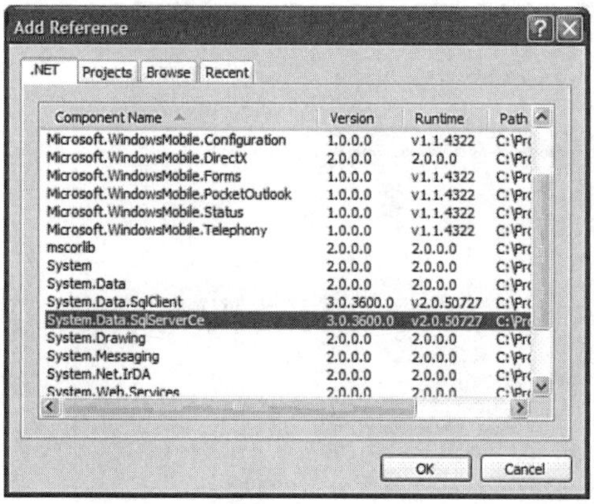

**FIGURE 3.39**   Add Reference Dialog Box

## Using Data Sources

Visual Studio 2005 provides great features for connecting to databases. In this section you will learn Visual Studio features that assist in developing applications using the SQL Server Compact Edition database. Using the Data Sources dialog box, you can create new data sources and view existing SQL Server Compact Edition data sources. Within the Data Source window you can add a new data source, edit an existing dataset, and configure a dataset with Wizard.

> **NOTE**
>
> The Data Source menu option becomes available after you open a project in Visual Studio 2005.

### The Data Source Window

You can  view data sources by clicking on Data I Show Data Sources options. The Data Source window is a central place to see the data available for a project. You can drag objects from a Data Source window onto forms to create data-bound controls.

### Configuration Wizard

Data Source Configuration Wizard helps manage the connection to Data Source. Using the Data Source Configuration Wizard, you can create and edit data sources. You can create a dataset consisting of one or more SQL Server Compact Edition tables. To connect to a data source click on Data I Add New Data Source. In Visual Studio you can create Data source from databases, Web Services, or Objects. You will get a dialog box similar to the one shown in Figure 3.40.

Click on Database and then click on the Next Button. The next dialog box as shown in Figure 3.41 allows you to choose the connection and connection string.

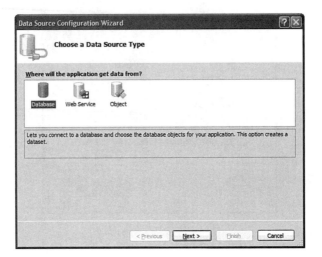

**FIGURE 3.40**    Choose a Data Source Type

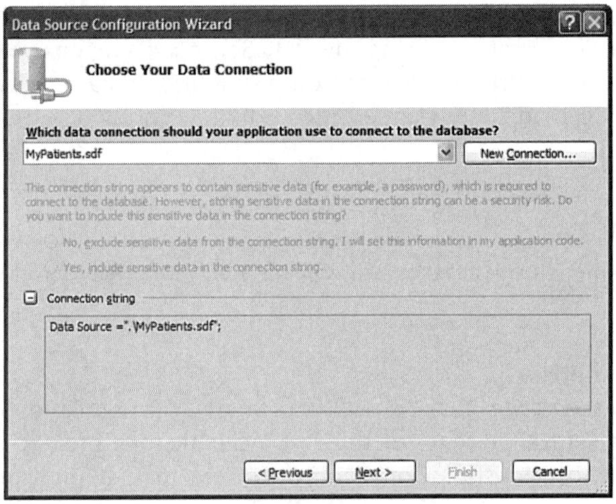

**FIGURE 3.41**    Choose Data Connection

Click on New Connection. The Add Connection dialog box shown in Figure 3.42 allows you to connect to a selected data source. You can also click on the Change button to choose a different data source. For SQL Server Compact Edition you will choose .NET Framework Data Provider.

You can click on browse and select a different database file or create a new SQL Server Compact Edition database file by clicking on the Create button.

The password field allows you to specify the password for a password protected SQL Server Compact Edition database.

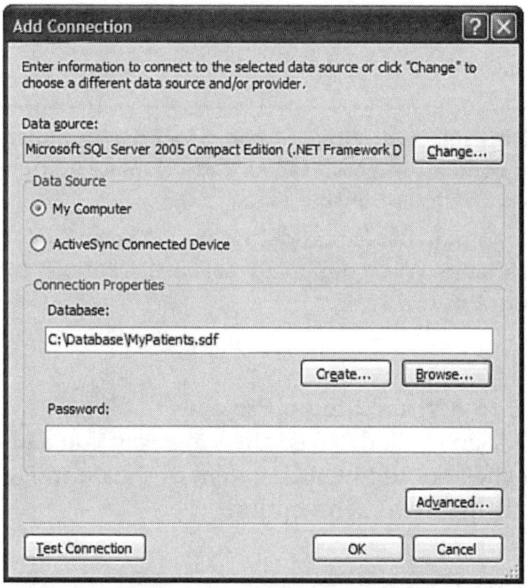

FIGURE 3.42    Add Connection Dialog Box

You can click on the Test Connection button to verify that connection to the database works.

Click the OK button.

The next dialog box shown in Figure 3.43 allows you to choose from the available objects that are displayed in a tree structure. After selecting the objects, you should provide a name for the dataset.

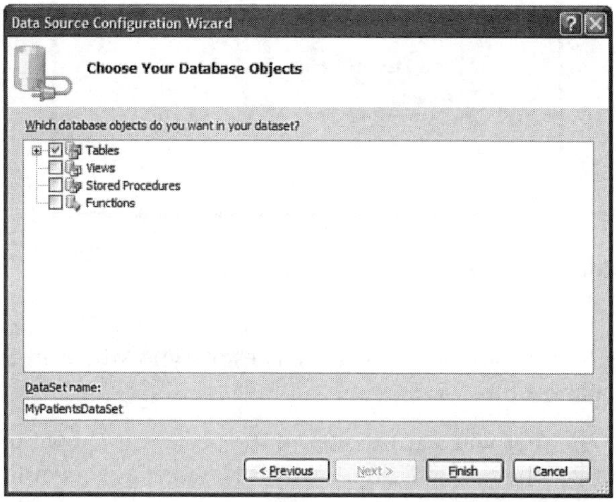

FIGURE 3.43    Choose Database Objects

On clicking Finish, a dataset schema will be added to Solution Explorer.

**NOTE**

**For the database objects selected, Visual Studio created a strongly typed dataset and adapater. The dataset contains selected tables and columns. A strongly typed dataset has columns and tables defined at design time.**

**The typed dataset allows data binding at design time. The strongly typed dataset will return all the rows in a table. When designing, select the dataset and add an SQL statement to retrieve a subset of rows.**

### Adding SQL Server CE to a Visual Studio Project

You can also add an SQL Server CE database the same way you add a C# or VB class. In Solution Explorer right click on Add | Existing Item as shown in Figure 3.44. You can also use the Project | Add Existing Item menu option.

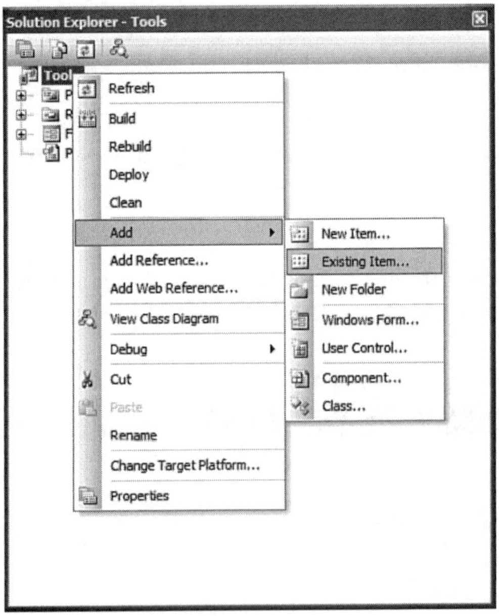


**FIGURE 3.44** Adding SQL Server CE Database to a Project

In the Add Existing Item dialog box, select the Files of Type Microsoft SQL Server 2005 Compact Edition database file.

Browse to a specific file that you want to add to the project as shown in Figure 3.45. You will notice that dataset schema file is added to your project as shown in Figure 3.46.

FIGURE 3.45     Add Database to a Project

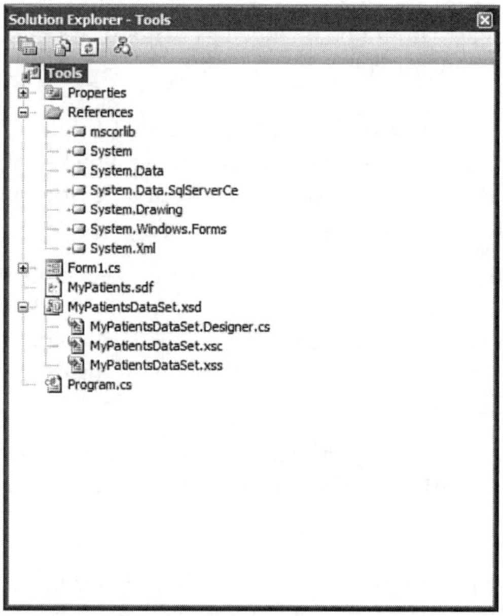

FIGURE 3.46     Data Set Schema in Solution Explorer

NOTE
_____

In the Data Source window you can click on Edit Data Source with the Designer option to modify a dataset schema.


By default Visual Studio set the Copy to Output Directory property to Copy if Newer and Build Action property value to Content.

You can choose one of three values for Copy to Output Directory.

- The Copy if Newer value copies the database file from the project folder to bin (output folder) if the database file in the project folder is newer.

- The Copy Always value always copies the database file from the project folder to a bin folder.

- The Do Not Copy value does not copy the database file. You should copy the database yourself.

You can choose one of following values for the Build Action property:

- Compile value to compile the element.

- Content to include the element as content.

- Embedded Resource to treat the element as embedded resource.

- Do nothing with the element.

The SQL Server CE database should be included as content in a project. Visual Studio 2005 does this automatically for you.

### Deploying Your Smart Device Application Using Visual Studio

Once you have built the application using Visual Studio, you will then want to execute it. For a desktop-based application you can run the executable from a command prompt or using the menu option Debug | Start without debugging.

For a device-based application you need to transfer the executable from a developer machine to a device. Visual Studio allows you to deploy the application directly on a device or on an emulator. You can use the following steps to deploy a smart device application onto a device or an emulator. You can also choose the device or emulator where you wish to deploy the application.

Emulators are virtual devices. Using Emulators available with Visual Studio 2005 you can develop and test the application on an emulator and you do not need a physical device.

1. Click Debug | Start without debugging.

2. The Deploy dialog box shown in Figure 3.47 is displayed. Choose whether to deploy an application on a device or on available emulators.

3. Select the device or emulator.

4. You can uncheck the button "Show me this dialog each time I deploy the application."

5. Click on the Deploy button.

If you opt not to get the Deploy dialog box, you will still choose whether to deploy on a device or on an emulator. From the Tool bar you can choose the option where to deploy your application. All the options in the Deploy dialog box are available in the Deployment Device combo box shown in Figure 3.48.

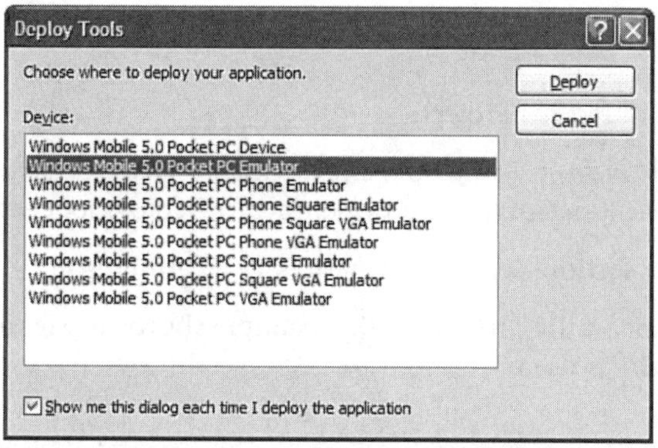

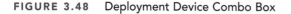

**FIGURE 3.47**    Deploy Dialog Box

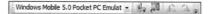

**FIGURE 3.48**    Deployment Device Combo Box

### Deploying Multiple Times

When you develop a program, it is likely that you will need to improve it over many iterations. You will deploy the application on a device or on an emulator, test it, make changes in the program, and then deploy it again. By default when you click X on a .NET Compact Framework application, it does not close. It simply becomes minimized and keeps on running in the background. As one instance of the application is already running and you are trying to deploy another instance, you will receive an error. To remove the error you need to close the already running instance of the application. You can go to running programs and close the application.

In most of the examples mentioned in this book, the Minimize Box property is set to false. When you set this property to false, an OK button appears on the right corner of the main form of application instead of an X mark. Clicking on the OK button closes the application instead of minimizing it. You can click the OK button and close the application. Once the application is closed, you can modify the application and deploy the application again. You do not need to go to the running program section to stop the previous instance of the application.

### Building a CAB File

Earlier versions of Visual Studio did not have support for building an installer project for .NET Compact Framework applications. Using Visual Studio 2005, you can build a Deployment project for Smart devices. Using Smart Device Cab Project you can drag and drop files, create folders, amend registry settings, and easily build the cabinet file for installation.

Cab files or Cabinet files are used to packages dll and executables. To build a CAB file for your application you should add a Smart Device CAB project to your solution. In the following steps you will learn how to create a Smart Device Cab project to install smart device applications.

1. Click on File | Add | New Project.

2. In the Add New Project dialog box, choose the Project type as Other Project Type and under Other Project type choose Setup and Deployment project.

3. In the template section, select the Smart Device CAB Project.

4. Specify the name of the project. In the example shown in Figure 3.49, the name SmartDeviceCab1 is used.

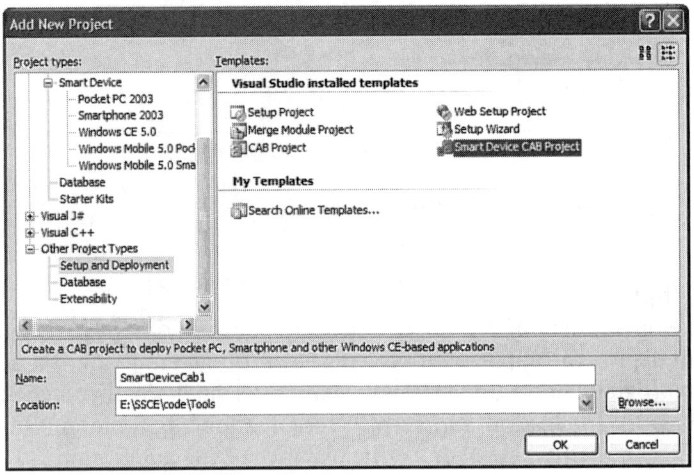

FIGURE 3.49    Setup and Deployment Project

5. Click OK.

6. Select the SmartDeviceCAB1 project.

7. Click on the View | Properties Window.

8. Change the ProductName as shown in Figure 3.50. In this example the name MyCAB is used.

9. To add the executable to the CAB file, open a file system editor. If it is not already open, right click on SmartDeviceCAB1 project, and click on View | File System option.

10. In the File System Editor, click on Application Folder.

11. Click on Action | Add | Project Output menu option as shown in Figure 3.51.

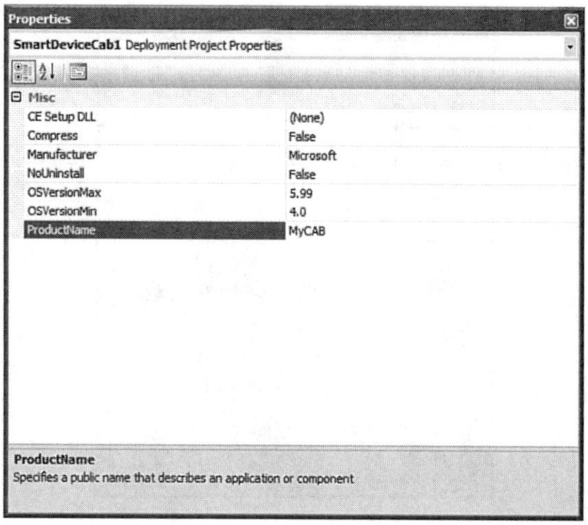

FIGURE 3.50    Properties of a CAB Project

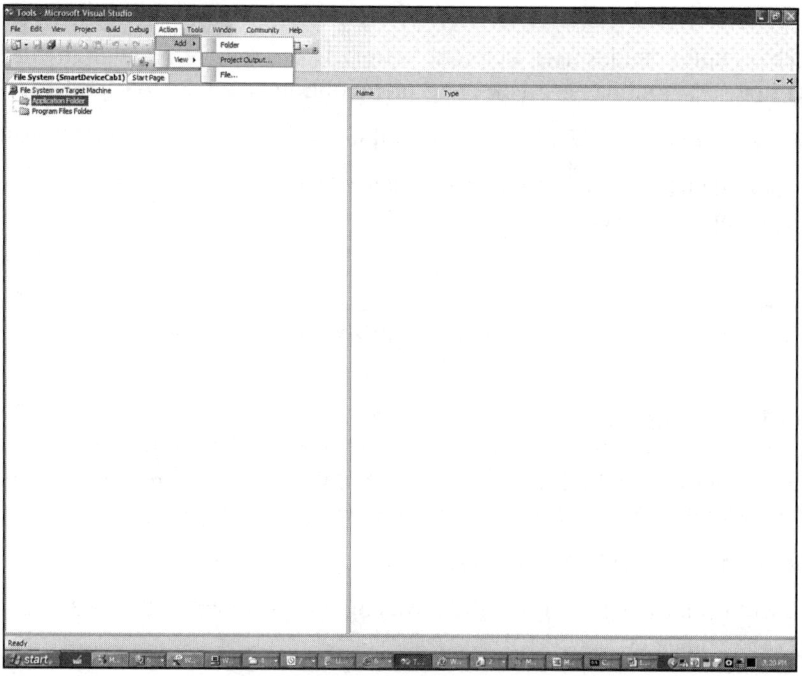

FIGURE 3.51    Project Output

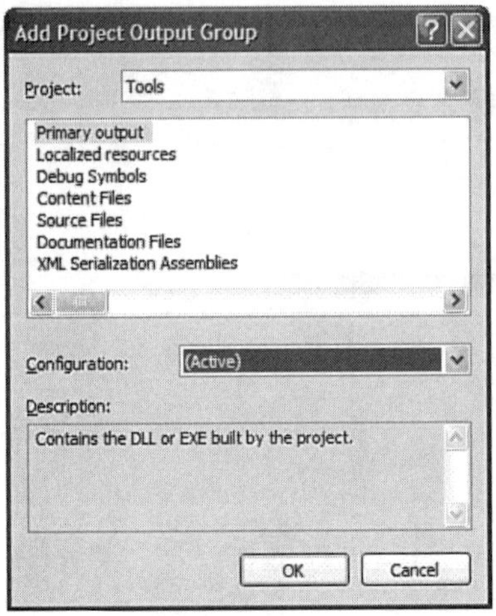

**FIGURE 3.52**    Add Primary Out

12. In the Add Project Output Group, click on Primary Output as shown in Figure 3.52 and click OK.

13. Click on Build | BuildsmartDeviceCab1. SmartDeviceCab1 is name of my deployment project. You may get a different menu option based on your project name.

14. Once you build the CAB file, you can find it under SmartDeviceCab1\Release folder.

You can copy the CAB file to a device or emulator. Just by clicking the file, the CAB file gets deployed on the device.

**NOTE**

For Smartphone you need to digitally sign the CAB file.

### Changing Target Platform

In Visual Studio it is possible for you to change the target platform For example, you can change the Windows Mobile 5.0 Pocket PC platform to Windows Mobile 5.0 Smartphone or Windows Mobile 6.0 platforms by simply following these steps:

1. Click on the Project | Choose Target Platform menu option.

2. You will get a Change Target Platform dialog box as shown in Figure 3.53.

3. Choose the New Platform in the Change to pop-up box.

4. Click OK after selecting the new platform.

5. A message box similar to one shown in Figure 3.54 is displayed telling you that the project will be closed and then reopened. Click Yes to continue.

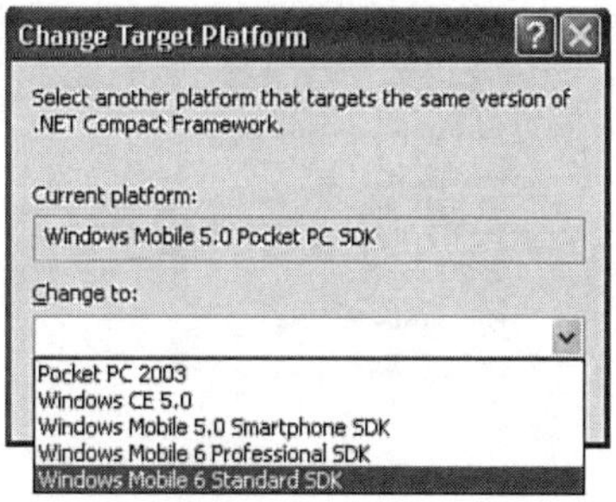

**FIGURE 3.53**    Change Target Platform

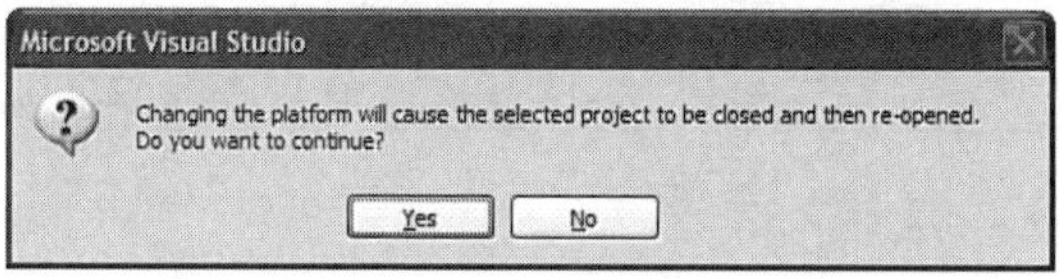

**FIGURE 3.54**    Information Message

Visual Studio 2005 and SQL Server Compact Edition integration have a number of features to develop, build, and deploy .NET Compact Framework applications. The Data Source window displays the data object for all types including the SQL Server Compact Edition data object. Data Source Configuration Wizard enables you to add the SQL Server CE database into a project.

Visual Studio 2005 has also added support for building an installer project for .NET Compact Framework based applications.

## Creating a Desktop Project

One of the main differences between SQL Server Compact Edition 3.1 and SQL Server Mobile Edition 3.0 is desktop support. Now you can use SQL Server Compact Edition to build a desktop-based application. Desktop support also enables you to develop applications in which desktop, laptop, and mobile devices can use the same database.

To use SQL Server Compact Edition in a desktop, you will create a Windows based project and add a reference to SqlServerCe dll installed for desktop. Follow these steps to create a Windows project using SQL Server Compact Edition

1. Start Visual Studio. Click on File | New Project as shown in Figure 3.55.

2. The New Project dialog box appears. The dialog box allows you to choose project types—Visual Basic, Visual C#, Visual J#, Visual C++, etc. In this example, the Visual C# node is selected as shown in Figure 3.55.

4. Select Windows Application from the templates.

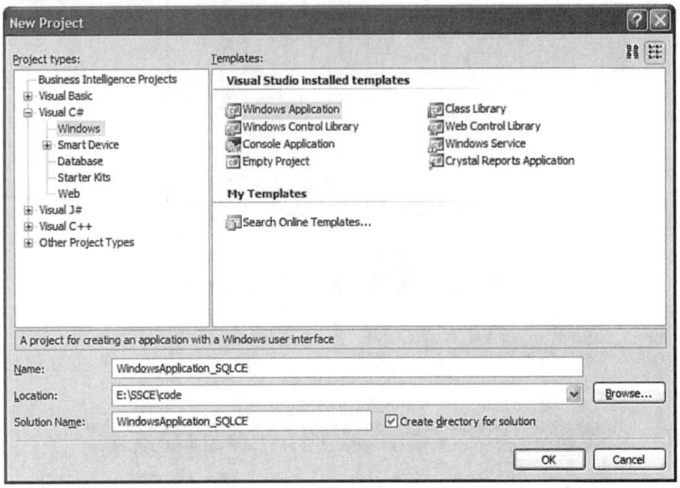

**FIGURE 3.55**    Desktop Project

5. Specify the name of the project and click OK to create the project. You will get a blank form. Using the Tool box you can add various controls to the form.

6. To use SQL Server Compact Edition you should add a reference to SqlServerCe dll. In Solution Explorer, click on References. Right click and choose Add References.

7. In the Add Reference dialog box, click on the Browse button.

8. Browse to locate where you have installed SQL Server Compact Edition. Earlier you learned that SQL Server Compact Edition for desktop gets installed at `<Disk>:\Program Files\Microsoft SQL Server Compact Edition\v3.1`.

9. Select System.Data.SqlServerCe.dll and click the OK button as shown in Figure 3.56.

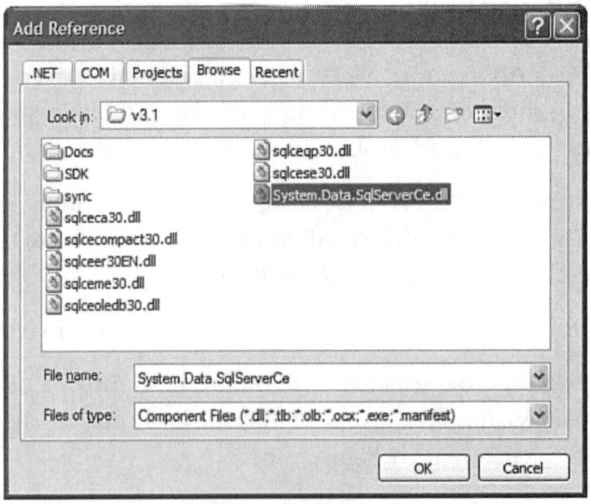

**FIGURE 3.56**    Add Reference to SQLServerCe Namespace

Once you have set up the reference, you need to add System.Data.SqlServerCe namespace in your program. At the top of the code include the SQLServerCe namespace as shown in Listing 3.2

**LISTING 3.2    Include namespace C#.NET**

```
using System.Data.SqlServerCe;
```

**LISTING 3.2    Include namespace VB.NET**

```
Imports System.Data.SqlServerCe
```

Now you can start writing code for a desktop application that uses SQL Server CE as a local store.

## Using DataDirectory

You have learned how to specify the full path of an SQL Server Compact Edition database file. Using the DataDirectory feature you can specify the path of database in DataDirectory. You can set the DataDirectory property using Application Domain as shown in Listing 3.3.

With the DataDirectory feature you do not need to hardcode the full path of the database in connection string.

**LISTING 3.3    DataDirectory C#.NET**

```
AppDomain.CurrentDomain.SetData ("DataDirectory",@"C:\Database");
```

**LISTING 3.3    DataDirectory VB.NET**

```
AppDomain.CurrentDomain.SetData("DataDirectory", "C:\Database")
```

Instead of specifying the full path in a connection string, you will specify DataDirectory enclosed in | (pipe) symbol and the SQL Server Compact Edition filename as shown in Listing 3.4.

**LISTING 3.4    DataDirectory C#.NET**

```
myConn = new SqlCeConnection
        ("Data Source=|DataDirectory|\\Email.sdf;");
myConn.Open();
```

**LISTING 3.4    DataDirectory VB.NET**

```
myConn = New SqlCeConnection _
        ("Data Source=|DataDirectory|\\Email.sdf;")
myConn.Open()
```

## Connecting to an Emulator

The device emulator is a desktop-based application that emulates the behavior of Windows Mobile or Windows CE based hardware. An emulator emulates an ARM processor. You can configure various properties of the emulator such as ROM size, orientation, and so on. Similar to a device, a partnership can now be created between ActiveSync and an emulator. The ActiveSync partnership is needed in applications that synchronize data between a desktop and a device.

There are three ways to connect to a device or an emulator:

- Develop a device project: Build and Deploy solution. A dialog box will appear where you can choose to develop or deploy the solution as shown in Figure 3.57.

- Click on the Tools | Connect to Device option. A dialog box similar to the one shown in Figure 3.57 will appear where you can choose the platform, the device/emulator, and select Connect.

- Click on Tools | Device Emulator Manager. A Device Emulator Manager dialog box appears showing a list of emulators. Select an emulator, right click, and select Connect.

### NOTE

You can also use the `dvcemumanager.exe` file to start the Device Emulator Manager. This executable is located in the `Program Files\Microsoft Device Emulator\1.0` folder.

The connected emulator is shown with a green arrow.

Once the emulator is connected, you can deploy an application and execute the application on an emulator. A connected, but not cradled, emulator is shown in Figure 3.57

### Cradling the Emulator

When the emulator starts, it acts as a device that is not cradled. A connected emulator can be used to execute an application locally on an emulator. If you need to synchronize data between a device and a server, the device needs to be cradled. Similar to a device, an emulator needs to be cradled. To cradle an emulator, you will choose the Cradle option in the Device Emulator Manager.

1. Select the emulator in Device Emulator Manager, right click, and select Cradle.

2. After the emulator is cradled, ActiveSync detects it, and the ActiveSync icon in the system tray will become green. You can also double click to start ActiveSync if it does not start automatically. Once the ActiveSync connection is established, it may display a dialog box to synchronize files. Click Cancel to establish a guest partnership between the emulator and the desktop as shown in Figure 3.58.

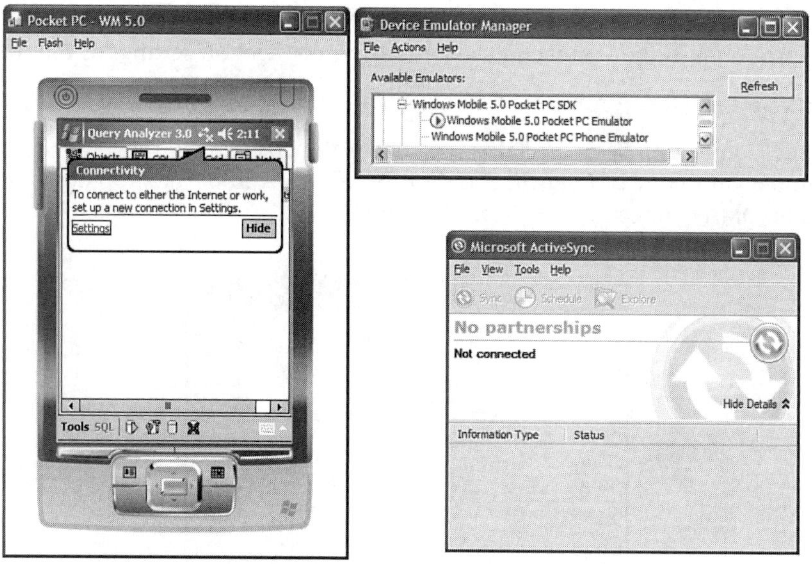

FIGURE 3.57    Not Cradled Emulator

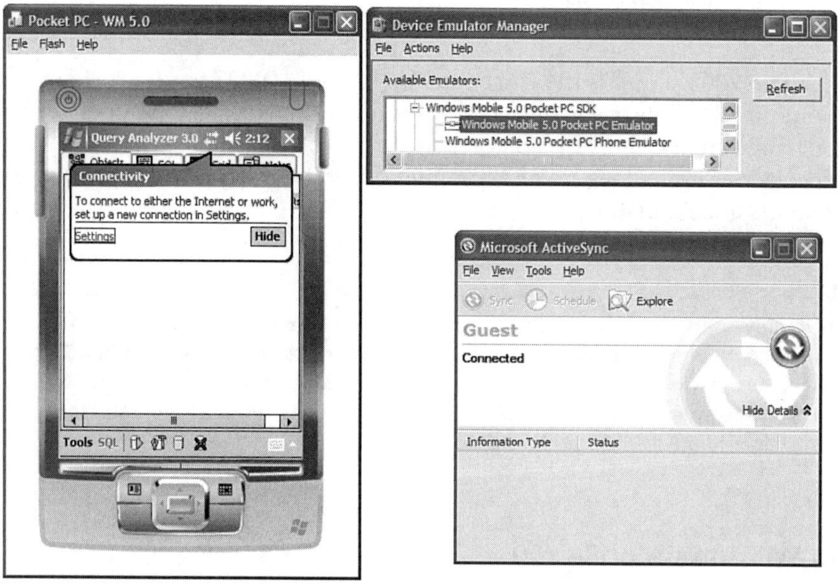

FIGURE 3. 58    Cradled Emulator

### Configuring ActiveSync for Emulator

The DMA option must be selected in the ActiveSync connection settings as follows:

1.  Click on the File | Connection Settings menu option.

2.  In the Connection Settings dialog box, check the box next to the "Allow Connection to one of following" option. Select DMA from the drop down box to enable DMA connections as shown in Figure 3.59.

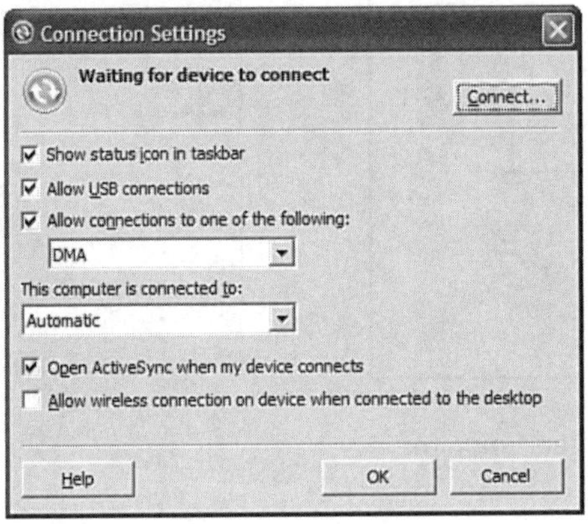

**FIGURE 3.59**    DMA Settings

Visual Studio 2005 supports the Direct Memory Access (DMA) transport channel to communicate with a device emulator. DMA is faster than TCP/IP and does not require network connectivity. DMA is also faster and more robust than transmitting over a network stack as it provides a direct communication between two Windows processes–Visual Studio and emulator.

**NOTE**

You do not need to use ActiveSync and you do not need to cradle the emulator if the application is running locally on an emulator. The emulator must be cradled through an ActiveSync connection if the application communicates to a backend server to exchange data. For example, Replication, RDA, or SqlClient usage requires an emulator to be cradled and connected through ActiveSync.

## Using Windows Mobile 6.0

Microsoft released Windows Mobile 6.0 SDK in the beginning of 2007. Windows Mobile 6.0 is built on top of Windows Mobile 5.0. The taxonomy is changed between Windows Mobile 5.0 and Windows Mobile 6.0

Windows Mobile 5.0 differentiates devices such as Windows Mobile Pocket PC and Windows Mobile Smartphone. Pocket PCs and Pocket PCs with the phone edition have touch screen capability and accept screen input whereas Smartphone does not.

Windows Mobile 6.0 SDKs does not target specific devices. Windows Mobile 6.0 has the following two SDK:

- Windows Mobile Professional Edition targets the devices that have touch screen capability.

- Windows Mobile Standard Edition targets devices that do not have touch screen capability.

Once you install the Windows Mobile 6.0 SDKs, you will be able to develop corresponding project types in Visual Studio. Windows Mobile SDKs are installed in the same fashion as Windows Mobile 5.0 SDK.

### New Features in Windows Mobile 6.0 SDK

Windows Mobile 6.0 devices include SQL Server Compact Edition and .NET Compact Framework in the ROM. Having these products in ROM have many benefits including:

- More remaining space available in RAM as .NET CF and SQL Server Compact Edition do not occupy RAM space.

- The reduction of the overall size of the installation package as it only contains the application component.

- A reduction in deployment effort and support level required for end users.

Windows Mobile 6.0 SDK provides Cellular Emulator. Using Cellular Emulator, you can test your application in various cellular communication situations from an emulator.

Using an emulator, you can also set the profile of your phone to headset, speaker phone, or car kit. The phone profile options and cellular emulator options in Emulator allow you to test your application in various real life scenarios.

Windows Mobile 6.0 provides a code signing utility, CABSignTool that signs together the Cab files and all of its constituent executables.

Windows Mobile 6.0 provides a Hopper unity to provide stress testing of mobile applications.

Windows Mobile 6 SDK provides Security Configuration Manager to configure the emulator with various security policies. Using these security policies, you can test the application with various security settings.

Windows Mobile 6.0 provides features and utilities to enhance the developer's experience. The inclusion of .NET CF and SQL Server compact Edition in ROM simplifies deployment. Device Emulator 2.0 included in Windows Mobile 6.0 allows you to test applications in real life scenarios without requiring a physical device.

You should consult the Windows Mobile documentation to get more details about Windows Mobile features.

## Summary

This chapter provided you with an overview of SQL Server Management Studio, Query Analyzer, and Visual Studio tools. You will use SQL Server Management Studio and Query Analyzer to manage databases on a desktop and a device. SQL Server Management Studio provides an integrated environment to manage SQL Server, Integration Service, Analysis Services, and an SQL Server Compact Edition database. You also learned how to use Visual Studio to connect to a database. SQL Server Management Studio and Visual Studio add a lot of flexibility to develop database applications. In the remaining chapters of this book you will be using these features to develop more powerful examples.

# Managing the SQL Server 2005 Compact Edition Database

This chapter describes the methods to create, secure, verify, compact, and shrink an SQL Server Compact Edition database. On server databases where the database is centrally located, these types of operations are done by Database Administrators (DBAs). On mobile and embedded databases that are deployed on a device or on a client, you may want a DBA to handle the data management operation or you can provide menu options in the application to verify, repair, compact, and shrink the database.

## Creating an SQL Server Compact Edition Database

To create an SQL Server Compact Edition database you will need to specify the path of the SQL Server Compact Edition database file and the database filename. You can later add other database attributes such as a password—a Boolean value for enabling encryption. While creating a new database file for one that already exists, you can specify an option to delete the existing file and create a new one.

You can create a database using SQL Server Management Studio, Visual Studio, or Query Analyzer. You can also create a database using Tools, a T-SQL statement, or programmatic ADO.NET and OLE DB interface.

## Creating a Database Using SSMS

SQL Server Management Studio (SSMS) provides an integrated environment for creating and maintaining SQL Server and SQL Server Compact Edition objects. When you start SQL Server Management Studio, it displays a dialog box to specify the Server type, Database file, etc. As shown in Figure 4.1, choose SQL Server Compact Edition for Server type. (SQL Server 2005 SP2 or a higher version will show Server type as SQL Server Compact Edition. An earlier version of SQL Server 2005 will show the Server type as SQL Server Mobile Edition.)

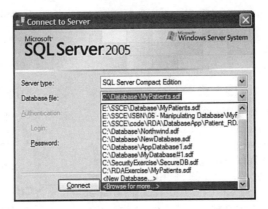

**FIGURE 4.1**    New Database Option in SSMS

You can choose any of the existing SQL Server Compact Edition database files or choose the New Database option to create a new SQL Server Compact Edition database. When you choose a New Database option, it asks you to specify the path and database filename.

Figure 4.2 demonstrates options that you can choose while creating a database. You can optionally select the check box, Overwrite existing database file. Other options include sorting language, encryption, and password protection.

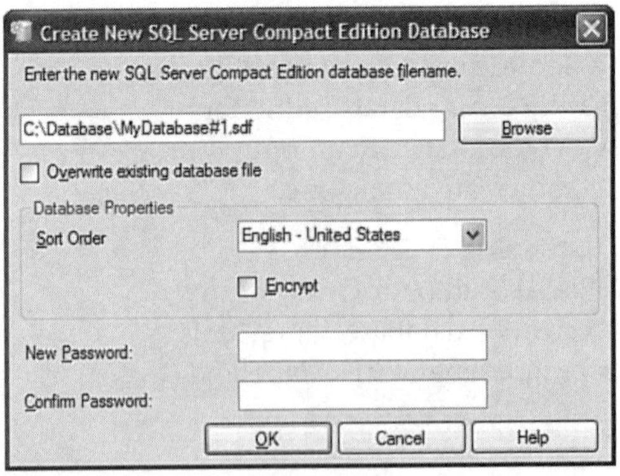

**FIGURE 4.2**    Create New Database Dialog Box

SQL Server 2005 SP2 or a higher version has SQL Server Compact Edition 3.1. Earlier versions of SQL Server 2005 (RTM or SP1) have SQL Server Mobile Edition.

This first exercise does not specify a password and does not use the encryption option. Not specifying a password displays a Warning dialog box as shown in Figure 4.3. Click Yes to continue and create a database without a password.

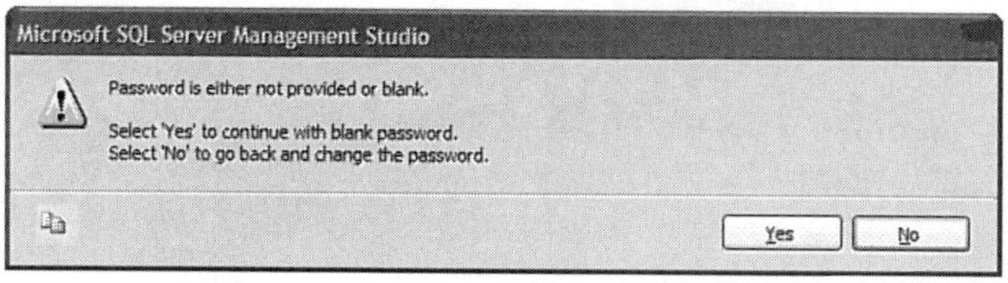

**FIGURE 4.3**    Warning for Missing Password

## Creating a Database Using Visual Studio

Visual Studio 2005 provides a complete development environment. Not only does it allow you to develop a client application, it also provides features to create and manage the SQL Server Compact Edition database. If you are a .NET developer, you do not need to install SQL Server Management Studio to create and manage an SQL Server Compact Edition database. Instead you create the database file the same way that you add any C# or VB.NET class—add a new item and choose the type, SQL Mobile Database, or the Database file option.

Visual Studio 2005 SP1 installs SQL Server Compact Edition 3.1. An earlier version of Visual Studio (RTM) installs SQL Server Mobile Edition. In Visual Studio 2005 SP1, the New Item dialog box will have the template Database file. Earlier versions will have the option SQL Mobile Database.

1. Right Click on the project.

2. Click on Add | New Item Option as shown in Figure 4.4.

3. In the New Item dialog box, select SQL Mobile Database (or Database File) as shown in Figure 4.5.

4. Specify the name of SQL Server Compact Edition file.

5. Click the Add button.

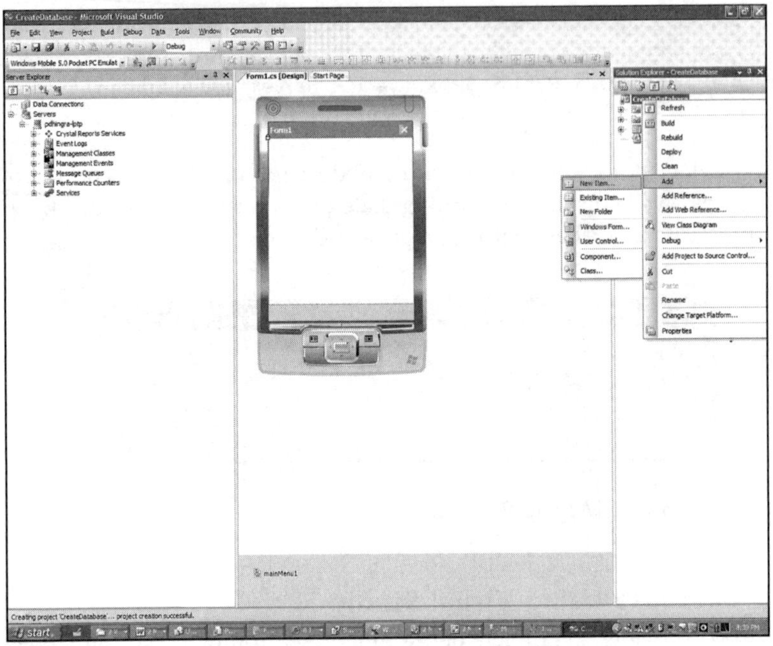

**FIGURE 4.4**    New Item Option for Database Creation

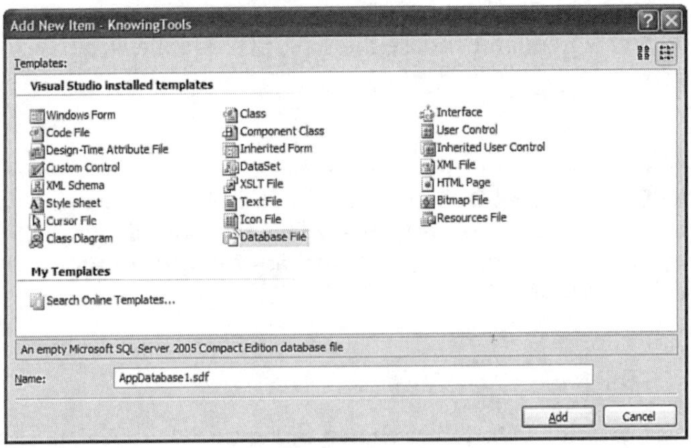

**FIGURE 4.5**    Add a New Database to a Visual Studio Project

6. The next dialog box allows you to choose which object you want to add to your dataset. When you add an SQL Server Compact Edition database in Visual Studio, you should select the Tables object as shown in Figure 4.6.

7. Click on the Finish button to complete the addition of a newly created database in Visual Studio.

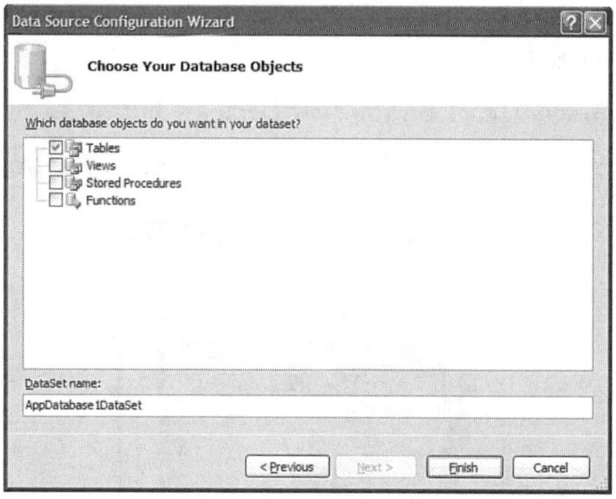

FIGURE 4.6    Choose Database Object

## Creating a Database Using Query Analyzer

You can use Query Analyzer on a device to create an SQL Server Compact Edition database. Click on the New Database icon in Query Analyzer, and then specify the path and filename. You can optionally choose to enable encryption and make the database password protected. Use the following steps to create the SQL Server Compact Edition database:

1. To start the Query Analyzer on a device or an emulator, click on Start | Query Analyzer as shown in Figure 4.7.

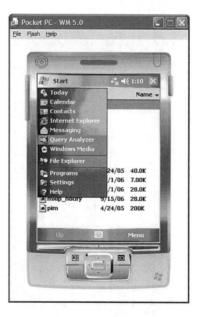

FIGURE 4.7    Query Analyzer Option

2. Click on the Database icon at the bottom of Query Analyzer. The Database icon is shown in Figure 4.8.

3. As shown in Figure 4.9, click on the New Database button to create a new database.

4. Specify the Path name of the database file. This exercise uses NewDatabase.sdf.

FIGURE 4.8    New Database Button

FIGURE 4.9    New Database Option in Query Analyzer

5. You can optionally check the Encrypt button. By enabling encryption, you need to specify a password in order to access the encrypted database.

6. Click on the Create button to create the database as shown in Figure 4.10.

7. As shown in Figure 4.11, the new database is created and Query Analyzer connects to the database.

FIGURE 4.10     Specify New Database Name

FIGURE 4.11     Objects Tab in Query Analyzer

## Creating a Database Using SQL

You can create a database using the following SQL Statement:

```
CREATE DATABASE "SecureDb.sdf"
```

When you create a database using an SQL statement, you can also specify the password creation. On a desktop, you execute the SQL statement in SQL Server Management Studio. On mobile devices, Query Analyzer can be used to execute SQL statements.

## Creating a Database Programmatically

To create an SQL Server Compact Edition database using ADO.NET, use the CreateDatabase method of SqlCeEngine class. Before calling the CreateDatabase method, you need to determine a connection string that specifies the path, filename, and other connection string properties. Listing 4.1 creates an SQL Server Compact Edition database named SecureDb.sdf.

LISTING 4.1    CreateDatabase C#.NET

```csharp
string myConnString = "Data Source='SecureDB.sdf';";
SqlCeEngine myEngine = new SqlCeEngine(myConnString);
myEngine.CreateDatabase();
```

LISTING 4.1    CreateDatabase Visual Basic.NET

```vbnet
Dim myConnString As String = "Data Source='SecureDB.sdf';"
Dim myEngine As New SqlCeEngine(myConnString)
myEngine.CreateDatabase()
```

# Deleting the Database

Since the SQL Server Compact Edition database is a file-based database, you can delete it by simply deleting the SQL Server Compact Edition file. The database file can be deleted using the operating system features.

Listing 4.2 demonstrates how the file can be deleted using an API.

### NOTE

The SQL Server Compact Edition file can be deleted if there is no open connection to the database.

LISTING 4.2     **Delete Database File C#.NET**

```
if (File.Exists("MyDatbase.sdf") )
{
    File.Delete("MyDatabase.sdf");
}
```

LISTING 4.2     **Delete Database File Visual Basic.NET**

```
If File.Exists("Northwind.sdf") Then
    File.Delete("Northwind.sdf")
End If
```

## Deleting the Database Using Query Analyzer

On a mobile device you can simply delete the SQL Server Compact Edition database file. The Query Analyzer also provides an option to delete the SQL Server Compact Edition file. Simply close the connection and click on the Delete icon to delete the database as demonstrated in the following steps:

1. Disconnect from the SQL Server Compact Edition database by clicking on the Disconnect button. As shown in Figure 4.12, the Disconnect button is highlighted in the rectangle.

FIGURE 4.12     Disconnecting from Database

2. After you are disconnected from database, click on the Delete button to delete the SQL Server Compact Edition database. Figure 4.13 highlights the Delete button by enclosing it inside a rectangle.

3. Click OK to delete the database.

**FIGURE 4.13**    Delete Database Using Query Analyzer

## Verifying a Database

The SQL Server Compact Edition database is made up of a single file consisting of logical pages. For each page, a checksum is calculated and written. You need to use the Verify method to verify a database. Unfortunately, the SQL Server Management Studio does not provide a dialog box to verify it.

The SQL Server Compact Edition database provides a Verify method to validate the database. The Verify method recalculates the checksum of each page. For a valid database, a checksum of each page will match the recalculated value for that page. If the recalculated checksums do not match the actual value, the verify method will return FALSE indicating that the database file is corrupted. If the checksum matches with the recalculated value, the Verify method returns TRUE.

## LISTING 4.3    Verify Database C#.NET

```
SqlCeEngine engine = new SqlCeEngine("DataSource=Northwind.sdf");
if (engine.Verify() == false)
    MessageBox.Show("Verification Failed. Please repair the database");
else
    MessageBox.Show("Verification Passed.");
```

## LISTING 4.3    Verify Database Visual Basic.NET

```
Dim myEngine As SqlServerCe.SqlCeEngine
myEngine = New SqlServerCe.SqlCeEngine("Data Source = Northwind.sdf")
If myEngine.Verify() = False Then
    MessageBox.Show("Verification Failed. Please Repair Database")
Else
    MessageBox.Show("Verification Passed.")
End If
```

# Repairing a Database

As discussed earlier, an SQL Server Compact Edition database can be validated by the Verify method. The Verify method will recalculate the checksum for a database page. For a corrupted database, the recalculated checksums do not match the actual value.

> **NOTE**
>
> SQL Server Compact Edition is a reliable and robust database. A database corruption is a rare scenario.

You can use the Repair method to repair a corrupted SQL Server Compact Edition database. Similar to the Verify method, the Repair method also recalculates the checksum of each page of the SQL Server Compact Edition database. If the page checksums do not match the calculated value, the page is considered corrupted. The Repair method will repair each corrupted page of an SQL Server Compact Edition database file.

There are two possible options for repairing an SQL Server Compact Edition database:

- The Delete Corrupted Rows option—deletes the pages having corrupted rows.
- The Recover Corrupted Rows option—reads and recovers data from corrupted pages.

When you choose the Delete Corrupted Rows option, you may lose a lot of data especially if the schema pages are corrupted. The advantage of the Recover Corrupted Rows option is that most of the data can be recovered; however, the downside is that recovered data may have logical inconsistencies.

## Repair a Database Using SQL Server Management Studio

The following steps demonstrate how SQL Server Management Studio uses the Repair Database option to repair a corrupted SQL Server Compact Edition database.

To repair the SQL Server Compact Edition database, follow these steps:

1. Open the corrupted database using SQL Server Management Studio.

2. Right click on the database and click on Properties.

3. On the Database properties dialog box, click on the Shrink and Repair tab (see Figure 4.14).

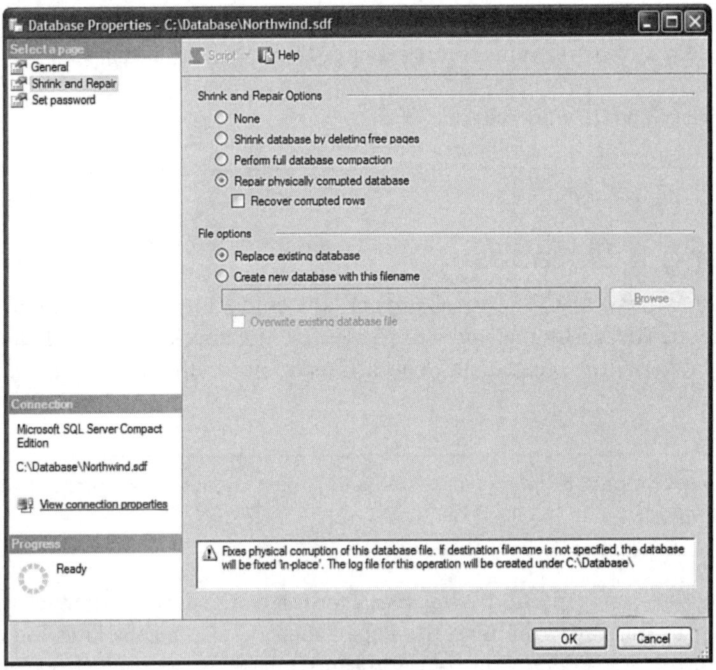

FIGURE 4.14    Repair Option in SSMS Dialog Box

4. Select the radio button, Repair physically corrupted database.

5. You can select the Recover corrupted rows option. If you do not select this option, the corrupted rows will be deleted.

6. Choose the radio button Replace existing database. By choosing this option, the original database file is repaired.

7. Choose the radio button, Create a new database with this filename, and specify a new file. When choosing this option, the original database file remains intact and a new database file is created in SQL Server Compact Edition.

8. Click OK to proceed with the repair.

As depicted in Figure 4.15, the log file is created in the same directory where the database exists. The following lists some of the example log file entries. The first example shows the Replace existing database option.

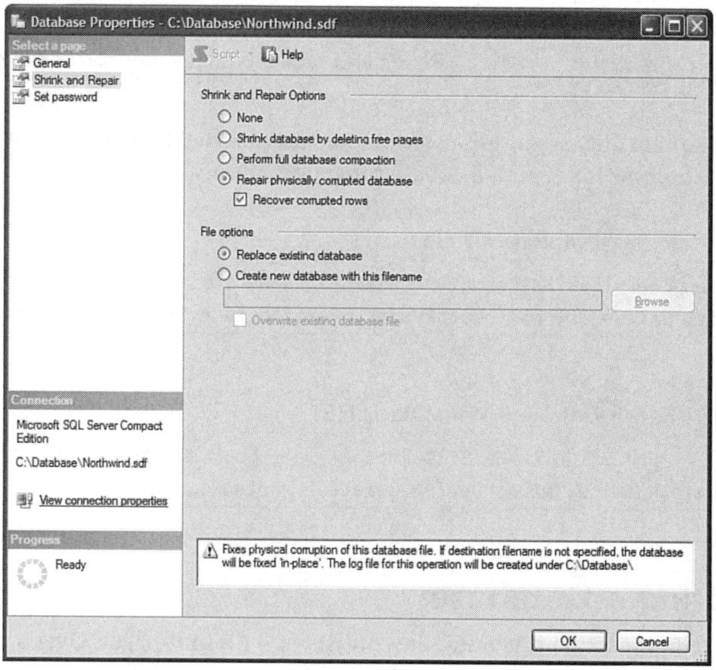

FIGURE 4.15    Repairing the Database with the Recover Option Using SSMS

Source: `C:\Database\Northwind.sdf`

Destination: `C:\Database\Northwind.sdf.F19823.tmp`

Time: `2006-22-12 00:03:07.781`

The second log file shows the option, Create new database with this filename.

Source: `C:\Database\Northwind.sdf`

Destination: `Northwindnew`

Time: `2006-24-12 21:45:40.953`

## Repair a Database Programmatically

SQL Server Compact Edition also provides an API to repair a database. The `SQLCeEngine` object has a Repair method to repair an SQL Server Compact Edition database. The Repair method takes two arguments: the first parameter is a connection string and the second parameter is an option specifying how the engine should repair the database.

The Repair option parameter can have one of two possible values as shown in Table 4.1.

TABLE 4.1    SQL Server Compact Edition Repair Options

| Repair Options | Description |
| --- | --- |
| DeleteCorruptedRows | Deletes the pages having corrupted rows. |
| RecoverCorruptedRows | Reads and recovers data from corrupted options. |

The two options are discussed in the section, Repairing a Database, on page 113. Listing 4.4 demonstrates how to repair a database programmatically.

LISTING 4.4    Repair Database C#.NET

```
SqlCeEngine engine = new SqlCeEngine("DataSource=Northwind.sdf");
engine.Repair("DataSource=Northwind2.sdf", RepairOption.DeleteCorruptedRows);
```

LISTING 4.4    Repair Database Visual Basic.NET

```
Dim myEngine As New SqlServerCe.SqlCeEngine("Data Source = Northwind.sdf")
myEngine.Repair(Nothing, RepairOption.DeleteCorruptedRows)
```

# Compacting a Database

An SQL Server Compact Edition database consists of 4 KB unit pages. Over a period of time, the internal structure of a database file can be fragmented. Fragmentation results in additional unused disk space and impacts performance. A Compact database mechanism reclaims the unused space from the database and removes the fragmentation.

Deleting a row from a database marks the row as deleted and available for new additions. The Delete operation does not physically reduce the database size. It results in the following types of unused space:

- Unused space in pages.

- Completely unused pages.

Unused spaces in pages can be claimed by the Compact method. The Compact operation creates a new SQL Server Compact Edition database and copies rows from an old database to a new database.

Completely unused pages can be reclaimed using the AutoShrink method. The next section, Shrink a Database, will describe the Shrink operation.

To compact the SQL Server Compact Edition database, all connections to the database should be closed. As a compact operation creates a new database, you should have additional space for a destination database. While compacting the database, you can change the encryption and password setting for the new database.

- The SQL Server Compact Edition database should be closed for compaction.

- You can change the collating order, encryption, and password setting while compacting the database.

- You need to have additional space—both for a source and a destination database for compacting.

## Compact the Database Using SQL Server Management Studio

SQL Server Management Studio provides a feature to compact an SQL Server Compact Edition database file. Open the database using SQL Server Management Studio and follow these steps:

1. Right click on the database and click on Properties.

2. On the Database properties dialog box, click on the Shrink and Repair tab.

3. Select the radio button, Perform the full database compaction option.

4. You can choose the file option, Replace existing database, as shown in Figure 4.16. This option compacts the original database file.

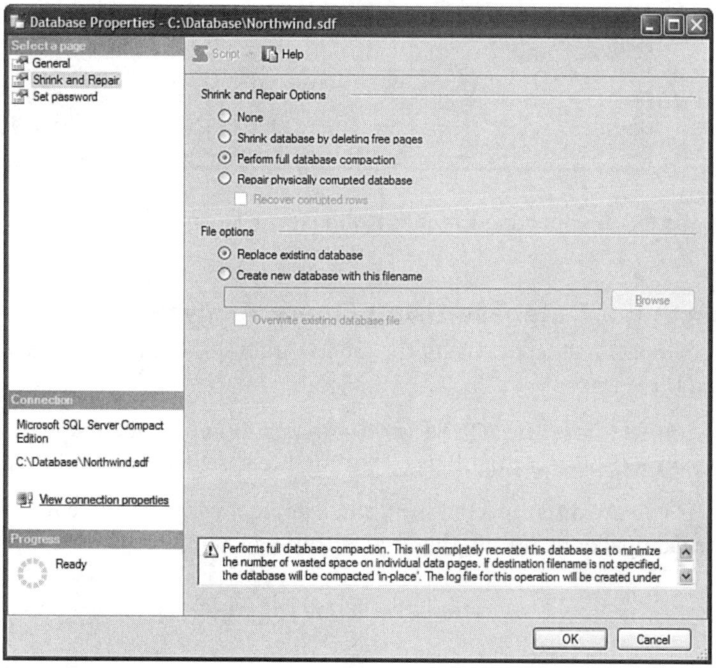

FIGURE 4.16    Compacting a Database Using SSMS

5. Or you can choose the file option, Create new database with this filename, as shown in Figure 4.17 and specify the new filename. When you use this option, the original database file remains intact and a compacted database is created into a new SQL Server Compact Edition file.

6. Click OK to proceed with compaction.

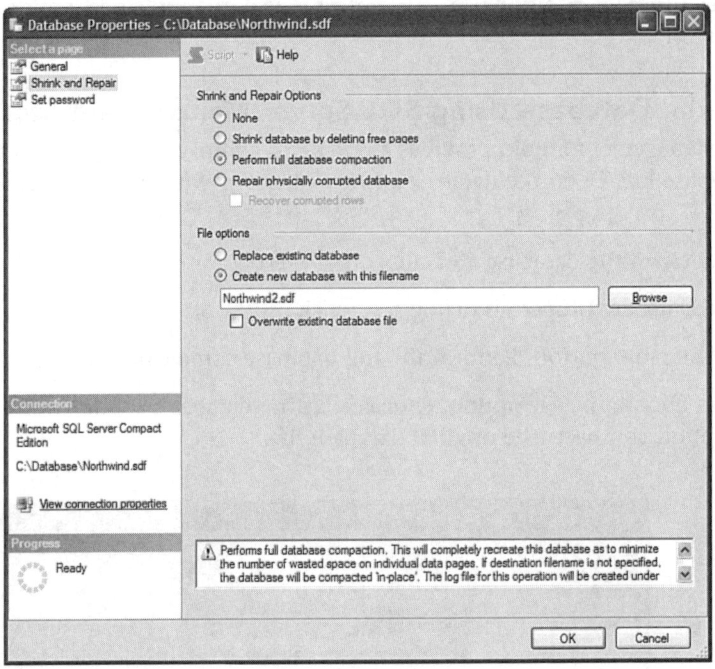

FIGURE 4.17    Compacting Database with New Filename Using SSMS

## Compacting a Database Using Query Analyzer

You can compact a database using the Query Analyzer tool on a device or an emulator by following these steps:

1. Disconnect from the SQL Server Compact Edition database by clicking on the Disconnect button (highlighted within a rectangle as shown in Figure 4.18).

2. After you are disconnected from the database, compact the database by clicking on the Compact button (highlighted within a rectangle as shown in Figure 4.19).

**FIGURE 4.18**    Disconnect Database from Query Analyzer

**FIGURE 4.19**    Compacting Database Using Query Analyzer

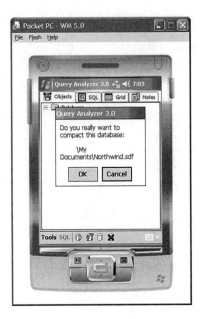

FIGURE 4.20    Warning Message for Compact

3. Clicking the Compact button triggers a pop-up message as shown in Figure 4.20.

4. Click the OK button to proceed with compaction.

Query Analyzer does not provide the option for specifying a database name destination.

## Compacting a Database Programmatically

To compact the database programmatically, you need to use the Compact method. This method does the compaction of the SQL Server Compact Edition database specified by the SqlCeEngine object. The Compact method only has one connection string argument. The connection string points to the destination database that will be created as a result of compaction. You can pass the empty destination string and the compacted database will overwrite the existing database. The Compact method will throw an exception if the destination database already exists. Listing 4.5 demonstrates how to compact the database programmatically.

LISTING 4.5    Compact Database C#.NET

```
string myConnectionStr = "DataSource=Northwind.sdf";
string dstConnectionStr = "DataSource=DstNorthwind.sdf";
SqlCeEngine engine = new SqlCeEngine(myConnectionStr);
engine.Compact(dstConnectionStr);
```

**LISTING 4.5    Compact Database Visual Basic.NET**

```
Dim srcConnectionStr As String = "Data Source = Northwind.sdf;"
Dim dstConnectionStr As String = "Data Source = Northwind.sdf;"
Dim myEngine As SqlServerCe.SqlCeEngine
myEngine = New SqlServerCe.SqlCeEngine()
myEngine.LocalConnectionString = srcConnectionStr
myEngine.Compact(dstConnectionStr)
```

# Shrinking a Database

Similar to the Compact method, the Shrink method helps to reclaim the unused database space by reclaiming the unused pages from the SQL Server Compact Edition database. Compact method copies the rows to a temporary database, and the Shrink method moves all the unused pages to the end of a file and then truncates the file.

## Shrinking a Database Using SQL Server Management Studio

To Shrink an SQL Server Compact Edition database, use the Shrink and Repair option to delete the free pages in a database:

1. Right click on Database and click on Properties.

2. On the Database properties dialog box, click on the tab Shrink and Repair.

3. Select the radio button, Shrink database by deleting free pages, as shown in Figure 4.21.

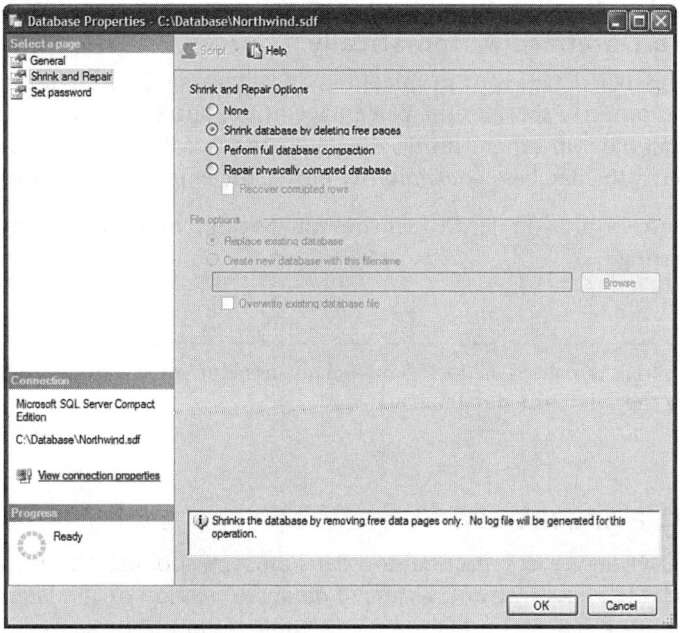

**FIGURE 4.21**    Shrink Database Using SSMS

**4.** Click OK.

## Shrinking a Database Programmatically

The Shrink method does not have any argument. This method shrinks the database pointed by the `SqlCeEngine` object. It does not use a destination database. Listing 4.6 demonstrates how to shrink an SQL Server Compact Edition database.

**LISTING 4.6    Shrink Database C#.NET**

```
string myConnectionStr = "DataSource=Northwind.sdf";
SqlCeEngine engine = new SqlCeEngine(myConnectionStr);
engine.Shrink();
```

**LISTING 4.6    Shrink Database Visual Basic.NET**

```
Dim myConnectionStr As String = "Data Source = Northwind.sdf;"
Dim myEngine As SqlServerCe.SqlCeEngine
myEngine = New SqlServerCe.SqlCeEngine(myConnectionStr)
myEngine.Shrink()
```

> **NOTE**
>
> The Shrink operation does not generate any log files.

## Shrinking a Database Automatically

You can configure a database to shrink automatically using the Auto Shrink threshold property. This property specifies the percentage of free space an SQL Server Compact Edition file can have and then shrinks the database accordingly. On setting the Auto Shrink property, the database continuously moves the empty pages to the end of the file.

To enable Auto Shrink, you need to set the Auto Shrink Threshold property as part of a connection string.

> **NOTE**
>
> The Auto Shrink threshold value 100 means no shrink. If you set the Auto Shrink but do not specify the value, the default value is 60.

## Securing a Database

To secure an SQL Server Compact Edition database, you should protect it with a password. You can specify the password at the time of database creation or at a later stage. To specify the password using SQL Server Management Studio, follow these steps:

1. Right click on Database and click on Properties.

2. On the Database properties dialog box, click on the tab, Set Password.

3. Specify the Old password.

4. Specify the new password and confirm the new password as shown in Figure 4.22.

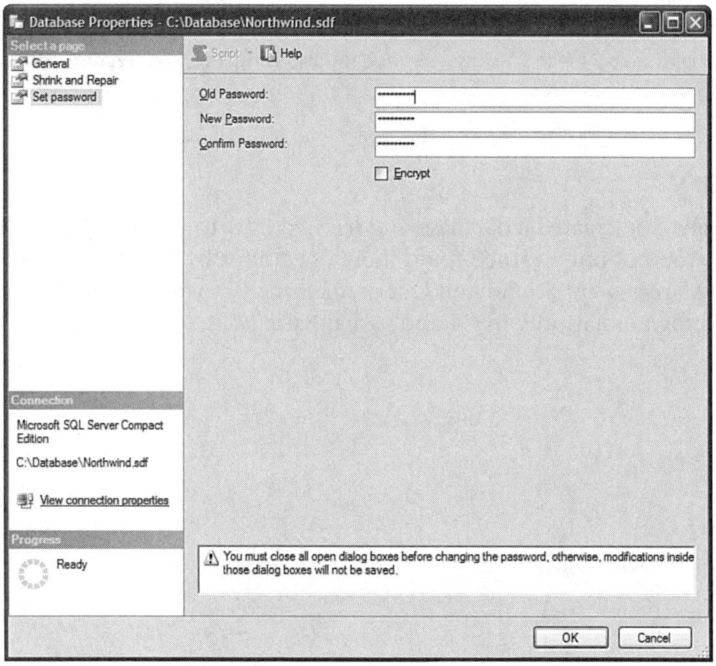

FIGURE 4.22     Password for SQL Server Compact Edition Database

5. You can choose to check the Encrypt option to enable encryption.

6. Click OK to set the password.

Security is discussed in detail in Chapter 14, *Securing the SQL Server Compact Edition Database*.

### NOTE

You should close all other open dialog boxes related to the database so that the password changes are reflected.

## Creating a Backup and Restoring the Database

The SQL Server Compact Edition database is a file-based database. For the sake of completeness, it contains a Backup and Restore section. The database can be backed up and restored simply by copying the database file. Similarly, you can restore the SQL Server Compact Edition database by copying the backed-up file.

> **NOTE**
>
> You can make a copy either programmatically by using the File System API or by using operating system features.

## Summary

In this chapter you created a database and learned how to verify, repair, shrink, and compact it. You not only learned to do these operations by using graphical tools such as SQL Server Management Studio and Query Analyzer, but you also implemented these operations programmatically in C# and Visual Basic.NET.

# Defining the Database Structure

Chapter 4, *Managing the SQL Server 2005 Compact Edition Database*, discussed management operations such as database creation, verification, repair, and compaction. These operations are generally done by DBAs. As a database designer and developer, you will most likely want to know the procedure and syntax for database object creation. In this chapter we will walk through the creation of SQL Server Compact Edition objects—tables and indexes. One major limitation of SQL CE 2.0 was that a database could only be managed on a mobile device. Two typical ways to create a database, tables, and columns was to run SQL statements on a device or to create database objects using ADO.NET code running on a device. SQL Server Compact Edition version 3.x and onwards made it possible to manage a database using SQL Server Management Studio and Visual Studio.

Both Visual Studio 2005 and SQL Server 2005 provide dialog boxes to maintain SQL Server Compact Edition database objects on a desktop. On a mobile device, Query Analyzer allows you to manage the SQL Server Compact Edition database objects.

This chapter introduces you to the SQL syntax to create SQL Server Compact Edition objects. Table 5.1 shows the conventions used to describe the syntax in this chapter. Examples in this chapter will walk you step by step in creating objects in SQL Server Management Studio.

TABLE 5.1    Syntax Convention

| Syntax Convention | Description |
|---|---|
| [,...n] | Item can be repeated n number of times. A comma separator will be used between items. |
| | Example: column [,...n] indicates n number of columns can be specified. The columns will be separated by commas. |
| [...n] | Item can be used n number of times. Blank space will be used between items. |
| | Example: `<column_constraint>[...n]` indicates n number of `column_constraint` separated by spaces. |
| ¦ | Specifies one of the options mentioned around the \| symbol. |
| | Example: PRIMARY ¦ UNIQUE indicates you can write a PRIMARY or UNIQUE constraint. |
| [] | Optional items are specified in square brackets. |
| | Example: [IDENTITY] indicates that you can optionally specify a column to be an IDENTITY column. |
| {} | Mandatory items are written in braces. |
| | Example: `{column_name data_type}` indicates that column name and data type must be specified. |
| <block> | Indicates a block item. |
| | Example: CREATE TABLE  table_name <column definition> indicates that a column definition will be specified as part of a table. |
| | The column definition detailed syntax should be explored. |
| <block> ::= | Indicates a block of index. |
| | Example:  `<column_definition>::=` indicates detailed `column_definition` syntax. |

# Creating a Table

Tables are the primary objects in an SQL Server Compact Edition database. A table name can have up to 128 characters and is unique within a database. Each table can have a maximum size of 512 MB and it consists of columns, column constraints, and table constraints.

This chapter will break down table creation into small steps. We will discuss how to write column definitions, column constraint definitions, and table constraint definitions.

## Creating a Table Using the SQL Statement

The CREATE TABLE command is used to create a table.

A table can have a maximum of 1024 columns and its name can be a maximum of 128 characters. Column names can also be a maximum of 128 characters. A table can have up to 249 constraints.

Listing 5.1 creates a Doctors table. The Doctors table has a column of type nchar and smallint.

**SYNTAX 5.1    Create Table**

```
CREATE TABLE table_name
(
    {<column_definition> | <table_constraint> }
    [ ,...n ]
)
```

**LISTING 5.1    Create Table**

```
CREATE TABLE [Doctors](
        [DoctorEmployeeNo] [nchar](10),
        [DoctorRegNo] [nchar](10) ,
        [FirstName] [nchar](20) ,
        [LastName] [nchar](20) ,
        [PhoneNo] [nchar](15) ,
        [CellNo] [nchar](15) ,
        [HighestQualification] [nchar](30) ,
        [Specialization] [nchar](30) ,
        [TotalExperienceInMonths] [smallint]
)
```

## Defining Columns

The table syntax shown in Syntax 5.1 uses the term < column _definition>. In Syntax 5.2, the column definition is expanded further. Column name and column data type are the two most important attributes in a column definition. A column name is unique in a table.

### Column Data Type

SQL Server Compact Edition Database supports a subset of data type supported by SQL Server. You should use the appropriate data type while defining a column. Table 5.2 describes the range and storage requirements of 17 data types supported in SQL Server Compact Edition. Only Unicode data types are supported in SQL Server Compact Edition.

**TABLE 5.2    SQL Server Compact Edition Data Type**

| Column Data Type | Data Type Description |
| --- | --- |
| Bigint | Bigint takes 8 bytes of storage. Values range from $-2^{63}$ to $2^{63} - 1$. |
| Integer | Integer takes 4 bytes of storage. Integer values range from $-2^{31}$ to $2^{31}-1$. |

TABLE 5.2    SQL Server Compact Edition Data Type

| Column Data Type | Data Type Description |
| --- | --- |
| Smallint | Smallint takes 2 bytes of storage. Values range from −32768 to 32767. |
| Tinyint | Tinyint takes 1 byte of storage. Values range from 0 to 255. |
| Bit | Stores 1 bit. Value is 1 or 0. |
| numeric (p,s) | Numeric takes 19 bytes of storage.<br>P indicates precision and range from 1 to 38.<br>S indicates scale and ranges from 0 to p.<br>Numeric fixed precision and scale-numeric data ranges from −10^38 to 10^38−1. |
| Money | Money takes 8 bytes of storage. Values range from −2^63/10000 to (2^63 − 1)/10000 having an accuracy of a ten thousandth of a monetary unit. |
| Float | Float takes 8 bytes of storage space. Values ranges from −1.79E +308 to 1.79E+308. |
| Real | Real takes 4 byte of storage. Values ranges from −3.40E+38 to 3.40E+38. |
| Datetime | Dates take 4 bytes of storage. Dates are internally stored as an integer. The first four bytes store the date. The last four bytes store the time.<br>The first four bytes stores the number of days before or after the base date.<br>The last four bytes stores the number of milliseconds after midnight.<br>The date value ranges from Jan 1, 1753 to Dec 31,9999. |
| nchar (n) | Nchar can have 1 to 4000 characters. Nchar is a fixed length Unicode data type. The storage required is double the number of characters. The default value of nchar is 1.<br>In SQL CE 2.0 the nchar data type range was 1 to 255 characters. |
| Nvarchar | Nvarchar is similar to nchar and unicode data type, but the data type is variable length data type. Nvarchar can also have 1 to 4000 characters<br>In SQL CE 2.0 the nvarchar data type range was 1 to 255 characters. |
| Ntext | Ntext is variable length Unicode data type. The ntext can have a maximum of (2^30−2)/2 characters. The storage space requirement is twice the number of characters. |

**TABLE 5.2     SQL Server Compact Edition Data Type**

| Column Data Type | Data Type Description |
|---|---|
| binary(n) | The length of binary data can be from 1 to 8000. The storage requirement in bytes is equal to the length declared. |
| | In SQL CE 2.0 the maximum length for binary was 510 bytes. |
| Varbinary | Varbinary is similar to binary data type but it's a variable length data type. The length of binary data can be from 1 to 8000. The storage requirement in bytes is equal to the length of data type. |
| | In SQL CE 2.0 the maximum length for binary was 510 bytes. |
| Image | Image consists of variable length binary data. Maximum length is 2^30 −1 bytes. Image takes storage equal to length in bytes. |
| Uniqueidentifier | Global Unique Identifier takes 16 bytes of storage. |

With column name and data type, you can specify whether a column is an identity column, contains a default value, or will have an automatically generated GUID. You can also specify constraints for every column.

**SYNTAX 5.2     Column Definition in Create Table**

```
< column_definition > ::=
    { column_name data_type }
    [ { DEFAULT constant_expression ¦ [ IDENTITY [ ( seed , increment ) ]
      ]
    }
    [ ROWGUIDCOL ]
    [<column_constraint> […n] ]
```

### Column Constraint

You can specify a constraint for every column by using a constraint key word. You can also provide a name for the constraint. If you do not provide a name for the constraint, SQL Server Compact Edition database will generate one.

In a column constraint, you can specify whether or not a column is a *Primary Key*, a *UNIQUE* column, or has a *NULL* value. You can also specify a *Foreign Key* using a column constraint. These constraints will be discussed in upcoming sections.

**SYNTAX 5.3     Column Constraint Definition in Create Table**

```
<column_constraint> :: =
  [CONSTRAINT constraint_name ]
  {
    [ NULL ¦ NOT NULL ]
  ¦ [ PRIMARY KEY ¦ UNIQUE ]
```

```
¦ REFERENCES ref_table [ ( ref_column ) ]
      [ ON DELETE { CASCADE ¦ NO ACTION } ]
      [ ON UPDATE { CASCADE ¦ NO ACTION } ]
}
```

The constraint name is optional. SQL Server Compact Edition will generate a constraint name if it is not specified.

### NULL or NOT NULL
You can specify this constraint to indicate whether a column can contain a NULL value or not. Adding a NOT NULL constraint will ensure that the column does not contain NULL values as demonstrated in Listing 5.2.

**LISTING 5.2    Create Table with NOT NULL Column constraint**

```
CREATE TABLE [PatientHistory](
        [PatientHistoryID] [int] IDENTITY(1,1) NOT NULL,
        [PatientRegNo] [nchar](10) NOT NULL,
        [DiseaseIdentified] [nvarchar](200) ,
        [DateIdentified] [datetime] NOT NULL,
        [Treatment] [nvarchar](200) ,
        [TreatmentStartDate] [datetime] ,
        [TreatmentEndDate] [datetime] NULL


)
```

### Column Level PRIMARY KEY Constraint
The Primary Key constraint is specified to indicate that a column will be a Primary key for a table. Only one Primary key can be specified for a table. Listing 5.3 creates a table named Doctors. The table has nine columns. The first column DoctorEmployeeNO is a Primary key.

**LISTING 5.3    Create Table with Primary Key Column Constraint**

```
CREATE TABLE [Doctors](
        [DoctorEmployeeNo] [nchar](10) PRIMARY KEY,
        [DoctorRegNo] [nchar](10) ,
        [FirstName] [nchar](20) ,
        [LastName] [nchar](20) ,
        [PhoneNo] [nchar](15) ,
        [CellNo] [nchar](15) ,
        [HighestQualification] [nchar](30) ,
        [Specialization] [nchar](30) ,
        [TotalExperienceInMonths] [smallint] NULL
)
```

## Column Level UNIQUE Constraint

Unique constraint ensures that a column contains unique values. A column with a Unique constraint can have NULL value however, a column can only contain one unique value. Listing 5.4 specifies the DoctorRegNo column as unique. It means no two rows can have the same DoctorRegNo.

**LISTING 5.4     Create Table with UNIQUE Column constraint**

```
CREATE TABLE [Doctors](
        [DoctorEmployeeNo] [nchar](10) PRIMARY KEY,
        [DoctorRegNo] [nchar](10) UNIQUE ,
        [FirstName] [nchar](20) ,
        [LastName] [nchar](20) ,
        [PhoneNo] [nchar](15) ,
        [CellNo] [nchar](15) ,
        [HighestQualification] [nchar](30) ,
        [Specialization] [nchar](30) ,
        [TotalExperienceInMonths] [smallint] NULL
)
```

## Identity Column

The Identity property is used to specify a column as an *Identity* column. For an Identity column, a user does not need to specify a value in the INSERT operation. The database adds a unique incremental value in the column at the time a row is inserted. An Identity column is only used for integer and bigint data type. Only one Identity column can be created for a table. Identity columns are generally created with a Primary Key constraint.

For an Identity column, the SQL Server Compact Edition database generates a new value. The first row will have the value specified as seed. The new row will have a value of the last row plus an incremental value. The default value of seed and increment is 1 and 1.

**NOTE**

If you do not have a column that can act as a key and narrow index, you can create one using an Identity column and use an index on it.

Listing 5.5 shows how to create the PatientHistory table. The column PatientHistoryID is the Identity column.

**LISTING 5.5     Create Table with IDENTITY Column Constraint**

```
CREATE TABLE [PatientHistory](
        [PatientHistoryID] [int] IDENTITY(1,1),
        [PatientRegNo] [nchar](10) ,
        [DiseaseIdentified] [nvarchar](200) ,
        [DateIdentified] [datetime] NOT NULL,
```

```
        [Treatment] [nvarchar](200) ,
        [TreatmentStartDate] [datetime] ,
        [TreatmentEndDate] [datetime] NULL


)
```

## Default Value

You can specify a default value for a column. During the INSERT if you do not specify the value for a column default, a value will be inserted automatically. You cannot use the default value and Identity property together for a column.  .

LISTING 5.6     **Create Table with DEFAULT Column Constraint**

```
CREATE TABLE [PatientHistory](
        [PatientHistoryID] [int] IDENTITY(1,1),
        [PatientRegNo] [nchar](10) ,
        [DiseaseIdentified] [nvarchar](200) ,
        [DateIdentified] [datetime] NOT NULL,
        [Treatment] [nvarchar](200) ,
        [TreatmentStartDate] [datetime] Default GETDATE(),
        [TreatmentEndDate] [datetime] NULL


)
```

## Defining a Table Constraint

You can specify a Primary Key, Unique constraint with any column. In a table, it is possible to have a Primary key on a combination of two columns. Whenever you need to apply a constraint on a combination of columns, you will use a Table constraint instead of a Column constraint.

### NOTE

Table Level constraint and Column Level constraint meet similar objectives. The main difference is where you specify them. Table constraint allows you to specify multiple columns in Unique, Primary Key, and Foreign Key constraints. Column Level constraint applies to only one column.

SYNTAX 5.4     **Table Constraint Definition in Create Table**

```
<table_constraint> ::=
  [CONSTRAINT constraint_name]
  { [ { PRIMARY KEY ¦ UNIQUE} { (Column [,…n]}]
```

```
¦ FOREIGN KEY (Column [,…n])
 REFRENCES ref_table [(ref_column[,…n])]
[ ON DELETE {CASCADE ¦ NO ACTION}]
[ ON UPDATE{CASCADE ¦ NO ACTION}]
}
```

The example statement shown in Listing 5.7 creates a Primary Key table constraint on a combination of Order ID and Product ID fields.

## Table Level PRIMARY KEY Constraint

**LISTING 5.7    Create Table with PRIMARY KEY Table Constraint**

```
CREATE TABLE [OrderDetails](
       [OrderID] [int] ,
       [ProductID] [int]   ,
       Qty [int],
CONSTRAINT JointKey PRIMARY KEY (OrderID, ProductID)
)
```

The next example statement shown in Listing 5.8 creates a Unique constraint on a combination of FirstName and LastName fields.

## Table Level UNIQUE Constraint

**LISTING 5.8    Create Table with UNIQUE Table Constraint**

```
CREATE TABLE [Doctors](
       [DoctorEmployeeNo] [nchar](10) PRIMARY KEY,
       [DoctorRegNo] [nchar](10) UNIQUE ,
       [FirstName] [nchar](20) ,
       [LastName] [nchar](20) ,
       [PhoneNo] [nchar](15) ,
       [CellNo] [nchar](15) ,
       [HighestQualification] [nchar](30) ,
       [Specialization] [nchar](30) ,
       [TotalExperienceInMonths] [smallint] NULL,
CONSTRAINT UniqueName UNIQUE (FirstName, LastName)
)
```

## Foreign Key

In a relational database, Foreign Key is a column(s) that matches a Primary Key column in a parent table. SQL Server Compact Edition database also supports Foreign Key constraints. For a new table, you can define the Foreign key using the *References* key word.

**REFERENCES, ref_table, ref_column**

Foreign Key and Reference constraints are used to add referential integrity to a column. The ref_table specifies the name of *Reference* table. The ref_column specifies one or more columns referenced in ref_table.

Listing 5.9 creates the tables, Patients and PatientHistory. The Patient table has a Primary key, PatientRegNo. In the PatientHistory table there is also a PatientRegNo column. Using the references keyword, the column has been made a Foreign key.

**LISTING 5.9    Create Table with FOREIGN KEY Table Constraint**

```
CREATE TABLE [Patients](
        [PatientRegNo] [nchar](10)  PRIMARY KEY ,
        [DoctorEmployeeNo] [nchar](10)  NOT NULL,
        [FirstName] [nchar](20) ,
        [LastName] [nchar](20) ,
        [PhoneNo] [nchar](15) ,
        [CellNo] [nchar](15) ,
        [DOB] [datetime] NOT NULL,
        [Age] [smallint] NULL,
        [GuardianFirstName] [nchar](20) ,
        [GuardianLastName] [nchar](20) ,
        [Martial Status] [nchar](1) ,
        [NoOfChildren] [smallint] NULL,
        [Education] [nchar](20) ,
        [Smokes] [nchar](1) ,
        [Drinks] [nchar](1)
);
— PatientHistory Table has a foreign key PatientRegNo
CREATE TABLE [PatientHistory](
        [PatientHistoryID] [int] IDENTITY(1,1),
        [PatientRegNo] [nchar](10) references Patients(PatientRegNo) ,
        [DiseaseIdentified] [nvarchar](200) ,
        [DateIdentified] [datetime] NOT NULL,
        [Treatment] [nvarchar](200) ,
        [TreatmentStartDate] [datetime] Default GETDATE(),
        [TreatmentEndDate] [datetime] NULL

)
```

The main objective of a Foreign key is to ensure referential integrity. A Foreign Key column in a child table can only have values present in a Primary Key column in a parent table. It is possible to update or delete rows in a parent table. ON DELETE and ON UPDATE constraints specify what to do with child table rows when rows in the parent table get deleted or updated.

## ON DELETE

The ON DELETE constraint specifies what happens to a child table when a row is deleted from the parent table. You can specify two types of action with the ON DELETE constraint: CASCADE and NO ACTION.

TABLE 5.3     ON DELETE Constraint Values

| ON DELETE Constraint Values | Description |
| --- | --- |
| CASCADE | The CASCADE option allows you to delete rows from a parent table where the parent primary column matches with a child table Foreign key column. |
| | This option cascades the deletion to the child table as well and the corresponding rows are deleted from the child table. The reference integrity is maintained even after deletion. |
| NO ACTION | The NO ACTION option does not allow you to delete rows from a parent table where the parent primary column matches with a child table Foreign key column. The Delete operation on the parent table fails and an error is returned if there are corresponding rows in the child table. |

Listing 5.10 creates a Patients table with PatientRegNo as a Primary key. The listing creates a PatientHistory table that sets the Foreign Key relationship using the keyword references after the Foreign Key column.

The database prevents you from deleting rows from the Patients (parent) table if there are corresponding rows in the PatientHistory (child) table. You will have to first delete a Patient History and then you will be able to delete the Patient record.

On specifying the ON DELETE CASCADE option, the database allows you to delete rows from Patients table and also deletes the corresponding rows in the PatientHistory table.

## LISTING 5.10     FOREIGN KEY with ON DELETE Option

```
CREATE TABLE [Patients](
        [PatientRegNo] [nchar](10)  PRIMARY KEY ,
        [DoctorEmployeeNo] [nchar](10)  NOT NULL,
        [FirstName] [nchar](20) ,
        [LastName] [nchar](20) ,
        [PhoneNo] [nchar](15) ,
        [CellNo] [nchar](15) ,
        [DOB] [datetime] NOT NULL,
        [Age] [smallint] NULL,
        [GuardianFirstName] [nchar](20) ,
        [GuardianLastName] [nchar](20) ,
```

```
        [Martial Status] [nchar](1) ,
        [NoOfChildren] [smallint] NULL,
        [Education] [nchar](20) ,
        [Smokes] [nchar](1) ,
        [Drinks] [nchar](1)
) ;
CREATE TABLE [PatientHistory](
        [PatientHistoryID] [int] IDENTITY(1,1),
        [PatientRegNo] [nchar](10) references Patients(PatientRegNo) ON DELETE
CASCADE ,
        [DiseaseIdentified] [nvarchar](200) ,
        [DateIdentified] [datetime] NOT NULL,
        [Treatment] [nvarchar](200) ,
        [TreatmentStartDate] [datetime] Default GETDATE(),
        [TreatmentEndDate] [datetime] NULL
)
```

The following example shows the structures of the Patients and PatientsHistory tables to demonstrate the Foreign key. Table 5.4 shows the Patients table content and Table 5.5 shows the PatientHistory table content. These tables show only the first few columns of each table as the remaining columns are not required to understand the Foreign key relationship.

TABLE 5.4    Patients Table Structure

| Column Name | Value |
| --- | --- |
| PatientRegNo | PER100051 |
| DoctorEmployeeNo | 1993243232 |
| FirstName | Adam |
| LastName | Smith |
| ... | |
| ... | |

TABLE 5.5    PatientsHistory Table Structure

| Column Name | Value |
| --- | --- |
| PatientHistoryID | 2 |
| PatientRegNo | PER100051 |
| DiseaseIdentified | Short sight |
| DateIdentified | 2005.03-24 |
| ... | |
| ... | |

## ON UPDATE

The ON UPDATE constraint specifies what happens to a child table when a row is modified in the parent table. Similar to the ON DELETE constraint, the ON UPDATE constraint also provides CASCADE and NO ACTION options as shown in Table 5.6.

**TABLE 5.6    ON UPDATE**

| Constraint values | Description |
| --- | --- |
| CASCADE | The CASCADE option allows you to modify the Primary Key column from a parent table where the parent primary column matches with a child table Foreign Key column. |
| | This option cascades the update to the child table. The child table's Foreign Key column is also modified and matched with the parent table primary column. The reference integrity is maintained even after modification. |
| NO ACTION | The NO ACTION option does not allow you to update Primary Key columns in a parent table where there is a matching Foreign Key column in the child table. |
| | The Update operation on parent table fails and an error is returned if there are corresponding rows in the child table. |

Listing 5.11 enhances Listing 5.10 by adding the ON UPDATE clause.

ON UPDATE NO ACTION would prevent operations such as:

```
Update Patients Set PatientRegNo = 'PER999999' where PatientRegNo = 'PER1000051'
```

This operation would fail if a PatientHistory table had rows with `PatientRegNo = 'PER1000051'`.

**LISTING 5.11    Foreign Key with ON DELETE and ON UPDATE Options**

```
CREATE TABLE [Patients](
        [PatientRegNo] [nchar](10)  PRIMARY KEY ,
        [DoctorEmployeeNo] [nchar](10)  NOT NULL,
        [FirstName] [nchar](20) ,
        [LastName] [nchar](20) ,
        [PhoneNo] [nchar](15) ,
        [CellNo] [nchar](15) ,
        [DOB] [datetime] NOT NULL,
        [Age] [smallint] NULL,
        [GuardianFirstName] [nchar](20) ,
        [GuardianLastName] [nchar](20) ,
        [Martial Status] [nchar](1) ,
        [NoOfChildren] [smallint] NULL,
        [Education] [nchar](20) ,
        [Smokes] [nchar](1) ,
```

```
        [Drinks] [nchar](1)
) ;
CREATE TABLE [PatientHistory](
    [PatientHistoryID] [int] IDENTITY(1,1),
        [PatientRegNo] [nchar](10) references Patients(PatientRegNo) ON DELETE CAS-
CADE ON UPDATE NO ACTION ,
        [DiseaseIdentified] [nvarchar](200) ,
        [DateIdentified] [datetime] NOT NULL,
        [Treatment] [nvarchar](200) ,
        [TreatmentStartDate] [datetime] Default GETDATE(),
        [TreatmentEndDate] [datetime] NULL
)
```

Consider the following: You are trying to update the Patient table and the row you are trying to update has a corresponding row in a child table. For a Patient with RegNo PER1000151, a patient history exists.

### LISTING 5.12    Update Patient Table

```
Update Patients Set PatientRegNo = 'PER1000151' where PatientRegNo = 'PER1000051' ;
```

When you execute the update statement, the update fails and you get the following error message:

```
Major Error 0x80040E2F, Minor Error 25025
> Update Patients Set PatientRegNo = 'PER1000151' where PatientRegNo = 'PER1000051'
```

The Primary key value cannot be deleted because references to this key still exist.
[ Foreign key constraint name = FK__PatientHistory__00000000000002A2 ]

Figure 5.1 shows this update statement and error message.

Next you will delete the row from the Patients table. There is a corresponding row in the PatientHistory table. As the ON DELETE CASCADE has been set, the Delete operation does not return an error message. The Delete operation successfully deletes the row from the Patients Table.

Now check the PatientHistory table. You will notice that the earlier Delete operation has not only deleted the row from the Patients table but also deleted the corresponding row from the PatientHistory table.

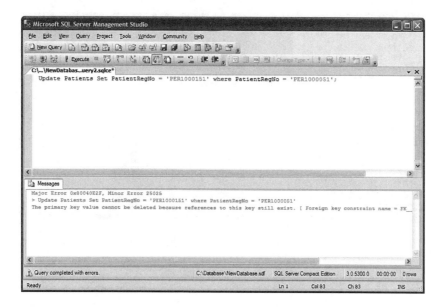

FIGURE 5. 1    ON UPDATE Constraint

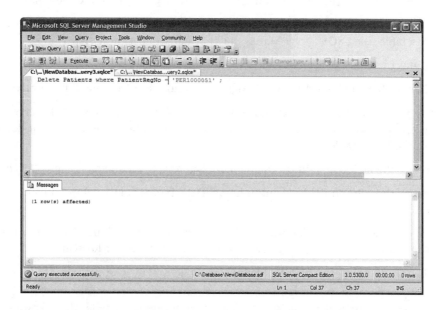

FIGURE 5.2    ON DELETE Constraint

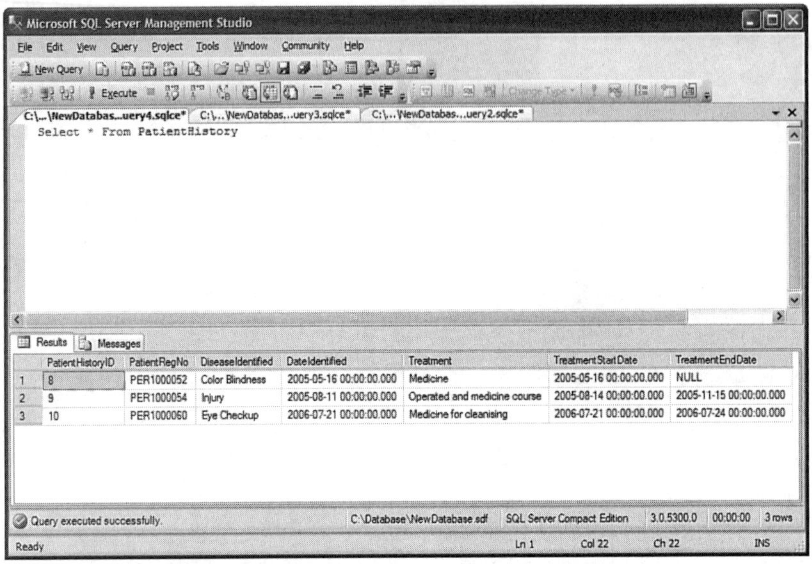

**FIGURE 5.3**    Child Table

## Creating a Table Using SQL Server Management Studio

As discussed, a table consists of columns, column constraints, and table constraints. SQL Server Management Studio provides an easy-to-use dialog box to define these table components.

To create a table using SQL Server Management Studio, follow these steps:

1. Connect to the SQL Server Compact Edition database.

2. Click on Table in Object Explorer. Right click and select the New Table option.

3. The New Table dialog box, as shown in Figure 5.4, is specific to the SQL Server Compact Edition database. SQL Server Management Studio uses a different design for SQL Server tables.

4. Specify the table name in the Name field. Figure 5.4 uses the table name Doctors.

5. Specify the column fields: Column name, Data Type, Length, Allow Nulls, Unique, and Primary Key.

6. You can also specify an Identity field in the lower section of the dialog box. The example shown in Figure 5.4 does not use an Identity key or RowGuid.

7. Click OK to complete the table definition.

Creating a table using SQL Server Management Studio is much simpler than writing a complicated Create Table statement.

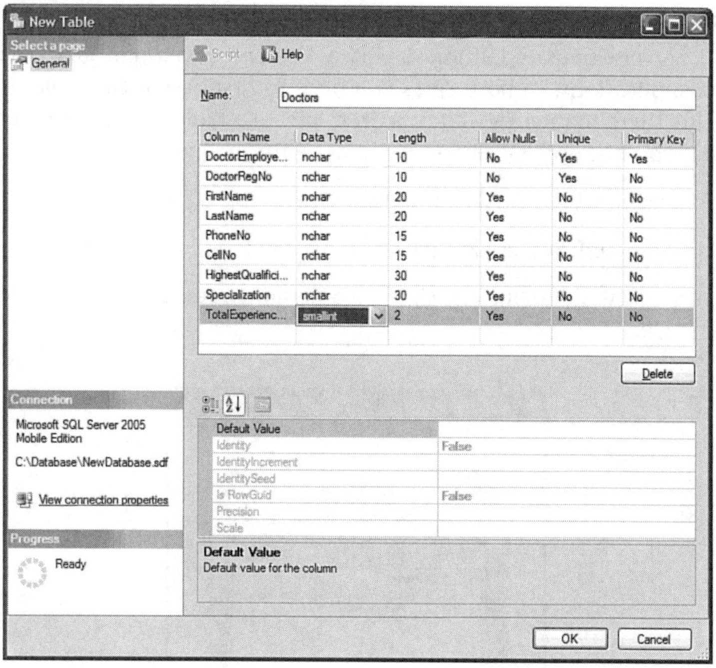

**FIGURE 5.4**    New Table Dialog Box

## Creating a Table Using Visual Studio

If you are a .NET developer and Visual Studio fan, you can also use Visual Studio to define table structures by following these steps:

1. Open the Visual Studio project that has the SQL Server Compact Edition database. (In Chapter 4, *Managing the SQL Server 2005 Compact Edition Database*, you learned how to add a new or existing database to a Visual Studio project.)

2. In Visual Studio, click on the View | Server Explorer option to start Server Explorer.

2. Expand the Database node and select the Tables node.

3. Right click and click on Create table.

4. The next dialog box is the New Table dialog box. This is the same dialog box that you used in SQL Server Management Studio. You can create the table the same way that you created one using SQL Server Management Studio.

SQL Server 2005, Visual Studio 2005, and SQL Server Compact Edition are tightly integrated with each other. The user experience is similar between SQL Server Compact Edition and SQL Server 2005. In addition, the user-friendly dialog boxes that manage database objects are used in Visual Studio as well.

## Creating a Table Using Query Analyzer

Using the SQL Server Compact Edition database, you can develop mobile device or desktop-based applications. In both cases you need to first design the tables on a desktop and then deploy them to devices. If you wish to create a table directly on a mobile device or an emulator, you can use SQL Server Compact Edition Query Analyzer.

To create a table using Query Analyzer, follow these steps:

1. Connect to the SQL Server Compact Edition database.

2. Click on the New Table button. Figure 5.5 demonstrates the button by enclosing it in a rectangle.

**FIGURE 5.5**    New Table Option in Query Analyzer

3. The New Table Definition dialog box appears.

4. Specify the table name in the Name field. Figure 5.6 specifies the table name of Doctors.

5. Click on the Insert column button to start inserting the columns as shown in Figure 5.6.

6. In the column definition dialog box, specify Column Name, Type, Length, and whether a column is Unique or a Primary key. You can also specify column properties in the Properties section of the Column Definition dialog box. The example shown in Figure 5.7 does not use Identity Key or RowGuid.

FIGURE 5.6    Table Definition in Query Analyzer

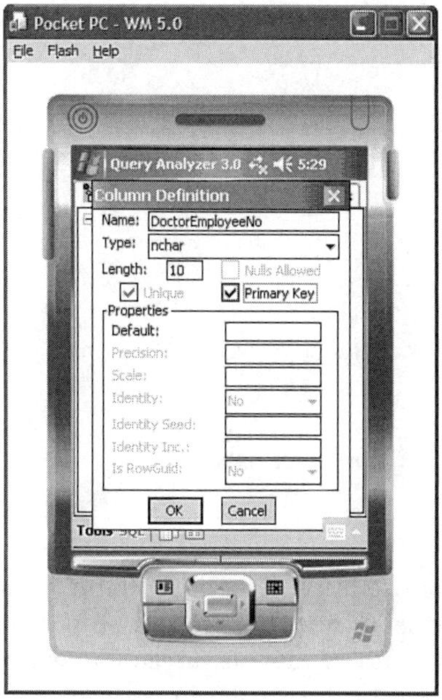

FIGURE 5.7    Column Definition in Query Analyzer

7. Click OK to complete the column definition.

8. Repeat steps 5, 6 and 7 for inserting the remaining columns of the table.

9. After you complete inserting all the columns, click OK on Table Definition dialog box.

## Updating a Table Definition

When designing a database, it is likely that it will take many iterations to complete. You will add new columns, modify columns, or decide to delete columns from a table. Similarly you will add, modify, and delete columns and table constraints.

The SQL Server Compact Edition database allows you to add, modify, and delete columns as well as table constraints. However, it is not possible to update a table name. Use the ALTER TABLE command to update a table. Similar to the CREATE TABLE syntax, the ALTER TABLE syntax also uses column definition, column constraint, and a table constraint block. The syntax of column definition, column constraint, and table constraint block remains the same.

To update a table definition, specify the ALTER TABLE command with the name of the table. Then specify the ADD, ALTER, or DROP operation for the column or constraint. The syntax of ALTER table demonstrates it with the ALTER COLUMN, ADD, and DROP sections.

**SYNTAX 5.5    Alter Table**

```
ALTER TABLE table_name
{[ALTER COLUMN column_name
    {
        IDENTITY [(seed, increment)]
        ¦ SET DEFAULT constant_expression
        ¦ DROP DEFAULT
    }
¦
ADD
    {<column definition> ¦ <table_constraint.} [,….n]
¦
DROP
    {[ CONSTRAINT] constraint_name ¦ COLUMN column}
]}
```

To use ALTER COLUMN, you need to specify the column name that you wish to alter. Within this section, you can set or reset the column properties. You can add an IDENTITY constraint or change the seed and increment value of an existing IDENTITY constraint. You can also specify a default value for a column or drop an existing default value.

The column definition block is the same as discussed in the CREATE TABLE section on page 135. You can specify the column name, data type, and define the column constraint. Similarly The column constraint block is exactly similar to the column constraint block we studied in the CREATE TABLE section on page 136.

**SYNTAX 5.6    Column Definition**

```
< column_definition > ::=
   { column_name data_type }
   [ [ DEFAULT constant_expression ]
      ¦ IDENTITY [ ( seed , increment ) ]
   ]
   [ROWGUIDCOL]
   [<column_constraint>] […n]]
```

**SYNTAX 5.7    Column Constraint**

```
<column constraint > :: =
   [NULL ¦ NOT NULL ]
   [CONSTRAINT constraint_name ]
   { ¦ { PRIMARY KEY ¦ UNIQUE }
      ¦ REFRENCES ref_table [ (ref_column) ]
      [ON DELETE {CASCADE ¦ NO ACTION} ]
      [ON UPDATE {CASCADE ¦ NO ACTION} ]
   }
```

**SYNTAX 5.8    Table Constraint**

```
<table_constraint> :: =
  [CONSTRAINT constraint_name]
  { [ {PRIMARY KEY ¦UNIQUE}
    {(column [,….n])}]
     ¦ FOREIGN KEY (column[,….n])
    REFERENCES ref_table [(ref_column[,….n])]
      [ON DELETE {CASCADE ¦ NO ACTION}]
      [ON UPDATE {CASCADE ¦ NO ACTION)]
}
```

Listing 5.13 modifies the Doctors table and adds the column Remarks.

**LISTING 5.13    Alter Table to Add a Column**

```
ALTER TABLE Doctors
ADD Remarks ntext
```

Listing 5.14 modifies the data type for column Specialization. To modify the data column, the statement first deletes the existing column and then re-creates the column with a new data type.

Dropping a column and then re-creating a column results in the loss of data. Listing 5.15 changes the default value of a column.

**LISTING 5.14    Alter Table to Modify a Column Data Type**

```
ALTER TABLE Doctors
DROP COLUMN Specialization ;
ALTER TABLE Doctors
ADD Specialization nvarchar(30) NULL;
```

**LISTING 5.15    Alter Table to Modify a Column Default Value**

```
ALTER TABLE Doctors
ALTER Column Specialization SET DEFAULT 'MS' ;
ALTER Table PatientHistory
Alter column PatientHistoryID IDENTITY (3000,1);
```

The above statement to alter the identity column works in SQL Server Compact Edition. A similar statement is not allowed in SQL Server.

## Updating a Table Using SQL Server Management Studio

To update a table definition using SQL Server Management Studio, follow these steps:

1. Connect to the SQL Server Compact Edition database.

2. Expand the Table node and click on the table that you wish to modify. The example modifies the Doctors table. Right click and select the Edit Table option.

3. The Edit Table dialog box appears displaying all column definitions and properties.

4. The example shown in Figure 5.8 modifies the Specialization column. The data type is modified as nvarchar. The column is also given a default value of MS in the Specialization field.

5. Add a Remarks column to the table.

6. Click OK once you finish updating the table definition.

## Updating the Table Using Visual Studio 2005

If you are developing an application using Visual Studio 2005, you do not need to go outside the Visual Studio environment to modify the table structure. Visual Studio provides an easy-to-use dialog box for changing the table design. You can update the table definition from Visual Studio as follows:

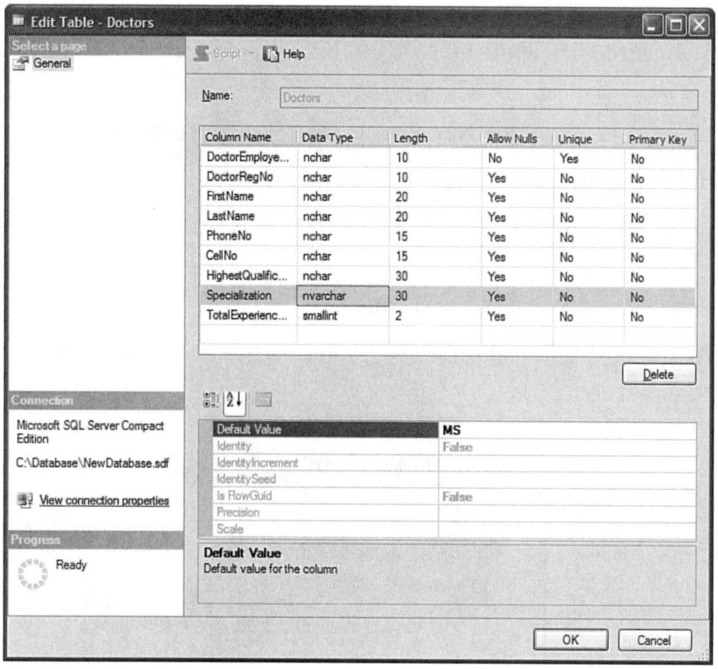

**FIGURE 5.8**    Edit Table Dialog

1. Start the Visual Studio project that has the SQL Server Compact Edition database. (Chapter 4, *Managing the SQL Server 2005 Compact Edition Database*, explained how to add a new or existing database to a Visual Studio project.)

2. In Visual Studio, click on the View | Server Explorer option to start the Server Explorer.

3. In Server Explorer, select the table and click on the Edit Table Schema option.

4. The same Edit Table dialog box appears that you saw earlier in SQL Server Management Studio.

5. Modify the table the same way as described previously.

## Updating a Table Definition Using Query Analyzer

With SQL Server 2000, Microsoft released an SQL Query Analyzer tool. Similar to the SQL Server Query Analyzer, Microsoft developed a device version of Query Analyzer to manage the SQL CE 2.0 database on a device. With SQL Server Compact Edition 3.x you can manage the database using SQL Server Management Studio on a desktop.

Even if the database can be managed on a desktop, with SQL Server Compact Edition 3.0, you also get the Query Analyzer tool to manage the database on a device and an emulator. If you have not installed SQL Server Management Studio or if you want to modify a database structure while you are mobile, Query Analyzer can be a very useful tool.

To update a table using Query Analyzer follow the following example:

1. Connect to the SQL Server Compact Edition database.

2. Expand the Table node and select the table you wish to edit. Figure 5.9 selects Doctors table.

3. Expand the column tabs of Doctors table.

4. In Query Analyzer, you will drop the column that you wish to edit and then re-create it.

FIGURE 5.9    Table Columns in Query Analyzer

5. Figure 5.10 demonstrates deleting the Specialization column by clicking on the Delete button. Clicking OK on the message box deletes the column.

6. Click on the Add Column button that is highlighted in a rectangle in Figure 5.11.

FIGURE 5.10    Drop Column in Query Analyzer

FIGURE 5.11    Table Columns in Query Analyzer

7. In the Column Definition dialog box, specify the new column definition and default value as shown in Figure 5.12.

8. Click OK to add the column.

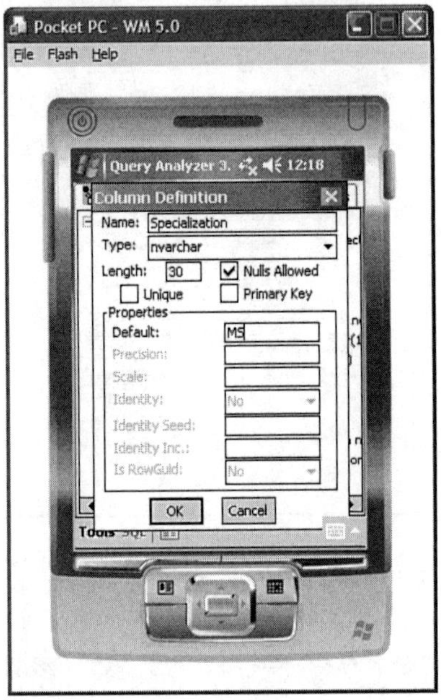

FIGURE 5.12     Column Definition in Query Analyzer

# Dropping a Table

You have learned the syntax and procedure for creating and modifying a table. Similar to create and modify, you can delete or drop a table using an SQL statement or by using SQL Server Compact Edition tools.

## Dropping a Table Using an SQL Statement

Deleting or dropping a table is quite simple—just use the DROP TABLE command with the table name as shown in Listing 5.16.

SYNTAX 5.9     Table Constraint Definition in Create Table

```
DROP TABLE <table name>
```

LISTING 5.16     Drop Table

```
DROP TABLE Doctors
```

## Dropping a Table with a Foreign Key Constraint

When you drop a table, you need to remember the rules for a Foreign key. If the table you are trying to delete is referenced by a Foreign key, then the DROP statement will result in an error. This is because if you delete a parent table, then the corresponding child table will not have any matching rows that are required to maintain referential integrity.

Listing 5.17 executes a DROP TABLE command on a Patients table. The Patients table has a child table, PatientHistory. Figure 5.13 shows the message you get while deleting Parent Table that has a foreign key constraint.

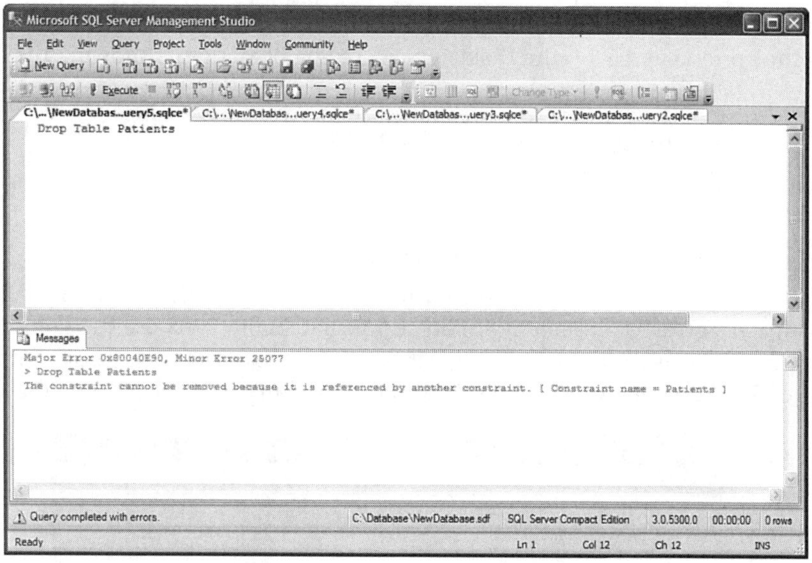

**FIGURE 5.13**    Foreign Key Constraint

**LISTING 5.17    Drop Table**

```
DROP Table Patients
Major Error 0x80040E90, Minor Error 25077
> DROP Table Patients
The constraint cannot be removed because it is referenced by another constraint.
[ Constraint name = Patients ]
```

To drop a table that is referenced by a Foreign key, you first need to drop the child table. After you drop the child table, then you can drop the parent table.

## Dropping a Table Using SQL Server Management Studio

SQL Server Compact Edition objects can be deleted using SQL Server Management Studio. In Object Explorer, select the object and delete it. The Delete Object dialog box will allow you to confirm the object that you want to delete. If the table you are trying to delete is referenced by a Foreign key, then you first need to delete the child table. After the child table is deleted, the SQL Server Compact Edition database will allow deletion of the parent table.

To delete a table definition using SQL Server Management Studio:

1. Connect to the SQL Server Compact Edition database.

2. Select the table you wish to delete. Right click and select the Delete option.

3. As shown in Figure 5.14, the Delete Object dialog box appears showing the selected Doctors table.

4. Click the Remove button to remove the object.

5. Click OK to complete the deletion.

## Dropping a Table Using Visual Studio

SQL Server Compact Edition is available for installation with SQL Server and Visual Studio 2005. Both SQL Server Management Studio and Visual Studio 2005 use the same set of dialog boxes to manage SQL Server Compact Edition objects. The dialog box that you used earlier in SQL Server Management Studio is also available in Visual Studio 2005.

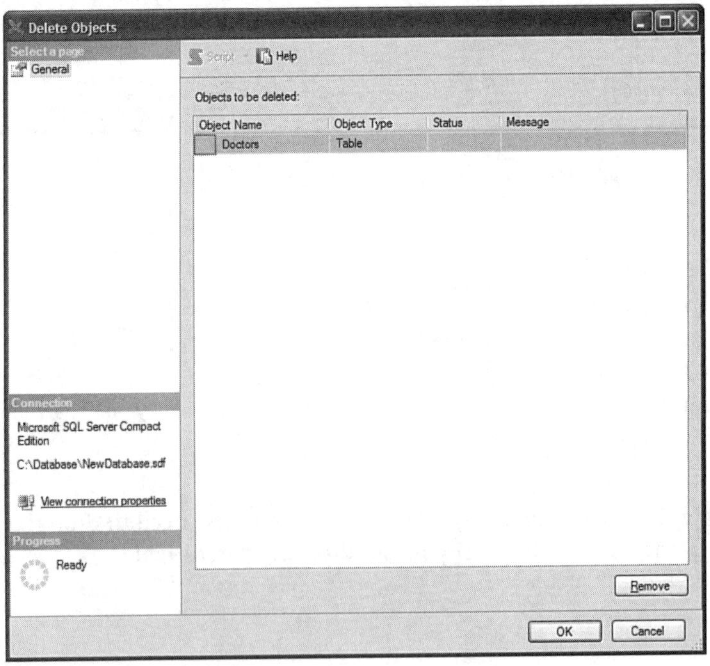

FIGURE 5.14    Delete Objects Dialog Box

Visual Studio 2005 also provides you a Drop Table option to delete a table from the database. Use the Server Explorer in Visual Studio to access the database. Choose the table and click on the Drop Table menu option. Visual Studio displays the SQL Server Compact Edition Delete Object dialog box to confirm deleting the table. Proceed with deleting the table as mentioned in a previous section.

## Dropping a Table Using Query Analyzer

Query Analyzer on a mobile device also allows deleting SQL Server Compact Edition objects. Query Analyzer has Object, SQL, Grid, and Notes tabs. The Object tab in Query Analyzer is similar to Object Explorer in SQL Server Management Studio. The Object tab shows the tree view of database objects. At the top of the tree is the Database node. The Database node shows the available connection. An open database connection will have a green icon and a closed database icon will be red. Under each database there are tables, columns, and indexes objects. To delete a table object, select the table and click on the Delete button.

To delete a table using Query Analyzer:

1. Connect to the SQL Server Compact Edition database.

2. Expand the Table node and select the table you wish to delete.

3. Click on the Delete button. Figure 5.15 highlights the Delete button by highlighting it in a rectangular box.

4. A message box is displayed to confirm the deletion. Click OK to confirm deletion.

**FIGURE 5.15**    Drop Table in Query Analyzer

# Creating Indexes

The proper use of an index can significantly improve the performance of the SQL Server Compact Edition database. In the absence of an index, the database engine has to scan all the rows in a table. With the help of an index engine, you can get the required data without scanning full tables.

SQL Server Compact Edition provides clustered and nonclustered indexes. A clustered index stores the data in order of key values. In a nonclustered index, the physical order of rows can be different from the order of the index. If you need to frequently access the rows sorted by a particular column, consider using a clustered index on the column.

> **NOTE**
> You can only create one cluster index on a table.

Once you have created the tables, you will focus on creating the indexes for the tables. Similar to tables, you can create, modify, and drop indexes using an SQL statement and easy-to-use tools.

## Create an Index Using an SQL Statement

**SYNTAX 5.10    Create Index**

```
CREATE [UNIQUE] INDEX index_name
ON table_name (column_name [ASC ¦ DSC] [,…n])
```

You create an index with `CREATE INDEX` keywords and the index name. An index can be made unique by adding the `UNIQUE` keyword between the `CREATE` and `INDEX` keywords.

> **NOTE**
> In a unique index, no two rows can have the same value on a column on which the index is created. Update and insert operations will return an error if you try to insert, update, or duplicate a value on a column having a unique index.

After the command and index name, specify the table name and column name on which you need to create an index. Optionally, you can add `ASC` or `DESC` keywords to indicate whether the index is in ascending or descending order. The default value is ascending order. The last part, [,…n], indicates that you can have an index on a set of columns separated by commas.

Listing 5.18 creates an index on the FirstName column.

**LISTING 5.18    Create an Index on Single Column**

```
CREATE INDEX IndName
ON Doctors (FirstName ASC)
```

Listing 5.19 creates an index on a combination of FirstName and LastName columns.

**LISTING 5.19    Create an Index on Two Columns**

```
CREATE INDEX IndJointName
ON Doctors (FirstName, LastName)
```

## Create an Index Using SQL Server Management Studio

SQL Server Compact Edition provides a New Index dialog box enabling you to create a new index on an SQL Server Compact Edition database table. Using the New Index dialog box, you specify the Index name, the Table name, and whether the Index is unique. You can also specify multiple columns that participate in the index key. The New Index dialog box can be invoked from SQL Server Management Studio. To create an index using SQL Server Management Studio, follow these steps:

1. Connect to the SQL Server Compact Edition database.

2. Expand the Tables node. Select the Table on which you wish to create an index.

3. Click on the Index node. Right Click and select New Index.

4. The New Index dialog box appears. Enter the index name as shown in Figure 5.16.

5. Click on the Add button.

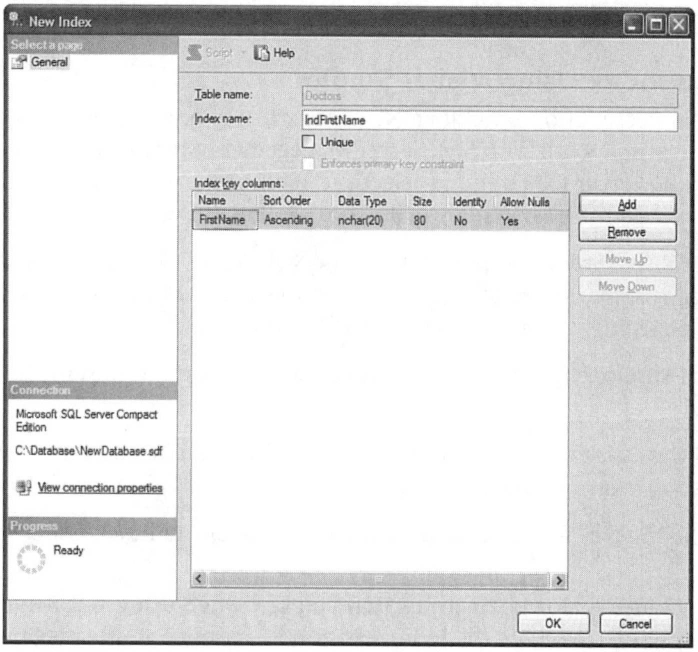

**FIGURE 5.16    New Index Dialog Box**

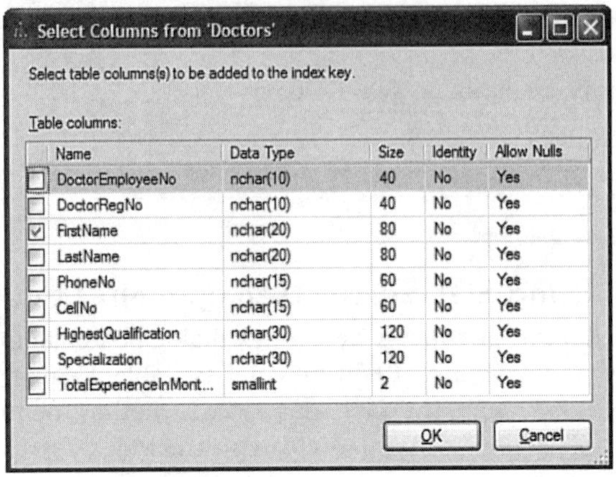

**FIGURE 5.17    Select Columns Dialog Box**

6. The next dialog box appears and allows you to choose the column on which you wish to create an index as shown in Figure 5.17.

7. Click the OK button on the Select Columns dialog box.

8. The selected column is displayed in the Index Key columns sections. You can add or remove columns to modify the index.

9. Once you are done, click OK.

## Creating an Index Using Visual Studio

SQL Server Compact Edition provides a New Index dialog box to create a new index. The dialog box is available both with SQL Server Management Studio and Visual Studio 2005. Use Visual Studio Server Explorer and select the Table and Index node. Use the Create Index option to open the New Index dialog box. Follow these steps to create a new index:

1. Start the Visual Studio project that has the SQL Server Compact Edition database. (Chapter 4, *Managing the SQL Server Compact Edition Database*, explained how to add a new or existing database into a Visual Studio project.)

2. In Visual Studio, click on the View I Server Explorer option to start the Server Explorer.

3. Expand the Database and Tables node. Select Tables and expand the Table node on which you wish to create an index.

4. Select the Indexes node. Right click and click the Create Index node.

The same New Index dialog box appears that you saw when using SQL Server Management Studio. Complete the index creation as specified in the previous exercise.

## Create an Index Using Query Analyzer

There may be a number of instances when you would like to create an index directly onto a mobile device. After you build and deploy an application on a mobile device, the application performance may diminish. It is useful to create and modify indexes on a device and see the impact on performance.

On a mobile device, Query Analyzer can be used to create an index. Select the table in the Object tab and use the New Index button to create an index.

To create an index using Query Analyzer:

1. Connect to the SQL Server Compact Edition database.

2. Expand the Tables node. Select the table on which you wish to create an index.

3. Click on the New Index button as shown in Figure 5.18.

FIGURE 5.18    New Index Option in Query Analyzer

4. The Index Definition dialog box appears as shown in Figure 5.19.

5. Specify the name of the index.

6. Add the columns on which you wish to create an index.

7. You can optionally select the Unique button if you want the index to be unique. For a unique index, no two rows in a column can have the same value. Click OK once you are done specifying the columns.

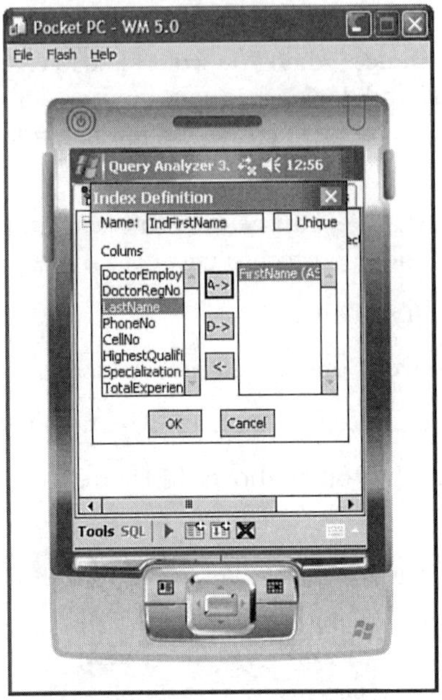

**FIGURE 5.19**    Index Definition in Query Analyzer

8. Click OK to confirm the creation of index.

# Viewing and Modifying Index Properties

> **NOTE**
>
> Creating effective indexes is an art. Although indexes help in querying and sorting, they slow down the performance of INSERT, UPDATE, and DELETE operations. During the performance tuning exercise, you will evaluate whether indexes are useful. You will modify the indexes to match queries that users are executing. You can also view and update the index properties.

## Viewing and Modifying Index Properties Using SQL Server Management Studio

SQL Server Compact Edition provides an Index Properties dialog box that enables you to view and modify an index on an SQL Server Compact Edition database table. Use the following steps to invoke the Index Properties dialog box from SQL Server Management Studio:

1. In SQL Server Management Studio Object Explorer, expand the Tables node. Select the table for which you need to view index properties.

2. Expanding the Indexes node allows you to see the various indexes available in a table. Figure 5.20 shows four indexes. IndName is the index that was created in a

previous exercise. Other indexes are created by the system as a result of Primary Key and Unique constraints.

3. To update the index property, select the index and double click. The example as shown in Figure 5.21 uses the IndName index. The Index name field is read-only and the index name cannot be modified.

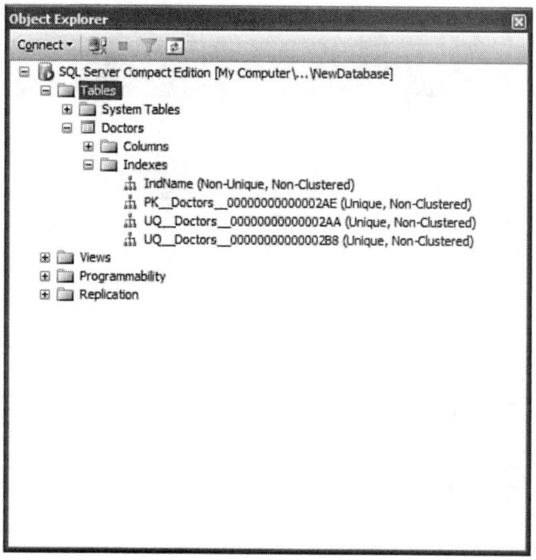

**FIGURE 5.20**    Indexes in SSMS Object Explorer

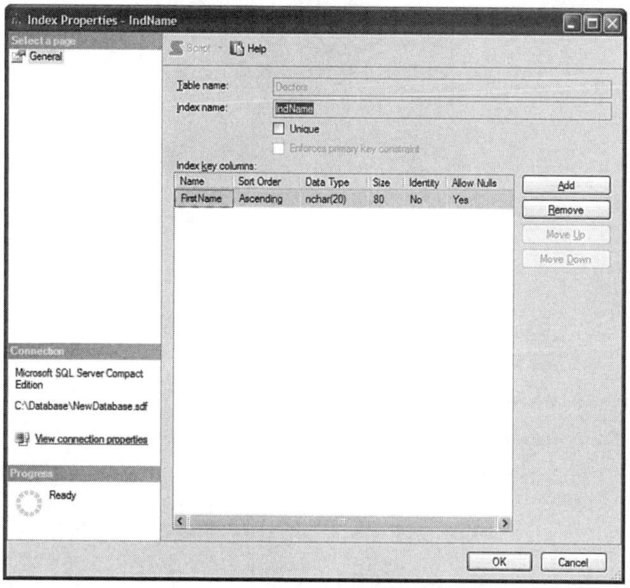

**FIGURE 5.21**    Index Properties Dialog Box

4. Click on the Remove button to remove the `FirstName` column name from the index.

5. Click on the Add button. The Select Columns dialog box appears as shown in Figure 5.22.

6. Select the `LastName` column and click OK on the Select Columns dialog box.

7. Click OK.

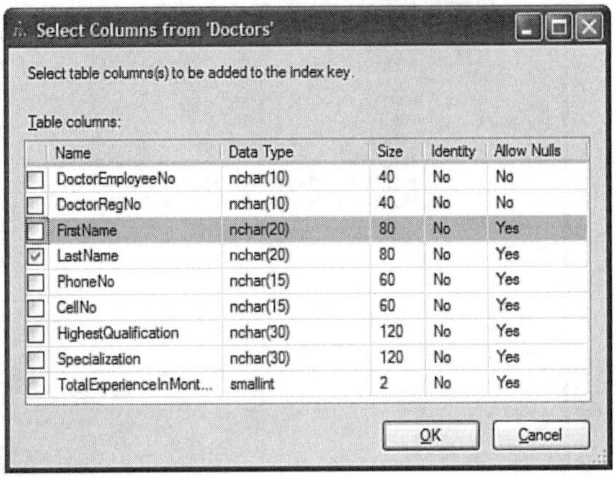

FIGURE 5.22    Select Column Dialog Box

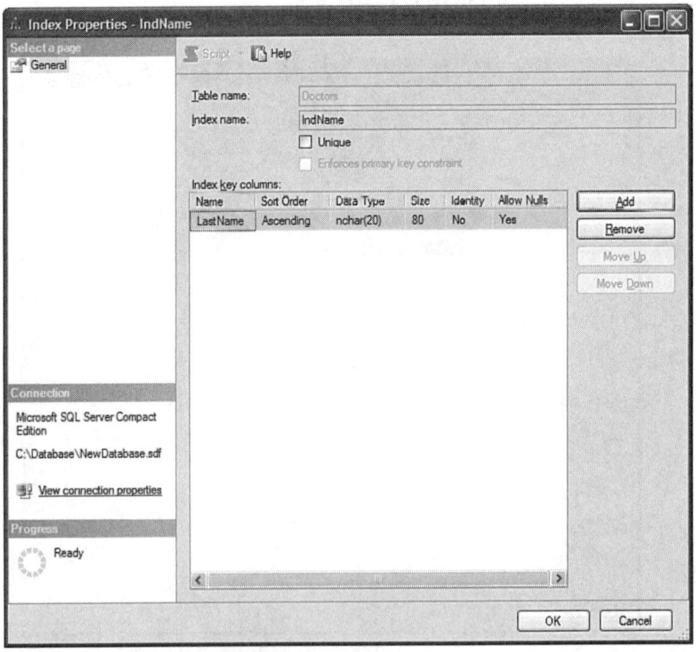

FIGURE 5.23    Index Properties Dialog Box

On refreshing the Object Explorer, you will see the IndName is changed. The index is now on LastName.

### Viewing and Modifying Index Properties Using Visual Studio

The Index Properties dialog box can also be used in Visual Studio 2005. Use Visual Studio Server Explorer to browse the SQL Server Compact Edition database object. Select the index and view properties as shown in the following steps:

1. Start the Visual Studio project that has the SQL Server Compact Edition database. (Chapter 4, *Managing the SQL Server Compact Edition Database*, explained how to add a new or existing database into a Visual Studio project.)

2. In Visual Studio, click on the View | Server Explorer option to start Server Explorer.

3. Expand the Database and Tables node. Select Tables and expand the Table node on which the index exists. Expand Indexes and select the index. The example as shown in Figure 5.23 uses the IndName index.

4. Right click and choose Index Properties.

5. The Index Properties dialog box appears. This is the same SQL Server Compact Edition dialog box that was displayed using SQL Server Management Studio. You can modify and save the properties as you did earlier.

# Deleting an Index

During the performance tuning exercise, you will evaluate whether indexes are useful. You will test the queries performance with and without indexes.

To drop an index, you use the DROP INDEX command. With the DROP INDEX command you specify the index name. As an index name is unique to a table, you need to specify the table name as well.

**SYNTAX 5.11    Create Table**

```
DROP INDEX <table_name>.<index_name>
```

The Drop Index statement deletes the index created by the user. It does not delete the index created by the Primary key or the Unique constraint. Listing 5.20 shows the statement used to delete the IndFirstName index on the Doctors table.

**LISTING 5.20    Delete Index**

```
DROP INDEX Doctors.IndFirstName
```

## Deleting an Index Using SQL Server Management Studio

The SQL Server Compact Edition database has a Delete Object dialog box. To delete the index, follow these steps:

1. In SQL Server Management Studio Object Explorer, expand the Tables node. Select the table for which you need to view index properties.

2. Expand the Indexes node and you will see various indexes available on the table. Figure 5.24 shows four indexes. IndName is the index that was created in a previous exercise; the other indexes were created by the system as a result of the Primary key and Unique constraint.

3. Right click on the IndName index and select Delete.

4. The Delete Object dialog box appears. Click on Remove to delete the index object as shown in Figure 5.24.

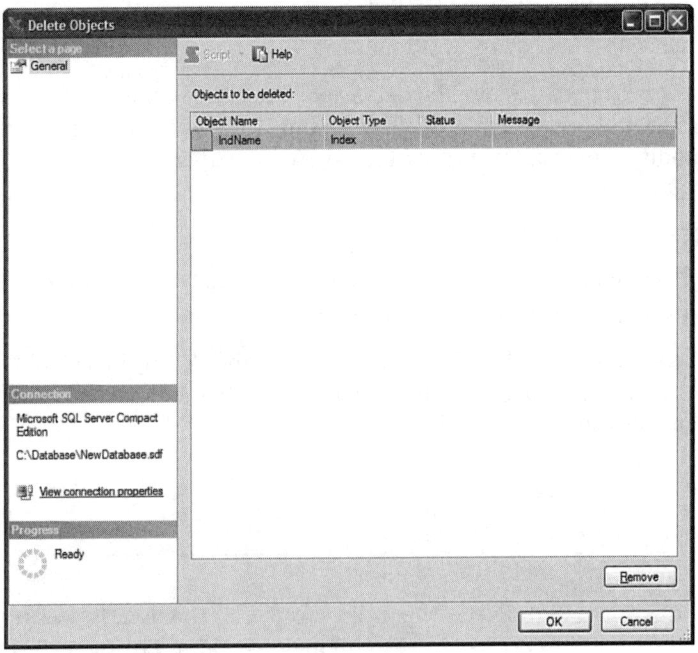

FIGURE 5.24    Delete Objects Dialog Box

## Deleting an Index Using Visual Studio

As discussed previously, SQL Server Compact Edition provides a set of dialog boxes to manage the database. The same set of dialog boxes are available from both SQL Server Management Studio and from Visual Studio 2005. To use Visual Studio, follow these steps:

1. Start the Visual Studio project that has the SQL Server Compact Edition database. (Chapter 4, *Managing the SQL Server Compact Edition Database*, explained how to add a new or existing database into a Visual Studio project.)

2. In Visual Studio, click on the View | Server Explorer option to start Server Explorer.

3. Expand the Database and Tables node. Select Tables and expand the Table node on which the index exists. Expand Indexes and select the index. The example as shown in Figure 5.25 uses the IndName index.

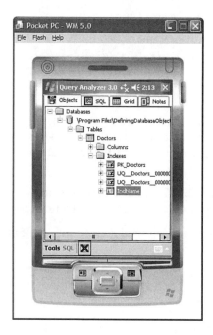

**FIGURE 5.25** Delete Index Option in Query Analyzer

4. Right click and choose the Drop Index option.

5. You are presented with the Delete Object dialog box. This dialog box has the IndName index selected. This is the same dialog box described in the previous section, Deleting an Index Using SQL Server Management Studio. Click on Remove and then OK to confirm the deletion.

The Delete Object dialog box is common. Both SQL Server Management Studio and Visual Studio invoke this dialog box when you choose to delete an object.

## Deleting an Index Using Query Analyzer

As previously discussed, there may be a number of instances when you need to modify or delete an index on a device. On a device, Query Analyzer can be used to delete an index by selecting the index and clicking on the delete button.

To delete an index using Query Analyzer, follow these steps:

1. Connect to the SQL Server Compact Edition database.

2. Expand the Tables node. Select the table on which you wish to delete an index. Figure 5.25 chooses the Doctors table.

3. Expand the Indexes section for Tables. Figure 5.25 shows four indexes. `IndName` is the index that was created in a previous exercise; the other three indexes were created as a result of Primary key and a Unique constraint. Select `IndName` as shown in Figure 5.25.

4. Click on the Delete button to delete the index.

5. A message box is displayed asking you to confirm the deletion. Click OK.

## Using Templates

Using templates, you can easily create SQL statements. Templates contain the SQL statements in which you can place query values. To access templates for the SQL Server Compact Edition database, you must start the template browser and select the template type.

Click on the View | Template Browser menu option to access the template browser. In Template Explorer, select the SQL Server Compact Edition icon.

SQL Server Compact Edition templates are divided into the following folders:

• Database

• Index

• Table

To create a new folder, right click on the parent folder, SQL Server Compact Edition, and select the New option.

To use an existing template, simply click the template. The template will be opened in SQL Server Management Studio. The template queries have parameter placeholders that can be replaced with actual values.

## Using Metadata

SQL Server Compact Edition exposes the metadata using INFORMATION_SCHEMA views. Using INFORMATION_SCHEMA views you can query the SQL Server Compact Edition database metadata without directly accessing its system tables. INFORMATION_SCHEMA views are easy to understand compared to system tables and they require less joins. There are seven information schema views that you can use to retrieve information: tables, columns, key columns, indexes, data types, table constraints, and referential constraints.

Listing 5.21 retrieves a list of tables that are accessible to the current user in a current database. If you need to retrieve the list of tables in a database programmatically, use the INFORMATION_SCHEMA view.

### LISTING 5.21   Table Metadata

```
SELECT * FROM INFORMATION_SCHEMA.TABLES
```

Listing 5.22 retrieves a list of columns that are accessible to the current user in a current database. The view returns one row for each column.

### LISTING 5.22   Columns Metadata

```
SELECT * FROM INFORMATION_SCHEMA.COLUMNS
```

Listing 5.23 retrieves a list of keys in a current database. The list will return one row for each key in a database. The columns in a row describe the table name, constraint_name, key ordinal position, and so on.

### LISTING 5.23   Keys Metadata

```
SELECT * FROM INFORMATION_SCHEMA.KEY_COLUMN_USAGE
```

Listing 5.24 retrieves a list of indexes in a current database.

### LISTING 5.24   Index Metadata

```
SELECT * FROM INFORMATION_SCHEMA.INDEXES
```

Listing 5.25 retrieves a list of 17 supported data types in SQL Server Compact Edition.

### LISTING 5.25   Provider Types

```
SELECT * FROM INFORMATION_SCHEMA.PROVIDER_TYPES
```

Listing 5.26 retrieves the table constraints in a current database. The list will return one row for each constraint. The columns will describe the table name, constraint name, constraint type, and so on.

### LISTING 5.26   Table Constraints Metadata

```
SELECT * FROM INFORMATION_SCHEMA.TABLE_CONSTRAINTS
```

Listing 5.27 retrieves the referential constraints in a current database. The list will return one row for each referential constraint. The columns will describe the constraint name, the parent table, and child table. Each row also has Update_Rule and Delete_Rule columns. These columns contain the values CASCADE or NO ACTION.

**LISTING 5.27**   **Referential Constraint Metadata**

```
SELECT * FROM INFORMATION_SCHEMA.REFERENTIAL_CONSTRAINTS
```

# Creating a Database Project Using Visual Studio

Visual Studio 2005 allows you to create a database project. A database project is used to design, modify, and view SQL scripts. A database project is not specific to .NET language such as C#.NET or VB.NET. Similar to frontend objects, backend objects can be stored in a single solution. In a development team, all developers can continue to add their database objects into a single solution. All scripts, queries, and database references are stored in a Visual Studio solution and can be checked into a source control system.

A database project in Visual Studio enables a developer to manage database objects without the use of SQL Server Management Studio. Multiple scripts can be executed in a project and multiple scripts can be combined into a logical group and executed as a command file.

### Create a Database Project

1. Start Visual Studio 2005 from the Start menu.

2. Click File | New | Project.

3. Click on Other Project Types | Database projects.

4. Click on Database Project Template.

5. Enter the Name and Location of the project as shown in the Figure 5.26

6. In the Add Database Reference dialog box, specify the path of the new database and the SQL Server Compact Edition provider.

7. The project is created with three folders: Changed Scripts, Create Scripts, and Queries.

It is possible to rename the folder and to add new folders.

8. To add an SQL script, right click on the folder and choose Add New Item or Add SQL Script. You can click on the sql script pane. Right click and select INSERT SQL to open a Query Builder as shown in Figure 5.27.

9. You can also generate a script for an existing database object by selecting the database object in Server Explorer. Right click and select the Generate Script option. The script will be stored in a folder selected in Solution Explorer.

The Create Script folder is required for the Create Database and Create Table scripts for a database. The Change Script folder contains the required updates needed after database

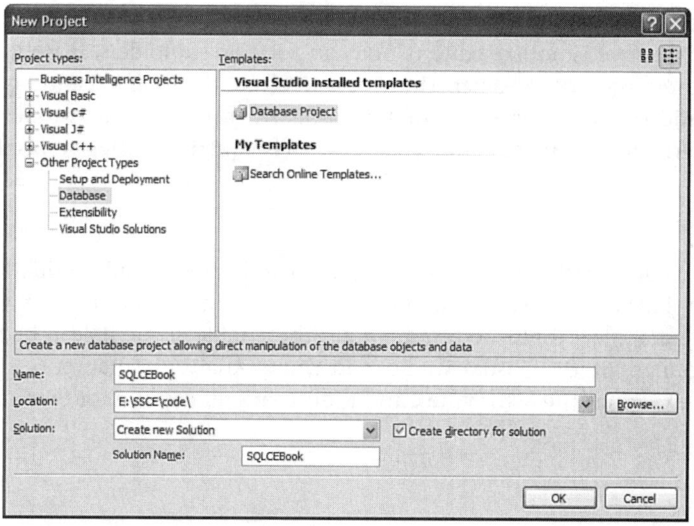

**FIGURE 5.26**   Database Project

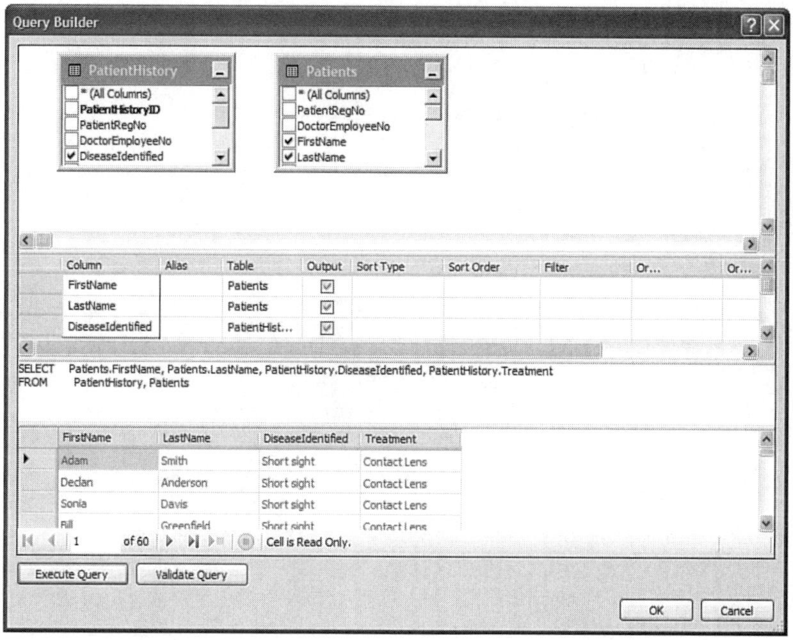

**FIGURE 5.27**   Query Builder Project

creation. For example, this book uses a Hospital database in SQL Server and a MyPatients database in SQL Server Compact Edition. You can add two subfolders, Hospital and MyPatients, under the Create Folder. The scripts to create the Hospital and MyPatients databases can be added in their respective folders. Similarly, you can create various subfolders under the Queries folder and store the chapter exercise queries in their respective folders.

## Summary

Defining the database structure correctly is similar to laying a solid foundation for a building. The skills to define and maintain tables, columns, and indexes have been discussed. The graphical tools used to maintain these table elements can be found in SQL Server Management Studio, Visual Studio, and Query Analyzer. Chapter 6, *Manipulating the Database*, examines the SQL syntax and tools that you can use for data manipulation.

# Manipulating the Database

In the previous chapters you learned how to define a database structure and manage database operations such as repair and compact. In this chapter you will learn how to access and manipulate data in the SQL Server Compact Edition database. There are two main scenarios in which you will be querying or updating a database:

1. Executing the SQL Queries on an SQL Server Compact Edition database either using tools or programmatically.

2. Using ADO.NET or OLE DB provider for SQL Server Compact Edition to execute queries programmatically.

While developing applications for SQL Server Compact Edition, you use SQL Server Management Studio, Visual Studio 2005, or the Query Analyzer tool to query data.

In a runtime environment, managed or native applications will execute queries on an SQL Server Compact Edition database.

This chapter introduces the syntax of common SQL statements. Also it demonstrates the data manipulation by using the MyPatients database that you created in a the example in Chapter 5, *Defining Database Structure*. Other examples will use the Northwind database available with the SQL Server Compact Edition installation.

# Connecting to the Database

To retrieve or update information from the SQL Server Compact Edition database, you need to connect to the database. In this section you will connect to the SQL Server Compact Edition database both using tools and programmatically.

When you connect to the SQL Server Compact Edition database and access and update it programmatically, you need to consider the mode to open the database. You also need to be aware of the isolation level and the locking mechanism that SQL Server Compact Edition uses.

## Connecting to the Database Using SQL Server Management Studio (SSMS)

SQL Server Management Studio is the most preferred tool for database developers. You will use this tool to initially populate the empty database. To connect to the SQL Server Compact Edition database, start SQL Server Management Studio and specify the server type, filename, and password to connect to the database.

1. Start SQL Server Management Studio.

2. Select SQL Server Compact Edition Server Type.

3. Specify the name of the SQL Server Compact Edition database file to open an existing database. You can choose the Browse for More option to browse the database file.

4. If you have created a password protected database, specify the password.

5. Click on the Connect button to connect to the database.

Now you are connected to an SQL Server Compact Edition database. In Object Explorer you can browse the SQL Server Compact Edition tables.

Click on the New Query tab. It will start an Editor window to write a new query. You are all set to write a query. Once you have written the query, click on the Execute button to run the query.

## Connecting to the Database Using Query Analyzer

You can enter the data manipulation and access query on your Smart device or on an emulator.

1. To connect to an SQL Server Compact Edition database using Query Analyzer, click on the Connect button. Figure 6.1 shows this button inside the rectangle.

2. Specify the path of the database and click Connect.

The database is now open. It has Objects, SQL, Grid, and Notes tabs. Click on the SQL tab and you are set to write queries. After writing a query, click on the Execute button to run the query.

FIGURE 6.1    Connect to an SQL Server Compact Edition Database Using Query Analyzer

## Connecting to the Database Using Visual Studio

If you are not a fan of writing SQL queries, you can manipulate the data in Visual Studio by opening a project that has an SQL Server Compact Edition database file. One of Visual Studio's goal is to provide a single development environment for building an SQL Server Compact Edition based application. Using Visual Studio, it is possible to create and manage an SQL Server Compact Edition database. Visual Studio Server Explorer allows you to make connection to the database. You can view table structure, table content and even insert or edit data without writing SQL queries.

1. Click on View Server Explorer.

2. In Server Explorer, right click on the database and click the Refresh button.

3. Expand the Table node. Now you see all the tables in your database.

4. Select the table from which you want to access or modify data.

5. Right click and click the Open option.

The table contents are displayed in a grid. You can directly modify the content of the database without writing the SQL queries.

6. To add a new row, right click and select New. A new row will be added and you can make entries. To delete a row, right click the selected row and select Delete as shown in Figure 6.2.

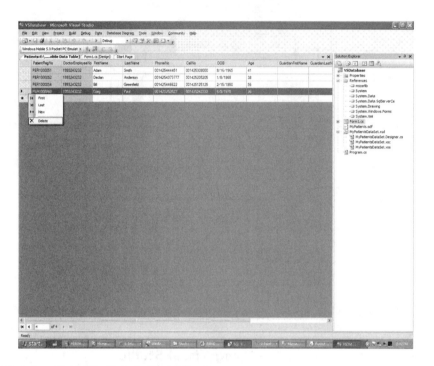

**FIGURE 6.2**   Updating Data in Visual Studio

Manipulating data through Visual Studio is an extremely useful feature. If you are a .NET developer, you may need to change the database frequently for unit testing. It would be more productive to make changes in a database using Visual Studio. As a .NET developer you do not need to install SQL Server or write SQL Queries to manipulate the data.

## Connecting to the Database Programmatically

To access or update a database programmatically, you need to set up a connection. To do this for ADO.NET, add a reference to the `System.Data.SqlServerCe` namespace in your project. You create a connection using the `SqlCeConnection` object and provide a connection string. Listing 6.1 demonstrates how to establish a connection using ADO.NET.

Once a connection is created, call the open method of the connection object. After opening the connection, execute the SQL statements. After you are done executing the statements, close the connection.

**LISTING 6.1    Connection Object C#**

```csharp
SqlCeConnection myConnection = null;
myConnection = new SqlCeConnection("Data Source=\\Mobile\\Northwind.sdf;");
myConnection.Open();
..

..
myConnection.Close();
```

**LISTING 6.1    Connection Object VB.NET**

```vbnet
Dim myConn As SqlCeConnection = New
SqlCeConnection("DataSource=\Mobile\Northwind.sdf")
myConnection.Open()
..

..
myConnection.Close()
```

At the time of creating a connection, you can set various properties in a connection string. In the connection, the string name/value pair can be specified to include the optional properties and their value. Table 6.1 lists the `SqlCeConnection` properties.

**TABLE 6.1    Connection Properties**

| Connection Property | Description |
|---|---|
| Data source | Path and filename for SQL Server Compact Edition database file. |
| Password | Password to access database file. |
| Encrypt database | Boolean value to indicate whether SQL Server Compact Edition database is encrypted or not. |
| Max buffer size | Maximum buffer size that SQL Server Compact Edition uses after which database flushes change to disk. The buffer size is described in kilobytes. The default value is 640 KB. |
| Max database size | Maximum size of a database in megabytes. The default value is 128 MB. |
| Mode | The mode for opening the database file. |
| | Read Write—Allows multiple processes to read and write on the database. |
| | Read Only—Opens the database file in read-only mode. |
| | Exclusive—Does not allow other processes to access the database. |

**TABLE 6.1    Connection Properties**

| Connection Property | Description |
| --- | --- |
| | Shared Read—Allows other processes to read but does not allow other processes to modify while it is opened by the current process. |
| | Read Write is the default mode. |
| Temp path | The temporary path specified by the location of the temporary database. |
| | The default option is to use the same path as the SQL Server Compact Edition database. |
| Temp file max size | Maximum size of temporary database file in megabytes. The default value is 128 MB. |
| Auto-shrink threshold | The percentage of free space the SQL Server Compact Edition database file can have. |
| Default lock timeout | The time in milliseconds up to which a transaction can wait for a lock. The default value is 2000. |
| Default lock escalation | The number of locks a transaction will have before escalating a lock from row to page. |
| Flush interval | This property specifies the time in seconds. After this time, committed transactions are committed to disk. |
| | The default value is 10 seconds. |
| Locale identifier | This property specifies the locale ID to use with a database. |
| Persist security info | The default value of the persist security information is false. Making it false means a password is not returned as part of the connection information. |

## Temporary Database

In the connection string you can specify the `temp file directory` and the `temp file max size` property to indicate the path and size of the temporary database file. A temporary database is useful for storing interim results during a query execution. A temporary database is also useful for storing interim results while executing SORT BY, ORDER BY, and GROUP BY clauses.

# Considerations for Multiuser Access

The SQL Server Compact Edition database supports a multiuser access feature. The SQL Server CE 2.0 was a single user database. In SQL Server Compact Edition 3.0 and higher versions you can open multiple connections on a database. Multiuser access enables scenarios such as data synchronization in the background while a client application is accessing the SQL Server Compact Edition database.

This section highlights the factors related to Locking, Concurrency, and Isolation that you should consider while building a solution that allows multiuser access on a database.

## Single Connection

This is the simplest way. One at a time, a single application opens a single connection to the database. On a Smart device this is the most commonly used method for accessing the SQL Server Compact Edition database.

## Multiple Connections

In many scenarios you will allow a user to continue working on an application accessing the SQL Server Compact Edition database. In the background, you may wish to trigger data synchronization using Replication, RDA, or Web Services. You can accomplish this by opening multiple connections to the SQL Server Compact Edition database.

## Multiple Applications

You can also allow multiple applications to access the same SQL Server Compact Edition database. You can do this by using the application to access the SQL Server Compact Edition database or by opening the database using SQL Server Management Studio or Query Analyzer.

### NOTE

You can open up to 256 connections on the SQL Server Compact Edition database.

## Locking, Concurrency, and Isolations

When multiple applications or processes are allowed to read the data, it becomes important that only one application change the data at any one point in time. Like other databases, an SQL Server Compact Edition database achieves this by locking. You do not need to lock the database explicitly; instead the SQL Server Compact Edition database applies the lock as needed. The SQL Server Compact Edition database automatically locks rows and corresponding index pages when you modify data. If more and more locks are used, the database automatically escalates the lock level and will lock the whole table instead of individual rows.

### Lock Granularity

The amount of data that a lock controls is termed *granularity* of lock. You can increase the currency control with granular locks but having granular locks means more overhead. SQL Server Compact Edition applies lock at the following levels:

1. Rows

2. Tables

3. Pages

4. Database

---
**NOTE**
---

By default SQL Server Compact Edition uses row-level locking for data pages and  page-level locking for index pages.

### Resources for Locking

SQL Server Compact Edition database locks the following types of resources:

- Row identifier to lock a single row in a table.

- Data pages or index pages to lock pages.

- Whole table including data, schema, and indexes.

- Table metadata to lock the table schema.

- Whole database.

### Mode for Locking

SQL Server Compact Edition determines which lock mode to use when concurrent transactions are accessing the database. In the previous section you learned the five types of resources that the SQL Server Compact Edition database locks. Based upon the operations to be performed and resources to be locked, the SQL Server Compact Edition database chooses the lock.

### Shared (S)

Other processes can read the data but other transactions can't modify the data.

### Update (U)

In this lock, transactions can obtain an Update lock one at a time. At the time of modification, the Update lock changes to an Exclusive lock.

### Exclusive (X)

This mode is used to ensure that only one update is made to a resource at a time. This lock is used at the time of Insert, Update, and Delete operations.

### Schema (Sch-M, Sch-S)

For some operations, SQL Server Compact Edition locks the schema of a table. There are two types of schema locks. These are Schema Modification (Sch-M) and Schema Stability (Sch-S). Schema Stability is required for a Select statement as schema should not be changed while a Select statement is executing.

### Intent

Intent lock mode is used to specify the lock hierarchy. An intent lock in the hierarchy means that a transaction is updating resources in the hierarchy.

### Setting Mode

When you allow multiple applications or multiple connections to access the same database, you need to handle the concurrency issues. There will be instances when you want an exclusive connection to a database. To specify the mode, you can set the Mode property while opening a connection to the database. The SQL Server Compact Edition database supports the following four modes.

### (1) Read Write
Read Write mode allows multiple processes or applications to access and modify the database. Listing 6.2 demonstrates how to use Read Write mode.

**LISTING 6.2     Read Write Mode C#**

```
SqlCeConnection myConn = new SqlCeConnection("DataSource=\\Program
Files\\Modes\\MyPatients.sdf; Mode='Read Write';");
```

### (2) Read Only
Setting the mode property to Read Only means you can only open the database for reading and not for updating. Listing 6.3 demonstrates how to use the Read Only mode.

**LISTING 6.3     Read Only Mode C#**

```
SqlCeConnection myConn = new SqlCeConnection("DataSource=\\Program
Files\\Modes\\MyPatients.sdf; temp path=\\Program Files\\Modes\\MyPatients2.sdf;
Mode='Read Only';");
```

### (3) Exclusive
When you open a database in Exclusive mode, other processes or applications cannot access the database. No other application or tool can access the SQL Server Compact Edition database when it is open with exclusive access. To open a database with exclusive access, specify the Mode property value as Exclusive in a connection string as shown in Listing 6.4.

**LISTING 6.4     Exclusive Mode C#**

```
SqlCeConnection myConn =
new SqlCeConnection("DataSource=\\Program Files\\Modes\\MyPatients.sdf; Mode=
Exclusive");
```

### (4) Shared Read
The Shared Read mode allows other processes to open the database for reading but they are not allowed to write. Listing 6.5 demonstrates usage of the Shared Read mode.

**LISTING 6.5     Shared Read Mode C#**

```
SqlCeConnection myConn =
new SqlCeConnection("DataSource=\\Program Files\\Modes\\MyPatients.sdf;
Mode='Shared Read';");
```

## Setting Isolation Level

Isolation is a property that ensures the changes made by one operation are not known to other simultaneous operations. You can set the isolation level using the SQL command SET TRANSACTION ISOLATION LEVEL. You can also set the isolation level in the ADO.NET program. To set the isolation level programmatically you can specify the isolation level property of the BeginTransaction method.

### Serializable

In Serializable isolation all transactions occur in a completely isolated way as if all transactions were executed serially. Listing 6.6 demonstrates setting the isolation level.

LISTING 6.6    Serializable Isolation level

```
SET TRANSACTION ISOLATION LEVEL SERIALIZABLE;
```

### Repeatable Read

Using the Repeatable Read isolation level, a transaction retrieves and updates the same rows of data until the task is completed. During this time no other transaction can manipulate the data. This isolation level prevents other transactions from reading dirty data. Listing 6.7 demonstrates how to set the isolation level to REPEATABLE READ.

LISTING 6.7  Repeatable Read Isolation Level

```
SET TRANSACTION ISOLATION LEVEL REPEATABLE READ;
```

### Read Committed

In a Read Committed isolation level, the Select query only receives data before the query starts. In this isolation level, it neither sees the uncommitted data nor the changes committed during query execution. Listing 6.8 sets the isolation level to READ COMMITTED.

LISTING 6.8    Read Committed Isolation Level

```
SET TRANSACTION ISOLATION LEVEL READ COMMITTED;
```

**NOTE**

The SQL Server Compact Edition database does not support the Read Uncommitted isolation level. SQL Server Compact Edition ensures that one transaction cannot read the uncommitted data of another transaction.

# Querying the Database

SQL Server Compact Edition Data Manipulate language allows you to retrieve, insert, update, and delete data from a database. This section discusses the syntax and parameters needed to use DML operations. Examples of retrieving, inserting, and updating data using Data Manipulation Language are provided.

## Retrieving Data from a Table

Use the Select statement to retrieve data from tables in a database. The two most important keywords are SELECT and FROM. You specify SELECT to start the statement. FROM specifies the table from which you want to retrieve data.

### SELECT

The following structure shows you how to retrieve rows from tables. The first part of the syntax demonstrates how to optionally provide ADD or DISTINCT in a select statement.

**SYNTAX 6.1    Select**

```
SELECT [ALL ¦ DISTINCT] select_list
[ FROM table_source ]
[ WHERE search_condition ]
[ GROUP BY group_by_expression ]
[ HAVING search_condition ]
[ ORDER BY order_expression [ ASC ¦ DESC ] ]
```

The second part, select_list, demonstrates how to specify the columns you want to retrieve from the table.

**SYNTAX 6.2    Select List**

```
< select_list > ::=
    { *
    ¦ { table_name ¦ table_alias }.*
    ¦ { column_name ¦ expression } [ [ AS ] column_alias ]
    } [ ,...n ]
```

### ALL

By default all rows, whether they are duplicate or not, return in the result set by a select statement. You can use the keyword ALL to explicitly specify that all rows should be returned.

## DISTINCT
Using a distinct keyword means that only unique rows can appear in the result set.

## *
You can either specify the column name that you wish to retrieve from a table or list of tables explicitly, or you can use a * word to denote that you want to retrieve all columns. If you are retrieving data from multiple tables and use a * keyword, then it means all columns from all tables will be returned.

The statement below is an example of the simplest Select statement. Here you retrieve all rows and columns from a Customers table as shown in Listing 6.9.

LISTING 6.9    **Examples of Select Statements**

```
SELECT * FROM Customers;

SELECT * FROM Patients;
```

## { column_name | expression } [ [ AS ] column_alias ]
Instead of specifying *, you can specify the column names you wish to retrieve from the tables. You can retrieve columns in a result set or specify an alias.

## Column Name
To select a subset of columns from Customers tables you can replace * with a list of column names. Listing 6.10 shows how to retrieve specific columns instead of all columns.

LISTING 6.10    **Examples of Select Statements with Column Names**

```
SELECT FirstName, LastName FROM Patients;

SELECT 'Contact Name', 'Contact Phone' From Customers
```

## Column Alias
You can also specify the column alias using the AS keyword. Instead of the actual column name, the column alias will be shown as demonstrated in Listing 6.11. Using alias, the logical column name can be specified.

LISTING 6.11    **Select Statement with Column Alias**

```
SELECT FirstName As Name, LastName As "Family Name" FROM Patients
```

## { table_name | table_alias }.*
If you are retrieving the data from multiple tables, there is a possibility that two tables may have the same column name. In these scenarios you will add the table name or table alias and add . (dot) in front of the column name.

Column alias can be used in an ORDER BY clause. Column alias can't be used in a WHERE, GROUP BY, and HAVING clause.

## Table Name

This is the name of the table from which you are retrieving data. Listing 6.12 demonstrates the usage of table names for qualifying column names.

**LISTING 6.12    Specifying Table Name with Column Name**

```
SELECT Patients.FirstName , Patients.LastName  FROM Patients
SELECT Employees.City , Customers.City FROM Employees, Customers
```

## Table Alias

If you have specified an alias with a table in the From clause, then the alias should be used with the column name too. Listing 6.13 shows the usage of the table alias..

**LISTING 6.13    Specifying Table Alias with Column Name**

```
SELECT A.City , B.City FROM Employees A, Customers B
```

## WHERE

To select a subset of rows, you can filter the data and specify the condition as shown in Listing 6.14. The rows meeting the filtering criteria will be returned by statement.

**LISTING 6.14    Examples for the Where Clause**

```
SELECT 'Contact Name', 'Contact Phone', City FROM Customers WHERE City = 'London' ;
SELECT FirstName, LastName, Age FROM Patients WHERE Age > 40;
```

You have learned how to retrieve data from a single table. The SQL Server Compact Edition database supports the Join operation and you can retrieve data from multiple tables using Join. With Join you will specify the tables to join and the type of join.

You can also put a Where condition to compare data from two columns from two tables. Listing 6.15 returns the matching rows from Patients and PatientHistory tables.

**LISTING 6.15    Examples for the Where Clause**

```
SELECT FirstName, LastName, DiseaseIdentified FROM Patients, PatientHistory
WHERE Patients.PatientRegNo = PatientHistory.PatientRegNo;
```

## JOIN

In the previous example you returned data from multiple tables. Whenever you need to return data from multiple tables you can specify the table names with the FROM keyword. You can also use the JOIN keyword.

The syntax demonstrates that you can retrieve the data from multiple table sources. The table sources should be specified by a comma.

**SYNTAX 6.3    From Clause**

```
[ FROM { < table_source > } [ ,...n ]
```

Each table source can be a table name. You can also optionally specify an alias with a table name. The OR symbol indicates that you can also have a result set that is a join of multiple tables.

**SYNTAX 6.4    Table Source**

```
< table_source > ::= table_name [ [ AS ] table_alias ] ¦ < joined_table >
```

The syntax of a Joined table indicates that it will consist of two table sources and the join type. You will specify the ON keyword followed by a search condition.

**SYNTAX 6.5    Joined Table**

```
< joined_table > ::=
        < table_source > < join_type > < table_source > ON < search_condition >
        ¦ ( < joined_table > )
```

Join types can be specified as an Inner join or Outer join. The outer join can be a Left Outer join or a Right Outer join.

**SYNTAX 6.6    Join Type**

```
< join_type > ::=[ INNER ¦ { { LEFT ¦ RIGHT } [ OUTER ] } ] JOIN ]
```

**Inner Join**

This is a default join. In the Inner join, all matching rows from both tables are retrieved. In the previous section you have retrieved rows from Patient tables where there is a corresponding row in the PatientHistory table. Listing 6.16 fetches the matching rows.

**LISTING 6.16    Where Clause**

```
SELECT A.FirstName, A.LastName, B.DiseaseIdentified FROM Patients A, PatientHistory B
WHERE A.PatientRegNo = B.PatientRegNo
```

You can achieve the same results using Inner join as demonstrated in Listing 6.17.

**LISTING 6.17    Inner Join**

```
SELECT FirstName, LastName, DiseaseIdentified FROM Patients INNER JOIN
PatientHistory ON Patients.PatientRegNo = PatientHistory.PatientRegNo
```

### Left [Outer] Join

In the Left Outer join, the matching rows from both tables are returned as well as the nonmatching rows from the left tables as shown in Listing 6.18. The OUTER keyword is optional.

**LISTING 6.18    Left Outer Join**

```
SELECT FirstName, LastName, DiseaseIdentified FROM Patients LEFT OUTER JOIN
PatientHistory ON Patients.PatientRegNo = PatientHistory.PatientRegNo
```

### Right [Outer] Join

In the Right Outer join, the matching rows from both tables are returned as well as nonmatching rows from the right table. The second table specified after the FROM keyword will be the right table as demonstrated in Listing 6.19. The OUTER keyword is optional.

**LISTING 6.19    Right Outer Join**

```
SELECT FirstName, LastName, DiseaseIdentified FROM Patients RIGHT OUTER JOIN
PatientHistory ON Patients.PatientRegNo = PatientHistory.PatientRegNo
```

### On

While joining tables you use the ON keyword to specify the condition. Generally you will compare the table columns that you are joining.

### Sorting Data

You use the ORDER BY statement to sort the data you retrieve from a table. Without sorting, the data is retrieved in the same order in which it is present in the table. The ORDER BY clause can have items not present in the SELECT list. Listing 6.20 demonstrates the usage of the Order By clause.

**SYNTAX 6.7    Order By**

```
ORDER BY OrderByExpression [ASC ¦ DESC] [,…n]
```

**LISTING 6.20    Order By**

```
SELECT "First Name", "Last Name" FROM Employees
ORDER BY "First Name"
```

---

**NOTE**

Columns of data type `ntext` and `image` can't be used in the Order By clause.

---

## Grouping Data

Using the Group By clause you can divide the table into groups. You can use aggregate functions like SUM or AVG to get the sum of group or rows. Columns included in the `GROUP BY` clause must be included in the `SELECT` list. Listings 6.21 and 6.22 show the usage of the Group By clause.

**SYNTAX 6.8    Group By**

```
GROUP BY GroupByExpression [,…n]
```

**LISTING 6.21    Group By Clause**

```
SELECT  "Category ID", AVG ( "Unit Price") FROM PRODUCTS GROUP BY "Category ID"
```

**LISTING 6.22    Group By Clause on Multiple Columns**

```
SELECT  "Category ID", "SUPPLIER ID", AVG ( "Unit Price") FROM PRODUCTS GROUP BY
"Category ID", "SUPPLIER ID"
```

## HAVING

The Having clause is similar to the Where clause. The difference between Where and Having is that Where works on individual rows and Having acts on groups. Use Having always with the Group By clause. Listing 6.23 shows the usage of the Having clause.

**SYNTAX 6.9    Having**

```
HAVING HavingCondition
```

**LISTING 6.23 HAVING CLAUSE**

```
SELECT  "Category ID", AVG ( "Unit Price") FROM PRODUCTS
GROUP BY "Category ID" HAVING COUNT(*) > 2
```

---

**NOTE**

You cannot use the Image or NText data type in a Having clause.

# Modifying a Database

Modifying data is the most important part of Data Manipulation Language. How to design tables is discussed in Chapter 5, *Defining the Database Structure*.

## Inserting Data into Tables

To insert rows into a table you will use the Insert statement. With this statement you provide a table name and values for the columns.

### INSERT

The following syntax demonstrates the options and parameters you need to specify with the Insert statement.

**SYNTAX 6.10     Insert**

```
INSERT [INTO] table_name  [ ( column_list ) ]
      { VALUES
( { DEFAULT ¦ NULL ¦ expression } [ ,...n] ) ¦ derived_table
        }
```

### INTO

INTO is an optional keyword that can be specified between the INSERT keyword and the table name.

### Table Name

This is the name of the table where you need to insert the data.

### Column List

List the columns to which you wish to add data. The list of columns is separated by a comma and the column list is enclosed in parentheses. The column list is optional. If you choose not to specify the column list, the database assumes that list of values consists of the value for each column as shown in Listing 6.24. If you wish to specify values in a different order, you should specify a column list.

**LISTING 6.24     Insert Statement Without Column Names**

```
INSERT INTO Patient2
     VALUES
            ('PER1000091'
            ,'1993243232'
            ,'Adam'
            ,'Smith'
            ,'001425444450'
            ,'001425309000'
            ,'1965-08-16'
            ,41
```

```
          ,Null
          ,Null
          ,'R'
          ,'R'
                    );
```

If your table has many columns for which you want to specify Default or null value, you can simply provide a column list for which you want to specify values.

## VALUES

The VALUES keyword is used to specify the list of values for a column. The list of values is enclosed in parentheses as shown in Listing 6.25.

**LISTING 6.25    Insert Statement**

```
INSERT INTO Patients
          (PatientRegNo
          ,DoctorEmployeeNo
          ,FirstName
          ,LastName
          ,PhoneNo
          ,CellNo
          ,DOB
          ,Age
          ,GuardianFirstName
          ,GuardianLastName
          ,Smokes
          ,Drinks
          )
     VALUES
          ('PER1000091'
          ,'1993243232'
          ,'Adam'
          ,'Smith'
          ,'001425444450'
          ,'001425309000'
          ,'1965-08-16'
          ,41
          ,Null
          ,Null
          ,'R'
          ,'R'
                    );
```

## DEFAULT | NULL | Expression

Default value indicates the column value when a column value is not explicitly specified during the Insert operation. Default value is specified as a constant value or a string.

A Default column value can be specified as NULL. Specifying NULL means the column will contain NULL if the Insert statement does not include a column value.

### NOTE

The Identity column can't be given a Default value.

Listing 6.26 demonstrates an Insert statement. The example statement does not specify the value of the four columns: GuardianFirstName, GuardianLastName, Smokes, and Drinks. The null values are entered in GuardianFirstName, and GuardianLastName. Smokes, and Drinks columns have a default value of N. The database adds N in these columns when you do not specify explicit values.

Expressions can consist of characters, numbers, variables, constants, or expressions.

**LISTING 6.26    Insert Statement**

```
INSERT INTO Patients
            (PatientRegNo
            ,DoctorEmployeeNo
            ,FirstName
            ,LastName
            ,PhoneNo
            ,CellNo
            ,DOB
            ,Age
            )
    VALUES
            ('PER1000094'
            ,'1993243232'
            ,'Prash'
            ,'Dhingra'
            ,'001425444450'
            ,'001425309000'
            ,'1971-08-25'
            ,35
            );
```

### Derived Table

A derived table can be any Select statement that returns rows to be inserted. Instead of inputting the values of rows, you input a Select statement that returns rows as shown in Listing 6.27.

**LISTING 6.27    Derived Table**

```
INSERT INTO Patient2 SELECT * FROM Patient1
```

## Updating Data in Tables

Once you have inserted data into tables you will want to update it as well. With Update statements you don't have to specify all the columns; instead you specify the column you wish to update. You can also do a bulk update for all rows that satisfy a condition.

### Update

To modify the existing data in a table you will use the Update statement. The syntax below demonstrates the structure and parameter you require for the Update statement. Listings 6.28 and 6.29 demonstrate the usage of the Update statement.

After the UPDATE keyword you will specify the table name.

**Syntax 6.11    Update**

```
UPDATE table_name
   [ WITH ( < table_hint > ) ]
   SET
   { column_name = { expression ¦ DEFAULT ¦ NULL } } [ ,...n ]
   [ WHERE < search_condition > ]
   [ OPTION ( <query_hint> [ ,...n ] ) ]
```

**LISTING 6.28    Update Statement**

```
UPDATE Patients SET PatientRegNo = 'PER1000151' WHERE PatientRegNo = 'PER1000051' ;
```

**LISTING 6.29    Update Statement with Default Values**

```
UPDATE Patient2 SET GuardianFirstName = NULL, Smokes = DEFAULT WHERE PatientRegNo =
'PER1000091'
```

### With

You can specify the table hint with the WITH keyword. In the absence of hint, Query Optimizer can pick the best optimization method. However you can modify the default behavior by specifying the following locking hints.

### Set

Use the SET keyword to specify the column name that you wish to update.

## Column Name

This is the name of the column that you wish to update. You can specify N number of columns separated by a comma. With each column name you specify the value that you want to update the column. This can be the expression NULL or DEFAULT.

The expression can be a value, a variable, or expression that returns a value. When you specify a DEFAULT keyword instead of an expression, it means that the default value specified for the expression will be used. When you specify a NULL value, the column value is set to NULL.

## Where

You can filter the set of rows to be updated. In the absence of the Where clause, all rows will be updated.

## OPTION

The Option clause is also optional and you use it rarely. With the OPTION keyword, you specify the hint that Query Optimizer can use. The hints you specify here can override the execution plan optimizer generally selected for the query.

# Deleting Data from Tables

To delete one or more rows from a table use the Delete statement.

## DELETE

The Delete statement consists of the DELETE keyword, table name, and Where clause. You can optionally specify the FROM keyword as well. Listing 6.30 shows the usage of the Delete statement..

### SYNTAX 6.12   Select

```
DELETE
    [ FROM ] table_name
    [ WHERE < search_condition > ]
```

### LISTING 6.30   Delete Statement

```
DELETE Patients WHERE PatientRegNo = 'PER1000051' ;
```

## FROM

The FROM keyword is optional in the Delete statement. In a Select statement, FROM is used after the * or column name. In a Delete Statement it is not necessary to specify the FROM keyword.

## WHERE

The WHERE keyword is used to specify the condition. All rows satisfying the condition will get deleted.

# Using SQL Server Integration Services

SQL Server Integration Services (SSIS) in SQL Server 2005 is the successor of SQL Server Data Transformation Service (DTS) in SQL Server 2000. Integration Services is commonly known as ETL (extract–transform–load). Traditionally, ETLs are used in a datawarehousing environment to move large quantities of data from nonhomogenous data sources. SSIS goes beyond the standard ETL traditional role.

## NOTE

SSIS is available in the Standard and Enterprise Editions of SQL Server 2005.

You can use the SSIS package to extract and transform data from SQL Server Compact Edition. Using SQL Server Integration Services, developers can export or import data from various data sources such as XML, flat files, MS Access, SQL Server, Oracle, IBM DB2, and so on.

The exercise example in this section demonstrates how to read a flat file into an SQL Server Compact Edition database using SSIS. The example creates an Integration Service project. In the project, a data flow task is created. The data source for the data flow task is defined as a flat file and the data destination is defined as an SQL Server Compact Edition table. The example also creates a connection manager for the flat file and the SQL Server Compact Edition database.

The example uses a flat file as the source. The flat file has patient data. The example also uses the SQL Server Compact Edition database, MyPatients, as the destination. The MyPatients database has an empty Patients table. The Patient table structure is defined in Chapter 5, *Defining the Database Structure*.

## NOTE

You can use a similar procedure to transform data from an XML file, Excel File, or OLE DB source into an SQL Server Compact Edition table on a desktop or on a mobile device.

## Create a Project

With SQL Server 2005, you get Business Development Studio built on top of Visual Studio 2005. You can use Business Intelligence Studio or Visual Studio to build SSIS packages.

1. Start Visual Studio 2005 from the Start menu.

2. Click File | New | Project.

3. Click on Business Intelligence Project.

4. Click on Integration Service Project Template.

5. Enter the Name and Location of the project as shown in the Figure 6.3.

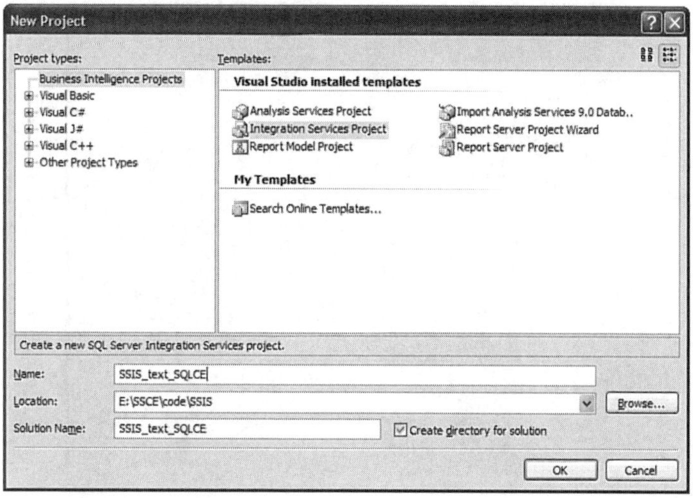

**FIGURE 6.3**   Integration Services Project

6. Click OK on the New Project dialog box.

## Define Data Flow Source

Data flow tasks move and transform data. In this section you will identify a flat file source.

7. From the toolbox, drag Data Flow Task onto Control Flow Canvas.

8. Click on Data Flow Canvas. Drag Flat File Source to Data Flow Task.

To fetch data from SQL Server, Oracle, Outlook search, and so on, use the OLE DB source. Choose the appropriate provider from the native OLE DB provider list. You can choose to fetch the whole table or provide a select statement to filter the table and upload it into the SQL Server Compact Edition destination.

9. Double click on Flat File Source. Click New to add a new connection manager for the flat file.

10. A Flat File Connection Manager Editor opens. Use a General_Tab in Editor. Give a name to the Connection Manager. The example uses the name "SSIS Connection Manager for Flat File" as shown in Figure 6.4.

11. Select the file that you wish to read into SQL Server Compact Edition. The example file is `E:\SSCE\code\SSIS\Patients.txt`.

12. Select `{CR}{LF}` in the header row delimiter.

13. Select `Columns name in first data row` to indicate that the first row of text file contains the name of the columns.

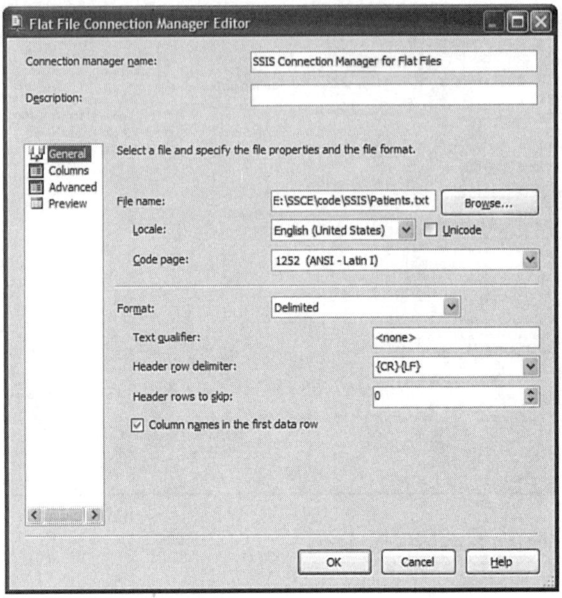

FIGURE 6.4    Specify File Properties

14. Select the Columns tab in the Flat File Connection Manager Editor.

15. Select {CR}{LF} in the row delimiter. Select Tab {t} in the Column delimiter. It indicates that the columns are separated by tabs.

16. The table in the Preview section shows the column name and data. Check the table columns and data in the Preview section as shown in Figure 6.5.

17. Click on the Advanced tab in the Flat File Connection Manager Editor and configure the properties for each column. You should change the Output Column Width and Data Type to match the table structure of the SQL Server Compact Edition table as shown in Figure 6.6. Initially, all the columns are defined as a DT_STR column. The nvarchar column in SQL Server Compact Edition will correspond to the DT_STR column. Change the DOB column data type to DT_DBTIMESTAMP. Similarly change the Age and NoOfChildren columns to DT_I2. Age and Number of Children are defined as smallint in the SQL Server Compact Edition table. SmallInt takes two bytes of storage. DT_I2 also takes two bytes of storage.

NOTE
You can select multiple columns and assign them each a data type, for example, select all DT_STRING columns of length 20 and assign each a value.

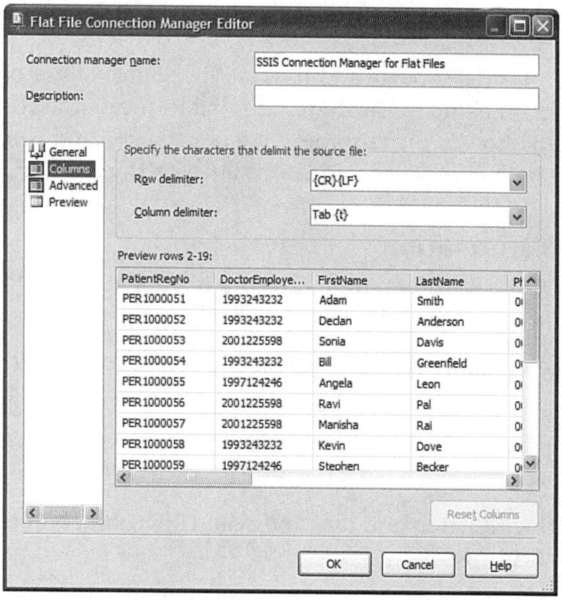

**FIGURE 6.5**   Specify Delimiting Characters

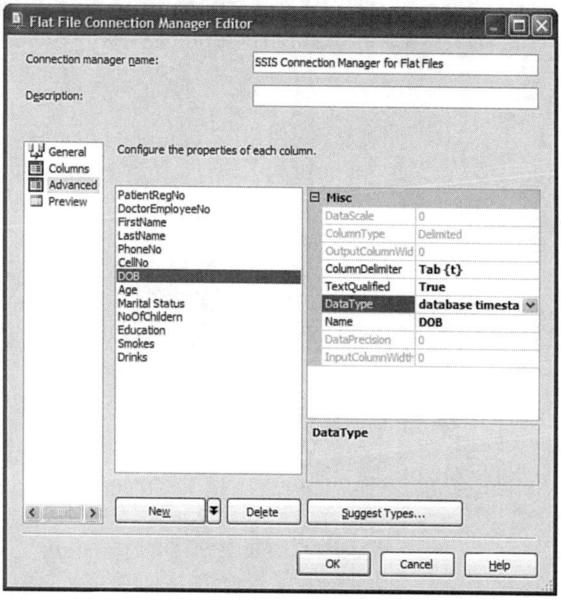

**FIGURE 6.6**   Configure Properties of Each Column

18. See the Data preview that shows up to 200 rows. Click OK on the File Connection Manager dialog boxes.

19. Double click on Flat File Source and the Flat File Source Editor opens. If you want to change the column name in the destination table, locate the column names in the Flat File Source Editor. In the example, ParentFirstName and ParentLastName are changed to GuardianFirstName and GuardianLastName.

## Define Data Transformation

20. From the Data Flow Transformation category in Toolbox, drag the Derived Column Data transformation to the Data Flow canvas.

21. Stretch the green output arrow of the Flat File Source to the Derive Column transform.

22. Double click on Derive Column transform. The Derive Column Transformation Editor will open.

23. Expand the String function and drag the SUBSTRING function to the Expression column of the first row.

24. Expand the Columns folder on the left. Drag Marital Status to the character expression field inside the SUBSTRING expression. Replace <<start>> and <<length>> with 1 and 1 as shown in Figure 6.7.

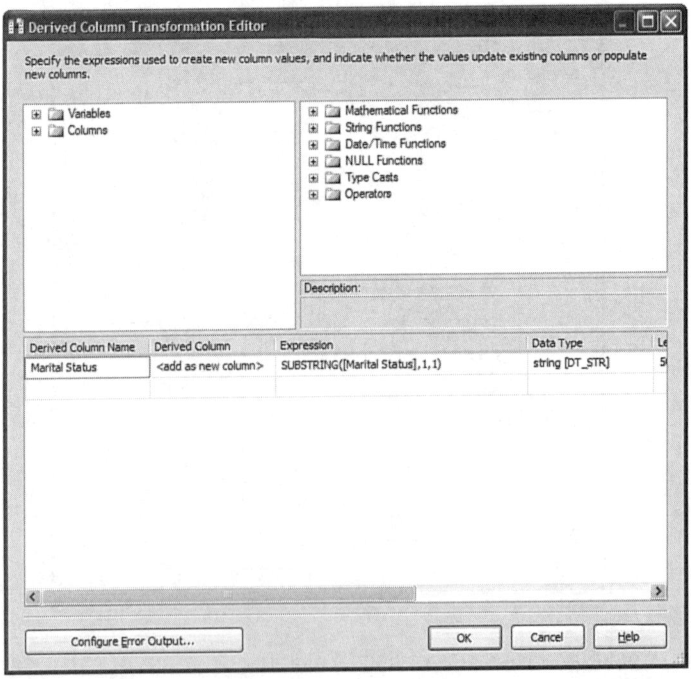

FIGURE 6.7    Derived Column Transformation Editor

## NOTE

If you have entered it correctly, the red expression will turn to a black expression once you click outside the row.

## Define Data Flow Destination

Data flow ends with one or more data sources. In this section you will define an SQL Server Compact Edition Destination database.

25. From the Data Flow Destination category in Toolbox, drag an SQL Server Compact Edition (or SQL Server Mobile Destination for version 3.0).

26. Stretch the green output arrow of the Derived Column Transformation to the SQL Server Compact Edition destination.

27. Click on the SSIS | New Connection menu option.

28. Choose Connection Manager for SQL Server Compact Edition from the Add SSIS Connection Manager dialog box.

Connection Manager defines the connection string and its properties. The connection manager is defined once and can be referenced at other places in the package.

29. In the SQL Server Connection Manager Edition dialog box, specify the path of the SQL Server Compact Edition file. The example uses the name MyPatients_SSIS. A connection manager, MyPateints_SSIS, is created.

30. Double click on SQL Server Compact Edition Destination. The Advance Editor for SQL Server Compact Edition will open.

31. In the Connection Manager tab. choose the connection manager you created earlier.

32. Select the Component Properties tab. In Custom Properties, specify the name Patients table.

33. Click on the Mapping tab to validate the mapping between the flat file table and the SQL Server Compact Edition table. If you need to ignore columns or change the mapping, you can do so using the Mapping tab as shown in Figure 6.8.

## Execute Package

In this section you will execute the package to read the data from the flat file, do the defined transformation, and copy it to the SQL Server Compact Edition database.

34. Click on the Execute button or click the Debug | Start without Debugging menu option.

35. Package executes successfully and the three tasks—Flat File Source, Derived Column, and SQL Server Compact Edition become green as shown in Figure 6.9.

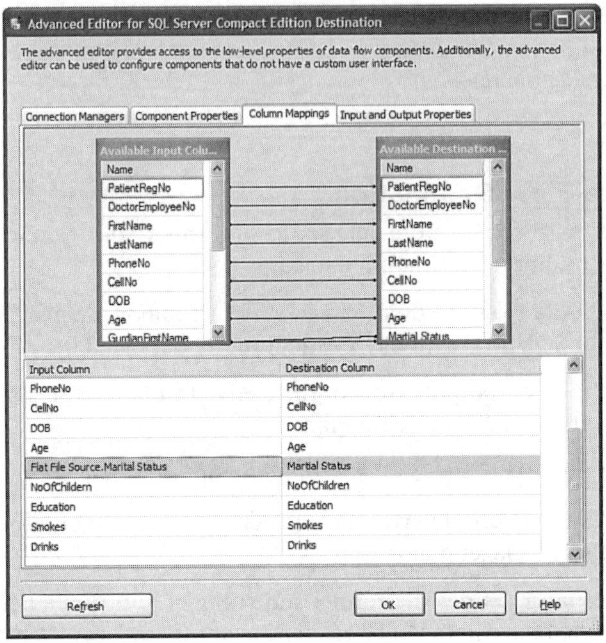


FIGURE 6.8 Columns Mapping

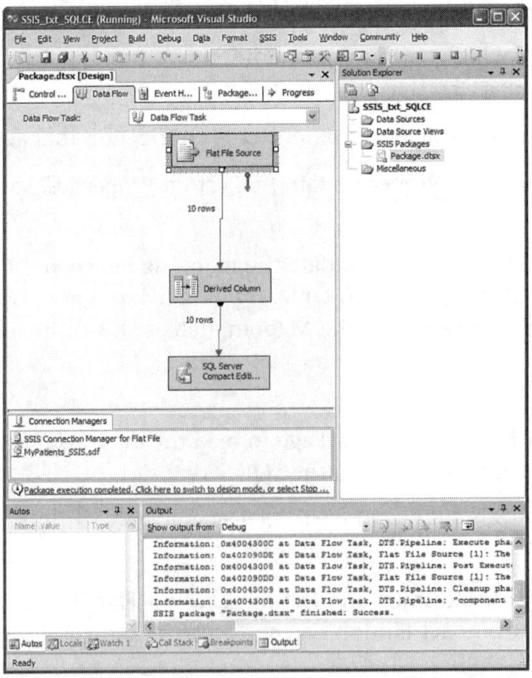


FIGURE 6.9 SSIS Package

36. To validate that the table in SQL Server Compact Edition is populated, open the SQL Server Compact Edition database. The Patients table is populated with data given in the flat file. The Marital Status column is populated with first characters as described in the Data Transformation Task.

This example demonstrates converting flat file data into SQL Server Compact Edition. Similarly, you can fetch data from other data sources such as Excel, MS Access, SQL Server, and other OLE DB sources.

**NOTE**

To learn more about SSIS, go to http://msdn2.microsoft.com/en-us/sql/aa336312.aspx.

## Summary

In this chapter you have seen how to connect to the SQL Server Compact Edition database using tools and programmatically. You have learned the syntax and parameters for the data manipulation language. Isolation level, concurrency, and locking SQL Server Compact Edition uses were also discussed. In the following chapters you will learn the SQL Server Compact Edition Built In operators and functions.

# Programming SQL Server 2005 Compact Edition with ADO.NET

SQL Server Compact Edition allows you to store data on a desktop or mobile device. A majority of application code consists of retrieving data from a database, updating it, and storing it back to the database. You can use an OLE DB Provider for accessing or manipulating the database or you can use an ADO.Net provider for managed access.

In this chapter, you will learn how to use ADO.NET to connect to the SQL Server Compact Edition database as well as how to read, update, and merge the changes back to the SQL Server Compact Edition database.

## Introducing ADO.NET

ADO.NET is the data access component for .NET Framework and .NET Compact Framework. Using the namespace and classes available in ADO.NET, you can access, manipulate, and update the SQL Server Compact Edition database.

ADO.NET provides a standardized mechanism to access a database. It is independent of the data source. Once you have referred to a database namespace, you will use a consistent set of API objects and properties to access the database. If you have used ADO.NET to access an SQL Server database, then you will find accessing SQL Server Compact Edition very similar. Instead of referring to System.Data.SqlClient namespace, you will be referring to System.Data.SqlServerCE namespace.

The data access architecture consists of a physical data store and ADO.NET classes. ADO.NET classes are divided into two categories. The first category communicates with the physical data store and is called *Data Provider*. The second category represents the in-memory representation of data.

- The physical data store can be an SQL Server database, XML file, or an SQL Server Compact Edition database.

- The data provider layer consists of a connection object and a command object to create in-memory representation of data.

- The uppermost layer is an in-memory representation of data consisting of tables and relationships.

The data provider layer is an abstract layer between the physical store and the in-memory representation on which the application works. Once the data set is created, it does not matter which is the physical data store. This is termed a *connectionless* or a *disconnected solution*.

## Namespace

ADO.NET provides its classes, methods, and properties through a set of namespaces. The classes combined together in these namespaces are termed *ADO.NET*. You should refer to the appropriate namespace to use classes in the respective namespace.

### System.Data

The ADO.NET objective is to provide data-access functionality. `System.Data` is perhaps the most important namespace among all the namespaces in ADO.NET. This namespace also contains the most important classes related to Data Access, such as, DataSet, DataTable, DataColumn, DataRow, and DataView.

### System.Data.Common

As discussed earlier there are three layers—data source, data provider, and in-memory representation of the data layer. The `System.Data.Common` namespace consists of classes related to the data provider layer. This namespace has providers for ODBC, OLDB, SQL Server, and so on.

### System.Data.SqlClient

The `System.Data.SqlClient` is the data provider for SQL Server. The SQL Server data provider exists both in .NET Framework and .NET Compact Framework. For desktop-based applications. use a .NET Framework data provider for SQL Server. For a Smart device-based application, use a .NET Compact Framework data provider for SQL Server.

The `System.Data.SqlClient` namespace in .NET Compact Framework corresponds to the `System.Data.SqlClient` namespace in .NET Framework.

The SQL Server Data Provider has classes to access the SQL Server database with managed code using .NET Compact Framework. You can use SQL Server Data Provider to connect, execute the command, and retrieve the data from the SQL Server database.

The System.Data.SqlClient classes in .NET Compact Framework match with the System.Data.SqlClient classes in .NET Framework except for a few limitations including:

- Connection pooling is not supported.

- Distributed transactions are not supported.

- Encrypted connections to SQL Server are not supported.

- Connection string properties related to connection pooling, encryption, network library, and so on are not supported.

- Windows Authentication should be used to connect to SQL Server from Smart devices. SQL Server authentication to connect to SQL Server from Smart device is not supported.

- SqlClientPermission and SqlClientPermissionAttribute classes are not supported.

For complete details you should refer to the System.Data.SqlClient documentation.

The System.Data.SqlClient namespace consists of a data provider for SQL Server. The SQL Server Data Provider has classes to access the SQL Server database. You can use the SQL Server Data Provider to access the database to fill data into the DataSet.

### System.Data.SqlServerCe

The System.Data.SqlServerCe namespace is the data provider for SQL Server Compact Edition. The SQL Server Compact Edition Data Provider contains classes that are specific to the SQL Server Compact Edition data source. You should add the reference to SqlServerCe namespace in the program using SQL Server Compact Edition classes as shown in Figure 7.1.

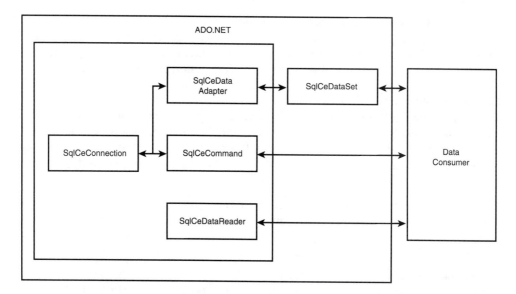

**FIGURE 7.1    ADO.NET Object Model**

**LISTING 7.1    SqlServerCe Namespace C#**

```
Using System.Data.SqlServerCe
```

**LISTING 7.1    SqlServerCe Namespace VB.NET**

```
Imports System.Data.SqlServerCe
```

## Introducing the ADO.NET Object Model

This section starts with a simplified model of ADO.NET. Figure 7.1 depicts the primary objects in ADO.NET.

The classes are divided into two categories:

- Data provider that communicates with the SQL Server Compact Edition data source.

- DataSets that store the memory representation of data.

### Understanding Data Providers

The data provider category of classes interacts with a physical data store and provides the data to a DataSet category of classes. The data provider category of classes interacts directly with a physical store. This is the reason a data provider is specific to a data source. For SQL Server Compact Edition, .NET Framework and .NET Compact Framework provide two data providers:

- OLE DB Data Provider

- SQL Server Compact Edition Data Provider

As shown in Figure 7.1, a connection object connects to a data source. The Data Consumer can call the Execute Reader method to execute the Data Reader against the connect object. You can execute the command object independently or use it with Data Adapter. Data Adapter acts like glue between the connection object and DataSet.

### Connection Object

The connection object represents the unique connection to the data source. The SqlCeConnection object manages the connection to the physical data store. The connection string that determines the path of the SQL Server Compact Edition database is the property of the connection object. Listing 7.2 describes the usage of Open and Close methods to open and close connections to the database.

The connection to the database does not close if the SqlCeConnection object goes out of scope. You must explicitly close the connection.

**LISTING 7.2    Connection Object C#**

```
SqlCeConnection myConnection = null;
myConnection = new SqlCeConnection("Data Source=\\Mobile\\Northwind.sdf;");
```

```
myConnection.Open();
..
..
myConnection.Close();
```

### LISTING 7.2    Connection Object VB.NET

```
Dim myConn As SqlCeConnection = New
SqlCeConnection("DataSource=\Mobile\Northwind.sdf")
myConnection.Open()
..
..
myConnection.Close()
```

### NOTE

SQL Server Compact Edition 3.x supports multiple simultaneous connections to a database.

Table 7.1 lists the connection object methods.

### TABLE 7.1    Commonly Used Connection Object Methods

| Method | Method Description |
| --- | --- |
| BeginTransaction | Begins a database transaction. |
| ChangeDatabase | Changes the current database. |
| Close | Closes a database connection |
| CreateCommand | Creates an `SqlCeCommand` object. |
| Dispose | Releases the resources used by the connection object. |
| Equals | Compares two connection objects and returns TRUE if objects are equal. |
| GetHashCode | Serves as a hash function for a particular type. |
| GetSchema | Returns schema information for its data source. |
| GetType | Gets type of current instances. |
| Open | Opens a database connection. |
| ReferenceEquals | Compares two connection objects and returns TRUE if objects are the same. |
| ToString | Returns a string that represents the current object. |

Table 7.2 lists the connection object properties.

**TABLE 7.2    Commonly Used Connection Object Properties**

| Properties | Property Description |
| --- | --- |
| ConnectionString | Gets or sets the string used to open a database. |
| ConnectionTimeOut | Gets the amount of time to wait while attempting to open a connection before generating an error. |
| DataBase | Gets the name of the database. |
| DataSource | Gets the physical file name including path of data source. |
| ServerVersion | Returns SQL Server Compact Edition version number. |
| Site | Gets or sets the ISite of a component. |
| State | Gets the current state of a connection. |

In the connection string, you can specify the location and size of the temporary database. To specify the temporary database, the `temp file directory` and `temp file max size` properties must be specified in the connection string.

## Command Object

The `SQLCeCommand` object allows you to execute an SQL command against the SQL Server Compact Edition database. A data command object is simply an SQL command that is executed against a connection object. Like most of the object, the data command object can be created at design time or at runtime in code. Listing 7.3 describes how a command object can be created.

**NOTE**

Multiple commands can share the same connection object.

**LISTING 7.3    Command Object C#**

```
SqlCeCommand myCmd = myConnection.CreateCommand();
```

**LISTING 7.3    Command Object VB.NET**

```
Dim myCmd As SqlCeCommand = myConn.CreateCommand()
```

Commonly used command object methods are listed in Table 7.3.

## Command Object Properties

The data command commonly used properties are described in Table 7.4. The CommandText property contains the actual text of the SQL command to be executed. The Connection property contains a reference to a connection object. The Parameters property contains a collection of parameters required for the SQL command. The Command object properties will be validated for syntax errors. Final validation occurs when a command is executed by a data source.

TABLE 7.3    Commonly Used Command Object Methods

| Method | Method Description |
|---|---|
| Cancel | Cancels execution. |
| CreateParameter | Creates a new parameter. |
| ExecuteNonQuery | Executes the query and returns the number of rows affected. |
| ExecuteReader | Builds a Data Reader. |
| ExecuteScalar | Executes the query and returns the first column of the first row of the result set. |
| ExecuteXMLReader | Builds an XML Reader. |
| Prepare | Builds a compiled version of command on data source. |
| ResetCommandTimeout | Sets the timeout to its default value. |

TABLE 7.4    Commonly Used Command Object Properties

| Properties | Property Description |
|---|---|
| CommandText | Gets or sets the SQL command that executes on a database. |
| CommandTimeOut | Gets or sets the amount of time to wait while executing a command before returning an error. |
| CommandType | Gets or sets a value that determines how CommandType is interpreted. |
| | Text—when passing a query. |
| | TableDirect—returns all rows and columns of a table. Command Text is the name of the table. |
| Connection | Gets or sets the SqlCeConnection. |
| IndexName | Specifies the index to be opened. |
| Parameters | Gets the SqlCeParameterCollection. |
| Site | Gets or sets the ISite of a component. |
| Transaction | Gets or sets the transaction that SqlCeCommand executes. |

NOTE

SQL Server Compact Edition Data Provider does not support batched queries.

ExecuteReader, ExecuteScalar, and ExecuteNonQuery are the most import methods to execute an SQL command against a connection object.

The following section discusses the SqlCeDataReader class. Using Data Reader the above methods can be executed.

## Data Reader

SQL Server Compact Edition provides an `SqlCeDataReader` class to implement Data Reader. A Data Reader is like a forward-only cursor for reading a data source. To use Data Reader, you need to create an `SqlCeDataReader` object and execute an `ExecuteReader` method of the object. To retrieve the rows, use the read method in a loop. Each iteration in a loop will read a row.

Listing 7.4 opens an `SQLCeConnection`. It creates a command. A command type property is set to `TableDirect`, and the `CommandText` property is set to a table name. A TableDirect command is similar to a Select statement that returns all rows of a table.

When you define a `CommandType` property to `TableDirect`, you use a base table cursor. You do not use a base table cursor with a Select statement. Instead, you can use it with Data Reader and a result set by setting the `CommandType` property to `TableDirect`.

The code creates the Data Reader by the `ExecuteReader` method while the loop reads the rows and populates the listbox.

### LISTING 7.4    Data Reader C#

```
// Code
SqlCeConnection myConnection = null;
myConnection = new SqlCeConnection("Data Source=\\Program Files\\DataReader\\North-
wind.sdf");
myConnection.Open();
SqlCeCommand myCmd = myConnection.CreateCommand();
SqlCeDataReader myDataReader ;
myCmd.CommandText = "Products";
myCmd.CommandType = CommandType.TableDirect;
myDataReader = myCmd.ExecuteReader();
while (myDataReader.Read()){
listbox1.Items.Add(myDataReader.GetValue(0));
}
myDataReader.Close();
}
```

### LISTING 7.4    Data Reader VB.NET

```
Dim myConnection As SqlCeConnection
myConnection = New SqlCeConnection("Data Source=\Program Files\DataReader\North-
wind.sdf;")
myConnection.Open()
Dim myCmd As SqlCeCommand = myConnection.CreateCommand()
myCmd.CommandText = "Products"
myCmd.CommandType = CommandType.TableDirect
Dim myDataReader As SqlCeDataReader = myCmd.ExecuteReader()
While myDataReader.Read()
```

```
    listbox1.Items.Add(myDataReader.GetValue(0))
End While
myDataReader.Close()
myConnection.Close()
```

The method exposed by Data Reader is shown in Table 7.5.

The Open method is used to open the DataReader. The DataReader is positioned at the beginning of a result set, before the first row. The Read method reads the row from the result. Any subsequent Read method will read the next row from the result set.

**TABLE 7.5    Commonly Used Data Reader Object Methods**

| Method | Method Description |
| --- | --- |
| Close | Closes the Data Reader object. |
| Equals | Returns TRUE if two object instances are equal. |
| GetBoolean | Gets the value of a specified column as Boolean. |
| GetByte | Gets the value of a specified column as Byte. |
| GetBytes | Reads a stream of bytes from a column offset. |
| GetChars | Reads a stream of characters from a column offset. |
| GetData | Returns a DBDataReader object. |
| GetDataTypeName | Gets the name of a data source type |
| GetDateTime | Gets the specified column as a DateTime object. |
| GetDecimal | Gets the specified column as a Decimal object. |
| GetDouble | Gets the specified column as a Double object. |
| GetFieldType | Gets the type of the object. |
| GetFloat | Gets the specified column as a Float object. |
| GetGuid | Gets the specified column as a Globally Unique Identified (GUID). |
| GetInt16 | Gets the specified column as a 16-bit integer. |
| GetInt32 | Gets the specified column as a 32-bit integer. |
| GetInt64 | Gets the specified column as a 64-bit integer. |
| GetName | Gets the name of a column. |
| GetOrdinal | Gets the ordinal of a column whose name is specified. |
| GetSchemaTable | Returns a Data Table specifying the structure of DataReader. |
| GetSqlBinary | Gets the value of a given column as SqlBinary. |
| GetSqlBoolean | Gets the value of a given column as SqlBoolean. |
| GetSqlByte | Gets the value of a given column as SqlByte. |
| GetSqlDateTime | Gets the value of a given column as SqlDateTime. |
| GetSqlDecimal | Gets the value of a given column as SqlDecimal. |
| GetSqlDouble | Gets the value of a given column as SqlDouble. |
| GetSqlGuid | Gets the value of a given column as SqlGuid. |
| GetSqlInt16 | Gets the value of a given column as SqlInt16. |

TABLE 7.5    Commonly Used Data Reader Object Methods

| Method | Method Description |
|---|---|
| GetSqlInt32 | Gets the value of a given column as SqlInt32. |
| GetSqlInt64 | Gets the value of a given column as SqlInt64. |
| GetSqlMoney | Gets the value of a given column as SqlMoney. |
| GetSqlSingle | Gets the value of a given column as SqlSingle. |
| GetSqlString | Gets the value of a given column as SqlString. |
| GetType | Gets the type of a current instance. |
| GetValue | Gets the value of a column. |
| IsDBNull | Gets the value to indicate whether a column contains nonexistent value. |
| Read | Advances the SqlCeDataReader to the next row. |
| Seek | Puts the SqlCeDataReader to a given record whose index is specified. |
| ToString | Converts the object to String and returns the string. |

### NOTE

The SQL Server Compact Edition Data Provider does not support the GetChar and Next ResultSet methods. These methods are supported by the SQL Server Data Provider.

Table 7.6 lists the SqlCeDataReader object properties.

TABLE 7.6    Commonly used Data Reader Object Properties

| Properties | Property Description |
|---|---|
| Depth | Indicates the depth of nesting for the current row. |
| FieldCount | Gets the number of columns in a current row. |
| HasRows | Gets a value to indicate whether Data Reader contains at least one row. |
| HiddenFieldCount | Gets the number of a hidden field. |
| IsClosed | Indicates whether Data Reader is closed. |
| Item | Gets the value of a column in its native format. |
| RecordsEffected | Gets number of rows affected by insert, delete, update operation. |
| VisibleFieldCount | Gets number of fields that are not hidden. |

## Data Adapter

Data Adapter sits between the Connection object and DataSet and provides a gateway between the SQL Server Compact Edition Connection object and the DataSet object. Data Adapter receives the data from the Connection object and passes it to DataSet. After updates are done, it passes the changes back from the DataSet to the connection that updates the data in the database. Instead of looping through a set of rows with Data Reader, Data Adapter fills the DataSet with data.

DataAdapter contains four command objects:

- `SelectCommand`
- `UpdateCommand`
- `InsertCommand`
- `DeleteCommand`

`SelectCommand` is used to fill a DataSet. The other three command objects are used to transmit changes back to the data source.

You can create the Data Adapter at design time and at runtime.

Listing 7.5 demonstrates the usage of `DataAdapter`. The listing creates a command. It creates `DataAdapter` and `DataSet`. The `Fill` method loads the data from a database into `DataTables` of a `DataSet`.

**LISTING 7.5    Data Adapter and DataSet Object C#**

```csharp
SqlCeConnection myConnection = null;
myConnection = new SqlCeConnection("Data Source=\\Program
Files\\ParameterQuery\\AppDatabase1.sdf;");
myConnection.Open();
SqlCeCommand myCmd = myConnection.CreateCommand();
myCmd.CommandType = CommandType.Text;
myCmd.CommandText = "Select * From Books";
SqlCeDataAdapter myDataAdapter = new SqlCeDataAdapter(myCmd);
DataSet myDataSet = new DataSet();
myDataAdapter.Fill(myDataSet);
dataGrid1.DataSource = myDataSet.Tables[0];
```

**LISTING 7.5    Data Adapter and DataSet Object VB.NET**

```vbnet
Dim myConnection As SqlCeConnection = New SqlCeConnection("DataSource=\Program
Files\ParameterQuery\AppDatabase1.sdf")
Dim myCmd As SqlCeCommand = myConnection.CreateCommand()
myConnection.Open()
myCmd.CommandType = CommandType.Text
myCmd.CommandText = "Select * From Books"
Dim myDataAdapter As SqlCeDataAdapter = New SqlCeDataAdapter(myCmd)
Dim myDataSet As DataSet = New DataSet()
myDataAdapter.Fill(myDataSet)
DataGrid1.DataSource = myDataSet.Tables(0)
```

Table 7.7 describes the usage of SqlCeDataAdapter methods.

**TABLE 7.7    Commonly Used Data Adapter Object Public Methods**

| Method | Method Description |
|---|---|
| Equals | Returns TRUE if two object instances are equal. |
| Fill | Fills data from a data source into one or more tables of DataSet. |
| FillSchema | Adds a DataTable to DataSet and configures the schema to match in data source. |
| GetType | Gets the type of instance. |
| ReferenceEquals | Returns TRUE if specified object instances are equal. |
| ToString | Returns a string having the name of component. |
| Update | For each row in DataSet that has changed, the Update method calls the InsertCommand, DeleteCommand or UpdateCommand. |

Table 7.8 shown below lists the SqlCeDataAdapter properties you can set.

**TABLE 7.8    Commonly Used Data Adapter Object Public Properties**

| Properties | Property Description |
|---|---|
| AcceptChangesDuringFill | Gets or sets a value to indicate whether AcceptChange is called for the DataRow added to the DataTable during Fill operations. |
| AcceptChangesDuringUpdate | Gets or sets a value to indicate whether AcceptChange is called for the DataRow added to the DataTable during Update operations. |
| DeleteCommand | Data command to delete a data row. |
| InsertCommand | Gets or sets the data command to insert rows in data source. |
| MissingMappingAction | Specifies the action to be taken when incoming data does not match an existing table/column. |
| MissingSchemaAction | Specifies the action to be taken when incoming data does not match an existing DataSet schema. |
| SelectCommand | Gets or sets the data command to select rows from the data source. |
| Site | Gets or sets the ISite of the component. |
| TableMappings | Collection of DataTableMapping between the source table and DataTable. |
| UpdateBatchSize | Gets or sets a value to indicate the number of commands that can be executed in a batch. |
| UpdateCommand | Gets or sets data command to update rows in the data source. |

## Understanding DataSet

DataSet is a memory resident structure consisting of relational data. `DataSet` consists of the collection of `DataTable` objects as shown in Figure 7.2. The `DataTable` object contains the actual data. You can use the `DataRelation` object in `DataSet` to relate the collection of tables in `DataSet`. For ensuring data integrity you can use the `UniqueConstraint` and `ForeignKeyConstraint` objects.

You can create DataSet interactively in Visual Studio or programmatically.

To use DataSet, follow these setps.

1. Create tables in DataSet and fill data in the tables from the data source.

2. Insert, update, or delete the data in the data table.

3. Call the GetChanges method. This method creates a DataSet with modified data.

4. Call the Update method of Data Adapter with the DataSet created in the previous step as an argument.

5. Call the Merge method.

Call the AcceptChanges or RejectChanges methods of DataSet.

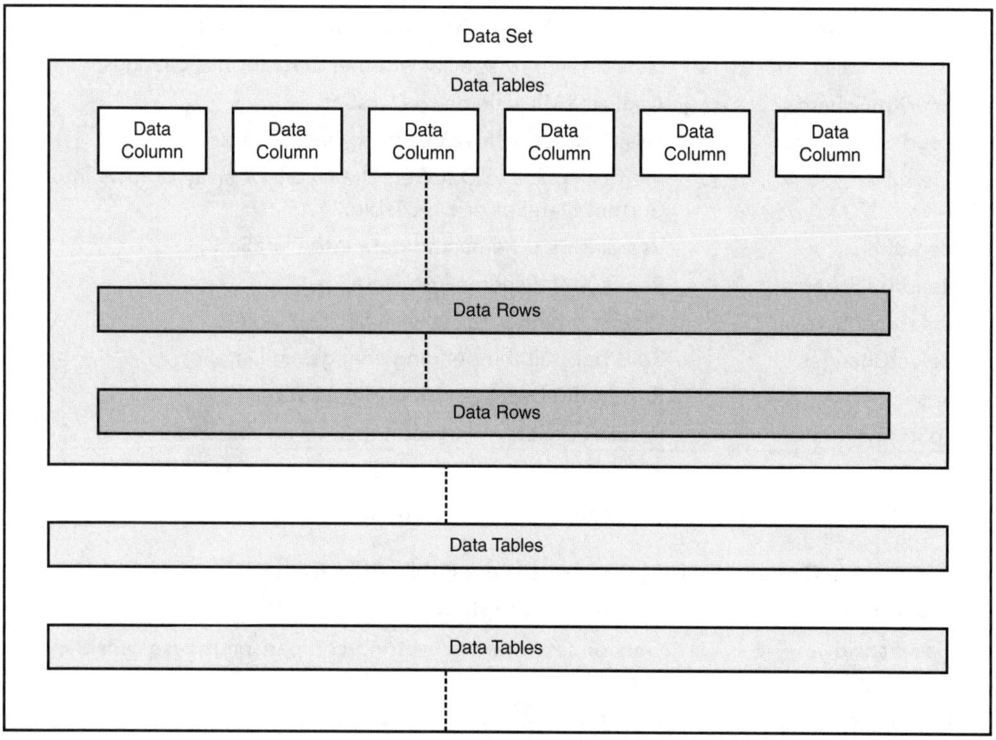

**FIGURE 7.2**  DataSet

Table 7.9 describes the SqlCeDataSet methods.

**TABLE 7.9    Commonly Used DataSet Object Public Methods**

| Method | Method Description |
|---|---|
| AcceptChanges | Commits all changes to DataSet. |
| BeginInit | Begins the initialization of the DataSet. |
| Clear | Empties all tables in DataSet. |
| Clone | Copies the structure of DataSet. |
| Copy | Copies the structure and content of DataSet. |
| CreateDataReader | Returns a DataTableReader with one result set for each data table. The result set is returned in the same sequence as tables appear in the tables collection. |
| EndInit | Ends the initialization of DataSet. |
| Equals | Determines whether two object instances are equal. |
| GetChanges | Gets a copy of DataSet containing only the changed rows in all the tables in DataSet. |
| GetDataSetSchema | Gets the Schema of DataSet. |
| GetType | Gets the Type of current instance. |
| GetXml | Gets the XML representation of DataSet. |
| GetXmlSchema | Gets the XML representation of data stored in DataSet. |
| HasChanges | Gets a value to specify whether DataSet has changes. |
| InferXmlSchema | Applies XML schema to DataSet. |
| Load | Fills DataSet with values from Data Source. |
| Merge | Merges specified DataSet, DataTable or array of rows into Current DataSet or DataTable. |
| ReadXml | Reads XML schema and data into DataSet. |
| ReadXmlSchema | Reads XML Schema into DataSet. |
| ReferenceEquals | Checks whether there is a specified object. |
| RejectChanges | Rolls back all the pending changes in DataSet. |
| Reset | Resets the DataSet to its original state. |
| ToString | Returns the string name. |

Table 7.10 lists the SqlCeDataSet properties that can be set.

**TABLE 7.10    Commonly Used DataSet Object Public Properties**

| Properties | Property Description |
|---|---|
| CaseSensitive | Gets or sets whether a string comparison is case sensitive or not. |
| Container | Gets the container for a component. |
| DataSetName | Gets or sets the name of DataSet. |

**TABLE 7.10     Commonly Used DataSet Object Public Properties**

| Properties | Property Description |
| --- | --- |
| DefaultViewManager | Defaults sorting and filtering for DataSet. |
| DesignMode | Gets a value to specify if component is in Design Mode. |
| EnforceConstraints | Gets or sets values to specify whether constraint rules are followed during update. |
| ExtendedProperties | Gets the custom user information. |
| HasErrors | Gets a value to indicate whether there are any errors in any DataTable objects in DataSet. |
| IsInitialized | Gets a value to specify whether DataSet is initialized or not. |
| Locale | Gets or sets the locale information to be used for a string comparison. |
| Namespace | Gets or sets the namespace for DataSet. |
| Prefix | Gets or sets the XML prefix used as an alias for namespace for DataSet. |
| Relations | Gets collection of DataRelations objects that relate the DataTables from DataSet. Using this you can navigate from parent table to child tables. |
| RemotingFormat | Gets or sets the SerializeFormat. |
| SchemaSerializationMode | Gets or sets the SchemaSerializationMode for DataSet. |
| Site | Gets or sets System.ComponentModel.ISite for DataSet. |
| Tables | Gets the collection of tables in DataSet. |

DataSet is capable of representing multiple tables like a relational database. The DataSet object uses a collection of dependant objects. A DataSet object can be comprised of one or more `DataTable` objects. `DataTable` consists of a collection of `DataRows` objects. `DataRow` is similar to a row in a database table except there is no concept of a *Current row*.

The attributes of each column such as data type, length, etc., are represented by a collection of `DataColumn` objects.

Listing 7.6 describes an addition of a data row in an existing DataSet. Using the code, a new row will be added in the DataSet described in Listing 7.5.

**LISTING 7.6     Data Row Object C#.NET**

```
DataRow myDataRow = myDataSet.Tables[0].NewRow();
myDataRow ["Title"] = "New Title";
myDataRow["Price"] = 25;
myDataRow["Publisher"] = "My Publisher";
myDataRow["Description"] = "New Book Description";
myDataSet.Tables[0].Rows.Add(myDataRow);
```

LISTING 7.6    Data Row Object VB.NET

```
Dim myDataRow As DataRow = myDataSet.Tables(0).NewRow()
myDataRow("Title") = "New Title"
myDataRow("Price") = 25
myDataRow("Publisher") = "My Publisher"
myDataRow("Description") = "New Book Description"
myDataSet.Tables(0).Rows.Add(myDataRow)
```

### Using a DataSet Relationship

It is also possible to define a relationship between multiple DataTables in DataSet. To define a relationship between two DataTables you will use a DataRelation object. The DataRelation object is similar to a Foreign key in a database and it can enforce referential integrity.

For example, you might have two tables, Product and Part, that have a master–detail relationship. Using the DataRelation object, you can enable a cascading delete of all part rows when the product is deleted.

### Using DataView Object

DataSet also provides a DataView object. A DataView object is a layer on top of the DataTable object. You can define multiple DataView objects on a single DataTable. DataView provides Databinding, sorting, filtering, etc. DataView can be created and configured both at design and runtime.

For example, you might have lot of tasks in DataTable. You can define views such as Task with status closed, Task with status open, etc.

### Updating Data with DataSet

We have discussed the various ADO.NET objects that you can use to fetch data. Now we will describe the sequence and objects that you will use to manipulate the data.

Fetch the data from SQL Server Compact Edition database and the data is placed in local memory. Use the Fill method of Data Adapter to populate the tables of DataSet. You can update the data programmatically or by using Data Binding control. Once you have made changes in the local memory, use the Update method Adapter to send the changes back to the data source.

Listing 7.7 describes the usage of DataAdapter Update method. The Update method checks each row and executes the appropriate command—insert, update, or delete.

LISTING 7.7    Update Data Source C#.NET

```
myDataAdapter.InsertCommand = myConnection.CreateCommand();
myDataAdapter.InsertCommand.CommandText = "INSERT INTO BOOKS (Title,Price, Pub-
lisher, Description) values (@Title,@Price,@Publisher, @Description)";
myDataAdapter.InsertCommand.Parameters.Add("@Title", SqlDbType.NChar, 100);
myDataAdapter.InsertCommand.Parameters.Add("@Price", SqlDbType.Money);
```

```
myDataAdapter.InsertCommand.Parameters.Add("@Publisher", SqlDbType.NChar, 50);
myDataAdapter.InsertCommand.Parameters.Add("@Description", SqlDbType.NVarChar,
2000);
// Insert a row
myDataAdapter.InsertCommand.Parameters["@Title"].Value = "New Title";
myDataAdapter.InsertCommand.Parameters["@Price"].Value = 25;
myDataAdapter.InsertCommand.Parameters["@Publisher"].Value = "My Publisher";
myDataAdapter.InsertCommand.Parameters["@Description"].Value = "New Book Descrip-
tion";
myDataAdapter.Update(myDataSet);
```

**LISTING 7.7    Update Data Source VB.NET**

```
myDataAdapter.InsertCommand = myConnection.CreateCommand()
myDataAdapter.InsertCommand.CommandText =
    "INSERT INTO BOOKS (Title,Price, Publisher, Description)
    values (@Title,@Price,@Publisher, @Description)"
myDataAdapter.InsertCommand.Parameters.Add
            ("@Title", SqlDbType.NChar, 100)
myDataAdapter.InsertCommand.Parameters.Add("@Price", SqlDbType.Money)
myDataAdapter.InsertCommand.Parameters.Add(
            "@Publisher", SqlDbType.NChar, 50)
myDataAdapter.InsertCommand.Parameters.Add
        ("@Description", SqlDbType.NVarChar, 2000)
myDataAdapter.InsertCommand.Parameters("@Title").Value = "New Title"
myDataAdapter.InsertCommand.Parameters("@Price").Value = 25
myDataAdapter.InsertCommand.Parameters("@Publisher").Value =
        "My Publisher"
myDataAdapter.InsertCommand.Parameters("@Description").Value =
        "New Book Description"
myDataAdapter.Update(myDataSet)
```

The Update method calls the AcceptChanges method automatically.

**NOTE**

The DataAdapter Update method is an easy way of saving data. However, Update method is not always the best choice. Use command objects to update the database when you are not using DataAdapter or you need to save changes in a particular order.

## Considering ADO.NET Additional Features

Now that we have discussed the various ADO.NET objects in Data Provider and DataSet categories, we will explore the features of ADO.NET that enable you to build multitier applications. ADO.NET is connectionless, based on XML, and provides data binding.

## Understanding Data Binding

Binding the ADO.NET object to the UI controls on your application creates a link between control and the data source. The main advantage of data binding is that a developer can focus on application writing and can use a built-in data binding mechanism to get data, store it locally, and display it in UI control. If the data value changes, then the corresponding changes are reflected in UI.

You can have two text boxes—First Name and Last Name—in your application. You can bind these text boxes to columns in your tables to display the values. To bind the values, specify the Text property in Data Bindings as shown in Figure 7.3.

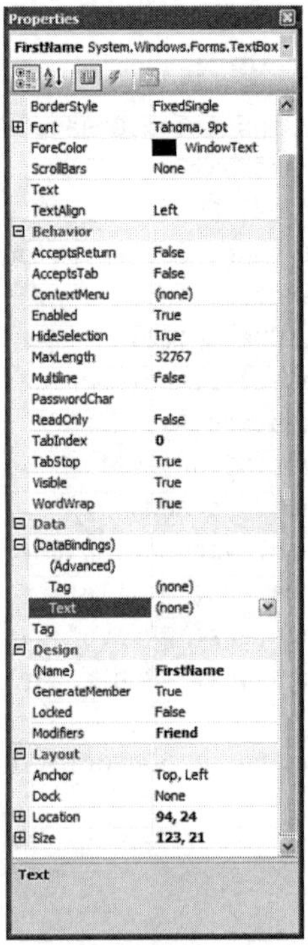

FIGURE 7.3    Data Bindings Properties

Specify the data source and Table and Column names from where the Text property will bind as shown in Figure 7.4.

## Understanding Connectionless

ADO.NET is connectionless and also enables data binding. This means that the ADO.NET object does not require live connections to a data source. You can connect to a data source to get the data. You can disconnect from a data source after getting the data and can manipulate the data offline. Later on, you can reestablish the connection and update the local store with data. ADO.NET has mechanisms to manage the details of data

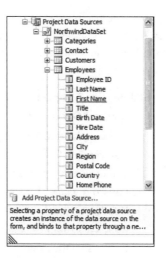

**FIGURE 7.4** Add Project Data Source

versions and status. It uses these details to merge the changes to a local store.

## Understanding Updateable Cursor

In the beginning of the chapter we discussed SqlCeConnection, SqlCeCommand, SqlCeDataAdapater, and SqlCeDataReader classes. You will always use SqlCeConnection to connect to a database. Once you are connected, you can use SqlCeDataReader to fetch and display data in the application. You can also use a combination of Data Adaptor and DataSet to fetch and display data.

SqlCeDataReader provides a forward read only cursor. SqlCeDataSet allows you to update data but first it loadsgets the data in local memory. SqlCeResultSet is a new player in this domain. Result Set class is only available for the SQL Server Compact Edition database. There is no corresponding class for the SQL Server database.

### SqlCeResultSet

SQL Server Compact Edition provides an updatable scrollable cursor. SQLCEResultSet derives from SQLCeDataReader and it is updatable, scrollable, and bindable. Using this cursor, you can get the performance of Data Reader and functionality similar to DataSet. It also requires less memory as it does not perform double buffering of the database as DataSet does.

### NOTE

In a traditional central database, the data is fetched from a central server into DataSet. SQL Server Compact Edition is used as an embedded database on a mobile device or desktop. As the database is already in memory, there is no need to make additional buffering of data in memory.

In .NET Framework, all DML operations are done through a query processor. As the database is on a local store, SQLCEResultset provides DML operations against base tables as well as a Query Processor Updatable cursor. Table 7.11 describes the methods exposed by SQLCeResultSet.

TABLE 7.11    Commonly Used SQL Server Compact Edition ResultSet Object Methods

| Method | Method Description |
|---|---|
| Close | Closes the Data Reader object. |
| Equals | Returns TRUE if two object instances are equal. |
| GetBoolean | Gets the value of a specified column as Boolean. |
| GetByte | Gets the value of a specified column as Byte. |
| GetBytes | Reads a stream of bytes from a column offset. |
| GetChars | Reads a stream of characters from a column offset. |
| GetData | Returns a DBDataReader object. |
| GetDataTypeName | Gets the name of a data source type. |
| GetDateTime | Gets the specified column as DateTime object. |
| GetDecimal | Gets the specified column as Decimal object. |
| GetDouble | Gets the specified column as Double object. |
| GetFieldType | Gets the type of the object. |
| GetFloat | Gets the specified column as Float object. |
| GetGuid | Gets the specified column as Globally unique identified (GUID). |
| GetInt16 | Gets the specified column as a 16-bit integer. |
| GetInt32 | Gets the specified column as a 32-bit integer. |
| GetInt64 | Gets the specified column as a 64-bit integer. |
| GetName | Gets the name of a column. |
| GetOrdinal | Gets the ordinal of a column whose name is specified. |
| GetProviderSpecifiedFieldType | Gives an object corresponding to a provider-specific field type. |
| GetProviderSpecificValue | Gets the value of a specified column. |
| GetProviderSpecificValues | Gets provider-specific columns for the current row. |
| GetSchemaTable | Returns a Data Table specifying the structure of DataReader. |
| GetSqlBinary | Gets the value of a given column as SqlBinary. |
| GetSqlBoolean | Gets the value of a given column as SqlBoolean. |
| GetSqlByte | Gets the value of a given column as SqlByte. |
| GetSqlDateTime | Gets the value of a given column as SqlDateTime. |
| GetSqlDecimal | Gets the value of a given column as SqlDecimal. |
| GetSqlDouble | Gets the value of a given column as SqlDouble. |
| GetSqlGuid | Gets the value of a given column as SqlGuid. |

**TABLE 7.11     Commonly Used SQL Server Compact Edition ResultSet Object Methods**

| Method | Method Description |
|---|---|
| GetSqlInt16 | Gets the value of a given column as SqlInt16. |
| GetSqlInt32 | Gets the value of a given column as SqlInt32. |
| GetSqlInt64 | Gets the value of a given column as SqlInt64. |
| GetSqlMetaData | Returns the MetaData information for a column. |
| GetSqlMoney | Gets the value of a given column as SqlMoney. |
| GetSqlSingle | Gets the value of a given column as SqlSingle. |
| GetSqlString | Gets the value of a given column as SqlString. |
| GetType | Gets the type of current instance. |
| GetValue | Gets the value of a column. |
| GetValues | Gets array of all the fields for a record. |
| Insert | Inserts the SqlCeUpdateableRecord. |
| IsDBNull | Gets the value to indicate whether a column contains a nonexistent value. |
| IsSetAsDefault | Returns TRUE if the field at a specified position will use the underlying default value. |
| Read | Advances the SqlCeDataReader to the next row. |
| ReadAbsolute | Moves the reader to a specified record. |
| ReadFirst | Positions the reader at first record. |
| ReadLast | Positions the reader at the last record. |
| ReadPrevious | Positions the reader to the previous cursor. |
| ReadRelative | Moves the reader from the current position. |
| ReferenceEquals | Returns TRUE if the specified object instances are the same. |
| Seek | Puts the reader to a given record whose index is specified. |
| SetBoolean | Sets the value of a given column with passed Boolean value. |
| SetBye | Sets the value of a given column with passed Bye value. |
| SetBytes | Sets the value of a given column with set of bytes in a buffer. |
| SetChar | Sets the value of a given column with passed Char value. |
| SetChars | Sets the value of a given column with a set of characters in a buffer. |
| SetDateTime | Sets the value of a given column with passed DateTime value. |

**TABLE 7.11    Commonly Used SQL Server Compact Edition ResultSet Object Methods**

| Method | Method Description |
| --- | --- |
| SetDecimal | Sets the value of a given column with passed Decimal value. |
| SetDefault | Sets the given column with a Default value. |
| SetFloat | Sets the value of a given column with passed Float value. |
| SetGuid | Sets the value of a given column with passed Guid value. |
| SetInt16 | Sets the value of given column with passed SetInt16 value. |
| SetInt32 | Sets the value of a given column with passed SetInt32 value. |
| SetInt64 | Sets the value of a given column with passed SetInt64 value. |
| SetSqlBinary | Sets the value of a given column with passed SqlSqlBinary value. |
| SetSqlBoolean | Sets the value of a given column with passed SqlBoolean value. |
| SetSqlByte | Sets the value of a given column with passed SqlByte value. |
| SetSqlDateTime | Sets the value of a given column with passed SqlDateTime value. |
| SetSqlDecimal | Sets the value of a given column with passed SqlDecimal value. |
| SetSqlDouble | Sets the value of a given column with passed SqlDouble value. |
| SetSqlGuid | Sets the value of a given column with passed SqlGuid value. |
| SetSqlInt16 | Sets the value of a given column with passed SqlInt16 value. |
| SetSqlInt32 | Sets the value of a given column with passed SqlInt32 value. |
| SetSqlInt64 | Sets the value of a given column with passed SqlInt64 value. |
| SetSqlMoney | Sets the value of a given column with passed SqlMoney value. |
| SetSqlSingle | Sets the value of a given column with passed SqlSingle value. |
| SetSqlString | Sets the value of a given column with passed SqlString value. |
| SetString | Sets the value of a given column with passed string value. |
| SetValue | Sets the value of a given column with value. |
| SetValues | Sets values of all fields in record. |
| ToString | Converts the object to a String and returns the string. |
| Update | Updates changes on the current row on the database. |

**NOTE**

The NextResult method is not supported.

Table 7.12 describes the usage of SqlCeResultSet properties.

**TABLE 7.12    Commonly Used SQL Server Compact Edition ResultSet Object Properties**

| Properties | Property Description |
| --- | --- |
| Depth | Indicates the depth of nesting for the current row. |
| FieldCount | Gets the number of columns in the current row. |

**TABLE 7.12    Commonly Used SQL Server Compact Edition ResultSet Object Properties**

| Properties | Property Description |
|---|---|
| HasRows | Gets a value to indicate whether Data Reader contains at least one row. |
| HiddenFieldCount | Gets the number of hidden fields. |
| IsClosed | Indicates whether Data Reader is closed. |
| Item | Gets the value of a column in its native format. |
| RecordsEffected | Gets the number of rows affected by insert, delete, update operations. |
| ResultSetView | Useful to bind a UI control with SqlCeResult. |
| Scrollable | Returns TRUE if SqlCeResultSet is scrollable. Default value is FALSE. |
| Sensitivity | The property determines the sensitivity of ResultSet. Sensitivity specifies whether ResultSet is aware of changes to the data source. |
| Updatable | Returns TRUE if SqlCeResultSet is updatable. |
| VisibleFieldCount | Gets the number of fields that are not hidden. |

**LISTING 7.8    SqlCeResultSet C#**

```
//Fetch Data using Result Set
          SqlCeCommand myCmd = myConn.CreateCommand();
          myCmd.CommandText = "SELECT BookID, Title FROM Books";
          myResultSet = myCmd.ExecuteResultSet(ResultSetOptions.Updatable |
ResultSetOptions.Scrollable);
          while (myResultSet.Read())
          {
              listBox1.Items.Add(myResultSet.GetInt32(0).ToString() + " " +
myResultSet.GetString(1));
          }
// Insert new record
          SqlCeUpdatableRecord myRec = myResultSet.CreateRecord();
          myRec.SetString(1, txtTitle.Text);
          myResultSet.Insert(myRec);
//Update Record
          myResultSet.SetString(1, txtTitle.Text.ToString());
          myResultSet.Update();
          txtTitle.Text = "";
//Delete  Record
          myResultSet.Delete();
```

LISTING 7.8    SqlCeResultSet VB.NET

```
' INSERT RECORD
        Dim myRec As SqlCeUpdatableRecord = myResultSet.CreateRecord
        myRec.SetString(1, txtTitle.Text)
        myResultSet.Insert(myRec)
        txtTitle.Text = ""
' UPDATE RECORD
        myResultSet.SetString(1, txtTitle.Text.ToString())
        myResultSet.Update()
        txtTitle.Text = ""
' DELETE RECORD
      myResultSet.Delete()
```

### SqlCeUpdateableRecord

You will use SQLCeUpdateableRecord with SqlCeResultSet. The SqlCeUpdateableRecord object represents a row. The SqlCeResultSet consists of one or more SqlCeUpdateableRecord objects. Table 7.13 shows the methods exposed by SqlCeUpdatableRecord. Table 7.14 describes the properties exposed by SqlCeUpdatableRecord.

TABLE 7.13    Commonly Used SqlCeUpdatable Object Public Methods

| Method | Method Description |
| --- | --- |
| Equals | Returns TRUE if the specified two object instances are equal. |
| GetFieldType | Returns the CLR data type for a given field. |
| GetOrdinal | Return the ordinal for a given field. |
| GetType | Gets the type of a current instance. |
| GetValue | Returns the value of a given record. |
| GetValues | Returns the value of all fields in a record. |
| IsDBNull | Returns TRUE if field is NULL. |
| IsSetAsDefault | Returns TRUE if a given field is marked to use the Default value. |
| ReferenceEquals | Returns TRUE if a specified instance is the same as a given instance. |
| ToString | Returns a string having the name of the object. |

TABLE 7.14    Commonly Used SqlCeUpdatableRecord Public Properties

| Property | Property Description |
| --- | --- |
| FieldCount | Number of fields in a record. |
| Updatable | Returns TRUE if field is updatable. |

## SqlCeEngine

The `SqlCeEngine` class represents the SQL Server Engine object. This class cannot be inherited. You can use this class to create an instance of an SQL Server Compact Edition database. You can also use this class to Compact, Repair or Shrink SQL Server Compact Edition Database programmatically. Table 7.15 and Table 7.16 provide details of `SqlCeEngine` method and properties.

**TABLE 7.15    Commonly Used SqlCeEngine Object Public Methods**

| Method | Method Description |
| --- | --- |
| Compact | This method reclaims the wasted space created by fragmentation. You should have a temporary space available to compact the database. The Compact mechanism creates a new database file and copies the database content to a new file. |
| CreateDatabase | This method creates an empty SQL Server Compact Edition database file. |
| Equals | Returns TRUE if the specified object instances are equal. |
| Repair | This method repairs a corrupted SQL Server Compact Edition database file. |
| Shrink | Similar to compact, Shrink also reclaims the wasted space and moves empty pages toward the end of a file and truncates the file. |
| ToString | Returns a string having the name of the component. |
| Verify | This method validates the SQL Server Compact Edition database. The Verify method recalculates the checksum for all pages in the database and compares the checksum with the actual value to validate it. |

**TABLE 7.16    Commonly Used SqlCeEngine Object Public Properties**

| Method | Method Description |
| --- | --- |
| LocalConnectionString | Gets or sets a connection String to the SQL Server Compact Edition database. |

**LISTING 7.9    SqlCeEngine C#**

```
if (File.Exists("MyDatabase.sdf"))
    File.Delete("MyDatabase.sdf");
string myConnectionStr = "Data Source = MyDatabase.sdf;";
SqlCeEngine engine = new SqlCeEngine(myConnectionStr);
engine.CreateDatabase();
```

**LISTING 7.9    SqlCeEngine VB.NET**

```
If File.Exists("MyDatabase.sdf") Then
    File.Delete("MyDatabase.sdf")
End If
Dim myConnectionStr As String = "Data Source = MyDatabase.sdf;"
Dim myEngine As SqlCeEngine
```

```
myEngine = New SqlServerCe.SqlCeEngine()
myEngine.LocalConnectionString = myConnectionStr
myEngine.CreateDatabase()
```

## Understanding Parameterized Queries

SQL Server Compact Edition supports parameterized queries. Parameterized queries give better performance as the queries are compiled once. Each time you execute an SQL Statement through ADO.NET, SQL Server Compact Edition will create a query plan. If you are executing the same query continuously with varying parameter values, you should consider using SqlCeParameterCollection. Parameterized queries also help protect against Sql Injections. You will create an SqlCeParameterCollection and add various parameters using the SqlCeParameter class. Parameterized statements will compile the query once and execute the same compiled plan on each execution.

### NOTE

Preparing a command has overhead. If a statement is executed only once, there is no need to prepare it.

ExecuteScalar, ExecuteReader, or ExecuteNonQuery commands can be prepared.

### SqlCeParameterCollection

The SqlCeParameterCollection object contains all SqlCeParameters and their respective mappings for SqlCeCommand. The number of parameter placed in SqlCeCommand should match with the parameters in the parameters collection.

TABLE 7.17    Commonly Used SqlCeParameterCollection Object Public Methods

| Method | Method Description |
|---|---|
| Add | Adds an SqlCeParameter object to anSqlCeCommand object. |
| AddRange | Adds an array of SqlCeParameter objects to anSqlCeCommand object. |
| AddWithValue | Adds a new SqlCeParameter object to an SqlCeCommand object. The method also sets the value of a new SqlCeParameter object. |
| Clear | Removes all SqlCeParameters from SqlCeParameterCollection. |
| Contains | Returns TRUE if the SqlCeParameter exists in an SqlCeParameterCollection. |
| CopyTo | Copies SqlCeParameter objects from SqlCeParameterCollection to an array. |
| Equals | Returns TRUE if specified two object instances are equal. |
| GetType | Gets the type of an object instance. |
| IndexOf | Gets the index location of a specified SqlCeParameter in an SqlCeParameter collection. |

**TABLE 7.17    Commonly Used SqlCeParameterCollection Object Public Methods**

| Method | Method Description |
| --- | --- |
| Insert | Adds the SqlCeParameter in an SqlCeParameterCollection at a specified location. |
| ReferenceEquals | Returns TRUE if the specific object instances are the same. |
| Remove | Removes the given SqlCeParameter from SqlCeParameterCollection. |
| RemoveAt | Removes the SqlCeParameter from a specified position in SqlCeParameterCollection. |
| ToString | Returns a string having the name of the object. |

**TABLE 7.18    Commonly Used SqlCeParameterCollection Object Public Properties**

| Property | Property Description |
| --- | --- |
| Count | Returns the count of SqlCeParameter in the SqlCeParameterCollection. |
| Item | Gets or sets the SqlCeParameter with a given value. |

**SqlCeParameter**

Use the SqlCeParameter class to create an instance of parameters to be used in SQL Server Compact Edition queries. You can populate the SQLCeParameter object associated with the SqlCeCommand.

First define the parameters in an SQL query with a parameter name. Table 7.19 and Table 7.20 define the SqlCeParameter object methods and properties. Then use the Add method of the parameter property to add the value of the parameter. The Add method accepts the name of the parameter and the value of the parameter. Add values of all parameters one by one.

**TABLE 7.19    Commonly Used SqlCeParameter Object Public Methods**

| Method | Method Description |
| --- | --- |
| Equals | Returns TRUE if the specified two object instances are equal. |
| GetType | Gives the type of a current instance. |
| ReferenceEquals | Returns TRUE if the specified instance is the same as the given instance. |
| ResetDbType | Resets the type of SqlCeParameter. |
| ToString | Returns a string having the name of the component. |

Use the Prepare method of SqlCeCommand to prepare the execution plan. Finally, execute the query.

TABLE 7.20    Commonly Used SqlCeParameter Object Public Properties

| Property | Property Description |
|---|---|
| DbType | Gets and sets the DbType of the parameter. |
| IsNullable | Gets or sets a value to specify whether a parameter can have NULL values. |
| ParameterName | Gets or sets the name of the SqlCeParameter. |
| Precision | Gets or sets the maximum number of digits to represent Value Property. |
| Scale | Gets or sets the number of decimal places. |
| Size | Gets or sets the maximum data length. |
| SourceColumn | Gets or sets the source column corresponding to DataSet. |
| SourceVersion | Gets or sets the version of row. The possible values are Current, Default, Original, and Proposed. |
| SqlDbType | Gets or sets the SqlDbType parameter. |
| Value | Gets or sets the parameter value. |

---

**NOTE**

The SQLCeParameter class cannot be inherited.

SQL Server CE 2.0 does not support named parameters. Named parameter support is added to SQL Server Compact Edition 3.x.

The same command object needs to be used for running all queries. If not, Destroy the Object and Create New Object queries will be compiled again.

---

Listing 7.10 describes the usage of a parameterized query. The code opens a connection and creates a command object. The code sets the CommandText property with SQL statements. Instead of defining the actual values, you define the parameters in command text. Then the code adds values to the parameter collection using the Add method. In conclusion, you prepare the command and execute the query.

LISTING 7.10    ParameterQuery  C#

```
SqlCeConnection myConn = new SqlCeConnection("DataSource=\\Program Files\\
ParameterQuery\\AppDatabase1.sdf");

SqlCeCommand myCmd = myConn.CreateCommand();

myCmd.CommandType = CommandType.Text;
myCmd.CommandText = "INSERT INTO BOOKS (Title,Price, Publisher, Description)
values (@Title,@Price,@Publisher, @Description)";

myCmd.Parameters.Add("@Title", SqlDbType.NChar, 100);
```

```
myCmd.Parameters.Add("@Price", SqlDbType.Money);
myCmd.Parameters.Add("@Publisher", SqlDbType.NChar, 50);
myCmd.Parameters.Add("@Description", SqlDbType.NVarChar, 2000);

myConn.Open();
myCmd.Prepare();

// First Insert
myCmd.Parameters["@Title"].Value = "Integration Services 2005";
myCmd.Parameters["@Price"].Value = 35;
myCmd.Parameters["@Publisher"].Value = "My Publisher";
myCmd.Parameters["@Description"].Value = "Insert 1";
myCmd.ExecuteNonQuery();
// Second Insert
myCmd.Parameters["@Title"].Value = "Analysis Services 2005";
myCmd.Parameters["@Price"].Value = 45;
myCmd.Parameters["@Publisher"].Value = "My Publisher";
myCmd.Parameters["@Description"].Value = "Insert 2";
myCmd.ExecuteNonQuery();
// Third Insert
myCmd.Parameters["@Title"].Value = "Reporting Services 2005";
myCmd.Parameters["@Price"].Value = 55;
myCmd.Parameters["@Publisher"].Value = "My Publisher";
myCmd.Parameters["@Description"].Value = "Insert 3";
myCmd.ExecuteNonQuery();
myConn.Close();
```

**LISTING 7.10    ParameterQuery Visual Basic .NET**

```
Dim myConn As SqlCeConnection = New SqlCeConnection("DataSource=\Program
Files\ParameterQuery\AppDatabase1.sdf")
Dim myCmd As SqlCeCommand = myConn.CreateCommand()
myCmd.CommandType = Data.CommandType.Text
myCmd.CommandText = "INSERT INTO BOOKS (Title,Price, Publisher, Description) values
(@Title,@Price,@Publisher,@Description)"

myCmd.Parameters.Add("@Title", SqlDbType.NChar, 100)
myCmd.Parameters.Add("@Price", SqlDbType.Money)
myCmd.Parameters.Add("@Publisher", SqlDbType.NChar, 50)
myCmd.Parameters.Add("@Description", SqlDbType.NVarChar, 2000)
myConn.Open()
myCmd.Prepare()
' First Insert
myCmd.Parameters("@Title").Value = "Integration Services 2005"
myCmd.Parameters("@Price").Value = 35
```

```
myCmd.Parameters("@Publisher").Value = "My Publisher"
myCmd.Parameters("@Description").Value = "Insert 1"
myCmd.ExecuteNonQuery()
' Second Insert
myCmd.Parameters("@Title").Value = "Analysis Services 2005"
myCmd.Parameters("@Price").Value = 45
myCmd.Parameters("@Publisher").Value = "My Publisher"
myCmd.Parameters("@Description").Value = "Insert 2"
myCmd.ExecuteNonQuery()
'// Third Insert
myCmd.Parameters("@Title").Value = "Reporting Services 2005"
myCmd.Parameters("@Price").Value = 55
myCmd.Parameters("@Publisher").Value = "My Publisher"
myCmd.Parameters("@Description").Value = "Insert 3"
myCmd.ExecuteNonQuery()
myConn.Close()
```

## Understanding Transactions

Transaction is used when you want multiple SQL statements to act as one unit. The set of statements are committed if all queries execute successfully. SQL Server Compact Edition supports the transactions.

### SqlCeTransaction

The SqlCeTransaction object provides the ability to pack multiple SQL statements and works with SqlCeConnection and the SqlCeCommand object. You use the BeginTransaction method of the SqlCeConnection object to start the transaction. After the transaction is initiated, any subsequent query execution happens as part of the transaction. Tables 7.21 and 7.22 describe the commonly used SqlCeTransaction object methods and properties.

**TABLE 7.21   Commonly Used SqlCeTransaction Object Public Methods**

| Method | Method Description |
|---|---|
| Commit | Commits the transaction. |
| Equals | Returns TRUE if the specified two object instances are equal. |
| GetType | Gets the type of the object instance. |
| ReferenceEquals | Returns TRUE if the specified object instances are the same. |
| Rollback | Rolls back a transaction. |
| ToString | Returns a string having the name of the object. |

TABLE 7.22    Commonly Used SqlCeTransaction Object Public Properties

| Property | Property Description |
|----------|---------------------|
| Connection | Connection object associated with transaction. |
| Isolation Level | Gives the Isolation level for a transaction. The possible values are ReadCommitted, ReadRepeatable, and Serializable. |

## SqlCeTransactionInProgressException

The SqlCeTransactionInProgressException object is created when a transaction is already in progress and you attempt to modify a database. Tables 7.23 and 7.24 describe the commonly used SqlCeTransactionInProgressException object methods and properties.

TABLE 7.23    Commonly Used SqlCeTransactionInProgressException Object Public Methods

| Method | Method Description |
|--------|-------------------|
| Equals | Returns TRUE if the specified two object instances are equal. |
| GetBaseException | Returns the root cause Exception. |
| GetType | Gives the type of current instance. |
| ReferenceEquals | Returns TRUE if the specified instance is the same as a given instance. |
| ToString | Returns a string having the name of the component. |

TABLE 7.24    Commonly Used SqlCeTransactionInProgressException Object Public Properties

| Property | Property Description |
|----------|---------------------|
| Data | Gets a collection of key/value pairs to provide additional information. |
| Errors | Gets a collection of SqlCeError objects. |
| HelpLink | Gets or sets a link to help a file corresponding to the exception. |
| InnerException | Gets the inner exception of the current exception. |
| Message | Provides the text corresponding to the first SqlCeError. |
| NativeError | Gives the native error number of the first SqlCeError |
| Source | Gets the name of the OLE DB Provider that generated the error. |
| StackTrace | Provides a string representation of the call stack. |
| TargetSite | Gets the method that has thrown the current exception. |

Transaction is closed by Commit or Rollback.

Listing 7.11 creates and opens a connection to the SQL Server Compact Edition database. A Data Command object is created.

The transaction is completed in three steps: (1) the transaction is assigned to command; (2) the database commands are executed; and (3) the transaction is closed by calling the Commit method.

**LISTING 7.11    SqlCeTransaction C#**

```
// C#.NET
SqlCeConnection myConnection = null;
myConnection = new SqlCeConnection("Data Source=\\Mobile\\Northwind.sdf;");
myConnection.Open();
SqlCeCommand myCmd = myConnection.CreateCommand();
// Transaction steps
SqlCeTransaction myTrans = myConnection.BeginTransaction ();
myCmd.Transaction = myTrans;
// do Database updated here
...
...
...
myTrans.Commit();
```

**LISTING 7.11    SqlCeTransaction VB.NET**

```
        Dim myConnection As SqlCeConnection
        myConnection = New SqlCeConnection("Data Source=\Program Files\SqlCeExcep-
tionError\Northwind.sdf;")
        myConnection.Open()
        Dim myCmd As SqlCeCommand = myConnection.CreateCommand()
        Dim myTrans As SqlCeTransaction
        myTrans = myConnection.BeginTransaction()
        myCmd.Transaction = myTrans
        ' do database updates here
        '...
        '...

        myTrans.Commit()
```

## Using Error and Exceptional Classes

Things can go wrong when you access data using ADO.NET. SQL Server Compact Edition Provider throws SqlCeException in case of error.

You will be using a *try-catch-finally block* to trap and catch exceptions. If an exception is thrown inside the *try block*, the code in the *catch block* gets executed. In the catch block, you can handle the exception. The code in the *finally block* always executes regardless of whether the exception is thrown into the try block.

You can also write a custom Data Access component that catches SqlCeException and throws a more specific exception.

## SqlCeException

The SqlCeException object is created when Data Provider for SQL Server Compact Edition gets an error generated by the SQL Server Compact Edition engine. The SqlCeException class contains at least one instance of SqlCeError. Tables 7.25 and 7.26 list the SqlCeException class methods and properties.

TABLE 7.25    Commonly Used SqlCeException Object Public Methods

| Method | Method Description |
| --- | --- |
| Equals | Returns TRUE if the specified two object instances are equal. |
| GetBaseException | Returns the root cause exception. |
| GetType | Gives the type of current instance. |
| ReferenceEqual | Returns TRUE if the specified instance is the same as a given instance. |
| ToString | Returns a string having the name of the component. |

TABLE 7.26    Commonly Used SqlCeException Object Public Properties

| Property | Property Description |
| --- | --- |
| Data | Gets a collection of key/value pairs to provide additional information. |
| Errors | Gets a collection of SqlCeError objects. |
| HelpLink | Gets or sets a link to help the file corresponding to an exception. |
| InnerException | Gets the inner exception of the current exception. |
| Message | Provides the text corresponding to the first SqlCeError. |
| NativeError | Gives the native error number of the first SqlCeError |
| Source | Gets the name of the OLE DB Provider that generated the error. |
| StackTrace | Provides a string representation of call stack. |
| TargetSite | Gets the method that has thrown the current exception. |

The SqlCeException class cannot be inherited.

## SqlCeError

The SqlCeError class collects error and warning information from the data source and returns it to the calling program.  Tables 7.27 and 7.28 describe the methods and properties of the SqlCeError class.

**TABLE 7.27    Commonly Used SqlCeError Object Public Methods**

| Method | Method Description |
| --- | --- |
| Equals | Returns TRUE if the specified object instances are equal. |
| GetType | Gives the type of current instance. |
| ToString | Returns a string having the name of the component. |

**TABLE 7.28    Commonly Used SqlCeError Object Public Properties**

| Property | Property Description |
| --- | --- |
| ErrorParameters | Gets the last three error parameters. |
| HResult | Return the HResult value for an error. |
| Message | Gets the error message that specifies the error. |
| NativeError | Gets the native error number for SQL Server Compact Edition error. |
| Source | Gets the source of the error. |

**NOTE**

The SqlCeError class cannot be inherited.

## SqlCeErrorCollection

The SqlCeErrorCollection class collects all errors generated by the SQL Server Compact Edition Data Provider. SQLCeErrorCollection will have at least one instance of the SqlCeError class and cannot be inherited.

Tables 7.29 and 7.30 describe the methods and properties exposed by the SqlCeErrorCollection class.

**TABLE 7.29    Commonly used SqlErrorCollection Object Public Methods**

| Method | Method Description |
| --- | --- |
| CopyTo | Copies the SqlCeCollection object into an array. |
| Equals | Returns TRUE if the specified two object instances are equal. |
| GetType | Gives the type of current instance. |
| ReferenceEquals | Returns TRUE if the specified instance is the same as a given instance. |
| ToString | Returns a string having the name of a component. |

**TABLE 7.30    Commonly Used SqlError Object Public Properties**

| Property | Property Description |
| --- | --- |
| Count | Gets the count of SqlCeError objects in a collection. |
| Item | Gets the specific error. |

## NOTE

The SqlCeErrorCollection class cannot be inherited.

Listing 7.12 describes the usage of the SqlCeException class. The listing uses the try-catch-finally block. The catch block displays all the error messages in an exception. In the finally block, connection to the database is closed.

**LISTING 7.12    SqlCeException C#**

```
try
{
SqlCeConnection myConnection = null;
myConnection = new SqlCeConnection("Data Source=\\Mobile\\Northwind.sdf;");
myConnection.Open();
SqlCeCommand myCommand = myConnection.CreateCommand();
SqlCeDataReader myDataReader ;
myCommand.CommandText = "Products";
myCommand.CommandType = CommandType.TableDirect;
myDataReader = myCommand.ExecuteReader();
while (myDataReader.Read()){
listbox1.Items.Add(myDataReader.GetValue(0));
}
myDataReader.Close();
}
catch (SqlCeException MyExp)
{
    foreach (SqlCeError MyError in MyExp.Errors)
    {
        MessageBox.Show(MyError.Message);
    }
}
finally
{
    myConnection.Close();
}
}
```

**LISTING 7.12    SqlCeException VB.NET**

```
        Dim myConnection As SqlCeConnection
        Try

        myConnection = New SqlCeConnection("Data Source=\Program Files\
SqlCeExceptionError\Northwind.sdf;")
        myConnection.Open()
```

```
        Dim myCommand As SqlCeCommand = myConnection.CreateCommand()
        myCommand.CommandText = "Products"
        myCommand.CommandType = CommandType.TableDirect
        Dim myDataReader As SqlCeDataReader = myCommand.ExecuteReader()
        While myDataReader.Read()
            listbox1.Items.Add(myDataReader.GetValue(0))
        End While
        myDataReader.Close()

    Catch MyExp As SqlCeException
        Dim myError As SqlCeError
        For Each myError In MyExp.Errors
            MessageBox.Show(myError.Message)
        Next
    Finally
        myConnection.Close()
    End Try
```

# Building Applications

This section explains the following types of solutions that you can build using the SQL
Server Compact Edition data provider (System.Data.SqlServerCe) and the SQL Server data
provider (System.Data.Sqlclient ) in .NET Compact Framework:

- Desktop applications using local cache in an SQL Server Compact Edition database.

- Smart device applications using local cache in an SQL Server Compact Edition database.

- Smart device applications connected to a backend SQL Server using SQL Server Data
  Provider (SqlClient namespace).

- Smart device applications that use an SQL Server Compact Edition database as a
  local store and occasionally connect to a backend SQL Server to synchronize data.

NOTE
_____
You should use the .NET Framework provider for connecting desktop applications to an
SQL Server.


## Developing Desktop Applications with SQL Server Compact Edition

SQL Server Compact Edition is ideal for many desktop-based applications where an application is needed to store data locally. For example, Outlook stores email in a .pst file. In
the future, an email client can download data to an SQL Server Compact Edition database
file (.sdf) instead of using a .pst file. The advantage of using a .sdf file is that you can use

database relational capabilities to find database information. The .sdf file can also be transferred to a mobile device where emails can be viewed.

### Create an Email .sdf File

To demonstrate this scenario, the following example uses an Email.sdf file that contains emails.

| Column | Data Type | Nullability | Description |
|--------|-----------|-------------|-------------|
| ID | bigint | Not Null | Email identity column Primary key |
| Sent | datetime | Not Null | Date/time that email was sent |
| Sub | Nvarchar (100) | Null | Email subject |
| Content | Nvarchar (2000) | Null | Email message body |
| Flag | bit | Null | A flag to indicate an urgent email |
| FromEmail | Nvarchar (100) | Null | Email address of person who sent email |
| ToEmail | nvarchar (100) | Null | Email address in the To list |
| CCEmail | nvarchar (100) | Null | Email address in the CC list |
| BccEmail | nvarchar (100) | Null | Email address in Bcc list |

Create the Emails table in the Email database. Fill the table with a set of emails.

Store the Email.sdf file and note down the path it uses in a Windows application. In the following example, the Email.sdf file path is `C:\Database\Email\Email.sdf`.

### Create a Windows Project

1. Start Visual Studio 2005 from the Start menu.

2. Click File | New | Project.

3. Click on Visual C# or Visual Basic.

4. Click on Windows Project and select Windows Application.

5. Enter the Name and Location of the project.

6. Click OK on the New Project dialog box.

7. Design the user interface for an email project as shown in Figure 7.5

Add a reference to the System.Data.SqlServerCe namespace in the project. In Solution Explorer, right click on References and select the Add Reference option. In the Add Reference dialog box, select System.Data.SqlServerCe dll.

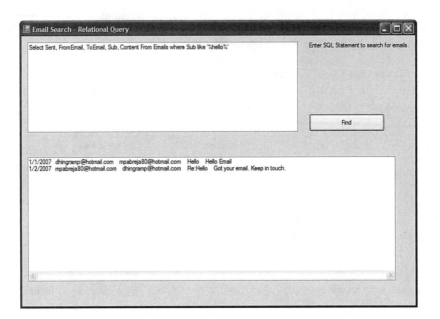

**FIGURE 7.5**    Desktop Email Application

Listing 7.9 has a complete code for this exercise. The code has the following methods:

- The Form_Load method loads the form and sets the initial query to select all emails.

- The btnFind_Click method triggers when a user clicks the Find button. This method opens a connection to the Email database and calls the FillEmailList method.

- The FillEmailList method executes a query given by the user. The result set of the query is shown back to the user in the List box.

**LISTING 7.13    Desktop Email   C#.NET**

```csharp
using System;
using System.Collections.Generic;
using System.ComponentModel;
using System.Data;
using System.Drawing;
using System.Text;
using System.Windows.Forms;
using System.Data.SqlServerCe;
namespace Email
{
    public partial class Form1 : Form
    {
```

```
SqlCeConnection myConn;
public Form1()
{
    InitializeComponent();
 }
private void Form1_Load(object sender, EventArgs e)
{
    txtSQL.Text = "Select Sent, FromEmail, ToEmail, Sub, Content From
Emails";
    // Use the DataDirectory macro to get database path.
    AppDomain.CurrentDomain.SetData("DataDirectory", @"C:\Database\Email");
}
private void btnFind_Click(object sender, EventArgs e)
{
    myConn = new SqlCeConnection
      ("Data Source=¦DataDirectory¦\\Email.sdf;");
    myConn.Open();
    FillEmailList();
    myConn.Close();
}
private void FillEmailList()
{
    SqlCeDataReader myEmailDataReader;
    // Opens a data reader and fetch the rows
    listEmail.Items.Clear();
    SqlCeCommand myCmd = myConn.CreateCommand();
    myCmd.CommandText = txtSQL.Text;
    myEmailDataReader = myCmd.ExecuteReader();
    while (myEmailDataReader.Read())
    {
        listEmail.Items.Add
            (myEmailDataReader.GetDateTime(0).ToShortDateString() + " "
            + myEmailDataReader.GetSqlString(1) + " "
            + myEmailDataReader.GetSqlString(2) + " "
            + myEmailDataReader.GetSqlString(3) + " "
            + myEmailDataReader.GetSqlString(4) + " "
            );
    }
}
    }
 }
}
```

**LISTING 7.13   Desktop Email   VB.NET**

```vb.net
Imports system.Data
Imports System.Data.SqlServerCe
Public Class Form1
    Dim myConn As SqlCeConnection
    Private Sub Form1_Load(ByVal sender As System.Object, ByVal e As System.Even-
tArgs) Handles MyBase.Load
        'Set the initial query.
        txtSQL.Text = _
            "Select Sent, FromEmail, ToEmail, Sub, Content From Emails"
        ' Use the DataDirectory macro to get database path.
        AppDomain.CurrentDomain.SetData _
            ("DataDirectory", "C:\Database\Email")
    End Sub
    Private Sub btnFind_Click(ByVal sender As System.Object, ByVal e As
System.EventArgs) Handles btnFind.Click
        'Open a connection to local .sdf file that contains Emails
        myConn = New SqlCeConnection _
         ("Data Source=¦DataDirectory¦\\Email.sdf;")

        myConn.Open()
        'Find the matching emails and fill the list box.
        FillEmailList()
        'Close the connection
        myConn.Close()
    End Sub
    Private Sub FillEmailList()
        Dim myEmailDataReader As SqlCeDataReader
        Dim myCmd As SqlCeCommand
        'Opens a data reader and fetch the rows
        listEmail.Items.Clear()
        myCmd = myConn.CreateCommand()
        'Read the query types by user
        myCmd.CommandText = txtSQL.Text
        myEmailDataReader = myCmd.ExecuteReader()
        'Display the matching rows in a listbox.
        While (myEmailDataReader.Read())
            listEmail.Items.Add( _
            (myEmailDataReader.GetDateTime(0).ToShortDateString() + " " _
                + myEmailDataReader.GetSqlString(1) + " " _
                + myEmailDataReader.GetSqlString(2) + " " _
                + myEmailDataReader.GetSqlString(3) + " " _
                + myEmailDataReader.GetSqlString(4) + " " _
                ))
```

```
        End While
    End Sub
End Class
```

To execute the email program, type an SQL statement to find an email and press the Find button. The emails matching the specified criteria will be displayed in a list box as shown in Figure 7.5.

## Developing Disconnected Smart Device Applications with SQL Server Compact Edition

You will use the same code to develop an email application for a mobile device. Create a Smart device project using a Windows mobile platform. First develop a user interface for a mobile device application. Copy the code used in Listing 7.14 into your device project. Change the path in the code to point to the database file.

**LISTING 7.14    Device Email   C#.NET**

```
myConn = new SqlCeConnection
    ("DataSource=\\Program Files\\Email_Device\\Email.sdf")
```

**LISTING 7.14    Device Email   VB.NET**

```
myConn = New SqlCeConnection _
    ("DataSource=Program Files\Email_Device\Email.sdf")_
```

Using these simple steps, you can use an email application on a Smart device as well.

Transfer the Email.sdf file that you created in the previous section to your Smart device and note down the path it uses in the device application. In the following example, the Email.sdf file path is \Program Files\Email_Device\Email.sdf.

Build and deploy the program onto a Smart device or emulator. To execute the email program, type an SQL statement to find an email and press the Find button. The emails matching the specified criteria will be displayed in a list box as shown in Figure 7.6.

The application that you created for a desktop and a device uses the local data store in SQL Server Compact Edition. The enterprise applications need to synchronize the data with a backend SQL Server. In Chapter 12, *Synchronizing Data with Merge Replication*, you will create an application that synchronizes data with a backend SQL Server.

The application that works on a local SQL Server Compact Edition database and synchronizes data with a backend Server is termed as an *occasionally connected* application. From a device, you can directly access and manipulate data on a backend server. These types of applications are called *connected solutions* as they require connectivity to a server while accessing the database. Chapter 12 will also demonstrate how to use an Sqlclient namespace of the .NET Compact Framework to develop a connected solution.

FIGURE 7.6    Device Email Application

## Summary

ADO.NET consists of a set of objects. One way to learn ADO.NET is to learn all the objects together. Instead of describing all the objects together, we first discussed the main objects that are needed to connect to the SQL Server database and execute SQL Commands to fetch data. We discussed Data Set in detail. After understanding the framework of ADO.NET, we discussed objects that use parameterized queries, transactions, and exception handling.

This chapter will not make you an ADO.NET expert. However, it will give you a fundamental understanding of ADO.NET objects for SQL Server Compact Edition.

# Introducing Native Access

.NET based applications are called *managed applications* because they are controlled by Common Language Runtime. Non-.NET based applications are said to execute as *unmanaged code* or *native code*. Using Microsoft Visual C++ you can write native applications that use SQL Server Compact Edition 3.0 or a later version.

In this chapter, first we will show you how to manage the SQL Server Compact Edition storage engine. Then, we will show you how to use OLE DB provider for SQL Server Compact Edition to manage and access data from the SQL Server Compact Edition database.

## Understanding the Difference between Managed and Unmanaged Access

Before you start writing native code, you should carefully evaluate whether native code is the right choice for your application. .NET Framework provides a Common Language Runtime (CLR) to execute code. Code that executes on CLR is called *managed code*. Managed code has advantages such as cross-language integration, cross-language exception handling, automatic memory management, version management, and enhanced security.

### Memory Management

.NET Framework provides a CLR environment that executes the code and manages memory. Automatic memory management takes care of issues such as memory leakage. In unmanaged applications, the application itself manages the memory. An unmanaged application developer needs to write code to perform memory management tasks. The common problems in managed applications include forgetting to free an object after use and causing a memory leak. Another common issue in unmanaged applications is the attempt to access an object that has already been freed.

In managed applications, memory allocation and de-allocation are done by .Net runtime. The CLR garbage collector manages the allocation of memory.

## Intermediate Language

In managed applications, the compiled executables are in Microsoft Intermediate Language format (MSIL). The compiled MSIL format is not dependent on a processor. These executables are converted to native code by the Just-in-Time compiler. The unmanaged applications are complied into a processor-specific machine code.

## No Garbage Collection

.NET platform performs the garbage collection in managed applications. The garbage collector determines when to release memory for objects that are no longer in use. There is no automatic garbage collection mechanism in native language applications. The developer needs to write code to free an object. Forgetting to free an object will result in a memory leak.

## Language Interoperability

Managed code is compiled into intermediate language. This allows interoperability between programs developed in different languages such as C#.NET and VB.NET. The different languages use a common type system defined by CLR. CLR allows the developing of applications whose objects interact to cross languages. In native language, the interoperability between different languages can be used within limits.

## Error Handling

The .NET Compact Framework data provider returns objects of type SqlCeException class when the SQL Server 2005 Compact Edition engine generates an error. Similarly, in native code, the error from the SQL Server 2005 Compact Edition engine is collected as an ErrorRecords property.

# Managing the Database

In this section you will learn the methods available to create, compact, and repair the SQL Server Compact Edition database. You have already learned how you can accomplish these operations using SQL Server Management Studio, Visual Studio, Query Analyzer, and ADO.NET programming. As you are already familiar with the concept, here we will discuss the syntax and parameters of functions.

The objects, methods, and properties of managed applications are similar to objects, methods, and properties in a native application.

## The CreateDatabase Method

The `CreateDatabase` method is used to create an SQL Server 2005 Compact Edition database. This method accepts a connection string as a parameter.

```
HRESULT CreateDatabase(BSTR LocalConnection);
```

### Local Connection String Properties

A connection string needs to be specified in order to access a database. The connection string is only set when the connection to the database is closed. You can specify various connection properties in a connection string. Consider the following rules while building a connection string:

- The connection string consists of a database path, filename, and other properties.

- The connection string consists of a name value pair for properties.

- The values are enclosed in single or double quotes.

- A property name and value pair are separated by semicolons.

- An escape sequence is not supported.

- Blank characters (except those in values or within quotations) are ignored.

### NOTE

The connection string syntax is also an application to another method of the engine object.

The section below describes the properties that you can specify as a connection string.

### Data Source

The Data Source property specifies the path and filename of the SQL Server Compact Edition database.

### Database Password

To secure the SQL Server Compact Edition database, create a password for the database. Once a password is set, you need to specify the password for accessing the database. A password string is specified by alphabets, digits, and nonalphanumeric characters. The password string can be up to 40 characters long. The property keyword name is `ssce: database password`.

### Encrypt Database

Without the password, no one will be able to access the database programmatically or with tools such as Query Analyzer or SQL Server Management Studio. However, one can open the database file as clear text and see the database content. The encryption feature provides protection against this vulnerability.

Encrypting data means converting the data into a format that can only be read with a special key. You can also choose to encrypt a database. Once you choose the encryption option, the database engine will encrypt the data and you will have to specify the password to decrypt and get the data. If the password is lost, you will never be able to encrypt data. The property keyword name is `ssce: encrypt database`. The property should be set to TRUE to enable encryption.

### NOTE
If you specify a password the database will be encrypted.

### MAX Buffer Size
The buffer size indicates the size of memory in kilobytes before SQL Server Compact Edition starts flushing changes to disk. The property keyword name is `ssce: max buffer size`. The default value of the max buffer size is 640 KB.

### Max Database Size
This property specifies the maximum size of the SQL Server Compact Edition database in megabytes. The default value is 128 MB. The property keyword name is `ssce: max database size`.

### Mode
This property defines the file mode to open SQL Server Compact Edition files. The default value is Read/Write. Table 8.1 specifies the modes in which the SQL Server Compact Edition database file can be opened. The property keyword name is `ssce: mode`.

**TABLE 8.1    SQL Server Compact Edition Mode for Database Access**

| Mode | Description |
| --- | --- |
| Read Write | Multiple processes can access and modify the database. |
| Read Only | Opens the database in Read Only mode. |
| Exclusive | Exclusive locks do not allow other processes to access or modify the database. |
| Shared Read | Allows other process to read the database but do not allow it to modify while the database is open. |

### Default Lock Timeout
The default lock timeout property specifies the time in milliseconds that a transaction will wait for a lock. The default value of the timeout period is 2000. The property keyword name is `ssce: default lock timeout`. If you wish to use a different timeout, specify the timeout value in the connection string.

### Default Lock Escalation

SQL Server Compact Edition escalates the row lock and page lock into a table lock when a transaction exceeds the limit. The limit is defined as the default lock escalation property. The default value of the lock escalation property value is 100. You can change the default value by specifying a different value in the connection string using the property keyword `ssce: default lock escalation`.

### Flush Interval

The flush interval property specifies the time interval in seconds after which the transactions are flushed to a disk. The default value of the flush interval is 10 seconds. The property keyword name is `ssce: flush interval`.

### Auto Shrink Threshold

This property indicates the percentage of free space in the SQL Server Compact Edition file after which the auto shrink will start. A value of 0 means that auto shrink will never happen The default value of the auto shrink threshold is 60. The property keyword name is `ssce: autoshrink threshold`.

### Temp File Directory

Use the temp file directory property to specify the location of a temporary database. An interim database is used to store a result set during query execution. The interim data can also be created into intermediate sort tables while executing the ORDER BY, GROUP BY, or DISTINCT clauses. The property keyword name is `ssce: temp file directory`.

### Temp File Maximum Size

The temp file maximum size property specifies the maximum size of a temporary file. The default value is 128 MB. The property keyword name is `ssce: temp file max size`.

### Locale Identifier

The locale identifier property specifies the locale ID that should be used with the database. The property keyword name is `locale identifier`.

## Compact Database

The SQL Server Compact Edition database consists of 4 KB unit pages. When rows are deleted from the SQL Server Compact Edition database, the database marks the rows available for new additions. As updates, inserts, and deletions are made in the database, the structure of the database file can become fragmented. Fragmentation results in additional unused disk space and performance degradation. The compact database mechanism reclaims the unused space from the database and removes the fragmentation.

Unused spaces in pages can be claimed by the `CompactDatabase` method. The Compact operation creates a new SQL Server Compact Edition database and copies rows from the old database to the new database. While copying the rows from an old database, the spaces used by earlier deleted rows are reclaimed. Same tables pages are placed adjacent to each other to reduce fragmentation. The rules for the CompactDatabase method are as follows:

- The SQL Server Compact Edition database should be closed before compacting.

- You can change the collating order, encryption, and password setting while doing the compaction on the database.

- You need to have additional space for both the source and the destination database before compacting. Listing 8.1 describes the usage of the CompactDatabase method.

**LISTING 8.1    Compact Database VC++**

```
HRESULT CompactDatabase(BSTR SourceConnection, BSTR DestConnection);
```

**TABLE 8.2    SQL Server Compact Edition Connection Properties**

| Property | Description |
|---|---|
| Provider | The provider property specifies the name of the provider to connect to the data source. An error occurs if the names of the provider in the source connection string and in the destination connection string are different. |
| | By default, the provider name is OLE DB provider for SQL Server Compact Edition. |
| Data Source | The data source property should specify the database file. It must be specified for both the source and destination databases. |
| Locale Identifier | Locale identifier is an optional property for the destination database. If the property is not specified for the destination database, the source database locale identifier is used in the destination database. |
| Temporary File directory | Temporary file specifies the path of a temporary database. If the path of the temporary database is not specified, then the current database location is used as the location of the destination database. |
| Password | The password must be specified if the source database is password-protected or encrypted. |
| | You can specify a password if you want to make the destination database encrypted or password-protected. If a password is not specified for the destination database, the source database password is assumed and applied to the destination database. If the source database has a password and you do not want to have a password in the destination database, you must specify an empty string in the destination password. |
| Encrypt Database | Using this property you can specify whether you wish the destination database to be encrypted or not. If you do not specify the encrypt property, then the destination database will have encryption similar to the source database. |

The CompactDatabase method requires two parameters: SourceConnection and DestinationConnection. The source connection and destination connection strings specify the path and filename of the source and destination databases respectively. The source database should not be open when you compact the database. You will get an error if the database is already open. You will also get an error if the destination database already exists.

As discussed, a password needs to be specified in order to open a password-protected or encrypted database. If the source database is password-protected or encrypted, then you should specify a password as part of the source connection string. By default, the destination database will be created with the same encryption and password as the source database. If you wish to choose a different password, then you need to specify the password as part of the destination database connection string. If the source database has a password and you do not want to have a password in the destination database, then you need to set the password property in the destination database connection string to empty string.

Even if the source database is not password-protected, you can protect the destination database. Simply specify the Password and Encryption property in the destination database connection string.

To change the collating order, temporary file location, encryption, and password settings while compacting the database, you can use Locale Identifier, Temporary File Directory, and Password and Encrypt database options as part of the connection string.

## The Repair Method

As discussed earlier, the SQL Server Compact Edition database can be validated by the Verify method. The Verify method will recalculate the checksum for a database page. For a corrupted database, the recalculated checksums do not match the actual value.

---
**NOTE**

SQL Server Compact Edition is a reliable and robust database. Database corruption is a rare scenario.

---

You will use the Repair method to repair the SQL Server Compact Edition database if the database is corrupted. Similar to the Verify method, the Repair method also recalculates the checksum of each page of the SQL Server Compact Edition database. If the page checksum does not match the calculated value, the page is considered corrupted. The Repair method will repair each corrupted page of the SQL Server Compact Edition database file.

The SQL Server Compact Edition database is made of a single file. The database file consists of logical pages. For each page a checksum is calculated and written to a page. The Repair method recalculates the checksum of each page of the SQL Server Compact Edition database. If the page checksum does not match the calculated value, the page is considered corrupted.

The Repair method will repair each corrupted page of the SQL Server Compact Edition database file. The Repair method uses one of two possible options to describe how the SQL Server Compact Edition engine should repair the database:

- Delete Corrupted Rows option—deletes the pages having corrupted rows.
- Recover Corrupted Rows option—read and recover data from corrupted pages.

Listing 8.2 describes the Repair method. The Repair method requires three parameters: `SourceConnection`, `DestinationConnection`, and `RepairOption`. The source connection and destination connection strings specify the path and filename of the source and destination databases, respectively. The `RepairOption` can have one of two possible values: DELETECORRUPTED and RECOVERCORRUPTED. These two options are described in Table 8.3 and can be used to describe how the SQL Server Compact Edition Engine should repair the database.

**LISTING 8.2    Repair Database VC++**

```
HRESULT Repair(BSTR SourceConnection, BSTR DestinationConnection, REPAIROPTION
RepairOption);
```

When you choose the DELETECORRUPTED option, you may lose a lot of data, especially if schema pages are corrupted. The advantage of the RECOVERCORRUPTED option is that most of the data can be recovered; however, the downside is the recovered data may have logical inconsistencies.

**TABLE 8.3    SQL Server Compact Edition Repair Options**

| Repair Options | Description |
| --- | --- |
| DeleteCorrupted | Delete corrupted rows. A repaired database will only have rows that were not corrupted before. |
| RecoverCorrupted | This option tries to recover the corrupted rows. A repaired database will have rows that were not corrupted originally as well as those rows that were corrupted. |

## Using Error Records

This section describes the collection and objects that you will use for error handling in VC++ for developing SQL Server Compact Edition database-based applications.

**NOTE**

Similar to the Engine object, RDA and Replication objects also use the SSCEError collection to send error information.

### SSCEErrors Collection

The SSCEErrors collection object contains a collection of SSCEError objects and has only one property.

### Count

The count property is a count of the number of SSCEError objects in the SSCEErrors collection.

### SSCEError

The SQL Server Compact Edition database reports an error in the form of an SSCEError object. When an SQL Server Compact Edition method call is not successful, it returns an SSCEErrors collection. The SSCEErrors collection consists of one or more SSCEError objects. You can read the SSCEError records to determine the cause of the errors. Table 8.4 shows a list of SSCEError object properties and their descriptions.

**TABLE 8.4    SSCEError Properties**

| Property | Description |
| --- | --- |
| Description | Provides you with a meaningful message. |
| Error Number | Provides the OLE DB HResult error number reported by the data source. |
| Native Error | Returns the native error number. |
| Source | Contains the source of the error. |
| Params | Contains a descriptive element for an error. |
| SSCEParams Collection | A collection of SSCEParam objects. It has only one property. |
| Count | A count of the number of SSCEParam objects in the SSCEParams collection. |
| SSCEParam | Gives you the details of error parameters. |
| Params | Contains a descriptive element for an error. |

## Understanding OLE DB

The Object Linking and Embedding Database (OLE DB) is an API set designed by Microsoft to access different types of data stores. A set of interfaces is implemented using a component object model (COM). OLE DB separates the data store from the application and consists of consumers and providers. Consumers are the applications that consume the data, and providers are components that implement the OLE DB interface and provide access to the data.

As different databases can have different capabilities, an OLE DB provider may not implement all the interfaces available in OLE DB. Also the provider may add an additional interface to utilize the functionality of the database.

---

**NOTE**

This chapter assumes that you have documentation available for the standard OLE DB interface. Refer to the `http://msdn2.microsoft.com/en-gb/library/ms714272.aspx` page for an OLE DB overview. This chapter will highlight the properties and interfaces specific to the SQL Server Compact Edition database.

---

## Introducing the OLE DB Object Model

OLE DB provides abstractions such as Datasource, Session, Command, Rowset, Table, Views, etc. As a developer, you use these abstractions as well as other interfaces.

### Understanding the Data Source Object

The data source object represents the underlying data store. You need to create and initialize an instance of the data source before using the data store. Use the CoCreateInstance function to create the data source object as shown in Listing 8.3. You need to pass the OLE DB provider for SQL Server Compact Edition as a class identifier.

**LISTING 8.3    CoCreateInstance VC++**

```
hr = CoCreateInstance( CLSID_SQLSERVERCE_3_0, 0,
                       CLSCTX_INPROC_SERVER,
                        IID_IDBInitialize,
                        (void**)&pIDBInitialize);
```

CLSID_SQLSERVERCE_3 indicates the OLE DB provider for SQL Server Compact Edition.

CLSCTX_INPROC_SERVER indicates that you want to use SQL Server Compact Edition as an in-process server. The possible values are CLSCTX_INPROC_SERVER, CLSCTX_INPROC_HANDLER, CLSCTX_LOCAL_SERVER, or a combination of these values. The constant CLSCTX_ALL is defined as the combination of all three.

You will use the DBPROP_INIT_DATASOURCE property to specify the full path of the database file. The steps include specifying the data source with a database filename and then initializing the data source object. Once the data source is initialized, you need to create a session object. The session object enables you to create commands, rowsets, and transactions.

### Differences in Data Source Object

Consider the following differences for OLE DB provider for SQL Server Compact Edition.

### Changing the Current Data Source

The SQL Server Compact Edition database OLE DB provider does not allow you to change the data source object. To change the data source object, you need to un-initialize the data source object. Then you can set the DBPROP_INIT_DATASOURCE to new data source name and initialize it again.

### Current Catalog

The catalog concept is not used in OLE DB provider for SQL Server Compact Edition. The initialized data source with property DBPROP_INIT_DATASOURCE is treated as a current catalog.

### Knowing the Session Object

Once you have initialized the data source, then you should create a session object. The session object enables you to define commands, rowsets, and transactions. You use the ISessionProperties interface to set the session properties.

From the Session object, you can create command object, rowset object, and initiate and close transactions. We will discuss the details of these operations later in the chapter.

The Session object has SQL Server Compact Edition provider-specific properties. These properties include DBPROP_SSCE_TRANSACTION_COMMIT_MODE.

> **NOTE**
>
> You will learn all provider specific properties in later sections.

### Knowing the Command Object

Use the Command object to execute SQL statements on the SQL Server Compact Edition database. To use an SQL statement, you should create a command object, specify the SQL Statement as Command Text, and execute the SQL statement as shown in Listing 8.4. If you are running a query for a number of times, it is recommended to use Prepare Command.

Use an IDBCreateCommand::CreateCommand method to create a command object.

**LISTING 8.4    Comand Object VC++**

```
// Create the command object.
hr = pIDBCrtCmd->CreateCommand(NULL, IID_ICommandWithParameters,
    (IUnknown**) &pICmdWParams);
```

You can specify the SQL Statement using the ICommandText interface as shown in Listing 8.5.

**LISTING 8.5    Using Command Text VC++**

```
hr = pICmdWParams->QueryInterface(IID_ICommandText, (void**) &pICmdText);
```

Preparing the command parses the query; compile the query and prepare the execution plan as shown in Listing 8.6.

**LISTING 8.6    Preparing the Command VC++**

```
hr = pICmdWParams->QueryInterface(IID_ICommandPrepare, (void**) &pICmdPrepare);
// Specify the command text with parameter markers.
hr = pICmdText->SetCommandText(DBGUID_DBSQL, L"INSERT INTO BOOKS \
(Title,Price, Publisher, Description) VALUES (?, ?, ?,?)");
// Prepare the command.
hr = pICmdPrepare->Prepare(1);
```

## Using the Rowset Object

A rowset object consists of a set of rows each containing columns of data. Providers present the data to the consumer in the form of a rowset. You can use Rowset objects to access data in a tabular format. Once you have a Rowset object, then you can retrieve rows one at a time in a sequential manner or directly access a specific row.

You create a rowset object by directly calling the IOpenRowset::OpenRowset method or by executing a command through ICommand::Execute. Use the IRowset::GetNextRows method to access rows. You can also use the IRowset interface to insert, update, and delete rows.

### NOTE

The OLE DB provider for SQL Server Compact Edition also supports the IRowsetPosition interface. The IRowsetPosition interface is specific to SQL Server Compact Edition.

## Knowing the Cursors Object

The SQL Server Compact Edition OLE DB provider supports the following cursor types:

- Forward only cursors
- Base table cursors
- Scrollable cursors

### Forward Only Cursor

The forward only cursor is used to read a forward only stream of data. The cursor runs against a query processor and allows you to scroll the data one row at a time. A forward only cursor requires little memory as only a single row of data is stored in memory. It does not allow you to update the data. If scrollability is the only requirement for your application, then you should use the forward only cursor.

### Base Table Cursor

The base table cursor executes directly on a base table. This cursor bypasses the query processor and fetches the data directly from the columns of a table. It interacts with the storage engine and supports update, bookmark, and index functionality.

You can also use the Seek and SetRange methods. Open a base table cursor against an index while using the Seek and Set Range methods. Using SetRange, you define a range of indexes; using Seek, you can position the cursor on rows in a range.

In base table cursor, you set the following properties to TRUE:

- DBPROP_BOOKMARKS
- DBPROP_OWNUPDATEDDELETE
- DBPROP_OWNINSERT
- DBPROP_OTHERUPDATEDELETE
- DBPROP_OTHERINSERT
- DBPROP_CANFETCHBACKWARDS
- DBPROP_QUICKRESTART

### Scrollable Cursor

The scrollable cursor provides the maximum functionality. This cursor catches the data from the Rowset object.

In scrollable cursor, the following properties are set to TRUE:

- DBPROP_BOOKMARKS
- DBPROP_CANFETCHBACKWARDS
- DBPROP_QUICKRESTART

### Using the Index Object

The SQL Server Compact Edition OLE DB provider supports interfaces for indexes. You can use the CreateIndex method of IIndexDefinition to create indexes. Similarly, you can use the AlterIndex method of the IAlterIndex interface to modify an index name.

You should be aware of the following restrictions that apply when a client application tries to change the current index using IrowsetCurrentIndex:

- All accessor handles must be released.
- All row handles must be released.
- No outstanding changes should exist.

### Using the Parameters Object

Each time you execute a query in your application and you pass the parameters, SQL Server Compact Edition creates a query plan and then executes the query. In case you need to execute a query multiple times with different sets of parameters, then you should use a parameterized query. Parameterized queries are discussed in Chapter 7, *Programming SQL Server Compact Edition with ADO.NET.*

With SQL Server Compact Edition OLE DB provider, you can specify parameters and obtain parameter information. You can also specify parameters of a query with the Execute method of the ICommand interface.

```
// Create command to uses parameters.
hr = pIDBCrtCmd->CreateCommand(NULL, IID_ICommandWithParameters,
    (IUnknown**) &pICmdWParams);
```

You can get information about a parameter with the GetParameter method of the ICommandWithParameters interface.

### Using the Constraint Object

Use the ITableDefinitionWithConstraints interface to add constraints to columns. You should set the matchType element of DBCNSTRAINTDESC to DBMATCHTYPE_FULL

### Using the Transaction Object

The following methods manage transactions in the ITransactionLocal interface:

- StartTransaction

- Commit

- Abort

### Understanding the Difference in Transaction Support

The SQL Server Compact Edition transaction support is different from the SQL Server transaction support. Due to transaction feature difference, the corresponding OLE DB interface has differences too. You should consider following differences while programming transactions.

1. Absence of Nested Transactions—A nested transaction is started inside an already existing transaction. SQL Server Compact Edition does not support nested transactions.

2. Single Phase Commit—SQL Server Compact Edition does not support two-phase commit transactions which are more useful for a Server database where distributed databases may exist on a network and updates need to occur simultaneously on multiple databases. As two-phase transactions are not supported, OLE DB provider for SQL Server Compact Edition does not support the ITransactionJoin interface.

3. Exclusive Lock—The SQL Server Compact Edition database makes an exclusive lock on a table that gets modified in a transaction. It means that the value of the DBPROP_SUPPORTEDTXNDDL property gets set to DBPROPVAL_TV_ALL.

## Understanding the OLE DB Data Type

Table 8.5 shows the mapping between SQL Server Compact Edition data types and OLE DB data types. You need to understand this mapping in order to execute SQL statements and process the results using OLE DB provider.

**TABLE 8.5    SQL Server Compact Edition and OLE DB Data Types**

| SQL Server Compact Edition Data Type | OLE DB Data Type |
| --- | --- |
| Bigint | DBTYPE_I8 |
| Binary | DBTYPE_BYTES |
| Bit | DBTYPE_BOOL |
| Datetime | DBTYPE_DBTIMESTAMP |
| Float | DBTYPE_R8 |
| Image | DBTYPE_BYTES |
| Integer | DBTYPE_I4 |
| Money | DBTYPE_CY |
| Nchar | DBTYPE_WSTR |
| Nvarchar | DBTYPE_WSTR |
| Ntext | DBTYPE_WSTR |
| Numeric | DBTYPE_NUMERIC |
| Real | DBTYPE_R4 |
| Smallint | DBTYPE_I2 |
| uniqueidentifier | DBTYPE_GUID |
| Tinyint | DBTYPE_UI1 |
| Varbinary | DBTYPE_BYTES |

## Standard OLE DB Interfaces for SQL Server Compact Edition

Table 8.6 gives a brief description of the OLE DB interfaces supported by SQL Server Compact Edition. Although, the complete details of the OLE DB interface are outside the scope of this chapter, the followings sections provide information on the interfaces that are different in OLE DB provider for SQL Server Compact Edition along with the provider-specific properties.

**TABLE 8.6    OLE DB Interfaces supported for SQL Server Compact Edition**

| OLE DB Interface | Description |
| --- | --- |
| IColumnsInfo | Exposes information about columns of a rowset. |
| ICommand | Contains a method to execute a command. |
| ICommandPrepare | Exposes Prepare and Unprepare methods. Using the Prepare method you can optimize a query execution by first generating an execution plan. |
| ICommandProperties | Returns or sets a list of properties in a rowset property group. |
| ICommandText | Returns or sets the command text. |
| ICommandWithParameters | Exposes methods to provide and obtain a list of parameters and their type. |
| IConvertType | Exposes a method to provide information about the availability of type conversions. |

TABLE 8.6    OLE DB Interfaces supported for SQL Server Compact Edition

| OLE DB Interface | Description |
| --- | --- |
| IDBCreateCommand | Creates a new command when used in a session. |
| IDBCreateSession | Used on a data source to create a new session when used on a data source. |
| IDBInfo | Exposes methods to provide information about keyword and literal database support. |
| IDBInitialize | Exposes methods to initialize and un-initialize data source objects and enumerators. |
| IDBProperties | Exposes methods to get and set values of properties on a data source object. Also provides a method to get information about properties supported by provider. |
| IDBSchemaRowset | Exposes a method to return advanced schema information about a rowset. |
| IGetDataSource | Exposes a method to obtain an interface pointer on a data source object. |
| IIndexDefinition | Exposes a method to create and drop indexes from a data source. |
| IRowset | Exposes methods for fetching rows in a sequential fashion. |
| IRowsetBookmark | Exposes the method to support the bookmark for the next fetch position. |
| IRowsetChange | Exposes the methods to update the values of columns in rows. Also provides a method to insert rows and delete existing rows. |
| IRowsetIndex | Exposes index functionality in OLE DB. Exposes a method to define a range and set the position within a range. |
| IRowsetInfo | Exposes methods to provide information about Rowset. |
| IRowsetUpdate | Allows transmission delay of the changes made with IRowsetChange. Enables the undo functionality. |
| ISequentialStream | Exposes a method to read and write binary large object data in OLE DB. |
| ISessionProperties | Gets and sets the properties in a session property group. |
| ISupportErrorInfo | Determines whether a particular OLE DB interface can return an OLE DB error object. |
| ITableCreation | Exposes methods to provide complete table definition. |
| ITableDefinition | Exposes methods to create, drop, and alter tables. |
| ITableDefinitionWithConstraints | Exposes methods to create and drop a table and column constraints on a table. |

## Understanding the OLE DB Interfaces Differences

In the previous section we discussed the interfaces supported by OLE DB provider for SQL Server Compact Edition.

### Accessor Performance

The OLE DB provider for the SQL Server Compact Edition database has an IAccessor interface. The CreateAccessor method of the IAccessor interface ignores the DBACCESSOR_OPTIMIZED flag. The SQL Server Compact Edition database does not use internal row cache; therefore, using DBACCESSOR_OPTIMIZED has no impact.

### Changing Table Properties

The OLE DB provider for SQL Server Compact Edition provides the IAlterTable interface. The interface enables consumers to modify table properties allowed by the database. With IAlterTable interface, you can modify the DBPROP_COL_DEFAULT, DBPROP_COL_SEED, DBPROP_COL_INCREMENT properties for a column. These properties change the default values of column, seed value, and incremental value.

To understand this concept better, consider the dialog box shown in Figure 8.1 to define table structure. At the time of defining table columns, you set the Identity property to TRUE or FALSE. If the Identity property is set to TRUE, then you can specify the IdentityIncrement and IdentitySeed values.

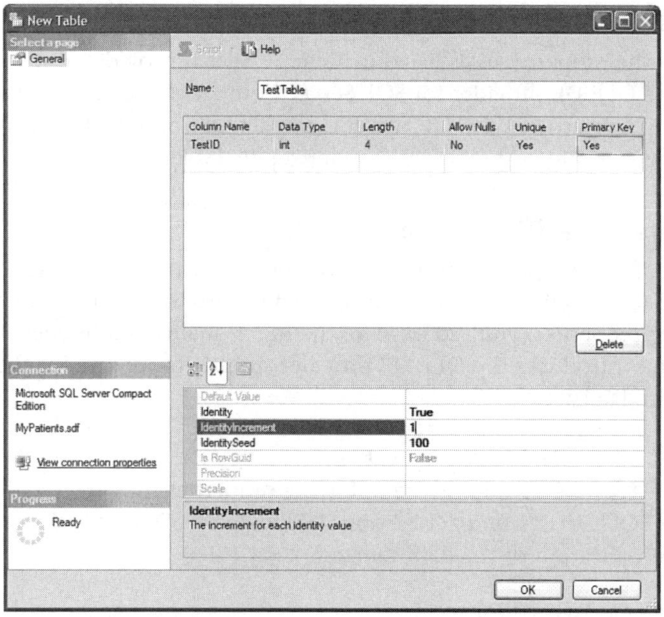

FIGURE 8.1     New Table Dialog

You can change the seed or incremental values for a column that already has the Identity property set to TRUE. Using OLE DB provider, you cannot change the Identity property from TRUE to FALSE or vice versa.

### Managing Database
The OLE DB provider has an IDBDataSourceAdmin interface. The OLE DB provider for SQL Server Compact Edition does not support modifying and deleting a database using this interface. You can create a new database using the CreateDataSource method.

### Using Views
The SQL Server Compact Edition OLE DB provider allows you to use the IOpenRowset interface to open base tables and indexes. You cannot use this for views.

### Setting the Transaction Level
Using the ITransactionLocal interface for OLE DB provider, you can specify the transaction level. Read Committed is the lowest level of transaction in the SQL Server Compact Edition database. If you specify a transaction level lower than Read Committed, then the provider will change the setting to Read Committed.

### IAlterIndex
Using IAlterIndex interface, you can only modify the name of the index.

## The OLE DB Property Set
OLE DB defines the property set as listed in Table 8.7. Each provider also specifies its own property set. The OLE DB provider for SQL Server Compact Edition database supports the standard OLE DB properties. The SQL Server Compact Edition OLE DB provider also supports provider-specific properties as summarized in Table 8.7.

## Using Provider-Specific Properties
The SQL Server 2005 Compact Edition supports the following properties that are specific to its provider. OLE DB allows implementing provider-specific properties. Using these provider-specific properties, you can execute the functionality that is specific to the database. This section introduces the OLE DB provider-specific properties for the SQL Server Compact Edition database.

### DBPROPSET_SSCE_DBINIT Property Set
DBPROPSET_SSCE_DBINIT contains the following properties that are specific to the OLE DB provider for SQL Server Compact Edition. DBPROPSET_SSCE_DBINIT contains properties related to initialization of the data source.

### DBPROP_SSCE_MAXBUFFERSIZE
Use the DBPROP_SSCE_MAXBUFFERSIZE property to specify the maximum size of the SQL Server Compact Edition database. The default size is 640 KB.

**TABLE 8.7   Property Set**

| Property Set | Description |
|---|---|
| DBPROPSET_DATASOURCE | This group has all the OLE DB properties defined in the Data Source property group. |
| DBPROPSET_DATASOURCEINFO | This group has all the OLE DB properties defined in the Data Source Information property group. |
| DBPROPSET_DBINIT | This group has all the OLE DB properties defined in the Initialization property group. |
| DBPROPSET_SESSION | This group has all the OLE DB properties defined in the Session property group. |
| DBPROPSET_TABLE | This group has all the OLE DB properties defined in the Table property group. |
| DBPROPSET_VIEW | This group has all the OLE DB properties defined in the View property group. |
| DBPROPSET_ROWSET | This group has all the OLE DB properties defined in the Rowset property group. |
| DBPROPSET_COLUMN | This group has all the OLE DB properties defined in the Column property group. |
| DBPROPSET_INDEX | This group has all the OLE DB properties defined in the Index property group. |
| DBPROPSET_PROPERTIESINERROR | This property set is used to return all properties that were in error when called by various methods. Example: If ICommand::Execute returns DB_E_ERRORSOCCURED, then the consumer application can call ICommandProperties::GetProperties with the DBPROPSET_PROPERTIESINERROR property set to return all properties that were in error. |

## DBPROP_SSCE_DBPASSWORD

To make an SQL Server Compact Edition database password protected, use the DBDROP_SSCE_DBPASSWORD property. You can specify the password with the property. No password will be used if you do not specify this property.

## DBPROP_SSCE_DEFAULT_LOCK_ESCALATION

By utilizing lock escalation, many fine-grained locks are converted into a few coarse-grained locks. SQL Server Compact Edition escalates the row lock and page lock into a table lock when a transaction exceeds the limit. You specify this limit using the DBDROP_SSCE_DEFAULT_LOCK_ESCALATION property. The default value of the lock escalation property value is 100.

### DBPROP_SSCE_ENCRYPTDATABASE

The DBPROP_SSCE_ENCRYPTDATABASE property has a Boolean value. This property determines whether a database will be encrypted or not.

### DBPROP_SSCE_TEMPFILE_DIRECTORY

You can use the DBPROP_SSCE_TEMPFILE_DIRECTORY property to specify the location of a temporary database. The SQL Server Compact Edition database creates a temporary database to store intermediate data. The intermediate data can be created as an interim result set during query execution. The interim data can also be created as intermediate sort tables while executing the ORDER BY, GROUP BY, or DISTINCT clauses.

This property can be set when initializing a database or at the time of executing an IISSCECompact::Compact method as shown in Listing 8.7.

LISTING 8.7    Specify the Temporary File Directory VC++

```
sscedbprop[0].dwPropertyID = DBPROP_SSCE_TEMPFILE_DIRECTORY;
sscedbprop[0].vValue.vt = VT_BSTR;
sscedbprop[0].vValue.bstrVal = SysAllocString(L"\\NewTempDir");
```

### DBPROP_SSCE_DEFAULT_LOCK_TIMEOUT

The DBPROP_SSCE_DEFAULT_LOCK_TIMEOUT property is used to specify the time in milliseconds up to which a transaction will wait for a lock. The default value of the timeout period is 2000.

### DBPROP_SSCE_AUTO_SHRINK_THRESHOLD

The DBPROP_SSCE_AUTO_SHRINK_THRESHOLD property specifies the percentage of free space in the SQL Server Compact Edition file after which the auto shrink will start. A value of 00 means auto shrink will never happen. The default value of this property is 60.

### DBPROP_SSCE_FLUSH_INTERVAL

The DBPROP_SSCE_FLUSH_INTERVAL property specifies the time interval in seconds after which transactions are flushed to disk. The default value of the flush interval is 10 seconds. If another client has already opened the database and specified the flush interval, then the next definition of the flush interval is ignored.

### DBPROP_SSCE_MAX_DATABASE_SIZE

The DBPROP_SSCE_MAX_DATABASE_SIZ property specifies the maximum size of a database in megabytes. The default value is 128 MB.

### DBPROP_SSCE_TEMPFILE_MAX_SIZE

The DBPROP_SSCE_TEMPFILE_MAX_SIZE property specifies the maximum size of a temporary file. The default value is 128 MB.

## DBPROPSET_SSCE_SESSION

The DBPROPSET_SSCE_SESSION property set contains the following properties that are specific to the SQL Server Compact Edition OLE DB provider.

## DBPROP_SSCE_LOCK_TIMEOUT

The DBPROP_SCE_LOCK_TIMEOUT property specifies an interval in milliseconds that a transaction will wait for a lock. The default value is 2000 milliseconds.

## DBPROP_SSCE_LOCK_ESCALATION

With lock escalation, many fine-grained locks are converted into a few coarse-grained locks. The default value of the lock escalation property is 100. In a session, you can specify the lock escalation using the DBPROP_SSCE_LOCK_ESCALATION property.

## DBPROP_SSCE_TRANSACTION_COMMIT_MODE

Using DBPROP_SSCE_TRANSACTION_COMMIT_MODE, you specify whether an engine should flush the buffer pool or not. The default value of the DBPROP_SSCE_TRANSAC-TION_COMMIT_MODE property is a deferred pool.

## DBPROP_SSCE_COLUMN

The DBPRO_SSCE_COLUMN property set contains properties that are specific to the SQL Server Compact Edition OLE DB provider.

## DBPROP_SSCE_COL_ROWGUID

The DBPROP_SSCE_COL_ROWGUID property is used to specify a column as a ROWGUID column.

## DBPROPSET_SSCE_ROWSET

The DBPROPSET_SSCE_ROWSET property set contains properties that are specific to OLE DB provider for the SQL Server Compact Edition database.

## DBPROP_SSCE_LOCK_HINT

DBPROP_SSCE_LOCK_HINT property specifies the level of locking done by rowset. You can use one of the following combinations of these eight values:

- DBPROPVAL_SSCE_LH_NOLOCK
- DBPROPVAL_SSCE_LH_HOLDLOCK
- DBPROPVAL_SSCE_LH_TABLOCK
- DBPROPVAL_SSCE_LH_DBLOCK
- DBPROPVAL_SSCE_LH_ROWLOCK
- DBPROPVAL_SSCE_LH_UPDLOCK
- DBPROPVAL_SSCE_LH_PAGLOCK
- DBPROPVAL_SSCE_LH_XLOCK

The default value is DBPROPVAL_SSCE_LH_NOLOCK.

## Using OLE DB Properties

The OLE DB provider for SQL Server Compact Edition database supports the standard OLE DB properties. This section describes the common property group used in the OLE DB provider.

## Using Column Properties

OLE DB allows you to use the following properties in DBPROPSET_COLUMN.

### DBPROP_COL_AUTOINCREMENT

The DBPROP_COL_AUTOINCREMENT property has a Boolean value to indicate whether the column is an Identity column or not.

For an Identity Column, the user does not need to specify a value in the INSERT operation. The database adds a unique incremental value in the column when inserting a row. The Identity column is only used for integer and bigint data types. Only one Identity column can be created for each table. Identity columns are generally created with a Primary Key constraint.

For an Identity column, the SQL Server Compact Edition database generates a new value. The first row will have the value specified as seed. A new row will have the value of the last row plus an incremental value. The default values of seed and increment are 1 and 1.

### DBPROP_COL_DEFAULT

To specify the default value for a column, you can use the DBPROP_COL_DEFAULT property. If you do not specify a value for a column during the INSERT operation, then the database will automatically fill the column with the default value.

### DBPROP_COL_FIXEDLENGTH

Get or set the Boolean value in order to specify whether or not a column is fixed in length. Fixed-length columns have the property set to TRUE.

### DBPROP_COL_INCREMENT

You use the DBPROP_COL_INCREMENT value to specify the incremental value for an auto-increment column.

### DBPROP_COL_ISLONG

The property is set to TRUE if the column can contain a long value.

### DBPROP_COL_NULLABLE

The property is set to TRUE if the column accepts NULL values.

### DBROP_COL_SEED

DBPROP_COL_SEED specifies the initial value of an auto-increment column. The default value is 1.

## Using the Data Source Information Property Group

The following section explains properties in the DBPROPSET_DATASOURCEINFO property set. For SQL Server Compact Edition OLE DB provider, all the properties in the group are Read Only.

### DBPROP_ALTERCOLUMN

DBPROP_ALTERCOLUMN alters the column definition. For SQL Server Compact Edition, you can update the DBPROP_COL_DEFAULT, DBPROP_COL_INCREMENT and DBPROP_COL_SEED properties.

### DBPROP_COLUMNDEFINITION

DBPROP_COLUMNDEFINITION is used to specify a column as not–nullable. For SQL Server Compact Edition OLE DB provider, the value is always set to DBPROPVAL_CD_NOTNULL.

### DBPROP_DBMSNAME

The DBPROP_DBMSNAME property returns the database product name. For SQL Server Compact Edition, it returns SQL Server for Windows CE.

### DBPROP_DBMSVER

The DBPROP_DBMSVER property returns the database product version. For SQL Server Compact Edition, it returns 3.00.0000.

### DBPROP_DSOTHREADMODEL

DBPROP_DSOTHREADMODEL returns the data source object-threading model. For SQL Server Compact Edition, it returns DBPROPVAL_RT_SINGLETHREAD.

### DBPROP_IDENTIFERCASE

The DBPROP_IDENTIFERCASE property returns the identifier case sensitivity of the database. For SQL Server Compact Edition, it returns DBPROPVAL_IC_MIXED.

### NOTE

The SQL Server Compact Edition identifiers are stored in mixed case.

### DBPROP_MULTIPLESTORAGEOBJECTS

DBPROP_MULTIPLESTORAGEOBJECTS returns a Boolean value specifying whether or not multiple storage objects are supported. For SQL Server Compact Edition, it returns a FALSE value (VARIANT_FALSE).

### DBPROP_NULLCOLLATION

DBPROP_NULLCOLLATION specifies the collation order of NULL values. In SQL Server Compact Edition, the NULL values are stored at the beginning of a list and return the value DBPROPVAL_NC_LOW.

### DBPROP_OLEOBJECTS

The DBPROP_OLEOBJECTS property specifies the type of support access to BLOB and COM objects. For SQL Server Compact Edition, it returns DBPROPVAL_OO_BLOB to indicate that the provider support accesses to BLOBs as structured objects.

### DBPROP_OPENROWSETSUPPORT

DBPROP_OPENROWSETSUPPORT returns the open rowset support provided by the database. For SQL Server Compact Edition, the possible values are DBPROPVAL_ORS_TABLE and DBPROPVAL_ORS_INTEGRATED_INDEX.

### DBPROP_PROVIDERFILENAME

The DBPROP_PROVIDERFILENAME property specifies the filename of the provider.

### DBPROP_PROVIDEROLEDBVER

The DBPROP_PROVIDEROLEDBVER property returns the OLE DB version. For the current version, it will return 02.50.00.

### DBPROP_PROVIDERVER

DBPROP_PROVIDERVER returns the provider version. For the current version, it will return 03.00.0000.

### DBPROP_STRUCTUREDSTORAGE

The DBPROP_STRUCTUREDSTORAGE property returns the bitmask that specifies which storage objects interface is supported by rowset. The OLE DB provider for SQL Server Compact Edition returns a zero, a combination of DBPROPVAL_SS_ISEQUENTIALSTREAM, or DBPROPVAL_SS_ILOCKBYTES.

### DBPROP_SUPPORTEDTXNDDL

The DBPROP_SUPPORTEDTXNDDL property specifies whether DDL statements are supported within transactions. SQL Server Compact Edition supports DDL and DML operations within a transaction. For SQL Server Compact Edition OLE DB provider, the return value is always DBPROPVAL_TC_ALL.

### DBPROP_SUPPORTEDTXNISOLEVELS

The DBPROP_SUPPORTEDTXNISOLEVELS property returns the bitmask specifying the supported transaction levels. For SQL Server Compact Edition, the supported isolation levels include:

- Read Committed
- Repeatable Read
- Serializable

This provider returns a bitmask consisting of DBPROPVAL_TI_READCOMMITTED, DBPROPVAL_TI_REPEATABLEREAD, and DBPROPVAL_TI_SERIALIZABLE.

## DBPROP_SUPPORTEDTXNISORETAIN

The DBPROP_SUPPORTEDTXNISORETAIN property returns a bitmask specifying the supported transaction isolation retention levels. SQL Server Compact Edition OLE DB provider returns DBPROPVAL_TR_COMMIT_DC.

### Using Initialization Properties

## DBPROP_INIT_DATASOURCE

The DBPROP_INIT_DATASOURCE property gets or sets the name of a data source.

## DBPROP_INIT_LCID

The DBPROP_INIT_LCID property gets or sets the locale ID of consumers. If a consumer does not specify the locale ID at initialization, then SQL Server Compact Edition will use a system locale ID.

## DBPROP_INIT_MODE

DBPROP_INIT_MODE returns the file mode that the storage engine will use for opening a database file.

### Using Rowset Properties

DBPROPSET_ROWSET property set has properties in a rowset group.

> **NOTE**
>
> DBPROPSET_SSCE_ROWSET contains additional properties related to rowset.

## DBPROP_ABORTPRESERVE

The DBPROP_ABORTPRESERVE property returns a Boolean value VARIANT_TRUE or VARIANT_FALSE. VARIANT _TRUE means that even after aborting a transaction, the rowset remains active. VARIANT_FALSE means that after aborting a transaction, the rowset does not remain active. The only operation allowed is to release the row and then the accessor handles the release to rowset.

OLE DB provider for SQL Server Compact Edition always returns VARIANT_FALSE for this property.

## DBPROP_ACCESSORDER

The DBPROP_ACCESSORDER property returns the order in which columns are accessed. For SQL Server Compact Edition, the property always returns DBPROPVAL_AO_RANDOM.

## DBPROP_BLOCKINGSTORAGEOBJECTS

OLE DB provider for SQL Server Compact Edition always returns VARIANT_TRUE for the DBPROP_BLOCKINGSTORAGEOBJECTS property. This property indicates whether the storage object might prevent the use of other methods on the rowset.

## DBPROP_BOOKMARKS

The DBPROP_BOOKMARKS property gets or sets a Boolean value indicating whether rowset supports bookmarks or not.

VARIANT_TRUE means the rowset supports bookmarks. VARIANT_FALSE means bookmarks are not supported. When bookmarks are supported, column 0 contains the bookmark value. When bookmarks are not supported, the DBPROP_LITERALBOOKMARKS and DBPROP_ORDEREDBOOKMARKS properties are ignored.

### DBPROP_BOOKMARKTYPE
The DBPROP_BOOKMARKTYPE property returns the bookmark type supported by a rowset. OLE DB provider for SQL Server Compact Edition always returns DBPROPVAL_BMK_NUMERIC. DBPROPVAL_BMK_NUMERIC stands for a numeric bookmark. The numeric bookmark is not based on a column's value in a row but rather on the absolute position or row ID assigned by the storage engine.

### DBPROP_CANFETCHBACKWARDS
DBPROP_CANFETCHBACKWARDS gets or sets the value indicating that the rowset can fetch backwards or not.

VARIANT_TRUE means that IRowset::GetNextRows, IRowsetLocate::GetRowsAt, and IRowsetScroll::GetRowsAtRatio can fetch backwards from the specified row by having negative values in cRows.

VARIANT_FALSE means that the cRows value cannot be negative and that IRowset::GetNextRows, IRowsetLocate::GetRowsAt, and IRowsetScroll::GetRowsAtRatio cannot fetch rows backwards.

### DBPROP_CANHOLDROWS
The DBPROP_CANHOLDROWS property returns a Boolean value indicating whether or not the rowset allows a consumer to fetch more rows while holding previously fetched rows with pending changes.

SQL Server Compact Edition OLE DB provider always returns VARIANT_FALSE.

### DBPROP_CANSCROLLBACKWARDS
DBPROP_CANSCROLLBACKWARDS indicates whether a rowset can scroll backwards. OLE DB provider for SQL Server Compact Edition is always VARIANT_FALSE.

### DBPROP_CHANGEINSERTEDROWS
The DBPROP_CHANGEINSERTEDROWS property gives a Boolean value indicating whether or not a consumer can call the DeleteRows and SetData methods of the IRowSetChange interface for newly inserted rows. OLE DB provider for SQL Server Compact Edition is always VARIANT_TRUE.

### DBPROP_COMMITPRESERVE
DBPROP_COMMITPRESERVE gives a Boolean value indicating that after committing a transaction, the rowset remains active or not. OLE DB provider for SQL Server Compact Edition is always VARIANT_TRUE.

### DBPROP_DEFERRED

The DBPROP_DEFERRED property gives a Boolean value. VARIANT_TRUE means that data in a column is not fetched until an the accessor is used on the column. VARIANT_FALSE means that data in a column is fetched when the row containing it is fetched.

OLE DB provider for SQL Server Compact Edition is always VARIANT_TRUE.

### DBPROP_DELAYSTORAGEOBJECTS

The DBPROP_DELAYSTORAGEOBJECTS property is always VARIANT_TRUE for SQL Server Compact Edition. This means that storage objects are used in a delayed update mode.

### DBPROP_IACCESSOR

For SQL Server Compact Edition, the DBPROP_IACCESSOR property value is always VARIANT TRUE. This means that the rowset supports the IAccessor interface.

### DBPROP_ICOLUMNSINFO

For SQL Server Compact Edition, the DBPROP_ICOLUMNSINFO property value is always VARIANT TRUE. It means that the rowset supports the IColumnsInfo interface.

### DBPROP_ICONVERTTYPE

For SQL Server Compact Edition, the DBPROP_ICONVERTTYPE property value is always VARIANT TRUE. This means that the rowset supports the IConvertType interface.

### DBPROP_ILOCKBYTES

The DBPROP_ILOCKBYTES property has a Boolean value. VARIANT_TRUE indicates that the rowset is capable of manipulating the column as a storage object.

### DBPROP_IROWSET

For SQL Server Compact Edition, the DBPROP_IROWSET property value is always VARIANT TRUE. This means that the rowset supports the IRowset interface.

### DBPROP_IROWSETUPDATE and DBPROP_IROWSETCHANGE

The property value indicates whether the corresponding interface is supported or not. VARIANT_TRUE means the interface is supported. If you set DBPROP_IROWSETUPDATE to VARIANT_TRUE, it will automatically set DBPROP_IROWSETCHANGE to VARIANT_TRUE.

### DBPROP_IROWSETINFO

For SQL Server Compact Edition, the DBPROP_IROWSETINFO property value is always VARIANT TRUE. This means the rowset support the IRowsetinfo interface.

### DBPROP_IROWSETINDEX and DBPROP_IROWSETCURRENTINDEX

The property value indicates whether the corresponding interface is supported or not. VARIANT_TRUE means the interface is supported. If you set DBPROP_IROWSETINDEX to VARIANT_TRUE, it will automatically set DBPROP_IROWSETCURRENTINDEX to VARIANT_TRUE.

### DBPROP_IROWSETBOOKMARK

The DBPROP_IROWSETBOOKMARK property value indicates whether the IRowsetBookmark interface is supported or not. A value of VARIANT_TRUE indicates that the interface is supported.

### DBPROP_ISEQUENTIALSTREAM

A VARIANT_TRUE value indicates that the rowset is capable of manipulating the content of a column as storage object.

### DBPROP_ISUPPORTERRORINFO

For SQL Server Compact Edition, the property value is always VARIANT TRUE. This means the rowset supports the ISupportErrorInfo interface.

### DBPROP_IMMOBILEROWS

The OLE DB provider for SQL Server Compact Edition will always have a VARIANT_FALSE. This means that if the rowset is ordered, inserted, and updated, then the rows follow the ordering criteria for rowset.

### DBPROP_LOCKMODE

The DBPROP_LOCKMODE property specifies the level of locking performed by rowset. The OLE DB provider for SQL Server Compact Edition will always have the value DBPROPVAL_LM_SINGLEROW.

### DBPROP_MAXOPENROWS

The DBPROP_MAXOPENROWS property specifies the maximum number of open rows. For SQL Server Compact Edition, the value is 1.

### DBPROP_MAXROWS

DBPROP_MAXROWS specifies the maximum number of rows that can be returned in a rowset. If there is no limit, the value of the property would be 0. For SQL Server Compact Edition, the property value is always 0.

### DBPROP_OTHERSINSERT

The DBPROP_OTHERSINSERT property specifies the visibility of rows inserted by a consumer or process other than a consumer of rowset.

### DBPROP_OTHERSUPDATEDELETE

The DBPROP_OTHERSUPDATEDELETE is a Boolean property that indicates whether updates and deletes made by others are visible to the rowset consumer.

VARIANT_TRUE indicates that changes made by users other than the consumer are visible to the rowset.

VARIANT_FALSE indicates that changes made by users other than the consumer are not visible to the rowset.

### DBPROP_OWNINSERT
The DBPROP_OWNINSERT property specifies a Boolean value VARIANT_TRUE or VARIANT_FALSE.

VARIANT_TRUE means that if a consumer of rowset inserts a row, then that row would be visible to other consumers the next time they fetch data.

VARIANT_FALSE means the changes to the rowset would not be visible to other consumers unless the command is re-executed.

### DBPROP_OWNUPDATEDELETE
The DBPROP_OWNUPDATEDELETE property specifies whether or not the update and delete changes to a rowset made by a consumer of rowset are visible or not.

### DBPROP_QUICKRESTART
DBPROP_QUICKRESTART indicates whether IRowset::RestartPosition is relatively quick to execute or not.

VARIANT_FALSE means it is expensive to execute and requires re-executing the command that created the rowset.

### DBPROP_REMOVEDELETED
The DBPROP_REMOVEDELETED property is a Boolean value indicating whether or not the provider removes the row it detects as deleted from the rowset. For SQL Server Compact Edition, this property is always VARIANT_TRUE.

### DBPROP_REPORTMULTIPLECHANGES
DBPROP_REPORTMULTIPLECHANGES specifies whether an update or delete can impact multiple rows or not. For SQL Server Compact Edition, the value is always VARIANT_TRUE.

### DBPROP_ROWTHREADMODEL
The DBPROP_ROWTHREADMODEL property specifies the bitmask of a threading model supported by rowset. For the SQL Server Compact Edition OLE DB provider, the value is always DBPROPVAL_RT_SINGLETHREAD.

### DBPROP_SERVERDATAONINSERT
DBPROP_SERVERDATAONINSERT specifies whether or not after an insert is transmitted to the server that a consumer can retrieve the actual values from the data store including the calculated columns and default columns.

For SQL Server Compact Edition, the property is always VARIANT_TRUE.

### DBPROP_UPDATABILITY
The DBPROP_UPDATABILITY property specifies the bitmask for the supported method on IRowsetChange.

### Using Index Properties

The DBPROPSET_INDEX property set has properties in the index property group.

### DBPROP_INDEX_AUTOUPDATE

The DBPROP_INDEX_AUTOUPDATE Boolean property specifies whether indexes are automatically maintained or not. For SQL Server Compact Edition, the property value is always VARIANT_TRUE.

### DBPROP_INDEX_NULLCOLLATION

The DBPROP_INDEX_NULLCOLLATION property indicates how NULLs are collated in an index. For SQL Server Compact Edition, the value is always DBPROPVAL_RT_SINGLETHREAD indicating that NULLs are collated at the low end of the list.

### DBPROP_INDEX_NULLS

The DBPROP_INDEX_NULLS property specifies whether NULL keys are allowed. For the SQL Server Compact Edition OLE DB provider, this value is always DBPROPVAL_IN_DISALLOWNULL. The DBPROPVAL_IN_DISALLOWNULL value indicates that the index does not allow entries where key columns are NULL.

### DBPROP_INDEX_TYPE

The DBPROP_INDEX_TYPE property specifies the type of index. For SQL Server Compact Edition the value is DBPROPVAL_IT_BTREE indicating that it uses a B+ tree.

### DBPROP_INDEX_UNIQUE

The DBPROP_INDEX_UNIQUE property indicates whether an index key must be unique or not. The SQL Server Compact Edition OLE DB provider can have VARIANT_TRUE and VARIANT_FALSE values.

VARIANT_TRUE indicates that the index keys must be unique.

VARIANT_FALSE indicates that duplicate index keys are allowed.

## Managing the Database with OLE DB

We have described the interfaces supported by the SQL Server Compact Edition OLE DB provider and discussed the specific properties. In the following section, you will use OLE DB provider to perform common tasks such as create, secure, encrypt, and delete a database.

### Creating a Database Using OLE DB

To create a database, first specify a database name with the DBPROP_INIT_DATASOURCE property as shown in Listing 8.8.

**LISTING 8.8    Specify Name of Database VC++**

```
dbprop[0].dwPropertyID  = DBPROP_INIT_DATASOURCE;
dbprop[0].dwOptions     = DBPROPOPTIONS_REQUIRED;
dbprop[0].vValue.vt     = VT_BSTR;
dbprop[0].vValue.bstrVal = SysAllocString(L"MyPatients.sdf");
```

Once you have set up the properties, you call the CreateDataSource function as described in Listing 8.9.

### LISTING 8.9    Create Date Source VC++

```
// Create and initialize the database.
hr = pIDBDataSourceAdmin->CreateDataSource(sizeof(dbpropset)/sizeof(dbpropset[0]),
    dbpropset, NULL, IID_IUnknown, &pIUnknownSession);
```

### Securing the Database Using OLE DB

In previous chapters we discussed how you can secure an SQL Server Compact Edition database with a password by using SQL Server Management Studio and Query Analyzer tools. Chapter 4, *Managing the SQL Server 2005 Compact Edition Database*, showed you how to create a password-protected database programmatically.

To make an SQL Server Compact Edition database password-protected using OLE DB, you set the DBPROP_SSCE_DBPASSWORD property as shown in Listing 8.10.

### LISTING 8.10    Specifying Password VC++

```
sscedbprop[1].dwPropertyID = DBPROP_SSCE_DBPASSWORD;
sscedbprop[1].dwOptions = DBPROPOPTIONS_REQUIRED;
sscedbprop[1].vValue.vt = VT_BSTR;
sscedbprop[1].vValue.bstrVal = SysAllocString(L"mypassword");
```

### Encrypting Database Using OLE DB

To make an SQL Server Compact Edition database encrypted using OLE DB provider, you use the provider-specific property DBPROP_SSCE_ENCRYPTDATABASE. Set this property to VARIANT_TRUE and specify the password with the DBPROP_SSCE_DBPASSWORD property as shown in Listing 8.11.

### LISTING 8.11    Specifying Encryption VC++

```
sscedbprop[0].dwPropertyID = DBPROP_SSCE_ENCRYPTDATABASE;
sscedbprop[0].dwOptions = DBPROPOPTIONS_REQUIRED;
sscedbprop[0].vValue.vt = VT_BOOL;
sscedbprop[0].vValue.boolVal = VARIANT_TRUE;
sscedbprop[1].dwPropertyID = DBPROP_SSCE_DBPASSWORD;
sscedbprop[1].dwOptions = DBPROPOPTIONS_REQUIRED;
sscedbprop[1].vValue.vt = VT_BSTR;
sscedbprop[1].vValue.bstrVal = SysAllocString(L"mypassword");
```

### Deleting a Database

To delete an SQL Server Compact Edition database, you should physically delete the SQL Server Compact Edition database file.

**NOTE**

IDBDataSourceAdmin::DestroyDataSource is not supported for SQL Server Compact Edition.

## Summary

In Chapter 7, *Programming SQL Server 2005 Compact Edition with ADO.NET,* we introduced ADO.NET programming for SQL Server Compact Edition. In this chapter we discussed how you can also utilize your VC++ skills to develop unmanaged applications based on the SQL Server Compact Edition database. First, we used the Engine Object method in VC++ to do common database management tasks. Then, we explained the specific properties and interfaces for OLE DB provider for SQL Server Compact Edition. Your existing OLE DB knowledge and specific details of the SQL Server Compact Edition OLE DB provider equip you to develop VC++ applications based on SQL Server Compact Edition.

# Using Operators in SQL Server 2005 Compact Edition

Operators have the ability to compare, manipulate, and filter data. You will be using operators in expressions or in conditional statements. SQL Server Compact Edition supports most of the operators supported by SQL Server. Both operator and expression are common to many programming languages. If you are already familiar with mathematical operators and expressions, you will see that SQL operators and expressions generally follow the same rules.

Expression consists of constants, functions, and other expressions, and returns a single value. An expression can be as simple as a single value and as complex as a formula consisting of various functions and expressions. SQL Syntax Expression can be used in place of a value. Expression can't be used in place of a table or column name.

This chapter demonstrates the syntax and examples of each operator that the SQL Server Compact Edition database supports.

Operators can be divided into the following categories:

- Arithmetic
- Assignment
- Bitwise
- Logical
- Comparison

- String Concatenation
- Unary

# Arithmetic Operators

You will use the Arithmetic operators to perform mathematical calculation. SQL Server Compact Edition supports operators for computations such as adding, subtracting, multiplying, and dividing. Arithmetic operators perform addition, subtraction, multiplication, and division on numeric operators.

## The + (Add) Operator

The + operator adds two numbers and can also be used to add a number of days to a date. The + operator is also used for string concatenation as shown in Listing 9.1.

### Syntax
expression + expression

### LISTING 9.1    Add Operator

```
Select OrderPrice + DeliveryCharge As TotalPrice from Orders
Select (DATEPART(day, OrderDate) + 5) As DeliveryDate From Orders
Select "First Name" + "Last Name" As FullName From Employees
```

## The – (Subtraction) Operator

Similar to the + operator, the – operator is used for subtraction. Using this operator you can subtract a number from another number or subtract a number of days from a date as described in Listing 9.2.

### Syntax
expressions – expressions

### NOTE

+ and – operators can be used with Datetime and SmallDateTime datatype.

### LISTING 9.2    Subtraction Operator

```
SELECT OrderPrice - Discount AS TotalPrice FROM Orders
SELECT (DATEPART(day, DeliveryDate) - 5) AS ProductionDate FROM Inventory
```

## The * (Multiply) Operator

The * arithmetic operator multiplies two numeric expressions together as shown in Listing 9.3.

NOTE

* Operator cannot be used with the datetime data type.

**Syntax**

expressions * expressions

**LISTING 9.3    Mulitply Operator**

```
SELECT ProductPrice * Quantity AS TotalPrice FROM Orders
```

## The / (Divide) Operator

The / operator divides one numeric expression by another. The data type or numeric expression to be divided is called the dividend. The data type or numeric expression used to divide the dividend is called the divisor. Similar to the * operator, the / can't be used with a datetime data type. Listing 9.4 demonstrates the usage of the Divide operator.

**Syntax**

dividend / divisor

**LISTING 9.4    Divide Operator**

```
SELECT CasePrice / NoofItem AS EachItemPrice FROM Orders
```

## The % (Modulo) Operator

The % (modulo) operator returns the integer remainder of one numeric expression divided by another. Listing 9.5 demonstrates the usage of the % (modulo) operator.

**Syntax**

dividend / divisor

**LISTING 9.5    Modulo Operator**

```
SELECT HouseNo FROM Property WHERE HouseNo % 2 = 0
```

Multiplication, division, and modulo have high precedence and are followed by subtraction and then addition.

Operators are executed from left to right if multiple operators in an expression have the same level of precedence.

You can use parentheses to change the order of execution. Expressions in parentheses take precedence over other operators.

# The Assignment Operator

You will use the Assignment operator to assign a value to a variable or to assign a result column with an alias. There is only one operator in each assignment category.

## The = (Equal To) Operator

The Equal To operator is used to compare the values of two expressions. It returns TRUE when the expressions are equal, otherwise it returns FALSE. Listing 9.6 demonstrates this.

LISTING 9.6    Equal To Operator

```
SELECT * From Emails where FromEmail = 'dhingramp@hotmail.com'
```

# Bitwise Operators

Use bitwise operators to perform bit manipulations between any two expressions whose data types are in the integer category. These operators temporarily convert numeric values to integers and do bitwise operations. Bitwise operators are very useful when you want to store multiple values in a single column. For example, an email application needs to store multiple flags—Urgent, Attachment, Follow up required, Replied, and so on. Instead of storing these flag in multiple bit columns, they can be stored as integers. Each flag value can be determined based on an integer bit.

## The & (And) Operator

To perform a bitwise logical And operation, you will use the & operator. This operator works with numeric expressions of an integer data type category. In the logical And operation the result bit will be 1 if the bits in both input expressions are 1. Otherwise the result bits will be 0. Listing 9.7 demonstrates this.

Syntax
expression & expression

LISTING 9.7    Bitwise & Operator

```
SELECT Column1 & Column2 FROM MyTable
```

## The | (Or) Operator

You will use the | symbol to perform a bitwise logical Or operation. In the logical Or operation, the result bit will be 0 if the bits of both input expressions are 0, otherwise the result bit will be 1. Listing 9.8 demonstrates this.

Syntax
expression | expression

LISTING 9.8    Bitwise Or Operator

```
SELECT Column1 | Column2 FROM MyTable
```

## The ^ (Exclusive Or) Operator

You will use the ^ symbol to perform a bitwise Exclusive Or operation. In an Exclusive Or operation the resultant bit is set to 0 if both the bits on corresponding expressions are 0 or 1. If one of the input bits is 0 and the other input bit is 1, then the resultant bit will be 1. Listing 9.9 shows the usage of the Exclusive OR operator.

### Syntax
expression ^ expression

**LISTING 9.9    Bitwise Exclusive Or Operator**

```
SELECT Column1 ^ Column2 FROM MyTable
```

## The ~ (Not) Operator

You will use the ~ operator to perform a bitwise logical Not operation. The bitwise Not operator only uses one operand. Listing 9.0 shows the usage of ~ operator.

### Syntax
~ expression

**LISTING 9.10    Bitwise Not Operator**

```
SELECT ~Column1 FROM MyTable
```

---

**NOTE**

Bitwise operators &, |, ^ work on Int, Smallint, and Tinydata. Bitwise operator ~ also works on Bit data type.

---

For bitwise operators you can use the data type integer or binary data type categories. Table 9.1 shows the data type you can use on the right-hand side of an operator based on the left-hand side operator.

**TABLE 9.1    Left and Right Operand**

| Left Operand | Right Operand |
|---|---|
| Binary | int, smallint, tinyint |
| Bit | int, smallint, tinyint, bit |
| Int | int, smallint, tinyint, binary, varbinary |
| Smallint | int, smallint, tinyint, binary, varbinary |
| Tinyint | int, smallint, tinyint, binary, varbinary |
| Varbinary | int, smallint, tinyint |

# The Comparison Operator

The Comparison operator is used to test individual values. Using the Comparison operator you can compare values for equality, nonequality, less than, and greater than. Comparison operators return bit data type—TRUE or FALSE.

## The = (Equals) Operator

The Equals operator compares two expressions as shown in Listing 9.11. If two values are equal, the return value will be TRUE, otherwise the return value will be FALSE. When comparing non-null expressions, the result is true if they are equal, otherwise it is FALSE.

**Syntax**

expression = expression

**Example**

LISTING 9.11    Equals Operator

```
SELECT * FROM Orders WHERE OrderID = 100;
```

## The < > or ! = (Not Equal To) Operator

You can use either symbol < > or symbol ! = for the Not Equal To operator. The Not Equal To operator returns TRUE if the expression on the left is not equal to the expression on the right. Listing 9.12 demonstrates this.

**Syntax**

expression ! = expression

expression < > expression

LISTING 9.12    Not Equal To Operator

```
SELECT * FROM Cinema WHERE Ticket != 10
SELECT * FROM Employee WHERE Education <> 'Graduate'
```

## The > (Greater Than) Operator

The Greater Than operator returns TRUE if the expression on the left has a higher value than the one on the right as shown in Listing 9.13.

**Syntax**

expression > expression

LISTING 9.13    Greater Than Operator

```
SELECT * FROM Employees where Salary > 5000
```

## The > = (Greater Than or Equal To)

This combination of Greater Than and Equal To operators returns TRUE if the expression on the left has a higher or equal value than the one on the right as shown in Listing 9.14.

**Syntax**

expression > = expression

**LISTING 9.14     Greater Than or Equal To Operator**

```
SELECT * FROM Employees where Salary >= 5000
Select * From Emails where SentDate >= '03-21-2007'
```

## The ! > (Not Greater Than) Operator

The Not Greater Than operator is the opposite of the Greater Than operator. It returns FALSE if the expression on the left has a higher value than the one on the right, otherwise it returns TRUE. Listing 9.15 demonstrates this.

**Syntax**

expression ! > expression

**LISTING 9.15     Not Greater Than Operator**

```
SELECT * FROM Employees where Salary !> 5000
```

## The < (Less Than) Operator

The Less Than operator returns TRUE if the expression on the left has a lower value than the one on the right. It returns FALSE if the expression on the left has a value equal to or higher than the one on the right. Listing 9.16 demonstrates this.

**Syntax**

expression < expression

**Example**

**LISTING 9.16     Less Than or Equal To Operator**

```
SELECT * FROM Employees where Salary > 5000
```

## The < = (Less Than or Equal To) Operator

The Less Than or Equal to operator is a combination that returns TRUE if the expression on the left has a lower or equal value than the one on the right. Listing 9.17 demonstrates this.

**Syntax**

expression < = expression

**LISTING 9.17    Not Less Than Operator**

```
SELECT * FROM Employees WHERE Salary <= 5000
```

## The ! < (Not Less Than) Operator

The Not Less Than operator is opposite of the Less Than operator. It returns FALSE if the expression on the left has a lower value than the one on the right, otherwise it returns TRUE. Listing 9.18 demonstrates this.

**Syntax**

expression ! < expression

**LISTING 9.18    Not Less Than Operator**

```
SELECT * FROM Employees where Salary !< 5000
```

# Logical Operators

You use a Logical operator to test whether the result of a condition is TRUE or FALSE. The result of a logical operation is a Boolean value, TRUE or FALSE.

## And Operator

The And operator returns a TRUE value if both Boolean expressions are TRUE as shown in Listing 9.19.

**Syntax**

Boolean Expression AND Boolean Expression

**LISTING 9.19    Logical And Operator**

```
SELECT * FROM OrderDetails where UnitPrice < 100 AND Discount < 10;
```

## Or Operator

The Or logical operator returns a TRUE value if either of the Boolean expressions is TRUE as shown in Listing 9.20.

**Syntax**

Boolean Expression AND Boolean Expression

**LISTING 9.20    Logical OR Operator**

```
SELECT * FROM OrderDetails where UnitPrice < 100 OR Discount < 10;
```

## Not Operator

The Not operator only works on one operand. With the Not operator you can toggle the value of a Boolean expression. If the value of a Boolean expression is TRUE with a Not operator, it becomes FALSE and vice versa.

The Not operator is useful when it is easier to express a condition in a negative way. Listing 9.21 demonstrates the usage of the Not operator.

**Syntax**
NOT Boolean Expression

**LISTING 9.21    Logical Not Operator**

```
SELECT * FROM Employee where NOT EducationMajor = 'Computer Science';
SELECT * From Orders where OrderDate NOT LIKE '2005%';
```

You will generally use Not with the Like, In, and Between operators. The first example can be better written with a Not Equal To operator

```
SELECT * FROM Employee where EducationMajor != 'Computer Science';
```

## In Operator

The In operator is used to check whether the argument specified as an expression exists in the values specified in a list. You can directly specify the list of values as an argument or you can specify a subquery that returns a list of values. The In operator returns TRUE if the test expression matches with any of the values returned by a subquery or in the list, otherwise it returns FALSE.

You can combine the In operator with the Not operand to check that expressions do not exist in the list.  Listing 9.22 demonstrates the usage of In operator.

**Syntax**
Test_expression IN (subquery)

Test_expression NOT IN (subquery)

Test_expression IN (expression [,...n])

Test_expression NOT IN(expression [,...n])

**Subquery**
A subquery should get one column. A subquery checks the existence that a row and duplicate rows do not impact the result.

## Example

**LISTING 9.22    In Operator**

```
SELECT * FROM Orders WHERE ShipCity IN ( SELECT City FROM Country WHERE CityType =
'Capital')
SELECT * FROM Orders WHERE ShipCity NOT IN ( SELECT City FROM Country WHERE City-
Type = 'Capital')
SELECT * FROM Orders WHERE ShipCity IN ('London', 'Portland','Seattle','Vancouver')
SELECT * FROM Orders WHERE ShipCity NOT IN ('London', 'Portland','Seattle',
'Vancouver')
```

## Exists Operator

As the name suggests, the Exists operator tests the existence of a row in the result of a subquery. It returns a TRUE value if the subquery returns one or more rows; if the subquery does not return a row, the operator returns a FALSE value. Listing 9.23 demonstrates the usage of the Exists operator.

**Syntax**
Exists subquery

**Subquery**
The subquery must be a Select statement and it cannot use the Into and Compute clauses. It can use the Order By clause.

## Example

**LISTING 9.23    Exists Operator**

```
SELECT * FROM Customers WHERE Exists
( SELECT * FROM Orders,Customers where 'Orders.Customer ID' = 'Customers.Customer
ID' );
DELETE FROM Customers WHERE EXISTS (SELECT *  FROM Orders where 'Customers.Customer
ID' = 'Orders.Customer ID');
```

## Like Operator

Use the Like operator to find values in a column that match the pattern you specify. The Like operator returns TRUE if the pattern matches value and returns FALSE if the pattern does not match with value.

**Syntax**
Match_expression LIKE pattern [ESCAPE escape_character]

Match_expression NOT LIKE pattern [ESCAPE escape_character]

## Pattern

The pattern you specify with the Like operator can include both regular and wild card characters. In a regular character you specify the complete value. This is similar to using = or ! = value. You can use _ or % wildcard characters.

_ matches single character

% matches zero or more characters

\ removes the significance of % or – character

### NOTE

An Escape character indicates that the character following it takes alternative interpretation. The Escape Sequence refers to an escape character and subsequent character(s) to be interpreted differently.

With the _ character in a pattern it will return a match if the string characters in a column match with a pattern string except the character at _ position. The string in a column can contain any value at a position where _ is specified.

With the % wildcard character you can specify a string of zero or more characters. You can place the % at the beginning of a string, at the end of a string, and both at the beginning and end of a string. Listing 9.24 shows the usage of the LIKE operator.

### LISTING 9.24    LIKE Operator

```
SELECT "First Name", "Last Name", "Postal Code" From Employees
where "Postal Code" Like '98%'
```

**Result**

| First Name | Last Name | Postal Code |
|---|---|---|
| Nancy | Davolio | 98122 |
| Andrew | Fuller | 98401 |
| Janet | Leverling | 98033 |
| .. | .. | .. |

```
SELECT "First Name", "Last Name", "Postal Code" From Employees
where "Postal Code" NOT Like '98%'
```

**Result**

| First Name | Last Name | Postal Code |
|---|---|---|
| Steven | Buchanan | SW1 8JR |
| Michael | Suyama | EC2 7JR |
| Robert | King | RG1 9SP |
| .. | .. | .. |

## Between and And Operators

The Between and And combination is used to test whether an expression is within or outside range. The operator returns TRUE if the expression value is within range and it return FALSE if the value is outside range. Listing 9.25 uses the Between and AND operators.

### Syntax

Test expression BETWEEN begin_expression AND end_expression

Test expression NOT BETWEEN begin_expression AND end_expresssion

LISTING 9.25    Between Operator

```
SELECT * From ServiceRequest WHERE CreatedDate BETWEEN '01/01/2005' AND
'12/31/2006' ;
SELECT * From Employee WHERE NOT Salary BETWEEN 50000 AND 900000 ;
```

## Some/Any Operator

The Some/Any operator is used to compare a scalar value with a single-column set of values. You will use a Where clause to compare a single value from a column. The column value will be compared with a subquery result. You can use any one of the comparison operators defined in the comparison operator section.

> NOTE
>
> The Some and Any operators can be used interchangeably.

### Syntax

Scalar expression {=, < >,!=, >, > =, <, < =,! >,! <} SOME (subquery)

Scalar expression {=, < >,!=, >, > =, <, < =,! >,! <} ANY (subquery)

### Comparison Operator

You can use any of these operators for comparison: =, < >,! =, >, > =, <, < =,! >,! <}.

### Subquery

Use a subquery that returns a result set of one column. The subquery must be a Select statement and it cannot use the Order By, Into, or Compute clauses. Listing 9.26 shows the usage of Subquery.

LISTING 9.26    Some/Any Operator

```
Select * From Products where  "Units On Order"  = SOME
(SELECT "Product ID" FROM Products WHERE "Category ID" =  1);
```

## All Operator

You will use the All operator to compare a scalar value with the single-column set of values. You can use any of the comparison operators specified previously. You will get the result TRUE when the comparison is true for all pairs (scalar expression, val). Val is the value in a single-column set.

### Syntax
Scalar expression {=, <>,!=, >, >=, <, <=,!>,!<}ALL (subquery)

### Comparison Operator
You can use any scalar expression {=, <>,!=, >, >=, <, <=,!>,!<}.

### Subquery
You use a subquery that returns a result set of one column. The subquery cannot use Order By, Into, and Compute clauses. The result of the subquery is compared with the value of the column specified in the Where clause. Listing 9.27 shows the usage of the ALL operator with Subquery.

**LISTING 9.27    All Operator**

```
Select * From Products where  "Units On Order"  > ALL
(SELECT "Product ID" FROM Products WHERE "Category ID" =  1);
```

# String Concatenation Operator

Use the String Concatenation operator to combine two strings into one. There is only one String Concatenation operator +. Listing 9.28 shows how to concatenate strings.

## The + (Add) Operator

Use this operator to concatenate multiple strings into one.

### Syntax
String  + String

**LISTING 9.28    String Concatenation Operator**

```
SELECT Address + City As "Full Address" From Customers
```

# Unary Operators

You will use the Unary operator on a single operator to make it positive, negative, or complement.

---

**NOTE**

Unary operator can be used on any data type in a numeric category except a datetime data type.

---

## The + (Positive) Operator

The + operator returns the positive value of an expression as shown in Listing 9.29.

### Syntax
+ Numeric Expression

**LISTING 9.29    UNARY Positive Operator**

```
SELECT  +("Units In Stock" - "Reorder Level")  As "Final Units" From Products
SELECT +(DATEPART(day, "Order Date") - DATEPART(day, "Shipped Date")) FROM Orders
```

## The – (Negative) Operator

The – operator returns the negative value of an expression as shown in Listing 9.30.

### Syntax
– Numeric Expression

**LISTING 9.30    UNARY Negative Operator**

```
SELECT  -("Units In Stock" - "Reorder Level")  As "Final Units" From Products
SELECT -(DATEPART(day, "Order Date") - DATEPART(day, "Shipped Date")) FROM Orders
```

# Precedence Rules

An expression can have multiple operators. Expressions can also have operands of multiple data types or of different lengths and precision. Of course it is important for you to understand the result value, result data type, precision, scale, and length of a result. The result of an operation that has different data types depends upon the following factors:

- Operator precedence
- Data type precedence
- Precision, scale, and length of input operand

## Operator Precedence

It is possible to use multiple operators in a complex expression. Operator precedence determines the sequence in which operations are performed. Knowing the order of operator execution will help you to write correct expressions. In this section we will specify the precedence of all operators. According to precedence rules, the operator with lower precedence gets converted to a higher precedence operator. Following is the precedence order for SQL Server Compact Edition:

1. ~

2. *, /, %

3. +, –, &

4. =, <,<=, !<, >,> =,! >, < >,

5. ^, |

6. Not

7. And

8. All, Any, Between, Like, Or, Some/Any

9. =

A higher-level operator is evaluated first and a lower-level operator is evaluated later. If operators in an expression have the same precedence, then operators are evaluated from left to right. You can use parentheses to change the order. The expression in parentheses will be evaluated first. You can also use nested parentheses. The expression in the innermost parentheses will be evaluated first.

## Data Type Precedence

In the previous section we discussed operators. Most operators require multiple operands. In the examples shown, the same data type was used with the operator. When you use the same data, the operation result has the same data type as both operators. When you add two integers, the result is an integer.

You can also use two different data types with the operators. When doing so, the lower-precedence data type is converted to a higher-precedence data type. In the following section the precedence of various data types is discussed. The data type precedence and precedence rules will help you to determine how data type is converted to a different data type.

SQL Server Compact Edition uses the following preference order for data types:

1. datetime (highest)

2. float

3. real

4. money

5. bigint

6. int

7. smallint

8. tinyint

9. bit

10. ntext

11. image

12. uniqueidentifier

13. nvarchar

14. nchar

15. varbinary

16. binary (lowest)

## Precision, Scale, and Length

Precision refers to number of digits in a numeric data. Scale refers to the number of digits to the right of a decimal. Length refers to the number of bytes used to store the field.

The following rules determine the precision, scale, and length of a result:

- When two of the same data types are used with an arithmetic operator, the result will be the same data type. The precision and scale will remain the same as the two data types.

- When an arithmetic operator has two different numeric data types, the rules of data precedence define the type of result. The result will get data type and precision defined for the data type having the higher precedence. For example, if a decimal and integer are added, the result will be a decimal data type. The result will have precision of decimal as a decimal has higher precision than integer.

- When you concatenate nchar or nvarchar operands, the resulting expression will have the sum length of two operands or 4000 characters, whichever is less.

- When you concatenate binary or varbinary operators, the result expression will have the sum length of two expressions or 8000 characters, whichever is less.

# Summary

In this chapter we discussed the operators that are used in expressions or in conditional statements. The operators allow you to manipulate and filter data that is retrieved from tables. A reference of all operators that are available in SQL Server Compact Edition is provided. The meaning of many of these operators is self explanatory but some require special attention. You should use the reference and examples to ensure that you are writing the expressions in your application properly.

Chapter 10, *Using the Built-In Functions*, will continue the progression and discuss the built-in function that you can use in SQL statements.

# Using the Built-In Functions

SQL Server Compact Edition supports built-in functions for counting, calculations, strings, and date manipulations. These functions are a subset function that SQL Server 2005 supports. The best way to learn the SQL Server Compact Edition built-in functions is to run the functions yourself and see the results.

## Mathematical Functions

Use the mathematical functions to operate numerical expressions. Mathematical functions operate on a numerical category data type. You can input float, real, integer, smallint, tinyint, and money.

### ABS (Absolute)

The ABS (Absolute) mathematical function takes a numeric expression as input and returns a positive and absolute value. The input expression can be of any data type that can be implicitly converted to float. Listing 10.1 describes the usage of ABS function.

**Syntax**
ABS (numeric expression)

**LISTING 10.1    Absolute Function**

```
SELECT ABS("Units In Stock"-"Units On Order") As
AbsoluteDifference,
"Units In Stock","Units On Order" From Products
```

**Result**

| AbsoluteDifference | Units In Stock | Units On Order |
| --- | --- | --- |
| 39 | 39 | 0 |
| 23 | 17 | 40 |
| 57 | 13 | 70 |
| .. | .. | .. |

## ACOS

ACOS, the inverse of cosine, returns the angle in radians for a cosine specified as a float expression as shown in Listing 10.2. The input expression is a float data type or a data type that can be implicitly converted to float.

**Syntax**
ACOS (float expression)

**LISTING 10.2    ACOS Function**

```
SELECT ACOS (.90)
```

**Result**
0.451026811796262

## ASIN

ASIN, also referred to as arcsine or the inverse of sine, returns the angle in radians whose sine is given as a float expression as shown in Listing 10.3. The input expression is a float data type or a data type that can implicitly be converted to float.

**Syntax**
ASIN (float expression)

**LISTING 10.3    ASIN Function**

```
SELECT ASIN (.90)
```

**Result**
1.11976951499863

## ATAN

ATAN is also known as arctangent. The ATAN mathematical function returns the angle in radians whose tangent is specified as a float expression as shown in Listing 10.4. The float expression can be a float data type or any data type that can implicitly be converted to float.

**Syntax**
ATAN (float expression)

### LISTING 10.4     ATAN Function

```
SELECT ATAN(.90)
```

**Result**
0.732815101786507

## ATN2

The ATN2 mathematical function returns the angle in radians whose tangent is the quotient of two float expressions as shown in Listing 10.5.

**Syntax**
ATN2 (float expression, float expression)

### LISTING 10.5     ATAN2 Function

```
SELECT ATN2(.90, 2)
```

**Result**
0.422853926132941

## CEILING

The CEILING mathematical function returns the smallest integer that is greater than or equal to a given numeric expression parameter as shown in Listing 10.6.

**Syntax**
CEILING (numeric expression)

### LISTING 10.6     CEILING Function

```
SELECT CEILING ("Unit Price" - "Discount") As Price,
"Unit Price", "Discount"  From "Order Details"
```

**Result**

| Price | Unit Price | Discount |
|-------|-----------|----------|
| 27 | 27 | 0 |
| 10 | 9.8 | 0.15 |
| 13 | 12.8 | 0 |
| .. | .. | .. |

## COS

The COS function returns the cosine of an angle as shown in Listing 10.7. The angle is specified in radians that can be specified as a float data type or any data type that can implicitly be converted to float.

**Syntax**
COS (float expression)

**LISTING 10.7    COS Function**

```
SELECT COS(0)
```

**Result**
1

## COT

The COT mathematical function returns the trigonometric cotangent of an angle as shown in Listing 10.8. Specify the radian angle as a float expression.

**Syntax**
COT (float expression)

**LISTING 10.8    COT Function**

```
SELECT COT(90)
```

**Result**
-0.501202783380153

## DEGREES

The DEGRESS function takes an angle in radians as input parameter and returns the angle in degrees as shown in Listing 10.9.

**Syntax**
DEGREES (numerical expression)

**LISTING 10.9    DEGREES Function**

```
SELECT DEGREES (PI())
```

**Result**
180

## EXP

The EXP mathematical function returns the exponential value of a given float expression as shown in Listing 10.10. The input expression can be a float data type or a data type that can implicitly be converted to float.

**Syntax**
EXP (float expression)

**LISTING 10.10 EXPONENTIAL FUNCTION**

```
SELECT EXP (1.5)
```

**Result**
4.48168907033806

## FLOOR

The FLOOR function is used to round a float expression down to a whole number as shown in Listing 10.11. The function accepts a float expression as input and returns the largest integer expression less than or equal to a given numeric expression.

**Syntax**
FLOOR (numeric expression)

**LISTING 10.11    FLOOR Function**

```
SELECT FLOOR ("Unit Price" - "Discount") As Price
, "Unit Price", "Discount" From "Order Details"
```

**Result**

| Price | Unit Price | Discount |
|-------|-----------|----------|
| 27    | 27        | 0        |
| 9     | 9.8       | 0.15     |
| 12    | 12.8      | 0        |
| ..    | ..        | ..       |

## LOG

The LOG mathematical function returns the natural logarithm of a given float expression as shown in Listing 10.12. The float expression can be a float data type or a data type that can implicitly be converted to float.

**Syntax**
LOG (float expression)

LISTING 10.12    LOG Function

```
INSERT INTO AlgorithmTable Values (Log(2), Log (10))
```

Value 0.693147180559945 and 2.30258509299405 will be inserted into AlgorithmTable.

## LOG10

The LOG10 functional returns the base 10 logarithm of an input float expression as shown in Listing 10.13.

### Syntax

LOG10 (float expression)

LISTING 10.13    Logarithm Base 10 Function

```
INSERT INTO AlgorithmTable Values (Log10(10), Log10(100))
```

Values 1 and 2 will be inserted into AlgorithmTable.

## PI

The PI function returns the constant value of PI. Listing 10.14 shows the usage of the PI function.

### Syntax

PI ()

LISTING 10.14    PI Function

```
INSERT INTO FormulaTable Values (PI ())
```

Value 3.14159265358979 will be inserted into FormulaTable.

## POWER

The POWER mathematical function returns the value of a given expression to the specified power. The numerical expression is specified as the first parameter and the second parameter indicates the power as shown in Listing 10.15.

### Syntax

POWER (numeric expression, y)

LISTING 10.15    Power Function

```
INSERT INTO DegreesTable VALUES (DEGREES(PI()), DEGREES(PI()/2))
```

**Result**

Values 180 and 90 will be inserted into FormulaTable.

## RADIANS

The RADIANS mathematical function takes the angle in degrees as input parameter and return the angle in radians as shown in Listing 10.16.

**Syntax**

RADIANS(numeric expression)

**LISTING 10.16     RADIANS Function**

```
INSERT INTO AngleTable VALUES (RADIANS(30), RADIANS(90))
```

**Result**

Values 0 and 1 will be inserted into FormulaTable.

## RAND

The RAND mathematical function returns a random float value between 0 and 1 for a specified integer seed value as shown in Listing 10.17.

**Syntax**

RAND ( [SEED] )

**LISTING 10.17     Random Function**

```
INSERT INTO Game Values (RAND(5), RAND(20), RAND (50)
```

**Result**

The random value generated will be inserted.

## ROUND

The ROUND mathematical function returns a numerical expression rounded to a given length. If the length specified is a positive number, the function rounds the expression to a number of decimal places given as length. If the specified length is a negative number, then the expression is rounded on the left side of the decimal point. Listing 10.18 demonstrates the usage of the ROUND function.

**Syntax**

ROUND(numeric expression, length [, function])

**LISTING 10.18    ROUND Function**

```
SELECT "Unit Price", ROUND("Unit Price", 0) as Price0,
ROUND("Unit Price", 1) As Price1,
ROUND("Unit Price", 2) As Price2
From "Order Details"
```

**Result**

| Price | Price0 | Price1 | Price2 |
|-------|--------|--------|--------|
| 27    | 27     | 27     | 27     |
| 9.8   | 10     | 9.8    | 9.8    |
| 12.8  | 13     | 12.8   | 12.8   |
| ..    | ..     | ..     | ..     |

## SIGN

The SIGN mathematical function returns a positive, zero, or negative sign for a given expression. Listing 10.19 shows the usage of the SIGN function.

**Syntax**

SIGN (numeric expression)

**LISTING 10.19    SIGN Function**

```
SELECT SIGN (SALARY - EMI) From SalaryAccount
```

**Result**

1

## SIN

The SIN function returns the trigonometric sine of a given angle. The angle is specified in radians as a float expression as shown in Listing 10.20.

**Syntax**

SIN (float expression)

**Listing 10.20 SIN Function**

```
SELECT SIN(45)
INSERT INTO FormulaTable Values (SIN(0), SIN(45), SIN(180))
```

## SQRT

The SQRT mathematical function returns the square root of a given float expressionas described in Listing 10.21.

**Syntax**
SQRT (float expression)

**LISTING 10.21    SQRT Function**

```
SELECT SQRT (65536)
SELECT Maxsize, SQRT (Maxsize) FROM DataSize
```

## TAN

The TAN mathematical function returns the tangent of a given float expression as shown in Listing 10.22.

**Syntax**
TAN(float expression)

**LISTING 10.22    TAN Function**

```
SELECT TAN(45)
INSERT INTO FormulaTable Values (TAN(0), TAN(45), TAN(180))
```

# Aggregate Functions

Aggregate functions work on a set of values and return a single value. You will mostly be using the aggregate functions in the Group By clause of a Select statement.

> **NOTE**
>
> Aggregate functions do not work on Image on an ntext data type.

## AVG

The AVG function returns the average value of a set of numeric values as well as the average value of a column in a selection. The NULL values in a selection will be ignored. Listing 10.32 shows the usage of the AVG function.

**Syntax**
AVG ([ALL] expression)

**LISTING 10.23    AVG Function**

```
Select AVG("Unit Price") From Products
```

**Result**

28.8663

On executing the statement, the average unit price of all products from the Northwind database is 28.8663.

## COUNT

The COUNT function returns the number of items in a group as shown in Listing 10.24. You can use COUNT with * to get the total number of rows in a group.

**Syntax**

COUNT ({ [ALL] expression *})

**LISTING 10.24    COUNT Function**

```
Select COUNT(*) As "Total Products" From Products
```

**Result**

77

On executing the statement, the total count of products in the Product table is returned. The result shown from the Northwind database is 77.

> **NOTE**
>
> Count function does not ignore NULL values.

## MAX

The MAX function returns the maximum value from a set of values as shown in Listing 10.25. For a numeric category data type it returns the highest value. For character category values, MAX returns the highest value as specified by a collating sequence.

**Syntax**

MAX ([ALL] expression)

**LISTING 10.25    MAX Function**

```
Select MAX ("Unit Price") From Products
```

**Result**

263.5

On executing the statement, the maximum product price is displayed. The result shown from the Northwind database is 263.5.

The MAX function works on dates. The statement below determines the Date of Birth of the youngest employee.

```
Select MAX("Birth Date") From Employees
```

> **NOTE**
>
> The MAX function does not work with bit data types.

## MIN

The MIN aggregate function is the opposite of the MAX function. It returns the minimum value from a set of values as shown in Listing 10.26. For character category values, MIN returns the lowest value in a collating sequence.

The collation sequence is used to compare the value of a column.

> **NOTE**
>
> The MIN function cannot be used for bit columns.

**Syntax**
MIN ([ALL] expression)

**LISTING 10.26     MIN Function**

```
Select MIN ("Unit Price") From Products
```

**Result**
2.5

On executing the statement, the minimum product price is displayed. The result shown from the Northwind database is 2.5.

The MIN function works with dates. The statement below determines the Date of Birth of the eldest employee.

```
Select MIN("Birth Date") From Employees
```

## SUM

The SUM aggregate function adds all values in the set of values and returns the SUM of values as shown in Listing 10.27.

**Syntax**
SUM ([ALL] expression)

**LISTING 10.27    SUM Function**

```
Select SUM ("Unit Price") From Products
```

**Result**

2222.71

The SQL statement aggregates the sum of the unit price of all products. On executing the result it shows a value of 2222.71.

> **NOTE**
>
> A Bit column cannot be used with a SUM function.

# String Functions

The String function operates on string and integer values. The string value is a data type of nchar, nvarchar, or ntext. String functions are used to manipulate strings or convert an integer value to a character value.

## NCHAR

The NCHAR function takes an integer expression as input and returns the Unicode character. The integer expression should be a number between 0 and 65535. A value outside the range will result in a return value of NULL. Listing 10.28 demonstrates the usage of the NCHAR function.

**Syntax**

NCHAR (integer_expression)

**LISTING 10.28    NChar Function**

```
SELECT NCHAR (UNICODE ("First Name")) As Initials From Employees;
```

**Result**

| Initials |
| --- |
| N |
| A |
| J |
| M |
| .. |

# CHARINDEX

The CHARINDEX function returns the starting position of a string expression in a string. You can also optionally specify the start position to search for a string. The first parameter expression is the string that you wish to search. The second parameter is the column name for a specified search. The first and second parameters are NText or a type that can be implicitly converted to NVarchar. The third optional parameter type is tinyint, smallint, int, or bigint. Listing 10.29 shows the usage of the CHARINDEX function.

### Syntax
CHARINDEX (expression1, expression2, [, start_location])

### LISTING 10.29    CHARINDEX Function

```
SELECT "Postal Code" , CHARINDEX ('980',"Postal Code")
As "Starting Position" From Employees;
```

### Result

| PostalCode | Starting Position |
| --- | --- |
| 98122 | 0 |
| 98401 | 0 |
| 98033 | 1 |
| 98052 | 1 |
| .. | .. |

```
SELECT "Postal Code" , CHARINDEX ('80',"Postal Code", 1) As "Starting Position"
From Employees
```

### Result

| PostalCode | Starting Position |
| --- | --- |
| 98122 | 0 |
| 98401 | 0 |
| 98033 | 2 |
| 98052 | 2 |
| .. | .. |

# LEN

The LEN function returns the length of a string expression as shown in Listing 10.30. The string expression can be any data type that can be implicitly converted to nvarchar. It returns the number of character strings including blanks.

**Syntax**

LEN (string_expression)

**Listing 10.30 LEN Function**

```
SELECT "First Name", LEN("First Name") As Length FROM Employees
```

**Result**

| First Name | Length |
|------------|--------|
| Nancy | 5 |
| Andrew | 6 |
| Janet | 5 |
| Margaret | 8 |
| .. | .. |

## LOWER

As the name suggests, the LOWER function takes a character expression as input and converts its uppercase letters into lowercase characters as shown in Listing 10.31. The function takes the input parameter as a data type that can implicitly be converted to nvarchar or ntext.

## Syntax

LOWER (character_expression)

**LISTING 10.31    LOWER Function**

```
SELECT "First Name", LOWER("First Name") As LowerCaseName FROM Employees
```

**Result**

| First Name | LowerCaseName |
|------------|---------------|
| Nancy | nancy |
| Andrew | andrew |
| Janet | janet |
| .. | .. |

## LTRIM

The LTRIM string function takes a character expression as input and returns the character expression after removing its leading blank spaces as shown in Listing 10.32. You can specify a column name in a character expression in a Select query. LTRIM will remove the blank spaces for all rows.

**Syntax**

LTRIM (character_expression)

**LISTING 10.32    LTRIM Function**

```
SELECT LTRIM(Address) As Address From Employees
```

**Result**

| Address |
| --- |
| 507 - 20th Ave. E.  Apt. 2A |
| 908 W. Capital Way |
| 722 Moss Bay Blvd. |
| .. |

# PATINDEX

The PATINDEX function returns the starting position of the first occurrence of a pattern. It returns a zero if the pattern is not found in a character expression. As it is a pattern you can input a string. You can also specify a wild character as part of a string. Listing 10.33 show the usage of the PATINDEX function.

**Syntax**

PATINDEX('%pattern%', expression)

**LISTING 10.33    PATINDEX Function**

```
SELECT "Postal Code" , PATINDEX ('980%',"Postal Code") StartPosition From Employees
```

**Result**

| Postal Code | Start Position |
| --- | --- |
| 98122 | 0 |
| 98401 | 0 |
| 98033 | 1 |
| 98052 | 1 |
| SW1 8JR | 0 |
| .. | .. |

```
SELECT "Postal Code" , PATINDEX ('%80%',"Postal Code") StartPosition From Employees
```

**Result**

| Postal Code | Start Position |
|-------------|----------------|
| 98122 | 0 |
| 98401 | 0 |
| 98033 | 2 |
| 98052 | 2 |
| SW1 8JR | 0 |

## REPLACE

The REPLACE function takes three string expressions as input. It finds the occurrence of a second string in a first string and replaces the second string expression occurrence with a third string expression. Listing 10.34 shows the usage of the REPLACE function.

All three string expressions can be a data type that can implicitly be converted to nvarchar or ntext.

**Syntax**
REPLACE ('string_expression1', 'string_expression2', 'string_expression3')

**LISTING 10.34     REPLACE Function**

```
SELECT "Company Name", Phone, REPLACE( Phone, '(91)', '(912)') As NewPhone From
Customers
```

**Result**

| Company Name | Phone | NewPhone |
|--------------|-------|----------|
| Ernst Handel | 7675-3425 | 7675-3425 |
| Familia Arquibaldo | (11) 555-9857 | (11) 555-9857 |
| FISSA Fabrica Inter. Salchichas S.A. | (91) 555 94 44 | (912) 555 94 44 |
| .. | .. | .. |

## REPLICATE

With the REPLICATE function you can repeat an alphanumeric character expression a specified number of times. The first parameter to function is an alphanumeric character expression that can implicitly be converted to the nvarchar or ntext data type. The second parameter is a data type that can implicitly be converted to int. Listing 10.35 shows the usage of the REPLICATE function.

**Syntax**
REPLICATE (character_expression, integer_expression)

**LISTING 10.35    REPLICATE Function**

```
SELECT Replicate (TitleSong, 5) From Music;
```

## RTRIM

The RTRIM string function takes a character expression as input and returns the character expression after removing its trailing blank spaces. This function is similar to LTRIM that removes leading spaces from a character expression. The string expression is any data type that can implicitly be converted to nvarchar or ntext. Listing 10.36 shows the usage of the RTRIM function.

**Syntax**

RTRIM (character_expression)

**LISTING 10.36    RTRIM Function**

```
SELECT "Contact Name", RTRIM(Address) As Address FROM Customers;
```

**Result**

| Contact Name | Address |
| --- | --- |
| Maria Anders | Obere Str. 57 |
| Ana Trujillo | Avda. de la Constitución 2222 |
| Antonio Moreno | Mataderos  2312 |
| Thomas Hardy | 120 Hanover Sq. |
| .. | .. |

## SPACE

The SPACE function has one argument of data type that can implicitly be converted to int. The function returns a repeated sequence of spaces specified by an integer expression. Listing 10.37 demonstrates the usage of the SPACE function.

**Syntax**

SPACE (integer_expression)

**LISTING 10.37    SPACE Function**

```
SELECT "Contact Name" + SPACE(2) + Address + SPACE(2) + City As CompleteAddress
FROM Customers
```

**Result**

| CompleteAddress |
| --- |
| Maria Anders  Obere Str. 57  Berlin |
| Ana Trujillo  Avda. de la Constitución 2222  México D.F. |
| Antonio Moreno  Mataderos  2312  México D.F. |
| .. |

# STR

The STR function returns the numerical data into character data. The function takes the input parameter of a data type that can implicitly be converted to float. You can also provide additional optional parameters to specify the total length including decimal point, sign, digit, and spaces as shown in Listing 10.38. The decimal parameter specifies the number of places to the right of a decimal point.

**Syntax**
STR (float_expression [, length [, decimal]])

**LISTING 10.38    STR Function**

```
SELECT STR(Freight, 8,1) From Orders;
SELECT Freight, STR(Freight, 8,1)As NewFreight From Orders;
```

**Result**

| Freight | NewFreight |
| --- | --- |
| 4.45 | 4.5 |
| 79.45 | 79.5 |
| 36.18 | 36.2 |
| .. | .. |

# STUFF

The STUFF function removes the specified length of a character and inserts a new character string from a specified starting position as shown in Listing 10.39. The input character string/expressions can be of any data type that can implicitly be converted to nvarchar or ntext. The length parameter and start position parameter can be a data type that can implicitly be converted to int.

**Syntax**
STUFF (character_expression, start, length, character_expression)

**LISTING 10.39    STUFF Function**

```
SELECT  "Postal Code", STUFF("Postal Code", 2,2,'XXX') As "New Postal Code"
From Customers
```

**Result**

| Postal Code | New Postal Code |
|-------------|-----------------|
| WA1 1DP | WXXX 1DP |
| S-958 22 | SXXX58 22 |
| 68306 | 6XXX06 |
| .. | .. |

## SUBSTRING

Using the SUBSTRING function you can get part of a string as shown in Listing 10.40. With SUBSTRING you will specify the character expression string, start position of a substring, and the length of substrings. The length and start position can be a data type that can implicitly be converted to integer. The character expression can be a string, binary string, image, text, or an expression that includes a column.

**Syntax**
SUBSTRING (expression, start, length)

**LISTING 10.40    SUBSTRING Function**

```
SELECT "First Name", SUBSTRING("First Name", 1,1) AS Initial From Employees
```

**Result**

| First Name | Initials |
|------------|----------|
| Nancy | N |
| Andrew | A |
| Janet | J |
| .. | .. |

## UNICODE

The UNICODE function returns the integer value as defined by a Unicode standard for the first character of input expression as shown in Listing 10.41.

**Syntax**
UNICODE ('ncharacter_expression')

**LISTING 10.41    UNICODE Function**

```
SELECT "Customer ID", UNICODE ("Customer ID") From Orders
```

**Result**

| Customer ID | Column1 |
|---|---|
| FRANS | 70 |
| MEREP | 77 |
| FOLKO | 70 |
| .. | .. |

## UPPER

The UPPER function takes an input character expression, converts the lowercase equivalents, and returns the uppercase string as shown in Listing 10.42.

**Syntax**
UPPER (character_expression)

**LISTING 10.42    UPPER Function**

```
SELECT "Product Name", UPPER("Product Name") As NewProductName From Products
```

**Result**

| Product Name | NewProductName |
|---|---|
| Chai | CHAI |
| Chang | CHANG |
| Aniseed Syrup | ANISEED SYRUP |
| .. | .. |

# DATETIME Functions

SQL Server Compact Edition has built-in functions to do operations on the date and time. The result of Date/Time functions can be date/time, string, or numeric values.

The DateTime function uses a DatePart parameter. You can specify the date part with the abbreviations given in Table 10.1.

**TABLE 10.1    Date Part Abbreviations**

| Date Part | Abbreviations |
|---|---|
| Year | yy, yyyy |
| Quarter | qq, q |
| Month | mm,m |
| Day Of Year | dy, y |
| Day | dd, d |
| Week | wk, ww |
| Hour | Hh |
| Minute | mi, n |
| Second | Ss, s |
| Millisecond | Ms |

# DATEADD

Use the DATEADD function to add a specific interval to a date. The result of the DATEADD function will be a valid date. You can add an interval to any part of a date—year, month, or day as shown in Listing 10.43.

The DATEADD function has three parameters:

- Interval—the interval that you want to add.

- Number—the number of intervals you want to add.

- Date—the date to which an interval is added.

**Syntax**
DATEADD (datepart, number, date)

**LISTING 10.43    DATEADD Function**

```
SELECT "Hire Date", DATEADD (month, 1, "Hire Date") As "Project StartDate" From
Employees
SELECT "Hire Date", DATEADD (mm, 1, "Hire Date") As "Project StartDate" From
Employees
SELECT "Hire Date", DATEADD (m, 1, "Hire Date") As "Project StartDate" From
Employees
```

**Result**

| Hire Date | Project Start Date |
|---|---|
| 1991-03-29 00:00:00.000 | 1991-04-29 00:00:00.000 |
| 1991-07-12 00:00:00.000 | 1991-08-12 00:00:00.000 |
| 1991-02-27 00:00:00.000 | 1991-03-27 00:00:00.000 |
| .. | .. |

## DATEDIFF

The DATEDIFF function returns the number of date parts between a given period. The DATEPART function accepts a start date, end date, and a date part option as shown in Listing 10.44. A date part option can have values such as year, quarter, month, day of year, day, week, hour, minute, second, and millisecond. These options were discussed in the DATEADD function section.

### Syntax
DATEDIFF (datepart, startdate, enddate)

**LISTING 10.44    DATEDIFF Function**

```
SELECT  "Order Date", "Required Date", DATEDIFF (d, "Order Date", "Required Date")
AS "Days Left" FROM Orders ;
SELECT  "Order Date", "Required Date", DATEDIFF (dd, "Order Date", "Required Date")
AS "Days Left" FROM Orders ;
```

### Result

| Order Date | Required Date | Days Left |
|---|---|---|
| 1992-10-20 00:00:00.000 | 1992-12-01 00:00:00.000 | 42 |
| 1992-10-21 00:00:00.000 | 1992-11-18 00:00:00.000 | 28 |
| 1992-10-22 00:00:00.000 | 1992-12-03 00:00:00.000 | 42 |
| .. | .. | .. |

```
SELECT  "Hire Date", DATEDIFF (m, "Hire Date", '2007-05-01') AS "Month Completed"
FROM Employees ;
SELECT  "Hire Date", DATEDIFF (mm, "Hire Date", '2007-05-01') AS "Month Completed"
FROM Employees ;
```

### Result

| Hire Date | Months completed |
|---|---|
| 1991-03-29 00:00:00.000 | 194 |
| 1991-07-12 00:00:00.000 | 190 |
| 1991-02-27 00:00:00.000 | 195 |
| .. | .. |

```
SELECT  "Hire Date", DATEDIFF (yy, "Hire Date", '2007-05-01') AS "Years Completed"
FROM Employees ;
SELECT  "Hire Date", DATEDIFF (yyyy, "Hire Date", '2007-05-01') AS "Years
Completed"
FROM Employees ;
```

**Result**

| Hire Date | Years |
|---|---|
| 1991-03-29 00:00:00.000 | 16 |
| 1991-07-12 00:00:00.000 | 16 |
| 1991-02-27 00:00:00.000 | 16 |

## DATEPART

The DATEPART function returns the date part of a given date as shown in Listing 10.45.

**Syntax**

DATEPART (datepart, date)

**LISTING 10.45    DATEPART Function**

```
SELECT DATEPART(d, "Order Date") As "Day of Month" From Orders;
SELECT DATEPART(m, "Order Date") As "Order Month" From Orders;
SELECT DATEPART(mi, "Birth Date") From Employees;
SELECT "Order Date",DATEPART(d, "Order Date") As "Day of Month" From Orders;
```

**Result**

| Order Date | Day of Month |
|---|---|
| 1991-05-10 14:58:17.347 | 10 |
| 1991-05-13 00:00:00.000 | 13 |
| 1991-05-14 00:00:00.000 | 14 |
| .. | .. |

```
SELECT "Order Date",DATEPART(m, "Order Date") As "Month" From Orders;
```

**Result**

| Order Date | Month |
|---|---|
| 1991-05-10 14:58:17.347 | 5 |
| 1991-05-13 00:00:00.000 | 5 |
| 1991-05-14 00:00:00.000 | 5 |
| .. | .. |

```
SELECT "Order Date",DATEPART(mi, "Order Date") As "Minute" From Orders;
```

**Result**

| Order Date | Minute |
|---|---|
| 1991-05-10 14:58:17.347 | 58 |
| 1991-05-13 00:00:00.000 | 0 |
| .. | .. |

## DATENAME

The DATENAME function has two input parameters—datepart and date. The DATENAME function returns the string name of a specified date part of a given date. The date part values have already been specified. Listing 10.46 descries the usage of the DATENAME function.

**Syntax**
DATENAME (datepart, date)

**LISTING 10.46    DATENAME Function**

```
SELECT "Hire Date", DATENAME(month, "Hire Date") As "Hire Month"
From Employees;
```

**Result**

| Hire Date | Hire Month |
|---|---|
| 1991-03-29 00:00:00.000 | March |
| 1991-07-12 00:00:00.000 | July |
| 1991-02-27 00:00:00.000 | February |
| .. | .. |

```
SELECT "Hire Date", DATENAME(qq, "Hire Date") As "Hire Quarter"
From Employees;
```

**Result**

| Hire Date | Hire Quarter |
|---|---|
| 1991-03-29 00:00:00.000 | 1 |
| 1991-07-12 00:00:00.000 | 3 |
| 1991-02-27 00:00:00.000 | 1 |
| .. | .. |

## GETDATE

The GETDATE function returns the current system's date and time as shown in Listing 10.47.

**Syntax**
GETDATE()

**LISTING 10.47   GETDATE Function**

```
INSERT INTO "Orders Details" ("Order ID", OrderDate) VALUES (512,          ());
```

The statement will add "Order Details" with Order Date as System Date.

# System Functions

The system functions available in SQL Server Compact Edition return and operate on SQL Server Compact Edition objects and settings.

## @@IDENTITY

The @@IDENTITY function returns the last inserted identity value generated by an insert statement. When a record is inserted into a table with an identity column, the @@IDENTITY function returns the value last inserted into the column.

Identity Columns are AutoNumber columns. The values in Identity Columns are inserted by the SQL Server Compact Edition database and not by the user.

**Syntax**
@@Identity

Listing 10.48 demonstrates the @@IDENTITY function. The Table PatientsHistory has an Identity column PatientHistoryID. A user does not need to specify the value of PatientHistoryID.

The PatientHistoryID value will be the addition of a previous row and increment value; for example, if the PatientHistory table has 5 rows and PatientHistoryID values are 2001 to 2005.

**LISTING 10.48   @@IDENTITY Function**

```
INSERT INTO [PatientHistory]

            ([PatientRegNo]
            ,[DiseaseIdentified]
            ,[DateIdentified]
            ,[Treatment]
            ,[TreatmentStartDate]
            ,[TreatmentEndDate]
            )
     VALUES
```

```
        ('PER1000051'
        ,'Short sight'
        ,'2005-03-24'
        ,'Contact Lens'
        ,'2005-03-24'
        ,null
        );
SELECT @@IDENTITY AS NewIdentity;
```

After executing the above statement, you will get the result 2006 as the value of NewIdentity.

## COALESCE

You can specify the n expression to the COALESCE function as shown in Listing 10.49. The function returns first a NONNULL expression. The function returns a NULL if all input expressions are NULL.

**Syntax**
COALESCE(expression[,.....n])

**LISTING 10.49    COALESCE Function**

```
SELECT COALESCE (HomePhone, WorkPhone, CellPhone) From Contact
```

Executing the above statement will give the first available phone number.

## DATALENGTH

The DATALENGTH function returns the number of bytes used to represent any given expression. Listing 10.50 describes the usage of the DATALENGTH function.

**Syntax**
DATALENGTH(expression)

The next statement will return 40 for all rows in a table as the HomePhone column is a data type NChar and has a fixed length of 20.

**LISTING 10.50    DATELENGTH Function**

```
Select Datalength (HomePhone) From Contact
```

Similarly using the DATALENGTH function with numeric and date fields will provide the same result for all rows as the length of the numeric and date fields are fixed.

The DATALENGTH function is more useful for variable length data type columns. The second statement returns the number of bytes for the City field. City field is a Nvarchar type.

```
Select City , DataLength(City) As ColumnLength From Customers
```

**Result**

| City | ColumnLength |
|------|--------------|
| London | 12 |
| Paris | 10 |
| Redmond | 14 |

The code statement below gives the size of employee photos. The photo field is an image type. By knowing the total number of photos and their size, the application can indicate to the user how much time it will take to transfer/copy the photos.

```
Select DataLength(Photo) From Employees
```

# Others

## CASE

The CASE function is similar to the Case statement of programming languages. The function evaluates a list of conditions and returns one possible outcome as shown in Listing 10.51.

You can use CASE function in two modes:

- Comparing an expression with a set of expressions to return a result.

- Searching CASE evaluates a set of boolean expressions to determine a result.

Both these options can have ELSE arguments.

Case expressions allow conditional processing within SQL statements. Without a Case statement, the same logic will be applied in a managed or native application.

**Syntax**

**Mode 1 Syntax**
CASE input expression

```
WHEN when_expression THEN Result

_expression

      [....n]
[
      ELSE else_Result
_espression
]
END
```

**Mode 2 Syntax**

```
CASE

WHEN Boolean_expression THEN Result

_expression

    [....n]
[
    ELSE else_Result
_espression
]
END
```

**LISTING 10.51    CASE Function**

```
SELECT "Product Name", "Category ID", CASE "Category ID"
    WHEN 1 THEN 'Category 1'
    WHEN 2 THEN 'Category 2'
    WHEN 3 THEN 'Category 3'
        ELSE 'Unknown'
        END
As CategoryName
FROM Products
```

**Result**

| Product Name | Category ID | Category Name |
| --- | --- | --- |
| Chai | 1 | Category 1 |
| Chang | 1 | Category 1 |
| Aniseed Syrup | 2 | Category 2 |
| .. | .. | .. |

```
SELECT
CASE
WHEN GetDate () < '07/01/2007'
    Then 'First Half of year'
ELSE 'Second Half of year'
END
```

**Result**

```
First Half of year
```

# CONVERT

The CONVERT function converts an expression of one data type to another data type. The first argument to function is the target data type that you want to convert. The second data type is the actual expression that you wish to convert. With the first argument you can specify the optional length parameter. With the second argument you can specify the optional style argument. Tables 10.2, 10.3, and 10.4 describe the styles for Float and Real, Money, and Date data types. The style parameter converts the style of data types. Listing 10.52 describes the usage of the CONVERT function.

## Syntax
CONVERT (data type [(length)], expression [, style])

**TABLE 10.2    Styles for Float and Real**

| Value | Output |
|---|---|
| 0 | Maximum of 6 digits. It can be used in scientific notation. This is the default value. |
| 1 | 8 digits. Used in scientific notation. |
| 2 | 16 digits. Used in scientific notation. |

**TABLE 10.3    Styles for Money**

| Value | Output |
|---|---|
| 0 | With this option:<br>There will be 2 digits after the decimal point.<br>There will be no commas to the left of the decimal point.<br>Example: 54985.62 |
| 1 | With this option:<br>There will be 2 digits after the decimal point.<br>There will be a comma every 3 digits to the left of the decimal point.<br>Example: 54,985.62 |
| 2 | With this option:<br>There will be 4 digits after the decimal point.<br>There will be no commas to the left of the decimal point.<br>Example: 54985.6208 |

TABLE 10.4    Styles for Dates

| Without Century (YY) | With Century (YYYY) | Standard | Input/Output | Example |
|---|---|---|---|---|
| - | 0 or 100 | Default | Mon dd yyyy hh:miAM(or PM | May 10 1991 2:58PM |
| 1 | 101 | USA | mm/dd/yy | 05/10/1991 |
| 2 | 102 | ANSI | yy.mm.dd | 1991.05.10 |
| 3 | 103 | British/French | dd/mm/yy | 10/05/1991 |
| 4 | 104 | German | dd.mm.yy | 10.05.1991 |
| 5 | 105 | Italian | dd-mm-yy | 10-05-1991 |
| 6 | 106 | | dd mon yy | 10 May 1991 |
| 7 | 107 | | Mon dd,yy | May 10, 1991 |
| 8 | 108 | | hh:mm:ss | 14:58:17 |
| - | 9 or 109 | Default + milliseconds | Mon dd yyyy hh:mi:ss:mmmmAM (or PM) | May 10 1991 2:58:17:347PM |
| 10 | 110 | USA | mm-dd-yy | 05-10-1991 |
| 11 | 111 | JAPAN | yy/mm/dd | 1991/05/10 |
| 12 | 112 | ISO | Yymmdd | 19910510 |
| - | 13 or 113 | Europe Default + milliseconds | dd mon yyyy hh:mm:ss:mmm(24h) | 10 May 1991 14:58:17:347 |
| 14 | 114 | | hh:mi:ss:mmm(24h) | 14:58:17:347 |
| - | 20 or 120 | ODBC canonical | yyyy-mm-dd hh:mi:ss(24h) | 1991-05-10 14:58:17 |
| - | 21 or 121 | ODBC canonical (with milliseconds) | Yyyy-mm-dd hh:mi:ss.mmm(24h) | 1991-05-10 14:58:17.347 |
| - | 126 | ISO8601 | yyyy-mm-ddThh:mm: ss.mmm(no spaces) | 1991-05-10T14: 58:17.347 Use for XML. |
| - | 130 | Hijri | dd mon yyyy hh:mi:ss:mmmAM | Month will be written in Arabic language. |
| - | 131 | Hijri | dd/mm/yy hh:mi:ss:mmmAM | 26/10/1411 2:58:17:347PM |

NOTE

SQL Server Compact Edition uses a Kuwaiti algorithm for the Hijri calendar.

**LISTING 10.52     CONVERT Function**

```
SELECT "Order Date", CONVERT (nvarchar(10), "Order Date", 101) As ConvertedDate
From Orders
```

**Result**

| Order Date | ConvertedDate |
| --- | --- |
| 1991-05-10 14:58:17.347 | 5/10/1991 |
| 1991-05-13 00:00:00.000 | 5/13/1991 |
| 1991-05-14 00:00:00.000 | 5/14/1991 |
| .. | .. |

```
SELECT "Order Date", CONVERT (nvarchar(30), "Order Date", 114) From Orders
```

**Result**

| Order Date | Time |
| --- | --- |
| 1991-05-10 14:58:17.347 | 14:58:17:347 |
| 1991-05-13 00:00:00.000 | 00:00:00:000 |
| 1991-05-14 00:00:00.000 | 00:00:00:000 |
| .. | .. |

## NEWID

The NEWID function creates a unique type value of uniqueidentifier as shown in Listing 10.53.

**Syntax**
NEWID()

**LISTING 10.53     New ID Function**

```
INSERT INTO PARTS VALUES (NEWID,'New Value')
```

# Summary

This chapter provides a complete reference to all Mathematical, Aggregate, String, Date, and System functions. It is important that you are aware of the built-in functions provided by your database and utilize these functions to implement functionality that otherwise would require multiple SQL and procedural language statements.

# Upgrading from a Previous Version

SQL Server 2005 Compact Edition replaces the Microsoft SQL Server 2000 Windows CE Edition (SQL Server CE version 2.0). The SQL Server Compact Edition 3.x database file is not compatible with the SQL Server CE 2.0 database file. If you have used this previous version, you may find a need to upgrade your database file to the new format before leveraging this database engine.  Although the binary format of some of the previous databases is not supported in this release, a tool is available to aid in the migration of schema and data to the new database format. The upgrade tool can be used to upgrade SQL Server CE 1.0, 1.1, or 2.0 database files, and there is no need to upgrade an SQL Server 2005 Mobile Edition 3.0 database as this database file format is compatible.

## Options for Upgrade

There are a few different way to approach a migration of a database file. If the application and all of the data in your client database is synchronized using replication or remote data access, you can simply migrate your application and database using the replication technologies. To do this you will need to first ensure that the client side database is synchronized, and then proceed to remove the subscription, upgrading your application and database engine, and then create a new subscription. You will find more details on how to create and remove an SQL Server subscription in Chapter 12 *Synchronizing Data with Merger Replication*. If you have data local to the device that must be migrated, you can either roll your own migration application or leverage the command-line upgrade tool available with SQL Server Compact. The environment necessary to complete the migration of a database file using the upgrade tool (upgrade.exe) will, however, require both database engines installed on a device or device emulator, since the previous version is only supported on mobile devices.

### Upgrade Options Overview

- Use replication technologies with distributed applications.

- Roll your own upgrade library or tool.

- Use the SQL Server 2005 Compact Edition upgrade tool.

Your development environment for a client application includes Visual Studio, .NET Compact Framework, and SQL Server Compact Edition. When you migrate from SQL CE 2.0 to SQL Server Compact Edition 3.0, you will also want to migrate your development environment. This chapter will take you through the following three simple tools that you can use to migrate SQL CE, Visual Studio Project, and .NET Compact Framework version:

- Upgrade utility to migrate SQL CE 2.0 to SQL Server Compact Edition 3.0.

- Conversion Wizard to migrate Visual Studio 2003 Solutions and Projects to Visual Studio 2005 Solutions and Projects.

- Upgrade Project option to convert .NET Compact Framework 1.0 projects to .NET Compact Framework 2.0 projects.

Rolling your own upgrade application or library is well outside the scope of this book— instead we will discuss upgrading a distributed application that leverages SQL Server Compact Edition replication technologies using the SQL Server Compact Edition upgrade tool.

## Upgrading a Database Using Replication or RDA

If your application is distributed and all the data stored in SQL Server CE 2.0 uses Merge Replication or Remote Data Access with SQL Server 2000 as a connectivity solution, upgrading a client application database can be very straightforward. SQL Server Compact Edition can synchronize the data with SQL Server 2000 and SQL Server 2005. The new database should synchronize the data with a backend server.

- Set up a Replication between the new SQL Server Compact Edition 3.x database and the earlier SQL Server 2000 database.

- Upgrade SQL Server 2000 to SQL Server 2005 and set up a Merge Replication or RDA between the SQL Server Compact Edition 3.x database and the SQL Server 2005 database.

You are going to want to configure your server environment for replication with SQL Server Compact Edition as it is covered in Chapter 12, *Synchronizing Data with Merge Replication,* and Chapter 13, *Synchronizing Data with Remote Data Access.* As you deploy

SQL Server Compact Edition client components, you are going to then need to update your application replication property **InternetURL**, so that it points to the SQL Server Compact Edition Server Agent, sqlcesa30.dll.

A path specified by **InternetURL** is a virtual directory and it contains Server Agent dll. As Server Agent dlls are different for SQL CE 2.0 and SQL Server Compact Edition (3.0 and 3.1), you need to modify this property to point to a path where sqlcesa30.dll exists.

### Database Upgrade Process

To upgrade the SQL Server Compact Edition database using Replication or RDA, synchronize the data and transfer the SQL CE content to a backend server. Set up IIS Web Server to synchronize data with the newer version of SQL Server Compact Edition. Finally synchronize data to bring data from SQL Server to SQL Server Compact Edition. Perform the following steps to complete the upgrade of your application.

1. Synchronize your client application.

2. Back up or remove the database file.

3. Install the Server Agent component appropriate for SQL Server Compact Edition and backend SQL Server version.

4. Update the application to use SQL Server Compact Edition (3.0 or 3.1) and change the **InternetURL** replication property to use the correct server agent.

5. Re-create the subscription and synchronize or repull

6. Ensure the upgrade application is functioning and remove the old client components and application.


## How the Upgrade Tool Works

The upgrade tool will connect to the source database using SQL Server CE 2.0; if that is not available, it will attempt SQL Server 1.1 and then 1.0. If those database engines or their OLE DB providers are unavailable, then upgrade.exe will fail with an error, "SQL Server CE 1.1 or higher must already be installed." The upgrade tool then reads the schema information from the source database and uses that schema to create a new SQL Server Compact Edition (3.0 and 3.1) database as depicted in Figure 11.1. Also note that if a unique constraint is specified on a column without specifying NULL or NOT NULL attributes, the upgrade utility will create the column with a NOT NULL attribute in the new database. The upgrade utility then reads data from the source database using the previous SQL Server CE database engine and writes that data to the destination database using the SQL Server Compact Edition database engine, as depicted in Figure 11.1. The upgrade utility does generate a log file named upgrade.log which is stored in the same location as upgrade.exe and will be overwritten every time the upgrade utility runs. The SQL Server Compact Edition database upgrade utility does not upgrade tracking or subscription information. If you are using SQL Server replication to synchronize data, you will need to re-create the subscription with the new database after running the upgrade utility.

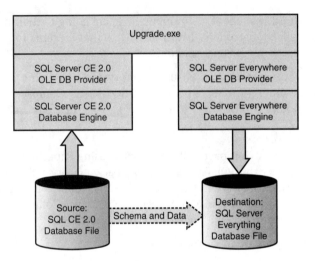

FIGURE 11.1    Upgrade Utility Architecture

### Database Upgrade Tool Prerequisites

- Must perform the upgrade on the device.

- SQL Server CE 2.0, 1.1, or 1.0 must be installed on the device.

- SQL Server Compact OLE DB Provider must be installed and registered.

- SQL Server 2005 Compact Edition must be installed on the device.

### Platform Consideration for Upgrade

To use the upgrade tool, both versions of SQL Server Compact Edition should exist on the same machine. The previous version of SQL CE (version 2.0) is supported on devices running Windows CE and Windows Mobile platform. SQL Server CE is supported on Windows CE.NET 4.2 but SQL Server Compact Edition 3.1 is not supported on Windows CE.NET 4.2. This means that you can't use the upgrade utility on the Windows CE.NET 4.2 version. To use the upgrade utility you need to choose Windows Mobile 2003, Windows Mobile 5.0, or Windows CE 5.0 platform.

### Using the Upgrade Tool

To upgrade a database you will first need to understand how to configure the environment, and then discuss using the tool to complete the migration as well as the upgrade log file that is generated. If you do not already have a previous version of SQL Server CE installed matching the source database file and application be it version 2.0, 1.1, or 1.0, you will need to install this to use the upgrade utility.

If your device does not already have the SQL Server Compact Edition client components installed, you will need to do this. The default location of this file, as shown in Figure 11.2, is `<drive>:\Program Files\Microsoft Visual Studio 8\SmartDevices\SDK\SQL Server\Mobile\v3.0\[platform]\[processor]\sqlce30.ppc.[platform].[processor].`

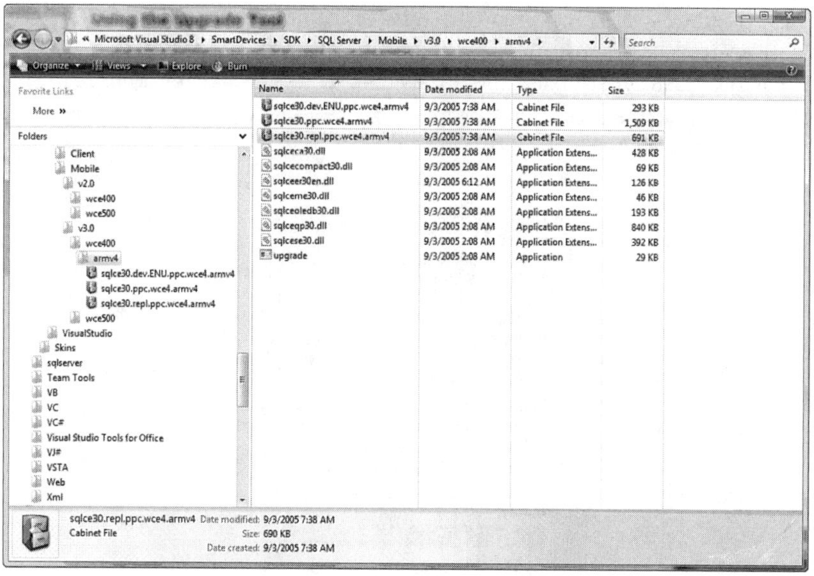

**FIGURE 11.2**    Upgrade Utility Location

cab. You are also going to need to either install the replication components or install and register the OLE DB provider for SQL Server Compact Edition to use the upgrade tool. You can find the replication components in the same directory named sqlce30.repl.ppc.[platform].[processor] as shown in Figure 11.3.

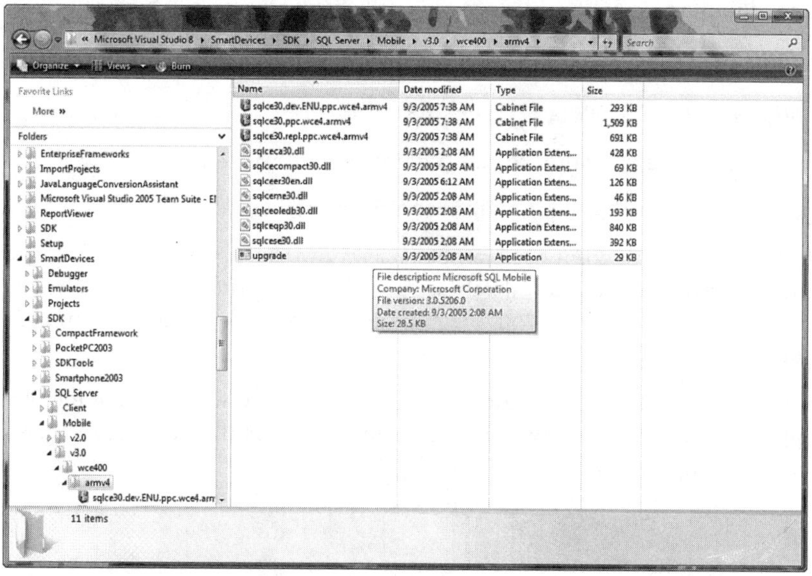

**FIGURE 11.3**    SQL Server Compact Edition Location

The database upgrade tool is installed with Visual Studio 2005 as part of SqlMobile30DevTools[lang].msi file. The default location of the file is `<drive>:\Program Files\Microsoft Visual Studio 8\SmartDevices\SDK\SQL Server\Mobile\v3.0\[plat-form]\[processor]\upgrade.exe` as shown in Figure 11.4. You can copy upgrade.exe to the device using activesync.

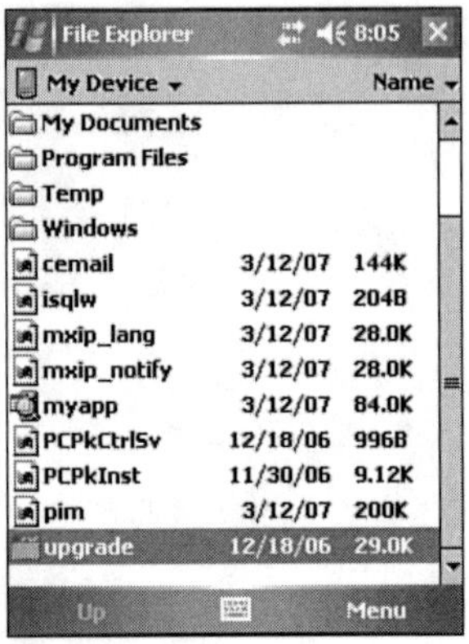

**FIGURE 11.4    Running the Upgrade Utility**

The SQL Server Compact Edition upgrade tool is a command line tool, so you may need to use one of the many utilities available for download to run this or create your own application to run it.

**Options for Running Command Line Applications on Windows Mobile Devices**

- Visual Studio 2005: Device Command Shell found on gotdotnet.

- Windows Mobile Developer Power Toys.

- Write your own application to call the upgrade utility.

- Open the command prompt window on supported devices.

The upgrade tool has a handful of parameters, as shown in Table 11.1, allowing you to specify the source and destination database as well as passwords. You can even specify a silent upgrade which is handy if you are going to be invoking the utility from another application.

If you have a source database file named myapp.sdf and you want to upgrade that to mynewapp.sdf, you would simply call upgrade.exe and pass the necessary values for the required parameters as shown in Figure 11.5.

**TABLE 11.1     Upgrade Utility Parameters**

| Parameter | Description |
| --- | --- |
| /s | The path of the source database file (required). |
| /sp | The password for the source database file (optional). |
| /d | The path of the destination database file. If you specify an existing file, the file will be overwritten (required). |
| /dp | The password for the destination database file (optional). |
| /e | If specified, the destination database will be encrypted. If you specify the /e parameter, you must also specify /dp and provide a password (optional). |
| /q | Perform the upgrade silently without any UI (optional). |
| /? | Displays this list of parameters (optional). |

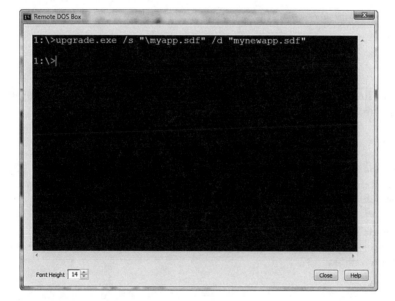

**FIGURE 11.5**   Upgrade Utility Command Line

Figure 11.6 shows the output message displayed by the Upgrade utility.

The upgrade tool does not make any changes in the source database file. It creates a new database file with the destination database name that you specified. You can use the parameters mentioned in Table 11.1 to specify the password for a source or destination database.

After running the upgrade tool, you should open and review the log file, upgrade.log, for potential errors or changes that might be of concern. Now that you have completed the upgrade for the database file, you should now be able to open the database file with your

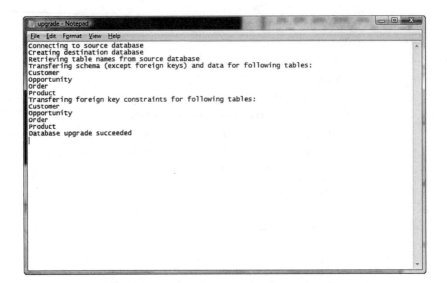

**FIGURE 11.6**    Upgrade Utility Log File

application using SQL Server Compact Edition. If you are using replication or RDA you will now re-create your subscription or repull.

---
**NOTE**
---

The upgrade program only upgrades schema and data of an older version of SQL CE. It does not upgrade a subscription or RDA tracking information. If the SQL Server CE database has subscriptions or tracked tables, you should upload your changes before doing the upgrade.

The upgrade utility creates another database and uses approximately 300 KB of memory in the process of creating it. Make sure that you have enough storage for the source and destination database.

## Upgrading the Application

Use .NET Compact Framework version 2.0 to develop a .NET based application for SQL Server Compact Edition 3.0 or later. Use .NET Compact Framework 1.0 for an SQL CE 2.0 based application.

After doing the migration of database from SQL CE 2.0 to SQL Server Compact Edition 3.0 or later, you need to migrate the .NET CF 1.0 based application to a .NET CF 2.0 based application.

## Using Conversion Wizard of Visual Studio 2005

The purpose of the Conversion Wizard is to convert Visual Studio 2003 solution and projects into Visual Studio 2005 solutions and projects. If you have developed a solution earlier using Visual Studio 2003 and now your development environment has Visual Studio 2005, you can upgrade the solutions and project using the Conversion Wizard.

To convert a Visual Studio 2003 solution, simply open a solution in Visual Studio 2005. It will automatically start the Conversion Wizard to walk you through the conversion process.

1. As shown in Figure 11.7, the first dialog in the Conversion Wizard asks you to start the conversion process. Click Next.

2. The next dialog box advises you to back up your current solution. Specify the path for backup and click Next as shown in Figure 11.8.

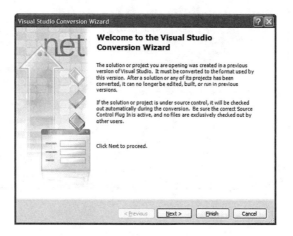

**FIGURE 11.7**   Conversion Wizard

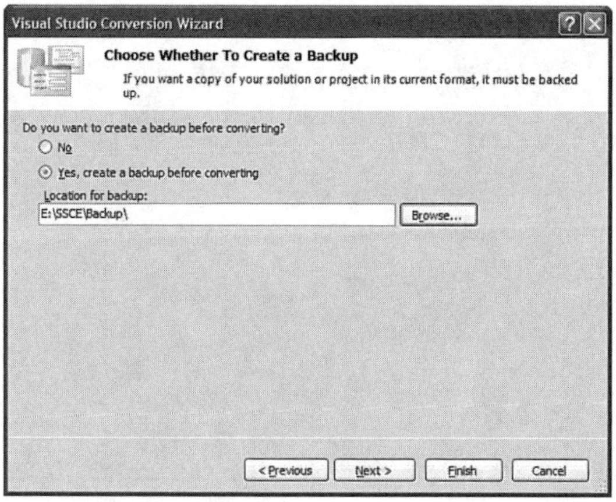

**FIGURE 11.8**   Create Backup of Project

3. The next dialog box lists the project under the solution that must be converted as shown in Figure 11.9. Click Next.

4. The last dialog box displays the completion message as shown in Figure 11.10 and displays a list of warnings if any. Click Close.

**NOTE**

With this set of steps you have migrated a VS 2003 project to a VS 2005 project. Your project is still a .NET CF 1 project and uses an SQL CE 2.0 database.

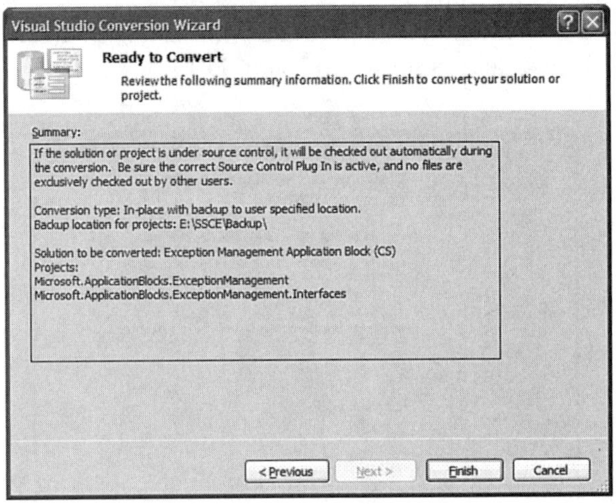

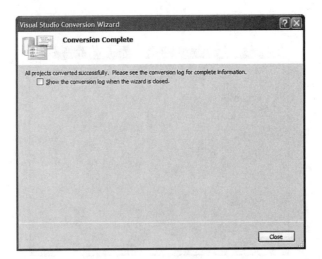

FIGURE 11.9    Summary information

FIGURE 11.10    Complete Conversion

## Using the Upgrade Project Option of Visual Studio 2005

The objective of the upgrade project option in Visual Studio is to upgrade the .NET Compact Framework 1.0 project to a .NET Compact Framework 2.0 project.

Once you have the new project open in Visual Studio 2005, you need to change it to a .NET Compact Framework 2.0 project and references should point to the Compact Framework 2.0 dll.

The example shown in Figure 11.11 is a .NET Compact Framework project using SQL CE 2.0. As shown in Figure 11.11, the SQL CE assembly is placed in location.

Figure 11.12 demonstrates the version of System.Data assembly. The assembly is .NET Compact Framework version 1.0.

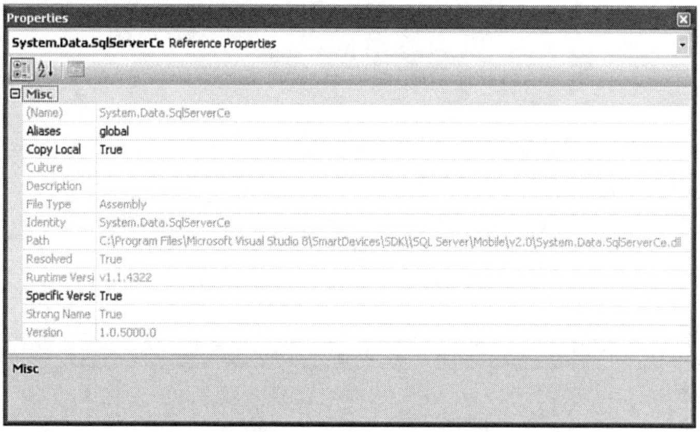

**FIGURE 11.11**    SQL ServerCE 2.0 Reference

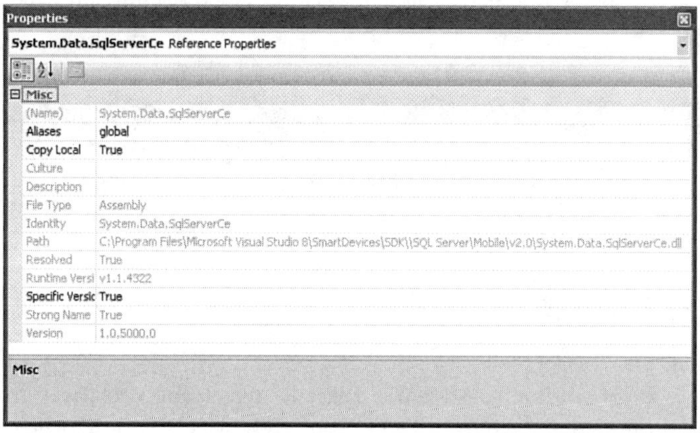

**FIGURE 11.12**    .NET CF 1.0 References

To convert the project into a .NET CF 2.0 project, click on the menu option Project |
Upgrade Project as shown in Figure 11.13.

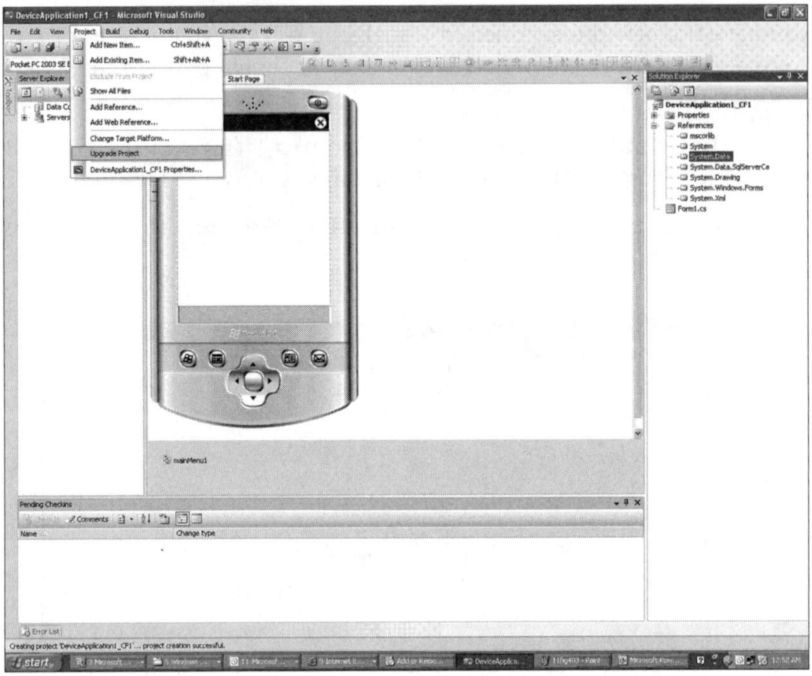

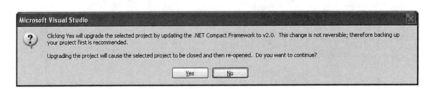

**FIGURE 11.13    Upgrade Project Menu Option**

A message box will appear suggesting that you make a backup of your project as shown
in Figure 11.14. If you have already made a backup, click Yes and proceed with the
upgrade process.

**FIGURE 11.14    Upgrading to .NET CF to 2.0**

The project upgrade is complete. After the upgrade, check the version of .NET Compact
Framework assemblies such as System.Data. The references to a new project point to .NET
Compact Framework 2.0 dll as shown in Figure 11.15.

The version of SQL CE assembly is still the same as SQL CE 2.0 as shown in Figure 11.16.

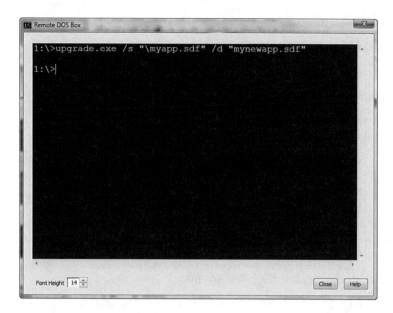

**FIGURE 11.15**    .Net CF 2.0 Assemblies References

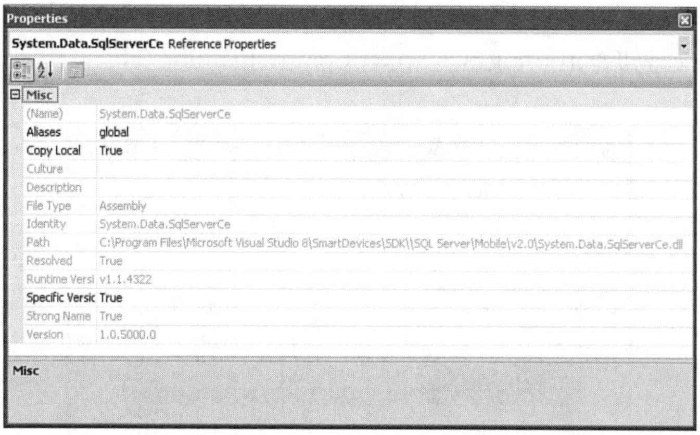

**FIGURE 11.16**    SQL CE 3.0 Reference

## Changing the SQL CE Assembly Reference

After you upgrade your project to .NET Compact Framework 2.0, your SQL CE namespace still points to an older version of SQL CE. To change the reference to a newer SQL CE, you need to remove the reference from the SQL CE 2.0 assembly.

The SQL CE 2.0 assembly is located at

```
<Disk>:\Program Files\Microsoft Visual Studio 8\SmartDevices\SDK\SQL
Server\Mobile\v2.0
```

The SQL CE 3.x assembly is located at

```
<Disk>:\Program Files\Microsoft Visual Studio 8\SmartDevices\SDK\SQL
Server\Mobile\v3.0
```

or

```
<Disk>:\Program Files\Microsoft SQL Server Compact Edition\v3.1
```

To change the reference to an SQL Server Compact Edition 3.x assembly, remove the reference to the older assembly and add the reference to point to the SQL Server Compact Edition 3.x assembly.

1. In Visual Studio, expand the reference node.

2. Right click on System.Data.SqlServerCe to remove the reference to assembly.

3. Click on the Reference | Add Reference menu option.

4. The Add Reference dialog box allows you to choose the assembly. Select System.Data.SqlServerCe version 3.0 assembly as shown in Figure 11.17 and click OK.

Now your project will start using SQL Server Compact Edition 3.0.

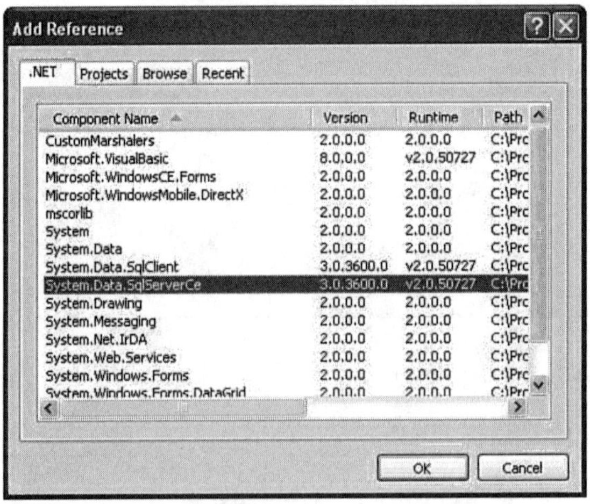

**FIGURE 11.17**    SQLServerCE 2.0 Reference

# Planning the Migration

In the last four sections you have learned how to migrate the SQL Server Compact Edition database, Visual Studio, .NET Compact Framework, and the SQL Server Compact Edition assembly in your project.

Table 11.2 shows a summary of the upgrade tool.

**TABLE 11.2    Upgrade Tools**

| Tools for Upgrade | Upgrade |
|---|---|
| Upgrade.exe | Migrate Database and Schema from SQL CE 2.0 to SQL Server Compact Edition (3.0 or later). |
| Conversion Wizard | Upgrade Visual 2003 project to Visual 2005 project. |
| Project \| Upgrade menu option | Upgrade .NET CF 1 application to .NET CF 2 application. |
| Manually change the reference | Upgrade SqlServerCe namespace from Version 2.0 to version 3.0. |

Based upon your migration scenario, you can choose the component you want to migrate.

## Migrating Development Environment

An enterprise has a .NET CF 1.0 project developed using Visual Studio 2003. The project uses an SQL CE 2.0 database. The development team wants to use Visual Studio 2005 for further development. You do not wish to migrate to SQL Server Compact Edition 3.0. Follow these steps to migrate your development environment from Visual Studio 2003 to Visual Studio 2005:

1. Open the project in Visual Studio 2005.

2. The Conversion Wizard will walk you through the migration to 2005.

With these two steps you have migrated a VS 2003 project to a VS 2005 project. Your project is still a .NET CF 1 project and uses an SQL CE 2.0 database as summarized in Table 11.3.

**TABLE 11.3    Migrating to Visual Studio 2005**

| Previous Platform | Target Platform |
|---|---|
| Visual Studio 2003 project | Visual Studio 2005 |
| .NET CF 1.0 | .NET CF 1.0 |
| System.Data.SqlServer.CE dll (2.0 version) | System.Data.SqlServer.CE dll (2.0 version) |
| The database file (.sdf) is a version 2 database file. | The database file (.sdf) is a version 2 database file. |

## Migrating Runtime Environment

An enterprise has a .NET CF 1.0 project developed using Visual Studio 2005. The project uses an SQL CE 2.0 database. The goal is to start using SQL Server Compact Edition 3.0 or later with .NET CF 2.0 as described in Table 11.4. The enterprise design team decides to migrate to .NET CF 2.0.

First use the Upgrade utility to convert the SQL Server CE 2.0 database into SQL Server Compact Edition 3.x database format. Then use the Upgrade Project option in Visual Studio to convert the .NET CF 1.0 project to a .NET CF 2.0 project.

1. Use the Upgrade utility to migrate schema and data from SQL Server CE 2.0 to an SQL Server Compact Edition 3.x database.

2. Open the project in Visual Studio 2005. As the original project is in VS 2005, the Conversion Wizard will not start.

3. Use the Upgrade project option to upgrade the .NET CF 1.0 project to a .NET CF 2.0 project.

4. Change the reference to SqlServerCe dll. Instead of using version 2.0 dll, use version 3.0 dll.

TABLE 11.4    Migrating .NET CF 2.0 and SQL CE 3.0 Database

| Previous Platform | Target Platform |
|---|---|
| Visual Studio 2005 project | Visual Studio 2005 |
| .NET CF 1.0 | .NET CF 2.0 |
| System.Data.SqlServer.CE dll (2.0 version) | System.Data.SqlServer.CE dll (3.0 version) |
| The database file (.sdf) is a version 2 database file. | The database file (.sdf) is a version 3.x database file. |

## Migrating Development and Runtime Environment

An enterprise has a .NET CF 1.0 project developed using Visual Studio 2003. The project uses an SQL CE 2.0 database. The architect wants to start using a new feature of SQL Server Compact Edition 3.x. The design and development team also decide to start using .NET CF 2.0 and develop the project in Visual Studio 2005. Table 11.5 summarize the current and target platforms for migration.

1. Use the Upgrade utility to migrate schema and data from SQL Server CE 2.0 to the SQL Server Compact Edition 3.x database.

2. Open the project in Visual Studio 2005. The Conversion Wizard will start and walk you through migrating the VS 2003 project to a VS 2005 project.

3. Use the Upgrade project option to upgrade the .NET CF 1.0 project to a .NET CF 2.0 project.

4. Change the reference to SqlServerCe dll. Instead of using version 2.0 dll, use version 3.0 dll.

**TABLE 11.5    Migrating to VS 2005, .NET CF 2.0, and an SQL CE 3.0 Database**

| Previous Platform | New Platform |
| --- | --- |
| Visual Studio 2003 project | Visual Studio 2005 |
| .NET CF 1.0 | .NET CF 2.0 |
| System.Data.SqlServer.CE dll (2.0 version) | System.Data.SqlServer.CE dll (3.0 version) |
| The database file (.sdf) is a version 2 database file. | The database file (.sdf) is a version 3.x database file. |

SQL Server Compact Edition 3.1 is the next generation database in the SQL Server CE family. The database file format of SQL Server Compact Edition 3.x is different than SQL CE 2.0. The SQL CE 2.0 database can be upgraded to SQL Server Compact Edition 3.x format using the Upgrade utility.

You can also upgrade a .NET CF 1 application to a .NET CF2 application using the Upgrade Project option available in Visual Studio 2005. If you have developed an application in an earlier version of Visual Studio 2003, it can simply be upgraded to a Visual 2005 environment.

Microsoft has provided a complete suite of upgrade options to migrate your design and runtime environment using SQL CE.

**NOTE**

If you wish to change the target platform of a device application such as Windows Mobile 5.0 to Windows Mobile 6.0, you can use the Change Target Platform option in Visual Studio. The detailed steps are given in Chapter 3, *Getting to Know the Tools*.

## Summary

There are a few strategies for upgrading solutions from SQL Server CE (2.0, 1.1, and 1.0). You can leverage Replication if all the data in your database is replicated to a central data store, you can roll your own, or you can leverage the upgrade tool, upgrade.exe, which ships with SQL Server Compact Edition. The steps and prerequisites for using the upgrade tool, as well as some tips and potential caveats to this process, have all been covered. The Conversion Wizard and the Visual Studio option to upgrade to Visual Studio 2005 and .NET Compact Framework 2.0 have also been discussed. The upgrade utility and tools equip you to migrate your development environment. As with any other upgrade of an application, proper testing is an important step in each process.

# Synchronizing Data with Merge Replication

This chapter introduces you to using SQL Server Compact Edition in a synchronization relationship with SQL Server. The chapter discusses creating a .NET Compact Framework application to use the SQL Server Compact Edition database. The data entered into the device needs to be synchronized with the backend SQL Server database. Microsoft SQL Server 2005 Compact Edition provides two powerful mechanisms to synchronize data between the SQL Server database and the SQL Server Compact Edition database: Remote Data Access and Merge Replication.

Using Remote Data Access (RDA), you can retrieve data from an SQL Server table and store it in a local table in the SQL Server Compact Edition on a device. You can update the table locally and later on update the modified records back to the SQL Server table. Using Merge Replication, you can update the data both on the server and the device, and synchronize the data between SQL Server Compact Edition and SQL Server. Merge Replication functionality is extremely useful when multiple clients or devices need to subscribe data, make offline changes, or need to subscribe data back to the backend server.

This chapter discusses the architecture of Merge Replication. It also demonstrates how to use Merge Replication to transfer data from SQL Server to SQL Server Compact Edition. You will also see how data modified in SQL Server 2005 Edition is synchronized again with SQL Server data.

# Merge Replication Scenarios and Features

Replication allows copying and synchronizing the database from one SQL Server to another. SQL Server 2005 provides Snapshot Replication, Transactional Replication, and Merge Replication to replicate data. You can use Merge Replication to synchronize data between SQL Server and SQL Server Compact Edition.

> **NOTE**
>
> Merge Replication is the only replication option available to synchronize data between SQL Server and SQL Server Compact Edition. Transactional Replication and Snapshot Replication are not supported in SQL Server Compact Edition.

In a simple scenario, a user is connected to a network and downloads data from a backend server to a client device. He disconnects from the network after getting the data. He then uses the device application to make transactions on a local database onto the device. Later, he will again connect to the network and upload the transaction to the backend server.

In a slightly more complex scenario, data on the backend server may change while the user is not connected to the network. In an enterprise, many mobile workers will retrieve the data. It would be useful for clients to filter data according to their needs instead of receiving all the rows. It is also possible that a different client may modify the same subset of data. At the time of synchronization, this will lead to conflict.

Merge Replication supports data synchronization, filtering rows, and conflict resolution. Merge Replication is useful when a client database needs to receive data from the server. Different clients may require different subsets of data; multiple clients can update the data offline and send the changes back to the server database. During synchronization, the replication mechanism should be able to identify conflicts and facilitate resolving conflicts. In Merge Replication terminology the server database is called *Publisher* and the client database is called *Subscriber*.

## Scenarios

You will be using Merge Replication to exchange data between a backend database and client applications. The client applications can be on mobile devices, laptops, Tablet PCs, ATMs, a kiosk, or any other Windows-based machines as shown in Figure 12.1.

A Route Sales application supports day-to-day activities of a company's sales force. The company's sales force visits customer stores in individual territories. During their visit to a customer store, they deliver goods and take new orders. Each sales person carries a mobile device or Tablet PC. The application on each sales person's device uses an SQL Server Compact Edition database whereas the central application uses an SQL Server database.

Enterprise agents visit remote areas. They survey the area and record their findings on handheld devices. These handheld devices have SQL Server Compact Edition databases. At regular intervals they transfer the recorded data to the central SQL Server database using Merge Replication.

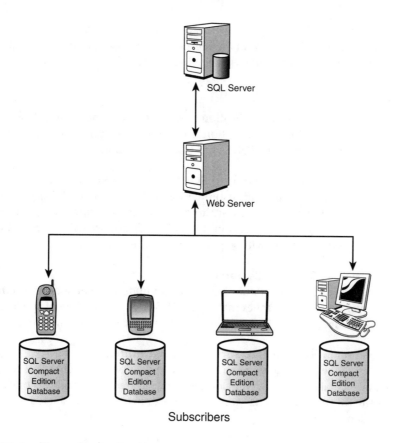

**FIGURE 12.1**   Merge Replication Usage

A hospital can develop an application for doctors. Doctors should enter the details of their observations and prescriptions when visiting patients. At regular intervals, the doctors' information on their handheld devices can be synchronized with the central system.

An electronic machine can have an embedded database. Everyday or every week a list of available TV and radio programs can be downloaded on it. The machine's user can check the programs anytime.

These are some sample scenarios in which you may use Merge Replication to synchronize data between SQL Server and SQL Server Compact Edition. You can transfer data in the following ways:

- Data is only downloaded from SQL Server to SQL Server Compact Edition. The download happens at regular intervals. Data on SQL Server Compact Edition is only used for browsing.

- Data is created on SQL Server Compact Edition. At regular intervals data is uploaded to SQL Server.

- Data is downloaded from SQL Server to SQL Server Compact Edition. Data is updated both on SQL Server and on SQL Server Compact Edition. At regular intervals, the server and client databases synchronize the data.

## Features

SQL Server 2005 provides various replication mechanisms to synchronize data between multiple database servers. Merge Replication is the only mechanism available to synchronize data between SQL Server and SQL Server Compact Edition.

### Download Database from SQL Server to SQL Server Compact Edition

After you set up the replication relationship between SQL Server and SQL Server Compact Edition, you can specify whether you want to create a new database on SQL Server Compact Edition. During synchronization, the published articles will be created on the client database and the database will be populated with initial data.

### Data Manipulation at Central SQL Server

After you set up the replication relationship, you can update the data on the central SQL Server. SQL Server tracks the changes made on SQL Server. At the time of synchronization it transfers the changes to the client's SQL Server Compact Edition database.

### Data Manipulation at Remote SQL Server Compact Edition

After you set up the replication, you can also update data on the client's SQL Server Compact Edition database. SQL Server Compact Edition tracks the changes on the client database. At the time of synchronization the updated, inserted, and deleted records participate in synchronization.

### Data Synchronization Capability Between SQL Server and SQL Server Compact Edition

Merge Replication applies the initial snapshot to a Subscriber during the first synchronization between SQL Server and SQL Server Compact Edition. Merge Replication tracks the changes on published data at both Publisher and Subscriber. At regular intervals, synchronization is used to combine the changes done at both Publisher and Subscriber.

For example, in a sales application a user will download product details, customer details, price, promotion, and so on, from a central SQL Server to a client's SQL Server Compact Edition database that is deployed on a mobile device, laptop, and so on. The sales person will take the customer's order and create a new sales order. Later, the sales person will synchronize the data. The synchronization process will send the new sales order to the central server. At the same time, new products, updated product prices, and new promotions will get downloaded from the central SQL Server to the client's SQL Server Compact Edition database.

### Programmable Data Synchronization

Merge Replication provides a Synchronize method to synchronize the data between SQL Server Compact Edition and SQL Server 2005. Using the Synchronize method you can trigger the synchronization at the click on event. An application user can trigger synchronization at the beginning and end of each day.

## Schema Changes

Using replication, it is possible to synchronize some of the schema changes from a central database to a client database. If you add or drop a column on a Published Table, the changes are synchronized with SQL Server Compact Edition Subscriber. It is possible to add a Table to Publication. The newly added Table in Publication can have foreign key constraints to other tables in publication.

If you modify the table indexes, the referential integrity constraints on the table's modifications are transmitted to a client's SQL Server Compact Edition database at the time of synchronization.

### NOTE

The subscriber must be reinitialized if an Identity column is added in a Published Table. Schema changes at Subscriber are not allowed in Merge Replication.

## Conflict Resolution at the Time of Synchronization

Merge Replication allows Publisher and Subscribers to update the data at the same time and synchronize data at regular intervals. A conflict occurs during synchronization when more than one Subscriber or Publisher updates the same record. SQL Server 2005 supports built-in Conflict Resolvers to resolve the conflict. It is also possible to write custom Conflict Resolvers.

## Data Filtering

Merge replication provides a data filtering feature. Using this feature you ensure that each client database receives a different set of rows at the time of synchronization and download. For example, the Central database will have a list of all customers. During synchronization, each salesperson's database will receive data pertaining to his or her own customers. Data filtering is extremely useful for applications where a large number of mobile devices synchronize data with a backend server. The filtered data is not shared across the devices and results in an increase in scalability.

## Applying Additional Business Logic for Synchronization

You can define a custom business logic that will be executed at the time of synchronization. For example, your application may upload a new sales order from a client to a server database. At the time of synchronization you may want to update additional tables on the central SQL Server for order backlog.

## Tools and Wizards

Before using Merge Replication, you need to provide configuration details—central database, remote database, Snapshot agent folder, security mechanism, and so on. You can set up this configuration either using programmability or wizards. SQL Server Management Studio provides tools and wizards to set up Publication, Subscription, and Snapshot folders. It even generates a template code that can be used for data synchronization.

### Compression

To reduce the amount of transfer, SQL Server Compact Edition provides a compression feature. If you choose to compress data, only compressed data needs to be transmitted and then uncompressed at the receiving end.

### Encryption

You can choose to use encryption while transferring data between device and Web Server. To use encryption you can use the Secure Socket Layer protocol for transferring data.

### Security

In an enterprise production environment, you must secure the data transmission. SQL Server Compact Edition uses the http or https protocol to transfer the data between Subscriber and Web Server. You can specify the authentication and authorization mechanism to specify the client who can communicate with the SQL Server Compact Server Agent. The SQL Server Compact Edition Server Agent communicates with the backend SQL Server. You can configure authentication and authorization mechanisms for backend SQL Server and publications.

### Synchronization Recovery

To complete the synchronization, Subscriber and Publisher establish connectivity. If communication breaks during communication, you do not need to restart the synchronization from scratch. Synchronization can start from the point where the communication break occurred. To ensure success, the next connection should be established within the connection retry timeout period.

### GPRS Connectivity

You will most likely use GPRS to establish connectivity between client and Subscriber. SQL Server Compact Edition provides you settings that can be helpful for GPRS. Using these settings you can set the timeout property that is suitable for GPRS connectivity.

## Merge Replication Architecture Components

SQL Server 2005 provides Merge Replication functionality. You can use Merge Replication for Server to Server Replication and Server to Client Replication. The Replication model is similar to the publishing industry. Even replication components responsibilities are similar to the publishing industry. A publishing company publishes a weekly magazine. The magazine is sent to Subscribers. Distributor distributes the magazine. The publisher also can act as Distributor and distribute the magazine.

In Merge Replication, the SQL Server database acts as Publisher and Distributor. The SQL Server Compact Edition database acts as Subscriber. This is called the *Server to Client* model of Merge Replication. Merge Replication allows Subscriber to make changes in the database and send the changes back to Publisher. Figure 12.2 demonstrates the Merge Replication architecture.

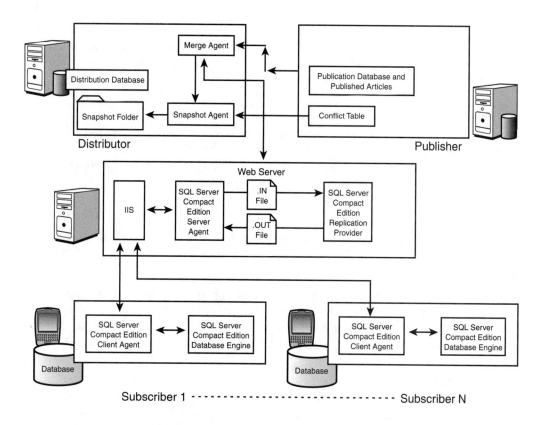

**FIGURE 12.2**    Merge Replication Architecture

## Distributor

Distributor Server is an SQL Server that contains a distribution database to store metadata, statistics, snapshots, and so on. Distributor Server is responsible for synchronizing the data between Publisher and Subscribers. Distributor manages the flow of data between Publisher and Subscribers. It is common to have the Publisher SQL Server instance act as Distributor too. However, for scalability purposes, Distributor and Publisher should be separate SQL Servers.

## Publisher

The Publisher database is a source database that defines publications. The publication process specifies which articles are published and available for synchronization. Publication is a grouping of articles that should be replicated as a unit.

You can define separate publications for different sets of users. For example, a set of tables related to orders and sales can be published to Sales and another set of tables can be published to the Billing Department.

> **NOTE**
>
> SQL Server Publisher can publish other objects such as stored procedures, views, and so on. These articles are ignored during synchronization as these types of objects are not available in SQL Server Compact Edition.

## Subscriber

The SQL Server Compact Edition instance that synchronizes the data with server is called *Subscriber*. Subscriber needs to subscribe to published data either programmatically or by using the Subscription Wizard. Upon creation of the initial subscription, the initial snapshot from the Distributor is applied to the device database.

> **NOTE**
>
> SQL Server Compact Edition Subscriber can subscribe data from multiple Publishers.

## Client Agent

SQL Server Compact Edition Client Agent is the most important component. You will be using the Client Agent method and properties to implement Merge Replication. Client Agent sits between the device-based application and the SQL Server Compact Edition database. Client Agent will interact with the SQL Server Compact Edition Server Agent and database.

## Server Agent

SQL Server Compact Edition Server Agent is a primary component to manage connectivity between SQL Server Compact Edition and SQL Server. The SQL Server Compact Edition Server Agent runs as ISAPI DLL on a machine running the IIS. The SQL Server Compact Edition Server Agent handles all http requests made by SQL Server Compact Edition Client Agent. Server Agent handles these requests and invokes the SQL Server Replication provider.

## SQL Server Reconciler

During synchronization, the replication mechanism should be able to identify conflicts and facilitate resolving conflicts. SQL Server Reconciler is a component used to resolve any conflicts that occur during synchronization. It is deployed on the server running IIS.

## SQL Server Replication Provider

SQL Server Replication Provider is also installed on the server running IIS. SQL Server Reconciler triggers the SQL Server Replication Provider that in turn starts a Merge Agent. It associates a Merge Agent at Publisher with Subscription.

## Snapshot Agent

The Snapshot Agent component is available in the snapshot.exe executable file. The Snapshot Agent component prepares the snapshot files that contain the schema and data of published tables. The Snapshot Agent runs at Distributor.

## Merge Agent

The Merge Agent component is available in the `replmerge.exe` executable file. Merge Agent applies the initial snapshot to Subscribers. Merge Agent merges the incremental changes done at Publisher and Subscriber and reconciles conflict using either defined rules or a `Custom Resolver`.

## The SQL Server Compact Edition Database Engine

The database engine manages the data. In Merge Replication, the perspective engine provides a tracking mechanism to track inserted, updated, or deleted records. The database engine is optimized for mobile devices and embedded applications.

# Using Merge Replication

In the previous section we discussed sample scenarios in which you will use SQL Server as a central database server and SQL Server Compact Edition as a client database. The client database will be deployed on mobile devices, laptops, Tablet PCs, and so on. The features that SQL Server Compact Edition provides to implement the above mentioned scenarios were also discussed.

This section describes the overview of steps that you need to execute in order to use the SQL Server Compact Merge Replication feature.

### Installing SQL Server Compact Server Components

The SQL Server on the server machine and the SQL Server Compact Edition on the client machine need to communicate to each other in order to do replication. The communication happens using IIS. The IIS Web Server and SQL Server can be on the same machine or they can be on different machines.

Deploy the SQL Server Compact Edition database on the client machine. SQL Server Compact Edition also has a server side component. You need to deploy this component on the machine running IIS. This component is called the *SQL Server Compact Edition Server Agent* component. This component is installed using `SqlCe30Setup[lang].exe` executable. The file is installed both with SQL Server 2005 and Visual Studio 2005. You can find the installer for SQL Server Compact Edition Server Agent at one of the following locations:

- With Visual Studio 2005 the file is installed at `<Disk>\Program Files\Microsoft SQL Server\90\Tools\Binn\VSShell\Common7\IDE\`.

- With SQL Server 2005 the file is installed at `<Disk>\Program Files\Microsoft Visual Studio 8\SmartDevices\SDK\SQL Server\Mobile\v3.0`.

---

**NOTE**

SQL Server Compact Server Agent components are installed on a computer running IIS.

### Configuring the Web Server

To configure the replication, you will specify that you wish to set up a replication between SQL Server and the SQL Server Compact Edition type database. You will specify the Web Server and virtual directory details. You will choose the security mechanism, and specify the security and authentication requirements.

### Data Publishing

In Data Publication, you specify articles in the database that you wish to make available for replication. Your server database can be very large and consist of hundreds of database objects. During publication, you specify which tables and columns will participate in replication.

Your publication steps start by specifying the Distributor server, Publisher database, the tables and columns that will participate in replication, row and column filtering, and the name of the publication. You will also specify where you wish to store snapshot files, the account that the Snapshot Agent will use, and at what point in time the Snapshot Agent will run.

### Distributor Server Details

While setting up Merge Replication, you define the Distributor server that stores the distribution database. You can choose to make the Publisher server act as Distributor or specify a different server as Distributor server. The distribution database stores the meta-data and history information.

### Snapshot Folder

You will specify a folder in which snapshots of publications will be stored. The Merge Agents that run on Subscriber will access the snapshots of publications. The Merge Agents should have sufficient permission to access the Snapshot folder.

> **NOTE**
> Local paths are not accessible from agents running at Subscriber. You should set up the Snapshot folder as a Network share.

The Snapshot Agent will store the snapshot in the default Snapshot folder located on Distributor.

### Publication Database

Here you select the database that will act as the central server. If you are using a wizard, the wizard will show you all the databases that are available on the database server. You will choose the database that you want to act as the central database.

When you select a database as the Publication database, the SQL Server sets the Merge Publish property to TRUE.

### Type of Publication

You will always choose Merge Replication for SQL Server Compact Edition. The wizard shows other options—Snapshot publication, Transactional Publication, and Transaction

Publication with updatable subscription. This wizard is part of SQL Server Management Studio. You can use all of these options if you are using Merge Replication between two SQL Server databases.

### Articles

The SQL Server database will have various objects such as tables, stored procedures, and views, and so on. While selecting articles for Merge Replication, you select the object type and then within each object type you can choose which article you would like to publish.

### Filtering

SQL Server Replication supports Row and Column filtering. Using Column filtering, a subset of columns is published. Using Row filtering, you can publish rows that meet the given criteria.

For example, you may want to develop an application for a hospital that sends patients' histories to doctors' laptops or mobile devices. A hospital database will contain histories of all patients. The various doctors working in a hospital would like to receive the histories of patients that they are going to see the next day.

Similarly your Subscriber does not need to receive all the columns of the Publisher database tables. For example, the Publisher database table of patients may contain information about patient employer, marital status, number of children the patient has, and so on. The doctor's application that subscribes patient data does not require these columns.

Filtering allows you to select a subset of rows and columns that a Subscriber is interested in subscribing.

After you have selected the tables you would like to publish, you can choose columns that are required from Subscribers. If there are columns that won't be needed by Subscribers, then you would not like these columns to participate in replication. Restricting the set of columns will reduce the time and network bandwidth of synchronization and help increase the performance. It will also reduce the storage space requirement by the Subscriber.

After you have selected the tables and columns, you can specify whether or not the Subscriber needs all the rows of a published table. You can add row filters and specify the condition for filtering. The rows satisfying the condition will participate in replication. You can use the Parameterized filter to send a different subset of data to different Subscribers. To use the parameter filters, you can use the SUSER_SNAME () and HOST_NAME() functions. These functions help identify the login id of a subscription or the computer name of a Subscriber. You can partition data according to Subscriber. In a Publisher database, you can have a column containing a login name or a computer name of a Subscriber. During data synchronization each Subscriber will receive the data matching his or her login or computer name.

Listing 12.1 demonstrates how to match a Subscriber login id with DoctorLoginID in the Publisher table. The rows matching the condition will get synchronized.

### LISTING 12.1    Login ID for Filtering C#.NET

```
DoctorLoginID = SUSER_SNAME()
```

At the time of synchronization, Merge Agent will specify the login we used for subscription. It will download only those rows where the login id of Subscriber matches the Doctor Login id.

Similarly you can use Listing 12.2.

### LISTING 12.2    Machine Name for Filtering C#.NET

```
DoctorComputerName = HOST_NAME()
```

In this case, Merge Agent will return the computer name we are using for subscription. It will only download those rows where the computer name of Subscriber matches the doctor's computer name.

### Snapshot Agent Schedule

Merge Replication creates a file containing a snapshot of schema and data for new subscriptions. Snapshot Agent creates the snapshot.

In this step you specify when the Snapshot Agent should run to create a snapshot of publication schema and data. The Snapshot Agent can be run immediately or at a specific time. It can also be scheduled to run at regular intervals. You can also choose to run Snapshot Agent manually instead of running it at a specified time.

In the previous section you learned how to use filtering on rows and columns. Merge Replication does not generate the snapshot containing schema and data if you are using parameterized filters to send different sets of rows to different Publishers. Instead it creates the snapshot containing schema and scripts. This snapshot is called a *schema snapshot*. After a schema snapshot is created, it then generates a snapshot for each Subscriber. To create this snapshot, it copies schema from the schema snapshot and data that belong to the Subscriber.

### Account Name for Snapshot Agent

Snapshot Agent runs on Distributor and makes a connection to Publisher. In this step you specify the account name under which Snapshot Agent will run at Distributor. You will also specify the setting which Snapshot Agent will use to connect to Publisher.

You can run Snapshot Agent as a Windows Service account or an SQL Server Service Account. Here you specify the account under which Snapshot Agent runs on Distributor and creates the initial file containing schema and data for Subscriber. The account you specify should have at least a db_owner permission fixed database on the distribution database. The Snapshot Agent should have permission to read/write snapshot folders.

Snapshot Agent can connect to Publisher by impersonating the process account or by using the SQL Server login. The process account is the account you have chosen for running Snapshot Agent at Distributor. The account you chose for making a connection to Publisher should have at least a db_owner permission fixed database on the distribution database.

## Publication Name

At this point you have specified all the steps to create a publication. You can specify a publication name and complete the publication. If you are using a Publication wizard, it will show you a summary of all the options that you have chosen. It will also allow you to generate a script for the required steps. You can save this script and reuse it later if you need to re-create the publication.

## How to Create a Publication

You can create a publication programmatically or by using a wizard. SQL Server Management Studio provides a wizard to set up a publication.

## Publication Wizard

By using the SQL Server 2005 Publication Wizard you can specify the Publisher, publication type, Snapshot folder, and articles to publish. In the previous section you have already read what a Publisher is. You will use Merge Replication as the publication type.

### NOTE

SQL Server provides various methods of replication; however, Merge Replication is the only method used between SQL Server and SQL Server Compact Edition.

The Snapshot folder contains the snapshot files consisting of schema and data for published articles.

## Stored Procedure

The other method to create a publication on SQL Server 2005 is to use the sp_addmerge-ereplication stored procedure.

In the later part of this chapter you will create an exercise. The exercise will require you to create a publication using Publication Wizard.

## Data Subscribing

You have installed and Configured SQL Server Compact Server components on a Web Server. You have created a publication and specified Publisher and Distributor databases.

## Specify Publication and Publisher Database

To create a subscription you will first need to choose the publication. You will specify the publication name you have chosen and select the Publisher database.

## Specify Subscriber or Subscriber Host Name

In this step you will choose a name for Subscriber. In case you have chosen parameterized row filtering, you need to consider the following:

- In a Pull subscription, HOST_NAME () returns a different value for a different computer. In a Push subscription, HOST_NAME() returns the same value for all Subscribers. HOST_NAME () is useful for filtering in a Pull subscription only.

- You can override the HOST_NAME() value. After override, HOST_NAME() will return the value you specify. You need to consider what the dependencies are on HOST_NAME().

### Specify Authentication Mechanism for Web Server

For the authentication mechanism you will specify the URL of a virtual directory on a Web Server. You will also specify the authentication mechanism that the Subscriber client will use to connect to a Web Server. The options available are anonymous authentication that does not require a user id and password, or choosing to use a user id password for authentication.

At this point you can test whether the Subscriber is able to connect to the Web Server. Once the connection is working, you can specify the authentication mechanism that will be used when the Subscriber client connects to the Publisher SQL Server. Here the options are to use either Windows authentication or SQL Server authentication.

### Copying a Subscription to Multiple Clients

When you use SQL Server Compact Edition, you will have multiple clients that subscribe to an SQL Server publication. You will most likely be using Parameterized filers and a Join filter together. This will allow you to create a single publication instead of multiple publications for each Subscriber.

When you are using multiple devices and each device uses a similar subscription, it is better to create a subscription on one device. After a subscription is created on one device, then you can deploy the application and subscription.

SQL Server Compact Edition automatically determines which device is a new Subscriber when the device is synchronized for the first time and creates a new subscription.

### Subscribing to Multiple Publications

The SQL Server Compact Edition allows a Subscriber to subscribe to multiple publications. For example, a hospital can have a patient database and a medicine database. The client application can subscribe data from a patient database and a medicine database.

When an SQL Server Compact Edition database subscribes to multiple publications, you need to consider the following constraint while designing the table structure.

You cannot have referential integrity between tables that come from different databases. For example, if you get the EmployeeDetail table from the employee database and the CustomerDetail table from the customer database, you can set up a referential integrity between the two tables on the SQL Server Compact Edition database. In fact, they are not considered restrictions as the tables on these two databases on the server are updated independently. Allowing referential integrity at a Subscriber database means that both databases should be updated first and the client database should synchronize first with the database having the parent table and then with the database having the child table.

## How to Create a Subscription

In this section you will learn how to create a subscription. When you create a subscription, three system tables are added to the SQL Server Compact database. At the same time, a user table is published with a few extra columns for replication. You can create an SQL Server Compact Edition subscription using two methods.

### Subscription Wizard

You can access the Subscription Wizard using SQL Server 2005 Management Studio. Using the Subscription Wizard you will be able to choose the publication that you want to subscribe to, specify the name of the subscription, provide a URL for a virtual directory, and choose the SQL Authentication/Windows authentication mechanism.

You will be able to do these steps as part of the exercise given on page 361.

### AddSubscription Method

To create a subscription programmatically you will use the replication object and call the AddSubscription method of the replication object. You also need to set the properties for the Publisher database before invoking the AddSubscription method.

```
repl.InternetUrl =  @"http://pdhingra-lptp/hospitalpatient/sqlcesa30.dll";
repl.InternetLogin = "SQLCE";
repl.InternetPassword = "<password>";
repl.Publisher = "SQLServerPublisher";
repl.PublisherDatabase = "SQLServerPublisherDatabase";
repl.PublisherLogin = "SQLServerPublisherLogin";
repl.PublisherPassword = "<password>";
repl.Publication = "SQLServerPublication";
repl.Subscriber = "SQLCE";
repl.SubscriberConnectionString="DataSource=SQLCEDatabase.sdf";
repl.AddSubscription(EXISTING_DATABASE ¦ CREATE_DATABASE)
```

You should use the EXISTING_DATABASE value when SQL Server Compact Edition database is already created on a Subscriber. You should use the CREATE_DATABASE value when a new SQL Server Compact Edition database needs to be created on a Subscriber device.

When you use the wizard you can specify the values of these properties in wizard.

An SQL Server Compact Edition database can subscribe to multiple Publishers. This feature was not available in SQL CE 2.0. You can subscribe to multiple databases by invoking the AddSubscription method for each Publisher and setting the properties.

On page 361 you will create a step-by-step exercise for Merge Replication as well as create a publication and then create a subscription.

### Data Synchronizing

Create the subscription using the wizard programmatically or by copying an existing subscription and then  invoke the synchronization method of the replication object to trigger the replication.

```
repl.Synchronize();
```

The SQL Server Merge replication mechanism can be used as push or pull subscriptions. However, with SQL Server Compact Edition you generally will be using a pull subscription.

Merge Replication is based on a pull subscription. This means that the Subscriber requests when data between should be synchronized between Publisher and Subscriber. We generally use Merge Replication in a Server to Client replication. Many Subscribers subscribe to one Publisher database. The Subscribers are disconnected and each Subscriber decides at what time they want to synchronize data with the Publisher.

### ReinitializeSubscription
You will use the ReInitializeSubscription method of the SQL Server Compact Edition Replication object if you need to re-create the snapshot of the published database. You can specify the UploadBeforeInit option for uploading the subscription changes before the snapshot is re-created. If this option is not specified or false, the Subscriber changes will not be uploaded on the server.

```
repl.ReInitializeSubscription(UploadBeforeReinit)
```

### DropSubscription
You will use the DropSubscription method of the SQL Server Compact Edition Replication object to drop a subscription from the SQL Server Publisher. At the time of AddSubscription, you created an SQL Server Compact Edition database. Similarly at the time of dropping the subscription, you can use DBDROPOPTION to delete an SQL Server Compact Edition database.

DBDROPOPTION can have two possible values: LEAVE_DATABASE or DROP_DATABASE.

LEAVE_DATABASE only drops the subscription by deleting the system tables that are specific to replication and the columns in user tables that are added for replication.

## Merge Replication Exercise

As discussed in the previous section, the setup of Publication and Subscription are the main steps for setting up Merge Replication. Before using Merge Replication you need to install SQL Server Compact Edition Replication components.

This section will demonstrate the above mentioned steps using a simple exercise. The objective of the exercise is to develop an application that provides up-to-date information to doctors about their patients on their laptop, Tablet PC, or mobile device. The application synchronizes the data with the hospital backend database on SQL Server 2005. You will execute steps to use Microsoft SQL Server Compact to synchronize data between a Microsoft Windows Mobile™–based device application and a Microsoft SQL Server 2005 backend database. You will set up and configure SQL Server 2005, Internet Information Services (IIS) and develop a .NET based application to view and update the data. On completion of these steps, you will know how to easily build a mobile application designed to keep mission-critical data synchronized with a backend database.

To make things simple in the following exercise you will use a single SQL Server 2005 instance that acts as Distributor and Publisher. You will use a single computer that hosts IIS and SQL Server.

**NOTE**

In a production environment, it is not recommended that you use IIS and SQL Server on the same computer due to concerns about security and scalability. In this chapter, however, you will use IIS and SQL Server 2005 on the same computer.

The exercise demonstrates how to use Merge Replication to synchronize data between SQL Server and SQL Server Compact Edition. In the exercise you will install the SQL Server Compact Edition Server Tool component. You will set up Publication on the SQL Server database. You will set up Subscription for the SQL Server Compact Edition database. You will build an application using Visual Studio that will update the data on an SQL Server Compact Edition database and synchronize the changes back to SQL Server.

To complete this exercise you will need the following software:

- Microsoft Windows XP SP2/ Microsoft Windows 2000/ Microsoft Windows 2003
- Internet Information Services (IIS)
- Microsoft SQL Server 2005
- Microsoft Visual Studio 2005
- Microsoft SQL Server Compact Edition

**NOTE**

You can test your application on a computer, laptop, Tablet PC, mobile device, or on an emulator. If you are using a device, you can develop a Pocket PC 2003 or Pocket PC 2005 device. You will require Active Sync 4.0 or later if you are using Mobile Device as a client.

The entire exercise is divided into the following steps:

1. Set up a backend SQL Server 2005 database.
2. Install SQL Server Compact Server components using SQL Server Compact Edition Server Tools Setup.
3. Create a publication on SQL Server 2005 using New Publication Wizard.
4. Configure the SQL Server Compact Server components using Configure Web Synchronization Wizard.
5. Create a subscription on SQL Server Compact Edition using New Subscription Wizard.

6. Develop an application using Visual Studio 2005 to view and update the patient data.

7. Synchronize the updated data with a backend SQL Server database.

## Setting Up a Backend SQL Server 2005 Database

In this first step you will set up a database on SQL Server 2005.

To demonstrate the Merge Replication exercise use Hospital database. The database will have the following tables:

- Doctor

- Patients

- PatientHistory

The Doctor table structure is shown in Table 12.1. The table includes the doctor's first name, last name, hospital employee number, and so on.

**TABLE 12.1    Doctor Table**

| Column | Data Type | Nullability | Description |
| --- | --- | --- | --- |
| DoctorEmployeeNo | Nchar(10) | Not Null | Employee number in hospital |
| DoctorRegNo | NChar(10) | Not Null | Doctor registration number in medical council |
| FirstName | NChar(20) | Not Null | First name |
| LastName | NChar(20) | Not Null | Last name |
| PhoneNo | NChar(15) | Null | Phone number with country and city code |
| CellNo | NChar(15) | Null | Cell phone number with country and city code |
| HighestQualification | NChar(30) | Null | Highest degree of doctor |
| Specialization | NChar(30) | Null | Area of specialization |
| TotalExperienceInMonths | Smallint | Null | Total working experience of doctor |

Table 12.2 show the schema of the Patients table. This table includes the patient's first name, last name, contact details, and so on. The table also includes the patient's registration number. The Patients table has a foreign key relationship with the Doctor table. The doctor's employee number is the employee number of Patient GP (General Practitioner Doctor).

**TABLE 12.2    Patients Table**

| Column | Data Type | Nullability | Description |
| --- | --- | --- | --- |
| PatientRegNo | NChar(10) | Not Null | ID of patient Primary key |

**TABLE 12.2    Patients Table**

| Column | Data Type | Nullability | Description |
| --- | --- | --- | --- |
| DoctorEmployeeNo | Nchar(10) | Not Null | Employee number in hospital Foreign key on Doctor Table |
| FirstName | NChar(20) | Not Null | First name |
| LastName | NChar(20) | Not Null | Last name |
| PhoneNo | NChar(15) | Null | Phone number with country and city code |
| CellNo | NChar(15) | Null | Cell phone number with country and city code |
| DOB | DateTime | Not Null | Date of birth |
| Age | SmallInt | Null | Age of patient in years |
| GuardianFirstName | NChar(20) | Null | First name of guardian—for young patients |
| GuardianLastName | NChar(20) | Null | Last name of guardian—for young patients |
| Martial Status | Char(1) | Null | Martial status of patient: 'M'—Married 'U'—Not Married 'D'—Divorced |
| NoOfChildren | SmallInt | Null | Number of children |
| Education | NChar(20) | Null | Education qualification of patient |
| Smokes | Char(1) | Null | 'R'—Patient smokes regularly 'O'—Patient smokes occasionally 'N'—Does not smoke |
| Drinks | Char(1) | Null | 'R'—Patient drinks alcohol regularly 'O'—Patient drinks alcohol occasionally 'N'—Does not drink alcohol |

Table 12.3 stores a history of treatment given to a patient. It has details of disease and treatment.

**TABLE 12.3    PatientHistory Table**

| Column | Data Type | Nullability | Description |
| --- | --- | --- | --- |
| PatientHistoryID | Int | Not Null | ID of patient and history Auto generated key. |
| PatientRegNo | NChar(10) | Not Null | ID of patient Foreign key on Patients Table |
| DiseaseIdentifed | NVarChar(200) | Not Null | Description of disease and symptoms |

TABLE 12.3    **PatientHistory Table**

| Column | Data Type | Nullability | Description |
| --- | --- | --- | --- |
| DateIdentified | DateTime | Not Null | Date when disease identified |
| Treatment | NVarChar(200) | Null | Treatment prescribed by doctor |
| TreatmentStartDate | DateTime | Null | Date when treatment started |
| TreatmentEndDate | DateTime | Null | Last date of treatment |

You can create the tables manually or use the `CreateHospitalDB.sql` script to create the Hospital database.

Once you have created the database you can use the `InsertDoctorData.sql` and `InsertPatientData.sql` script to insert Doctor and Patient data into the tables.

Once you have created the Hospital Database, you can see the database in Object Explorer in SQL Management Studio.

## Installing SQL Server Compact Server Components

SQL Server Compact Server Tool components are needed to do replication between SQL Server 2005 and the SQL Server Compact Edition database. In the current section, you will install the server tools components on an IIS Web Server. These components allow communication between SQL Server Compact Edition and an SQL Server database.

Start the Server Tools Setup wizard. You need to run `SQL_CE30SetupEn.exe` file to install the SQL Server Compact Edition Server Tool components. The file is placed when you install it under the `\90\Tools\Binn\VSShell\Common7\IDE\` path where you installed Microsoft SQL Server. If you have installed SQL Server in `C:\Program Files\Microsoft SQL Server`, the file will be placed in `C:\Program Files\Microsoft SQL Server\90\Tools\Binn\VSShell\Common7\IDE\`.

Double click on the file to start the setup. The SQL Server 2005 Compact Edition Server Tool Setup wizard will start as shown in Figure 12.3. The wizard notifies you that the SQL Server Compact Edition Server Tool component will be installed. Click Next on the Microsoft SQL Server 2005 Compact Edition Server Tools Setup Wizard.

The next screen, as shown in Figure 12.4, will display the license agreement. Choose the radio button, I accept the terms in the license agreement, and click Next.

The next dialog box as shown in Figure 12.5 displays the results of the System Configuration Check. It will show you the following:

- Success for OS and user requirement.
- Success for .NET Framework requirement.
- Success for MDAC requirement.
- Success for IIS requirement.
- Success for SQL Server Requirement.

**FIGURE 12.3**   Server Tools Welcome Screen

**FIGURE 12.4**   Server Tools License Agreement

**FIGURE 12.5**   Server Tool System Configuration Check

You can click on the More button to get further details about the results.

You can click on the More button for the SQL Server Warning requirement. The warning is for SQL Server 2000 replication components. These components are needed if you want to synchronize data between SQL Server 2000 and SQL Server Compact Edition. As you are using SQL Server 2005 in our example, you can ignore this warning. Click OK on the System Configuration Check Warning message box.

### NOTE

You can ignore the Warning for the SQL Server requirement. This warning is for synchronizing with the SQL Server 2000 requirement. In this exercise, you will be synchronizing with SQL Server 2005. Therefore, it is safe to ignore the warning.

Click Next on the System Configuration Check dialog box. In the next dialog box, choose whether you wish to synchronize data with SQL Server 2000 or with SQL Server 2005. In this exercise you will use SQL Server 2005 as a backend database. Check the box option, Synchronize with SQL Server 2005, as shown in Figure 12.6. Click on the Next button.

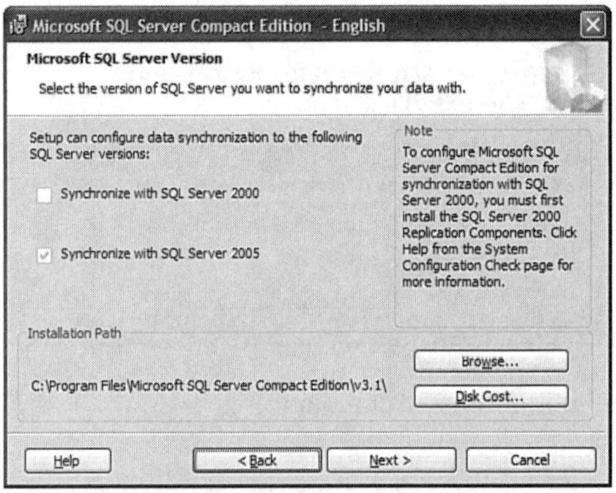

FIGURE 12.6    Server Tools to Select SQL Server Version

By this time you have accepted the license agreement, done the system check, and selected the backend database. The next dialog box shown in Figure 12.7 gives you a chance to change any of the settings or proceed with installation. Click on the Install button if you are ready to install the SQL Server Compact Edition Replication component.

The next screen displays the progress in installation.

On the completion of installation, the last dialog box, as shown in Figure 12.8, is displayed and informs you whether installation is successful or not.

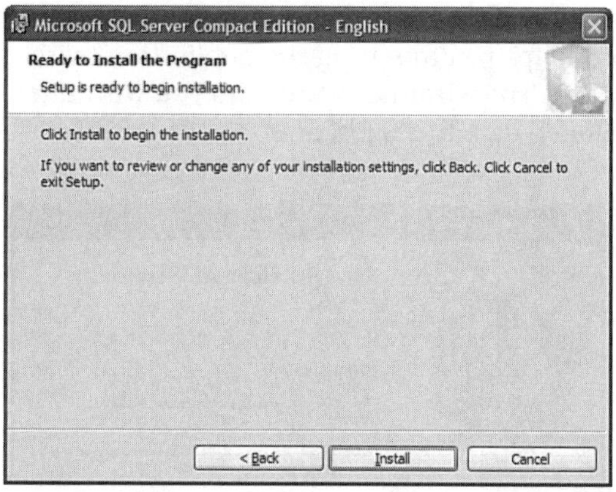

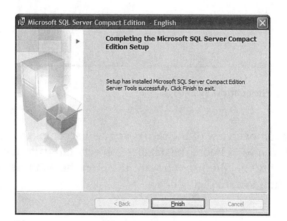

**FIGURE 12.7    Server Tools Ready to Install**

**FIGURE 12.8    Server Tools Installation Complete**

The last dialog box specifies that you have successfully installed the server-side components of SQL Server Compact Edition. Click on the Finish button as shown in Figure 12.8.
Now you have installed the SQL Server Compact Server Tools component. These components are needed to use Merge Replication between SQL Server and SQL Server Compact.

## Creating a Publication

In this section, you will create a publication on the Hospital database that you created on
SQL Server 2005. In the publication, you will publish a subset of tables in the SQL Server
database. To create a publication you will use Publication Wizard.

To start Publication Wizard, expand the Replication node in SQL Management Studio,
right click on the Local Publication node, and Click on New Publication.

Clicking on New Publication starts New Publication Wizard as shown in Figure 12.9. The New Publication Wizard helps you in setting the publication by selecting the database object you wish to publish. The wizard also provides you with filtering options to filter the articles and send filtered data to a Subscriber.

**FIGURE 12.9    New Publication Wizard**

The dialog box gives an overview of the things you will accomplish using New Publication Wizard. You will choose the database objects and data that you wish to publish. You will specify the filtering you want to do on the published data. Click Next on the New Publication Wizard dialog box.

### Specifying a Distributor

If this is the first time you have created a publication on this SQL Server, it will ask you to specify the Distributor. Remember in the beginning of the chapter we discussed that every Publisher needs to be associated with a Distributor. Here you can specify the Publisher server as Distributor or you can specify a different computer as Distributor. If you specify a different Distributor, you need to configure the Distributor in advance.

For the purpose of this exercise choose the first option as shown in Figure 12.10. Select your Publisher to act as Distributor and click Next on the Distributor dialog box.

### Specifying Snapshot Folder

In the next dialog box you will specify the location of the Snapshot folder. The Snapshot folder is the root location where a schema and snapshot file will be placed. The Subscriber will use this location to retrieve the database.

The wizard shows the Snapshot folder as shown in Figure 12.11. If you wish to change the Snapshot folder, you can specify the new folder here.

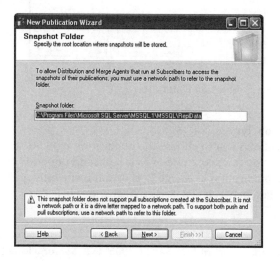

FIGURE 12.10   Distributor

FIGURE 12.11   Snapshot Folder

Before clicking Next, set the permission on the Snapshot folder (C:\Program Files\Microsoft SQL Server\MSSQL.1\MSSQL\repldata). Open Windows Explorer and select the folder C:\Program Files\Microsoft SQL Server\MSSQL.1\MSSQL\repldata. Right click and then click Sharing and Security and assign permission for FULL ACCESS to EVERYONE.

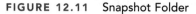

**NOTE**

In the production environment, specific users should be given read access. In this exercise, you are giving access to everyone.

Click the Customize tab and give access to the subfolders as well.

### Specifying Publication Database
You have selected Distributor and Snapshot folder. The next dialog box allows you to choose the publication database as shown in Figure 12.12. The SQL Server instance may have multiple databases. All the databases are shown in this dialog box. For this exercise select the Hospital database and click Next.

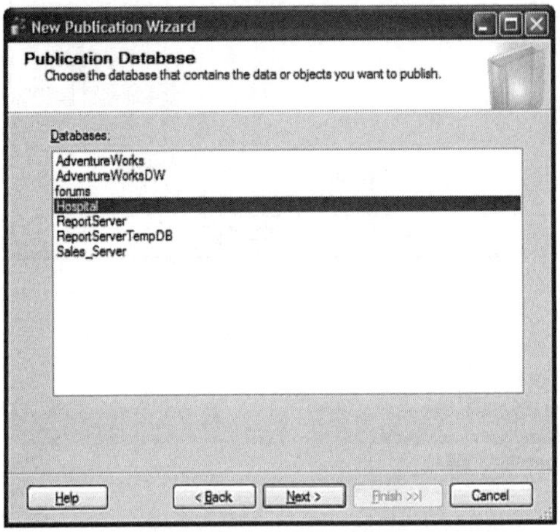

**FIGURE 12.12**    Select Publication Database

### Specifying Publication Type
The next dialog box allows you to choose the publication type. As shown in Figure 12.13, the dialog box allows you to choose one of four replication options available in SQL Server 2005. Choose Merge publication as Merge Replication is the only replication option available to synchronize data between SQL Server 2005 and SQL Server Compact Edition.

> **NOTE**
>
> The Publication Wizard is part of SQL Server 2005. SQL Server allows Snapshot publication, Transactional publication, Transactional publication with updatable subscriptions, and Merge Replication between two SQL Server databases. You can use only Merge Replication between SQL Server and SQL Server Compact Edition .

Click Next on Publication Type.

### Specifying Subscriber Type
The Subscriber Type dialog box allows you to choose various Subscriber types, such as SQL Server 2000, SQL Server 2005, SQL Server Compact Edition, and SQL Server CE 2.0. In this exercise you will choose the SQL Server Compact subscription. Select SQL Server 2005 Compact Edition as shown in Figure 12.14 and click Next.

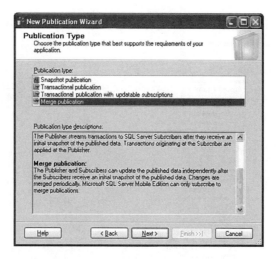

**FIGURE 12.13**    Select Publication Type

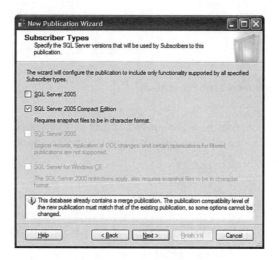

**FIGURE 12.14**    Select Subscriber Types

<hr>

**NOTE**

It is possible to select multiple Subscriber types.

### Specifying Articles

The Articles dialog box allows you to select SQL Server objects that you wish to publish. As shown in Figure 12.15, select the tables and columns that you wish to replicate to subscriber.

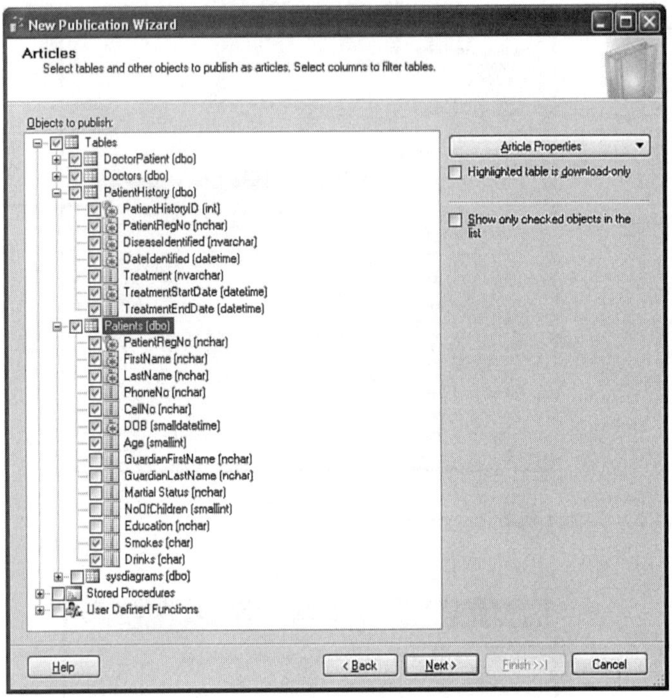

FIGURE 12.15    Select Tables for Publication

If you want to publish a subset of tables, only a subset can be selected. In this exercise, you will select all four tables. Within Patients table you will exclude the columns such as Marital Status, and so on.

1. Select Tables.

2. Expand Tables node.

3. Select Patients and PatientHistory tables and uncheck the other table boxes.

4. Expand the Patients table and see all columns available.

5. Uncheck the Marital Status, NoOfChildren, and Education columns. Select the Doctors table. Click on Article properties. For the Doctors table, change the synchronization direction from Bi-directonal to Download Only to Subscriber as shown in Figure 12.16.

After selecting Tables and columns, click Next. The next wizard reveals that the Uniqueidentifier columns will be added to the tables as shown in Figure 12.17. These columns are needed to track the changes that are happening on the SQL Server Publisher database. SQL Server adds these columns to each published table at the time of snapshot generation. This means that in Merge Replication you should have permission to change the schema on the server side.

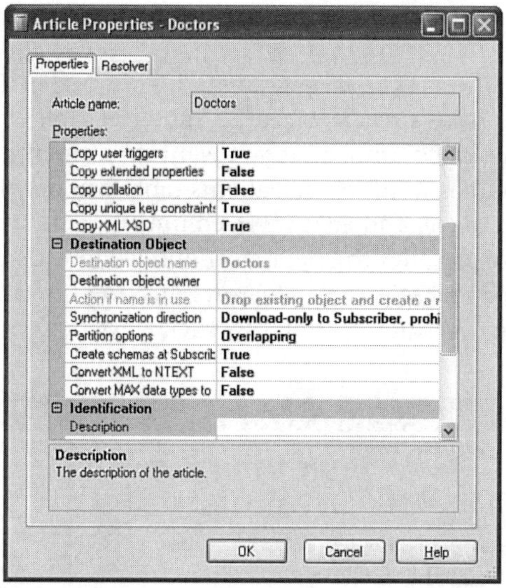

FIGURE 12.16    Article Properties

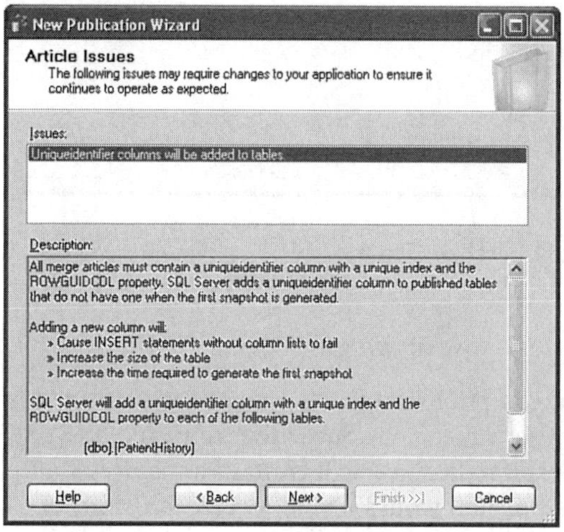

FIGURE 12.17    Unique Identifiers

**NOTE**

The Article Issues dialog box provides details of schema changes that will happen as a result of setting up a publication. If you have an existing production application with an SQL Server database and your enterprise wishes to extend it by setting Merge Replication between the central database and the client's SQL Server Compact Edition database, then you need to consider the factor that extra columns will be added at the central database.

Click Next to confirm that you agree to do schema changes at Publisher.

### Specify Rows Filtering

In the previous steps you have already selected a subset of tables for publication. You have also selected a subset of columns that you want on a client database. You have decided to publish four tables. Within the Patients table you decided not to publish Marital Status, NoOfChildren, and Education columns. As shown in Figure 12.18, the General Filters dialog box provides the next level of selection. Using this dialog box you can specify the criteria for row selection. The rows meeting the criteria will be published. If you do not wish to use row filtering, you can click Next.

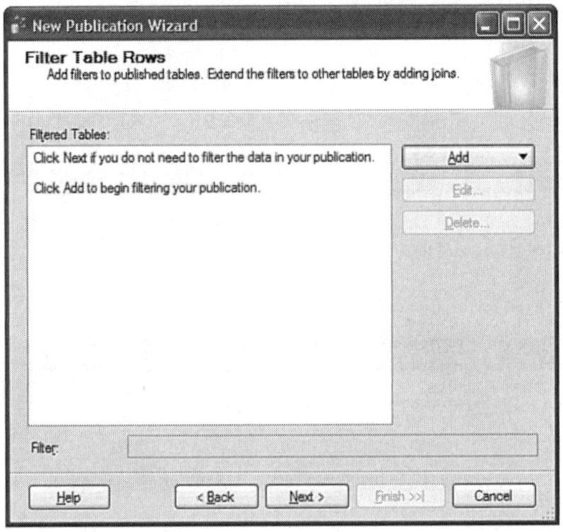

**FIGURE 12.18**    Specify Filter on Table

In this exercise you will use row filtering.

Using row filtering you can publish rows that meet a given criterion. Filtering propagates the rows that relate to the value at the Subscriber retrieved by SUSER_SNAME or HOST_NAME(). The Hospital database will contain a history of all patients. The various doctors working in the hospital would like to receive a history of each patient registered with them. You will specify a filter for the Patients table and choose an option to send patient data to his or her doctor.

To create a filter statement you will use a condition to return rows where DoctorEmployeeNo matches with HOST_NAME. HOST_NAME returns the hostname the user client device (subscriber). The rows in a Publisher database that have the same DoctorEmployeeNo as the Subscriber hostname will be synchronized with Subscriber.

   1. To specify the filter, click on Add and Filter. The Generate Filter dialog box is displayed.

### NOTE

If this is the the first time you are configuring Distributor, a dialog box will appear asking you to configure Distributor before generating the filters . If Distributor has already been configured, you will not receive this message.

2. As shown in Figure 12.18, select Add Filters.

3. Specify the condition for filtering. Select the `DoctorEmployeeNo` column and specify the condition where `[DoctorEmployeeNo]` = `HOST_NAME()` as shown in Figure 12.19.

4. Choose the radio button, A row from this table will go to only one subscription. In this exercise, each doctor row is going only to one doctor client database.

As shown in Figure 12.19, the next dialog box asks you to configure a Distributor before generating the filters you have specified. Click Yes to configure a Distributor.

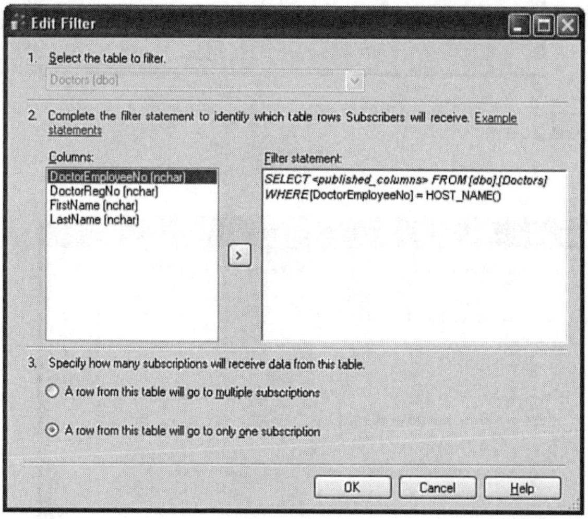

**FIGURE 12.19    Edit Filters**

5. Click on Add | Add Join to Extend the Selected Filter. Choose DoctorPatient as Joined Table and do the join on `DoctorEmployeeNo` as shown in Figure 12.20.

6. Select the DoctorPatient node in the filtered table and click on Add | Add Join to Extend the Selected Filter. Select Patient Table as Filtered Table. Select PatientRegNo as join column as shown in Figure 12.21 Click OK.

7. Select the Patient Table node in Filter Tables node. Click on Add | Add Join to Extend the Selected Filter. Select the PatientHistory table from the JoinTable drop

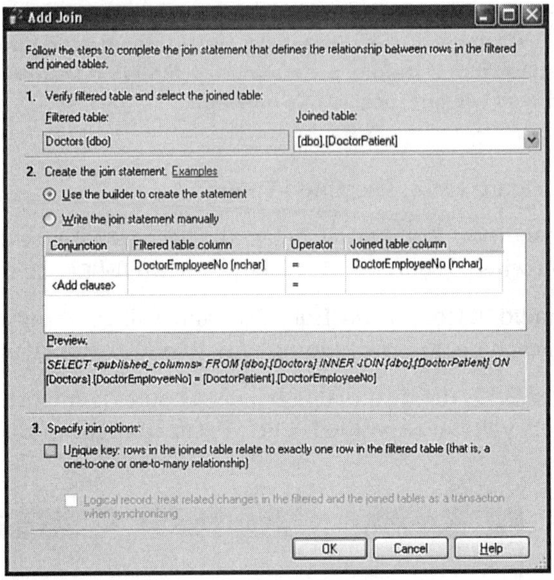

**FIGURE 12.20    Add Join**

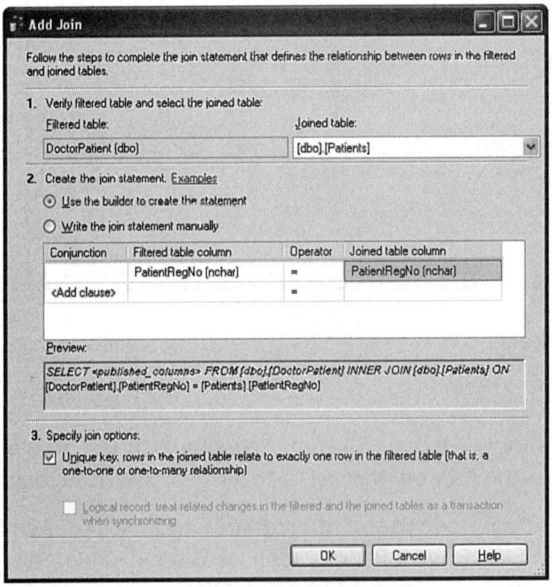

**FIGURE 12.21    Add Join to Filter Additional Tables**

down menu. Select PatientRegNo as a joined column as shown in Figure 12.22. Do not click on Unique Keys as for Each PatientRegNo as you can have multiple rows in PatientHistory Table.

8. Click on OK to add the Join dialog box.

9. Click Next on the Filter Table Rows dialog box.

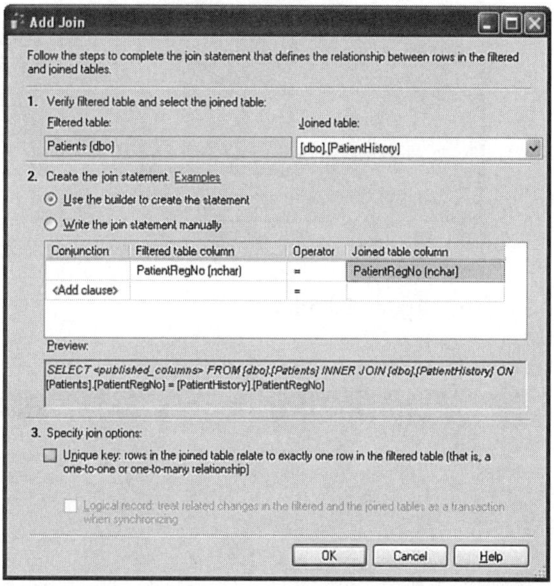

**FIGURE 12.22**    Filters for Related Tables

This completes the filtering rows of tables for publication. Using the above filters, each subscriber will receive one row in the Doctor table that matches the HOST_NAME of the subscriber. Corresponding to the doctor, the patients, and the patient's history will be sent to subscriber.

### Scheduling the Snapshot Agent
The next dialog box is the Snapshot Agent as shown in Figure 12.23. Select the Create a snapshot immediately option. It is possible to select both the options to Create immediately and Schedule to run later. In this exercise, you only need to select the first option.

You can click on the Change button. This will display the Job Schedule Properties dialog box as shown in Figure 12.24. Here you can specify the schedule on which you wish to run the Snapshot Agent. For this exercise click Cancel. Click Next on the Snapshot Agent dialog box.

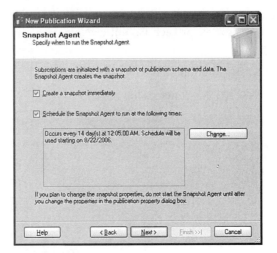

FIGURE 12.23    Snapshot Agent Schedule

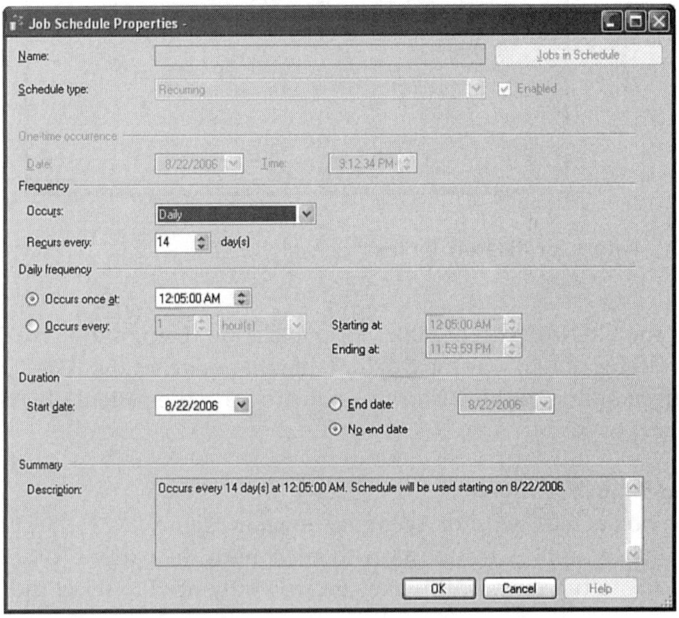

FIGURE 12.24    Snapshot Agent Job Schedule

## Configuring Snapshot Agent Security

You have specified when you wish to run Snapshot Agent. Now you are presented with the Agent Security dialog box as shown in Figure 12.25. Using the Agent Security dialog box for Snapshot Agent, you will specify the account under which Snapshot Agent will run.

The Agent Security Wizard is used to assign security rights to Snapshot Agent. Click the Security Settings button. It will start a new dialog box as shown in Figure 12.26.

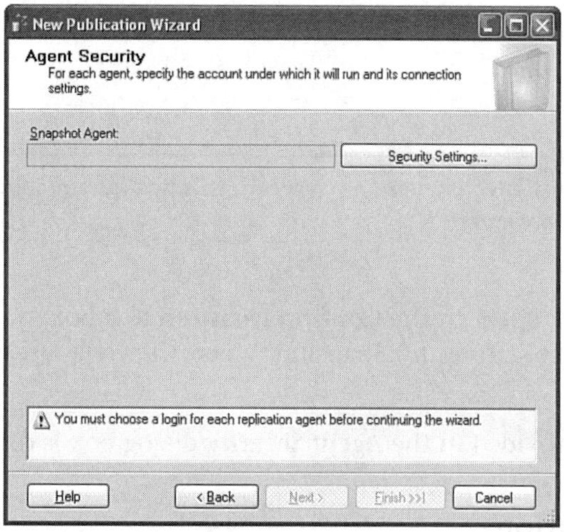

**FIGURE 12.25**   Snapshot Agent Security Account

**FIGURE 12.26**   Snapshot Agent Security

Type in the Process account name and Password. For this exercise, we have entered a sample account name and password.

> **NOTE**
>
> You should specify your account and password. The account used in this exercise is in Administrative group.

Under Connect to the Publisher, click the radio button, Using the following SQL Server login.

> **NOTE**
>
> For the purpose of this exercise use "sa" user id. It is not recommended to use "sa" user id in a production environment.

Type a password and retype it in the Confirm Password text box. In this exercise, you will also provide the security settings for Snapshot Agent. Click OK after you have added all the details.

The process account provided in the Agent Security dialog box is displayed. Click Next.

## Complete Publication

By this time you have specified all options for publication—Database, Publisher Types, Subscriber Types, Tables, Filters, and Snapshot Agent Security settings. The next dialog box allows you to create a publication or generate a script for creating a publication. You can select both options together. Select Create Publication and then select Generate a script file with steps to create the publication. Click Next.

Specify the path and name of the script to generate publication. Click Next.

The next dialog box allows you to verify the options that you have chosen and lets you specify the name of the publication. The wizard shows that you have selected to create a publication on the Hospital database. You have selected to use Patients and PatientHistory tables. You have done filtering on columns and on rows. As shown in Figure 12.27, Type Doctor_Patient as the Publication name and click Finish.

The create publication process runs and upon completion it displays the steps executed and their status. As shown in Figure 12.28, the next screen displays the success. You can click on Report to view the report.

At this point, you have created the database called *Hospital* in SQL Server 2005. You have also created a DoctorPatient publication in the SQL Server Compact database. While creating a publication you have specified a Snapshot folder on the Distributor. Access the

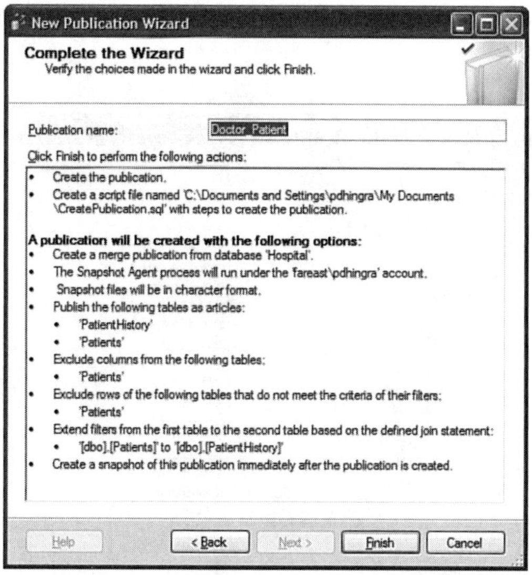

FIGURE 12.27   Verify Options and Specify Publication Name

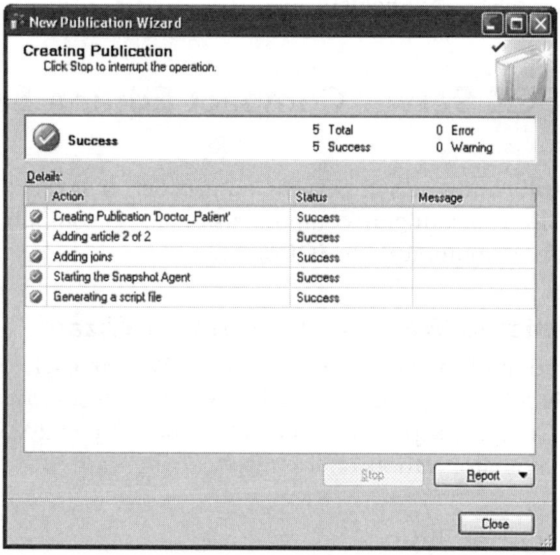

FIGURE 12.28   Create Publication Status

Snapshot folder. You will notice that the Snapshot folder contains snapshot files as shown in Figure 12.29.

**FIGURE 12.29**    Files in Snapshot Folder

# Configuring SQL Server Compact Edition Server Components

In this section, you will configure SQL Server Compact Server side components. You will use Web Synchronization to configure components on an IIS computer. This will allow SQL Server Compact to communicate to SQL Server.

## Starting the Configure Web Synchronization Wizard

To start the configuration of the Web Synchronization Wizard, click to expand the Replication folder. Under Local publication, select SQL Server Compact publication. Right click the SQL Server Compact Replication node of the SQL Server 2005 database, and then click Configure Web Synchronization.

## Choosing a Subscriber Type

The Configure Web Synchronization Wizard starts with a Welcome Page as shown in Figure 12.30 and provides you with a message that the wizard will help you to configure a virtual directory and set the access permission required for data synchronization. If you wish, you can disable the welcome screen for the future by clicking the option box at the bottom.

Click Next on the Welcome screen to start the configuration.

**FIGURE 12.30**   Welcome Screen for Configure Web Synchronization

The next screen allows you to choose the Subscriber type that will use the virtual direc-
tory on the IIS Server. You can use Merge Replication with SQL Server as Subscriber or SQL
Server Compact Edition as Subscriber. The same wizard is used both for SQL Server 2005
Subscribers and SQL Server 2005 Compact Edition Subscribers. For this exercise, choose
SQL Server Compact Edition as shown in Figure 12.31 and click Next.

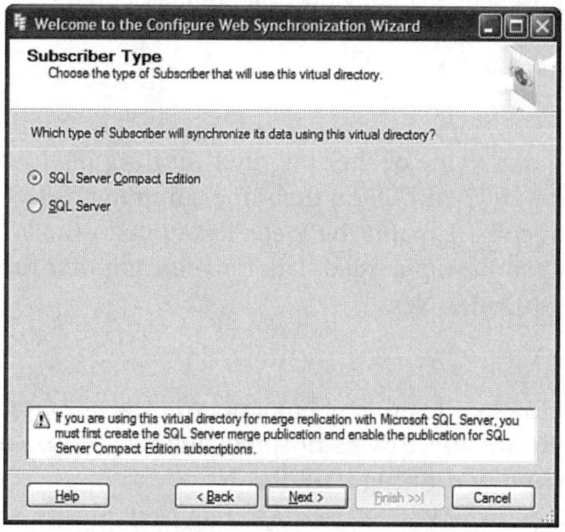

**FIGURE 12.31**   Select Subscriber Type

## Providing Web Server Details and Creating a Virtual Directory

In the next dialog box you need to identify the Web Server and virtual directory. Enter the name of your computer. In Figure 12.32, a sample computer is specified.

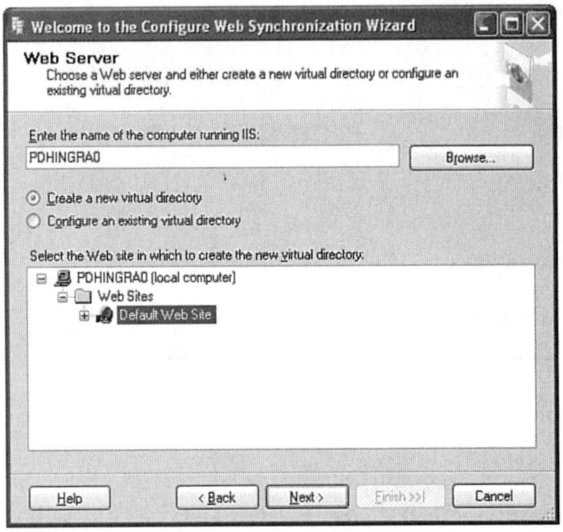

**FIGURE 12.32**    Specifying a Web Server and Virtual Directory

---

### NOTE

You can find out your machine name by doing a right click on My computer. Click on Start | My Computer. Right click on Properties and on the Computer Name tab you can see the name of your computer.

---

The field needs to know the name of the computer running IIS. In this chapter example, you are using SQL Server 2005 and IIS on the same computer. Select the radio button, Create a new virtual directory. Expand the Web Sites node in the Web Site pane and select Default Web Site. Now you have provided data for the computer running IIS and a virtual directory. Please verify and click Next.

### Specify Virtual Directory

As shown in Figure 12.33, the next dialog box asks you the alias for the virtual directory. Type the name of the virtual directory as HospitalPatient. This specified virtual directory will be created on a computer running IIS. Click Next.

You are prompted with a message that the HospitalPatient folder does not exist. Click Yes and allow the wizard to create a folder. This folder should have an SQL Server Compact Edition Server Agent. As this is a new folder you should allow wizard to copy Snapshot Agent into the HospitalPatient folder.

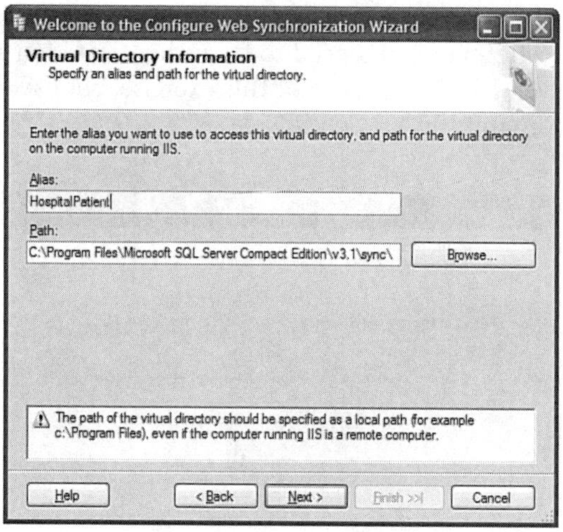

FIGURE 12.33  Alias and Path for Virtual Directory

### NOTE

The client connecting to the Web Server should have Execute permissions on the virtual directory content folder.

### Configuring Security and Authentication Requirements

As shown in Figure 12.34, the next dialog box allows you to specify whether you wish to use a secure channel or not. For the purpose of this exercise, click on the radio button, Do not require a secure channel and click the Next button.

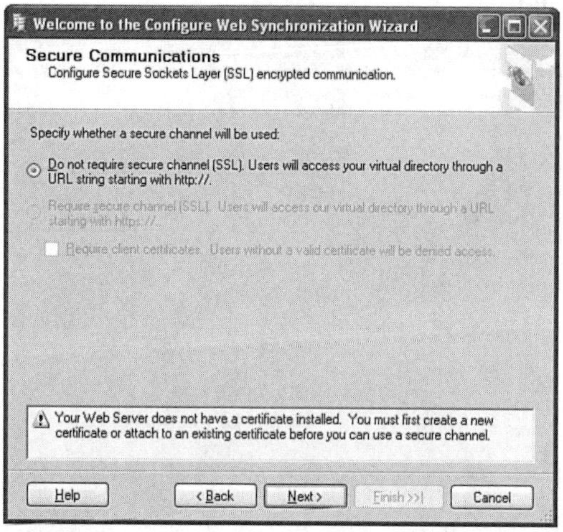

FIGURE 12.34  Secure Communication

As shown in Figure 12.35, the next dialog box asks for the authentication type. The dialog box asks you to specify whether clients need to be authenticated or not when they connect to the Web Server. For the purpose of this exercise, choose the radio button, Clients will connect anonymously, and click Next.

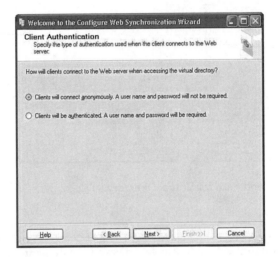

FIGURE 12.35    Client Authentication for Web Server

As you have chosen Anonymous Access in a previous dialog box, the next dialog box displayed is the Anonymous Access dialog box. This dialog box shows the account and password used for authentication as shown in Figure 12.36. Because anonymous access is chosen, there is no need to click Change to change the user account. Click Next on the Anonymous Access screen.

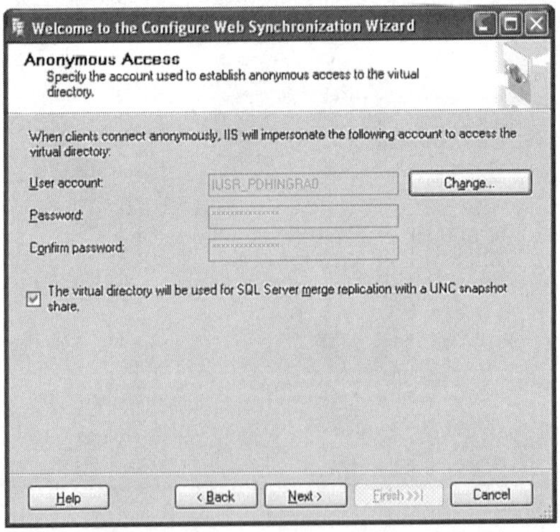

FIGURE 12.36    Account for Anonymous Access

In the next screen you will specify the path of Snapshot Share. The share you specify here should exist, be accessible, and you should have administrator privileges. Enter [your machine name]\repldata as a Snapshot folder. In the Figure 12.37 we have entered a sample machine name pdhingra0\repldata. After entering the Snapshot folder name, cick Next on the Snapshot Share Access dialog box.

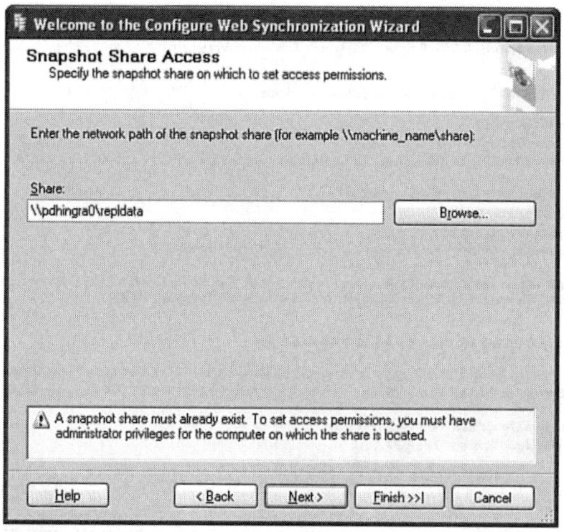

**FIGURE 12.37** Snapshot Share

## Completing the Web Synchronization Configuration

In the previous section you specified the IIS Server and virtual directory. You specified whether you wanted a secure access channel or not, and whether you wanted the client to connect to a Web Server anonymously or by providing a user name and password. The next dialog box in Figure 12.38 displays and allows you to verify the summary of options that you have specified. If you need to change any options you can go back and change them. If you are satisfied with your options, finalize your configuration of Web Synchronization Wizard by clicking the Finish button.

Figure 12.39 shows the last dialog box displaying the progress while executing the steps. Based upon the options you have specified, it displays these various steps and the results of their execution. If all the steps are successfully executed, it denotes that you have successfully configured the SQL Server Compact Server Tool for synchronization.

## Creating a Subscription

In this next part of the exercise, you will create a subscription on SQL Server Compact Edition. You will connect to an SQL Server Compact database, start the Subscription Wizard, and choose the Publisher to provide the Web Server details. In this exercise, you will also provide the security settings for Subscriber. We have discussed that you can use Subscription Wizard or the AddSubscription method to add a subscription. In this exercise you will use Subscription Wizard.

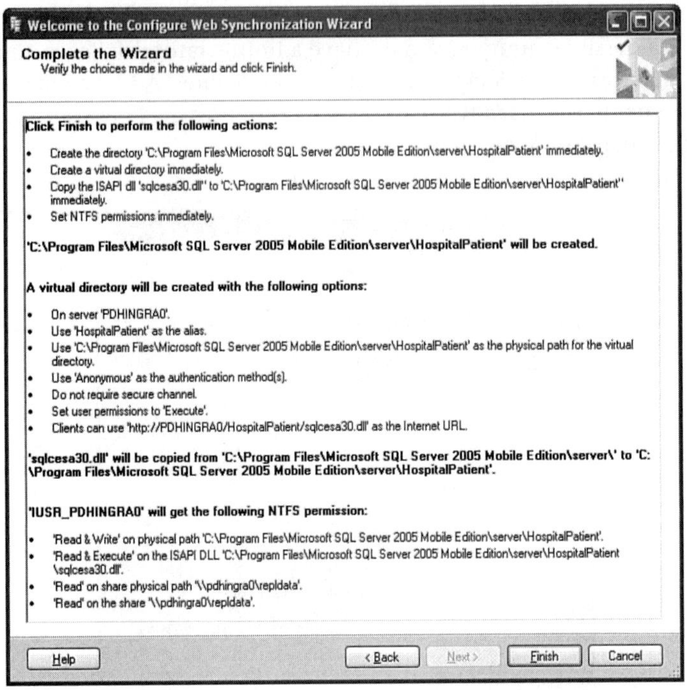

**FIGURE 12.38**    Verify Options for Configure Web Synchronization Wizard

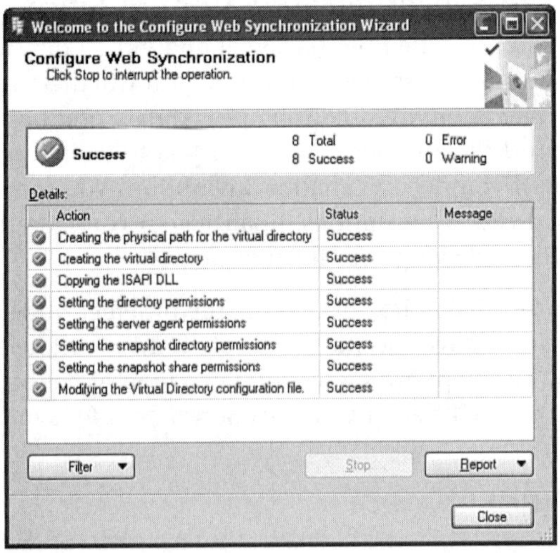

**FIGURE 12.39**    Configure Web Synchronization Progress

## Connecting to SQL Server Compact Database

You can use SQL Management Studio to open an SQL Server Compact database. In SQL Management Studio, click the Connect arrow, and then click SQL Server Compact in SQL Management Studio. You can browse to specify the name of an existing database or you can select New Database to create a new SQL Server Compact database. In this exercise, click on New Database in the database file.

The next dialog box asks for a file name for the new SQL Server Compact Edition database. The example uses the filename `C:\ReplicationExercise\MyPatients.sdf`. Click OK.

The next dialog box displays a warning that the SQL Server Compact Edition database is created without a password. For this exercise you can click Yes.

## Starting Subscription Wizard

SQL Server Management Studio now opens an SQL Server Compact Edition database. Click on the MyPatients database. In the Object Explorer expand the SQL Server Compact object and the Replication node.

Right click the Subscription node, and then click New Subscription.

Clicking on the New Subscription option opens the New Subscription Wizard. As shown in Figure 12.40, the wizard helps you to create an SQL Server Compact subscription. The wizard informs you that you should set up a publication and configure the Web Synchronization wizard before setting a subscription.

You have already created a publication named Doctor_Patient on the Hospital database and configured the Web Synchronization Wizard. Click Next on the New Subscription Wizard.

**FIGURE 12.40**    Welcome Screen for Subscription Wizard

**NOTE**

On a Server multiple SQL Server services can run. Each SQL Server service will have its own ports, logins, and databases. Each of these services is called SQL Server "instance."

The next dialog box, as shown in Figure 12.41, allows you to choose a Publisher. As SQL Server Distributor and Publisher are on the same database, the wizard can find the Publisher on SQL Server instance. Click on the Publisher option, <Find SQL Server Publisher...>.

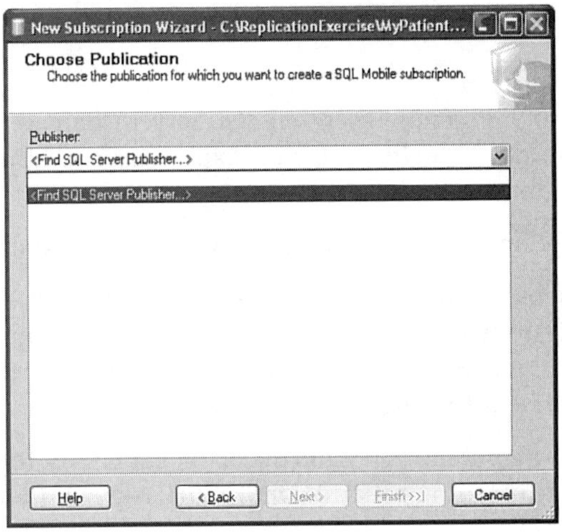

**FIGURE 12.41**    Choose Publication for Subscription

**NOTE**

You can use Subscription Wizard to create a subscription if SQL Server Publication and Distribution are on the same computer.

The next dialog box asks you to specify authentication for SQL Server instance. Choose Server Name and Authentication as Windows Authentication. Click the Connect button.

After clicking on the Find a Publisher option, you are presented with a dialog box to choose a Publisher on the SQL Server instance.

As shown in Figure 12.42, the example shows the Publisher as PDHINGRA0\BOOK. This is the publication you created in the Create Publication exercise. Expand the Hospital database node and Select the Doctor_Patient node.

After specifying the Publisher and Publication, click Next to display the Next Identify Subscription dialog box. Here you will specify the Subscription name. For this exercise, specify the Subscription name as PatientSubscription as shown in Figure 12.43.

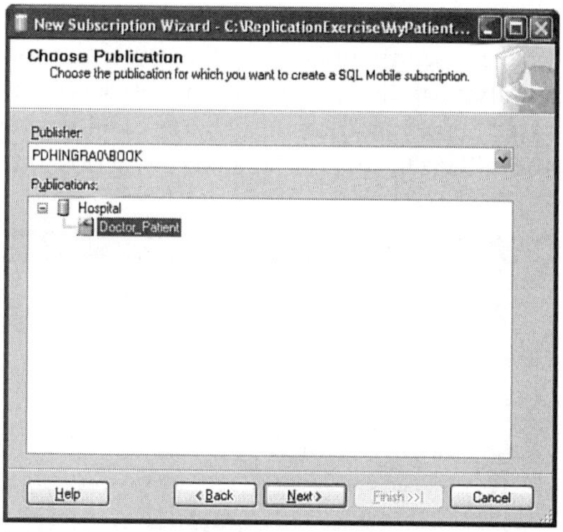

FIGURE 12.42    Specifying Database and Publication for Subscription

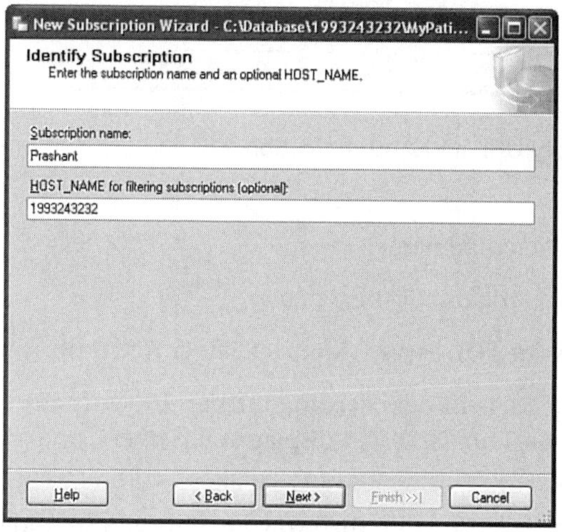

FIGURE 12.43    Specifying Subscription Name

Click Next on the Identify Subscription dialog box.

NOTE

The HOST_NAME field needs to be entered if filtering is used based on Subscriber host name devices in publication. Because you have used SUSER_SNAME() for  filtering while creating a publication, you should keep this field blank.

### Choosing the Authentication Mechanism for the Web Server

The next dialog box, Web Server Authentication, allows you to specify the authentication mechanism that the Subscriber will use to connect to Web Server. Enter the URL of the virtual directory on the Web Server. As shown in Figure 12.44 we have entered a sample virtual directory. Enter the URL as `http://pdhingra0/hospitalpatient/sqlcesa30.dll`:

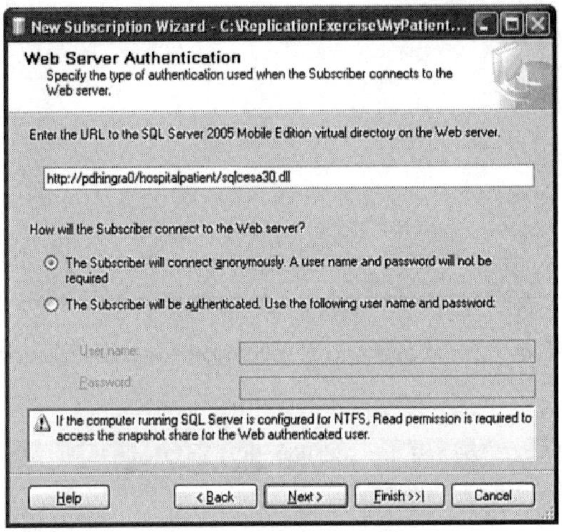

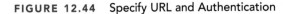

**FIGURE 12.44**    Specify URL and Authentication

- `Pdhingra0` is the machine name.
- `hospitalpatient` is the publication name.
- `sqlcesa30.dll` is the SQL Server Compact Server Agent dll.

You should verify this URL before proceeding further. To verify the URL, open a browser and enter the URL in the address. It will display SQL Server Compact Edition Server Agent with the version number.

After verifying the URL you can close the browser. Now you should choose the authentication mechanism. The wizard provides the following two options:

- Subscriber will connect anonymously.
- Subscriber will be authenticated.

For this exercise you can select the first option as shown in Figure 12.44. Click Next on the Web Server Authentication Wizard.

In the next dialog box you will specify how Subscriber will connect to SQL Server. To connect to SQL Server you can use Windows Authentication or SQL Server Authentication. In this exercise you will choose SQL Server Authentication and specify User name and Password as shown in Figure 12.45.

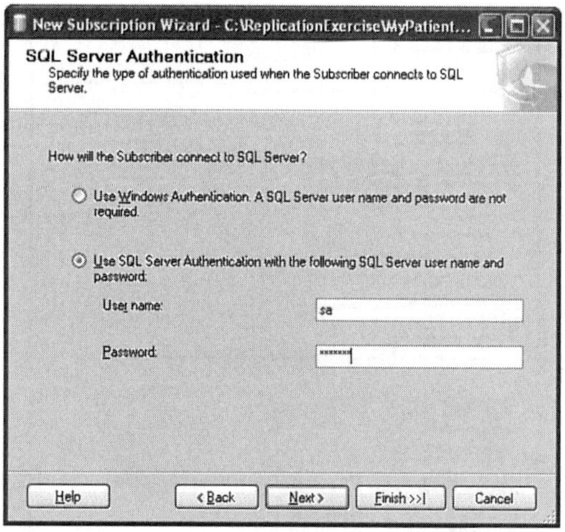

FIGURE 12.45   Authentication for Backend SQL Server

### NOTE

Windows authentication is recommended. For this exercise, you will use SQL Server authentication with sa as the user ID.

After providing authentication details, click Next.

### Completing the Subscription

As shown in Figure 12.46, the last dialog box allows you to view your subscription options. The dialog box shows that you have created PatientSubscription for the Doctor_Patient publication.

The wizard also displays sample code for setting up the subscription and synchronizing data. You should copy the code and save it into a file for later use in this exercise.

Once you are satisfied with all options, click Finish. SQL Server Compact Edition will create the subscription and begin synchronizing the data. A dialog box shows the status of various steps.

Once steps are completed successfully, you can view the Report.

Now you have completed the subscription, you can view the Subscriber database. Open MyPatient.sdf file in SQL Management Studio and see the tables. The tables you have specified in the publication are available in the Subscriber database. You should create more subscriptions for other subscribers. For example, the Doctors table contains three doctors. You can create two more subscriptions. While specifying the host name, specify the DoctorEmployeeNo of subscriber. The example uses 1993243232, 1997124246, 2001225598 Host_name, and DoctorEmployeeNo.

**FIGURE 12.46**    Verify Options and Complete Subscriptions

## Monitoring Replication

Replication Monitor is a tool that allows the user to see the status of Publications and Subscriptions. The Replication tool graphical interface provides you an overall picture about Publishers, Subscribers, and the Snapshot Agents. To use the Replication Monitor in SQL Server 2005, start SQL Server Management Studio and select the Publication you wish to monitor. Right click on the Publication and select the Launch Replication Monitor option. The Replication Monitor shows the Publication and Subscribers list. You can filter the list of subscribers by choosing the Show All Subscribers option, Show Errors only option, and so on ashown in Figure 12.47.

To see the Snapshot Agent status, choose the Warnings and Agents tab in the Replication Monitor.

To monitor a replication, a user should have a member of a sysadmin role at Distributor or a member of a replmonitor database role in the distribution database.

## Viewing Snapshot Agent Status

The snapshot agent is an executable that is responsible for generating snapshot files and also records synchronization jobs in the distribution database. Snapshot files contain published articles. To view the status of the Snapshot Agent, select the publication. Right

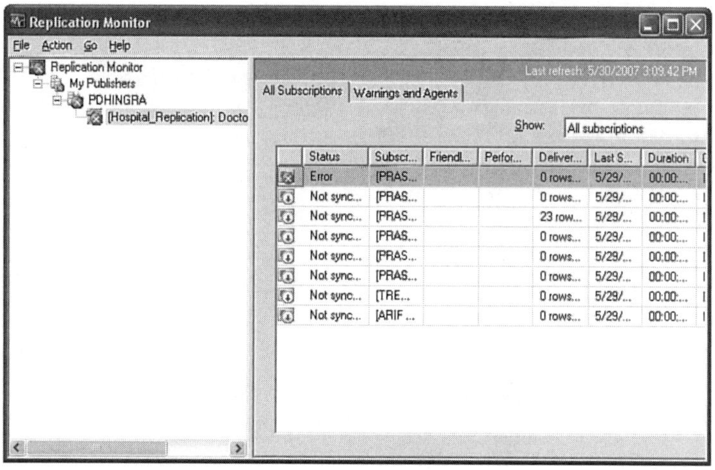

**FIGURE 12.47** Replication Monitor

click on Publication and select View Snapshot Agent status. The snapshot agent status appears as shown in Figure 12.48.

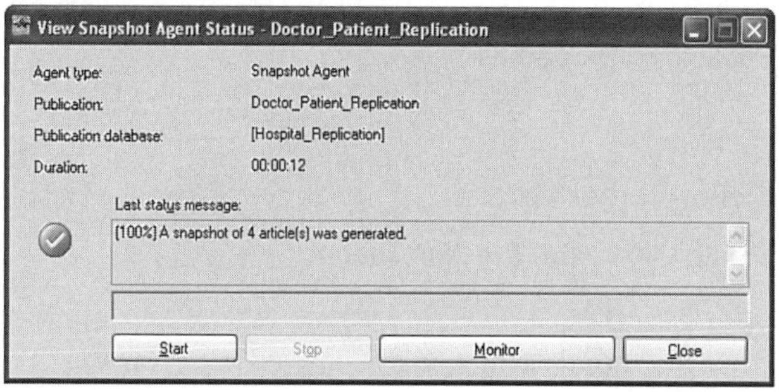

**FIGURE 12.48** View Snapshot Agent Status

## Viewing and Modifying Publisher Properties

To view or modify a publication, select the publication. Right click and select Properties. The Publication properties dialog box is displayed as shown in Figure 12.49. You can select various tabs on the left to access properties for Article, Filtering, Snapshot, and so on.

## Creating a Device Application in Visual Studio 2005

In this section you will create a .NET Compact Framework application using Visual Studio 2005. The application will fetch the patient data onto a doctor/client device. The application will inset, update, and delete data in the SQL Server Compact Edition database. Finally, the data will be synchronized with a backend SQL Server.

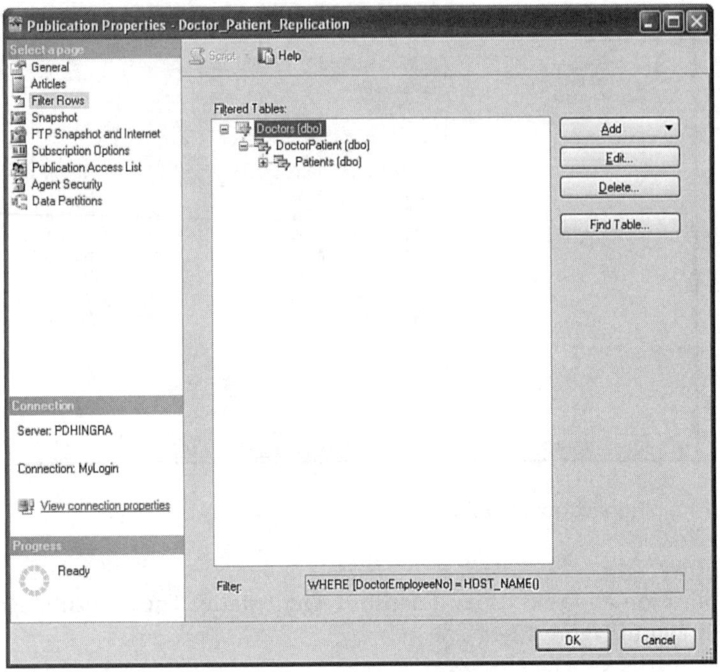

FIGURE 12.49    Publication Properties

## Creating a Project

To create a project follow these steps:

1. Start Visual Studio 2005 from the Start menu.

2. Click File | New | Project.

3. Click on Visual C# or Visual Basic.

4. Click on Smart Devices project and select Windows Mobile 5.0 Pocket PC. Select Device Application.

5. Enter the Name and Location of the project.

6. Click OK on New Project Dialog box.

## Add Database File

Right click on Project and Add Existing Item. Select the SQL Server Compact File that you generated.

It will start the Data Source Configuration Wizard. Select Tables and click Finish.

## Create the User Interface

Click on the Tool box. Select Tab Control, and then use a drag-and-drop operation to move it to Form. Click on the Tab Pages property.

Create four tabs: Patient, History, New Treatment, and Sync. On the first tab, create a list box, fields, and buttons as shown in Figure 12.50.

The second tab provides fields to enter new patient details as shown in Figure 12.51. On the History tab create a RegNo text box, listHistory text box, and a Refresh button

**FIGURE 12.50**    Synchronize Tab

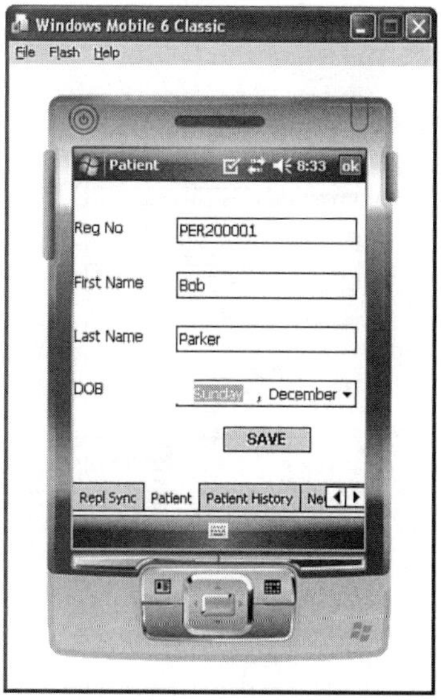

**FIGURE 12.51**    Patient Tab

as shown in Figure 12.52 to display the history of previous treatments given to a patient.

On the New Treatment tab, add the fields to enter treatment details as shown in Figure 12.53. This tab has Disease and Date Identified fields, as well as Treatment, Start, and End date fields.

**FIGURE 12.52    Patient History Tab**

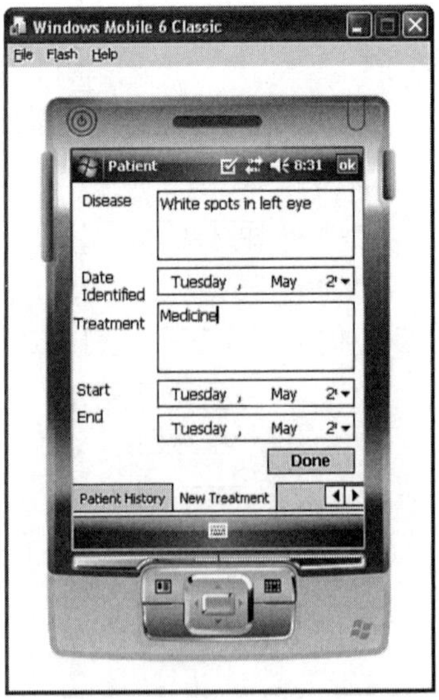

**FIGURE 12.53    New Treatment Tab**

Listing 12.3 illustrates how to view the data you retrieved into the SQL Server Compact database. The code also illustrates how to insert and update records. The `Patient_Load` function loads the form. It opens the database connection and displays a list of patients. Details of a new patient can be added in Patient tab. The btnSavePatient_Click method saves the patient's details. On entering a patient registration number and clicking on the Refresh button, the FillListHistory method is executed and it loads the history of the selected patient under the History tab. For new treatment, the doctor can click on the New Treatment tab and enter the details. On clicking the Done button, data entered is inserted into the PatientHistory table. The doctor can enter the details of treatment given to various patients and save it on a local device. Later, the doctor can synchronize the data by clicking the Sync button.

The synchronize method sets the various replication properties such as the URL for Web Server, Publisher, Publisher database, and so on, and then you invoke the synchronization method.

### LISTING 12.3    Hospital Application Based on Replication C#.NET

```csharp
using System;
using System.Collections.Generic;
using System.ComponentModel;
using System.Data;
using System.Drawing;
using System.Text;
using System.Windows.Forms;
using System.Data.SqlServerCe;

namespace Patient_Repl
{
    public partial class Patient : Form
    {
    SqlCeConnection myConn;
    SqlCeDataReader myPatientDataReader;
    SqlCeDataReader myHistoryDataReader;
    SqlCeCommand myCmd;
    string selectedPatientRegNo;
    string strDoctorEmployeeNo;
    string connStr;

    public Patient()
    {
        InitializeComponent();
    }

    private void Patient_Load(object sender, EventArgs e)
    {
```

```
        connStr =
            "DataSource=\\Program Files\\Patient_Repl\\MyPatients.sdf";
        myConn = new SqlCeConnection(connStr);
        myConn.Open();
        FillDoctorEmployeeNo();
        FillPatientList();



    }
    private void FillDoctorEmployeeNo()
    {



        SqlCeCommand myCmd = myConn.CreateCommand();
        myCmd.CommandText =
            "Select DoctorEmployeeNo" +
            " From Doctors";
        strDoctorEmployeeNo= (string)myCmd.ExecuteScalar();
        txtDoctorEmployeeNo.Text = strDoctorEmployeeNo;
        txtDoctorEmployeeNo.Enabled = false;


    }
    void FillPatientList()
    {
        // Opens a data reader and fetch the rows from Patient Table
        listPatient.Items.Clear();
        SqlCeCommand myCmd = myConn.CreateCommand();
        myCmd.CommandText =
            "Select PatientRegNo, FirstName, LastName " +
            " From Patients";

        myPatientDataReader = myCmd.ExecuteReader();
        while (myPatientDataReader.Read())
        {
            listPatient.Items.Add
                (myPatientDataReader.GetString(0) + " "
                + myPatientDataReader.GetString(1) + " "
                + myPatientDataReader.GetString(2));
        }
    }
    private void btnPatientRefresh_Click(object sender, EventArgs e)
    {
            FillPatientList();
    }
```

```
private void btnRefresh_Click(object sender, EventArgs e)
{
    // Gets detail of patient history for a given patient
    FillListHistory();
}

private void FillListHistory()
{
// Opens a data reader and fetch the rows from Patient History Table
listHistory.Items.Clear();
SqlCeCommand myCmd = myConn.CreateCommand();
selectedPatientRegNo = txtRegNo.Text;
myCmd.CommandText =
    "Select PatientRegNo, Treatment, TreatmentStartDate" +
    " From PatientHistory" +
    " where PatientRegNo = " + "'" + selectedPatientRegNo + "'";
myHistoryDataReader = myCmd.ExecuteReader();
while (myHistoryDataReader.Read())
{
   listHistory.Items.Add
      (myHistoryDataReader.GetDateTime(2).ToShortDateString() + " "
       + myHistoryDataReader.GetString(1));
}

}
```

The sample can be written using VB.NET. Listing 12.4 is given in VB.NET. It is similar to Listing 12.3 but uses an SqlClient namespace.

**Build and Deploy Application**
Click Build and compile the application. Click Debug | Start Without Debugging. Data Synchronization between a device or an emulator and a server requires that you cradle the emulator or device. The DMA option should be selected in ActiveSync for using Emulator.

Check the status of connectivity by clicking on the connectivity icon on emulator/device.

You can select the device or emulator for deployment. The first tab in the application displays a list of Patients as shown in Figure12.50 on page 397.

Click on the Patient Tab. Enter a Registration number, First name, Last name, and DOB for a new patient as shown in Figure 12.51 on page 397.

Click on the Patient History tab, enter a patient registration number, and click on the Refresh button. It will fetch the treatment details and fill the list box. The form displays a list of treatments given to the patient as shown in Figure 12.52 on page 398.

To enter details of a new treatment click on the New Treatment tab and enter the details as shown in Figure 12.53 on page 398.

Click the Done button. It will insert the new treatment details in the PatientHistory table. You can insert new treatment history rows and verify the data inserted into History by clicking on the Refresh button.

Clicking on the Sync button synchronizes the data with the backend SQL Server. Use SQL Server Management Studio to see the data in the PatientHistory table. The PatientHistory table now has up-to-date data that you entered into the device application.

**NOTE**

To see a conflict that may have occurred during synchronization, select the publication in Object Explorer. Right click and select the View Conflict menu option. Conflict View will display the conflicts that occurred.

In this exercise, you created an end-to-end scenario for a disconnected device application. You created the Hospital backend database on SQL Server 2005, created a publication and subscription, and received the data in the SQL Server Compact database using Merge Replication. Using .NET Compact Framework 2.0 and Visual Studio 2005, you created an application to access and update the local SQL Server Compact Edition Database on a client device. Finally, you synchronized the data back with SQL Server 2005.

## Synchronizing Data with SQL Server 2000

Many of you will be using SQL Server 2000 as a backend database. It is possible to set up a Merge Replication between SQL Server 2000 and SQL Server Compact Edition.

You need to install the Server Tool component on the Web Server. Based upon the version of SQL Server that you will be using, you will need one of the following Server Tool components:

- `sqlce30setupen.MSI`—Server Tool components to synchronize with SQL Server 2005.
- `sql2kensp3a.MSI`—Server Tool components to synchronize data with SQL Server 2000 SP3a.
- `sql2kensp4.MSI`—Server Tool components to synchronize data with SQL Server 2000 SP4.

The Install SQL Server Compact Components section discussed that you need to install SQL Server Compact Server Tool components to synchronize data with SQL Server 2005. To install the component for replication, you installed the `Sqlce30setupen.MSI` file. For replication between SQL Server 2000 and SQL Server Compact Edition, you need to install Server Tool components for SQL Server 2000. You may be using SQL Server 2000 Service Pack 3 or SQL Server 2000 Service Pack 4. Based upon the service pack version, you need to install the `sql2kensp3a.MSI` or `sql2kensp4.MSI` file.

Visual Studio 2005 also copies the following installer packages on a computer running Visual Studio 2005. These three packages are copied at `<Disk>\Program Files\Microsoft Visual Studio 8\SmartDevices\SDK\SQL Server\Mobile\v3.0`.

Once you set up the SQL Server 2005 Server Tools for SQL Server 2000, you can configure a Merge Replication between SQL Server 2000 and SQL Server 2005 Compact Edition.

# Developing Connected Smart Device Applications with SqlClient

In this section, you will create a .NET Compact Framework application using Visual Studio 2005. In this exercise, you are not required to create an SQL Server Compact Edition database. The .NET Compact Framework application will directly access the SQL Server. The application will fetch the patient data from the backend SQL Server and will input data to the SQL Server. As the application is directly accessing and updating the SQL Server, the solution does not require replication. However, your device requires connectivity with a backend server while working on this application.

From a device, you can connect to the SQL Server using a TCP/IP connection. You need to configure the SQL Server to accept remote connections over TCP/IP.

## Enable Remote Connections

SQL Server 2005 allows a local connection by default. To connect to SQL Server remotely, you should enable the remote connection. Use the following steps to enable a remote connection over TCP/IP:

1. Click on All Programs | Microsoft SQL Server 2005 | Configuration Tools | SQL Server Surface Area configuration.

2. In the surface area configuration dialog box, click on the Surface Area Configuration for Services and Connections option.

3. Click on the Remote Connections in Database Engine node.

4. Enable remote connections by clicking on Local and Remote Connections.

5. Select the suboption Using Both TCP/IP and Name Pipes.

## Configure a Firewall

If your system has a firewall, it should allow communication with an SQL Server executable. Use the following steps to allow communication with an SQL Server:

1. Start the Control Panel on a computer running SQL Server.

2. Double click on Windows Firewall.

3. Click on the Exceptions tab.

4. Click on the Add Program button.

5. Add the path of sqlsrvr.exe. The sqlsrvr.exe is installed at `<Drive>\Program Files\Microsoft SQL Server\MSSQL.1\MSSQL\Binn\sqlservr.exe`

6. Click OK.

### Create a Smart Device Project

1. Create a Smart device project in Visual Studio. Start Visual Studio 2005.

2. Design the user interface for the project as shown in Figure 12.50

3. Add a reference to the System.Data.SqlClient namespace in the project. In Solution Explorer, right click on References and select the Add Reference option. In the Add Reference dialog box, select System.Data.SqlClient dll.

Listing 12.4 has the complete code for this exercise. The code is similar to Listing 12.3 except that instead of using the SqlServerCe classes code it uses the SqlClient classes.

Here is the complete listing in VB with the SqlClient namespace.

### LISTING 12.4    Patient SqlClient   VB.NET

```vbnet
Imports System.Data
Imports System.Data.SqlClient
Public Class Form1

    Dim myConn As SqlConnection
    Dim connStr As String
    Dim myPatientDataReader As SqlDataReader
    Dim myHistoryDataReader As SqlDataReader
    Dim myCmd As SqlCommand
    Dim selectedPatientRegNo As String
    Dim strDoctorEmployeeNo As String


    Private Sub Form1_Load(ByVal sender As System.Object, ByVal e As System.Even-
tArgs) Handles MyBase.Load
        ' Use your machine name and credentials
        connStr = "Server='PDHINGRA';Initial Catalog=Hospital;User Id=MyLogin;Pass-
word=MyPassword"


    End Sub
    Private Sub FillDoctorEmployeeNo()

        myCmd = myConn.CreateCommand()
        myCmd.CommandText = _
            "Select DoctorEmployeeNo" + _
            " From Doctors"

        strDoctorEmployeeNo = Convert.ToString(myCmd.ExecuteScalar())
```

```
        txtDoctorEmployeeNo.Text = strDoctorEmployeeNo
        txtDoctorEmployeeNo.Enabled = False

End Sub
Private Sub FillPatientList()

    ' Opens a data reader and fetch the rows from Patient Table
    listPatient.Items.Clear()
    myCmd = myConn.CreateCommand()
    ' Fetch the patients for a given Doctor.
    ' In replication exercise such filtering is applied during synchronization.
    ' Each subbscriber gets its own patients.
    myCmd.CommandText = _
        "Select P.PatientRegNo, P.FirstName, P.LastName " + _
        " From Patients P, DoctorPatient D" + _
        " where P.PatientRegNo = D.PatientRegNo" + _
        " and D.doctoremployeeno = " + _
        "'" + txtDoctorEmployeeNo.Text + "'"

    myPatientDataReader = myCmd.ExecuteReader()
    While (myPatientDataReader.Read())

        listPatient.Items.Add _
           (myPatientDataReader.GetString(0) + " " _
            + myPatientDataReader.GetString(1) + " " _
            + myPatientDataReader.GetString(2))
    End While

End Sub
Private Sub FillListHistory()

    listHistory.Items.Clear()
    myCmd = myConn.CreateCommand()
    selectedPatientRegNo = txtRegNo.Text
    myCmd.CommandText = _
        "Select PatientRegNo, Treatment, TreatmentStartDate " & _
        "From PatientHistory " & _
        "where PatientRegNo = " & "'" & selectedPatientRegNo & "'"
    ' Read all records returned by Select statement
    myHistoryDataReader = myCmd.ExecuteReader()
    While (myHistoryDataReader.Read())
        listHistory.Items.Add( _
          myHistoryDataReader.GetDateTime(2).ToShortDateString() + " " + _
          myHistoryDataReader.GetString(1))
    End While
```

```
    End Sub
    Private Sub btnSave_Click(ByVal sender As System.Object, ByVal e As
System.EventArgs) Handles btnSave.Click

        'Save the new patient detail.
        If txtPatientRegNo.Text <> "" Then

            myConn = New SqlConnection(connStr)
            myConn.Open()
            'Command for adding new Patients
            myCmd = myConn.CreateCommand()
            myCmd.CommandText = _
            "INSERT INTO Patients " & _
            "(PatientRegNo, FirstName, LastName, DOB) " & _
            "VALUES " & _
            "(@PatientRegNo, " & _
            " @FirstName, @LastName, @DOB)"

            myCmd.Parameters.Add("@PatientRegNo", SqlDbType.NChar, 10)

            myCmd.Parameters.Add("@FirstName", SqlDbType.NChar, 20)
            myCmd.Parameters.Add("@LastName", SqlDbType.NChar, 20)
            myCmd.Parameters.Add("@DOB", SqlDbType.DateTime)

            myCmd.Parameters("@PatientRegNo").Value = txtPatientRegNo.Text

            myCmd.Parameters("@FirstName").Value = txtFirstName.Text
            myCmd.Parameters("@LastName").Value = txtLastName.Text
            myCmd.Parameters("@DOB").Value = dateTimeDOB.Value
            myCmd.ExecuteNonQuery()

            myCmd = myConn.CreateCommand()
            myCmd.CommandText = _
             "INSERT INTO DoctorPatient " & _
             "(DoctorEmployeeNo, patientRegNo)" & _
              "VALUES " & _
             "(@DoctorEmployeeNo, @PatientRegNo)"


            myCmd.Parameters.Add("@DoctorEmployeeNo", SqlDbType.NChar, 10)
            myCmd.Parameters.Add("@PatientRegNo", SqlDbType.NChar, 10)

            myCmd.Parameters("@PatientRegNo").Value = txtPatientRegNo.Text
            myCmd.Parameters("@DoctorEmployeeNo").Value = _
             txtDoctorEmployeeNo.Text
```

```
            myCmd.ExecuteNonQuery()
            myConn.Close()
        End If
        txtPatientRegNo.Text = ""
        txtFirstName.Text = ""
        txtLastName.Text = ""

        myConn.Close()
    End Sub
    Private Sub btnRefresh_Click(ByVal sender As System.Object, ByVal e As
System.EventArgs) Handles btnRefresh.Click
        'Gets detail of patient history for a given patient
        myConn = New SqlConnection(connStr)
        myConn.Open()

        FillListHistory()
        myConn.Close()

    End Sub
    Private Sub btnPatientRefresh_Click(ByVal sender As System.Object, ByVal e As
System.EventArgs) Handles btnPatientRefresh.Click
        myConn = New SqlConnection(connStr)
        myConn.Open()
        FillPatientList()
        myConn.Close()

    End Sub

    Private Sub btnDone_Click(ByVal sender As System.Object, ByVal e As
System.EventArgs) Handles btnDone.Click
        ' Save the Patient History
        If txtDisease.Text <> "" Then
            myConn = New SqlConnection(connStr)
            myConn.Open()
            ' SQL Command for adding new PatientHistory
            myCmd = myConn.CreateCommand()
            myCmd.CommandText = _
              "INSERT INTO PatientHistory " & _
              "(PatientRegNo,DiseaseIdentified," & _
              " DateIdentified,Treatment,TreatmentStartDate, " & _
              " TreatmentEndDate) " & _
              " VALUES " & _
              "(@PatientRegNo,@DiseaseIdentified,@DateIdentified, " & _
              " @Treatment, @TreatmentStartDate,@TreatmentEndDate) "
```

```
            myCmd.Parameters.Add("@PatientRegNo", SqlDbType.NChar, 10)
            myCmd.Parameters.Add("@DiseaseIdentified", SqlDbType.NVarChar, 200)
            myCmd.Parameters.Add("@DateIdentified", SqlDbType.DateTime)
            myCmd.Parameters.Add("@Treatment", SqlDbType.NVarChar, 200)
            myCmd.Parameters.Add("@TreatmentStartDate", SqlDbType.DateTime)
            myCmd.Parameters.Add("@TreatmentEndDate", SqlDbType.DateTime)


            myCmd.Parameters("@PatientRegNo").Value = selectedPatientRegNo
            myCmd.Parameters("@DiseaseIdentified").Value = txtDisease.Text
            myCmd.Parameters("@DateIdentified").Value = dateTimePicker1.Value
            myCmd.Parameters("@Treatment").Value = txtTreatment.Text
            myCmd.Parameters("@TreatmentStartDate").Value = dateTimePicker2.Value
            myCmd.Parameters("@TreatmentEndDate").Value = dateTimePicker3.Value


            myCmd.ExecuteNonQuery()
            myConn.Close()
        End If
        txtDisease.Text = ""
        txtTreatment.Text = ""
    End Sub
End Class
```

You can use the sample application in a similar way that you used the application in Listing 12.3.

In this exercise, you created an end-to-end scenario for a connected device application. You created the Hospital backend database on SQL Server 2005 and enabled a remote connection. Using .NET Compact Framework 2.0 and Visual Studio 2005, you created an application to fetch the data from a remote SQL Server and updated the SQL Server from a client device. You used SQL Server Data Provider to connect, execute a command, and retrieve data from an SQL Server database.

In the connected solution, you required a connection to a backend database while retrieving and saving the database. The alternate approach is to have a local SQL Server Compact Edition database on a device. The SQL Server Compact Edition database will store the transactions and synchronize with the backend database at regular intervals.

## Summary

In this chapter, you learned how to use Merge Replication between SQL Server and SQL Server Compact Edition. We discussed the various possible scenarios in which SQL Server on a backend and SQL Server Compact Edition on a client machine together can provide disconnected solutions. You learned how Merge Replication features enable such scenarios by synchronizing updates and resolving conflicts from multiple clients and a server. You also learned SQL Server Compact components that participate in Merge Replication. We discussed in detail the various steps you need to complete for setting up Merge Replication. At the end of the exercise, you developed a complete solution to demonstrate Merge Replication. In the solution you installed SQL Server Compact Server components; you created a publication, configured the Web synchronization, and then set up the subscription. You created a client application that allows updating the data. After updating the client data, you have synchronized the data again with the backend server.

# Synchronizing Data with Remote Data Access

CHAPTER **13**

Chapter 12, *Synchronizing Data with Merge Replication,* discussed the importance of transferring data from a desktop application to a mobile device. Merge Replication allows you to update data on both SQL Server and SQL Server Compact Edition. Merge Replication functionality is extremely useful when multiple clients or devices need to subscribe data, make offline changes, and need to subscribe data back to a backend server.

Remote Data Access (RDA) allows you to fetch data from SQL Server to an SQL Server Compact Edition database table. The table can be updated on a client and then those updates are sent back to the SQL Server table.

In this chapter, you are introduced to scenarios in which RDA is useful and then look at RDA architecture and features. This chapter focuses on RDA from a developer perspective and creates a sample application to pull data from SQL Server to SQL Server Compact Edition. The application will update data in the SQL Server Compact Edition database and then transfer the changes back to SQL Server 2005.

## Remote Data Access Scenarios

You will be using RDA to exchange data among a backend database and client applications. The client applications can be on mobile devices, laptops, Tablet PCs, ATMs, kiosks or any other Windows-based machines as shown in Figure 13.1.

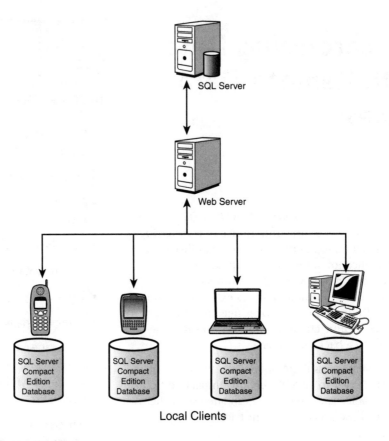

SQL Server

Web Server

Local Clients

**FIGURE 13.1**    RDA Usage

Using RDA, an application on a client device can pull a table from the SQL Server database. The changes can be made locally on the SQL Server Compact Edition database. After the data changes are complete, the client can push the changes back to the backend SQL Server. You can use RDA as a data exchange mechanism in the following scenarios.

## Download Only

An enterprise may have an application in which they download details of a TV Program from the SQL Server database to a local SQL Server Compact Edition database. The application using SQL Server Compact Edition can invoke the Pull method to get the table from SQL Server.

## Upload Only

An application may be used in surveys where the user goes in the field and collects people's names and addresses and record them locally on the SQL Server Compact Edition database on a device. Later, the application can push the data to the SQL Server backend.

## Download, Change, and Upload

An enterprise application can pull the detail of orders from the SQL Server database to the SQL Server Compact Edition on a mobile device. After the delivery is done, the user can change the status to "Delivered." SQL Server Compact Edition can track the rows that are updated. Later on, the user can exchange the updated data with the SQL Server.

## Submitting SQL Statements

RDA provides an additional method for executing an SQL Statement on the backend SQL Server. Using this technique, an SQL Server Compact Edition database can trigger an SQL Statement on an SQL Server database.

# Remote Data Access Features

In this section you will learn about the Remote Data Access features. The combination of these features allows you to synchronize the data between the backend SQL Server to a local SQL Server Compact Edition client.

### The Pull Feature

You will use the Pull feature to get a table from an SQL Server table to an SQL Server Compact Edition table. To use this feature you will use the Pull method of an RDA object. Invoking the Pull method will create the table, create the indexes on the table, and fetch the data in the table.

### Tracking the Changes

The Tracking feature allows you to track the changes in a table on SQL Server Compact Edition after you have pulled it from the SQL Server. In case you want to update the data locally and then send the updated changes back to the SQL Server backend, you should track the changes on the SQL Server Compact Edition database. The Pull method has an optional parameter to enable the tracking of changes.

### The Push Feature

RDA provides a feature to push the changes from SQL Server Compact Edition to SQL Server. To use this feature, first you need to track the changes done on SQL Server Compact Edition. Once the changes are tracked, you will use the Push method of the RDA object to send the completed updates on SQL Server Compact Edition to SQL Server.

### Batch Changes

When you push changes from SQL Server Compact Edition to SQL Server, changes are applied individually. Some changes may fail and an error is logged. If you want either all or none of the changes to succeed, you can use the SQL Server Compact Edition Batch feature. The Batch feature allows you to apply all changes as a transaction. You can switch on the Batching option in RDA to make all changes as part of a single transaction. With the Batch option on, the Push operation requires that all rows should be successfully updated on SQL Server. The Push operation will fail even if a single row is not applied successfully.

### Submitting SQL

There will be scenarios when you need to execute a statement and take an action on a remote SQL Server. You can do this by using the SubmitSQL method of the RDA object. Using the SubmitSQL method, you cannot return the rows. You can only execute an SQL Statement that does not return rows such as Insert, Update, Delete, etc.

### Error Logging

Errors that occur during RDA operations get logged in the Error table on the SQL Server Compact Edition database. The Error Table contains columns specified in the SELECT statement of Pull operations and three additional columns to indicate error number, error string, and date/time on which error occurred.

## Remote Data Access Architecture

You have previously learned the architecture component of Merge Replication. RDA also uses the same components for communication between the client and remote server. The communication from Client Agent to Server Agent happens over http. The Server Agent communicates with the Remote SQL Server using the Old DB Connection Provider. Figure 13.2 shows the architecture component of RDA.

The architecture is similar but simpler than Merge Replication as RDA does not have Distributor and Conflict Resolver components.

### Server Agent

The SQL Server Compact Edition Server Agent is the primary component to manage connectivity between an SQL Server Compact Edition database and an SQL Server database. The SQL Server Compact Edition Server Agent runs as ISAPI DLL on a machine running the IIS. The SQL Server Compact Edition Server Agent handles all http requests made by the SQL Server Compact Edition Client Agent. The Server Agent handles these requests and invokes an SQL Server Replication provider.

### Web Server

The SQL Server Compact Edition Server Agent is hosted on the Web Server. The Server Agent runs as an ISAPI extension under IIS. You can create a virtual directory on the Web Server and place Server Agent Dll sscesa30.dll under that directory.

### Client Agent

The SQL Mobile Client Agent is the most important component. As the name suggests, this component runs on a mobile device or desktop where SQL Server Mobile Edition is installed. You will be using the Client Agent method and properties to implement RDA. The client agent exposes Push, Pull, and SubmitSQL methods to use RDA.

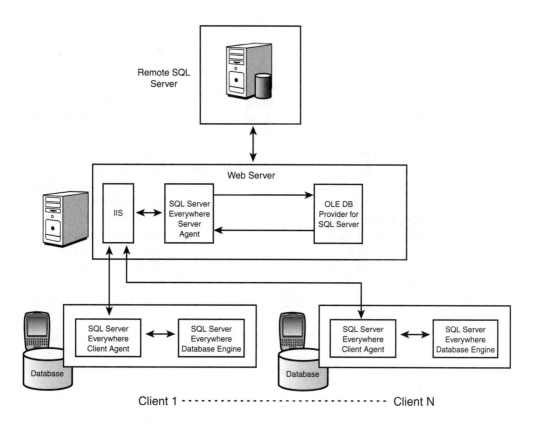

**FIGURE 13.2**    RDA Architecture

The Client Agent sits between the .NET/.NET CF based application and the SQL Server Compact Edition Database. The Client Agent will interact with the SQL Mobile Server Agent over http/https.

## The SQL Server Compact Edition Database Engine

The engine creates the tables, columns, and indexes as well as provides a tracking mechanism to track the changes on a database. The tracking changes then can be pushed back to the SQL Server using the Client and Server Agents.

Now let's see what happens between architecture components when you invoke Pull, Push, or SubmitSQL methods. Table 13.1 summarizes the sequence of steps in RDA operations.

TABLE 13.1    RDA Operations

| Method | Client Agent | Database Engine | Server Agent |
|---|---|---|---|
| Pull | Client Agent initiates the pull by sending the request for fetching a table.<br><br>On receiving a response from the Server Agent it gives the data to the database engine.<br><br>Client Agent enables the tracking on a pulled table if the tracking option is specified. | After receiving table details from the Client Agent, the database engine creates table, index, etc.<br><br>Inserts the records in the table. | On receiving the request from a Client Agent over http, the Server Agent opens a connection with a backend SQL Server.<br><br>It executes the SQL select statement sent by the Client Agent to fetch the data from the remote database.<br><br>Returns the data back to the SQL Server Compact Edition Client Agent; on error it returns the error back to the Client Agent. |
| Push | Client Agent initiates the Push by sending the updated (inserted/deleted/updated) record to the SQL Server Compact Server Agent. | On successful update on the SQL Server, the database engine updates the tracking info onto a local database. | On receiving the request from the Client Agent over http, the Server Agent opens a connection with backend SQL Server.<br><br>It updates (Insert/Modify/Delete) the record in the backend SQL Server.<br><br>On error, it returns the error back to the Client Agent. |
| SubmitSQL | Client Agent sends the SQL, statement specified to be executed on the backend Server. | | On receiving the request from the Client Agent over http, opens a connection with the backend SQL Server.<br><br>Executes the statement sent by the client.<br><br>On error, returns the error back to the Client Agent. |

# Using Remote Data Access

This section introduces you to the requirements needed to implement an RDA mechanism. RDA uses the IIS Web Server to transfer the data from the client database to the server database. This chapter presents an overview on how to configure the Web Server and the RDA operations—Push, Pull, and SubmitSQL. The SQLCERemoteDataAccess object and its properties are also discussed while providing the SQLCERemoteDataAccess method and its parameters.

## Installing the Server Agent Component

As discussed, the SQL Server Compact Edition Server Agent component on IIS Web Server communicates with the Client Agent component on a client machine.

You need to deploy the Server Agent component on the machine running IIS. This component is installed using `SqlCe30Setup[lang].exe`. The file is available both with SQL Server 2005 and Visual Studio 2005 at the following locations:

- Visual Studio 2005: the file is installed at `<Disk>\Program Files\Microsoft SQL Server\90\Tools\Binn\VSShell\Common7\IDE\`.

- SQL Server 2005: the file is installed at `<Disk>\Program Files\Microsoft Visual Studio 8\SmartDevices\SDK\SQL Server\Mobile\v3.0`

You can also get the SQL Server Compact Edition Server Agent component from the Microsoft Download Center.

> **NOTE**
>
> If your application needs to synchronize data using RDA or Merge Replication with a backend SQL Server, you will also set up an IIS Web Server. Also you need to install SQL Server Compact Edition Server Tools on a computer running IIS.

## Configuring the Virtual Directory

The SQL Server Compact Edition Server Agent on Web Server communicates with the Client Agent on a local client machine. It also communicates with the remote SQL Server. You need to configure the Web Server to establish connectivity. You can configure the Web Server manually or by using the Web Synchronization Wizard by following these steps:

1. Create a new virtual directory or use an existing one.

2. Specify the alias and location of the virtual directory.

3. Set the permission on the virtual directory.

4. Copy the SQL Server Compact Edition Agent into the virtual directory.

5. Register SqlCeRp30.dll.

6. Configure authentication for IIS Web Server and the virtual directory.

## Security Options

While using RDA, you will be using security at two levels. First you need to get authenticated at IIS to access the Web Server. After accessing IIS, you need to fulfill the security requirement to access data from a remote SQL Server. For IIS, you can choose among Anonymous Access, Basic Authentication, and Integrated Windows Authentication to authenticate a client. You can also choose to have Secure Socket Layer encrypt the data when it travels on the network.

These security options are discussed in detail in Chapter 14, *Securing the SQL Server 2005 Compact Edition Database*.

## Programming for RDA

To use RDA, you will be using the SQLCeRemoteDataAccess class of SqlServerCe namespace. This class provides Pull, Push, and Submit SQL operations.

### Setting the SqlCeRemoteDataAccess Project Properties

You will first create an instance of `SqlCeRemoteDataAccess` object. Table 13.2 has the properties that you need to set before calling the Pull, Push, or SubmitSQL methods.

**TABLE 13.2    RDA Object Properties**

| Property | Description |
|---|---|
| CompressionLevel | This property specifies the level of compression you wish to use during Push and Pull operations. |
| | Setting this value to 0 means no compression. |
| | By default the value of this property is 1. |
| | Based on your application need, you can customize the level of compression. Increasing the compression level means more processing time for compression but less transmission time. |
| ConnectionManager | You can set this value to use a client's connection manager to establish a network connection. |
| ConnectionRetryTimeout | Using this property you can specify the amount of time in seconds that the SQL Server Compact Edition will attempt to establish a failed connection during Push, Pull, and SubmitSQL methods. |
| InternetUrl | The URL to access the SQL Server Compact Edition Server Agent. |
| InternetLogin | The login name required to connect to the SQL Server Compact Edition Server Agent. |
| | You do not need to set this property if you are using Anonymous authentication access or Integrated Windows authentication. |
| InternetPassword | The password required with login name to connect to SQL Server Compact Edition Server Agent. |

**TABLE 13.2     RDA Object Properties**

| Property | Description |
| --- | --- |
| | You do not need to set this property if you are using Anonymous authentication access or Integrated Windows authentication. |
| InternetProxyServer | You need to specify a proxy server IP address and port in the format ProxyServer:Port. |
| | You do not need to set this property if you are not using Proxy Server. |
| InternetProxyLogin | This is the login name for the proxy server. |
| | You do not need to set this property if you are using a proxy server with Basic or Integrated authentication. |
| InternetProxyPassword | This password string is for a proxy server login name. |
| | You need to set this property if you are using proxy server with Basic or Integrated authentication. |
| LocalConnectionString | OLE DB connection string for accessing a local SQL Server Compact Edition database on a client's machine. |

Listing 13.1 demonstrates an example that describes how to create an SqlCeRemoteDataAccess object and set the properties.

**LISTING 13.1     SqlCeRemoteDataAccess C#.NET**

```csharp
SqlCeRemoteDataAccess myRDA = new SqlCeRemoteDataAccess();
myRDA.InternetLogin = "mylogin";
myRDA.InternetPassword = "mypassword";
myRDA.InternetUrl =
  @"http://pdhingra-lptp/hospitalpatient/sqlcesa30.dll";
myRDA.LocalConnectionString =
  "DataSource=\\Program Files\\Patient_RDA\\MyPatients.sdf";
```

**LISTING 13.1     SqlCeRemoteDataAccess VisualBasic.NET**

```vbnet
Dim myRDA As SqlCeRemoteDataAccess
myRDA = New SqlCeRemoteDataAccess()
myRDA.InternetLogin = "mylogin"
myRDA.InternetPassword = "mypassword"
myRDA.InternetUrl = _
  "http://pdhingra0/hospitalpatient/sqlcesa30.dll"
myRDA.LocalConnectionString = _
  "Data Source\Program Files\Patient_RDA\MyPatients.sdf"
```

## Pulling Remote Data into a Local Database

To pull data from a backend SQL Server into SQL Server Compact Edition you need to do the following:

1. Create an SQL Server Compact Edition database into which you want to pull data.

2. Connect to the database using the SqlCeConnection object.

3. Delete existing tables from SQL Server Compact Edition that are part of a pull.

4. Invoke the Pull method of the SqlCeRemoteDataAccess object from the client application.

When you invoke the Pull method, the Client Agent on SQL Server Compact Edition sends the request over http for fetching the table to the Server Agent. On receiving the request, the Server Agent opens a connection with the backend SQL Server and executes the Select statement to fetch the data. It sends the results of the Select statement to the SQL Server Compact Edition Client Agent. The Client Agent gives the data to the database engine which in turn creates a table on the client database. The tracking option is enabled if the option was specified as part of the Pull method.

### Using Pull Method

To use the Pull method of SqlCeRemoteDataAccess, you need to specify the parameters described in Table 13.3.

TABLE 13.3    Arguments for Pull Method

| Argument | Description |
| --- | --- |
| Local Table | This is the table that would be created on SQL Server Compact Edition as a result of a Pull operation. |
| Sql String | Sql query to fetch table content from SQL Server. |
| OLE DB Connection String | OLE DB connection string to connect to the remote SQL Server. |
| Tracking Changes Option | This option specifies whether or not to track changes done on the local SQL Server Compact Edition. |
| Error Table | The argument specifies the name of the Error table. All the errors are logged into the Error table. |

Local table is the table name you wish to create on SQL Server Compact Edition. This will generally be the same table name that you have on a remote SQL Server. You can retrieve all rows and columns from SQL Server or you can select a subset of rows and columns and fetch them into the local database. For retrieving all rows you will use a statement such as SELECT * FROM Table. For retrieving specific columns and rows you can add column names and a where condition in a SELECT query.

**NOTE**

The SELECT statement can refer to a View or Stored Procedure.

You need to specify the connection string to connect to the remote SQL Server. You will be using an OLE DB connection string for connection. In the connection string, you will specify the SQL Server, initial catalog, and user ID and password that are required for making the connection.

Listing 13.2 presents code to show the usage of the Push method of the RemoteDataAccess object. These lines are part of a bigger exercise that you will complete later in the chapter.

**LISTING 13.2    Pull Method C#.NET**

```
string sqlServerConnection =
    @"Provider=SQLOLEDB;Data Source=PDHINGRA-LPTP0\Book;
      Initial Catalog=Hospital_RDA;
     User Id=RDALoging; Password=RDAPasswordfareast\pdhingra";

SqlCeRemoteDataAccess myRDA = new SqlCeRemoteDataAccess();
//You need not have to set Login and Password for Anonymous Access

myRDA.InternetLogin = "mylogin";
myRDA.InternetPassword = "mypassword";
myRDA.InternetUrl =
  @"http://pdhingra-lptp0/hospitalpatient/sqlcesa30.dll";
myRDA.LocalConnectionString =
  "DataSource=\\Program Files\\Patient_RDA\\MyPatients.sdf";
myRDA.Pull ("Patients", "Select * From Patients",sqlServerConnection,
RdaTrackOption.TrackingOnWithIndexes,"ErrorTable");
```

**LISTING 13.2    Pull Method Visual Basic.NET**

```
Dim myRDA As SqlCeRemoteDataAccess
myRDA = New SqlCeRemoteDataAccess()
'You need not have to set Login and Password for Anonymous Access

myRDA.InternetLogin = "mylogin"
myRDA.InternetPassword = "mypassword"
myRDA.InternetUrl =
    "http://pdhingra-lptp0/hospitalpatient/sqlcesa30.dll"
myRDA.LocalConnectionString = _
    "DataSource=\\Program Files\\Patient_RDA\\MyPatients.sdf"
 myRDA.Pull("Patients", "Select * From Patients", sqlServerConnection, _
                   RdaTrackOption.TrackingOnWithIndexes, "ErrorTable")
```

## Tracking Changes

The Pull method of SQLCeRemoteDataAccess has an RDATrackingOption parameter. This option tells the SQL Server Compact Edition database engine whether to track the changes made on local tables pulled from the SQL Server or not. To push the changes back to SQL Server you first need to track the changes by enabling the RDATrackingOption. Table 13.4 provides values that can be assigned to the RDATrackingOption parameter.

**TABLE 13.4    RDA Tracking Option**

| Tracking Option Value | Description |
| --- | --- |
| TrackingOn | You will use the TrackingOn option when you want to push the changes on SQL Server Compact Edition back to SQL Server. |
| | The SQL Server Compact Edition database engine tracks all insert, update, and delete operations. |
| | When you use the TrackingOn option primary key, constraints are created on the pulled table. |
| TrackingOff | You will use this value when you want to download only tables from SQL Server and there is no need to push the changes back to the backend database. |
| TrackingOnWithIndexes | This option is similar to the TrackingOn option. With this option, the database engine also copies the indexes on SQL Server to SQL Server Compact Edition pulled tables. An index is copied if the column used in the index is pulled. |
| | You will be using this option if the SQL Server table has an index to implement unique constraints. This option will copy the index onto a local table too. |
| TrackingOffWithIndexes | This option is similar to the TrackingOff option. However in this option, Primary key and indexes are copied to local tables. |

## Restrictions on Tracking

- The resultset produced by SELECT statement must be updatable.

- Primary Key must be defined on updatable resocrdset returned by SELECT statement used in Pull method.

- Multi Table Query can't be tracked. You will receive an error at runtime if SELECT statement, View, or stored procedure refers to multiple tables.

## Data Type Conversion

When you use the Pull method, a table from the SQL Server is copied to the SQL Server Compact Edition database. To copy the table schema and table data, the source and destination database should have similar or compatible data types. SQL Server Compact Edition supports only a subset of data types supported by SQL Server. Most of the data types are directly supported in  SQL Server Compact Edition and data can be directly copied. Some other data types are compatible between SQL Server and SQL Server Compact Edition with size limits. Of these data types, size limit is applied at the time of the data pull. While planning to use RDA you should consider whether the data type supported in both is compatible or incompatible.

- The data types that are supported in both databases can be pulled directly.

- The data type is not supported in SQL Server Compact Edition but is a compatible data type. At the time of the pull data, it is converted from SQL Server data type to SQL Server Compact Edition data type.

- The data types in SQL Server are incompatible with SQL Server Compact Edition data types. These data types cannot be used for RDA pull.

Table 13.5 summarizes the data type compatibility between SQL Server and SQL Server Compact Edition.

**TABLE 13.5    Data Type compatibility**

| SQL Server | SQL Server Compact Edition | Remarks |
|---|---|---|
| Bigint | Bigint | |
| Binary | Binary | |
| Bit | Bit | |
| Char | NChar or NText | 4000 or fewer characters on SQL Server maps to NChar on SQL Server Compact Edition. For length greater than 4000, NText data type is used. |
| | | RDA push fails if length of NText on SQL Server Compact Edition is greater than length of Char on SQL Server. |
| Varchar | NVarChar or NText | 4000 or fewer characters on SQL Server maps to NVarchar on SQL Server Compact Edition. For length greater than 4000, NText data type is used. |
| Computed Columns | Not Supported | |
| DateTime | DateTime | |
| Decimal | Not Supported | You should use numeric instead of Decimal as Decimal is not supported in SQL Server Compact Edition. |
| Double Precision | Double Precision | |
| Float | Float | |
| Image | Image | |
| Int | Int | |
| Money | Money | |
| NChar | NChar | |

**TABLE 13.5    Data Type compatibility**

| SQL Server | SQL Server Compact Edition | Remarks |
|---|---|---|
| NText | NText | |
| Numeric | Numeric | |
| Nvarchar(n) | NVarchar(n) | |
| NVarchar(max) | NText | |
| Real | Real | |
| SmallDateTime | DateTime | |
| SmallInt | SmallInt | |
| SmallMoney | Money | RDA fails if precision of Money on SQL Server Compact Edition is more than precision of SmallMoney on SQL Server. |
| SQL_Varient | Not Supported | |
| Text | NText | RDA fails if length of text on SQL Server is more than 1,073,741,823 characters. |
| TimeStamp | TimeStamp | |
| TinyInt | TinyInt | |
| UniqueIdentifier | UniqueIdentifier | |
| VarBinary(n) | VarBinary(n) | |
| VarBinary(max) | Image | RDA fails if length of VarBinary(max) on SQL Server is greater than Image. |
| Xml | NText | |

### Error Logging

At the time of pushing changes back to a remote server, errors can occur and certain rows may not update on a remote server. All the errors will be logged in the Error table you specified as an argument while pulling data from SQL Server. The Error table contains the following information:

- All columns specified in the SELECT statement of the Pull operation contains data you entered.
- s_OLEDBErrorNumber column contains the error number.
- s_OLEDBErrorString column contains the error string
- s_ErrorDate column contains the date/time of error

Consider a scenario in which you have entered two rows in the PatientHistory table of SQL Server Compact Edition after pulling data from the SQL Server. If an error occurs, two newly entered rows will move to the ErrorHistory table. The ErrorHistory table will also have an Error number, Error string, and the date and time when the error occurred.

### Changing the Pulled Table

Once you have pulled the table locally on SQL Server Compact Edition, you can make changes programmatically using DDL SQL commands.

### Restrictions

There are a few restrictions on the type of changes you can make on the pulled table:

- You can't remove the Primary key from the table that you fetched using RDA Pull.

- You can't add columns on a pulled table.

- You can't rename a column on a pulled table.

- You can't delete a column from a pulled table.

- You can't rename the table that you fetched using RDA Pull.

### Allowed Changes

You can make the following schema changes in a Tracked Table pulled into SQL Server Compact Edition

- You can add or drop indexes on SQL Server Compact Edition tables after tables are pulled into SQL Server Compact Edition.

- Forgeign key can be added or dropped after pulling the tables.

- Identity Column increment and seed values can be changed after pulling tables. RDA does not do automatic management of the Identity column. By default Identity and Seed are assigned value of 1.

- Default constraint can be added or dropped in pulled table.

- Table can  be dropped after being pulled from SQL Server.

### Pushing Local Changes Back to Remote Database

To push data from SQL Server Compact Edition to a backend SQL Server, you need to do the following

1. Pull the table from the SQL Server.

2. Enable the tracking changes on the local SQL Server Compact Edition database.

3. Make changes and invoke the Push method of the `SqlCeRemoteDataAccess` object.

When you invoke the Push method, the Client Agent on SQL Server Compact Edition sends the changes to the Server Agent on the Web Server. The Server Agent opens a connection with the backend SQL Server and updates the changes to a remote SQL Server. After the successful updates, SQL Server Compact updates the tracking information on the local table.

### Using Push Method

To use the Push method of `SqlCeRemoteDataAccess`, you need to specify parameters as shown in Table 13.6.

TABLE 13.6    Parameter of Push Method

| Argument | Description |
| --- | --- |
| Local Table | This is the table name on SQL Server Compact Edition that you have pulled. After the changes, you will be sending the tracked changes from the local table to SQL Server. |
| Ole Db Connection String | The OLE DB Connection string to connect to the remote SQL Server. |
| Batch Option | This option specifies whether or not to treat all changes as part of single transaction or not. |

Listing 13.3 shows how to use the Push method of the `SqlCeRemoteDataAccess` object. Here the same code is used as part of a longer exercise appearing later in this chapter.

LISTING 13.3    Push Method C#.NET

```
SqlCeRemoteDataAccess myRDA = new SqlCeRemoteDataAccess();
// You need not have to set Login and Password for Anonymous Access
myRDA.InternetLogin = "mylogin";
myRDA.InternetPassword = "mypassword";
myRDA.InternetUrl =
    @"http://pdhingra0/hospitalpatient/sqlcesa30.dll";
myRDA.LocalConnectionString =
    "DataSource=\\Program Files\\Patient_RDA\\MyPatients.sdf";
myRDA.Push("Patients", sqlServerConnection,RdaBatchOption.BatchingOff);
```

LISTING 13.3    Push Method Visual Basic.NET

```
Dim myRDA As SqlCeRemoteDataAccess
myRDA = New SqlCeRemoteDataAccess()
myRDA.InternetLogin = "mylogin"
myRDA.InternetPassword = "mypassword"
myRDA.InternetUrl = _
    "http://pdhingra0/hospitalpatient/sqlcesa30.dll"
myRDA.LocalConnectionString = _
    "DataSource=\\Program Files\\Patient_RDA\\MyPatients.sdf"
myRDA.Push("Patients", sqlServerConnection, RdaBatchOption.BatchingOff)
```

### Batch Option

The Push method of SQLCeRemoteDataAccess has an RDA_BatchOption parameter. When you enable this option, the Push method sends all changes as part of the transactions. Either all changes are applied or none of the changes are applied on the backend SQL Server. By default this option is off. When the option is FALSE, all changes are applied individually. Table 13.7 summarizes the Batch option values.

**TABLE 13.7   RDA Batch Option Values**

| Value | Description |
|---|---|
| BatchingOn | You will use the BatchingOn value when you want to push the changes on SQL Server Compact Edition back as a transaction.<br><br>Either all rows succeed and are updated on SQL Server or none of the rows are updated on SQL Server. |
| BatchingOff | This is the default value of the Batch option. When you use this option, each change is treated as a separate transaction. It is possible that some changes are applied successfully and some fail and are logged in the Error table. |

### Handling of Conflict

When you push the changes back to a remote SQL Server, the changes get updated on the SQL Server. In case the same data was also updated on the SQL Server after you pulled the changes, the Push operation will overwrite the changes with the changes done on the SQL Server Compact Edition.

You should consider this scenario when choosing RDA as the mechanism for data synchronization.

### Executing SQL Statements on Remote Database

You can execute an SQL statement from SQL Server Compact Edition to a backend SQL Server. To execute the SQL statement, follow these steps:

1. Connect the local client to a remote server.

2. Invoke the SubmitSQL method of `SqlCeRemoteDataAccess` object.

3. Using the SubmitSQL method, you can execute an sql query or stored procedure. However, you can execute only those statements that do not require returning rows back to the local client.

When you invoke the SubmitSQL method, the Client Agent on SQL Server Compact Edition sends the statement to the Server Agent on the Web Server over http. The Server Agent opens a connection with the backend SQL Server and executes the SQL statement on a remote database.

### Using SubmitSQL Method

To use the SubmitSQL method of `SqlCeRemoteDataAccess`, you need to specify the parameters described in Table 13.8.

**TABLE 13.8    Parameters for SubmitSQL Method**

| Argument | Description |
| --- | --- |
| SQL String | SQL query or stored procedure that you want to execute on a remote SQL Server. |
| OLE DB Connection String | OLE DB Connection string that connects to a remote SQL Server. |

Listing 13.4 demonstrates how to use the SubmitSQL method. This same piece of code is also used in the Remote Data Access exercise presented later in this chapter.

**LISTING 13.4    SubmitSQL Method C#.NET**

```
SqlCeRemoteDataAccess myRDA = new SqlCeRemoteDataAccess();
// You need not have to set Login and Password for Anonymous Access
myRDA.InternetLogin = "mylogin";
myRDA.InternetPassword = "mypassword";
myRDA.InternetUrl =
  @"http://pdhingra-lptp/hospitalpatient/sqlcesa30.dll";
myRDA.LocalConnectionString = "Data Source=MyPatients.sdf";
string strCmd =
    @"Update Doctors set TotalExperienceInMonths = 160
      where doctoremployeeno = "
      + txtDoctorEmployeeNo.Text;

myRDA.SubmitSql(strCmd, sqlServerConnection);
```

**LISTING 13.4    SubmitSQL Method Visual Basic.NET**

```
myRDA = New SqlCeRemoteDataAccess()
'You need not have to set Login and Password for Anonymous Access

myRDA.InternetLogin = "mylogin"
myRDA.InternetPassword = "mypassword"
myRDA.InternetUrl = _
    "http://pdhingra0/hospitalpatient/sqlcesa30.dll"
myRDA.LocalConnectionString = _
        "DataSource=\Program Files\Patient_RDA\MyPatients.sdf"
strCmd = "Update Doctors set TotalExperienceInMonths = 160 " & _
            "where doctoremployeeno = " & _
            "'" & txtDoctorEmployeeNo.Text & "'"

myRDA.SubmitSql(strCmd, sqlServerConnection)
```

### Restrictions in RDA

You should consider following restrictons while designing an RDA solution:

- The Pull method gives an error if the recordset returned by the SELECT statement contains a computer column. You should exclude the computed column in the SELECT statement that pull data from the backend SQL Server.

- SQL Server Compact Edition can have 1024 columns in a table. Tracked RDA tables require 7 system columns. You can have up to 1017 columns in a tracked RDA table.

- SQL Server 2005 supports Triggers on a table. SQL Server Compact Edition does not support Triggers in a table. If you pull a table from SQL Server 2005 that has triggers, triggers will not be pulled into SQL Server Compact Edition. However Triggers will be executed when you push changes back to SQL Server 2005.

- If the pulled table contains an identity column, the management of identity columns should be done by your application. By default SQL Server Compact Edition assigns the value of the identity seed and identity increment value to 1. To manage the Identity column you should use ALTER TABLE to change the identity seed and identiy increment value.

- If you have set up Replication in SQL Server 2005 table, a rowguid column is added on Published tables. This column is not required in a local table on SQL Server Compact Edition.

- SQL Server 2005 is a case sensitive database. SQL Server Compact Edition is a case insensitive database.

- SQL Server Compact Edition supports only a subset of data types supported by SQL Server. You should consider the guidelines given in the Data Conversion section.

# Remote Data Access Exercise

Now that you have learned the Remote Data Access features, architecture, and methods. as well as the steps required to implement RDA, it is time to build the end-to-end exercise. You will use the Hospital_RDA database from Chapter 12 to build this RDA exercise. The Hospital_RDA database has five tables. To demonstrate these things in a simpler manner, the exercise application will fetch only the PatientHistory table.

The objective of the exercise is to develop an application for doctors that provides information about their patients on their laptop, Tablet PC, or mobile device. The application fetches the data from the backend Hospital_RDA database on SQL Server 2005. After making changes, the application will push the changes back to the remote SQL Server.

## Installing SQL Server Compact Server Components

Chapter 12, *Synchronizing Data with Merge Replication,* introduced you to steps for installing the SQL Server Compact Edition Server Agent Component. If you have already installed the Server Agent Component, you should skip this section. If you have not yet already installed the Server Agent Component, follow the steps given on page 353.

## Setting Up a Backend SQL Server 2005 Database

This RDA exercise uses the same Hospital_RDA database used earlier in Chapter 12 for the Merge Replication exercise. The database has the following tables:

- Doctors

- Patients

- PatientHistory

The Doctors table structure is shown in Table 13.9. The table has the doctor's first name, last name, etc. and also contains the doctor's hospital employee number.

**TABLE 13.9    Doctors Table Schema**

| Column | Data Type | Nullability | Description |
| --- | --- | --- | --- |
| DoctorEmployeeNo | Nchar(10) | Not Null | Employee number in hospital |
| DoctorRegNo | NChar(10) | Not Null | Doctor registration number in medical council |
| FirstName | NChar(20) | Not Null | First name |
| LastName | NChar(20) | Not Null | Last name |
| PhoneNo | NChar(15) | Null | Phone number with country and city code |
| CellNo | NChar(15) | Null | Cell phone number with country and city code |
| HighestQualification | NChar(30) | Null | Highest degree of doctor |
| Specialization | NChar(30) | Null | Area of specialization |
| TotalExperienceInMonths | Smallint | Null | Total working experience of doctor |

Table 13.10 shows the schema of the Patients table. This table has the patient's first name, last name, contact details, etc. as well as the patient's registration number. The Patients table has a foreign key relationship with the Doctors table as the doctor's employee number is the employee number of Patient GP (General Practitioner doctor).

**TABLE 13.10    Patients Table Schema**

| Column | Data Type | Nullability | Description |
| --- | --- | --- | --- |
| PatientRegNo | NChar(10) | Not Null | ID of patient Primary key |
| DoctorEmployeeNo | Nchar(10) | Not Null | Employee number in hospital Foreign key on Doctors table |
| FirstName | NChar(20) | Not Null | First name |
| LastName | NChar(20) | Not Null | Last name |

**TABLE 13.10    Patients Table Schema**

| Column | Data Type | Nullability | Description |
|---|---|---|---|
| PhoneNo | NChar(15) | Null | Phone number with country and city code |
| CellNo | NChar(15) | Null | Cell phone number with country and city code |
| DOB | DateTime | Not Null | Date of birth |
| Age | SmallInt | Null | Age of patient in years |
| GuardianFirstName | NChar(20) | Null | First name of guardian for young patients |
| GuardianLastName | NChar(20) | Null | Last name of guardian for young patients |
| Martial Status | Char(1) | Null | Martial status of patient: 'M'—Married 'U'—Not Married 'D'—Divorced |
| NoOfChildren | SmallInt | Null | Number of children |
| Education | NChar(20) | Null | Education qualification of patient |
| Smokes | Char(1) | Null | 'R'—Patient smokes regularly 'O'—Patient smokes occasionally 'N'—Does not smoke |
| Drinks | Char(1) | Null | 'R'—Patient drinks alcohol regularly 'O'—Patient drinks alcohol occasionally 'N'—Does not drink alcohol |

Table 13.11 shows the disease and history of treatment given to a patient.

**TABLE 13.11    PatientHistory Table Schema**

| Column | Data Type | Nullability | Description |
|---|---|---|---|
| PatientHistoryID | Int | Not Null | ID of patient history Auto generated key |
| PatientRegNo | NChar(10) | Not Null | ID of patient Foreign key on Patients table |
| DoctorEmployeeNo | NChar(10) | Not Null | Employee Number of Doctor who provided treatment. |
| DiseaseIdentifed | NVarChar(200) | Not Null | Description of disease and symptoms |
| DateIdentified | DateTime | Not Null | Date disease identified |
| Treatment | NVarChar(200) | Null | Treatment prescribed by doctor |
| TreatmentStartDate | DateTime | Null | Date when treatment started |
| TreatmentEndDate | DateTime | Null | Last date of treatment |

You can create the tables manually or use the `CreateHospitalDB.sql` script to create the database. Once you have created the database, you can use the `InsertDoctorData.sql` and `InsertPatientData.sql` script to insert data into the Doctors and Patients tables.

> **NOTE**
>
> It is not possible to include multiple tables in a SELECT statement to pull tracked tables. The database design is de-normalized and includes the DoctorEmployeeNo in PatientHistory table so that PatientHistory table can be pulled into SQL Server Compact Edition with the tracking option.

## Configuring the Web Server for RDA

In this section, you will use the Web Synchronization Wizard to configure components on an IIS computer. Using the wizard you will be able to:

- Configure a virtual directory on IIS. You can create a new virtual directory or use an existing one.

- Set permissions on the virtual directory.

- Specify whether you want a secure access channel or not.

Chapter 12, *Synchronizing Data with Merge Replication,* introduced steps for configuring a Web Server. Follow the same steps to configure a Web Server, create a virtual directory, and set the permission on virtual directory.

> **NOTE**
>
> This exercise uses Virtual Directory HospitalPatient.

## Creating a Device Application in Visual Studio 2005

### Create Database

As discussed in RDA, the Pull operation is used to fetch a table from SQL Server to the SQL Server Compact Edition database. Let's start the exercise by creating an empty SQL Server Compact Edition database.

Open SQL Server Management Studio and click on Connect and SQL Server Compact Edition. Select New Database in the Database file.

Specify the location of the database file. Click on the OK button to create a database.

In this section you will create a .NET Compact Framework application using Visual Studio 2005. The application will fetch the patient data onto a doctor client device. The application will insert, update, and delete data from the SQL Server Compact Edition database. Finally, the updates made will be sent back to the backend SQL Server.

**Create a Project**

1. Start Visual Studio 2005 from the Start menu.

2. Click File | New | Project.

3. Click on Visual C# or Visual Basic.

4. Click on Smart Devices Project and select Windows Mobile 5.0 Pocket PC. Select Device Application.

5. Enter the Name and Location of the project as shown in the Figure 13.3.

6. Click OK on the New Project dialog box.

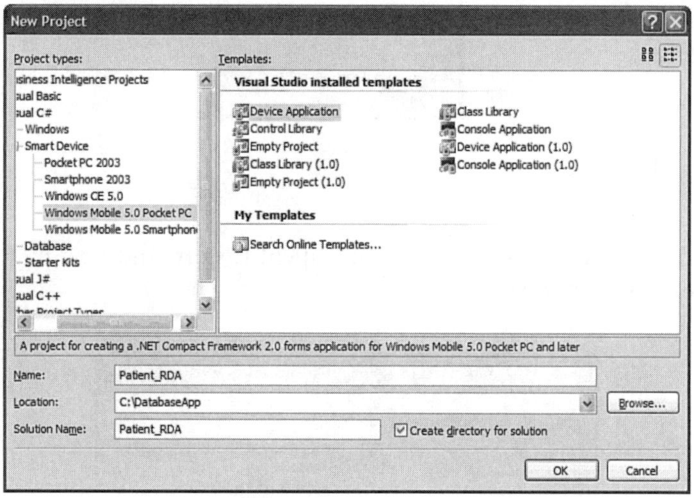

**FIGURE 13.3**   New Project

**Add Database File**

Right click on Project and Add Existing Item. Select the SQL Server Compact Edition File MyPatients.sdf that you created earlier.

It will start the Data Source Configuration Wizard. As there is no table in the database, click Finish.

You have created a Visual Studio project and added the MyPatients.sdf file into the project. Now you will create a user interface and write code to implement RDA methods.

**Create User Interface**

Click on the Tool box. Select the Tab Control, and then use a drag-and-drop operation to move it to Form. Click on the TabPages property as shown in Figure 13.4.

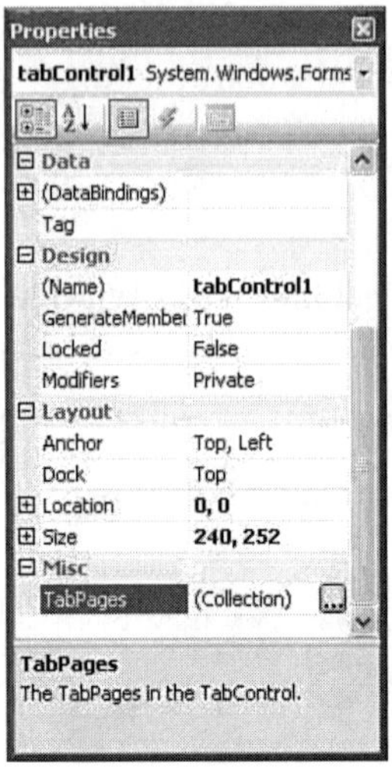

**FIGURE 13.4** Tab Control

Create four tab members—RDA Sync, Patient, Patient History, and New Treatment—on the Tab control as shown in Figure 13.5.

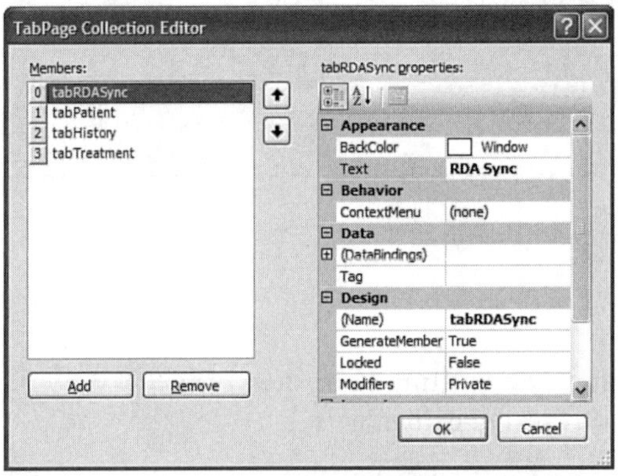

**FIGURE 13.5** Tab Design

On the RDA Sync tab, create three buttons—RDA Pull, RDA Push, and Submit SQL On the RDA sync tab also create a label and text field to enter DoctorEmployeeNo.

On the Patient tab create the fields to enter new patient PatientRegNo, First Name, Last Name, and date of birth. Also create a Save button to save patient details.

On the Patient History tab, create the fields to display the history of previous treatments given to a patient.

On the New Treatment tab, add the fields to enter treatment details.

Listing 13.5 has complete code for this exercise. The code has the following methods:

- `Patient_Load`
- `btnPull_Click`
- `AlterHistoryIdentity`
- `btnRefresh_Click`
- `FillListHistory`
- `btnDone_Click`
- `btnSave_Click`
- `btnPush_Click`
- `btnSubmitSQL_Click`

The `Patient_Load` method displays the Patient application.

The `btnPull_Click` method executes on clicking the Pull button. By executing the following steps, this method brings the Patients table from SQL Server to the SQL Server Compact Edition database:

1. Define a connection string for the backend SQL Server.
2. Create an `SqlCeRemoteDataAccess` object.
3. Set the `InternetLogin`, `InternetPassword`, `InternetURL`, and `LocalConnectionString` properties.
4. Execute the Pull method to fetch Patients table. It specifies table name, Select statement, Tracking Option parameter and Error Table.
5. Executes the Pull method to fetch PatientHistory table. It specifies table name, Select statement, Tracking Option parameter and Error Table.
6. Change the Identity and Seed value of Patient History Identity column.

After the Pull method is successfully executed, you can verify the tables in the SQL Server Compact Edition database. SQL Server Compact Edition will have pulled tables and error tables.

- The Patients table stores the list of the doctor's patients. It contains the column specified in the SELECT statement given in the Pull method. The Patients table also stores seven additional columns.

- The PatientHistory Table contains the patient's history of the doctor's patient. It contains the columns specified in the SELECT statement given in the Pull method. Similar to the Patients table, the PatientHistory table also stores seven additional columns. As RDA pulls individual tables, the Foreign key relationship between

Patient and PatientHistory does not exist in the SQL Server Compact Edition tables. You should set this up explicitly if your application requires it.

- The ErrorTable contains the columns of the patient table and three addition columns for error number, error string and date of error.

- The ErrorTableHistory contains the columns of the PatientHistory table and three additional columns for error number, error string and date of error.

The btnSave_Click method is executed after you add details to the Patients table. The method stores the information in the local SQL Server Compact Edition database.

The btnDone_Click method stores the details of Patient Disease and Treament into the PatientHistory table in the local SQL Server Compact Edition database.

The btnPush_Click method is executed on clicking the Push button. This method sends the changes made in the Patients table and PatientHistory table back to the SQL Server database by executing the following steps:

1. Defines a connection string for the backend SQL Server.

2. Creates an SqlCeRemoteDataAccess object.

3. Sets the InternetLogin, InternetPassword, InternetUrl, and LocalConnectionString property.

4. Executes the Push method and specifies table name, connection string for SQL Server, and BatchingOption parameter.

The btnSubmitSQL_ClickSQL method connects the backend SQL server and executes the query specified as a parameter of the SubmitSQL method. This method executes the following steps:

1. Defines a connection string for the backend SQL Server.

2. The code creates an SqlCeRemoteDataAccess object.

3. Sets the InternetLogin, InternetPassword, and InternetURL property.

4. Executes the SubmitSQL method.

Listing 13.5 has complete code for Patient application.

### LISTING 13.5    RDA Exercise C#.NET

```
using System;
using System.Collections.Generic;
using System.ComponentModel;
using System.Data;
using System.Drawing;
using System.Text;
using System.Windows.Forms;
using System.Data.SqlServerCe;
```

```
namespace Patient_RDA
{
    public partial class Patient : Form
    {
    SqlCeConnection myConn;
    SqlCeDataReader myPatientDataReader;
    SqlCeDataReader myHistoryDataReader;
    SqlCeCommand myCmd;
    string selectedPatientRegNo;
    string strDoctorEmployeeNo;

    public Patient()
    {
        InitializeComponent();
    }


    private void Patient_Load(object sender, EventArgs e)
    {
    }

    private void btnPull_Click(object sender, EventArgs e)
    {


    string sqlServerConnection =
      @"Provider=SQLOLEDB; Data Source='PDHINGRA-LPTP';
        Initial Catalog=Hospital_RDA;
        User Id=RDALoging;Password=RDAPassword";

  SqlCeRemoteDataAccess myRDA = new SqlCeRemoteDataAccess();

  // You need not have to set Login and Password for Anonymous access
      //myRDA.InternetLogin = "mylogin";
      // myRDA.InternetPassword = "mypassword";
      // myRDA.InternetProxyServer = @"itgproxy:80";
      // myRDA.InternetProxyLogin = @"";
  myRDA.InternetUrl =
      @"http://pdhingra-lptp/hospitalpatient/sqlcesa30.dll";
  myRDA.LocalConnectionString =
      "DataSource=\\Program Files\\Patient_RDA\\MyPatients.sdf";
  strDoctorEmployeeNo = txtDoctorEmployeeNo.Text;
  string strCmd = "Select * From Patients where DoctorEmployeeNo= "
                  + strDoctorEmployeeNo ;
```

```
myRDA.Pull ("Patients", strCmd,sqlServerConnection,
            RdaTrackOption.TrackingOnWithIndexes,"ErrorTable");

string strSQLCmd = @"Select PatientHistoryID, PatientRegNo,
                    DoctorEmployeeNo, DiseaseIdentified,
                    DateIdentified, Treatment, TreatmentStartDate,
                    TreatmentEndDate
                    From PatientHistory where DoctorEmployeeNo = "
                    + strDoctorEmployeeNo;

myRDA.Pull("PatientHistory", strSQLCmd, sqlServerConnection,
            RdaTrackOption.TrackingOnWithIndexes,
            "ErrorTableHistory");

 myRDA.Dispose();
 AlterHistoryIdentity();
 labelPull.Text = "Pull Complete";


}
private void AlterHistoryIdentity()
{
 myConn = new SqlCeConnection
         ("DataSource=\\Program Files\\Patient_RDA\\MyPatients.sdf");
 myConn.Open();
 myCmd = myConn.CreateCommand();
 myCmd.CommandText =
       @"ALTER TABLE PatientHistory
         ALTER COLUMN PatientHistoryID IDENTITY (3000,1)";
 myCmd.ExecuteNonQuery();
 myConn.Close();
}
private void btnPush_Click(object sender, EventArgs e)
{
 string sqlServerConnection = @"Provider=SQLOLEDB;
        Data Source='PDHINGRA-LPTP'; Initial Catalog=Hospital_RDA;
        User Id=RDALoging; Password=RDAPassword";

   // You need not have to set Login and Password for Anonymous Access
   SqlCeRemoteDataAccess myRDA = new SqlCeRemoteDataAccess();
   //myRDA.InternetLogin = "mylogin";
   //myRDA.InternetPassword = "mypassword";

    myRDA.InternetUrl =
        @"http://pdhingra-lptp/hospitalpatient/sqlcesa30.dll";
    myRDA.LocalConnectionString =
```

```
       "DataSource=\\Program Files\\Patient_RDA\\MyPatients.sdf";
    myRDA.Push("Patients", sqlServerConnection,
                RdaBatchOption.BatchingOff);
    myRDA.Push("PatientHistory", sqlServerConnection,
                RdaBatchOption.BatchingOff);
    myRDA.Dispose();
    labelPush.Text = "Push Complete";
}


private void btnRefresh_Click(object sender, EventArgs e)
{
    // Gets detail of patient history for a given patient
myConn = new SqlCeConnection
       ("DataSource=\\Program Files\\Patient_RDA\\MyPatients.sdf");
myConn.Open();
FillListHistory();
myConn.Close();
}

private void FillListHistory()
{
 // Opens a data reader and fetch the rows from Patient History Table
 listHistory.Items.Clear();
 SqlCeCommand myCmd = myConn.CreateCommand();
 selectedPatientRegNo = txtRegNo.Text;
 myCmd.CommandText =
       "Select PatientRegNo, Treatment, TreatmentStartDate" +
       " From PatientHistory" +
       " where PatientRegNo = " + "'" + selectedPatientRegNo + "'";
 myHistoryDataReader = myCmd.ExecuteReader();
 while (myHistoryDataReader.Read())
 {
   listHistory.Items.Add
       (myHistoryDataReader.GetDateTime(2).ToShortDateString() + " "
        + myHistoryDataReader.GetString(1));
 }

}
private void btnSubmitSQL_Click(object sender, EventArgs e)
{

 string sqlServerConnection = @"Provider=SQLOLEDB;
       Data Source='PDHINGRA-LPTP'; Initial Catalog=Hospital_RDA;
       User Id=RDALoging; Password=RDAPassword";
```

```
SqlCeRemoteDataAccess myRDA = new SqlCeRemoteDataAccess();

 // You need not have to set Login and Password for Anonymous Access
 // myRDA.InternetLogin = "mylogin";
 // myRDA.InternetPassword = "mypassword";
 myRDA.InternetUrl = @"http://pdhingra-lptp/hospitalpatient/sqlcesa30.dll";
 myRDA.LocalConnectionString = "Data Source=MyPatients.sdf";
 string strCmd =
  @"Update Doctors set TotalExperienceInMonths = 160
    where doctoremployeeno = "
    + txtDoctorEmployeeNo.Text;

   myRDA.SubmitSql(strCmd, sqlServerConnection);

   myRDA.Dispose();
   labelSubmit.Text = "Submit SQL Complete";
}

private void btnSave_Click(object sender, EventArgs e)
{
    // Save the new patient detail.
    if (txtPatientRegNo.Text != null)
    {
    myConn = new SqlCeConnection
        ("DataSource=\\Program Files\\Patient_RDA\\MyPatients.sdf");
    myConn.Open();

    // Prepare the command for adding new Patients
    myCmd = myConn.CreateCommand();

    myCmd.CommandText =
        @"INSERT INTO Patients
         (PatientRegNo,DoctorEmployeeNo, FirstName, LastName, DOB)
         VALUES
         (@PatientRegNo,@DoctorEmployeeNo,
          @FirstName, @LastName, @DOB)";

    myCmd.Parameters.Add("@PatientRegNo", SqlDbType.NChar, 10);
    myCmd.Parameters.Add("@DoctorEmployeeNo", SqlDbType.NChar, 10);
    myCmd.Parameters.Add("@FirstName", SqlDbType.NChar, 20);
    myCmd.Parameters.Add("@LastName", SqlDbType.NChar, 20);
    myCmd.Parameters.Add("@DOB", SqlDbType.DateTime);


    myCmd.Parameters["@PatientRegNo"].Value = txtPatientRegNo.Text;
```

```
    myCmd.Parameters["@DoctorEmployeeNo"].Value = "1993243232";
    myCmd.Parameters["@FirstName"].Value = txtFirstName.Text;
    myCmd.Parameters["@LastName"].Value = txtLastName.Text;
    myCmd.Parameters["@DOB"].Value = dateTimeDOB.Value;
    myCmd.ExecuteNonQuery();
    }
    txtPatientRegNo.Text="";
    txtFirstName.Text="";
    txtLastName.Text="";

    myConn.Close();

}

private void btnDone_Click(object sender, EventArgs e)
{
// Save the Patient History
if (txtDisease.Text != null)
{
    myConn = new SqlCeConnection
        ("DataSource=\\Program Files\\Patient_RDA\\MyPatients.sdf");
    myConn.Open();
    //  SQL Command for adding new PatientHistory
    myCmd = myConn.CreateCommand();
    myCmd.CommandText =
      @"INSERT INTO PatientHistory
      (PatientRegNo,DiseaseIdentified,
      DateIdentified,Treatment,TreatmentStartDate,
      TreatmentEndDate, DoctorEmployeeNo)
      VALUES
      (@PatientRegNo,@DiseaseIdentified,@DateIdentified,@Treatment,
       @TreatmentStartDate,@TreatmentEndDate, @DoctorEmployeeNo)";

    myCmd.Parameters.Add("@PatientRegNo", SqlDbType.NChar, 10);
    myCmd.Parameters.Add("@DiseaseIdentified", SqlDbType.NVarChar, 200);
    myCmd.Parameters.Add("@DateIdentified", SqlDbType.DateTime);
    myCmd.Parameters.Add("@Treatment", SqlDbType.NVarChar, 200);
    myCmd.Parameters.Add("@TreatmentStartDate", SqlDbType.DateTime);
    myCmd.Parameters.Add("@TreatmentEndDate", SqlDbType.DateTime);
    myCmd.Parameters.Add("@DoctorEmployeeNo", SqlDbType.NChar, 10);

    myCmd.Parameters["@PatientRegNo"].Value = selectedPatientRegNo;
    myCmd.Parameters["@DiseaseIdentified"].Value = txtDisease.Text;
    myCmd.Parameters["@DateIdentified"].Value = dateTimePicker1.Value;
    myCmd.Parameters["@Treatment"].Value = txtTreatment.Text;
```

```
    myCmd.Parameters["@TreatmentStartDate"].Value = dateTimePicker2.Value;
    myCmd.Parameters["@TreatmentEndDate"].Value = dateTimePicker3.Value;
    myCmd.Parameters["@DoctorEmployeeNo"].Value = txtDoctorEmployeeNo.Text;
    myCmd.ExecuteNonQuery();
    myConn.Close();

    txtDisease.Text = "";
    txtTreatment.Text = "";

    }

  }

}
```

## LISTING 13.5   RDA Exercise Visual Basic.NET

```
Imports System.Data
Imports System.Data.SqlServerCe

Public Class Patient
    Dim myConn As SqlCeConnection
    Dim myPatientDataReader As SqlCeDataReader
    Dim myHistoryDataReader As SqlCeDataReader
    Dim myCmd As SqlCeCommand
    Dim selectedPatientRegNo As String
    Dim strDoctorEmployeeNo As String

    Private Sub Patient_Load(ByVal sender As System.Object, ByVal e As System.Even-
tArgs) Handles MyBase.Load

    End Sub
    Private Sub btnPull_Click(ByVal sender As System.Object, ByVal e As
System.EventArgs) Handles btnPull.Click

        Dim sqlServerConnection As String
        Dim myRDA As SqlCeRemoteDataAccess
        Dim strCmd As String

        sqlServerConnection = _
            "Provider=SQLOLEDB;Data Source='PDHINGRA-LPTP';" & _
            "Initial Catalog=Hospital_RDA; " & _
            "User Id=RDALoging; Password=RDAPassword"
```

```
    myRDA = New SqlCeRemoteDataAccess()
    ' You need not have to set Login and Password for Anonymous access
    ' myRDA.InternetLogin = "mylogin"
    ' myRDA.InternetPassword = "mypassword"
    myRDA.InternetUrl = _
        "http://pdhingra-lptp/hospitalpatient/sqlcesa30.dll"
    myRDA.LocalConnectionString = _
        "DataSource=\Program Files\Patient_RDA\MyPatients.sdf"
    strDoctorEmployeeNo = txtDoctorEmployeeNo.Text
    strCmd = "Select * From Patients where DoctorEmployeeNo= " & _
            "'" & strDoctorEmployeeNo & "'"

    myRDA.Pull("Patients", strCmd, sqlServerConnection, _
            RdaTrackOption.TrackingOnWithIndexes, "ErrorTable")
    strCmd = "Select PatientHistoryID, PatientRegNo, " & _
            "DoctorEmployeeNo, DiseaseIdentified, " & _
            "DateIdentified, Treatment, TreatmentStartDate, " & _
            "TreatmentEndDate " & _
            " From PatientHistory where DoctorEmployeeNo = " & _
            "'" & strDoctorEmployeeNo & "'"

    myRDA.Pull("PatientHistory", strCmd, sqlServerConnection, _
     RdaTrackOption.TrackingOnWithIndexes, "ErrorTableHistory")
    myRDA.Dispose()
    AlterHistoryIdentity()
    labelPull.Text = "Pull Complete"

End Sub

Private Sub AlterHistoryIdentity()

    myConn = New SqlCeConnection _
            ("DataSource=\Program Files\Patient_RDA\MyPatients.sdf")
    myConn.Open()
    myCmd = myConn.CreateCommand()
    myCmd.CommandText = _
        "ALTER TABLE PatientHistory " & _
        "ALTER COLUMN PatientHistoryID IDENTITY (3000,1)"
    myCmd.ExecuteNonQuery()
    myConn.Close()
End Sub
Private Sub btnPush_Click(ByVal sender As System.Object, ByVal e As
System.EventArgs) Handles btnPush.Click
```

```
    Dim myPullCommand As SqlCeCommand
    Dim sqlServerConnection As String
    Dim myRDA As SqlCeRemoteDataAccess
    myPullCommand = myConn.CreateCommand()
    sqlServerConnection = _
        "Provider=SQLOLEDB;Data Source='PDHINGRA-LPTP';" & _
        "Initial Catalog=Hospital_RDA; " & _
        "User Id=RDALoging; Password=RDAPassword"

    myRDA = New SqlCeRemoteDataAccess()
    'You need not have to set Login and Password for Anonymous Access
    'myRDA.InternetLogin = "mylogin"
    'myRDA.InternetPassword = "mypassword"
    myRDA.InternetUrl = _
        "http://pdhingra-lptp/hospitalpatient/sqlcesa30.dll"
    myRDA.LocalConnectionString = _
        "DataSource=\Program Files\Patient_RDA\MyPatients.sdf"

    myRDA.Push("Patients", sqlServerConnection, RdaBatchOption.BatchingOff)
    myRDA.Push("PatientHistory", sqlServerConnection, RdaBatchOption.Batchin-
gOff)
    myRDA.Dispose()
    labelPush.Text = "Push Complete"
End Sub

Private Sub btnRefresh_Click(ByVal sender As System.Object, ByVal e As
System.EventArgs) Handles btnRefresh.Click

    myConn = New SqlCeConnection _
            ("DataSource=\Program Files\Patient_RDA\MyPatients.sdf")
    myConn.Open()
    FillListHistory()
    myConn.Close()
End Sub

Private Sub FillListHistory()
    Dim myCmd As SqlCeCommand
    listHistory.Items.Clear()
    myCmd = myConn.CreateCommand()
    selectedPatientRegNo = txtRegNo.Text
    myCmd.CommandText = _
        "Select PatientRegNo, Treatment, TreatmentStartDate " & _
        "From PatientHistory " & _
        "where PatientRegNo = " & "'" & selectedPatientRegNo & "'"
```

```
        myHistoryDataReader = myCmd.ExecuteReader()
        While (myHistoryDataReader.Read())
            listHistory.Items.Add(myHistoryDataReader.GetDateTime(2).ToShortDat-
eString() + " " + _
                              myHistoryDataReader.GetString(1))
        End While
    End Sub
    Private Sub btnSubmitSQL_Click(ByVal sender As System.Object, ByVal e As Sys-
tem.EventArgs) Handles btnSubmitSQL.Click

        Dim sqlServerConnection As String
        Dim myRDA As SqlCeRemoteDataAccess
        Dim strCmd As String

        sqlServerConnection = _
          "Provider=SQLOLEDB;Data Source='PDHINGRA-LPTP';" & _
          "Initial Catalog=Hospital_RDA; " & _
          "User Id=RDALoging; Password=RDAPassword"
        myRDA = New SqlCeRemoteDataAccess()
        'You need not have to set Login and Password for Anonymous Access
        'myRDA.InternetLogin = "mylogin"
        'myRDA.InternetPassword = "mypassword"
        myRDA.InternetUrl = _
                    "http://pdhingra-lptp/hospitalpatient/sqlcesa30.dll"
        myRDA.LocalConnectionString = _
            "DataSource=\Program Files\Patient_RDA\MyPatients.sdf"
        strCmd = "Update Doctors set TotalExperienceInMonths = 160 " & _
                "where doctoremployeeno = " & _
                "'" & txtDoctorEmployeeNo.Text & "'"
        myRDA.SubmitSql(strCmd, sqlServerConnection)

        myRDA.Dispose()
        labelSubmit.Text = "Submit SQL Complete"

    End Sub


    Private Sub btnSave_Click(ByVal sender As System.Object, ByVal e As
System.EventArgs) Handles btnSave.Click
    If txtPatientRegNo.Text <> "" Then
        myConn = New SqlCeConnection _
                ("DataSource=\Program Files\Patient_RDA\MyPatients.sdf")
        myConn.Open()
        myCmd = myConn.CreateCommand()
        myCmd.CommandText = _
```

```
    "INSERT INTO Patients " & _
    "(PatientRegNo,DoctorEmployeeNo, FirstName, LastName, DOB) " & _
    "VALUES " & _
    "(@PatientRegNo,@DoctorEmployeeNo, " & _
    " @FirstName, @LastName, @DOB)"

  myCmd.Parameters.Add("@PatientRegNo", SqlDbType.NChar, 10)
  myCmd.Parameters.Add("@DoctorEmployeeNo", SqlDbType.NChar, 10)
  myCmd.Parameters.Add("@FirstName", SqlDbType.NChar, 20)
  myCmd.Parameters.Add("@LastName", SqlDbType.NChar, 20)
  myCmd.Parameters.Add("@DOB", SqlDbType.DateTime)


  myCmd.Parameters("@PatientRegNo").Value = txtPatientRegNo.Text
  myCmd.Parameters("@DoctorEmployeeNo").Value = _
            txtDoctorEmployeeNo.Text
  myCmd.Parameters("@FirstName").Value = txtFirstName.Text
  myCmd.Parameters("@LastName").Value = txtLastName.Text
  myCmd.Parameters("@DOB").Value = dateTimeDOB.Value
  myCmd.ExecuteNonQuery()

  txtPatientRegNo.Text = ""
  txtFirstName.Text = ""
  txtLastName.Text = ""
  myConn.Close()
 End If
End Sub


 Private Sub btnDone_Click(ByVal sender As System.Object, ByVal e As
System.EventArgs) Handles btnDone.Click

 If txtDisease.Text <> "" Then
   myConn = New SqlCeConnection _
         ("DataSource=\Program Files\Patient_RDA\MyPatients.sdf")
   myConn.Open()
   myCmd = myConn.CreateCommand()
   myCmd.CommandText = _
   "INSERT INTO PatientHistory " & _
   "(PatientRegNo,DiseaseIdentified," & _
   " DateIdentified,Treatment,TreatmentStartDate, " & _
   " TreatmentEndDate, DoctorEmployeeNo) " & _
   " VALUES " & _
   "(@PatientRegNo,@DiseaseIdentified,@DateIdentified, " & _
```

```
    " @Treatment, @TreatmentStartDate,@TreatmentEndDate, " & _
    " @DoctorEmployeeNo)"

    myCmd.Parameters.Add("@PatientRegNo", SqlDbType.NChar, 10)
    myCmd.Parameters.Add("@DiseaseIdentified", SqlDbType.NVarChar, 200)
    myCmd.Parameters.Add("@DateIdentified", SqlDbType.DateTime)
    myCmd.Parameters.Add("@Treatment", SqlDbType.NVarChar, 200)
    myCmd.Parameters.Add("@TreatmentStartDate", SqlDbType.DateTime)
    myCmd.Parameters.Add("@TreatmentEndDate", SqlDbType.DateTime)
    myCmd.Parameters.Add("@DoctorEmployeeNo", SqlDbType.NChar, 10)

    myCmd.Parameters("@PatientRegNo").Value = selectedPatientRegNo
    myCmd.Parameters("@DiseaseIdentified").Value = txtDisease.Text
    myCmd.Parameters("@DateIdentified").Value = dateTimePicker1.Value
    myCmd.Parameters("@Treatment").Value = txtTreatment.Text
    myCmd.Parameters("@TreatmentStartDate").Value = dateTimePicker2.Value
    myCmd.Parameters("@TreatmentEndDate").Value = dateTimePicker3.Value
    myCmd.Parameters("@DoctorEmployeeNo").Value = txtDoctorEmployeeNo.Text

    myCmd.ExecuteNonQuery()
    myConn.Close()

    txtDisease.Text = ""
    txtTreatment.Text = ""

    End If
End Sub
```

## Build and Deploy Application

Click Build and compile the application. Click Debug | Start Without Debugging.

Select the device or emulator for deployment. The RDA Sync tab in the application displays three buttons for executing Pull, Push, or SubmitSQL statements as shown in Figure 13.6.

### NOTE

The emulator must be cradled and connected through active sync to connect to the remote SQL Server. To cradle an emulator, click on Tools | Device Emulator Manager to start Device Emulator Manager. Right click on the emulator and click Cradle.

Check the status of connectivity by clicking on the connectivity icon as shown in Figure 13.7.

Click on the RDA Pull button. It will fetch the PatientHistory table from the remote SQL Server.

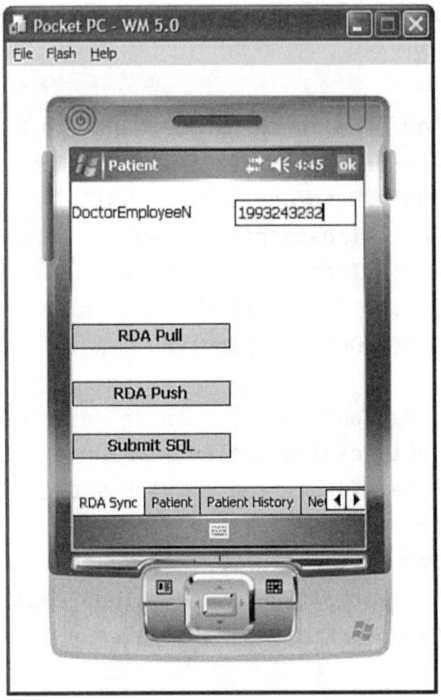

FIGURE 13.6    RDA Pull

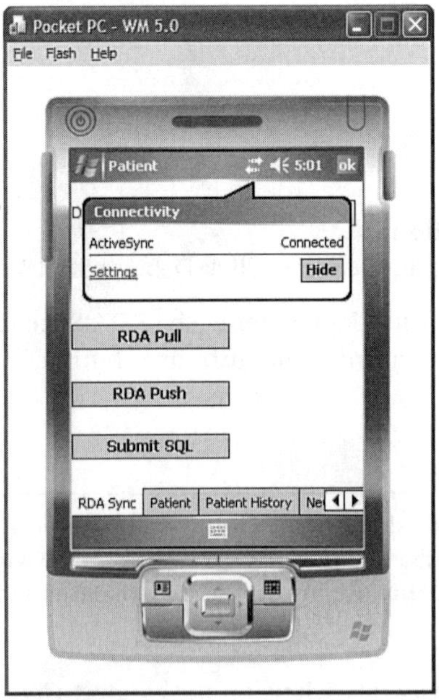

FIGURE 13.7    Active Sync Connectivity

Click on the Patient Tab. Enter a Registration number, First name, Last name, and DOB for new patient as shown in Figure 13.8. Click Save to add a new patient.

Click on the Patient History tab, enter a patient registration number, and click on the Refresh button. It will fetch the treatment details and fill the list box as shown in Figure 13.9.

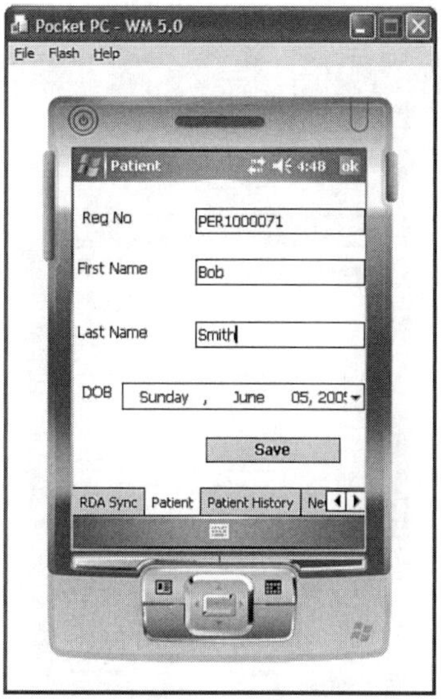

**FIGURE 13.8    Enter New Patient**

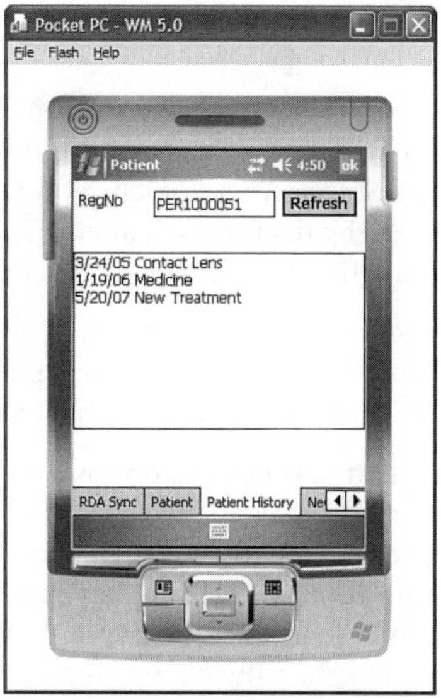

**FIGURE 13.9    View Patient's History**

To enter details of a new treatment, click on the New Treatment tab and enter the details as shown in Figure 13.10.

Click the Done button. It will insert the new treatment details into the PatientHistory table. You should insert a few treatment history rows and verify the inserted data into Patient History by clicking on the Refresh button.

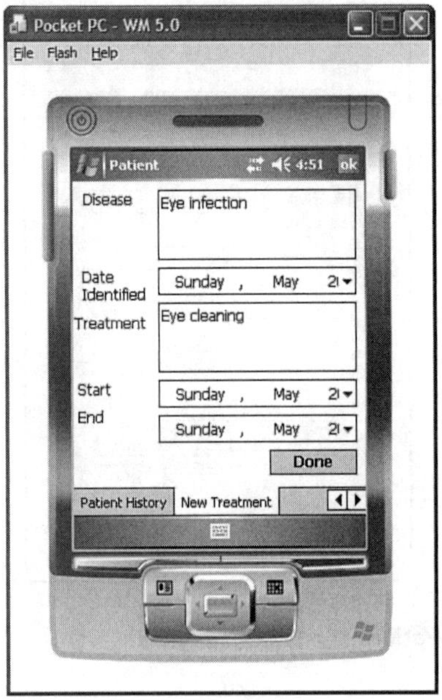

FIGURE 13.10    New Treatment

You should click on the RDA Sync button and click on the Push button to send the changes back to the remote SQL Server. After you click on the Push button, use SQL Server Management Studio to see the data in the PatientHistory table. The PatientHistory table now has the up-to-date data that you entered in the device application.

In this exercise we will also execute an SQL Statement on a remote server using the SubmitSQL method. Click on the SubmitSQL button to update the statement and execute it on the remote server. You can check the updated table in SQL Management Studio.

In this exercise, you created an end-to-end scenario for a disconnected device application. You created the Hospital_RDA backend database on SQL Server 2005, installed SQL Server Compact Edition Server Agent, and configured the Web Server. Using .NET Compact Framework 2.0 and Visual Studio 2005, you created an application to fetch the table from a remote SQL Server and updated the local SQL Server Compact Edition database on a client device. In conclusion, you pushed the changes back to the remote SQL Server 2005.

# Connectivity Options

You have learned how to use the Remote Data Access mechanism to synchronize data between SQL Server Compact Edition and SQL Server. In Chapter 12 you learned Merge Replication for synchronization. These are the two built-in mechanisms to synchronize data between SQL Server Compact Edition and a backend database. You can also write a custom synchronization methodology using Web Services. The following section compares features of Merge Replication and RDA and explains which connectivity solution is suitable for your project.

You can use three methods to exchange data between SQL Server Compact Edition and SQL Server 2005 database:

- Remote Data Access (RDA) Web Service

- Merge Replication

- Web Service

RDA provides the simplest method for a mobile application to access (pull) and send (push) data to and from a remote Microsoft SQL Server database table and a local SQL Server Mobile database table. RDA can also be used to issue SQL commands on a server running SQL Server.

Merge Replication allows a mobile application to make changes to replicated data, and at a later time, merge those changes with a Microsoft SQL Server database and resolve conflicts when necessary.

Web Service is the most complex method to implement as you need to write the implementation yourself. However, if you wish to synchronize data between SQL Server Compact Edition and any database other than SQL Server, Web Service is the option to choose.

# Feature Comparison

There are several factors that you should consider when choosing between Merge Replication and RDA for data exchange. Here we compare the feature-set and implementation techniques of Merge Replication and RDA.

## Conflicts

Both in Merge Replication and RDA, it is possible that conflicts can occur while transferring data to the SQL Server. A conflict can occur during synchronization when more than one client database or server updates the same record.

### Types of Conflict

To understand the differences between Merge Replication and RDA, consider the following reasons for conflict:

- The rows inserted, deleted, or updated on SQL Server Compact Edition failed to update on SQL Server.

- The rows updated on SQL Server Compact Edition are already updated on SQL Server. The rows are updated on SQL Server because a Publisher or another Subscriber updated the rows and synchronized them.

The main difference between Merge Replication and RDA is how each deals with a row being changed by different users. RDA does not consider this to be a conflict; the last user to transfer the data overwrites all other users' data. Only rows that fail to be updated on the SQL Server are considered a conflict in RDA and it is possible to ascertain which ones these are. On the other hand, Merge Replication detects these rows as conflicts and uses the Conflict Resolver to resolve them.

### Conflicts Logging
The conflicts in Merge Replication are logged at Publisher, the SQL Server database.

In RDA you can specify an Error table. This table contains all rows that fail to transfer to the SQL Server during the Push operation. You can write a Customer Conflict detection and report it using the Error table.

### Conflicts Resolution
RDA does not provide any built-in conflict resolution mechanism. Merge Replication provides Conflict Resolver. Merge Replication launches Conflict Resolver specific to the article. There are default, specified, and custom Resolvers.

## Single *Versus* Multiple Table Pull
RDA is designed to pull one table during data synchronization. If you want to pull multiple tables, you need to make multiple calls. On the other hand, Merge Replication allows multiple tables to be synchronized. You can create a publication and define multiple tables with filtering, and so on.

RDA is easy to program and configure compared to Merge Replication. However, if you have to make multiple RDA calls to synchronize multiple tables, the effort required will be less using Merge Replication.

## Referential Integrity Transfer
The Merge Replication referential integrity constraints are replicated from Publisher to Subscriber. Merge Replication replicates constraints between multiple tables on Subscriber and also transfers indexes on tables to Subscriber tables. However RDA is meant only for single table synchronization. Using RDA, only indexes can be transferred to the client side and constraints that define the rule between multiple tables are not replicated.

With Web service program the table, indexes, or referential integrity constraints need to be synchronized.

## Identity Columns
Merge Replication provides an Identity columns feature that generates incrementing numbers for newly inserted rows. In many applications, you may want to use an incremental

number to manage records inserted at a client database. For example, if your user is entering new orders into a table, you may want to assign an automatic incremental number to each order. When using such a system, you must ensure that the numbers do not conflict between clients. Merge Replication supports automatic identity range management for both `int` and `bigint` columns for publications and subscriptions. Using automatic identity, range management ensures that no rows will conflict, no matter how many clients you have.

When using RDA, automatic management of identity columns is not supported. To use this data type property you must manually manage the values for the entire system.

With Web service, you have to build such a mechanism yourself.

## Tools

To manage Merge Replication, SQL Server Management Studio provides wizards and Replication Monitor. You can use SQL Server Management Studio wizards to create publication, create subscription, configure the Snapshot folder, etc. There is also a wizard that generates template code that can be used to synchronize the data. Also, you can use Replication Monitor to check the status of subscriptions.

There are no special tools required for RDA—you just need to write code to set up RDA and transfer the data.

## Server Side Changes

To implement Merge Replication, you create a publication. Creating a publication adds system tables. It also adds a Unique Identifier column to tables in a publication.

Merge Replication executes schema changes on the backend SQL Server and provides a rich feature set for data exchange. If for some reason you can't change schema on the SQL Server side, Merge Replication is not available. You must consider in advance whether or not you will have permission to modify the SQL Server schema in a production environment.

RDA does not require changing schema on a backend SQL Server. It provides a limited feature set to exchange data between SQL Server Compact Edition and SQL Server.

## Configurations

Merge Replication requires configuring the server whereas RDA does not. For RDA, each client is configured individually and is suitable when you have a constraint on configuring a server.

## Synchronization Control

In an RDA-based solution, data exchange is initiated by a client application. The client application calls the Pull method or Push method to exchange data with the backend SQL Server. The backend SQL Server does not have to know the tables that participate in the data exchange.

On the other hand, in Merge Replication the backend Server acts as Publisher of data. The Publisher database publishes the tables and columns that you want to make available for the Subscriber SQL Server Compact Edition database.

## Server Side Schema Changes

RDA does not support schema change. Consequently, if schema on the server side is changed, you must drop the table and pull the data from the server again, otherwise the push to server will fail. Only minor schema changes are allowed and you may have to recompile the application.

In Merge Replication it is possible to do schema changes on the server side. You can add or drop a column and then synchronize the data. At the time of synchronization, first the schema changes will be replicated, and then corresponding data changes will be synchronized.

## Bidirectional *Versus* Single Directional Changes

Merge Replication supports bidirectional changes where data changes from Publisher to Subscriber and from Subscriber to Publisher are tracked and applied at the time of synchronization. In RDA, these changes are tracked only on SQL Server Compact Edition. RDA sends one of following:

- A pull request to retrieve data from SQL Server and store it in the SQL Server Compact Edition local database.

- A push request to update the data back on SQL Server.

- An SQL query to execute any query on the SQL Server. It does not return any rows back to SQL Server Compact Edition.

## Download Only Articles

Merge Replication provides a Download Only Article feature. Using this feature you can define tables that are only copied from SQL Server Publisher to SQL Server Compact Subscriber. As Merge Replication is meant for synchronizing multiple tables you can define a few tables as *Download Only Article* and the remaining can be standard article.

With RDA you synchronize each table separately. For tables that are only updatable at Publisher, you will use only the Pull method to get data and there is no need to use the Push method.

## Filtering Tables

It is possible in both RDA and Merge Rplication to get a subset of rows instead of bringing all rows from Publisher to Subscriber.

With RDA you will be using the criteria in the Sql query that you pass in the Pull method. Within Merge Replication you can use the filtering option. This option controls the flow of data between Publisher and Subscriber.

With RDA you synchronize each table separately. For tables that are only updatable at Publisher, you will use only the Pull method to get data and there is no need to use the Push method.

## Summary of RDA and Merge Replication Features

Table 13.12 summarizes the feature differences between Merge Replication and Remote Data Access.

**TABLE 13.12    RDA and Replication Comparision**

| RDA | Replication |
| --- | --- |
| Conflicts only include rows which did not apply because of an error. RDA does not detect if data was changed by a different user. | Conflicts include data changed by different users and rows which did not apply because of an error. |
| Conflicts not managed, but are optionally reported in an Error table on the client. | Resolution and management of conflicts on the server. |
| No conflict resolvers. | Built-in and custom conflict resolvers supported. |
| One table per RDA method. | Multiple tables—as many as defined in the publication. |
| Constraints are not transferred. Only indexes on a table can be transferred to SQL Server Compact Edition. | Constraint between multiple tables can be transferred to Subscriber. |
| RDA does not have data flow controls. Addition or removal of a table at the server is not automatically replicated to the client. | Different types of tables to control data flow. Addition or removal of a table in the publication (server) is replicated automatically without reinitializing the subscription on the client. |
| No tools supported. | Extensive tools to create and manage subscriptions, and monitoring tools to manage multiple subscriptions, watch performance, and sync times. |
| Pushes change from client to server only. Complete update of client data required to receive server changes. | Replicates changes to and from server and client. |
| Row-level tracking—whole row is transferred. | Column-level tracking—reduces the amount of data transferred by only transferring changed column data. Row-level tracking—whole row is transferred. |

TABLE 13.12    RDA and Replication Comparision

| RDA | Replication |
|---|---|
| Schema changes are not allowed. If the schema are changed, the client must drop the table at the client and pull all the data from the server again. Depending on the schema change, a push can fail. | Schema changes (such as add/drop columns, add/drop constraints, or changing column definition) can replicate. |
| Manual identity range handling. Bigint and Int columns supported. | Manual and auto identity range handling. BigInt and Int columns supported. |
| Data and schema definition occurs at the client when data is pulled from server to client. | Occurs at the server when the publication is configured and is automatically defined at the client when the subscription is created. |
| No changes made to database on server. | Tables and columns added to server database to manage replication. |

# Advantages and Disadvantages of Using Web Service as Synchronization Mechanism

As discussed, Merge Replication and RDA are two methods that synchronize data between a backend database and a client database. It is also possible for you to build a custom mechanism that you fully control. You will probably not want to spend a huge amount of time implementing the similar technology that SQL Server Compact Edition already provides. RDA and Merge Replication help you to synchronize data with Microsoft SQL Server only. You may want to build a custom mechanism yourself if you wish to synchronize the data with databases other than Microsoft SQL Server.

## Advantages

SQL Server Compact Edition provides RDA and Merge Replication to synchronize data. The built-in mechanism allows data to be synchronized with SQL Server. The advantage of using a Web Service is that you can synchronize the data between SQL Server Compact Edition and any data source.

Web Services use standard protocol and provide interoperability between disparate software and platforms.

## Disadvantages

You can use a Web Service to transfer the data between client and server. There is no built-in mechanism so you will need to implement a mechanism to synchronize data between server and client.

To use a Web Service as a synchronization method, you need to create a Web Service solution that creates and updates the server database. You also need to implement complex logic for transferring schema, indexes, and constraints from server to client or vice versa.

You need to handle the conflict resolution in a Web Service. For some applications, having a large number of clients may be very complex.

You can easily change the set of tables and columns to be synchronized in replication. But if you are using Web Services, these changes may be extremely complex and costly.

A Web Service uses SOAP to transfer data between client and server. Web Services uses http and XML for data transfer. This means that you need to convert the data into XML format at the time of synchronization.

# Synchronizing Microsoft Access Data with SQL Server Compact Edition

You can download and use the Microsoft SQL Server Compact Edition Database Access Synchronizer tool to synchronize data between Microsoft Access on a desktop and an SQL Server Compact Edition database on a device. The Access Database Synchronizer tool is written using RDA technology.

To synchronize data between Microsoft Access and SQL Server Compact Edition, install the Database Access Synchronizer onto a desktop, deploy the cab files on a device, use the wizard tool to specify the desktop and device database path, and synchronize the data.

## Installing the Data Access Synchronization Tool

To install the Data Access Synchronization tool, download the installer package from the Microsoft Download Center. The Data Access Synchronizer is free to install.

1. Download the Access Synchronizer tool (AccessDatabaseSynchronizer-EN.msi) from the Microsoft Download Center.

2. Install the Database Access Synchronizer tool. The installation will install a Sample Wizard (tool), source code, End-User License Agreement, and a Readme file on `<drive:>\Program Files\Microsoft SQL Server Compact Edition\v3.1\ Sync\Access`. Installation will also add registry entries on the desktop.

3. You can compile the source code and deploy it onto the device using Visual Studio or directly deploy the tool onto the device.

## Synchronizing Data

To synchronize the data between Access and SQL Server Compact Edition, the tool uses the RDA component `Client Agent` on the device (SQL Server Compact Edition) and adds a synchronization component on the desktop to communicate with the Access database. The synchronization component runs as a service and it starts when an ActiveSync connection is established between the device and the desktop.

1. Run the wizard tool on the device. The tool allows you to specify the path of Access and the SQL Server Compact Edition database. You will also specify the desktop name and the port used for communication as part of the desktop URL.

### NOTE

By default, port 1024 is used. You can change the port in the registry settings. Add the port used in the Firewall Exception list.

2. The tool offers a File I Connect option to connect to the Access database.

3. Use the File I Pull menu option to pull the tables from the Access database.

4. Similarly, use the File I Push option to send the tables back to the Access database.

### NOTE

Use the Readme file located at `<Drive>\Program Files\Microsoft SQL Server Compact Edition\v3.1\Sync\Access` to see detailed instructions for using the Data Access Synchronization tool.

You can use the Access Database Synchronizer tool to synchronize data directly or you can write custom applications using ssceas.dll. The ssceas.dll export function can be used by a custom application.

## Summary

Earlier in this chapter you learned how to use the Remote Data Access mechanism between SQL Server and SQL Server Compact Edition. You have seen how to set up and build an RDA-based solution as well as an end-to-end process by setting up a database at an SQL Server. Using RDA you retrieved a table onto the SQL Server Compact Edition and after updating the table, sent the changes back to the SQL Server. You have set up a Web Server for RDA as well as learned the details of the Push, Pull, and Submit SQL methods.

Later in the chapter, Merge Replication and RDA were compared. The comparison outlined the differences between features and constraints imposed by both functionalities. This comparison will help you to choose the appropriate architecture for your solution. Whether you choose RDA or Merge Replication, the decision should not be taken lightly. You must consider the points mentioned here to evaluate which mechanism is suitable for your enterprise application.

# Securing the SQL Server 2005 Compact Edition Database

Laptop, Tablet PC, and mobile devices enable information workers to access enterprise data from remote locations. The database is the most import asset for an organization. Enterprise databases are hosted on a server located in a secure building. Even for a database located in a building, data security is one of the biggest concerns for an organization. New risks are introduced due to the mobility of data outside the boundaries of the corpnet firewall. As more and more users become mobile, the number of security breaches increases. The misuse of confidential information increases when data travels outside the boundaries of an enterprise. With this recent trend, it is becoming more important for enterprise IT strategy to address security issues related to the mobile work force.

The SQL Server Compact Edition database is used as a local store for mobile workers. SQL Server Compact Edition has features to secure and encrypt data on a client device and also enables secure data transmission between a client device and the backend SQL Server.

This chapter explains the SQL Server Compact Edition features that you can use to address security issues and discusses the factors you should consider while planning to secure data for mobile workers. The security features explained in this chapter will help you to choose and implement the right solution for your application.

# Securing the Client Database

The SQL Server Compact Edition database is deployed on client machines—laptop, Tablet PC, mobile devices, etc. As each client is carrying a copy of the database and users of these databases are mobile, there are specific problems that need to be considered while designing database security. Some of the more common risks for a database on client machines include:

- A user can lose a database device while out in the field.

- Even if your client application requires a user ID and password, someone can directly open the database on the device.

You access an SQL Server Compact Edition database with client applications and your device and application have authentication and authorization to ensure that only authorized users have access. Even if unauthorized users do access your device, they should not be able to see the content of the database by using Query Analyzer or SQL Server Management Studio. This chapter focuses on the password and encryption features that SQL Server Compact Edition provides. The password feature ensures that anyone trying to access the database needs to supply the password.

## Using a Password

To secure the SQL Server Compact Edition database you should create a password for the database. Once a password is set, you need to specify the password for accessing the database.

### Password String

In a password string, you can specify alphabets, digits, and nonalphanumeric characters. The password string can be up to 40 characters long.

It is recommended that a password consist of letter, digit, and nonalphanumeric characters. SQL Server Compact Edition also recommends that the length of a password string should be a minimum six characters. SQL Server Compact Edition displays a warning message if you specify a password that does not meet the recommendation as shown in Figure 14.1.

You can still choose not to have a recommended password string by clicking Yes on the warning message dialog box.

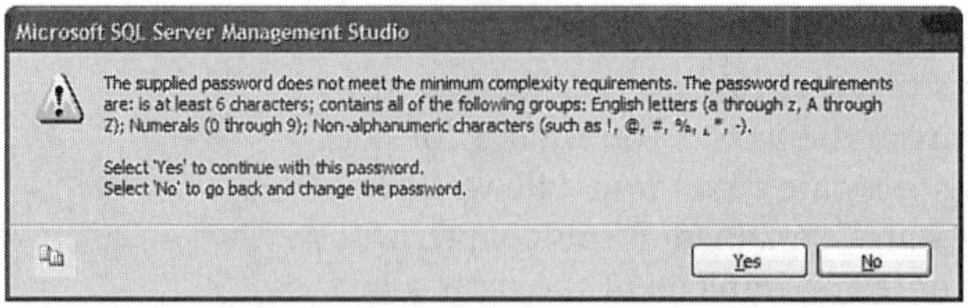

FIGURE 14.1    Password String

## Encryption

You can protect the database by using a password. Without a password, a user will not be able to access the database programmatically or with tools such as Query Analyzer or SQL Server Management Studio. However, a user will be able to open the database file as clear text and see the content. By using the Encryption feature, you can ensure that the database cannot be read without a password.

Encrypting data means converting data into a format that can be read only with a special key. When you choose to encrypt a database, the database engine encrypts the data and you will have to specify the password to decrypt and retrieve the data. If the password is lost, you will never be able to encrypt the data.

### NOTE
You must specify the password for encryption.

## Setting a Password and Encryption

A password is required to authenticate an SQL Server Compact Edition user. The password is specific to the SQL Server Compact Edition database, not to each user. A password is created when the database is created and it protects the database from unauthorized access. However, one can still read the database as clear text. If you store the database in an encrypted format, the encryption and password together will provide protection.

### Setting a Password with SQL Management Studio
You can set the password at the time you create the new database. As shown in Figure 14.2, you can specify the password in the Create New SQL Server dialog box of SQL Server Management Studio.

You can check the Encrypt box shown in Figure 14.2 to enable database encryption.

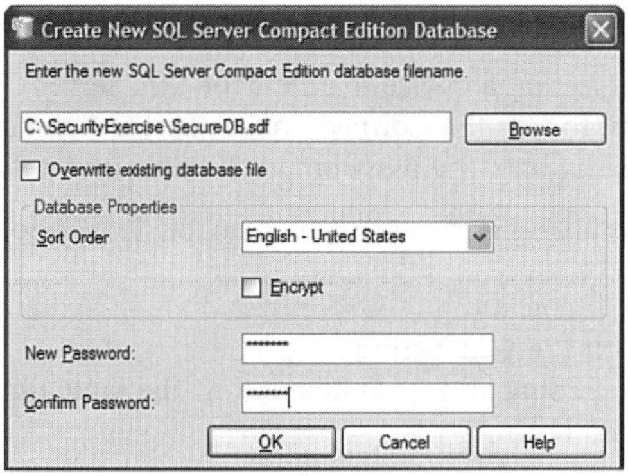

FIGURE 14.2   Create Database with a Password

You can also use SQL Management Studio to set the password for the database at a later stage. Select the Database, right click, and select Properties.

The Database Properties dialog box has a Set Password tab that allows you to create a new password or change a previous password. This dialog box also includes an Encrypt check box to enable database encryption as shown in Figure 14.3.

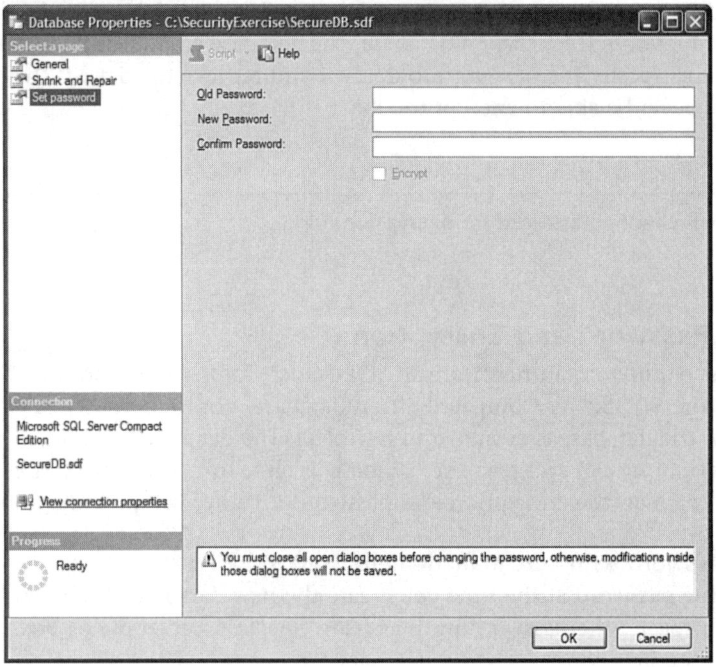

**FIGURE 14.3    Setting a Password with Database Properties**

### Setting a Password with Query Analyzer
You can use Query Analyzer on a device to access the SQL Server Compact database. Click on the New Database button on the Connect to SQL Server Compact Edition dialog box to create a new database. Specify the password at the time of database creation.

Query Analyzer also has an Encrypt check box to enable encryption as shown in Figure 14.4.

### Setting a Password with the SQL String
You can create a database using an SQL Statement. At the same time, you can also specify the password as shown in Listing 14.1.

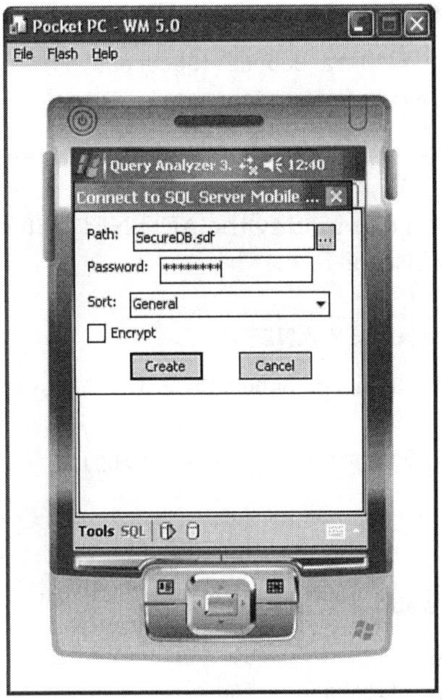

**FIGURE 14.4**    Create Database Using Query Analyzer

**LISTING 14.1    Create Database Using an SQL Statement**

```
CREATE DATABASE "SecureDb.sdf" DATABASEPASSWORD 'password'
```

To enable the encryption, you can specify it in an SQL statement as shown in Listing 14.2.

**LISTING 14.2    Encrypt Database SQL Statement**

```
CREATE DATABASE "SecureDb.sdf" DATABASEPASSWORD 'password' encryption on
```

### Setting a Password with ADO.NET

You can create a database using ADO.NET. You will be using the CreateDatabase method of the SqlCeEngine class. Before calling the CreateDatabase method, you specify a connection string to create an SqlCeEngine object. You can specify the password as part of a connection string as shown in Listing 14.3.

**LISTING 14.3    Create Database C#.NET**

```
string myConnString = "Data Source='SecureDB.sdf';  Password='password';";
SqlCeEngine myEngine = new SqlCeEngine(myConnString);
myEngine.CreateDatabase();
```

**LISTING 14.3     Create Database VB.NET**

```
Dim myConnString As String = "Data Source='SecureDB.sdf'; Password='password'"
Dim myEngine As New SqlCeEngine(myConnString)
engine.CreateDatabase()
```

To switch the encryption, you can modify the ADO.NET statement and add `encrypt database=TRUE` as shown in Listing 14.4.

**LISTING 14.4     Encrypt Database C#.NET**

```
string myConnString = "Data Source='SecureDB.sdf';  Password='password'; encrypt
database=TRUE";
SqlCeEngine myEngine = new SqlCeEngine(myConnString);
myEngine.CreateDatabase();
```

**LISTING 14.4     Encrypt Database VB.NET**

```
Dim myConnString As String = "Data Source='SecureDB.sdf';
Password='password';encrypt database = TRUE"
Dim myEngine As New SqlCeEngine(myConnString)
engine.CreateDatabase()
```

**Setting a Password with OLE DB**

Similar to ADO.NET, you can create a database and set the password using the OLE DB provider. To set the password, you need to set the value of `DBPROP_SSCE_DBPASSWORD`. To switch on the encryption you need to set `DBPROP_SSCE_ENCRYPTDATABASE` as `VARIANT_TRUE`.

## Accessing a Password-Protected Encrypted Database

Once you have set the password for the database, you need to supply the password for accessing the database. If you have enabled database encryption, the engine will decrypt and give you the data.

SQL Management Studio will prompt you to enter the password when you connect to the database as shown in Figure 14.5.

If you are using Query Analyzer on a device you can open a password-protected database. When you try to open it, Query Analyzer will prompt you to supply a password.

While accessing the database through ADO.NET, you need to specify the password as part of connection string as shown in Listing 14.5.

FIGURE 14.5   Specifying a Password in Management Studio

FIGURE 14.6   Specifying a Password Using Query Analyzer

LISTING 14.5   Accessing Database with a Password C#.NET

```
string myConnString = "Data Source='SecureDB.sdf';  Password='password';";
SqlCeConnection myConn = new SqlCeConnection(myConnString);
myConn.Open();
```

**LISTING 14.5    Accessing Database with a Password VB.NET**

```
Dim myConnString As String = "Data Source='SecureDB.sdf'; Password='password'"
Dim myConn As New SqlCeConnection (myConnString)
myConn.Open
```

If you are using an OLE DB provider to access the password-protected SQL Server Compact Edition database, you need to use the DBPROP_SSCE_DBPASSWORD property in the DBPROPSET_SSCE_DBINIT provider-specific property set to specify the password.

# Exploring the Web Server Security Options

Data synchronization between SQL Server Compact Edition and SQL Server is done through an IIS Web Server. You need to secure data transmission from end to end. SQL Server Compact Edition provides features to secure connectivity between the backend SQL Server and the client SQL Server Compact Edition database.

Before discussing the security planning for data transmission, this section will briefly discuss the security options available for Web Server and SQL Server. In this section, you will also be introduced to the Secure Socket Layer that enables secure transmission over http.

## IIS Authentication

SQL Server Compact Edition Server Agent runs on an IIS Web Server on behalf of a client under the identity of a supplied username. IIS supports the following three authentication mechanisms:

- Anonymous authentication
- Basic authentication
- Windows Integrated authentication

### Anonymous Authentication

Anonymous authentication means no authentication. This method gives access to a client on a Web Server and does not prompt for a username and password. Using this method, the Server Agent runs under the identity of Internet Guest Account. IUSR_computername is the default Internet Guest Account. When a client attempts to connect to a Web Server, it assigns the user to the Windows user account named IUSR_*computername*, where *computername* is the name of the server that IIS is running. The IUSR_*computername* account is included in the Windows user group Guests when IIS is installed on the server. This group has security restrictions, imposed by NTFS permission, that designate the level of access and the type of content available to public internet users.

**NOTE**

IUSR_*computername* is the default Internet Guest Account but you can designate another Windows account as the Internet Guest Account.

## Basic Authentication

In Basic authentication, your Web Server client application needs to specify credentials in the form of a username and password. This username should be a valid Windows account, meaning each SQL Server Compact Edition client should have a Windows user account. The SQL Server Compact Edition Server Agent on a Web Server runs under the identity of the account supplied.

### NOTE

By default the credentials are sent on a network as a string with base-64 encoding. It is not advisable to send the credentials as text with base-64 encoding and you should combine Basic authentication with SSL.

The steps to use Secure Socket Layer (SSL) are explained in the next section.

## Windows Integrated Authentication

In Windows Integration authentication, a client Windows domain account is used. The system sends your Windows username and password. In Integrated Windows authentication, SQL Server Compact Edition Server Agent runs under the identity of the client account. This method works if client and server are on the same domain. Integrated Windows authentication does not work with firewalls or proxy servers. It uses a hashing algorithm to encode the username and password.

# Secure Socket Layer

The purpose of the Secure Socket Layer (SSL) is to encrypt the information transmitted over http/https. If you transmit a user ID and password over http, then anyone can intercept the information. You can use an SSL Certificate to protect sensitive data transmitted over http. On the World Wide Web, SSL is a universally accepted method for establishing an encrypted connection.

An SSL certificate is provided in the form of an electronic file. The certificate is signed digitally by an authority. VeriSign is a major authority providing SSL certificates.

## Establishing a Secure Connection

To initiate the SSL connection, the client and server exchange information about the encryption information related to the SSL certificate. Once the initial handshake is completed, both client and server know the key for encryption and decryption. Anyone intercepting the information between client and server will see only the encrypted information. Once the information is encrypted it is extremely difficult to decrypt it.

The following steps establish a connection between client and server:

1. The client initiates the request.

2. The server sends its digital ID and may also ask the client for a certificate ID.

3. The client verifies the client's digital certificate and sends its digital certificate. This completes the authentication process.

4. After authentication is complete, the client sends a session key to the server. The session key is encrypted using the server public key.

5. After a session key is established between client and server, client and server can start secure communication.

## HTTPS

Https stands for http over SSL. Https provides authenticated and encrypted communication between client and server. When you use https, it encrypts the client request and it gets decrypted at the server. URLS starting with https indicate that you are using http protocol with an additional layer of encryption. A Web Server must have a server certificate to accept an https connection. Using the certificate server authenticates the sender.

---

**NOTE**

By default http uses port 80. url. For https url, the default port is 443.

---

## Using SSL

To set up a certificate for your Web Server, you need to create a Certificate Signing Request and send it to a signing authority such as VeriSign. The certificate authority will then send you the certificate.

### Creating a Certificate Signing Request File

To generate a Certificate Signing Request (CSR) file, go to control panel | Administrative Tool and double click on Internet Information Services as shown in Figure 14.7.

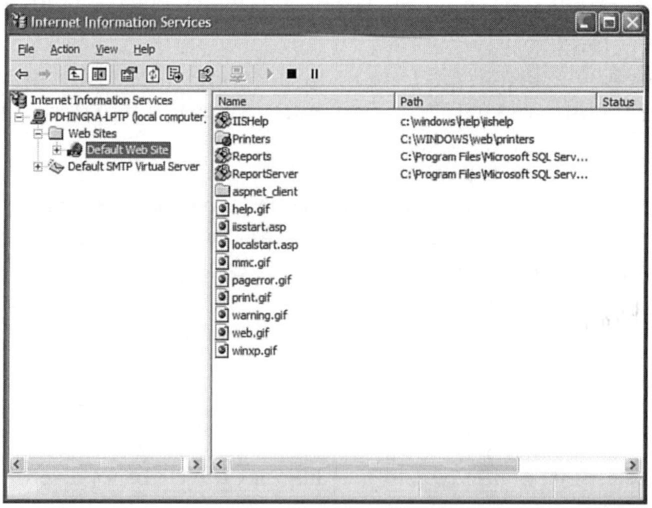

**FIGURE 14.7**    Internet Information Services

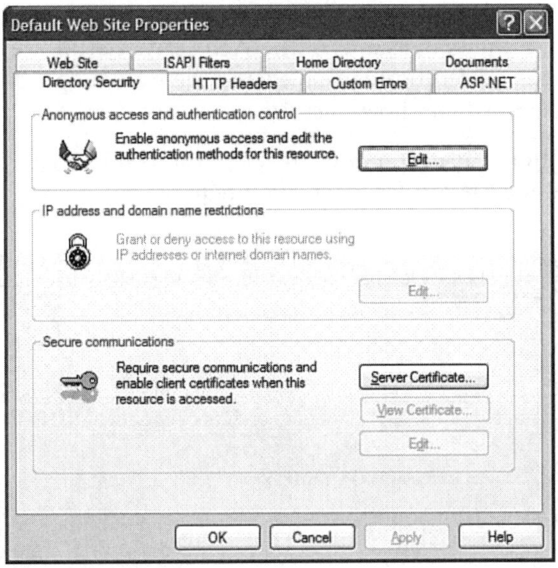

**FIGURE 14.8**    Directory Security

Click on Default Web Site and right click on Properties to start the Default Web Set Properties dialog box as shown in Figure 14.8. Click on the Directory Security tab.

Click on the Server Certificate button in the Secure communication section on the dialog box. Clicking on the Server Certificate button starts the wizard to create a Web Server Certificate as shown in Figure 14.9.

**FIGURE 14.9**    IIS Certificate Wizard

The Web Server Certificate wizard is a useful tool to create and administer certificates. The first page of the wizard shows the status of the Web Server Certificate on the Web Server. It tells you that there is no certificate installed and there are no pending requests. The following example demonstrates how to create a new certificate for the Web Server.

Choose the radio button, Create a new certificate, as shown in Figure 14.10 and click the Next button to continue the certificate creation request.

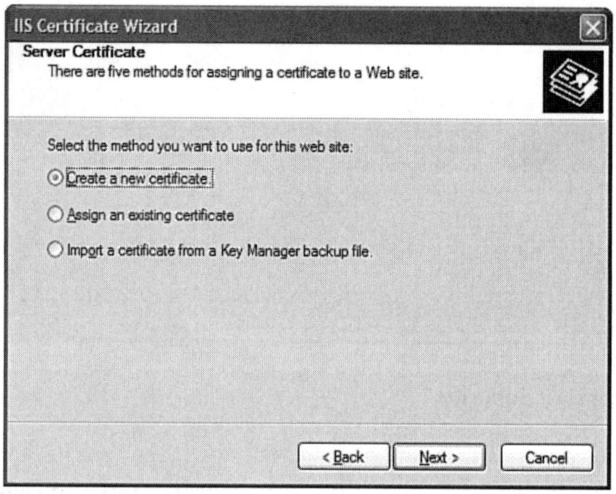

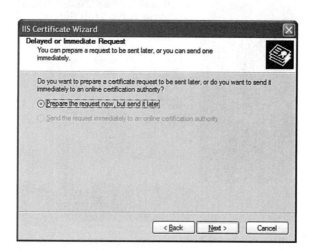

**FIGURE 14.10**    Create a New Certificate

The next dialog box asks if you want to prepare a certificate request to be sent later or immediately to an online certification authority. Choose the radio button, Prepare the request now, but send it later as shown in Figure 14.11. Click the Next button.

**FIGURE 14.11**    Prepare a Request for IIS Certificate

In the Name and Security Settings dialog box, as shown in Figure 14.12, specify the name of your certificate. The example here shows pdhingraCertificate. Type in the name of your certificate. The Bit length field on wizard allows you to enter the bit length. The example here chooses the default bit length 1024 which is quite strong for encryption. Click Next.

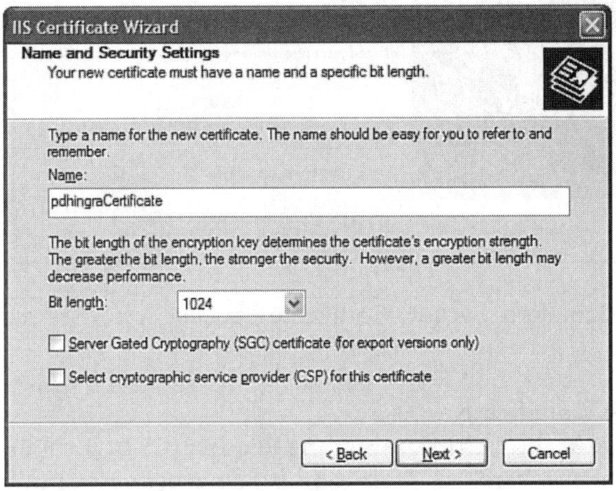

**FIGURE 14.12**    Name for Security Certificate

The next dialog asks you to enter your organization information. Type in the names of your organization and the organization unit.

Clicking Next on the Organization Information dialog box takes you to the Geographical Information dialog box.

After you have entered the details in the Organization Information dialog box, click the Next button. On the Certificate Request File Name dialog box, enter the path and file-name for your certificate request. You will be saving the request into a text file and then sending it to a certification authority that will then send you a certificate.

Specify the path and name of the file.

Click Next after you have specified the filename. The next dialog box presents a Summary of Request File. The dialog box shows you all the details that you have specified in the IIS Certificate Wizard. You should review the details—Web Server, Certificate Name, Geography Information, and Organization Information. Click the Next button if you are satisfied with the information .

The next dialog box, as shown in Figure 14.13, confirms that you have created a certificate request into a file. The dialog box advises you to send the request file to a certificate authority.

**FIGURE 14.13**    Complete Security Certificate Request

### Obtaining the SSL Certificate

After you have created the Certificate Signing Request (CSR), it should be sent to a certification authority such as VeriSign. The example below demonstrates the steps to obtaining a trial certificate from the VeriSign certification authority.

To enroll for a trial certificate, you need to have a CSR generated from the server where you want to test the certificate. During the enrollment process you also need to provide your contact information as the person responsible for maintaining the trial certificate. After you submit the CSR, you will receive the trial certificate and installation instructions via email. To use the trial certificate, you need to install CA Root with each browser that will be used to test the trial certificate.

Open a browser and navigate to the VeriSign certification page. The page prompts you to enter your contact information. Enter your information and click Continue to proceed further.

The next page, as shown in Figure 14.14, contains all the steps that you need to complete to get a certificate.

1. Enter Technical Contact Information.

2. Submit CSR.

3. Provide password for CSR.

4. Submit your order.

5. Install the Test CA root.

6. Install SSL Certificate.

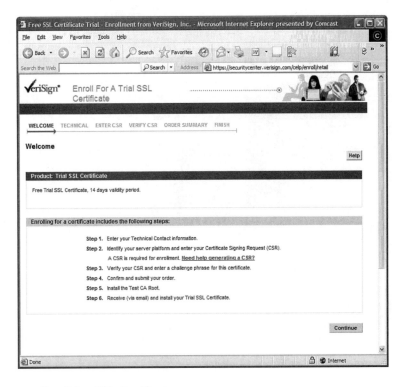

**FIGURE 14.14**    Enroll for  SSL Certificate

Click Continue to initiate the steps.

Enter the contact details and click Continue.

As shown Figure 14.15, paste the CSR you created earlier into the Enter Certificate Signing Request. To do this, open the CSR in a notepad and copy all the lines including the `Begin New Certificate Request` and the `End New Certificate Request` lines.

The next page, as shown in Figure 14.16, allows you to enter a password type phrase. You can use this phrase to renew your certificate.

Click Continue to display the next page which shows the summary of your order including the validity information of your certificate. Click Continue to proceed.

The next page confirms your order. This completes the steps for obtaining the certificate and shortly thereafter you will receive a confirmation email from VeriSign.

The confirmation email will include steps to install an attached certificate. Save this certificate including the `BEGIN CERTIFICATE` and `END CERTIFICATE` lines in a file named `ReceiveromEmail.Cer`.

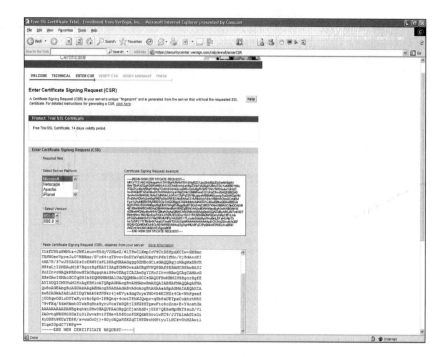

FIGURE 14.15    Add  Certificate Signing Request

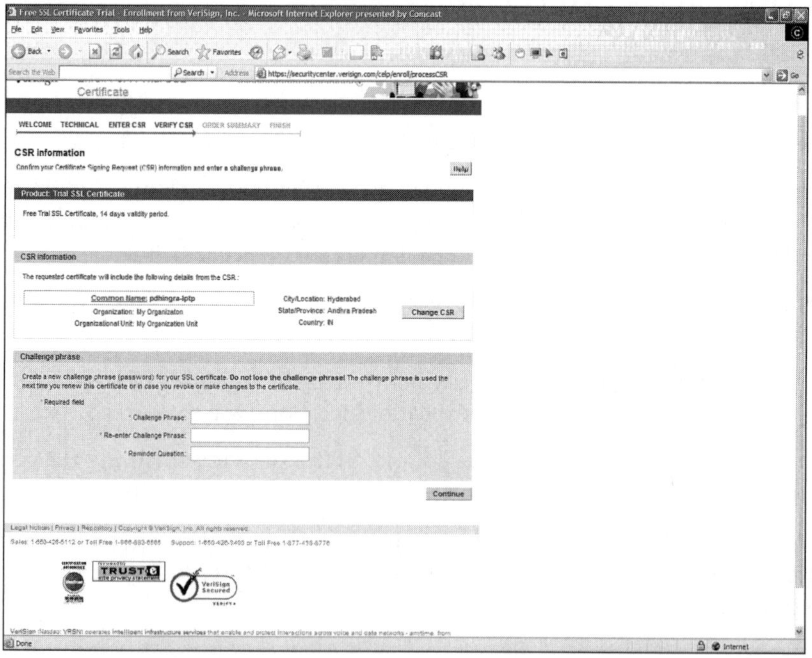

FIGURE 14.16    Password Phrase for CSR

## Installing Test CA Root Certificate

The example dialog box as displayed in Figure 14.17 shows a trial version of an SSL certificate. As per VeriSign guidelines, you need to install Trial CA Root with each browser that will be used to test the trial certificate.

The email you received from VeriSign will have a link to a page for installing the Test CA Root certificate.

---

**NOTE**

You need to install only the Test CA Root certificate if you are using a trial version of the SSL certificate. Install Test CA Root with each browser that will be used to test the trial certificate.

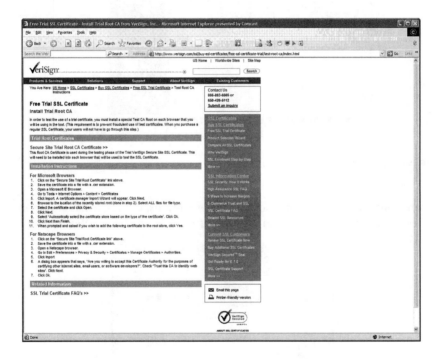

**FIGURE 14.17**    Trial CA Root Certificate

To install the Trial Root certificate, open the Secure Site Trial Root Certificate and save it into a file. Once the certificate is saved, you can import the certificate file using the Certificate Manager Import Wizard.

When you click on the link, the next page presents you with another certificate—the Root CA Certificate. Copy and paste the new certificate including the BEGIN CERTIFICATE and END CERTIFICATE lines as shown in Figure 14.18. Save the file with a .cer extension. In the example shown, the file is saved with the VeriSign.cer name.

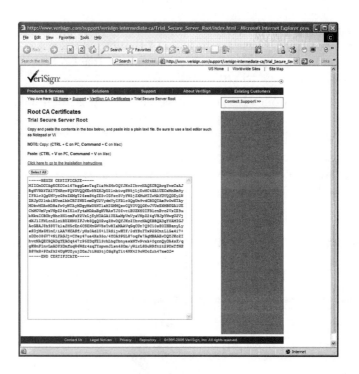

**FIGURE 14.18    Obtain Root CA Certificate**

Now open a browser and click on Tools | Internet Options. On the Internet option dialog, click on the Content tab as shown in Figure 14.19. Click on the Certificates button.

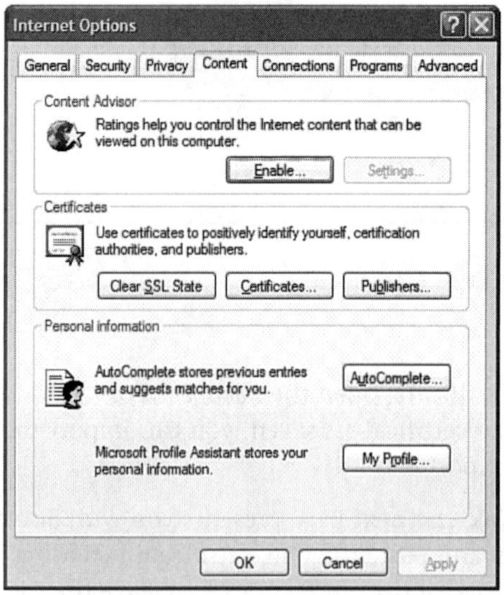

**FIGURE 14.19    Upload Root CA Certificate**

As shown in Figure 14.20, click on the Import button on the Certificates dialog box to import the CA Root certificate.

The Certificate Import Wizard helps you to upload the certificate. Click on the Next button as shown in Figure 14.21.

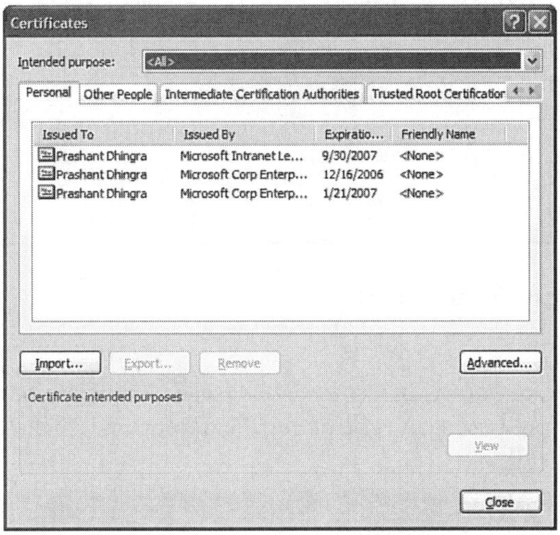

**FIGURE 14.20    Import Root CA Certificate**

**FIGURE 14.21    Start Certificate Import Wizard**

As shown in Figure 14.22, in the file import dialog box, specify the path and filename where you saved the Root CA certificate. Click on Next.

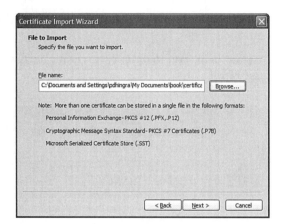

**FIGURE 14.22     Specify File to Import**

In the next dialog box, as shown in Figure 14.23, select the radio button, Automatically select the certificate store based on type of certificate option. Click Next.

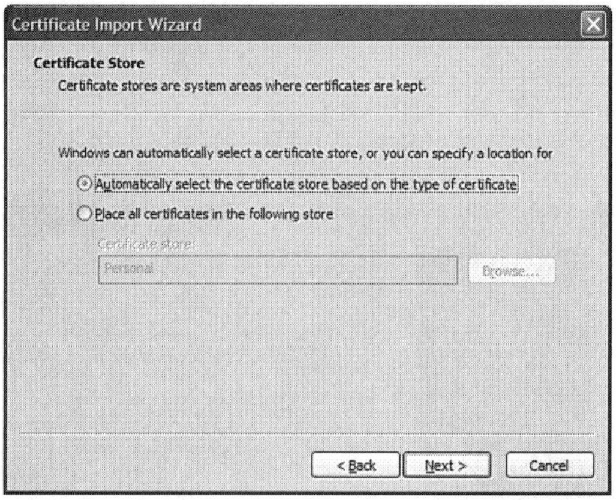

**FIGURE 14.23     Automatically Select the Certificate**

The next dialog box, as shown in Figure 14.24, confirms the specified file to import.

After you click the Finish button, you are shown a message that the import was successful.

### Installing SSL Certificate

The last example demonstrates how to install the Test CA Root Certificate that is needed for the trial version of the certificate. You can install the certificate that you received via email. To install the certificate again, start the IIS using the Control Panel and

**FIGURE 14.24** Complete Certificate Import

Administrative Tools. Select your Web Site, right click on it, and click Properties. Click on the Directory Security tab as shown in Figure 14.25.

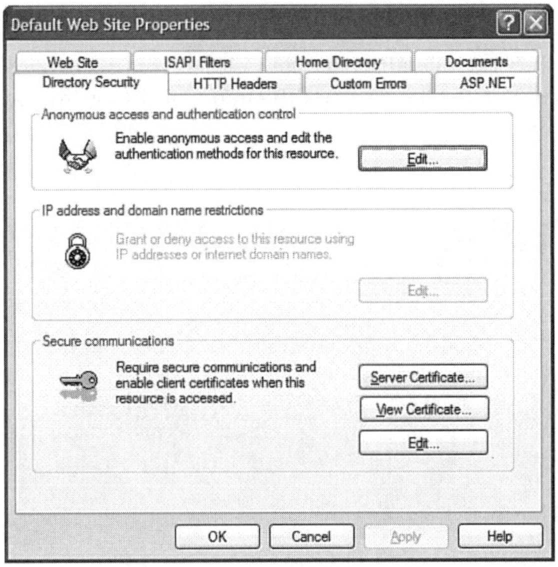

**FIGURE 14.25** Start Installing Server Certificate

In the Secure communication section, click on Server Certificate. It will start a Pending Certificate Request dialog box. Select the radio button, Process the pending request and install the certificate, as shown in Figure 14.26. This step applies the certificate against the pending CSR. Click Next.

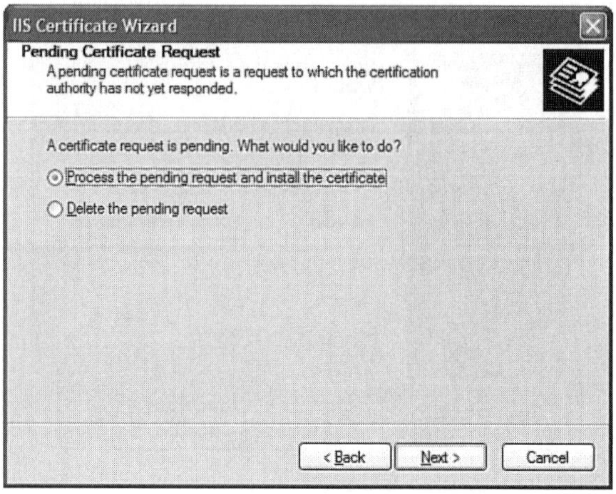

FIGURE 14.26    Processing a Pending Request

NOTE

The certificate file you receive is specific to the CSR sent to the certification authority.

The next dialog box, Process a Pending Request, allows you to enter the certificate you received from VeriSign. Specify the Path and filename of the certificate file as shown in Figure 14.27. Click Next.

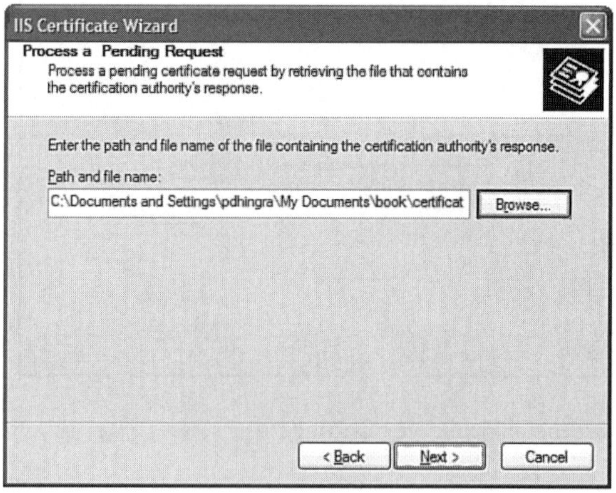

FIGURE 14.27    Specify the Path of the Certificate

**NOTE**

The pending request must match the response file. If you deleted the pending request in error, you must generate a new CSR and replace this certificate.

The Certificate Summary dialog box, as shown in Figure 14.28, displays a summary of the certificate that you are going to install. On clicking the Next button, the Complete Certificate Wizard is shown. This wizard confirms the completion. Click Finish.

This ends the certificate installation. You are set to use SSL over https.

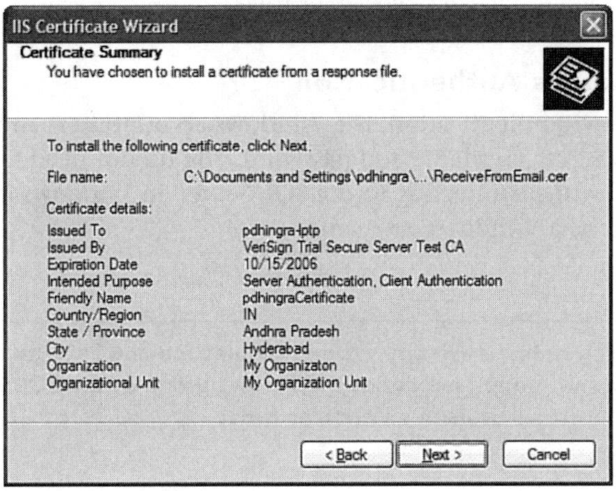

**FIGURE 14.28**    Certificate Summary

# SQL Server Security Options

Authentication determines the user identity by validating the user's credentials and also the level of privileges granted to the login associated with the credentials.

SQL Server supports following authentication mechanisms:

- Windows authentication
- SQL Server authentication

The SQL Server authentication mechanism has two parts: (1) It authenticates the user for the server, and (2) once the user is authenticated, the SQL Server grants access to the individual database. A user must be granted permission to database objects (tables, store procedure, and functions). You can define custom roles to a server as groups. The roles are granted permission and users are assigned to roles.

## SQL Server Authentication

At the time of SQL Server installation, you choose either Windows authentication mode or Mixed mode for access. Mixed mode allows the use of both Windows authentication and SQL Server authentication.

While making a connection to the SQL Server, you will specify the SQL Server authentication mode. In SQL Server authentication, you specify a username and password while connecting to the SQL Server. SQL Server validates the username and password combination with its registered username and password.

When you install SQL Server for Mixed mode, an sa user id is automatically created. An sa user is a member of a sysadmin fixed server role.

## Integrated Windows Authentication

In Integrated Windows authentication, the Windows account username and password are mapped to the SQL Server username and password. You do not need to supply the username and password while connecting to the SQL Server. In Windows authentication, a username must exist as a Windows username.

> **NOTE**
>
> In an enterprise, you define a Windows group by function and security level. A user belongs to a Windows group; you define a Windows group at the SQL Server login. SQL Server will authenticate all users in a Windows group.

Server users are known by their LoginID. For SQL Server authentication, you specify the SQL Server login and for Windows Authentication, you specify the Windows domain and username.

# Security Planning for Connectivity

We have discussed the fundamentals of client security, IIS security, and SQL Server Security. This section will put all the puzzle pieces together to plan for connectivity. When using Merge Replication or RDA, SQL Server Compact Edition and SQL Server are connected through IIS Web Server. The following lists security needs at multiple levels:

- How clients obtain authentication when they connect to an IIS Web Server.

- How a client should be authorized to execute Server Agent on a Web Server.

- Which identity should run the Server Agent.

- The credentials and permissions required sent to the Publisher/Backend SQL Server instance and access to permissions.

- The Additional credentials required sent to a Distributor SQL Server instance.

You have learned in Merge Replication and RDA, Chapters 12 and 13, that you need to install an SQL Server Compact Edition Server Agent on the Web Server and configure a virtual directory and NTFS permissions. In the first set of security permissions, you specified how a client gets authenticated and is able to invoke an SQL Server Compact Edition Server Agent. The second level of security authentication and authorization gives SQL Server Compact Agent access to the backend SQL Server and publications.

## Securing Web Server

SQL Server 2005 provides a Web Synchronization wizard to create and configure the Web Server for data synchronization. Using the wizard, you can do the following:

- Create a new directory or configure an existing directory.

- Configure a security and authentication requirement for a virtual directory.

- Set permissions on a Snapshot folder.

In the Merge Replication and RDA chapters, you configured a virtual directory using the Web Synchronization wizard. In both those chapter exercises you chose the Anonymous access option on the Web Server. You can also choose to have Basic or Integrated Windows authentication using the same Web Synchronization wizard.

---

**NOTE**

To start the Configure Web Synchronization wizard, right click the Replication node and click the Configure Web Synchronization option.

---

### Choose Channel for Transmission

The Configure Web Synchronization wizard allows you to create a virtual directory. After you specify the virtual directory details in the Web Synchronization wizard, the next dialog box, Secure Communications, allows you to specify whether you wish to use a secure channel or not. In the Merge Replication and RDA chapter exercises you selected the Do not require Secure Channel option. This section introduces you to the required steps for using SSL with Anonymous, Integrated Windows, and Basic authentication access.

### Using HTTP

The dialog box, as shown in Figure 14.29, is part of the Configure Web Synchronization wizard. You used the option shown in the previous Replication and RDA chapter exercises. If your Web Server does not have a certificate, the option to choose SSL would be disabled.

### Using HTTPS and Secure Socket Layer

For any enterprise application, you should be using a secure connection to transmit data over the Web. To establish a secure connection, you need to install a security certificate. If you have already installed the certificate using the procedure demonstrated earlier in this

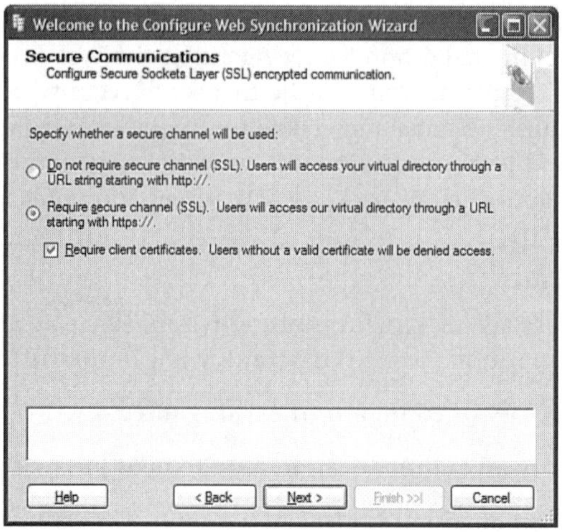

**FIGURE 14.29**    SSL Dialog Box with Security Certificate Installed on a Web Server

chapter, then you will see a dialog box with the available option to enable the use of SSL as shown in Figure 14.29.

Choose the radio button, Require secure channel, and also check the next box, Require client certificate. Click Next.

### Configuring Security and Authentication Requirements

In the Merge Replication and RDA chapter exercises, Anonymous access was used to authenticate a client while connecting to a Web Server. This is fine for a development exercise but for any enterprise application you will be using a Basic or Windows Integrated authentication.

This section demonstrates the steps for specifying the type of authentication using the Configuration Web Synchronization wizard.

As shown in Figure 14.30, the Client authentication dialog box asks you to specify whether a client needs to be authenticated or not when they connect to a Web Server.

### Setting for Anonymous Access

If you do not wish a client to be authenticated, choose the first option for Anonymous access and click Next. This will complete the client authentication part of Web Synchronization.

### Setting for Basic Authentication

For using a Basic or Windows Integrated authentication, choose the second option on the Client Authentication dialog box as shown in Figure 14.30 and click the Next button.

When choosing to authenticate a client, you also need to choose between Basic authentication or Integrated Windows authentication in the Authenticated Access dialog box. If you choose Basic authentication, specify the values and click the Next button.

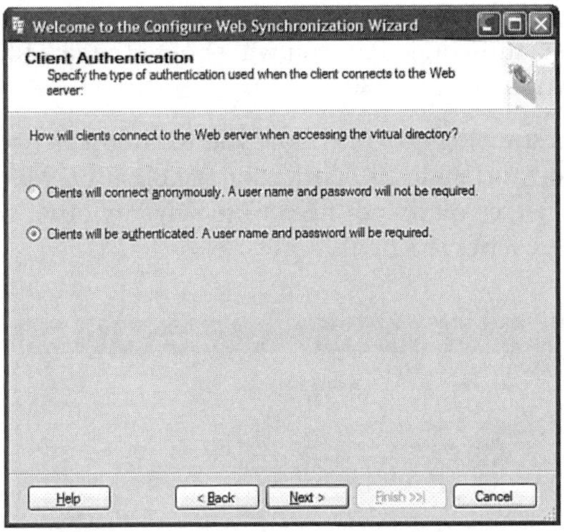

FIGURE 14.30    Basic Authentication

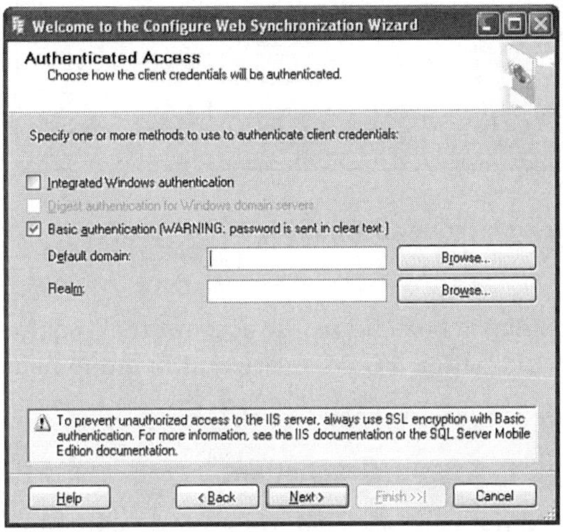

FIGURE 14.31    Basic Authentication Settings

Click on Add to add a client account and then click on the OK button.

Click Next on the Directory Access dialog box. The account you have added should have access to the virtual directory on the Web Server.

Clicking the Next button will complete the Web Server authentication setting to Basic Authentication.

## Setting for Integrated Windows Authentication

If you choose Integrated authentication, you will choose the radio button, Clients will be authenticated, as shown in Figure 14.30.

The Authenticated Access dialog box will allow you to choose between Integrated Windows authentication and Basic authentication. Choose Integrated Authentication as shown in Figure 14.32. Here you do not need to specify any other values as Integrated authentication uses the client credentials. Click Next.

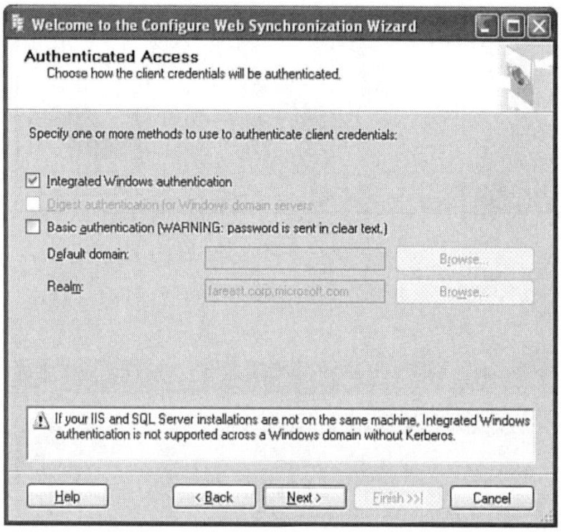

**FIGURE 14.32**    Selecting Integrated Windows Authentication

On the Directory Access dialog box choose the account that requires access to the virtual directory. Click on the Add button to add an account or group name.

You should be adding your account details. Click OK.

Once the details are added, click the Next button.

Now you have completed the steps required to specify an authentication mechanism that you wish to use. The Web Synchronization wizard will lead you to specify the path of snapshot share. You need to ensure that users accessing the Web Server have read and write permission on Snapshot folders.

## Virtual Directory Permission

The user ID that Server Agent uses to run should have Read and Write access on the virtual directory.

- For Anonymous access, the Internet Guest Account (IUSR_*computername* or other configured account) should have Read and Write access to the virtual directory folder.

- For Basic authentication, the valid user ID or corresponding group should have Read and Write permission on the virtual directory folder.

- For Integrated authentication, the client account or corresponding group should have Read and Write permission on the virtual directory folder.

The client connecting to the Web Server should have Execute permissions on the virtual directory content folder.

### Authorization for Accessing the Server Agent

The SQL Server Compact Edition Server Agent communicates with a backend SQL Server. The Server Agent acts as the client for SQL Server. A client must pass the Web Server authentication and should be authorized to execute Server Agent. The client that does not have permission to execute Server Agent cannot participate in connectivity between SQL Server and SQL Server Compact Edition.

It is possible for you to restrict Server Agent access to a particular computer, group of computers, or an entire network. You can restrict this access by specifying the IP address. If you have disabled the access to Server Agent, a client will not be able to execute the Server Agent and will not be able to synchronize data with the backend server.

### Setting Replication and RDA Object Properties for Web Server

In replication, you use the object `SqlCeReplication` and for RDA you use the `SqlCeRemoteDataAccess` object. Both Replication and RDA objects expose the same set of properties for an IIS Web Server as shown in Table 14.1.

**TABLE 14.1**    Replication and RDA Object Properties

| Replication Object Properties for Web Server | RDA Object Properties for Web Server | Description |
| --- | --- | --- |
| CompressionLevel | CompressionLevel | Describes the amount of compression. |
| ConnectionManager | ConnectionManager | Allows Replication and RDA to use smart device connection manager API. |
| ConnectionRetryTimeout | ConnectionRetryTimeout | Amount of time the client will continue retrying after the initial request has failed. |
| InternetUrl | InternetUrl | URL to connect to Server Agent on Web Server. |
| InternetLogin | InternetLogin | Login name for connecting to the Server Agent. |
| InternetPassword | InternetPassword | Password for connecting to the Server Agent. |
| InternetProxyServer | InternetProxyServer | Proxy server used for URL to connect to the Server Agent. |

**TABLE 14.1   Replication and RDA Object Properties**

| Replication Object Properties for Web Server | RDA Object Properties for Web Server | Description |
|---|---|---|
| InternetProxyLogin | InternetProxyLogin | Login name used for connecting to the Proxy Server that requires authentication. |
| InternetProxyPassword | InternetProxyPassword | Password for connecting to the Proxy Server that requires authentication. |

## Configuring the SQL Server Database

When you are using Replication or RDA, the SQL Server Compact Edition Server Agent acts as a client and the account under which the Server Agent is running is authenticated

- For Anonymous access at a Web Server, the Server Agent runs under Internet User Guest account (IUSR_*Computername* or other configured Internet guest account) and should be registered as a valid account on the SQL Server.

- For Basic authentication at a Web Server, the Server Agent runs under the identity of a Windows account that the client has specified. This Windows account should have access on the backend SQL Server.

- For Integrated authentication at a Web Server, the Server Agent runs under the identity of a client. The Windows account used by the client should be registered at the backend SQL Server.

### Setting Up Security for Merge Replication

In Merge Replication, a backend SQL Server database acts as Publisher and SQL Server Compact Edition database acts as Subscriber. In addition to Publisher, Merge Replication also uses a Distributor SQL Server instance.

Distributor is an SQL Server instance that holds all metadata, snapshots, and statistics. A Distributor instance is responsible for synchronizing data between Publisher and Subscribers.

> **NOTE**
>
> In a development environment, you can use a single SQL Server instance to act as Publisher and Distributor. For scalability reasons, it is better to use separate SQL Servers for Distributor and Publisher in a production environment.

The following section introduces you to the permission set needed by both Publisher and Distributor.

### Securing Publisher for Merge Replication

You need to grant access to a publication in order to synchronize data in Merge Replication. The Publication Access List (PAL) contains a list of all logins that have access to a publication. When you synchronize the data with the backend server, the server verifies that the valid user ID exists in PAL.

To grant access, you can add the user in the PAL. To update the PAL, select Publication in SQL Management Studio, and right click on Properties. Click on the Publication Access List tab on the Properties page. The Publication Access List page specifies the login and permissions as shown in Figure 14.33

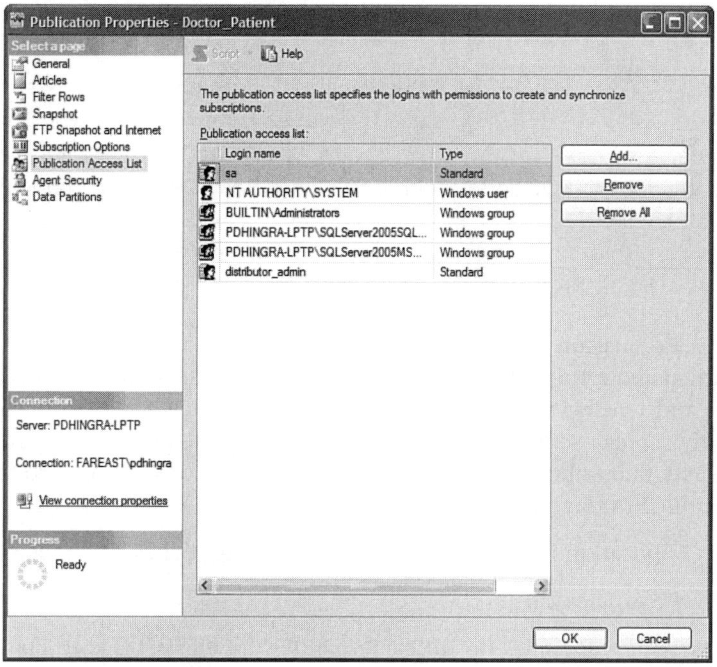

**FIGURE 14.33    Publication Properties**

Use the Add or Remove button to add more logins or reduce logins. You can only add those users that exist in the database. First grant login permission on the database and then grant access to publication. The user that you need to add in PAL depends upon the IIS and SQL Server authentication as shown in Table 14.2.

**TABLE 14.2    Authentication Combinations for Web Server and Backend SQL Server**

| Authentication at Web Server | Authentication at Backend SQL Server | Login to Add to PAL |
|---|---|---|
| Anonymous | Windows Integrated | *computername*\\`IUSR`_*computername* or other configured Internet Guest Account. |
| Basic | Integrated Windows | The user ID passed as `InternetLogin` property of the Replication object. |
| Integrated Windows | Integrated Windows | User ID of client. |
| Anonymous | SQL Server Authentication | Both IDs that are passed in `DistributorLogin` and `PublisherLogin` properties of the Replication object. |
| Basic | SQL Server Authentication | Both IDs that are passed in `DistributorLogin` and `PublisherLogin` properties of the Replication object. |
| Integrated Windows | SQL Server Authentication | Both IDs that are passed in `DistributorLogin` and `PublisherLogin` properties of the Replication object. |

**Verify Change Permission on Publisher**

You have learned about the PAL (Publication Access List) that specifies logins and permission to create and synchronize subscriptions. Additionally, SQL Server Publication has an option to verify that Subscriber has insert, update, and delete permissions on published tables. By default, Subscriber does not require these permissions as access to the published tables as controlled through PAL.

1. To select Publication in SQL Management Studio, right click on Properties.

2. Click on the Articles tab.

3. Select the Article and click on Article Properties. It will start the Article Properties dialog box as shown in Figure 14.34.

4. Under the Properties tab you can set these permissions in the Merge Changes section.

There are insert, update, and delete permission options. When you enable these options, SQL Server checks that Merge Agent is running under an identity and has permission to execute the operations that are TRUE.

When a client is successfully authenticated, the user or group name of the client is mapped to an SQL Server user account. The client must have a user account in each database that it wants to access. The user account is used to control access to the tables, views, stored procedures, and so on, in that database. The activities that a client can perform are controlled by the permissions applied to the user account through which the client gained access to the database.

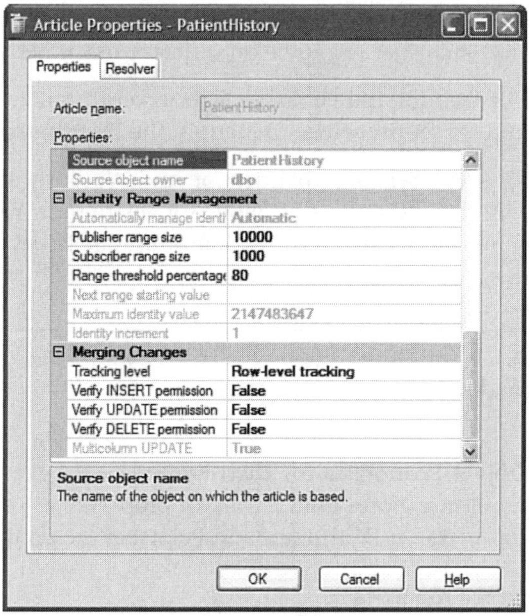

**FIGURE 14.34**    Insert, Update, Delete Permissions on Published Articles

### Setting Replication Object Properties for Publisher

The Merge Replication object exposes properties for Publisher as shown in Table 14.3.
These properties need to be set in the client program in order to synchronize the data.

**TABLE 14.3    Publisher Properties**

| Replication Object Properties for Publisher | Description |
|---|---|
| Publication | Name of SQL Server publication. |
| Publisher | Name of computer having SQL Server publication. |
| PublisherDatabase | Name of publication database. |
| PublisherLogin | Login name for connecting to Publisher. |
| PublisherPassword | Password for connecting to Publisher. |
| PublisherSecurityMode | Security mode for connecting to Publisher. Two possible values are NTAuthentication for Windows Integrated authentication and DBAuthentication for SQL Server authentication. |

### Securing Distributor for Replication

We have discussed that Replication requires a Distributor SQL Server instance. Merge
Replication Snapshot is stored at Distributor. All the logs related to Merge Replication
history and statistics are also kept at Distributor. In the Merge Replication exercise, the

Distributor and Publisher were both set up on the same SQL Server. In a production environment, Distributor and Publisher would be on different machines.

- When you have Distributor and Publisher SQL Server instances on different machines, you need to set properties to identify the Distributor SQL Server instance.

- SQL Server supports SQL Server authentication and Windows authentication modes. You need to specify the authentication mode for Distributor. You also need to specify a login name and password if Distributor uses SQL Server authentication.

**NOTE**

Distributor and Publisher are assumed to be on same server if none of the distributor properties are specified.

### Setting Replication Object Properties for Distributor

The Merge Replication object exposes the Distributor properties as shown in Table 14.4 . You need to set these properties if Distributor and Publisher are on different machines.

**TABLE 14.4    Distributor Properties**

| Replication Property | Description |
| --- | --- |
| Distributor | Specifies the name of Distributor. |
| DistributorAddress | You can set this property to define the network address of Distributor. This property is required when the DistributorNetwork property has a value other than `DefaultNetwork`. |
| DistributorLogin | Specifies the login name for connecting to the Distributor SQL Server instance. |
| | You need to set this property if `DistributorSecurityMode` is DBAuthentication (uses SQL authentication). |
| DistributorNetwork | Specifies the network protocol used for communication between Distributor and SQL Server Compact Edition Reconciler. |
| | You can set this to one of three values—`DefaultNetwork`, `MultiProtocol`, or `Tcpipsockets`. |
| DistributorPassword | Specifies the password for connecting to Distributor. |
| | You need to set this property for connecting to Distributor using SQL Server authentication. |
| DistributorSecurityMode | Specifies the security mode for connecting to the Distributor SQL Server instance. You can set this to one of two values: |
| | DBAuthentication—SQL Server authentication. |
| | NTAuthentication—Integrated Windows authentication. |
| | (DBAuthentication is the default value of the `DistributorSecurityMode` property.) |

You must set all necessary Distributor properties if any of the Distributor properties are set.

### Setting Up Security for RDA

In Remote Data Access (RDA), you use an OLE DB connection string to specify the information needed for making a connection to the SQL Server. The OLE DB connection string will have a user ID and password for SQL Server authentication. For Integrated Windows authentication, a user ID and password are not needed but you do need to specify `INTE-GRATED SECURITY="SSPI"`.

```
string sqlServerConnection = @"Provider=SQLOLEDB;Data Source=PDHINGRA0\Book;Initial
Catalog=Hospital; user ID = 'myuserid'; password='password'";
```

Based upon the permission given to a client, you can precisely control the database operations that RDA clients can perform:

- For SQL Server authentication, the user ID specified in the OLE DB string should have read access on the backend table.

- For Integrated Windows authentication, the Internet Guest Account should have read access to the SQL Server table.

There is no Publisher or Distributor in RDA; therefore you do not need to set specific configurations for RDA. You need to specify only the connection string to access the remote database. The OLE DB connection string specifies all the information that is needed to connect to the SQL Server.

## Programming for Secured Web Server and Backend Database

Now you know what things you need to consider for planning security for connectivity. Once you have decided the security options for Web Server and SQL Server, you can configure them using the Configure Web Synchronization wizard. You can set up the user ID, and so on, at the SQL Server using SQL Server Management Studio. Table 14.5 presents a  summary of various combinations that you can use at the Web Server and the backend SQL Server.

In the following section you will write a client-side code and set Replication and RDA properties.

Remember the following:

- The authentication method you want to use for a Web Server is defined at the time of setup. You use the Web Synchronization wizard to choose Anonymous, Windows Integrated, or Basic authentication. You also choose a secure or nonsecure channel at the time of setup.

TABLE 14.5    Web Server and SQL Server Authentication

| Mode of Authentication at IIS Server | Mode of Authentication at SQL Server | Remarks |
|---|---|---|
| Anonymous | SQL Server | No security to access for Web Server resources. You can use it for exercise, testing, developing POC, etc. |
| Anonymous | Windows Integrated | As you are using an anonymous account (IUSR_*machinename*) on the Web Server and Windows Integrated Account on SQL Server, the account used on the Web Server (IUSR_*machinename*) will be passed to the SQL Server. You should add this account in SQL Server. |
| Basic | SQL Server | You will be specifying a username and password for connecting to an IIS Server. Similarly, you will be specifying a separate username and password for connecting to the SQL Server. The username and password for SQL Server should be set in SQL Server. You can pass both sets of credentials as part of a Replication and RDA object. |
| Basic | Windows Integrated | You will be specifying a username and password for connecting to an IIS Server. The same username and password should be set up in SQL Server. |
| Windows Integrated | SQL Server | Client credentials will be used for the Web Server. However you will specify credentials for a backend server. |
| Windows Integrated | Windows Integrated | This method is secure but works on intranet only. |

- The authentication method that you want to use for the SQL Server is not defined at the time of setup. For Replication, you set the property PublisherSecurityMode to DBAuthentication or NTAuthentication.

- A client application uses InternetLogin and InternetPassword properties to set the user ID and password for the account that you wish to use on the Web Server.

- The client application uses PublisherLogin and PublisherPassword properties to describe the user ID and password for the publisher database.

- A client application uses DistributorLogin and DistributorPassword properties to set the user ID and password for an account that you wish to use on Distributor.

- In RDA, a client application specifies the user ID and password as part of a remote connection string if you wish to use SQL Server authentication.

### Setting Replication and RDA Properties for Client Database

In Replication, you use an object SqlCeReplication, and for RDA you use the SqlCeRemoteDataAccess object. To specify the connection information for a client database, you need to set the properties as shown in Table 14.6.

- For a Replication object, set Subscriber and SubscriberConnectionString properties. A Subscriber property is used to specify the subscriber name. The SubscriberConnectionString property contains all the connection information including the password for a client database.

- For an RDA object, use LocalConnectionString to specify connection information for a local database. If the local database is password protected, specify the password as part of the connection string.

**TABLE 14.6    Replication and RDA Object Properties**

| Replication Object Properties for Client Database | RDA Object Properties for Client database | Description |
|---|---|---|
| SubscriberConnectionString | LocalConnectionString | Full path of a client database. |
| Subscriber | Not Applicable | Subscription name. |

In an enterprise application you will develop a client application that contains a connection string including password. The password is embedded into an executable that is deployed on devices.

### NOTE

To authenticate and authorize a user of a device or client application, you need to build a security mechanism or use a third-party mechanism.

An SQL Server Compact Edition database can be accessed by a client application that has a connection string with a password. A user who knows the password can open the SQL Server Compact Edition database in Query Analyzer, Visual Studio, and in SQL Server Management Studio.

### Programming for Anonymous and SQL Server Access

To use Anonymous access for Replication and RDA, you specify it at the time of configuring the Web Server for synchronization. You can use the Configure Web Synchronization Wizard to specify that you want to use Anonymous access.

The Replication and RDA object has an InternetLogin and InternetPassword property. You do not need to set this property for Anonymous access.

## Replication

To specify that you want to use SQL Server authentication at the backend, you need to set the PublisherSecurityMode property in the client program. This property has two values: DBAuthentication and NTAuthentication. You will be selecting DBAuthentication for SQL Server authentication. With DBAuthentication, you need to specify PublisherLogin and PublisherPassword properties as shown in Listing 14.6. Similarly for Distributor, you need to provide values for DistributorLogin, DistributorPassword, and other Distributor properties.

**LISTING 14.6    Replication Properties for Anonymous and SQL Server Authentication C#.NET**

```
//code for Anonymous Access at IIS
// Internet Login and Internet Password are not needed.
repl.InternetUrl = @"http://pdhingra0/hospitalpatient/sqlcesa30.dll";
repl.Publisher = @"PDHINGRA0\BOOK";
repl.PublisherDatabase = @"Hospital";
repl.Publication = @"Doctor_Patient";
repl.Subscriber = @"PatientSubscription";


// code for SQL Server authentication.
// User ID and Password needed for SQL Server Authentication.
repl.PublisherSecurityMode = SecurityType.DBAuthentication;
repl.PublisherLogin = @"mylogin";
repl.PublisherPassword = @"mypassword";
```

## RDA

For RDA you also need to set up Anonymous access at the time of configuring the Web Server for synchronization. To implement SQL Server access at a remote database, you specify the user ID and password as part of a remote connection string as shown in Listing 14.7.

**LISTING 14.7    RDA Properties for Anonymous and SQL Server Authentication C#.NET**

```
// Access Client
// You need not have to enter password if no password is set for client database
myRDA.LocalConnectionString = "DataSource=\\Program Files\\Patient_RDA\\MyPa-
tients.sdf; Password ='mypassword'";

// Access Web Server
// You need not have to set Login and Password for IIS Anonymous Access
SqlCeRemoteDataAccess myRDA = new SqlCeRemoteDataAccess();
myRDA.InternetUrl = @"http://pdhingra0/hospitalpatient/sqlcesa30.dll";

// Access back end SQL Server
// Enter User ID and Password for SQL Server authentication in Sql connection
string.
```

```
string sqlServerConnection = @"Provider=SQLOLEDB;Data Source=PDHINGRA0\Book;Initial
Catalog=Hospital; User ID='mysqllogin'; Password='mypassword'";
```

### Programming for Anonymous and Windows Integrated Access

To use an Anonymous and Windows Integrated combination, you define Anonymous access at setup time. Using Anonymous access for Web Server, a client does not need to supply a username and password. Instead, the Server Agent runs under the identity of an Internet Guest Account. Using Windows Integrated access, you do not need to supply credentials. An IUSR_machinename account should be given access to the SQL Server where machinename is the name of the computer.

### Replication

As you are using Windows Integrated access to access the Publisher database, you do not need to specify the PublisherLogin and PublisherPassword properties as described in Listing 14.8. The Server Agent runs with an Internet Guest Account.

**LISTING 14.8    Replication Properties for Anonymous and Windows Integrated Access C#.NET**

```
//code for Anonymous Access
// Internet Login and Internet Password are not needed.

repl.InternetUrl = @"http://pdhingra0/hospitalpatient/sqlcesa30.dll";
repl.Publisher = @"PDHINGRA0\BOOK";
repl.PublisherDatabase = @"Hospital";
repl.Publication = @"Doctor_Patient";
repl.Subscriber = @"PatientSubscription";

// code for Windows Integrated Authentication.
// User ID and Password are not needed for Windows Integrated Authentication.
repl.PublisherSecurityMode = SecurityType.NTAuthentication;
```

### RDA

As in the previous example, Anonymous access is specified at the same time you set up the Web Server for synchronization. As you are using Integrated Windows authentication for the SQL Server, you do not need to specify a user ID and password as part of the remote connection string. However, you will use INTEGRATED SECURITY = "SSPI" as part of a connection string to indicate that you wish to use Windows Integrated security on the SQL Server as shown in Listing 14.8.

**LISTING 14.8    RDA Properties for Anonymous and Windows Integrated Access C#.NET**

```
// Access Client
// You need not have to enter password if no password is set for client database
myRDA.LocalConnectionString = "DataSource=\\Program Files\\Patient_RDA\\
```

```
MyPatients.sdf; Password ='mypassword'";

// Access Web Server
// You need not have to set Login and Password for IIS Anonymous Access
SqlCeRemoteDataAccess myRDA = new SqlCeRemoteDataAccess();
myRDA.InternetUrl = @"http://pdhingra0/hospitalpatient/sqlcesa30.dll";

// Access back end SQL Server
// You need not have to enter User ID and Password for Windows Authentication in
Sql connection string.
string sqlServerConnection = @"Provider=SQLOLEDB;Data Source=PDHINGRA0\Book;Initial
Catalog=Hospital; INTEGRATED SECURITY="SSPI";";
```

---

**NOTE**

An Internet Guest User Account will be passed to SQL Server. This should be added as a user to the SQL Server.

---

### Programming for Basic Authentication and SQL Server Authentication Access

You will choose Basic authentication access at the time of configuring the Web Server for Replication. In the client program, you need to set the `InternetLogin` and `InternetPassword` properties to specify the user ID and password. With Basic authentication, you should use SSL. Using SSL encrypts the user ID and password when they are sent over the network.

### Replication

In order to use SQL Server authentication at Publisher, you need to set `PublisherSecurityMode` to `DBAuthentication`. With a `DBAuthentication` value, you will use `PublisherLogin` and `PublisherPassword` properties to enter the user ID and password, respectively as shown in Listing 14.9. For Distributor, you will use `DistributorLogin` and `DistributorPassword` to enter user credentials.

**LISTING 14.9    Replication Properties for Basic Authentication and SQL Server Authentication C#.NET**

```
//code for Basic Authentication Access
// Internet Login and Internet Password are required.
// Login and Password are passed over the network.
repl.InternetUrl = @"http://pdhingra0/hospitalpatient/sqlcesa30.dll";
repl.InternetLogin = "myWebLogin" ;
repl.InternetPassword = "myWebPassword";
repl.Publisher = @"PDHINGRA0\BOOK";
repl.PublisherDatabase = @"Hospital";
repl.Publication = @"Doctor_Patient";
repl.Subscriber = @"PatientSubscription";
```

```
// code for SQL Server authentication.
// User ID and Password needed for SQL Server Authentication.
repl.PublisherSecurityMode = SecurityType.DBAuthentication;
repl.PublisherLogin = @"mylogin";
repl.PublisherPassword = @"mypassword";
```

### RDA

To use Basic authentication at a Web Server, you need to supply a username and password in order to connect to an IIS Server.

To use SQL Server authentication, you need to specify a separate username and password in order to connect to the SQL Server. You need to specify the user ID and password in the connection string for a remote SQL Server as shown in Listing 14.10.

**LISTING 14.10**    **RDA Properties for Basic Authentication and SQL Server Authentication Access C#.NET**

```
// Access Client
// You need not have to enter password if no password is set for client database
myRDA.LocalConnectionString = "DataSource=\\Program Files\\Patient_RDA\\MyPa-
tients.sdf; Password ='mypassword'";

// Access Web Server
// Set InternetLogin and InternetPassword for IIS Basic Authentication
SqlCeRemoteDataAccess myRDA = new SqlCeRemoteDataAccess();
myRDA.InternetLogin = "mylogin";
myRDA.InternetPassword = "mypassword";
myRDA.InternetUrl = @"http://pdhingra0/hospitalpatient/sqlcesa30.dll";

// Access back end SQL Server
// Enter User ID and Password for SQL Server authentication in Sql connection
string.
string sqlServerConnection = @"Provider=SQLOLEDB;Data Source=PDHINGRA0\Book;Initial
Catalog=Hospital; User ID='mysqllogin'; Password='mypassword'";
```

#### Programming for Basic and Windows Integrated Access

Choose Basic authentication access when you are using the Web Synchronization wizard to configure the Web Server for Replication. In the client program, you need to set the InternetLogin and InternetPassword properties.

#### Replication

Set PublisherSecurityMode to NTAuthentication in a client program choosing Windows Integrated authentication. When using Windows Integrated authentication, you do not need PublisherLogin and PublisherPassword as shown in Listing 14.11.

LISTING 14.11    Replication Properties for Basic Authentication and Windows
                 Integrated Authentication C#.NET

```
//code for Basic Authentication Access
// Internet Login and Internet Password are required.
// Login and Password are passed over the network.
repl.InternetUrl = @"http://pdhingra0/hospitalpatient/sqlcesa30.dll";
repl.InternetLogin = "myWebLogin" ;
repl.InternetPassword = "myWebPassword";
repl.Publisher = @"PDHINGRA0\BOOK";
repl.PublisherDatabase = @"Hospital";
repl.Publication = @"Doctor_Patient";
repl.Subscriber = @"PatientSubscription";


// code for Windows Integrated Authentication.
// User ID and Password are not needed for Windows Integrated Authentication.
repl.PublisherSecurityMode = SecurityType.NTAuthentication;
```

## RDA

The SQL Server Agent will run under the credentials that you specified for Basic authentication. The same credentials will be used to access the SQL Server. You do not need to
specify a user ID and password for accessing a backend SQL Server. In the connection
string, you need to mention INTEGRATED SECURITY = "SSPI" as shown in Listing 14.12.

LISTING 14.12    RDA Properties for Basic Authentication and Windows Integrated
                 Authentication C#.NET

```
// Access Client
// You need not have to enter password if no password is set for client database
myRDA.LocalConnectionString = "DataSource=\\Program Files\\Patient_RDA\\MyPa-
tients.sdf; Password ='mypassword'";


// Access Web Server
// Set InternetLogin and InternetPassword for IIS Basic Authentication
SqlCeRemoteDataAccess myRDA = new SqlCeRemoteDataAccess();
myRDA.InternetLogin = "mylogin";
myRDA.InternetPassword = "mypassword";
myRDA.InternetUrl = @"http://pdhingra0/hospitalpatient/sqlcesa30.dll";


// Access back end SQL Server
// You need not have to enter User ID and Password for Windows Authentication in
Sql connection string.
string sqlServerConnection = @"Provider=SQLOLEDB;Data Source=PDHINGRA0\Book;Initial
Catalog=Hospital; INTEGRATED SECURITY="SSPI";";
```

**Programming for Windows Integrated and SQL Server Authentication Access**
Choose Windows authentication access in the Web Synchronization wizard in order to configure the Web Server for Replication. No other setting is required in the client program.

### Replication
Set `PublisherSecurityMode` to `DBAuthentication` in the client program when choosing SQL Server authentication. Set `PublisherLogin` and `PublisherPassword` properties to specify user credentials as shown in Listing 14.13.

**LISTING 14.13    Replication Properties for Windows Integrated and SQL Server Authentication C#.NET**

```
//code for Windows Integrated Access
// Internet Login and Internet Password are not required.
repl.InternetUrl = @"http://pdhingra0/hospitalpatient/sqlcesa30.dll";
repl.Publisher = @"PDHINGRA0\BOOK";
repl.PublisherDatabase = @"Hospital";
repl.Publication = @"Doctor_Patient";
repl.Subscriber = @"PatientSubscription";


// code for SQL Server authentication.
// User ID and Password needed for SQL Server Authentication.
repl.PublisherSecurityMode = SecurityType.DBAuthentication;
repl.PublisherLogin = @"mylogin";
repl.PublisherPassword = @"mypassword";
```

### RDA
Client credentials are used for Web Server access in Windows Integrated authentication. You specify credentials for connecting to a backend SQL Server in SQL Server authentication. You specify the user ID and password in the connection string for remote SQL Server as shown in Listing 14.14.

**LISTING 14.14    RDA Properties for Windows Integrated and SQL Server Authentication C#.NET**

```
// Access Client
// You need not have to enter password if no password is set for client database
myRDA.LocalConnectionString = "DataSource=\\Program Files\\Patient_RDA\\MyPa-
tients.sdf; Password ='mypassword'";


// Access Web Server
// You need not have to set Login and Password for Integrated Windows Authentica-
tion
SqlCeRemoteDataAccess myRDA = new SqlCeRemoteDataAccess();
myRDA.InternetUrl = @"http://pdhingra0/hospitalpatient/sqlcesa30.dll";
```

```
// Access back end SQL Server
// Enter User ID and Password for SQL Server authentication in Sql connection
string.
string sqlServerConnection = @"Provider=SQLOLEDB;Data Source=PDHINGRA0\Book;Initial
Catalog=Hospital; User ID='mysqllogin'; Password='mypassword'";
```

**Programming for Windows Integrated Access Both at Web Server and SQL Server**
Choose Windows authentication access in the Web Synchronization wizard to configure
Web Server for Replication. No other setting is required in a client program.

### Replication

As you are using Windows Integrated access to access the Publisher database, you do not
need to specify the `PublisherLogin` and `PublisherPassword` properties as shown in
Listing 14.15. The Windows account used by a client should be registered at the backend
SQL Server.

**LISTING 14.15    Replication Properties for Windows Integrated Both at Web Server and
SQL Server C#.NET**

```
//code for Windows Integrated Acess
// Internet Login and Internet Password are not required.
repl.InternetUrl = @"http://pdhingra0/hospitalpatient/sqlcesa30.dll";
repl.Publisher = @"PDHINGRA0\BOOK";
repl.PublisherDatabase = @"Hospital";
repl.Publication = @"Doctor_Patient";
repl.Subscriber = @"PatientSubscription";

// code for Windows Integrated Authentication.
// User ID and Password are not needed for Windows Integrated Authentication.
repl.PublisherSecurityMode = SecurityType.NTAuthentication;
```

### RDA

In the OLE DB connection string, you need to specify only the backend database and
`INTEGRATED SECURITY="SSPI"` to use Windows Integrated security as shown in Listing
14.16.

**LISTING 14.16    Replication Properties for Windows Integrated Both at Web Server and
SQL Server C#.NET**

```
// Access Client
// You need not have to enter password if no password is set for client database
myRDA.LocalConnectionString = "DataSource=\\Program Files\\Patient_RDA\\MyPa-
tients.sdf; Password ='mypassword'";
```

```
// Access Web Server
// You need not have to set Login and Password for Integrated Windows Authentica-
tion
SqlCeRemoteDataAccess myRDA = new SqlCeRemoteDataAccess();
myRDA.InternetUrl = @"http://pdhingra0/hospitalpatient/sqlcesa30.dll";

// Access back end SQL Server
// You need not have to enter User ID and Password for Windows Authentication in
Sql connection string.
string sqlServerConnection = @"Provider=SQLOLEDB;Data Source=PDHINGRA0\Book;Initial
Catalog=Hospital; INTEGRATED SECURITY="SSPI";";
```

## Recommended Practices

- Integrated Windows Authentication can be used when a client machine, Web Server, and SQL Server are on the same Windows domain. This method of authentication is useful for intranet-based applications.

- In Basic authentication, credentials are sent over a network and there is a possibility that a malicious user could intercept them. Use an SSL type of mechanism to encrypt the credentials.

- Basic authentication with SSL on a Web Server and SQL Server authentication on an SQL Server are the most suitable for an Internet-based application.

- IIS authentication and authorization are done at the virtual directory level. You should create a virtual directory for each application.

- Having a separate virtual directory for each application allows you to configure access for each application.

- When you synchronize using Replication or RDA, the Server Agent allocates a worker thread pool consisting of worker threads. The thread pool is created per virtual directory. Having a separate virtual directory means a separate thread pool per application.

- You should create an NTFS content folder for each virtual directory. The content folder contains a copy of the Server Agent dll as well as input and output files for data transfer.

- Remove the default password and any unnecessary accounts.

- Review the Web Server logs regularly to monitor any suspicious activity.

- Use an encryption method such as SSL to ensure secure data transfer over a network.

- Using Windows Integrated Security is preferable. A user does not need to learn extra user IDs and passwords. The application does not need to embed a password in the connection strings.

- You can make a Window user group an SQL Server login. All users in the Windows group will have access to the SQL Server.

- Remove access to an Internet Guest Account from the SQL Server if you are not using Anonymous access at the Web Server.

- Ensure that you install the latest hot fixes and service packs for operating systems and databases.

- The Replication Merge Agent and Distribution Agent should be in a PAL (Publication Access List).

- the Merge and Distribution Agent should have read access on a snapshot share.

- Snapshot Agent should have write access on a snapshot share.

- If you are using parameterized filtering in Replication, ensure that each folder is only accessible to require the Merge Agent Account.

Like other aspects of architecture, security should be planned and designed from the start of a project. Implementing security minimizes risk. You need to evaluate risk and the potential for data exploitation. To design security, you need to consider various questions. The answers to these questions will vary based upon enterprise need. This chapter presented you with some security guidelines. You should evaluate and use them according to the needs of the enterprise application.

## Summary

You can secure enterprise solutions by firewalls, proxies, application authentication, etc. However, an attacker needs to find only one weakness in your solution to access valuable data. This chapter focused on the security features of the SQL Server Compact Edition database. You have learned in detail how to protect data on a client device. You have also learned how to configure a Web Server and SQL Server Compact Edition Server Agent so that it securely communicates with a client and a remote database.

As your client device contains not only the application but also the database file, you need to protect the database. You can use a password and encryption to protect the database. The client application synchronizes the data with the backend SQL Server. This chapter also discussed in detail how to secure the connectivity between the client and the server. The Server Agent on an IIS Web Server acts as a gateway to enable communication between client and server. The Server Agent runs under the identity of Internet Guest Account for Anonymous access and runs under the identity of the user ID supplied by a client program for Basic and Integrated Windows authentication on a Web Server. According to the Server Agent identity, you need to provide access to a user on a backend SQL Server. You have also learned how to set up for SSL. Information on Merge Replication, RDA, and security together will well equip you to choose the appropriate and secure design for your SQL Server Compact Edition based application that synchronizes data with an SQL Server.

# SQL Server 2005 Compact Edition Performance Tuning

This chapter highlights the tips that you can use to increase the performance of the SQL Server Compact Edition database. You will learn the internals of query optimization and how Query Optimizer uses indexes, statistics, and joins. We will also discuss the execution plan that tells you what is going on inside when the database engine is executing the query. These internals will provide you with the necessary clues to make the right trade-offs and help you to determine the appropriate choices for your database design.

The chapter also provides tips that you can utilize while programming and includes examples of how and when you should utilize the DataReader, base table cursor, and SQLCeResultSet to get faster access on a database.

The chapter also describes tips for faster synchronization.

SQL Server Compact Edition can be used on mobile devices and on desktop-based applications. This chapter will help you in understanding the platform factors such as memory, processing power available, etc., and help you in making the right trade offs for your applications.

Tables 15.1 through 15.5 describe performance issues and improvement guidelines. You should create these tables in the SQL Server Compact Edition database to follow along with the chapter exercises.

- Customers

- Products

- Orders

- Orders_Item

- RewardProgram

TABLE 15.1    Definition: Customers Table

| Column | Data Type | Nullability | Description |
| --- | --- | --- | --- |
| CustomerID | Int | Not Null | ID of customer |
| FirstName | NVarChar(50) | Null | First name |
| LastName | NVarchar(50) | Null | Last name |
| Route_Area | SmallInt | Null | Area ID |
| Address | NVarChar(50) | Null | Address |
| City | NChar(20) | Null | City |
| State | NChar(20) | Null | State |
| ZipCode | NChar(20) | Null | Postal Code |
| ProgramID | smallint | Null | ID of reward program |

TABLE 15.2    Definition: Products Table

| Column | Data Type | Nullability | Description |
| --- | --- | --- | --- |
| ProductID | Int | Not Null | ID of customer |
| ProductDesc | NVarChar(50) | Null | First name |
| ProductPrice | Money | Not Null | Selling price |

TABLE 15.3    Definition: Orders Table

| Column | Data Type | Nullability | Description |
| --- | --- | --- | --- |
| OrderID | Int | Not Null | ID of customer |
| OrderDate | DateTime | Null | Date on which order is placed |
| CustomerID | Int | Not Null | Foreign key to Customer table |
| DiscountOnOrder | Money | Null | Overall discount on order |
| OrderPrice | Money | Null | Overall price of order |
| Status | Nchar(1) | Null | Status—delivered or not |

**TABLE 15.4     Definition: Orders_Item Table**

| Column | Data Type | Nullability | Description |
|---|---|---|---|
| OrderID | Int | Not Null | Foreign key to Orders table |
| ProductID | Int | Not Null | Foreign key to Products table |
| Qty | Int | Null | Selling price |
| DiscountOnItem | Money | Null | Discount on item |
| ItemPrice | Money | Null | Price of item |

**TABLE 15.5     Definition: RewardProgram Table**

| Column | Data Type | Nullability | Description |
|---|---|---|---|
| ProgramID | smallint | Not null | Reward program ID |
| ProgramName | NVarChar | Null | Name of reward program |
| StartDate | DateTime | Null | Start date of program |
| AnnualCharge | Money | Null | Annual charge for reward program |

# Query Optimizer

The SQL Server Compact Edition has a cost-based Query Optimizer. The SQL Server Compact Edition Query Optimizer evaluates the options for executing a query and determines the execution plan. A number of possible ways to execute a query are generated, and their estimated execution time is calculated. The plan that is fastest is used for the actual query execution.

## Query Execution Plan

To improve the performance of your query, the most important thing to know is how SQL Server Compact Edition is executing your query. SQL Server Compact Edition allows you to see the query execution plan. Before executing a query, SQL Server Compact Edition compiles the query and puts it into a query plan. The compiled plan is stored in memory. The query plan gives you insight as to what goes on behind a query execution and is a useful source of information for performance tuning. You can use the estimated execution plan or the actual execution plan.

### Estimated Execution Plan

The estimated execution plan parses the query and then generates the execution plan. In this option, SQL Server Compact Edition does not execute the query. Instead, the estimated execution plan displays the query execution plan that the SQL Server Compact Edition database engine would most probably use for the query execution.

### Actual Execution Plan

The actual execution plan executes the query and then shows the plan used by the SQL Server Compact Edition engine.

You can view the estimated and actual plans using SQL Server Compact Edition Query Analyzer on a device as well as on the desktop using SQL Server Management Studio. After generating the plan on a device, you can save the plan into an XML file. You can then open the SQL Plan XML file in SQL Server Management Studio on the desktop.

**NOTE**

SQL Server Compact edition does not support the SHOWPLAN_ALL, SHOWPLAN_TEXT, SHOW-PLAN_XML options. These options are available in SQL Server 2005. In SQL Server 2005, you can use the graphical option.

To see the estimated execution plan of a query in SQL Management Studio, click on the Display Estimated Execution Plan query option under the Query menu option as shown in Figure 15.1.

**FIGURE 15.1**    Estimated Execution Plan Menu Option

To see the actual execution plan of a query in SQL Management Studio, click on the Display Include Actual Execution Plan query option under the Query menu option. When you execute the query using the Execute Query option, SQL Server Management Studio will display the actual execution plan as shown in Figure 15.2.

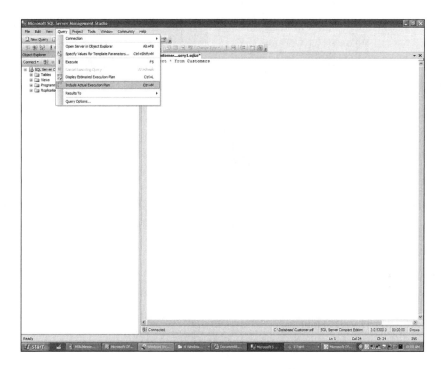

**FIGURE 15.2**    Actual Execution Plan Menu Option

The SQL Server Compact Edition Engine can execute a query in a number of ways. It can access the tables in a different order, do a table scan, or access the index. The database analyzes the various plans and executes the query in the most efficient way.

## Cost-Based Optimization

In a Cost based optimization Query Optimizer estimates the cost of various query plan. To estimate the cost it tries to determine the number of database read and sort operations.

The graphical execution plan shows various icons that demonstrate the cost of operations involved in executing a query as shown in Figure 15.3. The icons represent various operations that SQL Server Compact Edition can do to execute a query. By selecting icons, you can see the cost of items that contribute to the overall cost of executing a query.

By looking at the costs of various suboperations that contribute to query cost, you can focus on improving the performance of costly suboperations.

To interpret the Query Plan you should read the steps from right to left. Follow the arrows that connect various icons together. It will lead to the topmost left corner of theexecution plan that represents the root of the execution plan. The thickness of the arrow between two icons indicates the data transfer (number of rows and row length) between the corresponding suboperations. Click on arrow and select it. It will show:

**FIGURE 15.3** Execution Plan Attributes

- Actual number of rows
- Estimated number of rows
- Estimated Row Size
- Estimated Data Size

For performance tuning you should pay attention to suboperations that have a large percentage cost of execution. Similarly pay attention to thick arrows. The thick arrows should be toward the right of the query execution plan, If there are more thick arrows on the left it means a large number of data is transferred between suboperations.

To see the cost of an operation, right click or move the cursor over on the icon and see the attributes. Table 15.6 shows the attributes of an execution plan.

If you are executing multiple queries, the execution plan shows icons for all the queries. It also displays the cost of executing each query as a percentage of the total cost of the batch.

Queries having a JOIN operation will have a Join icon. The icon specifies the type of join and the inner and outer table used in the join. There would be two arrows pointing to the join icon. A lower arrow connects the inner table and an upper arrow connects the outer table to the join icon.

**TABLE 15.6     Execution Plan Attributes**

| Execution Plan Attributes | Description |
| --- | --- |
| Physical Operation | This item shows what a physical operation engine does. Examples: Table Scan, Index Scan, Cluster Index Scan, Sort, Filter, Compute Scalar, Stream Aggregate, etc. |
| Logical Operation | This is a logical operation that results in a physical operation. For some operations the names of the physical and logical operations are the same, for others they are different. Example: The logical operation Aggregate can result in a physical operation Stream aggregate. |
| Estimated I/O Cost | This represents the cost of an I/O operation. As I/O cost is important, you should try to keep this to a minimum. |
| Estimated CPU Cost | This item represents the cost of a CPU operation. |
| Estimated Operator Cost | This item represents the cost of an operation on the node/icon. It also shows the cost as a percentage of the total cost of executing the query. |
| Estimated Subtree cost | This items shows the sum cost of this operation and previous operations in the same subtree. |
| Estimated Number of Rows | Number of rows available through this suboperation. |
| Estimated Row Size | Size of a row in bytes. |
| Node ID | Node ID. |

**NOTE**

The SQL Server Compact Edition Query Optimizer chooses the most efficient plan and does not support query hints. These are supported in SQL Server 2005.

# Database Schema Design Considerations

Schema is the foundation of any database. You will be using SQL Server Compact Edition on a mobile device or on a desktop. Mobile devices have less space and less memory. You need to choose the schema design that suits your runtime environment. The information documented in the first part of this section will help you to design tables and columns. The second part of this section documents the criteria you should use to design indexes.

## Tables and Columns

Application performance depends on database design. It is easy to change indexes even after application development is complete. However, it is important that table structure and column types are chosen correctly from the beginning as changing the design at a later stage will result in rewriting client application code.

### Fixed- and Variable-Length Columns

Fixed-length columns take the full storage space allocated to the column. The advantage of a variable-length column is that they take space according to the value width entered in column.

Due to variable widths of columns in different rows, the operations on variable-length columns take more time than on fixed-length columns.

You need to consider the trade-offs between performance and storage efficiency in order to decide whether fixed-length or variable-length columns are appropriate for your application. The fields that are used to store comments, remarks, notes, etc., are likely candidates for variable-length columns. These are optional and wide columns that may have a smaller percentage of rows fully utilizing the column's width. Using variable-length columns saves space that would go to waste if these columns were fixed-length columns.

Columns that are not wide should be considered for fixed length. Columns that are wide but most of the space is filled (column size * rows) should be also considered for fixed length as well as columns that are frequently updated (more text is appended). Appending more text may cause fragmentation in data pages during runtime.

### Normalization *versus* De-normalization

The SQL Server Compact Edition has a small footprint. It is generally easy to query the database if a number of joins on tables is limited. With the increase in the number of tables in a join, the execution time increases significantly. Joins on more than five tables may lead to performance issues.

If your business logic needs to query multiple tables, you may want to consider de-normalizing your schema. De-normalizing schema will lead to some redundancy of information in multiple tables that not only increases the storage requirement but also makes the write/update operations more costly.

Based upon your storage needs and performance target (whether performance is an issue while making transactions or while querying data) you need to chose the right level of normalization and de-normalization.

### Row Length

In the previous section we talked about the usage of de-normalization for faster access. De-normalization generally leads to an increase in row size. Here is the opposite guideline. A large row size leads to performance degradation. The obvious question is, *How large should a row should be?* The factors to consider are the size of your page, the size of a row, and how many rows you want to get in one I/O operation. The larger the rows, the fewer rows on a data page, and the more I/O operations that need to be done to retrieve all the rows. Therefore, if your rows are large, you may want to split the table, meaning that you need to carefully consider the trade-off between join and row size.

## Store Computed Columns

The time needed to calculate a computed column depends upon processing power. As a mobile device has limited processing power, doing a lot of processing during querying will degrade performance.

If your queries return a computed value, it will take time to calculate the computed value. If the number of rows is large, then the time to calculate the computed column can be significant.

Under these circumstances, you may want to calculate the computed value once and store the computed values in a table. During querying, you can simply retrieve the value and return it to the client.

## Indexes

Indexes play a significant role in performance improvement. In the absence of an index, a database engine needs to scan all the rows in a table. With the help of an index engine, you can get the required data without scanning full tables. In this section, we will discuss the factors that you should consider while designing indexes. The proper use of an index can significantly improve the performance of an SQL Server Compact Edition database.

SQL Server Compact Edition provides clustered and nonclustered indexes. A clustered index can store the data in order of key values. In a nonclustered index, the physical order of rows can be different from the order of the index. If you need to frequently access the rows sorted by a particular column, consider using a clustered index on the column. You can only create one cluster index on each table.

---
#### NOTE

SQL Server Compact Edition automatically creates a clustered index on a Primary key. At the time of creation, you can change the option and make it a nonclustered index.

---

### Index Length

Indexes are used to access data faster. They use extra storage space, but help in accessing the reference rows in a much faster way. The index gets less effective as it gets wider. SQL Server Compact Edition stores indexes as B-Trees. A wider index means fewer rows on a page. Fewer rows on a page means more pages. Both for faster access and for storage, it is better to use a narrow index.

If you do not have a column that can act as a key and narrow index, you can create one using the identity column and use the index on it.

### What to Index

Indexes help in querying and sorting. However, indexes slow the performance of Insert, Update, and Delete operations because these operations need both the tables and the indexes to be updated.

First, you need to analyze the kind of operations that you are trying to improve. For query operations, indexes are useful for large tables. For very small tables it is better to scan the table instead of using indexes. You should consider indexing on Primary keys and other columns used in the WHERE clause of your queries.

Consider the following query as shown in Figure 15.4

```
SELECT * From Customers order by FirstName;
```

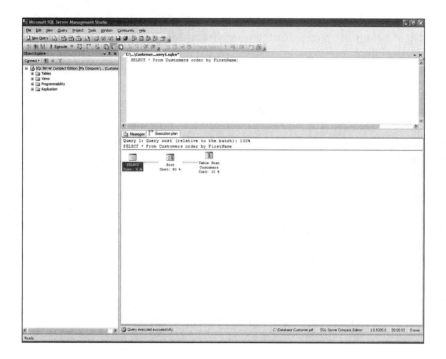

FIGURE 15.4    Execution Plan without Index on First Name

Get the estimated execution plan when there is no index on the FirstName column.

Now create an index on First Name and check the execution plan again as shown in Figure 15.5

The WHERE clause selects a subset of rows from a table. Creating an index on a column used in the WHERE clause improves the performance. The improvement depends on the selectivity of the index.

The ratio of qualified rows to total rows is called *density*. The number of distinct values in the index key is called *selectivity*. Lower the ratio, and the index will be more useful. A Unique index has the lowest ratio and highest selectivity as only one row is returned.

Consider the following example as shown in Figure 15.6.

```
SELECT * FROM Products WHERE ProductPrice > 40
```

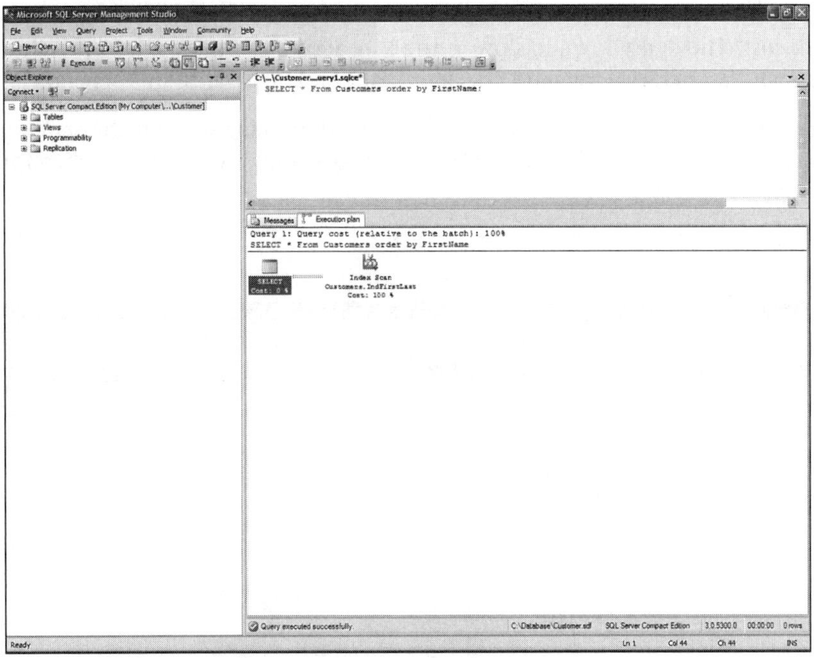

**FIGURE 15.5** Execution Plan with Index on First Name

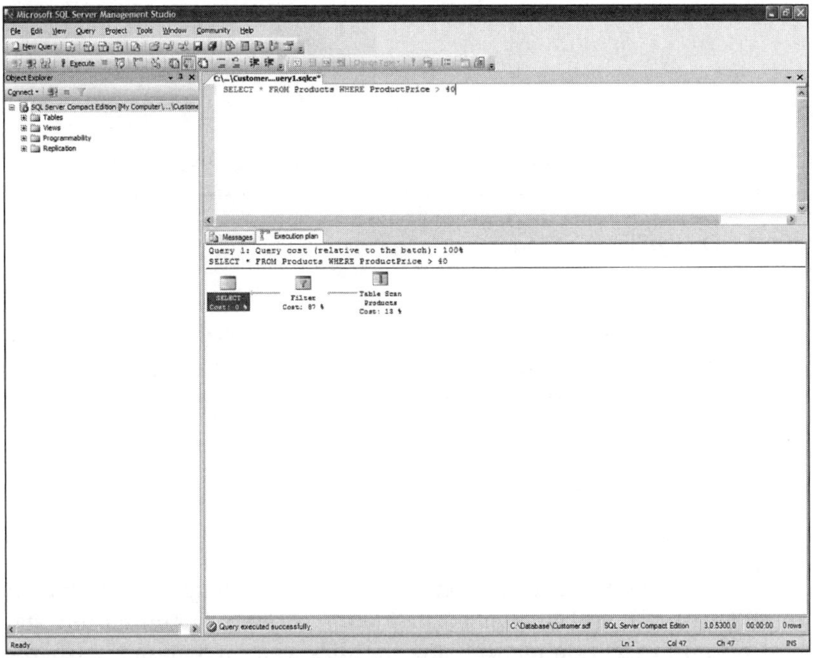

**FIGURE 15.6** Query Plan without index

There is no index on ProductPrice. On looking at the query execution plan, it shows an
87% filter cost. The query is quite slow as the SQL Server Compact Edition engine
analyzes each ProductPrice row and checks whether it is greater than 40 or not.

Now create an index on ProductPrice, see the execution plan, and run the same query
again as shown in Figure 15.7. The engine has to seek only the index and therefore runs
much faster.

```
SELECT * FROM Products WHERE ProductPrice > 40
```

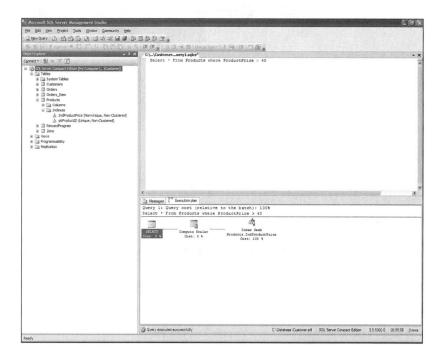

FIGURE 15.7    Query Plan with index

The SQL Server Compact Edition provides built-in stored procedures to determine the
selectivity of an index. You can use this stored procedure to know the selectivity of the
index. Following are the built-in stored procedures:

- sp_show_statistics
- sp_show_statistics_columns
- sp_show_statistics_steps

You use statistics to determine index selectivity. SQL Server Compact Edition maintains
the data on index keys. This data is called *statistics*. The Query Optimizer uses statistics
data to come up with execution plans. Using statistics, you can determine whether using
an index will provide performance improvement or not.

### sp_show_statistics

The SQL Server Compact Edition Query Optimizer uses statistical information to come up with an optimal query execution plan. The database engine creates the statistical information. Using the three stored procedures mentioned previously, you can determine the statistics and get insight as to why Query Optimizer chooses a particular execution plan.

sp_show_statistics displays the statistics for an index. To see the statistics of all indexes in a database, run the stored procedure without any parameters as shown in Figure 15.8. Specifying a table name with a stored procedure displays the statistics for all the indexes of a given table. Adding both table name and index name with a stored procedure shows the statistics of a given index.

FIGURE 15.8    sp_show_statistics Displays all Indexes

### Example:

```
sp_show_statistics
```

On executing sp_show_statistics, the procedure shows all indexes on a database. Figure 15.8 shows the following indexes: IndRouteArea, IndFirstLast, IndProductPrice, and IndOrderDate .

To see statistics for indexes on Customers table, execute the following statement as shown in Figure 15.9.

```
sp_show_statistics 'Customers'
```

FIGURE 15.9    sp_show_statistics Displays Indexes for One Specified Table

To see details of a specific index on a specific table, specify the table name and the index name. Execute the following statement to see details of the IndRouteArea index on Customers table as shown in Figure 15.10. Table 15.7 describes the table statistics attributes.

FIGURE 15.10    sp_show_statistics Displays One Specified Index for Specified Table

**TABLE 15.7    SQL Server Compact Edition Statistics Attributes**

| Statistics Attributes | Description |
|---|---|
| Table | Name of table on which index exists. |
| Index | Name of index. |
| Update | Date and time of statistics update. |
| Rows | Number of rows. |
| Rows Sampled | Number of rows that are used to generate statistics information. |
| Steps | Number of distribution steps. |
| Density | The selectivity of the first index column. |
| | Density of index is a ratio of the number of rows that would be returned by a key value to the total number of rows. |
| | The lower the density, the better it is. |
| | Density values range between 0 to 1. |
| Average Key Length | Average length of all indexes. |
| | The average key length of IndRoute area is 2. |
| | The average key length of ProductPrice is 8. |
| | IndRouteArea is smallint and each column and average is 2 bytes. Similarly, ProductPrice is of type Money and of 8 bytes. |
| | FirstName and LastName are of type NVarchar. Their average length is calculated by using the actual number of characters used in the keys. |
| Recompute | This variable denotes whether statistics will be automatically updated at the time of the next usage. This is determined by the Query Optimizer. |
| Stale | The Query Optimizer determines whether statistics must be updated. It implies that current statistics are stale. |

```
sp_show_statistics 'customers', 'IndFirstLast'
```

**sp_show_statistics_columns**

Sp_show_statistics_columns displays the data related to columns participating in an index. It is particularly useful when you have a multicolumn index.

To see the details of FirstLast index on the Customers table, execute the following statement as shown in Figure 15.11.

```
sp_show_statistics_columns 'customers', 'IndFirstLast'
```

The output shows FirstName and LastName columns.

The output displays two rows. Each row displays a set of indexes that Query Optimizer can use. The first row is for FirstName and the second row is for a combination of First and Last name. The result demonstrates that an index would be useful for Query

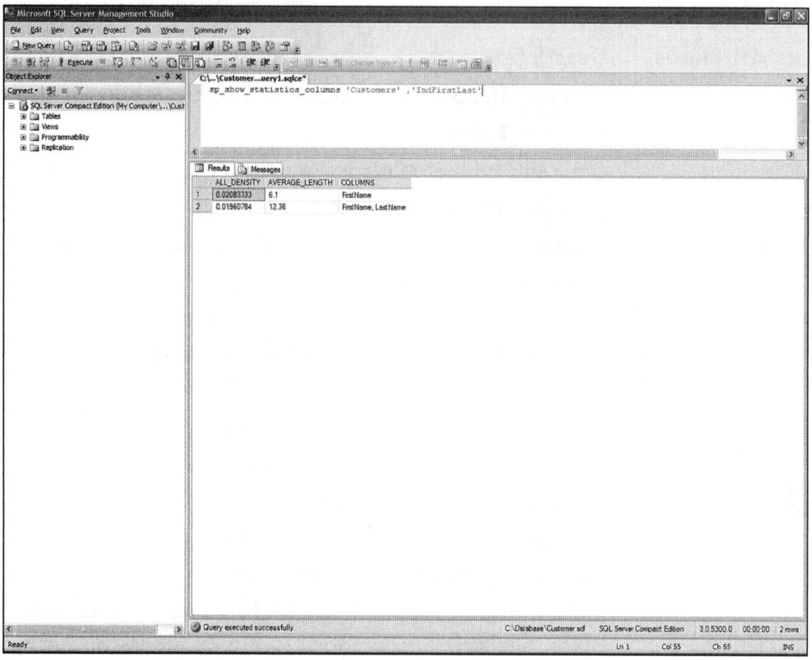

**FIGURE 15.11**    Output of sp_show_statistics_columns

Optimizer while selecting FirstName or on a set of FirstName and LastName. Table 15.8 describes the meaning of column statistics.

**TABLE 15.8    Column Statistics**

| Column Statistic Attribute | Description |
| --- | --- |
| Columns | It specifies the name of a column. In a multi-column index, it will specify one of the column names. The result set will show one row for each column. |
| All_density | Selectivity of a column. |
| Average_length | Shows the average length of a column. |
| | For FirstName, the average of all characters is 3.05. |
| | For FirstName and LastName, the average of all characters is 6.19. |
| | As NVarchar is 2 bytes, the average length is 6.1 and 12.38 bytes respectively. |

To see the distribution statistics details of IndProductPrice index on Products table, execute the following statement as shown in Figure 15.12.

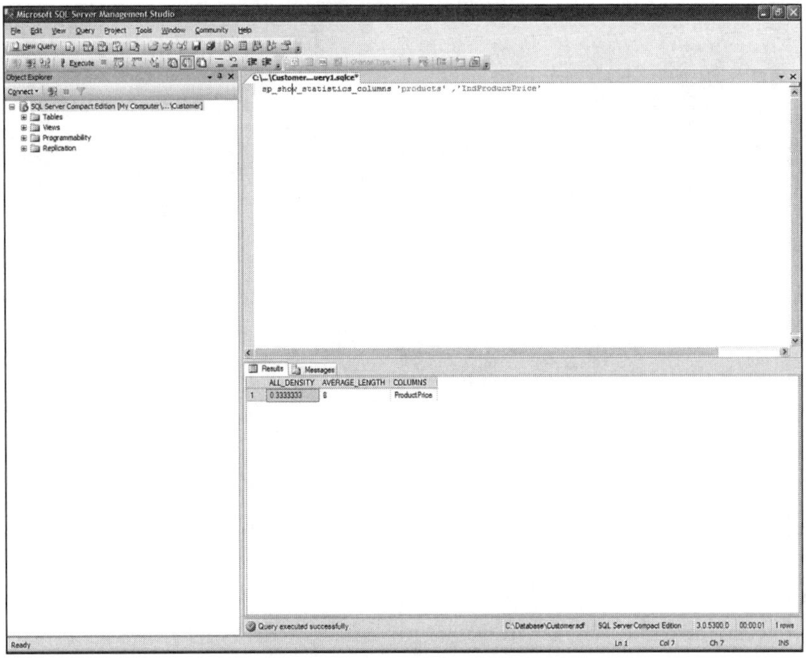

**FIGURE 15.12**    Density of IndProductPrice

```
sp_show_statistics_columns 'products' ,'IndProductPrice'
```

The Price table has only three prices—400, 40, and 600. One third of the rows have the price 400, one third have the price 40, and the remaining one third of rows have the price 600. For a given price, one third of the rows will be selected. Due to this reason, density of the IndProductPrice index is .33.

### Sp_show_statistics_steps

Sp_show_statistics_steps provides a histogram for the index.

Query Optimizer uses statistics to understand the distribution of key values in a table. The histogram consists of the sampling of 200 values for an index's first key column.

To see the histogram of FirstLast index on Customers table, execute the following query as shown in Figure 15.13:

```
sp_show_statistics_steps 'Customers','IndFirstLast'
```

Table 15.9 describes the Index Statistic field.

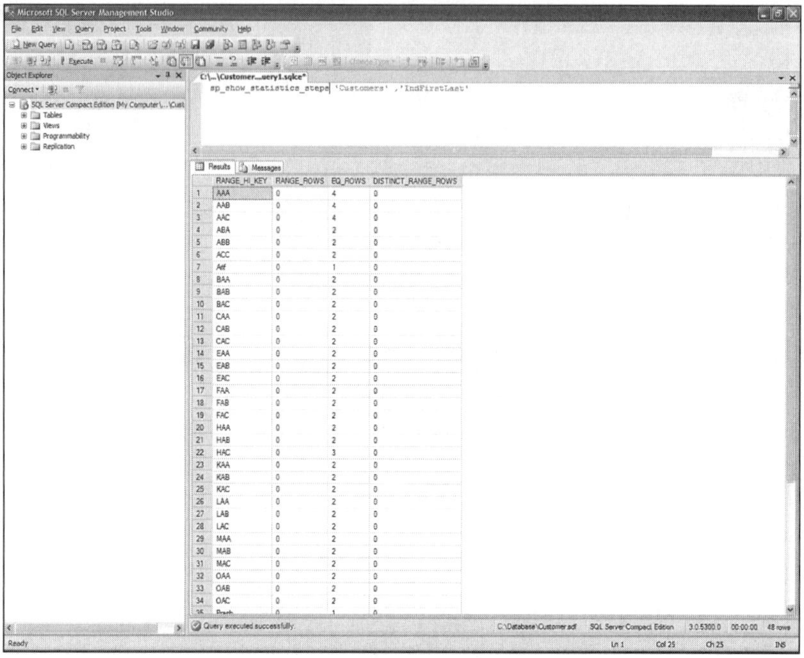

**FIGURE 15.13**    Output of sp_show_statistics_steps

**TABLE 15.9    Distribution of Keys**

| Index Statistic Attribute | Description |
| --- | --- |
| RANGE_HI_KEY | Upper bound value of a histogram step. |
| RANGE_ROWS | Number of rows that fall within each histogram step excluding the upper bound. |
| EQ_ROWS | Number of rows from a sample that are equal in value to the upper-bound of a histogram step. |
| DISTINCT_RANGE_ROWS | The number of distinct values within a histogram step excluding the upper-bound. |

**Read-Only Tables**

Indexes help when you try to read data from a table. When updating an indexed table, both table data and indexes have to be updated. Having too many indexes on a table that you frequently update means more overhead of updating indexes. You should carefully evaluate indexes on tables that frequently update data. In some cases, it is better to drop the index, update/add data in a table, and then re-create the index. If you have large read-only tables where you wish to sort data by different columns or by using different conditions, etc., you may want to consider more indexes.

### Multiple-Column Indexes

In multiple-column indexes, you define an index jointly on two columns. The order of a column in a multiple-column index is very important. To make a multiple-column index more useful, you should use the most selective column on the far-left side to improve the effectiveness of an index.

Consider the following example:

Index is on FirstName and LastName.

```
SELECT * FROM Customers Order By FirstName
```

SQL Server Compact Edition uses the index scan to return rows as shown in Figure 15.14.

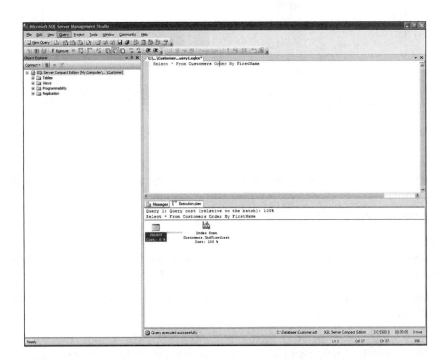

**FIGURE 15.14**    Multiple-Column Index, Most Selective Column on Left

Now change the Order By clause. Use LastName in the Order By clause instead of FirstName as shown in Figure 15.15.

```
SELECT * FROM Customers Order By LastName
```

In this case, SQL Server Compact Edition does not use the index and does the sorting in a temporary area. This is a costly operation for large tables as shown in Figure 15.15.

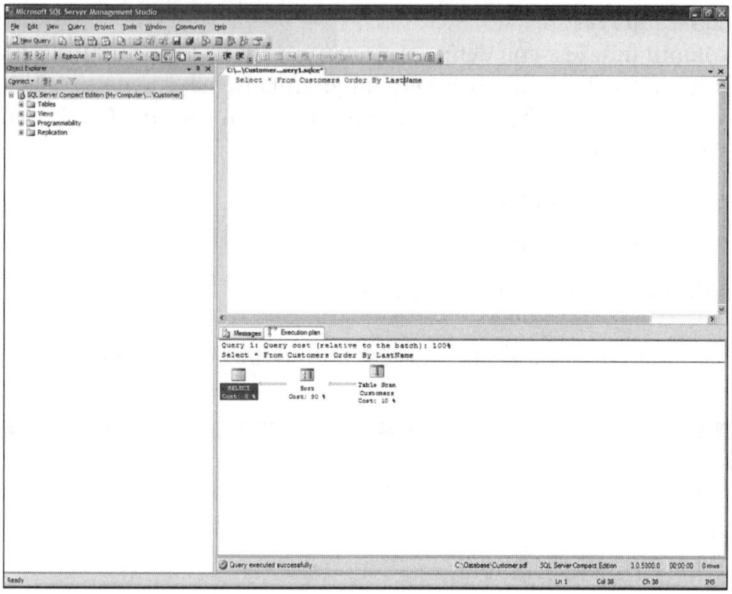

**FIGURE 15.15**    Multiple-Column Index, Selective Column on Right

### Keys

As Primary keys and Foreign keys are used in a join, it is generally useful to create an index on Primary keys. SQL Server Compact Edition automatically creates an index on Primary keys and Foreign keys.

### Filter Clauses

In the previous section we discussed that generally a column used in a WHERE clause is a potential indexing candidate. We also discussed index *selectivity*.

You should evaluate the expressions used in a WHERE clause and decide whether an index will help to reduce the scan on a table.

In an expression that has operators such as NOT, <>, NOT EXISTS, NOT IN, NOT LIKE, it would not be beneficial to use an index on a corresponding column as the entire table still needs to be scanned.

In an expression that has operators such as =, >, <, >=, <=, IN, BETWEEN, and, it would be beneficial to use an index on a corresponding column as it would limit the search.

Consider following example:

```
SELECT * FROM Products WHERE ProductPrice NOT IN (37,42);
```

Even if the index on ProductPrice exists, the execution plan does not use the index as shown in Figure 15.16. The plan shows that the entire table still needs to be scanned to determine whether a specific product price does not exist. Now instead of using NOT IN, use the IN operator as shown in Figure 15.17.

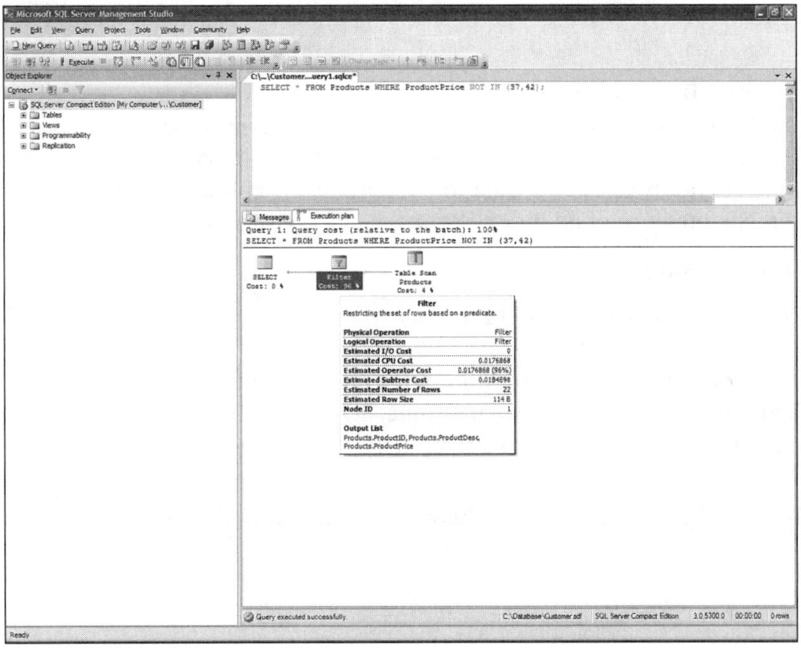

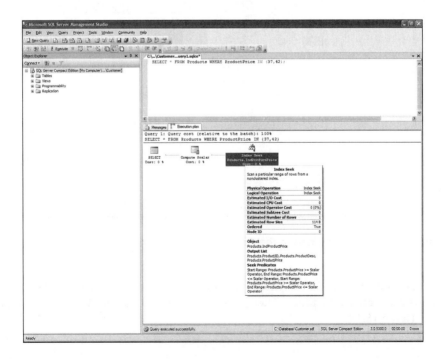

FIGURE 15.16     Full Table Scan for NOT IN Operator

FIGURE 15.17     Index Is Used for IN Operator

```
SELECT * FROM Products WHERE ProductPrice IN (37,42);
```

### Order-By, Group-By, and Distinct

Order-By and Group-By perform sorting. Having an index on these columns generally improves performance. In the absence of an index, the SQL Server Compact Edition Query Optimizer needs to put the data into a temporary table and arrange it according to a sort order. The presence of an index eliminates these costly steps.

Consider the following query:

```
SELECT * From Customers Order by FirstName
```

See the execution plans when there is no index on FirstName, and when there is an index on FirstName. Without an index on FirstName, SQL Server Compact Edition will spend 90% of cost on sorting the data into a temporary table as shown in Figure 15.18.

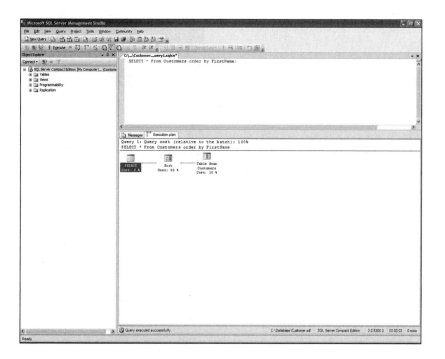

**FIGURE 15.18**    Cost of Sorting in the Absence of an Index

When you create an index and see the execution plan, the query execution plan is a straightforward scan on the index. There is no additional cost associated in querying as shown in Figure 15.19.

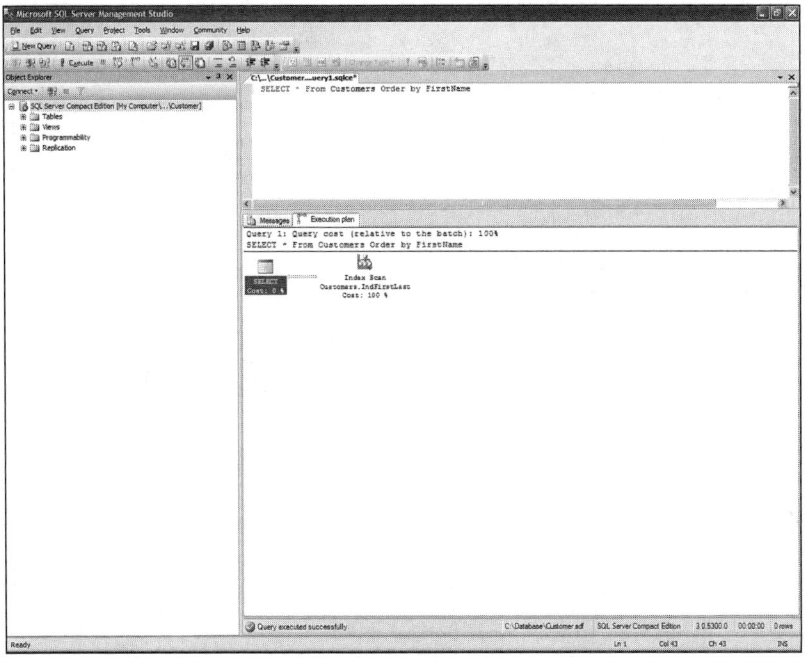

**FIGURE 15.19** Index Makes Sorting Faster

### MAX and MIN

If you are using Max () and Min () functions on a column, you should consider these columns for indexing.

Consider the following example:

```
SELECT MAX (ProductPrice) FROM Products;
```

There is no index on the ProductPrice column.

The execution plan shows four nodes: Stream Aggregate, Compute Scalar, Sort, and Table Scan. Sort and Table Scan are responsible for 99% of the cost as shown in Figure 15.20.

Now create an index on the ProductPrice column and see the execution plan.

Instead of four nodes, now there are three nodes as shown in Figure 15.21

### Table Size

Even if an index helps in searching and sorting by limiting the number of rows, there is overhead associated with index space as indexes need to be loaded into index pages. For a very small table, it is more efficient to scan the whole table instead of using an index. If you create an index, SQL Server Compact Edition Optimizer will use it. Therefore, for a small table, it is better not to create an index.

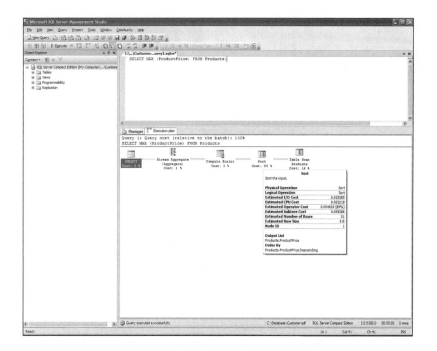

**FIGURE 15.20**    MAX Operation Requires Stream Aggregate, Compute Scalar, Sort, and Table Scan Operations in the Absence of an Index

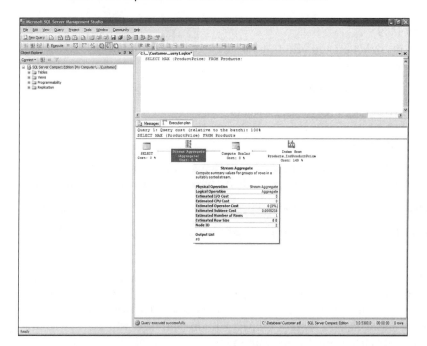

**FIGURE 15.21**    MAX Operation Runs Faster with an Index

### Low Density

Index density is the ratio of qualifying rows to the total number of rows in a table. When Query Analyzer uses an index, there is an overhead associated with the first using of a book mark and then accessing a row. If the number of rows is a large percentage of the total rows, then the overhead becomes significant. If the density of an index is high, it would be more appropriate to use a table scan. A lower density index means greater *selectivity*.

Let's consider a scenario in which the order table contains 1000 rows for 2 customers. Both customers have placed 500 orders each. If you write a query to select an order for a customer, you will get 500 rows. The density of index will be 500/1000 = .5 or 50%. In general if more than 10% of rows are selected, query optimizer may not use the index.

Similarly if the order table contains 1000 rows for 500 customers and each customer has 2 records each, on selecting orders for customer 2 rows will be returned. The density of the index will be 2/1000 or .02%. As the density is low and selectivity is high, the query optimizer will use the index.

> **NOTE**
>
> A unique index has lowest density and highest selectivity.

### Time to Create an Index

As mentioned previously, an index helps while reading from a table, but it needs to be updated at the time of data update. If there are scenarios where a lot of data is populated in a table, then you may want to consider first updating the table and then re-creating the index.

In some scenarios you may be refreshing or building the table every day of the week with new data. In those scenarios, you may want to drop the index first, then populate the table, and then create the index and use it in queries.

> **NOTE**
>
> Although it is possible to create multiple indexes on a table, the SQL Server Compact Edition Query Processor will consider all indexes but select only one index in the execution plan.

## Programming Considerations

To manage end-to-end performance for an application, you need to model the database for performance and then design application code for performance. This section describes performance-tuning tips for SQL queries and ADO.NET programs.

## Queries

You can optimize application performance by writing well-designed queries. A query plan will help you to fine-tune queries. Statistics can help you to understand why a particular plan is chosen.

### Subquery *versus* Join

A *subquery* is a query nested inside another query. You may be able to replace a subquery with a join. Query Optimizer has more plan options in join and can choose a better plan.

It is not possible to convert all subqueries into a join. The subqueries in which an inner query returns unique values are generally the right candidates for conversion.

```
—Sub Query
SELECT CustomerID FROM Customers WHERE CustomerID IN (SELECT CustomerID FROM
Orders)
```

```
—Join
SELECT Customers.CustomerID FROM Customers, Orders WHERE    Customers.CustomerID =
Orders.CustomerID ;
```

Compare the results of the previous two queries. As a customer can place multiple orders, the results of the two queries will differ. The result of an inner query is not unique and the previous subquery cannot be converted into a join.

> **NOTE**
>
> You cannot always replace a subquery with a join. Often the results of a subquery and join are different.

Here is another example: Get a list of all the customers who are participating in one of the reward programs. (Each customer can participate only in one program.) You can write this as a subquery and, in this instance, it is possible to convert this subquery easily into a join.

```
— Sub Query
SELECT CustomerID FROM Customers WHERE ProgramID IN (SELECT ProgramID FROM Reward-
Program );
```

```
— Join
SELECT Customers.CustomerID FROM Customers, RewardProgram WHERE Customers.ProgramID
= RewardProgram.ProgramID;
```

### Exists *versus* Count (*)

Exists is faster than using Count(*) to determine that no rows satisfy the criteria. Count (*) should be used when you actually want to count the rows that satisfy the criteria. Exist should be used when you wish to determine whether any rows exist or not.

### Outer Join

In Inner join, queries return results based on matching rows from both tables (left and right). However, in Outer join, the matching rows are returned and all other rows from the left table (for the Left Outer join) that do not meet the condition are also included in results. Similarly all other rows that do not match the condition from the Right table (for the Right Outer join) are included in the results.

In Inner join, the Query Optimizer can choose which table (left or right) to include first, but in Outer join, the Query Optimizer has to include Left table for Left Outer join and vice versa.

### Join on Multiple Tables

Joining large numbers of tables on SQL Server Compact Edition can degrade the performance. In general, you should avoid joining more than five tables in a query. If you need to join more than five tables to get the desired results, you may want to consider denormalization and combining the tables.

## Using Hints

Query Optimizer evaluates the various options for executing a query and choosing the best execution plan. Each database has an algorithm to determine the best execution plan.

Hints are an additional instruction you can provide with SQL queries. Using Hints you can override the execution plan Query optimizer might choose and specify the execution plan you wish to use. Using Hints you can specify join order, indexes, and type of access paths.

SQL Server Compact Edition supports two types of hints

- Table Hint

- Query Hint

### Table Hint

Within Table Hint you can specify whether Table scan or Index scan should be used. Table Hint also specifies the locking method to be used with a specified table.

Using Locking Hints you can suggest Lock duration, Lock modes, and Lock granularity.

You can specify the following lock duration as Hint:

- NOLOCK

- HOLDLOCK

The NOLOCK option in a SELECT statement specifies that the table won't be locked. The NOLOCK options turn off the locking. This is also the default behavior in SQL Server Compact Edition. In SQL Server 2005, NOLOCK hints enable the Read Uncommitted isolation level. In SQL Server Compact Edition, NOLOCK enables the Read Committed isolation level.

```
SELECT * From Patients with (NOLOCK)
```

---
**NOTE**

NOLOCK is applicable for SELECT statements, It does not apply to INSERT, UPDATE, or DELETE statements.

---

The HOLDLOCK hint suggests that the database will hold a lock until the completion of the transaction. The default granularity is ROWLOCK.

Using Table Hints you can specify the following lock modes:

- UPDLOCK

- XLOCK

SQL Server Compact Edition uses a Shared Lock in the SELECT statement. Update Lock is used while updating data. Using the UPDLOCK hint, you can force the database to use the update lock even in a SELECT statement. The UPDLOCK hint is useful in scenarios where you want to read records, have the ability to update these records later, and also be sure that these records are not updated in the meantime. The default granularity is ROWLOCK.

---
**NOTE**

UPDLOCK do not block other users from reading data.

---

The XLOCK hint is used to obtain an exclusive lock until the end of the transaction. The default granularity is ROWLOCK. If needed, XLOCK can be combined with PAGLOCK or TABLOCK.

You can specify the following lock modes as Hint:

- ROWLOCK

- PAGLOCK

- TABLOCK

- DBLOCK

Table lock and DB locks are held until the end of the statement.

### Query Hint

The Query Hint is applicable to the entire query. Query Hints are applied with the OPTION clause. SQL Server Compact Edition allows you to specify the FORCE ORDER option in a query hint. The FORCE ORDER option instructs the Query optimizer to join the table in an order specified in a query and not to reorder the join.

---
**NOTE**

SQL Server 2005 supports many argument options such as FORCE ORDER, RECOMPILE, ROBUST PLAN, and so on. SQL Server Compact Edition only supports FORCE ORDER argument option.

---

```
<query_hint> ::= { FORCE ORDER}
```

The following example demonstrates the Query Hint. The Master table has 3 rows and the Child table has 2000 rows. The first query joins a Master table and Child table. In the next query, the join order is reversed. In both cases, the query optimizer uses the optimized plan. Execute the queries and check their execution plan.

```
Select child_id, child_comment from Master inner join Child ON   Master.Master_id =
Child.Master_id;
```

```
Select child_id, child_comment from Child inner join Master ON   Child.Master_id =
Master.Master_id;
```

The third query is similar to the second query but it uses the FORCE ORDER option. Check out the plan. The plan in this case is different.

```
Select child_id, child_comment from Child inner join Master ON   Child.Master_id =
Master.Master_id OPTION (FORCE ORDER);
```

In a graphical execution plan, the Join icon will have two arrows pointing to it. The upper arrow pointing to the join refers to the outer table and the lower arrow refers to the inner table in a join. In the first two queries, the Child table was used as the inner table. In the third example, the Master table was used as the outer table and the Child table was used as the inner table.

> **NOTE**
>
> In a join, the upper arrow that refers to the outer table should return fewer rows than the lower arrow that refers to the inner table.

## ADO.NET Considerations

Similar to database design and query design, data access design is an essential part of application performance. This section provides guidance on optimizing data access design and also provides input on DataReader, DataSet, and ResultSet.

To explain this concept, we use a simple example in the SQL Server Compact Edition database. The name of the database file is AppDatabase1.sdf. The database has only one table—Books. The Books table has rows similar to those shown in Figure 15.22.

| BookID | Title | Price |
|--------|-------|-------|
| 101 | SQL Server 2005 Everywhe... | 100 |
| 102 | SQL Server Developer Guid... | 41 |
| 103 | SQL Server Administrator G... | 50 |
| 104 | Exam Guide ... | 51 |
| 105 | Architecture Guide ... | 70 |
| 106 | Integration Services 2005 ... | 90 |
| 107 | Analysis Services 2005 ... | 110 |
| 108 | Reporting Services ... | 99 |

**FIGURE 15.22**  Content of Books Table

## Use of Cursor

On mobile devices, memory is critical. If you are using SQL Server Compact Edition on mobile devices, you need to use a cursor when necessary. Moreover, you should try using a forward-only cursor if scrollability is not required. There is a significant difference in performance that can be obtained with a forward-only cursor.

## SqlCeDataReader

The DataReader object sequentially reads data from a data source. DataReader efficiently retrieves a forward-only stream of data from a data source. The DataReader is used when updatability and scrolling are not requirements. To access data from an SQL Server Compact database, use the SqlCeDataReader object.

The SQL Server Compact Edition DataReader provides faster access than DataSet and takes less memory. DataReader is a better choice to access data one record at a time

Internally, DataSet also uses DataReader to populate the data. DataReader acts between the .NET based application and the data source. Each read operation of DataReader brings the next record from the database to the application.

## SqlCeResultSet

The SQL Server Compact Edition provides an updatable, scrollable cursor. Using this cursor, you can get the performance of DataReader and a similar functionality of DataSet. It also requires less memory as it does not perform double buffering of the database as DataSet does.

The .NET Framework provides a forward- and read-only cursor to fill datasets. Users can manipulate these datasets and the changes are sent back to the data source.

### NOTE

SQLCEResultSet gives the performance of DataReader and the programmatic ease and functionality of DataSet.

If a developer needs to populate a data grid without writing custom code, DataSet is the natural choice. Developers use the same design concepts on a mobile device and use DataSet with SQL Server Compact Edition to implement positional access, updatability, and bindability. However, on SQL Server Compact Edition, the usage of DataSet should be minimized.

There is a fundamental difference between mobile applications and client-server applications. In a mobile device, the application database is on a local store and not on a separate server. As the database is available on a local store, instead of buffering the data in memory, the SQL Server Compact Edition provides a scrollable updatable cursor. This is faster than using a DataSet.

In .NET Framework, all DML operations are done through a query processor. As the database is on a local store, SQLCEResultSet provides DML operations against base tables as well as a query Processor updatable cursor.

SQLCEResultSet derives from SQLCeDataReader and it is updatable, scrollable, and bindable. To demonstrate the usage of SQLCEResult, use the sample code given in Listing 15.1.

## LISTING 15.1    ResultSet C#

```csharp
namespace ResultSet
{
    public partial class ResultSet : Form
    {
        SqlCeConnection myConn;
        SqlCeResultSet myResultSet;
        public ResultSet()
        {
            InitializeComponent();
        }
        private void ResultSet_Load(object sender, EventArgs e)
        {
            myConn  = new SqlCeConnection("DataSource=\\Program
Files\\ResultSet\\AppDatabase1.sdf");
            myConn.Open();
            FillListBox();
            listBox1.SelectedIndex = 0;
        }
        private void FillListBox()
        {
            listBox1.Items.Clear();
            SqlCeCommand myCmd = myConn.CreateCommand();
            myCmd.CommandText = "SELECT BookID, Title FROM Books";
            myResultSet = myCmd.ExecuteResultSet(ResultSetOptions.Updatable |
ResultSetOptions.Scrollable);
            while (myResultSet.Read())
            {
                listBox1.Items.Add(myResultSet.GetInt32(0).ToString() + " " + myRe-
sultSet.GetString(1));
            }
        }
        private void btnInsert_Click(object sender, EventArgs e)
        {
            if (txtTitle != null)
            {
                SqlCeUpdatableRecord myRec = myResultSet.CreateRecord();
                myRec.SetString(1, txtTitle.Text);
                myResultSet.Insert(myRec);
                txtTitle.Text = "";
            }
        }
        private void btnUpdate_Click(object sender, EventArgs e)
        {
            if (txtTitle.Text != null)
```

```
            {
                myResultSet.SetString(1, txtTitle.Text.ToString());
                myResultSet.Update();
                txtTitle.Text = "";
            }
        }
        private void btnDelete_Click(object sender, EventArgs e)
        {
                myResultSet.Delete();
        }
        private void btnRefresh_Click(object sender, EventArgs e)
        {
            FillListBox();
        }
        private void listBox1_SelectedIndexChanged(object sender, EventArgs e)
        {
            myResultSet.ReadAbsolute(listBox1.SelectedIndex);
        }
    }
}
```

**LISTING 15.1    ResultSet Visual Basic.NET**

```
Imports System.Data.SqlServerCe
Public Class Form1
    Dim myConn As SqlCeConnection
    Dim myResultSet As SqlCeResultSet
    Private Sub Form1_Load(ByVal sender As System.Object, ByVal e As System.Even-
tArgs) Handles MyBase.Load
    myConn = New SqlCeConnection("DataSource=\Program Files\ResultSet\AppData-
base1.sdf")
        myConn.Open()
        FillListBox()
        ListBox1.SelectedIndex = 0
    End Sub
    Private Sub FillListBox()
        ListBox1.Items.Clear()
        Dim myCmd As SqlCeCommand = myConn.CreateCommand
        myCmd.CommandText = "SELECT BookID, Title FROM Books"
        myResultSet = myCmd.ExecuteResultSet(ResultSetOptions.Updatable Or Result-
SetOptions.Scrollable)

        While myResultSet.Read()
            ListBox1.Items.Add(myResultSet.GetInt32(0).ToString() + " " + myResult-
Set.GetString(1))
```

```
        End While
    End Sub
    Private Sub btnInsert_Click(ByVal sender As System.Object, ByVal e As
System.EventArgs) Handles btnInsert.Click
        If txtTitle.Text <> "" Then

            Dim myRec As SqlCeUpdatableRecord = myResultSet.CreateRecord
            myRec.SetString(1, txtTitle.Text)
            myResultSet.Insert(myRec)
            txtTitle.Text = ""
        End If
    End Sub
    Private Sub btnUpdate_Click(ByVal sender As System.Object, ByVal e As
System.EventArgs) Handles btnUpdate.Click
        If txtTitle.Text <> "" Then
            myResultSet.SetString(1, txtTitle.Text.ToString())
            myResultSet.Update()
            txtTitle.Text = ""
        End If
    End Sub
    Private Sub btnDelete_Click(ByVal sender As System.Object, ByVal e As
System.EventArgs) Handles btnDelete.Click
        myResultSet.Delete()
    End Sub
    Private Sub btnRefresh_Click(ByVal sender As System.Object, ByVal e As
System.EventArgs) Handles btnRefresh.Click
        FillListBox()
    End Sub
    Private Sub ListBox1_SelectedIndexChanged_1(ByVal sender As System.Object,
ByVal e As System.EventArgs) Handles ListBox1.SelectedIndexChanged
        myResultSet.ReadAbsolute(ListBox1.SelectedIndex)
    End Sub
End Class
```

The code listing opens a connection to a database and fills a list book with BookID and Book names. The example uses SQLCeResultSet with an updatable and scrollable cursor option to fetch data from the Books table.

The sample application has a list box to display a list of books. The form has Insert, Update, Delete, and Refresh buttons. The Title field is used to enter the title for a new book. The field is also used to update the title of a selected book.

The listBox1_SelectedIndexChanged method sets the ResultSet cursor on a table to the record selected in the list box.

The btnInsert_Click method inserts a new record in the Books table. This method creates a new record. To insert the new record into the database, the Insert method of the ResultSet is called.

The btnDelete_click method deletes the record selected in the list box from the database.

The btnUpdate_click updates the Book name of the selected record with a new book name. The Update method updates the Book name with a string entered in the Title field. To update the record in a database, the Update method of the ResultSet is called.

Build the application and execute it. The application will show a list of books as shown in Figure 15.23.

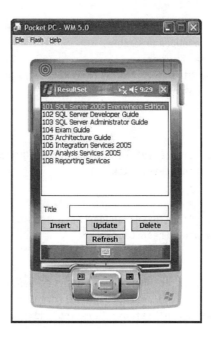

**FIGURE 15.23**    BookID and Title Value at Start

- Select a row from the list box

- Add a new title in the Title text box as shown in Figure 15.24.

- Click the Update button.

On selecting a list box, the listBox1_SelectedIndexChanged method is called. The method reads the row number selected in a list box. The list box row number starts from 0. On selecting the fourth row, listbox1.SelectedIndex will have a value of 3. The ReadAbsolute positions the SQLCEResultSet cursor on the specified row number. The

**FIGURE 15.24** Update Exam Guide to SQL Server Exam Guide

ReadAbsolute method is also 0-based. Passing 0 to a method will position the cursor on the first row of the table. If `listbox1.SelectedIndex` has a value 3, the ReadAbsolute will position the cursor on the fourth row of the Books table. On clicking the Update button, the second column value is changed to the new title specified in the text box. The Update method updates the data source.

- Select a row in the list box as shown in Figure 15.25.

- Click the Delete button.

On selecting a list box, the `listBox1_SelectedIndexChanged` method is called. It positions the cursor on the row selected. On clicking the Delete button, the record at the current cursor position is deleted.

- Enter New Title in the Title text box as shown in Figure 15.26.

- Click the Insert button.

On clicking the Insert button, a new record is created with a new book title. The new record is added to the database.

- Click Refresh.

FIGURE 15.25    Delete Architecture Guide

FIGURE 15.26    Insert New Title

**FIGURE 15.27**    Refresh the Screen with Updated Data

The screen is refreshed with the updated data as shown in Figure 15.27.

### Parameterized Queries

Each time you execute an SQL Statement through ADO.NET, SQL Server Compact Edition creates a query plan. If you are executing the same query continuously with varying parameter values, you should consider using parameterized queries. Parameterized statements will compile the query once and execute the same compiled plan on each execution. To create the execution plan once and use it multiple times, use the `Prepare` method. Preparing a command has overhead. If a statement is executed only once, there is no need to prepare it.

> **NOTE**
>
> Parameterized queries also help protect against SQL Injections.
>
> You can prepare ExecuteReader, ExecuteScalar, and ExecuteNonQuery commands.

You will use the parameter property and the Prepare method to implement the execution plan programmatically. You will need to keep the same command object to store the compiled command. If you destroy the object and create a new one, the object query will be compiled again.

Listing 15.2 describes the usage of a parameterized query. The code opens a connection and creates a command object. The code sets the CommandText property with SQL statements. Instead of defining the actual values, you define the parameters in the command text. The code adds values to the parameter collection using the Add method. You prepare the command once. A query plan is generated with the Prepare command.

Once the command is prepared, then you can fill values to command and execute the query. For any subsequent operations, you need to add only different values to the parameter.

### LISTING 15.2    ParameterQuery  C#

```csharp
SqlCeConnection myConn = new SqlCeConnection("DataSource=\\Program Files\\Parame-
terQuery\\AppDatabase1.sdf");

SqlCeCommand myCmd = myConn.CreateCommand();

 myCmd.CommandType = CommandType.Text;
 myCmd.CommandText = "INSERT INTO BOOKS (Title,Price, Publisher, Description) val-
ues (@Title,@Price,@Publisher, @Description)";

 myCmd.Parameters.Add("@Title", SqlDbType.NChar, 100);
 myCmd.Parameters.Add("@Price", SqlDbType.Money);
 myCmd.Parameters.Add("@Publisher", SqlDbType.NChar, 50);
 myCmd.Parameters.Add("@Description", SqlDbType.NVarChar, 2000);

 myConn.Open();
 myCmd.Prepare();

 // First Insert
 myCmd.Parameters["@Title"].Value = "Integration Services 2005";
 myCmd.Parameters["@Price"].Value = 35;
 myCmd.Parameters["@Publisher"].Value = "My Publisher";
 myCmd.Parameters["@Description"].Value = "Insert 1";
 myCmd.ExecuteNonQuery();

 // Second Insert
 myCmd.Parameters["@Title"].Value = "Analysis Services 2005";
 myCmd.Parameters["@Price"].Value = 45;
 myCmd.Parameters["@Publisher"].Value = "My Publisher";
 myCmd.Parameters["@Description"].Value = "Insert 2";
 myCmd.ExecuteNonQuery();

 // Third Insert
 myCmd.Parameters["@Title"].Value = "Reporting Services 2005";
 myCmd.Parameters["@Price"].Value = 55;
 myCmd.Parameters["@Publisher"].Value = "My Publisher";
```

```
myCmd.Parameters["@Description"].Value = "Insert 3";
myCmd.ExecuteNonQuery();
myConn.Close();
```

## LISTING 15.2    ParameterQuery Visual Basic .NET

```
Dim myConn As SqlCeConnection = New SqlCeConnection("DataSource=\Program
Files\ParameterQuery\AppDatabase1.sdf")
Dim myCmd As SqlCeCommand = myConn.CreateCommand()

myCmd.CommandType = Data.CommandType.Text
myCmd.CommandText = "INSERT INTO BOOKS (Title,Price, Publisher, Description) values
(@Title,@Price,@Publisher,@Description)"

myCmd.Parameters.Add("@Title", SqlDbType.NChar, 100)
myCmd.Parameters.Add("@Price", SqlDbType.Money)
myCmd.Parameters.Add("@Publisher", SqlDbType.NChar, 50)
myCmd.Parameters.Add("@Description", SqlDbType.NVarChar, 2000)

myConn.Open()
myCmd.Prepare()

' First Insert
myCmd.Parameters("@Title").Value = "Integration Services 2005"
myCmd.Parameters("@Price").Value = 35
myCmd.Parameters("@Publisher").Value = "My Publisher"
myCmd.Parameters("@Description").Value = "Insert 1"
myCmd.ExecuteNonQuery()

' Second Insert
myCmd.Parameters("@Title").Value = "Analysis Services 2005"
myCmd.Parameters("@Price").Value = 45
myCmd.Parameters("@Publisher").Value = "My Publisher"
myCmd.Parameters("@Description").Value = "Insert 2"
myCmd.ExecuteNonQuery()

'// Third Insert
myCmd.Parameters("@Title").Value = "Reporting Services 2005"
myCmd.Parameters("@Price").Value = 55
myCmd.Parameters("@Publisher").Value = "My Publisher"
myCmd.Parameters("@Description").Value = "Insert 3"
myCmd.ExecuteNonQuery()

myConn.Close()
```

## Open Objects

The amount of memory on a mobile device is limited. Every time you open an object, it takes memory and reduces performance. Therefore, you should open the object only when needed and close it as soon as you finish working with it.

## Number of Columns

This is an obvious tip—you should retrieve the required number of columns. This will be faster and will use less memory. The memory is especially important if you are running SQL Server Compact Edition on a device.

## Order By, Group By, and Distinct

Using operators such as Order By, Group By, and Distinct utilize more memory. The memory is limited on a device and may slow down the system. You need to use these operators when they are actually needed and when they improve the query performance. The performance gain in a query should be larger than the extra overhead of memory consumption.

## Usage of ExecuteScalar

If your query needs to return a single value, you should use the ExecuteScalar method. The Command object has the ExecuteScalar method to return the first column of the first row of the ResultSet. You can do the same operation using the ExecuteReader method as well but the ExecuteScalar method is better optimized for returning a single value.

## Base Table Cursor

SQL Server Compact Edition provides a query processor. A query processor parses, analyzes, optimizes, and prepares an execution plan for queries in an efficient way. Even if the query processor runs the query in an efficient way, there is a processing cost associated with all these steps.

On occasion, it is better to bypass the query processor and fetch the table column directly. Use the base table cursor to fetch all columns of a row.

A base table cursor is the fastest cursor in SQL Server Compact Edition. The Base table cursor does not use a query processor but works directly with the SQL Server Compact Edition storage engine. The cursor can move forward, backward, and is updatable. You do not use a base table cursor with a Select statement. Instead you can use it with DataReader and ResultSet by setting the command Type property to Table Direct as shown in Listing 15.3.

### LISTING 15.3    TableDirect C#

```
SqlCeConnection myConn = new SqlCeConnection("DataSource=\\Program Files\\TableDi-
rect\\AppDatabase1.sdf");
SqlCeCommand myCmd = myConn.CreateCommand();
myCmd.CommandText = "Books";
myCmd.CommandType = CommandType.TableDirect;
myConn.Open();
```

```
SqlCeDataReader myReader;
myReader = myCmd.ExecuteReader();
while (myReader.Read())
{
  listBox1.Items.Add(myReader.GetValue(1));
}
myReader.Close();
myConn.Close();
```

**LISTING 15.3    TabletDirect Visual Basic.NET**

```
        Dim myConn As SqlCeConnection = New SqlCeConnection("DataSource=\Program
Files\TabletDirect\AppDatabase1.sdf")
        Dim myCmd As SqlCeCommand = myConn.CreateCommand()
        myCmd.CommandText = "Books"
        myCmd.CommandType = CommandType.TableDirect
        myConn.Open()
        Dim myReader As SqlCeDataReader = myCmd.ExecuteReader()
        While myReader.Read()
            ListBox1.Items.Add(myReader.GetValue(1))
        End While
        myReader.Close()

        myConn.Close()
```

### Seek/Set Range

You can open a base table cursor directly on an index. The advantage of this is that it can be used to seek particular values. It can also be used to restrict the rows based on a range of values within an index.  Using SetRange, you define a range on an index; using Seek, you can position rows in a current range.

To use this method, follow these steps:

1. Set CommandType to TableDirect.

2. Set CommandText to base table.

3. Set IndexName to index on table.

On using SetRange, it will return the rows whose key values fall in the range. On using Seek on a DataReader that has a range, it positions the row in a specified range.

When you use the SetRange and Seek combination, you retrieve a set of rows based on index values. This provides a better performance than using the WHERE condition in a SELECT query.

Example: The database has the following rows as shown in Figure 15.28.

| BookID | Title | Price |
|--------|-------|-------|
| 101 | SQL Server 2005 Everywhe... | 100 |
| 102 | SQL Server Developer Guid... | 41 |
| 103 | SQL Server Administrator G... | 50 |
| 104 | Exam Guide      ... | 51 |
| 105 | Architecture Guide    ... | 70 |
| 106 | Integration Services 2005  ... | 90 |
| 107 | Analysis Services 2005   ... | 110 |
| 108 | Reporting Services    ... | 99 |
| * |  |  |

FIGURE 15.28  Content of Books Table

To access the list of books in a price range and then position them by price, you can use
the sample shown in Listing 15.29.

FIGURE 15.29  BookID and Title in Range 40 to 100 and Cursor Position on Value 50

Listing 15.4 shows the code to implement the functionality.

### LISTING 15.4    Seek C#

```
SqlCeConnection myConn = new SqlCeConnection("DataSource=\\Program
Files\\Seek\\AppDatabase1.sdf");
        SqlCeCommand myCmd = myConn.CreateCommand();
        myCmd.CommandText = "Books";
```

```
            myCmd.CommandType = CommandType.TableDirect;
            String BookDetail;
            myConn.Open();

            myCmd.IndexName = "IndPrice";
            myCmd.CommandText = "Books";
            SqlCeDataReader myReader =
myCmd.ExecuteReader(CommandBehavior.Default);
                // Choose a range for price specified
                myCmd.SetRange(DbRangeOptions.InclusiveStart | DbRangeOptions.Inclu-
siveEnd,
                    new object[] { txtStartRange.Text}, new object[] { txtEndRange.Text
});

            myReader = myCmd.ExecuteReader(CommandBehavior.Default);
            // Now set it to at price
            bool onRow = myReader.Seek(DbSeekOptions.FirstEqual, new object[] {
txtSeek.Text });
                // Now ,the reader will return rows with Price between
                // Seek start price and end range price
                if (onRow)
                {
                    listBox1.Items.Clear();
                    for (int i = 1; myReader.Read(); i++)
                    {
                        BookDetail = myReader["BookID"] + " " +
myReader["Price"].ToString() + " " + myReader["Title"] ;
                        listBox1.Items.Add(BookDetail);
                    }
                }
            myConn.Close();
```

## Get the First Response

In many applications, you want to return to a client the number of rows that are populated on a form. A subset of rows is displayed on the form. By using the Next button, a
user can view the next set of records. In these circumstances, instead of getting all the
rows and then displaying them on a form, you should consider getting the first response
and populating. While the form is being filled with the first set of rows, another set of
rows can be brought and populated in the background.

Even if the total time to bring data from the database is long, you can create the impres-
sion that the data was available when you received the first set of responses.

Based upon your application need, you need to decide whether response time or total
time is more important and design your queries accordingly.

## Materialization

Operations such as DISTINCT, ORDER BY, and GROUP BY require the sorting of data. The database engine sorts either by using an index or by storing the results in a temporary table. The query will return result faster if there is an appropriate index to use and usage of a temporary table can be avoided.

Operations such as selections and joins can be performed without requiring the storage of intermediate results. These are called pipelined operations. Operations such as SORT and GROUP BY need all data to be retrieved before applying SORT or Group By operations. This is called *materialization*. In these operations, there is an initial delay and then all the results come in quickly. These kinds of operations are not good for better response time but are useful for better total time.

When response time is important, materialization should be avoided. Appropriate indexing can help avoid materialization.

# Performance for Synchronization Considerations

An application with better performance provides a better user experience and increases user productivity. Improving the performance at synchronization not only provides a better user experience and increases productivity, but also reduces network traffic and the cost of connectivity.

## Publish Required Data

You should publish only the data that is needed by your Subscribers. Avoid publishing unnecessary data as that requires extra network bandwidth and slows down performance during replication.

You should consider avoiding a text column in a publication.

Publication tables have columns such as remarks, comments, notes, etc. These columns are not necessarily needed in a device-based application. Columns not used by client applications should not be downloaded to Subscriber.

## Download Only Article Type

The SQL Server Compact Edition has a Download Only Articles feature. Its purpose is to download only articles from Publisher to Subscriber. These articles are not synchronized back from Subscriber to Publisher.

There may be many scenarios where you want to get the latest version of a look-up table from Server to Subscriber, but these tables do not get updated at Subscriber.

Specifying the articles as Download Only has an advantage because there is no need to store metadata for synchronization on the device and there are fewer tables that need to be synchronized.

## Well-Partitioned Group

SQL Server 2005 provides well-partitioned articles. This is different from the previous version of SQL CE. With well-partitioned articles, the changes that are uploaded are mapped to a single partitioned ID, thus avoiding the recalculating of the partitioned ID.

## Filters and Index

You should consider creating an index on the Publisher filter's WHERE clause which will result in a faster scan.

For example, if you are using the filtering condition `where [DoctorEmployeeNo] = SUSER_SNAME()`, having an index on the DoctorEmployeeNo column will increase performance for replication.

## Complex Join

Having a complex join on the filter clause can degrade performance. You should consider moving the following types of tables out of a join:

- Small table

- Look-up table

- Table that does not change often

These tables can be part of a publication and the entire table can be sent to the Subscriber instead of using it in the filter clause.

## Interval of Replication

Appropriate intervals should be set to replicate the data between Publisher and Subscriber. Having a continuous replication, or running it at short intervals, is performance overhead. Similarly if the interval is very long, it may take more time to replicate and be unacceptable to users.

## Disk Drive for Logs

Writing a log for a Distributor database and a Publisher database is an I/O intensive operation. You can achieve performance gain if the Publisher database log and the Distributor database log are on separate disk drives.

## Considerations for Subscribers

Synchronizing data with a large number of Subscribers at the same time may result in performance issues. Consider synchronizing the Subscribers at different times.

# Storage Media Considerations

Storage is an important factor if you are using SQL Server Compact Edition on mobile devices. You can save SQL Server Compact Edition on a storage card. This feature was not available in SQL CE 2.0.

The performance of a database depends largely upon Read–Write operations. The performance overhead varies from storage card to storage card. If you are not getting the appropriate performance from the database, you need to evaluate whether this is due to your storage card or to other factors.

First measure the database performance by keeping SQL Server Compact Edition on a mobile device memory and then measuring the difference that occurs when moving it to a storage card. If the difference is great, you should try another type of storage card. After doing the benchmark, you should roll out your application to production.

## Summary

In this chapter you learned how to view and interpret an SQL Server Compact Edition query execution plan. We discussed various factors to consider while designing schema and how indexes play a critical role in performance improvement. This chapter documented in detail where and when indexes should be used.

Performance tips for programming were presented along with the functions of DataReader, DataSet, and SqlCeResultSet. The advantages of Parameterized query, Range, and the Seek mechanism were also discussed. In conclusion, we discussed performance improvement ideas for synchronization.

# Index

## Symbols

## A

*How can we make this index more useful? Email us at indexes@samspublishing.com*

# H

**hardware requirements**

SQL Server Compact Edition, 35-38

**HasChanges method (DataSet object), 218**

**HasErrors property (DataSet object), 219**

**HasRows (data reader object), 214**

**HasRows property (ResultSet object), 227**

**Having Clause listing (6.20), 190**

**HAVING keyword**

database queries, 190

**HelpLink property (SqlCeException object), 237**

**HelpLink property (SqlCeTransactionInProgressException object), 235**

**HiddenFieldCount (data reader object), 214**

**HiddenFieldCount property (ResultSet object), 227**

**Hints, 531-533**

Query Hint, 532-533

Table Hint, 531-532

**HResult property (SqlError object), 238**

**HTTP**

Web servers

securing with, 483

**Https (http over SSL)**

Web servers, 468-481

# I

**IDENTIFY column constraint, 137**

**identity columns**

Merge Replication

RDA (Remote Data Access), 452

**IIS**

platform support, 39

**IIS authentication**

Web servers, 466-467

**IIS Certificate Wizard, 469**

**IIS (Integrated Information Services), 468**

**IIS servers**

security

connectivity, 482-493, 495-504

**Include namespace C#.NET listing (3.1), 90**

**Include namespace C#.NET listing (3.2), 103**

**indexes, 513-516**

creating, 160, 529

CREATE INDEX keyword, 160

Query Analyzer, 163-164

SSMS (SQL Server Management Studio), 161-162

Visual Studio, 162

deleting, 167-170

metadata, 171

properties

modifying, 164-167

viewing, 164-167

schema design considerations, 513-529

density, 529

filter clauses, 524-525

keys, 524

length, 513

MAX() function, 527-528

MIN() function, 527-528

multiple-column indexes, 523-524

read-only tables, 522

sorting, 526-527

table size, 527

sp_show_statistics, 517-519

sp_show_statistics_columns, 519-522

sp_show_statistics_steps, 521-522

**Indexes view (Views node), 70**

**Index Metadata listing (5.24), 171**

# J

# K

# L

*How can we make this index more useful? Email us at indexes@samspublishing.com*

*How can we make this index more useful? Email us at indexes@samspublishing.com*

# M

# N

# R

Replication Properties for Windows Integrated and SQL Server Authentication C#.NET listing (14.13), 501

Replication Properties for Windows Integrated Both at Web Server and  SQL Server C#.NET listing (14.15), 502

Replication Properties for Windows Integrated Both at Web Server and  SQL Server C#.NET listing (14.16), 502

replication wizards

SQL Server Management Studio, 74-75

ResetDbType method (SqlCeParamter object), 231

Reset method (DataSet object), 218

restoring

database, 130

ResultSet, 534, 536-541

ResultSet C#/Visual Basic.Net listing (15.1), 535-536

ResultSetView property (ResultSet object), 227

Right Outer Join listing (6.17), 189

Rollback method (SqlCeTransaction object), 234

ROUND Function listing (10.18), 302

ROUND mathematical function, 301

rows

length

schema design, 512

rows filtering

Merge Replication

specifying, 374, 376-377

rowset object (OLE DB), 258

RTRIM Function listing (10.36), 311

RTRIM string function, 311

running

upgrade tool, 332

runtime environment

migration, 342-343

# S

saving

SQL statements

Query Analyzer, 85-87

Scale property (SqlCeParameter object), 232

scenarios

Merge Replication, 346-348

RDA, 411-413

scheduling

Snapshot Agent, 377-378

schema design considerations

database, 511

columns, 511-513

indexes, 513-529

tables, 511-513

Schema (Sch-M, Sch-S) locks, 182

SchemaSerializationMode property (DataSet object), 219

schema snapshots, 356

scrollable cursors, 259

Scrollable property (ResultSet object), 227

securing

database, 128-129

security

database, 460

encryption, 461-464

passwords, 460-464

Snapshot Agent

configuring, 379-380

SQL servers, 481-482

authentication, 482, 490

connectivity, 482-493, 495-504

Web servers, 466

authentication, 490

Https (http over SSL), 468-481

Safari®
BOOKS ONLINE
ENABLED

# THIS BOOK IS SAFARI ENABLED

## INCLUDES FREE 45-DAY ACCESS TO THE ONLINE EDITION

The Safari® Enabled icon on the cover of your favorite technology book means the book is available through Safari Bookshelf. When you buy this book, you get free access to the online edition for 45 days.

Safari Bookshelf is an electronic reference library that lets you easily search thousands of technical books, find code samples, download chapters, and access technical information whenever and wherever you need it.

**TO GAIN 45-DAY SAFARI ENABLED ACCESS TO THIS BOOK:**

- Go to **http://www.samspublishing.com/safarienabled**

- Complete the brief registration form

- Enter the coupon code found in the front of this book on the "Copyright" page

If you have difficulty registering on Safari Bookshelf or accessing the online edition, please e-mail customer-service@safaribooksonline.com.